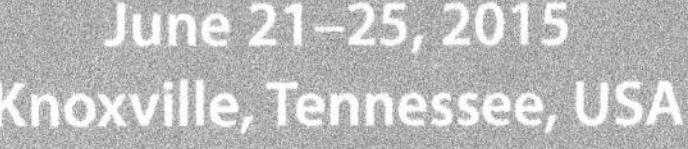

Advancing Computing as a Science & Profession

JCDL'15

Proceedings of the 15th ACM/IEEE-CS
Joint Conference on Digital Libraries

Sponsored by:

ACM SIGIR, ACM SIGWEB, IEEE and IEEE TCDL

Supported by:

Google, The University of Tennessee-Knoxville, NSF, The iSchool at Illinois, and University of North Carolina

Other Assistance:

CNI

Advancing Computing as a Science & Profession

The Association for Computing Machinery
2 Penn Plaza, Suite 701
New York, New York 10121-0701

ISBN: 978-1-4503-3594-2 (Digital)

ISBN: 978-1-4503-3877-6 (Print)

Additional copies may be ordered prepaid from:

ACM Order Department
PO Box 30777
New York, NY 10087-0777, USA

Phone: 1-800-342-6626 (USA and Canada)
+1-212-626-0500 (Global)
Fax: +1-212-944-1318
E-mail: acmhelp@acm.org
Hours of Operation: 8:30 am – 4:30 pm ET

Printed in the USA

JCDL 2015 Chairs' Welcome

It is our great pleasure to welcome you to the *2015 ACM/IEEE-CS Joint Conference on Digital Libraries – JCDL 2015.* When we originally put together the proposal and theme for this year's conference, we saw Big Data as a hot topic that we believed at the time was of vital importance to the Digital Libraries community. Two years later we feel that our original observations still hold and that our community has the ability to bring much to an exciting area. Big Data is everywhere – from Computational Science to Digital Humanities, from Web Analytics to traditional libraries. For many the biggest issues in big data are a digital libraries issues – How do we preserve big data collections? How do we provide access to big data collections? What new questions can we pose against our big data collections? How can we, the digital libraries community, stand up in the face of these challenges and inform collection builders, curators, and interface developers how to best solve their challenges? What assumptions have we been working under that no longer hold in light of Big Data? These are the questions we hope to address here.

The call for papers attracted submissions from thirty countries on six continents. The program committee reviewed and accepted the following:

Venue or Track	*Reviewed*	*Accepted*	*Percent*
Full Research Papers	60	18	30%
Short Research Reports	60	30	50%
Posters and Demos	21	18	85.7%

We also organized a series of exciting keynotes and panels:

Keynotes:

- *The Google Cultural Institute,* Piotr Adamczyk (Google Cultural Institute)
- *Moving the Needle: from Innovation to Impact*, Katherine Skinner (Educopia Institute)
- *The HathiTrust Research Center: Providing analytic access to the HathiTrust Digital Library's 4.7 billion pages,* J. Stephen Downie (University of Illinois at Urbana-Champaign)

Panels:

- *Lifelong Digital Libraries,* Frank Hopfgartner (University of Glasgow), Steve Whittaker (University of California at Santa Cruz), Cathal Gurrin (Dublin City University), Hideo Joho (University of Tsukuba)
- *The Future of Digital Preservation of Cultural Heritage,* Piotr Adamczyk (Google Cultural Institute), Leah Weinryb Grohsgal (National Endowment for the Humanities), Unmil Karadkar (University of Texas), Katherine Skinner (Educopia Institute)

Putting together *JCDL 2015* was a team effort. We first thank the authors for providing the content of the program. First we would like to recognize the organizing committee who have had a daunting task of arranging events often from the opposite side of the world. We are grateful to the program committee and the senior program committee, who worked very hard in reviewing papers and providing feedback for authors. We thank the University of Tennessee for hosting the conference. We would also like to thank our sponsors, ACM SIGIR, SIGWEB, and IEEE TC-DL, and our generous financial supporters, Research at Google and The University Libraries at the University of Tennessee. Finally, thanks to the Coalition for Networked Information for assistance with publicity.

We hope that you will find this program interesting and thought-provoking and that the conference will provide you with a valuable opportunity to share ideas with other researchers and practitioners from institutions around the world.

Paul Logasa Bogen II
Google, USA

Suzie Allard
University of Tennessee, USA

Holly Mercer
University of Tennessee, USA

Micah Beck
University of Tennessee, USA

JCDL 2015 Conference Co-Chairs' Welcome

We are pleased to welcome you to the 2015 ACM/IEEE Joint Conference on Digital Libraries. This year's conference theme, *Large, Dynamic and Ubiquitous–The Era of the Digital Library*, is inspired by nearby Oak Ridge National Laboratory (ORNL), where big data abounds. The program is reflective of the big data information challenges that DL researchers are confronting, be it with structured data, text, images, audio, video or other forms of information.

The Program Committee has created a program that we believe covers a broad spectrum of digital library topics in both depth and focus. We note an increased number of papers addressing issues of crowd sourcing and big data as these become more prevalent trends in our information landscape.

Our program starts with a full day of tutorials along with our Doctoral Consortium. The next two and a half days are filled with conference paper sessions, keynotes, and panels. The ever-popular Poster and Demonstration session will be held Tuesday evening, where 26 posters and demonstrations will be on display. Preceded by the light-hearted "minute madness," this is a time when you can interact one-on-one with the authors as well as mingle with your colleagues throughout the reception. The evening will be capped off with the *Best Poster Award.* The final day offers a series of workshops for more in-depth analysis of key topics in digital libraries.

In addition to the papers, posters, demos, tutorials and workshops, JCDL 2015 features two panels, *Lifelong Digital Libraries*, and *The Future of Digital Preservation of Cultural Heritage*, along with three thought-provoking keynote talks on Monday, Tuesday, and Wednesday that will round out the program. The first keynote is by Piotr Adamczyk discussing *The Google Cultural Institute.* Katherine Skinner will present the second keynote: *Moving the Needle: from Innovation to Impact.* Finally, the closing plenary keynote will be delivered during the banquet lunch by J. Stephen Downie, talking about *The HathiTrust Research Center: Providing analytic access to the HathiTrust Digital Library's 4.7 billion pages.* Now that's big data! Awards for the Vannevar Bush Best Paper and Best Student Paper will also be presented at the banquet lunch.

The quality of papers for JCDL 2015 remains high. As in years past, JCDL received a wealth of quality submissions. Each paper was read and rated by at least 3 reviewers. Each paper was then read by additional meta-reviewers who reconciled first level reviews and formulated a recommendation for the Program Committee as a whole. Final selections reflect the outcome of the overall paper scores and reviews submitted by the Program Committee members. For this year's conference 18 of 60 full paper submissions (30%) and 15 of 44 short paper submissions (34%) were accepted. We extend our congratulations to the accepted paper authors on their noteworthy accomplishments and acknowledge the many others who submitted strong paper proposals. An additional 22 papers submitted, a mix of both full and short, were converted to and accepted as Posters or Demonstrations on the advice of the Program Committee. Finally, we wish to thank our fellow Program Committee members for their thorough and thoughtful reviews of all of the submissions. Without their expert review of the papers, JCDL would not be possible.

Enjoy your time at JCDL as you find out about new digital library developments, explore new partnerships, meet new colleagues and renew relationships with friends from past DL conferences.

Sally Jo Cunningham
JCDL'15 Program Co-Chair
University of Waikato
New Zealand

Dion Goh
JCDL'15 Program Co-Chair
Nanyang Technological
University, Singapore

Geneva Henry
JCDL'15 Program Co-Chair
George Washington
University, USA

Table of Contents

Session 4: Working the Crowd

Session Chair: Dion Goh *(Nanyang Technological University)*

Session 5: User Issues

Session Chair: Pertti Vakkari *(University of Tampere)*

Session 6: Ontologies and Semantics

Session Chair: Min-Yen Kan *(National University of Singapore)*

Session 7: Non-text Collections

Session Chair: Geneva Henry *(George Washington University)*

Panels

Session Chair: Andreas Rauber (*TU Vienna*) and Hideo Joho *(University of Tsukuba)*

Tutorials

Workshop Summaries

JCDL 2015 Conference Organization

General Chairs: Paul Logasa Bogen II *(Google, USA)*
Suzie Allard *(School of Information Sciences, University of Tennessee, USA)*
Holly Mercer *(University Libraries, University of Tennessee, USA)*
Micah Beck *(University of Tennessee, USA)*

Program Chairs: Sally Jo Cunningham *(Waikato University, New Zealand)*
Dion Goh *(Wee Kim Wee School of Communication and Information, Nanyang Technical University, Singapore)*
Geneva Henry *(University Libraries, The George Washington University, USA)*

Panels Chairs: Hideo Joho *(University of Tsukuba, Japan)*
Andrea Rauber *(Vienna University of Technology, Austria)*

Poster and Demo Chairs: Kyumin Lee *(Utah State University, USA)*
Martin Klein *(University of California, Los Angeles, USA)*

Tutorial Chairs: Udo Kruschwirz *(University of Essex, UK)*
Line Pouchard *(Purdue University, USA)*

Workshop Chairs: Birger Larsen *(Aalborg University, Denmark)*
Jibonananda Sanyal *(Oak Ridge National Laboratory, USA)*

Doctoral Consortium Chairs: Kazunari Sugiyama *(National University of Singapore, Singapore)*
Catherine L. Smith *(Kent State University, USA)*

Doctoral Consortium Committee: George Buchanan *(City University London, UK)*
Huang-Hsuan Chen *(Industrial Technology Research Institute, Taiwan)*
Sally Jo Cunningham *(Waikato University, New Zealand)*
Richard Furuta *(Texas A&M University, USA)*
Liangcai Gao *(Peking University, China)*
Michael Nelson *(Old Dominion University, USA)*
Edie Rasmussen *(University of British Columbia, Canada)*
Laure Soulier *(University Paul Sabatier, France)*

Publications Chair: Liangcai Gao *(Peking University, China)*

Publicity Chair: Unmil Karadkar *(The University of Texas at Austin, USA)*

Continuity Advisor: Richard Furuta *(Texas A&M University, USA)*

Steering Committee Chair: Michael Nelson *(Old Dominion University, USA)*

Steering Committee: Edie Rasmussen *(University of British Columbia, Canada)*
Cathy Marshall *(Texas A&M University, USA)*
Richard Furuta *(Texas A&M University, USA)*
Shigeo Sugimoto *(University of Tsukuba, Japan)*
Jose Borbinha *(IST / INESC-ID, Portugal)*
Ed Fox *(Virginia Polytechnic Institute and State University, USA)*
Herbert Van de Sompel *(Los Alamos National Laboratory, USA)*
Maureen Henninger *(University of Technology Sydney, Australia)*
J. Stephen Downie *(University of Illinois, USA)*
Ron Larsen *(University of Pittsburgh, USA)*
Sally Jo Cunningham *(Waikato University, New Zealand)*

Senior Program Committee Members: Maristella Agosti *(University of Padua, Italy)*
Christoph Becker *(University of Toronto, Canada)*
Johan Bollen *(Indiana University, USA)*
Jose Borbinha *(IST / INESC-ID, Portugal)*
George Buchanan *(City University London, UK)*
Donatella Castelli *(CNR-ISTI, Italy)*
Fabio Crestani *(University of Lugano, Switzerland)*
J. Stephen Downie *(University of Illinois, USA)*
Schubert Foo *(Nanyang Technological University, Singapore)*
Edward Fox *(Virginia Polytechnic Institute and State University, USA)*
Luis Francisco-Revilla *(The University of Texas at Austin, USA)*
Ingo Frommholz *(University of Bedfordshire, UK)*
Richard Furuta *(Texas A&M University, USA)*
C. Lee Giles *(Pennsylvania State University, USA)*
Marcos Goncalves *(Federal University of Minas Gerais, Brazil)*
Maureen Henninger *(University of Technology, Sydney, Australia)*
Xiao Hu *(University of Hong Kong, China)*
Min-Yen Kan *(National University of Singapore, Singapore)*
Sarantos Kapidakis *(Ionian University, Greece)*
Martin Klein *(University of California, Los Angeles, USA)*
Carl Lagoze *(University of Michigan, USA)*
Ray Larson *(University of California, Berkeley, USA)*
Andrew MacFarlane *(City University London, UK)*
Catherine Marshall *(Texas A&M University, USA)*
Robert H. McDonald *(Indiana University, USA)*
Carlo Meghini *(CNR ISTI, Italy)*
Wolfgang Nejdl *(L3S and University of Hannover, Germany)*
Michael Nelson *(Old Dominion University, USA)*
Edie Rasmussen *(University of British Columbia, Canada)*
Robert Sanderson *(Los Alamos National Laboratory, USA)*
Heiko Schuldt *(University of Basel, Switzerland)*
Frank Shipman *(Texas A&M University, USA)*
Ingeborg Torvik Solvberg *(Norwegian University of Science & Technology, Norway)*

Senior Program Committee Members (Continued):

Nicolas Spyratos *(University of Paris South, France)*
Shigeo Sugimoto *(University of Tsukuba, Japan)*
Kazunari Sugiyama *(National University of Singapore, Singapore)*
Hussein Suleman *(University of Cape Town, South Africa)*
Herbert Van De Sompel *(Los Alamos National Laboratory, USA)*

Program Committee:

Piotr Adamczyk *(Google, USA)*
Robert Allen *(Yonsei University, South Korea)*
Ahmed Alsum *(Stanford University, USA)*
David Bainbridge *(University of Waikato, New Zealand)*
Thomas Baker *(DCMI Ltd., USA)*
Sean Bechhofer *(University of Manchester, UK)*
Maria Bielikova *(Slovak University of Technology in Bratislava, Slovakia)*
Tobias Blanke *(University of Glasgow, UK)*
Paul Bracke *(Purdue University, USA)*
Pável Calado *(IST/INESC-ID, Portugal)*
José H. Canós *(Universitat Politècnica de València, Spain)*
Vittore Casarosa *(ISTI-CNR, Italy)*
Jason Casden *(NCSU Libraries, USA)*
Lillian Cassel *(Villanova University, USA)*
Youngok Choi *(Catholic University of America, USA)*
Gregory Crane *(Tufts University, USA)*
Theodore Dalamagas *(IMIS-"Athena" R.C., Greece)*
Josep Lluis De La Rosa *(EASY Innovation Center, UdG & RPI, Spain)*
Lois Delcambre *(Portland State University, USA)*
Giorgio Maria Di Nunzio *(University of Padua, Italy)*
Ying Ding *(Indiana University, USA)*
Boris Dobrov *(Moscow State University, Russia)*
Fabien Duchateau *(Université Claude Bernard Lyon 1 - LIRIS, France)*
Erik Duval *(K.U. Leuven, Belgium)*
Kai Eckert *(University of Mannheim, Germany)*
Ricky Erway *(OCLC Research, USA)*
Pierluigi Feliciati *(Università degli studi di Macerata, Italy)*
Nicola Ferro *(University of Padua, Italy)*
Muriel Foulonneau *(Henri Tudor Research Center, Luxembourg)*
Nuno Freire *(The European Library, Netherlands)*
Stephane Gancarski *(Pierre et Marie Curie University, France)*
Manolis Gergatsoulis *(Ionian University, Greece)*
Jane Greenberg *(University of North Carolina at Chapel Hill, USA)*
Elke Greifeneder *(Humboldt-Universitat zu Berlin, Germany)*
Thomas Habing *(University of Illinois, Urbana-Champaign, USA)*
Martin Halvey *(University of Strathclyde, UK)*
Myung-Ja Han *(University of Illinois, Urbana-Champaign, USA)*
Bernhard Haslhofer *(University of Vienna, Austria)*
Bradley Hemminger *(University of North Carolina at Chapel Hill, USA)*

Program Committee (Continued):

Annika Hinze *(University of Waikato, New Zealand)*
Ingrid Hsieh-Yee *(Catholic University of America, USA)*
Jimmy Huang *(York University, Canada)*
Antoine Isaac *(Europeana & VU University Amsterdam, Netherlands)*
Adam Jatowt *(Kyoto University, Japan)*
Leslie Johnston *(NARA, USA)*
Jaap Kamps *(University of Amsterdam, Netherlands)*
Unmil Karadkar *(University of Texas, USA)*
Michael Khoo *(Drexel University, USA)*
Ross King *(Austrian Institute of Technology GmbH, Austria)*
Claus-Peter Klas *(Leibniz Institute for Social Sciences, Germany)*
Stacy Kowalczyk *(Indiana University, USA)*
Alberto Laender *(Federal University of Minas Gerais, Brazil)*
Ronald Larsen *(University of Pittsburgh, USA)*
Jonathan Leidig *(Grand Valley State University, USA)*
Daniel Lemire *(Université du Québec, Canada)*
Chern Li Liew *(Victoria University of Wellington, New Zealand)*
Ee-Peng Lim *(Singapore Management University, Singapore)*
Joan Lippincott *(Coalition for Networked Information, USA)*
Xiaozhong Liu *(Indiana University Bloomington, USA)*
Clare Llewellyn *(University of Edinburgh, UK)*
Fernando Loizides *(Cyprus University of Technology, Cyprus)*
Clifford Lynch *(Coalition for Networked Information, USA)*
Linaza Maria Teresa *(Visual Communication Technologies, Spain)*
Byron Marshall *(Oregon State University, USA)*
Patricia Martin *(California Digital Library, USA)*
Bruno Martins *(Instituto Superior Técnico, Portugal)*
Dana McKay *(Swinburne University of Technology, Australia)*
David Mimno *(University of Massachusets, Amherst, USA)*
Erich Neuhold *(University of Vienna, Austria)*
Glen Newton *(Natural Resources Canada, Canada)*
David Nichols *(University of Waikato, New Zealand)*
Kjetil Nørvåg *(Norwegian University of Science and Technology, Norway)*
Christos Papatheodorou *(Ionian University, Greece)*
Dimitris Plexousakis *(Institute of Computer Science, FORTH, Greece)*
Thomas Risse *(L3S Research Center, Germany)*
Seamus Ross *(University of Toronto, Canada)*
Stefan Rueger *(Knowledge Media Institute, UK)*
J. Alfredo Sánchez *(Universidad de las Américas Puebla, Mexico)*
Michalis Sfakakis *(Ionian University, Greece)*
Ali Shiri *(University of Alberta, Canada)*
Joan Smith *(Linear B Systems, USA)*
Lloyd Smith *(Missouri State University, USA)*
Julie Speer *(Virginia Tech Libraries, USA)*
Lisa Spiro *(Rice University, USA)*

Program Committee (Continued):

Besiki Stvilia *(Florida State University, USA)*
Tamara Sumner *(University of Colorado at Boulder, USA)*
Sue Yeon Syn *(The Catholic University of America, USA)*
Atsuhiro Takasu *(National Institute of Informatics, Japan)*
Nicholas Taylor *(Stanford University Libraries, USA)*
Manfred Thaller *(Universität zu Köln, Germany)*
Giannis Tsakonas *(University of Patras, Greece)*
Chrisa Tsinaraki *(European Union - Joint Research Center, Italy)*
Pertti Vakkari *(University of Tampere, Finland)*
Nicholas Vanderschantz *(University of Waikato, New Zealand)*
Andre Vellino *(University of Ottawa, Canada)*
Simeon Warner *(Cornell University, USA)*
Anne L. Washington *(George Mason University, USA)*
Michele Weigle *(Old Dominion University, USA)*
Michael Wright *(UCAR, USA)*
Iris Xie *(Universty of Wisconsin-Milwaukee, USA)*
Patrick Yott *(Northeastern University, USA)*
Maja Žumer *(University of Ljubljana, Slovenia)*

JCDL 2015 Sponsors & Supporters

Sponsors:

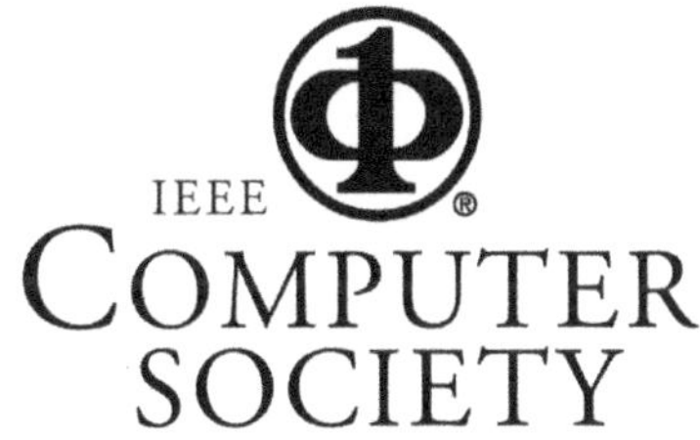

Supporters:

GRADUATE SCHOOL OF LIBRARY AND INFORMATION SCIENCE
The iSchool at Illinois

Other Assistance:

The Google Cultural Institute Tools for Libraries, Archives, and Museums

Piotr Adamczyk
Google Inc.
London, UK
pdadamczyk@google.com

ABSTRACT

1. In 2011, Google launched the Google Art Project, an ever-growing repository of artworks from Museums around the globe, quickly followed by the expanded Google Cultural Institute. Efforts like these with the cultural sector use a combination of Google technologies and expert information provided by partner institutions to create unique online experiences. Spurred on by our partners, we've been adding features to our platform - content hosting, embeddable image viewers, exhibit creation tools - and making Google technology work for Museums - high-resolution imaging, mobile publishing, and experiments in VR. Building these projects requires a deep understanding of library, archival, and museum practices and standards as well as providing tools that can be used by a wide array of partners at different stages of cataloging and digitization. So, how are we doing? We'll discuss reactions to the work so far, present some of our latest attempts to do more with cultural heritage online, and talk about how Google would like to further engage with cultural partners.

2. Categories and Subject Descriptors

H.3.7 [Digital Libraries]: Collection; Dissemination; User issues

J.5 [Arts and Humanities]: Fine Arts.

General Terms

Management, Design, Human Factors.

Keywords

Google Cultural Institute; Cultural Heritage; Digital Libraries

BIO

Starting with an analyst position at The Metropolitan Museum of Art, as the Data Lead for the Google Art Project, and now on the Content Team of the Google Cultural Institute, Piotr Adamczyk's work is focused on the use of open/linked data in cultural heritage institutions. With undergraduate degrees in Mathematics and Computer Science, Piotr holds graduate degrees in Human Factors and Library and Information Science from the University of Illinois at Urbana-Champaign. Piotr has authored papers, organized workshops, and served as a Program Committee member for Association for Computing Machinery and cultural heritage conferences, and his arts research includes residencies at the Banff New Media Institute, Medialab-Prado, and Eyebeam.

JCDL'15, June 21–25, 2015, Knoxville, Tennessee, USA.
© 2015 ACM. ISBN 978-1-4503-3594-2/15/06…$15.00
DOI: http://dx.doi.org/10.1145/2756406.2756909

Moving the Needle: From Innovation to Impact

Katherine Skinner
Educopia Institute
1230 Peachtree Street, Suite 1900
Atlanta, GA 30309
1-404-783-2534
Katherine@educopia.org

ABSTRACT

The digital library has been on a seemingly insatiable quest for "innovation" for decades. This focus permeates our field, usually in the guise of transforming digital library practices. The themes change over time (e.g., Federating library collections! Digital humanities! Digital preservation! Big data!), but dependably, digital library research projects on "innovation" topics are seeded in abundance each year. Researchers are rewarded (and funded) for their big, experimental ideas, not for successful applications of innovations in practice. Gearing resources toward "innovation" alone prizes the unique or novel approach above the cultivation of our field. Few innovations ever flower and thrive beyond their initial moments in the sun.

What might happen if digital libraries shift their focus from the innovative solution to the *process* of using innovations within networks to actively facilitate system-wide change? Drawing from the disciplines of sociology and economics, Skinner will explore both established and emergent models for system-wide transformation, ultimately asking what digital libraries could accomplish as a field if we shifted our focus from "innovation" to "impact."

Categories and Subject Descriptors

K.4.0 [**Computers and Society**]: General

General Terms

Management, Experimentation, Human Factors, Standardization.

Keywords

Digital preservation. Distributed. Community models. Innovation. Impact. Workflows. Standardization. Collective Impact. Funding models; Alignment

JCDL'15, June 21–25, 2015, Knoxville, Tennessee, USA.
ACM 978-1-4503-3594-2/15/06.
DOI: http://dx.doi.org/10.1145/2756406.2756408

The HathiTrust Research Center

Providing Analytic Access to the HathiTrust Digital Library's 4.7 Billion Pages

J. Stephen Downie
The University of Illinois at Urbana-Champaign
jdownie@illinois.edu

ABSTRACT

This lecture provides an update on the recent developments and activities of the HathiTrust Research Center (HTRC). The HTRC is the research arm of the HathiTrust, an online repository dedicated to the provision of access to a comprehensive body of published works for scholarship and education. The HathiTrust is a partnership of over 100 major research institutions and libraries working to ensure that the cultural record is preserved and accessible long into the future. Membership is open to institutions worldwide.

Over 13.1 million volumes (4.7 billion pages) have been ingested into the HathiTrust digital archive from sources including Google Books, member university libraries, the Internet Archive, and numerous private collections. The HTRC is dedicated to facilitating scholarship by enabling analytic access to the corpus, developing research tools, fostering research projects and communities, and providing additional resources such as enhanced metadata and indices that will assist scholars to more easily exploit the HathiTrust materials.

This talk will outline the mission, goals and structure of the HTRC. It will also provide an overview of recent work being conducted on a range of projects, partnerships and initiatives. Projects include Workset Creation for Scholarly Analysis project (WCSA, funded by the Andrew W. Mellon Foundation) and the HathiTrust + Bookworm project (HT+BW, funded by the National Endowment for the Humanities). HTRC's involvement with the NOVEL(TM) text mining project and the Single Interface for Music Score Searching and Analysis (SIMSSA) project, both funded by the SSHRC Partnership Grant programme, will be introduced. The HTRC's new feature extraction and Data Capsule initiatives, part of its ongoing work its ongoing efforts to enable the non-consumptive analyses of the approximately 8 million volumes under copyright restrictions will also be discussed. The talk will conclude with some suggestions on how the non-consumptive research model might be improved upon and possibly extended beyond the HathiTrust context.

Categories and Subject Descriptors

H.3.7 [Digital Libraries]: Collection; Dissemination; User issues

General Terms

Management, Design.

JCDL'15, June 21–25, 2015, Knoxville, Tennessee, USA.
ACM 978-1-4503-3594-2/15/06.
DOI: http://dx.doi.org/10.1145/2756406.2756909

Keywords

HathiTrust Research Center; Analytic Access; Digital Libraries

BIO

J. Stephen Downie is the Associate Dean for Research and a Professor at the Graduate School of Library and Information Science at the University of Illinois at Urbana-Champaign. Dr. Downie is the Illinois Co-Director of the HathiTrust Research Center. He is also Director of the International Music Information Retrieval Systems Evaluation Laboratory (IMIRSEL) and founder and ongoing director of the Music Information Retrieval Evaluation eXchange (MIREX). He was the Principal Investigator on the Networked Environment for Music Analysis (NEMA) project, funded by the Andrew W. Mellon Foundation. He was Co-PI on the Structural Analysis of Large Amounts of Music Information (SALAMI) project, jointly funded by the National Science Foundation (NSF), the Canadian Social Science and Humanities Research Council (SSHRC), and the UK's Joint Information Systems Committee (JISC). He represents the HTRC on the NOVEL(TM) text mining project and the Single Interface for Music Score Searching and Analysis (SIMSSA) project, both funded by the SSHRC Partnership Grant programme. All of these aforementioned projects share a common thread of striving to provide large-scale analytic access to copyright-restricted cultural data. Stephen has been very active in the establishment of the Music Information Retrieval (MIR) community through his ongoing work with the International Society for Music Information Retrieval (ISMIR) conferences. He was ISMIR's founding President and now serves on the ISMIR board. Along with Robert MacDonald of Indiana University he co-chaired the 2013 Joint Conference on Digital Libraries (JCDL). Dr. Downie currently serves on the JCDL steering committee. Professor Downie holds a BA (Music Theory and Composition) along with a Master's and a PhD in Library and Information Science, all earned at the University of Western Ontario, London, Canada.

Result List Actions in Fiction Search

Pertti Vakkari
School of Information Sciences
FIN-33014
University of Tampere, Finland
Pertti.Vakkari@uta.fi

Janna Pöntinen
School of Information Sciences
FIN-33014
University of Tampere, Finland
Janna.Pontinen@outlook.com

ABSTRACT

It is studied how users browse search results to find interesting novels for four search scenarios. It is evaluated in particular whether there are differences in search result page (SERP) browsing patterns and effectiveness between an enriched catalog for finding fiction compared to a traditional public library catalog. The data was collected from 30 participants by eye-tracking and questionnaires. The results indicate that the enriched catalog supported users to identify sooner and more effectively potentially clickable items on the results list compared to a traditional public library catalog. This is likely due to the more informative metadata in the enriched catalog like snippets of content description on the result list items. The discussion includes a theoretical and empirical comparison of findings in studies on fiction and non-fiction searching.

Categories and Subject Descriptors

H.3.7. [**Digital Libraries**]: User Issues; H3.4. [**Systems and Soft ware**]: Performance evaluation

General Terms

Performance, Human Factors

Keywords

Fiction Retrieval; Selecting Novels; Public Libraries; Catalogs; Metadata; Result List; Interest Grades; Eye Tracking; Relevance

1. INTRODUCTION

Fiction reading is a major leisure time interest among the adult population in many countries. E.g. in the U.S. in 2013, 81 % of adults had read a book in the previous year. They read on average 13 books per year [17]. Public libraries are among the major sources of fiction in the population. Borrowing books is the most popular activity among library users [17]. Enjoying reading books, fiction in particular, was clearly the major outcome of using the public library in Finland, Norway and the Netherlands [22].

The proportion of fiction books in electronic form is increasing. 26 % of the top 50 novels sold in 2012 in the U.K. were in electronic form [8]. In years to come, readers will increasingly enjoy fiction literature electronically. In bookshops such as Amazon, accessing and selecting books takes place totally in an electronic environment. In the near future, readers will face the same development in public libraries. Online catalogs have facilitated for a long time accessing fiction through metadata. When fiction is available in libraries in electronic form, accessing, identifying and selecting books to read based on metadata is linked with browsing and reading text in the books.

Therefore, it is necessary to study how readers access and select books by using metadata in order to inform the designing of metadata for fiction searching. E.g. Adkins and Bossaler [1] argue that online catalogs are effective in known author or known title searches, but not as effective in supporting browsing books for other purposes. They call for studies on actual fiction searching practices of readers using electronic access tools like catalogs to determine how those readers make book selection decisions in the absence of the physical book.

There are attempts to enrich catalogs in public libraries to better serve the needs of fiction readers e.g. by indexing fiction, enhancing browsing facilities or adding more content information to metadata [e.g. 13, 24]. However, there are only a handful of studies evaluating fiction search systems [e.g. 16, 21, 23], because almost all IR evaluation has focused on searching non-fiction. Thus, it is vital to study to what extent these enriched catalogs help readers to find fiction books compared to traditional ones.

The aim of this study is to analyze how users browse search result pages (SERP) to find interesting novels for various search scenarios. It is evaluated whether there are differences in SERP browsing patterns and effectiveness between an enriched catalog for finding fiction compared to a traditional public library catalog.

2. RELATED RESEARCH

There is a growing tradition of eye-tracking studies on user behavior on SERP and content pages when assessing the value of documents [6]. However, most of these studies focus on finding non-fiction instead of fiction [23]. In the following we briefly introduce eye-tracking studies on examining SERPs when searching for non-fiction and then for fiction books.

2.1 Examining SERP for Non-fiction

Eye-tracking experiments reveal that searchers fixate on the first few items in the result list; the higher the rank of the item, the shorter the arrival time and the more time is devoted on examining it [2, 7, 12]. Cutrell and Guan [2] reported that users examined the first eight results before reformulating a query. Liu et al. [9] observed that users inspected 1.6 SERPs during unsuccessful query reformulation intervals (QRI) and 2.6 SERPs during successful QRIs. They tend to view the results in a roughly linear order from top to bottom, although they may skip some items and scan backwards on SERP [2, 7, 12]. When browsing SERPs, users typically clicked more highly ranked results [7, 12].

Jian et al. [6] analyzed SERP browsing patterns in complex search tasks. They found out that in complex search tasks, results in lower rank positions of SERP can still get substantial visual attention after multiple SERP views. Moffat et al. [12] also observed that in complex search tasks users tend to explore the

JCDL'15, June 21–25, 2015, Knoxville, Tennessee, USA.

DOI: http://dx.doi.org/10.1145/2756406.2756911

result list in greater depth. Both Moffat et al. [12] and Jian et al. [6] observed that instead of scanning the whole page, users focus on an area of 3-4 results in a SERP view and usually skip results in browsing. Jian et al. [6] specified, that in an exploratory search task users browsed larger areas and skipped more results in a SERP compared to a factual known item search task. Thus, more complex tasks seemed to lead to more complex browsing behaviors, e.g. non-linear browsing and scanning larger areas.

Liu et al. [9] compared the characteristics of successful and unsuccessful query reformulation intervals (QRI). A QRI is successful if at least one page was saved for inspection. They found out that compared to unsuccessful QRI, successful QRI lasted significantly longer, and the number of both visited SERPs and content pages were significantly larger, but the mean time per SERP or content page was equal. During unsuccessful QRI users spent proportionally more time on SERPs compared to content pages, while during successful QRI proportionally most attention was devoted to content pages instead of SERPs.

Liu et al. [10] modeled user search behavior for predicting document usefulness. Users rated the usefulness of each page saved for tasks. The authors used binary recursive partitioning for identifying the most important predictors of useful pages. Dwell time on documents was the most important variable in the model, followed by time to the first click and the number of visits on a page. Long dwell time, more than one visit on a page, and short time to the first click predicted usefulness.

The above findings seem to show that when examining SERPs users typically focus on the top ranked results, which they also more likely click. Users scan items from top to bottom, although they may skip some items and also move upwards on the list. While examining results users tend to focus on a cluster of a few items on the list before skipping to the next one. In complex search tasks they browse the result list deeper, scan larger areas and skip more than on simpler searches. Studies also hint that compared to unsuccessful QRIs, in successful QRIs users examine and click more results and spend proportionally more time on content pages compared to SERPs.

2.2 Selecting Fiction

There is a total lack of studies on SERP examination behavior in searching for fiction books. Therefore we present findings on examining clicked book pages when selecting fiction in online catalogs.

Pöntinen and Vakkari [16] studied how readers explore metadata in clicked book pages when selecting fiction in two public library catalogs. They analyzed eye-movements of 30 participants selecting fiction for four search tasks. The results indicated, that although participants devoted most attention in book pages to content description and keywords, these had no bearing on selecting an interesting novel. Author and title information received less attention, but were significant predictors of selection.

Vakkari et al. [23] studied how searchers explore metadata in book pages when selecting novels of varying interest levels. 30 participants searched for interesting novels in four search tasks in two public library catalogs. The results showed that the associations of dwell time in clicked book pages and in many metadata types, and novels' interest grading were non-linear. Most time was used for assessing a somewhat interesting novel compared to a non-interesting or very interesting one. Therefore, the binary classification of interest grading hides and over-emphasizes the contribution of the "somewhat interesting" category in modeling interest by dwell time in book pages or metadata.

They found out also that searchers visited a larger number of metadata types and spent proportionally more time on interesting pages compared to non-interesting ones. It seems that more metadata types are used for selecting an interesting novel than excluding a non-interesting one. This hints that the inference that a novel is interesting is made based on more versatile metadata compared to a non-interesting one.

3. RESEARCH DESIGN

3.1 Research Questions

The aim of the study is to analyze users' actions on search result lists between the catalogs and how the actions are associated with the dwell time on book pages and books' interest grading in selecting fiction. The particular research questions are:

1) Are there differences in the behavior of users on result lists between clicked and not clicked book pages?

2) Is there an association between users' behavior on result lists and the decision to click a book page?

3) How users' behavior on the result list is associated to dwell time on book pages and books' interest grading?

3.2 Search Tasks

We designed four search tasks simulating typical situations in selecting fiction in public libraries [3, 15,18]:

1) Your friend, interested in reading, suggests that you should familiarize yourself with the work of the novelist Joel Haahtela. Select a novel by Haahtela, which appeals to you.

2) Search for a novel about friendship, which you would like to read.

3) You would like to familiarize yourself with authors and novels not known to you. Select two works by authors not familiar to you, which intrigue you.

4) You are about to leave for a vacation trip. Find a good novel to read during the trip.

In the first task the name of the author is known. *Author search* is the most common method of searching for novels in libraries [3, 11, 18]. Author search functioned also as an easy task for the participants to start with and familiarize with the system used.

The second task was a *topical search*, where the reader wishes to find a novel on a particular theme [15] The aim of the third task was to generate *browsing*, which is a popular method of choosing fiction [3, 11, 18]. By instructing participants to select works unfamiliar to them we tried to exclude the possibility that they would choose books already known to them in all of the tasks.

The fourth task simulated a situation when a reader tries to find a good read. The aim was to let the participant select a book of her/his liking without limiting it by author, theme or familiarity 15, 18]. We call this task *vacation reading*.

In usability tests it is recommended that the first task should be easy so that the participants relax and experience a feeling of success at the beginning of the test [14]. It is also recommended that the last task should be relatively easy, so that the participants remain motivated until the end of the test. Therefore, all our participants performed author search first. The third task was performed as third by all participants, because we did not want to place that kind of demanding task last. The order of topical search and vacation reading tasks was varied so that the former was the last task for 12 participants and the latter for 18 participants.

3.3 Library Catalogs

The catalogs used were Kirjasampo (http://www.kirjasampo.fi), which is an enriched networked service for fiction literature, and Satakirjastot (http://www.satakirjastot.fi), which is a traditional online public library system. Kirjasampo is a new national fiction portal for public libraries, whereas Satakirjastot represents an established catalog type in public libraries.

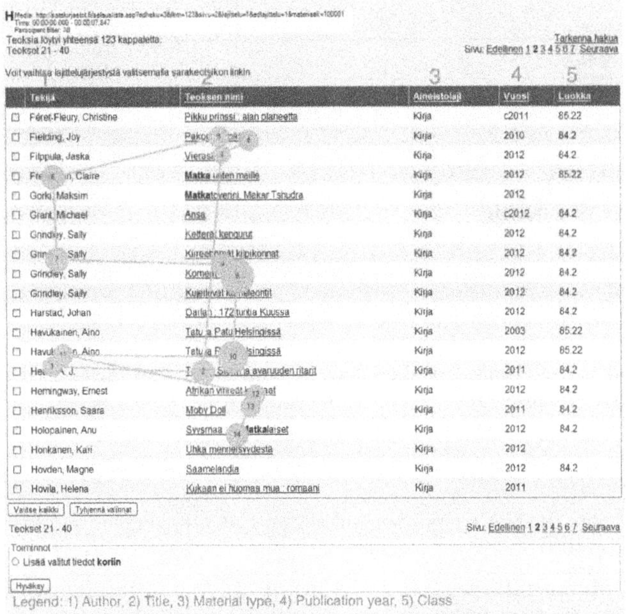

Legend: 1) Author, 2) Title, 3) Material type, 4) Publication year, 5) Class

Figure 1. A SERP in Sata

The result lists in both catalogs are ranked by matching keywords to metadata. In Sata the results are presented alphabetically by author name. In Sampo the results are presented in the ranking order. An item on a result list in Sata consists of author name, book title, material type (e.g. book, CD, etc.), publication year and class A SERP includes twenty items (figure 1). A result list item in Sampo includes book cover, title, a snippet of content description and author name. A SERP covers ten items (figure 2).

Kirjasampo (Sampo) is a fiction literature portal based on principles of the semantic web. In the database in addition to bibliographic information about the books, content and context information is indexed. The database employs functional content-centered indexing, ontological vocabularies and the networked data model of linked data [13]. The Finnish fiction ontology Kaunokki is used for indexing the works in the database.

Sampo has two basic functionalities, searching and browsing. Searching includes the possibility of using text or cover image queries. Users may also utilize book recommendations on the main page or select books through fellow users' bookshelves. As a result of text querying, a list of categories author, person or other actor, and various genres like novels or short stories are provided. After having clicked a category, the user is provided with brief information about the book including the title, author name, cover image and a snippet of content description. By clicking a book title the user is transferred to the information page of the book, which includes the following metadata: author, title, keywords from facets: genre, theme, figures, time and place and other keywords, a content description of the story (typically from the back of the book), a sample text passage, publication data, cover image, possible presentation by other readers, and "see also" recommendations.

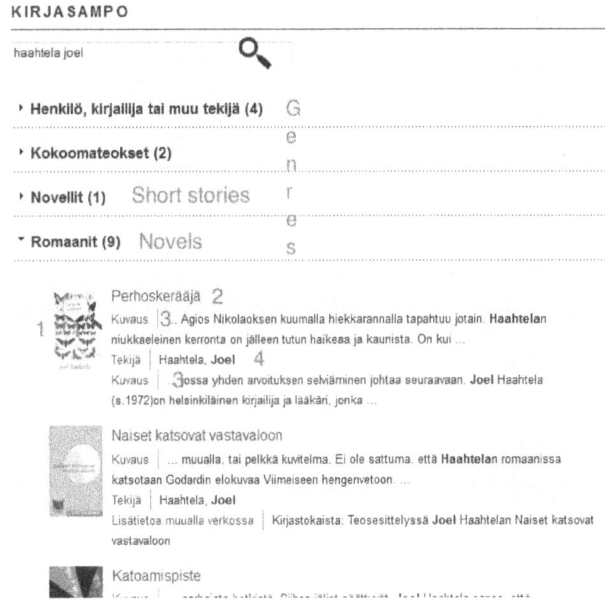

Legend: 1= Cover, 2 = Title, 3 = Content description, 4 = Author.

Figure 2. A SERP in Sampo

Satakirjasto (Sata) is a traditional public library online catalog providing users with quick search, advanced search and a browsing option. Searching starts with querying. In quick search users key in search terms in a textbox, whereas in advanced search in addition to that they may limit the search by the type of literature (fiction – non-fiction), author, title, keywords, or other bibliographic information.

The result list is organized by material type such as books or CDs. In the list the user should click the link "book" in order to explore the list of books retrieved. The list includes the following metadata from each book: author, title, material type, publication year and library class. A click on a book title leads to the book page containing metadata: title, author, publication data, keywords from the fiction thesaurus Kaunokki. The upper right corner includes more recent books, a cover image and a link to the content description of the story.

In general, result lists and book pages in Sampo include more information about the books compared to Sata. A more comprehensive introduction to both catalogs can be found in [23].

3.4 Data Collection

We recruited participants who were interested in fiction literature. We posted announcements on mailing lists for students of information studies and of literature. There were 30 participants in the experiment, of whom 24 were females and 6 males. The number of fiction books read during the last 12 months varied between 1-50, the average being 16.

We used between subjects design assigning 15 participants to Sampo and 15 to Sata. None of the participants had used Sata, whereas two had used Sampo. It is likely that this does not bias the results. A more detailed description of the participants can be found in [23].

Pilot tests were conducted to assess the usability of test arrangements and questionnaires. The actual tests took place in a gaze-tracking laboratory in September 2012. During searching, participants' eye movements were captured by the Tobii T60 eye-tracker. The device included a 17inch screen with the gaze-tracking mechanism. It allowed the users to have free head motion. Before each session participants' eyes were calibrated to the screen to ensure the accuracy of recording. Minimum duration for fixation was set to 100 milliseconds, because it is considered to be the minimum duration for cognitive processing. The sampling data rate was 60Hz. There was no time limit for performing the search tasks.

We collected information using three questionnaires. The first one, filled in before the test, elicited participants' background information such as gender, book reading and library use. After each search they rated on a four-point scale how interesting the novel selected was (very interesting, somewhat interesting, marginally interesting, not interesting, i.e. not selected), and indicated the most decisive metadata item influencing their selection. The test was finished by a questionnaire eliciting participants' assessments of the online catalogs used.

When a participant had filled in the first questionnaire, the purpose and the procedure of the test was introduced followed by the calibration. After that an introduction to the test was presented on the screen, which asked the participants to imagine themselves sitting at home without hurry looking for books to read. After the instruction for each task, the main page of the used catalog was shown automatically on the screen. After the task, the participants closed the browser window, which opened a popup window with two questions concerning the selection of the novel. After the four tasks they filled in the final questionnaire. At the end of the test, the participants received a cinema ticket as compensation.

3.5 Analysis

We focus in this study on the examination of result items on the SERPs. The unit of observation is a search result item on the SERP, which consists of surrogate information concerning a particular book.

We coded from the SERPs the following information: the number of queries producing the search result list, the rank of the search result item fixated from the beginning of the list, the fixation rank of the search result item, the number of unique items fixated prior to clicking, the number of all items fixated prior to clicking, time to the first fixation on an item, time to click, and dwell time on a clicked book page.

For the analysis the interest levels of somewhat interesting and marginally interesting were collapsed due to the small number of cases (n=4) in the latter category. Thus, the interest variable has three values, very, somewhat and not interesting.

4. RESULTS

4.1 Actions on Result List

Users devoted attention to 1855 search results in total, of which they clicked, i.e. opened 434 (23.4 %) book pages for a closer inspection. SERP browsing differs significantly between opened and not opened search results (table 1). Users tend to click results, which were retrieved by a significantly smaller number of queries. Users also clicked results on significantly higher ranks, their fixation rank was smaller, and they were fixated sooner, but on average more frequently compared to non-clicked results.

The results show that in selecting fiction, users tend to scan the result list extensively. The average rank of viewed, but not clicked results was 31.4. It is lower than the clicked ones, which was 23.3. This means that in Sampo users on average visited the third result page, and in Sata the second one. Users also devoted attention on average to 9.6 results before clicking one, and viewed 13.5 results, if they did not click. This seems to differ from the result list behavior in factual searches, where users typically visit only the first page of the result list and look only at the first items on the list [2, 7, 12].

Table 1. SERP behavior in clicked and not clicked results

Variable	Clicked (n=413)	Not clicked (n=1421)	t-test p
# of queries	2.3	2.6	.007
Result rank	23.3	31.4	.001
Fixation rank	9.6	13.5	.000
Time to fixation (sec)	35.6	39.7	.18
# of fixations	2.0	1.2	.000

We also calculated to what extent result rank (Rr) and fixation rank (Fr) differed from each other by subtracting fixation rank from result rank (Rr-Fr). Zero indicates that both ranks are identical. Positive value indicates downwards movement on the list, because users perceived rank of results were smaller than result rank. If the value is negative, it reflects upwards movements on the list. Users' fixation order of SERP items was smaller compared to result rank.

Table 2. The proportion of clicks and the average interest scores by SERP movement type

Movement type	Clicked %	Interest scores
Upwards (n=126)	34.1	0.16
Stabile (n=358)	27.7	0.51
Downwards (n=1271)	16.0	0.51
Total	19.7	0.46

Most of the SERP moves were down the list (72 %). Only a minority (7 %) was directed upwards. The proportion of clicked results among all fixated results differed significantly between movement types (Chi^2: p=0.000) (table 2). Although most of the clicks occurred when users browsed down the list, the chance to click an item was 16 % when browsing down, while 34.1 % in upward browsing. Interestingly, although the chance to click was greatest during upward browsing, the average interest scores were significantly lower when moving upwards compared to other move types (Dunnett C: p<0.05). The results of clicking were likely more disappointing in upward browsing than in downward browsing.

An elaboration indicated that author search differed significantly from other search types in the larger proportion of upward browsing (Dunnett C: p<0.05), in the larger proportion of clicks (author>topical, browsing; Dunnett C: p<0.05), but received lower interest scores (F=3.2; p=0.025). It is evident that it is difficult to find an interesting book among the limited number of titles by a given author likely not known to users. Therefore, they seemed to scan down and up the SERP containing a limited number of titles and to click a lot in order to identify an interesting title. This likely explains the differences in the chance to click and interest scores between SERP movement types.

Table 3. SERP behavior in clicked and not clicked results

Variable	Sata			Sampo		
	+click n=192	- click n=946	Total	+click n=221	- click n=475	Total
# queries	2.9	2.8	2.8	1.8	2.3**	2.2°°°
Result rank	36.5	41.6	40.7	7.8	11.8**	10.3°°°
Fixation rank	13.2	16.3**	15.8	5.5	7.9***	7.3°°°
Time to fixation (sec)	45.2	45.6	45.5	28.0	27.4	27.8°°°
# fixat-ns	2.2	1.2***	1.4	1.8	1.3***	1.4

Legend: * = p<.05, ** = p<.01, ***= p<.001 (within system), °= between systems

Compared to Sampo for finding an interesting novel, Sata users submitted significantly more queries (p=0.000), devoted attention to results lower on the list (p=0.000) fixated on more results (p=0.000), and used more time before the first fixation on a result (p=0.000) (table 3). However, there were no differences between the systems in the average number of fixations on a result (p=0.39). As a result of SERP exploration, users clicked 18 % of fixated items in Sata, while 32 % in Sampo (p=0.000). Thus, it seems that users needed more search actions and spent more time on the result list for identifying interesting results to click in Sata compared to Sampo. E.g. the average rank of results viewed was 41 in Sata, while 10 in Sampo. The average number of results fixated was 16 in Sata and 7 in Sampo. This is naturally reflected in the time of the first fixation on a result, which was 66 % longer in Sata compared to Sampo. This greater effort in Sata resulted in a significantly lower proportion of clicks compared to Sampo.

In Sata there were no differences between the clicked and not clicked results in the number of queries, the result rank and time to first fixation. Fixation rank and the number of fixations were significantly higher in clicked than not clicked items in Sata. In Sampo clicked results were found by significantly fewer queries on better result ranks viewing less results, but by more views per item.

Table 4. SERP behavior by the type of search task (Anova)

Variable	Author n=247	Topical n=602	Brows. n=781	Vacat. n=204	p
# of queries	1.1	2.4	3.3	1.9	.000
Result rank	6.3	34.6	37.5	14.3	.000
Fixation rank	5.0	15.5	14.9	5.4	.000
Time to fixation	19.0	53.7	40.8	11.2	.000
# of fixations	2.2	1.3	1.3	1.4	.000
%clicked/fixated	38	17	21	34	.000

Search tasks differed significantly in each result list action (p=0.000) (table 4). Compared to other search types, author search required significantly less effort in the form of queries, of the rank of viewed results, and of time to the first fixation on an item, but more views per result (Dunnett C: p<0.05). It required less effort in author search to identify a potentially clickable item, but more views to ascertain its worth to be clicked compared to other search types.

The vacation reading task required significantly less effort in all result list actions except in the number of views compared to topical search and browsing tasks (Dunnett C: p<0.05). The two search tasks requiring less effort resulted also in the largest proportion of clicks of all items viewed compared to other search tasks (Dunnett C: p<0.05). While during the inspection of SERP the change to click was 38 % in author search and 34 % in vacation reading, it was only 21 % in browsing and 17 % in topical search.

Topical search and browsing tasks required most effort to identify clickable items on the result list compared to other search types (Dunnett C: p<0.05). It is likely that in vacation reading users may identify titles from authors known to and liked by them, which may have reduced the amount of result list actions and the time spent on those actions. In topical search and browsing tasks it is much more unlikely that users would have run into a familiar author, which would have facilitated finding an interesting book with less effort. Identifying a truly unknown title seems to lead to formulating more queries, browsing the result list more deeply, and viewing more items. Interestingly, it seems that compared to browsing in topical search, users devoted more attention to items on the list, because the viewing rank was about the same in both, while it took significantly longer to the first view on an item in topical search. On the other hand, the browsing task required significantly more queries compared to topical search. Thus, topical search required less effort in the querying stage, while more effort in result list inspection compared to browsing.

4.2 Predicting Clicks

Next we analyze the associations between SERP behavior and the decision to click a book page by using binary logistic regression analysis. It allows the use of categorical variables as independent variables and does not require linear relationships between the independent variables and the dependent variables [5]. We include in the model only those variables, which contributed significantly to the decision to click. The category "not clicked" was used as a reference.

The Chi^2 of the omnibus test was significant (p=0.000) indicating that the final model predicts significantly better the odds of clicking compared to the model with only the intercept, which is the default model. The Hosmer and Lemeshow test of the model was significant (p=0.000) meaning that predicted and observed data matrixes did not resemble each other well, which is a drawback. Nagelkerke pseudo R^2 was 0.33, which means that the model explains about 33 % of the variation in clicks.

Table 5 shows that all the independent variables except the type of search task are significant and help predict the odds to click. The strongest predictor is the number of items viewed on a result list (Wald=212.9, p=0.000), followed by fixation rank (Wald=27.9, p=0.000), SERP movement type (Wald=19.7, p=0.000), time to the first fixation (Wald=19.2, p=0.000), result rank (Wald=17.8, p=0.000) and system (Wald=8.7, p=0.003).

Exp(B) is the odds ratio for the explanatory variables. Exp(B) = 1 means that an explanatory variable does not affect dependent variables. The number of items viewed on the result list decreases the odds of clicking about four times, while upwards browsing on the SERP increases the odds of clicking about three times compared to downwards browsing. Also using Sampo for searching instead of Sata increases the chance of clicking 1.7 times. Compared to author search vacation reading search increases 1.7 times the odds of clicking. Other variables, although contributing significantly, do not increase the odds of clicking much from one. Thus, devoting attention to a few items on the SERP before observing an item (a high fixation rank) and browsing upwards when using system Sampo, in particular increases the odds of clicking an item.

Table 5. Modeling clicks by logistic regression (n=1755)

Variable	Wald	Sig	Exp (B)
Rank	17.8	.000	1.01
Fixation rank	27.9	.000	0.93
# of items fixated prior the 1st fixation	212.9	.000	4.13
Time to the 1st fixation	19.2	.000	1.01
SERP movement	19.7	.000	
• Upwards	19.6	.000	3.09
• Stabile	0.45	.50	1.14
System: Sampo	8.7	.003	1.66
Search task	4.7	.20	
• Topical	0.41	.52	1.17
• Browsing	1.46	.23	1.32
• Vacation	4.1	.042	1.74

4.3 SERP Behavior on Clicked Pages

Next we will take a closer look at SERP actions on clicked book pages. Users clicked (opened) 445 book pages, of which they assessed 67 as very interesting, 78 as somewhat interesting and 268 as non-interesting (table 6).

Table 6. SERP behavior of clicked book pages by interest level

Interest/ Variable	Non (n=268)	Somewhat (n=78)	Very (n=67)	Anova p
# of queries	2.4	2.3	2.1	.90
Result rank	21.7	27.9	24.5	.54
Fixation rank	9.7	11.2	7.3	.21
# of items fixated	11.8	13.7	11.2	.46
Time to fixation (sec)	39.3	35.1	21.1[1]	.07
Time to click (sec)	63.0	59.8	35.2[2]	.007
# of fixations	2.0	2.1	1.8	.23
# of clicked items	3.8	3.8	3.0	.10
Time on a book page (sec)	14.7[3]	29.4	22.6	.000

Legend: [1)] Very < Not; [2)] Very < Somewhat, Non; [3)] Non < Somewhat, Very ($p<0.05$ Dunnett C).

There were no differences between opened book pages of various interest levels in the number of queries, in the average rank of viewed items, in fixation rank, in the number of items viewed prior to clicking, in the average number of views per clicked item and in the number of clicked items prior to opening the selected page. Although these differences were not statistically significant, they were systematic in the sense that users seemed to use more effort in observing somewhat interesting items compared to not interesting or very interesting ones.

Users viewed and clicked significantly sooner items on the list, which were later assessed as very interesting compared to not interesting or somewhat interesting ones (Dunnett C: $p<0.05$). Also dwell time on clicked, non-interesting book pages was significantly shorter compared to more interesting ones (Dunnett C: $p<0.05$). Thus, it seems that users devoted attention sooner to result list surrogates of very interesting book pages compared to less interesting ones. Opened, very interesting book pages were explored for longer after a rapid identification and inspection on the result list, compared to non-interesting, in particular.

4.4 Modeling the Selection of Novels

Next we analyze how various actions on the result list and the dwell time on the clicked book pages were associated with the interest scores of books. We wish to know which variables distinguish both very interesting and somewhat interesting books from non-interesting ones. For the analysis multinomial logistic regression was used. It is an extension of binary logistic regression allowing the use of more than two categories in the dependent variable [5]. We included in the model only those variables which contributed significantly to interest scores. The category "not interesting" was used as a reference.

Model fitting information was significant ($p=0.000$) indicating that the final model predicts significantly better the odds of interest levels compared to the model with only the intercept. The goodness of fit test of the model was not significant ($p=0.64$) meaning that predicted and observed data matrixes did resemble each other. Nagelkerke pseudo R^2 was 0.35, which hints that the model explains about 35 % of the variation in interest scores.

The independent variables significantly predicting both positive interest grades differ somewhat (table 7). The variables significantly distinguishing somewhat interesting novels from not interesting ones are dwell time on a book page (Wald=40.6, p=0.000), system type (Wald=8.38, p=0.004) and time to click (Wald=7.89, p=0.005). The variables significantly predicting very interesting novels compared to not interesting ones are dwell time on a book page (Wald=15.39, p=0.000), fixation rank (Wald=12.53, p=0.000), the number of items viewed on the result list (Wald=10.85, p=0.001), time to click (Wald=5.89, p=0.015) and search tasks author search (Wald=9.49, p=0.002) and browsing (Wald=0.51, p=0.043).

The model indicates that the shorter the time to click, the longer the dwell time is on a book page, using system Sampo for certain search task types increases the odds of selecting a novel as somewhat interesting instead of not interesting.

All variables except system type predicted significantly the odds of selecting a book as very interesting compared to a non-interesting one. The model indicates that the less items on a result list were viewed, and the higher the fixation rank and the less time to clicking a book page, and the longer the dwell time on a book page, the greater chance of selecting a very interesting novel. Also certain search task types increased the odds of selecting a very interesting novel instead of a non-interesting one. Thus, is seems that the sooner users find a potentially clickable item on a SERP and the sooner they click it, and the longer they devote attention to an opened book page, the greater the chance that the book is very interesting.

Table 7. Modeling interest grades by multinomial logistic regression (n=338)

Variable	Wald	Sig	Exp (B)
Somewhat interesting			
# of items fixated prior 1st fixation	1.50	.22	1.06
Fixation rank	0.13	.72	0.99
Time to click	7.89	.005	0.99
Time on a book page	40.60	.000	1.08
System: Sampo	8.38	.004	1.44
Search task			
• Author	2.64	.10	2.75
• Topical	0.20	.66	1.34
• Browsing	0.96	.33	1.82
Very interesting			
# of items fixated prior 1st fixation	10.85	.001	1.17
Fixation rank	12.53	.000	0.86
Time to click	5.89	.015	0.98
Time on a book page	15.39	.000	1.06
System: Sampo	3.13	.077	2.10
Search task			
• Author	9.49	.002	0.11
• Topical	1.48	.22	0.54
• Browsing	0.51	.043	0.35

5. DISCUSSION

There is a rich tradition of eye-tracking studies focusing on SERP behavior when assessing the value of non-fiction documents in information retrieval [6]. To our knowledge, this is the first study exploring how users examine SERP when selecting fiction. We analyzed how users inspected search results in two public library catalogs when searching for interesting novels in four search tasks.

The findings show that in selecting fiction, users tend to scan SERPs extensively. The average rank of viewed, but not clicked result was 31.4. It was lower than the clicked ones, which was 23.3. This means that in Sampo users visited on average the third result page, and in Sata the second one. Users examined on average 15.1 unique results, of which they clicked 3.5 items

Author search and vacation reading tasks required significantly less effort to identify a clickable item resulting in proportionally more clicks compared to topical search and browsing tasks. In the latter tasks users likely had a much smaller chance to run into a familiar author, whose work would have been easier to identify as an interesting novel. Moreover, in author search, the number of titles among which to select was notably limited compared to other search types. This evidently led in topical search and browsing tasks, the users to formulate more queries, browse the result list deeper, and fixate on more items.

We modeled by binary logistic regression the chances to click an item on the result list using SERP behavior variables. The SERP behavior variables explained about 33 % of the variance in clicks. Thus, variables outside the model covered two thirds of the variation in clicks. The less items scanned on the SERP before viewing an item (a high fixation rank) and browsing upwards when using the system Sampo, in particular increased the odds of clicking an item.

5.1 SERP behavior leading to book pages of varying levels of interest

Users devoted attention significantly sooner to the result list surrogates of very interesting book pages, which they also clicked sooner compared to less interesting ones. Opened, very interesting book pages were explored for longer after a rapid identification and inspection of the result list, compared to non-interesting book pages, in particular. Thus, it took less time to identify a potentially clickable item on the list and to decide to click it if the book page turned out to be very interesting compared to less or not interesting ones. Users, however, spent more time in assessing a book page as very interesting compared to a non-interesting one. The findings by Liu et al. [10] correspond to ours, when they found out that the shorter the time to click and the longer the dwell time on a document, the more likely the document is to be useful.

Our results confirm our previous finding [23] that users spend most time in assessing a book page as somewhat interesting compared to very interesting and not interesting ones. It takes least time to decide that a book page is not interesting. Our results correspond to the findings of an eye-tracking study by Gwidzka [4], that it requires most cognitive effort to identify a partially relevant document, and least effort to infer that a document is not relevant. Relevant documents were continuously read, while irrelevant ones were scanned. Although our results were based on book pages and not whole documents, it is likely that the same mechanism applies also in our case.

Our previous study indicated that the time spent on a book page was the strongest predictor of books' interest grading [23]. We were curious to know to what extent the SERP behavior in addition to the dwell time on a book page was associated with the books' interest scores. We were interested whether the pattern of SERP behavior variables differed between very interesting and somewhat interesting book pages compared to not interesting ones. Therefore, we modeled books' interest scores by multinomial regression analysis.

The models indicated that the sooner the users clicked an item on a SERP, and the longer they devoted attention to an opened book page, the greater the chance that the book was either somewhat interesting or very interesting. In addition, the odds that a page was very interesting increased the sooner users found a potentially clickable item on a SERP, and also if they used the system Sampo in certain search task types.

5.2 Comparing the Catalogs

There were significant differences between the two catalogs in SERP browsing patterns. The catalog designed for fiction search (Sampo) supported the users to find interesting novels much more effectively compared to a traditional public library catalog (Sata).

Users needed more SERP actions and spent more time on the result list for identifying interesting results to click in Sata compared to Sampo. E.g. the average rank of results examined was 41 in Sata, while 10 in Sampo. The respective figures of clicked items were 37 and 8. The proportion of clicked of all examined results was significantly larger in Sampo (32 % vs. 18 %). It seems that the SERP design in Sampo facilitated a much effective identification of clickable and likely more interesting novels to read. The SERP in Sata consisted of a listing of author names in alphabetical order with book titles, publication year and book class. The SERP in Sampo was ordered by the ranking of books. It included book cover, title, author name and a snippet of book description. Thus, the result description in Sampo contained notably more useful information like book cover and the snippet of content description, which made easier the selection of the item to click.

Our previous results showed that in selecting fiction users spent notably more time on clicked book pages in Sampo compared to Sata [16]. Because there were no differences between the catalogs in the number of opened book pages on various interest levels, it was concluded that a traditional public library catalog outperformed a catalog designed for fiction searching. Users spent more effort in Sampo for selecting an interesting book [16]. However, this conclusion should be smoothed by the observation that the metadata in book pages of Sampo included considerably more content information compared to Sata. Therefore, the difference in dwell time may be caused by richer content information. It may be that the decisions on books' interest level were more informed among Sampo users, despite that there were no differences in the average interest scores between the catalogs.

Our current findings indicate that Sampo users needed significantly less effort in SERPs for identifying a potentially clickable item and in deciding to click it. Due to the richer provision of information in result items, users were able to identify potentially interesting novels higher on the result list and by fewer queries. Also the average interest scores per query were significantly higher in Sampo compared to Sata. Thus, Sampo outperformed Sata in supporting SERP behavior for identifying potentially enjoyable books. It seems that among Sampo users the time saved in SERP actions was used for inspecting more closely the metadata in clicked book pages compared to Sata. The users of Sampo rated content description as the most decisive metadata influencing their decision to select a novel as interesting.

These results strongly suggest enriching SERP item descriptions in traditional public library catalogs with additional metadata like book cover image and the snippet of content description, in particular. This would significantly decrease the effort required in scanning SERPs to identify potentially interesting novels to read.

5.3 Selecting Fiction and Non-Fiction

Due to the large difference in the pattern of SERP actions between the catalogs, it is difficult to compare our findings with result list browsing in non-fiction search. The fiction search tasks in this study also differ from typical search tasks in interactive IR experiments. First, our tasks aimed at finding one interesting book, whereas in IR experiments typical aims vary from finding an item to answer a factual question or to find several topically relevant items [25]. Thus, our tasks were strictly precision-oriented, whereas IR tasks typically vary from precision oriented fact-finding to more recall oriented topical tasks. The second, and more essential difference is the nature of text genres accessed.

It is evident that selecting fiction differs from selecting non-fiction. Studies on relevance show, that topicality, what the document is about, is the major criterion in selecting non-fiction [20]. The topic of a novel plays a minor part in selecting fiction. Readers typically select unfamiliar novels of the authors they like [18]. The name of an author acts as an indicator of a set of criteria associated with a good novel. The name as such is a recommendation of a good read. If readers have no author in mind, they focus on the genre, plot, setting, characters or literary style of a novel [15, 18, 19]. They apply selectively these criteria in reading choices. The criteria vary by the type of readers [19]. Also the substitutability of books differs notably between fiction and non-fiction. Topicality restricts the section of non-fiction to certain items, whereas a novel can be of any theme if the major criterion like genre or literary style is appropriate.

If readers wish to find good reads from authors they do not know, traditional search systems do not help much [1]. If users invent keywords like in topical search, the system ranks the results by topical relevance. However, topical relevance is not among the typical criteria used in selection, but those characteristics in a novel that appeal to the reader [15,18,19]. These may be a compelling plot, interesting characters, a challenging worldview, skillful literary style or exotic setting. If readers are applying any of these criteria in selecting interesting novels on the result list, it is evident that they had to work really hard to find a potentially interesting novel of their liking. This suggests that for serving fiction readers better, current library catalogs have to be enriched in several ways.

One option is fiction indexing using a controlled vocabulary specifically designed for this purpose [cf. 13]. The challenge is, however, how to include e.g. attributes of a compelling plot or skillful literary style in index terms, i.e. those attributes of attracting books used by readers. An additional option is to include in the system command "search for similar books that I like". Naming a book title would spare the readers from troubling their head about articulating the attributes of the novel, but would leave the toil of inventing the attributes to the system. Again, there is no magic wand to produce the keywords for the system. It seems that building recommender systems based on public libraries' loan data would solve this problem. With libraries' big loan data it would be possible to produce and compare long interest profiles, and thus create solid recommendations. In this option, it is not necessary to articulate the attributes of interesting books, because a long interest profile includes them implicitly [19].

5.4 SERP Browsing for Fiction and Non-Fiction

The above limitations should be kept in mind in the following comparison between the two search genres. There are only a limited number of eye-tracking studies providing comparable results. Wu et al. [26] analyzed users' search behavior in six search tasks in which the number and pattern of relevant results were manipulated. They found out that across all search tasks the number of SERPs visited was 1.5, the deepest rank of items clicked was 17.3 and of items hovered 32.2. Jiang et al. [6] showed that users examined on average 16.1 unique results, while they clicked 9.3 results.

These results hint that the behavior in examining SERPs for identifying valuable documents differs between fiction and non-fiction searches depending on the system used for finding fiction. If a special system (Sampo) is used, less effort is required for identifying clickable items compared to non-fiction, whereas by using a traditional system (Sata) more effort is needed. On average, the depth of scanning in SERPs is greater in selecting fiction compared to non-fiction. In fiction search the average scanning depth of both examined and clicked results was about the same as the deepest respective ranks in non-fiction search [26]. Consequently, the extent of examined SERPs was greater in fiction search due to the greater number of results per page. In fiction search users also had to work harder to find clickable results. Although the number of examined results was about the same in both search genres (15.1 vs. 16.1), the number of clicked items was notably smaller in selecting fiction compared to non-fiction (3.5 vs. 9.3) [6]. The latter is naturally in part a consequence of the difference between precision and recall oriented searches.

When identifying interesting novels users tend to click results, which were retrieved by a significantly smaller number of queries than non-clicked ones. Users also clicked results on significantly higher ranks, their fixation rank was smaller, and they were viewed sooner as in Joachims et al. [7] and Moffat et al. [12], but on average more frequently compared to non-clicked results. However, the average rank of a clicked item was 23.3, which is notably lower than in Liu et al. [10]. They found out that the average rank of clicked documents was 7.4 in difficult search tasks and 9.4 in easy tasks.

As in non-fiction search, users tend to browse SERPs in a roughly linear order from top to bottom, although they skipped some results and browsed also upwards [2, 7, 12]. Proportionally most clicks occurred in upward browsing, but the opened book pages resulted mostly in disappointment compared to downward browsing. The reason for this pattern was the nature of author search. When seeking to identify an interesting novel by a given author, the result set is limited, in our case less than 10 titles. It is likely difficult to decide which of the few unknown titles would be interesting to read. This resulted in significantly more upward browsing when users scanned SERP back and forth in order to make their choice. There were no differences in these browsing patterns between other search types.

6. CONCLUSIONS

This was the first study analyzing how users examine SERPs when selecting fiction in two public library catalogs. We found out that the catalog specifically designed for fiction search supported users to identify more effectively clickable items and potentially interesting novels compared to a traditional catalog. Users of the former needed fewer queries, identified clickable items higher on the ranking and needed less time to click an item. This was due to the richer metadata in result items providing users with more information about the content of book and cover image. It evidently led to more rapid and informed decision making about examining the item closer. This suggests enriching the traditional public library SERPs by snippets of content descriptions and cover images.

7. REFERENCES

[1] Adkins, D. & Bossaller, J. E. 2007. Fiction access points across computer-mediated book information sources: a comparison of online bookstores, reader advisory databases, and public library catalogs. *Libr Inform Sci Res*, 29, 354-368. DOI = http://dx.doi.org/10.1016/j.lisr.2007.03.004.

[2] Cutrell, E., & Guan, Z. 2007. What are you looking for? An eye-tracking study of information usage in web search. In *Proceedings of the ACM HCI 2007 Conference on Human factors in computing systems*. ACM, New York, NY, 407-415.

[3] Goodall, D. 1989. *Browsing in the public libraries.* LISU Occasional paper No 1. Library and Information Statistics Unit, Loughborough.

[4] Gwizdka, J. 2014. Characterizing relevance with eye-tracking measures. In *Proceedings of the 5th Information Interaction in Context Symposium.* ACM, New York, NY, 58-67.

[5] Hair, J. F., Black, W. C., Babin, B. J. & Anderson, R. E. 2010. *Multivariate data analysis.* Prentice-Hall, New Jersey.

[6] Jian, J., He, H. & Allan, J. 2014. Searching, browsing, and clicking in a search session: Changes in user behavior by task and over time. In *Proceedings of the 37th ACM SIGIR Conference.* ACM, New York, NY, 607-616.

[7] Joachims, T., Granka, L., Pan, P., Hembrooke, H. & Gay, G. 2005. Accurately interpreting clickthrough data as implicit feedback. In *Proceedings of the 27th ACM SIGIR Conference.* ACM, New York, NY, 154-161.

[8] Jones, P. 2013. E-book sales data, the truth is out there. *Futurebook* 11/1/2013. Retrieved May 6, 2013: http://www.futurebook.net/content/e-book-sales-data-truth-out-there.

[9] Liu, C., Gwizdka, J. and Liu, J. 2010. Helping identify when users find useful documents: examination of Query Reformulation Intervals. In *Proceedings of the 4th Symposium for Information Interaction in Context.* IIiX2010, 215-224.

[10] Liu, C., Belkin, N.J. & Cole, M. 2012. Personalization of search results using interaction behaviors in search sessions. In *Proceedings of the 35rd ACM SIGIR Conference.* ACM, New York, NY, 205-214.

[11] Mikkonen, A. & Vakkari, P. 2012. Readers' search strategies for accessing books in public libraries. In *Proceedings of the 4th Information Interaction in Context Symposium.* ACM, New York, NY, 214-223.

[12] Moffat, A., Thomas, P. & Scholer, F. 2013. Users versus models: What observation tells us about effectiveness metrics. In Proceedings of CIKM 2013, ACM, New York, NY, 659-668.

[13] Mäkelä, E., Hypén, K. & Hyvönen, E. 2012. Improving Fiction Literature Access by Linked Open Data -Based Collaborative Knowledge Storage - the BookSampo Project. *78th IFLA General Conference and Assembly, Helsinki*, http://conference.ifla.org/ifla78

[14] Nielsen, J. 1993. *Usability Engineering.* Academic Press, Boston.

[15] Pejtersen, A. M. 1989. *The Bookhouse: Modeling user's needs and search strategies as a basis for system design.* Risø report M-2794. Risø National Laboratory, Roskilde.

[16] Pöntinen, J. & Vakkari, P. 2013. Selecting fiction in library catalogs: A gaze tracking study. *Proceedings of the 17th international conference on Theory and Practise of Digital Libraries.* LNCS 8092. Springer, 72-83.

[17] Rainie, L. 2014. *The next library and the people who will use it. November 2014.* Pew Research Internet Project. http://www.pewinternet.org/2014/11/13/the-next-library-and-the-people-who-will-use-it/.

[18] Ross, C.S. 2001. Making choices: What readers say about choosing books to read for pleasure. *The Acquisition Librarian,* 13, 5-21. DOI= http://dx.doi.org/10.1300/J101v13n25_02

[19] Saarinen, K. and Vakkari, P. 2013. A sign of a good book: Readers' means of accessing fiction in the public library. *JDoc*, 69, 5, 736-754. DOI: 10.1108/JD-04-2012-0041.

[20] Schamber, L. 1994. Relevance and information behavior. In *Annual Review of Information Science and Technology 29*, M. Williams Ed., Information Today, Medford, NJ, 3-48.

[21] Tang, M-C., Sie, Y-J. & Ting, P-H. 2014. Evaluating books finding tools on social media: a case study of aNobii. *Information Processing and Management* 50, 54-68.

[22] Vakkari, P., Aabø, S., Audunson, R., Huysmans, F., & Oomes, M. 2014a. Perceived outcomes of public libraries in Finland, Norway and the Netherlands. *Journal of Documentation, 70*(5), 927-944.

[23] Vakkari, P., Luoma, A. & Pöntinen, J. 2014b. Book's interest grade and dwell time in metadata in selecting fiction. *Proceedings of IIiX'14 conference* ACM, New York, NY, 28-37.

[24] Van Riel, R., Fowler, O. & Downes, A. 2008. *The Reader-friendly Library Service.* The Society of Chief Librarians, Newcastle.

[25] Wildemuth, B. & Freund, L. 2009. Search tasks and their role in studies of search behaviors. In *Proceedings of HCIR 2009.*

[26] Wu, W-C., Kelly, D. & Sud, A. 2014. Using information scent and need for cognition to understand online search behavior. In *Proceedings of the 37th ACM SIGIR Conference.* ACM, New York, NY, 557-566.

Where My Books Go: Choice and Place in Digital Reading

George Buchanan
City University London
Northampton Square
London EC1V 0HB, UK
+44 (0) 20 7040 8469
george.buchanan.1@city.ac.uk

Dana McKay
Swinburne University of Technology
John Street,
Hawthorn, VIC 3122, Australia
+61 123456789
dmckay@swin.edu.au

Joanna Levitt
City University London
Northampton Square
London EC1V 0HB, UK
Telephone number, incl. country code
joanna.levitt.1@city.ac.uk

ABSTRACT
Digital reading is a topic of rising interest in digital libraries, particularly in terms of optimizing the reading experience. However, there is relatively little data on the patterns of digital reading, including issues of where and what users read, and how they organize, plan and conduct their reading sessions. This paper reports the first data on mobile reading, combining insights from three different studies of users, including diary studies, interviews and ethnomethodological work. The data reveals that reading often depends on highly developed and rehearsed practices, especially when the reading is related to study or research. From this, we are able to identify a number of opportunities for further digital library research to better support the needs of users.

Categories and Subject Descriptors
H3.7. Digital Libraries: User issues;

General Terms
Design, Human Factors.

Keywords
Digital reading; digital libraries; tablet PCs.

1. INTRODUCTION
We know that readers read print in a variety of contexts: travelling, in the library, in bed, and on the beach [19, 20, 30]. Print is, in many ways, suited to a diversity of reading: it stands up reasonably well to the elements, it is relatively cheap to replace, it is easy to mark one's place, and to annotate. In contrast, much recent research notes the rising importance of reading on mobile devices (phones, tablets and ereaders) [7], asserts it as an axiomatic truth [6], or focuses on specific issues of tool design [6,24], there is a relative dearth of evidence about the detailed context in which reading occurs. A better understanding of the physical, social and temporal contexts of reading on mobile devices would better enable us to better design effective systems for mobile reading: from underlying digital library infrastructure to the interface of reading applications and software.

JCDL'15, June 21–25, 2015, Knoxville, Tennessee, USA.
 ISBN 978-1-4503-3594-2/15/06…$15.00
DOI: http://dx.doi.org/10.1145/2756406.2756917

Like work-related reading [1], the mobile reading environment is a complex tapestry of different types of reading, and involves a wide variety of content. It could be disputed, indeed what constitutes mobile reading: is email, twitter use or even social networking 'reading'? Our focus is on the reading of magazine article length or longer, which is more typical of DL content.

Besides questions of material length and type, the issue of how readers use different devices is of increasing interest. While particular attention has been paid to the rise of ereader devices [30] and tablet PCs [24], the increasing size of mobile phone displays, and the shrinking size of laptops, all serve to mean that reading on the move can involve a choice of devices at any one moment. Readers choose not only what material to read, but also on which device and in which context. Such devices *are* used within the home [8], so 'mobile' does not simply imply on-the-move, but also often occurs when seated in a café, or on the sofa. How influential device features, place, and context are on device choice, is an open question.

We draw on three sets of data in this paper. One dataset captures the repertoire of reading undertaken by British university students, including their leisure reading; a second draws on observations of students in a university library in Australia; and the third covers the work-related reading of academic researchers in the humanities, and was gathered over a ten-year period.

A number of common themes and distinct differences emerge, not only along the lines of the reader's background, but also across devices and physical places.

As we shall see, digital reading proves to be highly bounded with social, practical and technological constraints. Choices of what to read when, and on which device, suggest that there are marked differences in behaviors that set markedly different design constraints and goals for practical technology. In turn, digital libraries now face a reassessment of which needs each DL aims to serve, and the likely reading context its technology must serve.

The structure of the paper is as follows: we first briefly recap the broader history of DL research on reading; then we describe the study methods for the three investigations, before reporting the findings, drawing on common themes across all three studies; we then enter the discussion, comparing our insights with existing literature, and draw out our contribution; finally we reflect on directions for future work, and lessons for DL researchers and developers to consider when creating new DLs.

2. BACKGROUND
Reading has long been established as a key topic of research in digital libraries. Previous work spans the range of examining the high-level needs of particular reader groups [5], through investigating particular types of reading [14], to detailed

technological interventions to enhance reading [17, 23]. From the perspective of libraries in general, reading has also proved a long-standing interest, drawing on logs of both ebook reading [21] and borrowing behaviors [13], studies of the impact of library space on reading [32] and interviews with library patrons on their reading needs [32]. With the rise of the mobile reading device, researchers in human-computer interaction have returned to the topic with a level of interest last seen in the early 1980s, when the personal computer emerged as a potential reading tool.

Despite this broad span of investigation, many key gaps remain in our knowledge. Despite advances in digital reading technologies, readers still tend to print digital texts for close study [29], and paper retains a pivotal role in reading. However, there are many reasons why digital reading can be the medium of preference, including the oft-mentioned search [3, 13, 16, 20], cost [10], continuous access [10, 26], and mobile device portability [10, 11] particularly in comparison with books. At present, we have only a limited understand of how these decisions are made by users.

There are other, enduring contexts and issues of reading where we lack a detailed understanding. Reading occurs in different styles: from the close reading of academic scholars [29], through engaged leisure reading of novels [27], and the casual reading of magazines [19], to triage, when a potential reader assesses the relevance of a text [14]. Each of these may provide a reason for selecting a different reading medium. Perhaps more interestingly, these same differences likely occur in different reading contexts of physical and social place, physical space and time. While we have some localized insights into how reading locations are chosen in libraries [32], and indeed how physical library spaces have evolved over time [25], and various essayists have written about their design of their own formal libraries [15], the selection of personal reading spaces, particularly in the context of digital reading devices, is very thinly covered.

3. METHODOLOGY

In this section, we report the method for the three separate studies in turn, noting particularly techniques used in each to elicit insight into how users read. We characterize the participants in each part of the research, and set the context that led to each investigation.

3.1 The reading practices of academics

Humanities academics are regularly noted as voracious and sophisticated readers of long, complex material (e.g. [5,29]. In recent years, there has been an explosion of quality source materials in electronic form, e.g. from the HathiTrust, Google Books and LION. Following the User-Centred Interactive Search project [5], we have gathered three phases of interviews on the information practices of humanities scholars in 2004, '09 and '14.

These academics were recruited from a number of institutions in three countries: New Zealand, the United Kingdom and Canada. Two participants from the original 2004 study, and three from the 2009 study, have been re-interviewed for the current 2014 group. The initial cohort consisted of a total of 19 participants, with 17 in 2004 (three being second interviews), and 16 in 2014 (two being third, three being second interviews). Thus we have a total of 44 respondents, who are presented here as R1-R44. The year of interview is, for second interviews, added in parentheses.

We interviewed participants on a range of topics related to their reading, including the acquisition of documents, digital document access and use and organizing collections in the initial phases, which was analyzed using a grounded theory approach [5]. This coding scheme has been subsequently extended in response to data from the later phases. New themes included ereader devices, reading on the move and the effect of location. These changes reflect the increasing availability of both contemporary research output and period source documents in digital form, and the ready availability of digital reading technologies.

In contrast to the undergraduate diary study (Sec. 3.2), we have not sought to capture the wider reading behaviors of our respondents, but occasional reference will be made to respondents' reading behaviors, as reported by them.

3.2 Reading behavior of university students

We recruited fifteen undergraduates at a British university. Each participant maintained a diary of their reading across one week, supported with both entry and exit interviews. The diary recorded their daily reading, including the time, location, materials and devices used. Reading on paper was not directly asked for in the diaries, however use of paper alongside the devices was captured. Further context, including the use of paper, was elicited in exit interviews. The diary was informed by our previous work on search behaviors using mobile devices [2], and was piloted with two students for validation. As only minor adjustments were found to be necessary following the pilot test, we moved directly to the main study after making adjustments in light of the pilot.

In the entry interview, we took demographic details, the course of study the participant was currently following, their current range of reading devices and materials, and their intended reading goals for the week, if any formal ones existed. The exit interview was used, in contrast, to clarify any diary entries that were difficult to interpret, or to add additional detail in the most incomplete entries. We also invited the participants to reflect on any insights into their reading habits that they had gained from their work on the diaries, and to comment on their reading in general.

Participants were met two days after induction. In that discussion we reviewed their current entries with them, and provided guidance as to the level of detail we expected, and addressed any practical problems encountered by the participant. In three cases further contact was made to ensure that issues from the follow-up session were resolved. Participants received no financial reward.

All data was subsequently analyzed using the qualitative inductive coding method, using no a-priori codes or themes. The coding was conducted by one researcher, who first constructed an initial coding scheme, before proceeding to coding an initial sample and then a complete analysis. Both the coding scheme and the (10%) sample were inspected by a second researcher, the scheme being verified and the sample validated with an agreement rate of over 95%. As is typical for an initial sample on a novel topic, we did not aim to code to the complete exhaustion of themes, but rather we fully coded the most dominant themes found in the data.

3.3 Reading in the Library

The final study in this paper is a longitudinal ethnomethodological investigation of how patrons use academic library space.

In this study we counted, over the course of a semester from initial classes to exams, the number of patrons (mostly students) physically present in a busy academic library in Australia. The library is spread over five levels: the top two are dedicated to silent study and house the majority of the book collection, level 3 has significant social space with moveable furniture and an area of fixed computer desks, level 2 includes the entry and service point, the newspaper table, and fixed computer desks, level 1 includes a large area of fixed computer desks, a dedicated group study area.

Rather than simply counting patrons, we also noted which floor they were on; whether they were using laptops, tablets and books, and made special note when they were using only books. We developed an interest in group-work, thus ended up counting group size, what technologies were in use in groups (including paper) and what kind of seating groups were using over a shorter period. Next we developed a group typology, which included groups that were creating a shared artifact together, groups that were reading together, groups rehearsing talks, informal study groups and social groups. Finally, we conducted anonymous observations of these groups noting particularly their spatial arrangements, negotiations over work, and access to documents.

Our findings on the interactions of groups and space are reported elsewhere [23]. While this study was not dedicated to reading, the use of books and their combination with other devices can give us some insight into the reading ecologies of these students. Further to this our observations of groups provide additional insight into the nature of academic reading in the library. Data from this study is used to enhance and expand understandings gained from the other two studies presented here.

4. RESULTS

In reporting our results, we combine the insights from each of the three studies within the major common themes that emerged: time, material, location, and devices. For the two studies of individual people, we report on selected individuals, who are briefly described in the text. For identification, participants in the student diary studies are referenced by Pn (e.g. 'P6') while academic interviewees are indicated as Rn (e.g. 'R21').

4.1 Reading matter

Within the diary study, we gathered a total of 169 reading episodes from the 15 participants. Table 1 shows the breakdown of device versus reading matter.

Table 1. Device choice and reading activity

Device	Work-related	Pleasure
Mobile phone	6	48
Tablet PC	22	33
Laptop PC	31	22
ereader	0	7
Total	59	110

Only two of our respondents used an ereader device, hence its low apparent use. The data shows mobile phones were only occasionally used for study-oriented reading, but were frequently used for leisure reading, while in contrast laptops were relatively frequently used for work, but less regularly for pleasure. Excluding the few ereader cases, a chi-squared of relative frequencies produces $p<0.0001$ ($X^2=26.39$ df=2), indicating a strong interaction between device type and reading purpose—an issue discussed in the next section.

We are not able, with the academics, to discern such a clear division between devices, and of course the pattern has changed over the ten-year span of the study. Mobile reading devices were almost unknown in 2004, and laptops were the only cited technology then in use. Three respondents reported a reading device in 2009, including R26 already noted above, while by 2014 ten of our sixteen respondents said they now had one—four, like R26, having both an e-Ink device such as a Kindle, well as an iPad or similar LCD device. With this change in technology has flowed a change of material used—in 2009 no-one regularly read journal articles on their device, by 2014 it was universal.

Changes in convenience played a key role here, as one frustrated (2009) Kindle user stated that they "couldn't be bothered with the hassle" with uploading material to their device, and even R26, an enthusiastic use of her Sony Reader for novels, dismissed the idea of using it for reading journal articles due to screen size and the practicalities of installing the files onto the machine.

However, among the humanities researchers there are repeated patterns of allocation of reading particular types of material to chosen locations, either due to a co-incidence in time (e.g. R31's early evening reading of longer material was always at home), or due to more direct preferences of particular places for certain material. One example was the senior literature professor R22 who, while having a well-loved domestic library, preferred to read journals that he was reviewing in a nearby café.

In the library observations, there was a common trait in group reading for different, if related, materials to be read at the same time. An assignment handout (in digital or printed form) would often be read alongside content such as lecture material, textbooks or web sources. Leisure reading was almost exclusively limited to web browsing and occasional newspaper reading: even though the library does retain novels and other leisure material in a dedicated section next to the entrance.

For all three studies, and as amply demonstrated by Table 1's data on undergraduates, there was an interaction between reading purpose and the chosen device, and we now turn to that concern.

4.2 Reading throughout the day

One pattern that was particularly pronounced in the undergraduate diaries was the allocation of reading to particular parts of the day.

Five participants demonstrated a regular pattern of setting aside reading time within an overall plan for the day: e.g. reading in the morning before commuting, then undertaking further reading en route to university, but then reverting to leisure reading later in the day. For example, P2 read a PDF both on his laptop at home and on his iPhone during the commute to university in anticipation of a meeting with his tutor soon after arriving.

However, there were patterns that were more specific to parts of the day. P2 was also one of seven participants who regularly read first thing in the morning (36 entries). Typically this was brief leisure reading. In contrast to the 85 minutes P2 spent on their academic paper, before and during his commute, the morning spell of reading for pleasure seldom exceeded 10 minutes.

In contrast, the evening saw a repeated reading period for work (for 11 participants) and leisure (for ten), though this was usually interrupted on occasional days by social events. P6 was a typical evening reader, ending each day by reading a novel on her iPad.

Among the academic interviewees, reading was more often spread across the day, and in blocks defined by work or home commitments. R27, an English academic, did read at home in the evening, but this was constrained by having a young family. At work he has developed a regular pattern of reading across the week, but this varies from short periods in the morning to a "three hour marathon" on Wednesday afternoons. In contrast, his colleague, R31, regularly read each morning immediately after arriving at work as this was when she was least likely to be disturbed, and read again in the early evening when she returned home. Her morning reading was more focused on reviewing and reading journal articles, whereas she assigned the evening session for reading books and (long) manuscripts.

4.3 Reading location

The location of reading was a recurring and significant trend across all three investigations. We begin with our undergraduate diary studies, before reporting in detail the insights from our interviews with researchers and drawing on the ethno-methodological examination of a working academic library.

4.3.1 Reading at University

For the undergraduates, the university was a key base for their study-related reading. The library and student common rooms were two major locations, and there was almost no leisure reading on site (the one incident occurred when waiting to meet friends). Laptops, tables and mobiles were used with equal frequency, and the choice was often determined by the context of the exact moment of reading. When entirely controlled, laptops and tablets prevailed, and most of the documents had been previously downloaded and stored for reading at university.

Researchers' personal offices were similarly the focus of their academic reading. R23 explained "despite the occasional interruption, it's still the place I'm least likely to be disturbed".

In the 2005 cohort, reading of digital material was limited, and mostly circumscribed to (rare) professional digital transcriptions, supplemented by transcribed material from personal notes of printed texts. A personally maintained collection of print material in the academic office, including borrowed library books, photocopied papers and the researcher's personal collection of print books was their primary pool of reading matter.

R26, a professor of mediaeval history, demonstrated a particularly systematic approach. She noted that "all my writing really happens here"—despite sharing her home with another academic—and her office was carefully arranged with a large number of books, and three filing cabinets of indexed paper. She reported a tight process of managing the material kept in her office, insisting that "every book and paper has to earn its keep". Reading time was scheduled in her diary, in order to ensure that a regular of volume of new text was studied each week. She kept a specific notebook to use while reading at her desk, accompanied by a highlighter pen, pencil and two pens, all placed on a neat pile of current reading. This image of a well-regulated reading routine, carefully planned for with available supporting materials for writing and annotation was exceptionally visible in a thoroughly organized office, but the underlying preparedness was common.

For R26, digital content was—in 2009—an issue of rising importance, especially as her own research involved digitized material. Her own practice in her office with digital material was almost entirely of on-screen reading from her laptop; mostly of digital journals, but also of online scans of mediaeval material. This proved less satisfactory to her : "the online stuff…it's hard to keep organized; if you download it, it becomes a mess, and if you don't, you often lose track of here you got it from… which site you were reading". Thus, while the physical reading space was a well-oiled machine, the digital experience was more chaotic and was proving a source of frustration. As a result, she had developed a practice of printing important material so that it was more easily stored in the physical resources over which she had a better sense of control.

As R23—a U.K. based early career researcher in German literature—noted at the time "you need to be on campus to get the digital stuff" and so the office was in many cases the most convenient place to obtain digital material. In these situations—as was almost unanimously reported by that cohort—reading of secured material was accompanied by note-taking on their desktop or laptop PC, with in a few cases the use of a traditional notebook as well. Neither was particularly satisfactory: As R28 (modern historian) complained "you switch between Word and the web all the time" or "you jot stuff down just to type it in again later".

The office was, however, only part of a wider repertoire of place, and the connections between places varied, and also the type of reading done, in terms of both devices and content, also contrasted between venues. Printed books were reported as primarily residing in either the office or at home, but not often being moved around because of their physical size and weight.

4.3.2 Reading at Home

The second most common location for reading was at home. For the undergraduates, this was the predominant location, in which 68% of all reading sessions occurred. In contrast to university, at home leisure reading predominated, particularly early in the morning and last thing at night.

As with university, there was an equal distribution between laptop, mobile and tablet use. When work reading was done, mostly in the early evening, this was often from material downloaded when at university, or downloaded from the online learning environment when at home. As with reading at the university, paper was used in connection with digital reading, often in the course of textbooks, personal notebooks and occasional class handouts. Paper and electronic documents formed two different resources that were read together for an underlying task (e.g. revising the content of a particular lecture).

All bar two scholars reported reading at home, and for a sizeable minority, it was the primary location for reading. R35 reports one common story: "the office is too busy for me to work there, and I find it too… sterile a place to write, so I tend to read most of my reading—or my most productive reading—at home".

A domestic 'office' was reported by all bar five participants, though it varied from a 'cubbyhole' to an extensive library. R22, a senior English scholar, made a particularly clear distinction between office and home, scarcely reading in his work office, whereas his library "is my real office—the office at the university is only to read with or talk with students". As with R26's work office, the home office could be highly organized (as was the case with R22). However, it faced significant barriers with reading online material during 2004 and 2009, though in 2014 these were reported as being much less (a problem for 5 of 16 participants).

Twenty-eight researchers reported having a personal computer at home, rather than using a laptop that belonged to the university. Using a laptop—be it personal or a 'work' machine—was strongly associated with having different places to work around the house. While R22 kept almost strictly to his library, using a desktop, R24, a drama scholar, provided a more typical case. In addition to having a library-style office upstairs, she also used her living and dining rooms depending upon mood. The library was associated with more intense reading: close reading of plays, reviews of journal articles etc. ; while the living room was used for an occasional 'change of scenery' but more often for an initial reading of an article or book without taking longer notes. The dining room was even more turned towards more general reading.

This distinction between places at home for different reading purposes was mirrored in almost every researcher's reporting: one key reading 'station', well-equipped and organized, is supplemented by other sites for lighter reading or as a necessary retreat when other family members were noisy. R11's articulated another side to this story : "somehow my own home office can be hard to read at, when

I just want to get an overview—it's where I can concentrate, but it's .. it can be too much to read there when I just want to read over something". Hence, rather than there being a single 'ideal' style of reading place, there is a need for a variety of places that are associated with different reading work.

This overlaps, in 2009 and 2014, with a move towards new technologies. R24 was an early adopter of ereading devices, and now possesses both a Sony Reader and iPad. She explained "I loved the Reader for getting about … and the iPad has been better as I can put it on my easel and read from it while I type on my iMac". In this case, R24 had set up the site beside her iMac to optimize reading paper material, but then had co-opted that as a support for her iPad, treating the new device much like a large pad of paper. For R38, just like R24, the iPad occupied a place similar to paper: "I've always tended to read over photocopies and journal printouts on the sofa. More often I tend to that with the iPad now, though I do print to make any detailed notes and to scribble comments on once I know what I'm doing..".

R38 used his laptop in his upstairs office for final detailed readings that would lead to writing, and this was an almost ubiquitous pattern of the PC emerging as the reading device of choice as writing drew near.

Both iPads and laptop computers were reported as being common tools for transporting digital documents from work to home. R40 mirrored R38 and R24's practices, and those of five further tablet owners: "I download things onto the iPad at work now…then I take them home and read on it whenever I have time". One common problem encountered was managing the device's storage as R38 said "you can end up with so much" and "the filenames mean nothing—some number or other .pdf"—which mirrors again the problems with electronic material noted by the highly systematic R26. R39 showed the display of her preferred iPad reading software, exclaiming how "stupid" and "meaningless" the filenames were, and complaining about the fact she frequently had to "hunt out" what the latest document she had added was called.

The home is not a single space, but represents a patina of different devices and places, each providing better or weaker support for different styles of reading. Considerable effort was recorded in bringing the needed combination of print and digital material together to ensure the different content needed is present and usable at the moment of reading. The reading of materials flows from and returns to the academic office, from which most of the digital material is originally sourced. Devices are used both to transport material for reading, and to enable associated work once reading commences. We will address the choice of device once the moment for reading arrives later in this section.

4.3.3 Reading in third places

The home and office provided the two common points for our academics. For most, one or other location was their primary place for reading, but there was a recurring theme of other rehearsed sites that were regularly used. R21, an early career researcher in the social sciences, was one clear example, using a local café which "isn't that noisy, cheap, and they leave me alone". She contrasted the "bright" location where she sat with her small, north-facing, home office where "sometimes the darkness just…it kills me…particularly now, in mid-winter".

While in her case, physical shortcomings in her home proved a key factor in going elsewhere, for R27 and R41, getting away from distractions and noise was the primary reason, both having young families. R27, a new faculty member in 2009, had extended this practice by 2014, depending more on it, but also "I now find that I do my best work outside of the house—in the summerhouse in the garden, or down at the caff" while the home was now used for more functional reading and writing, such as reviews.

R27 again demonstrates the close association between reading and writing, but there are more subtle contexts at play: different resources and tools were to hand at the different locations. R27 kept her personal library at home, but with a dedicated stash of books in the summerhouse, complete with notebook and post-its, mirroring the reading pile in R26's office at work. There was also a separate bag that held materials that rotated between home, work and other locations, with a further notebook, pen and, in 2014, an iPad. R24, the drama academic, had created a similar toolset, as indeed had almost all the 2009 and 2014 cohorts.

The small, focused collection of most immediately valuable books follows the concept of the "handapparat" in (German) library science: a small collection of media brought together for individual use. While this was an established and visible resource in the respondents' working space, three interviewees in the 2009 and eight in the 2014 cohorts had developed a digital equivalent, including either an ereader or tablet PC. R24 initially used her Sony Reader as a mobile pool of original novels, but by 2014 had migrated to using their iPad to store not only novels, but also articles related to her ongoing research work. Two further academics used their laptop as their main digital reading device, having amassed a considerable volume of material over many years. The remainder of the group reported only occasional 'serious' digital reading, usually in a fixed place of work.

However, six of the eight who used tablets and ereaders reported problems in managing the content of their reading devices—noting that it was "easy to keep adding material willy-nilly until you can't…find what you're after". While digital files were easier to transport, the volume of material proved harder to master, and marshaling even smaller sets of documents was noted as being more difficult. R33, a mid-career literature faculty member explained: "with books and paper it is easier to bind and lock things together; to see where you are. With my [i]Pad, it's ordered for me, but in the wrong way"—in her case, the alphabetical ordering system of her preferred reader software could be circumvented by the use of folders and renaming of files but "I just don't have the time for that".

This digital material also had to co-exist as a set with printed and physical documents. All eight reading device users reported that concurrent reading of printed documents and books was a predominant part of their working practice. However, those using laptops would often use either paper on its own, or their laptop on its own, often due to the physical constraints of the weight they carried, or the physical bulk of the laptop in their working environment. Those using reading devices also reported such issues, but their treatment of their tablets was synonymous with the paper practice of their laptop-based colleagues, and the use of a paper 'handapparat' of working documents.

There were also connections between specific handapparat sets and location. Some sets resided in particular locations, such as a summerhouse or, more often, commonly were taken to regular reading locations like R21's café. R24's use of her iPad serves as a case in point: it being used in her kitchen with a set of 19th century novels, but also travelling in her satchel that contained material for a journal article she was completing which typically accompanied her to a favored café and her office. Between these venues, the material being read on the iPad changed, but each location emphasized a particular piece of work.

R33 had a satchel set that was reserved for use on a train, where she regularly worked on an ongoing project. This practice was shared with just over a third of the interviewees in 2009 and '14, who reported that working on trains was a regular, planned space for reading—and one where ereader and tablet users identified their devices as particularly useful. Similar notes about trains were found in the undergraduates, who did 18% of their reading while commuting. However, most of their reading was for leisure, drawing on pre-loaded ebook fiction and online reading of news and culture websites. Four explicitly stated that they would not use laptops on trains due to security concerns, and none recorded their use there. This may also mark a difference between long-distance travel and commuter trains as a working space: with the students reporting use during commuting, while the academics planned reading was rarely during commuting.

4.3.4 Reading in the library

Libraries have themselves been termed 'third places'; and are, of course, understood as places to read within. Over half of our undergraduate diarists reported using their university library as a reading location. In contrast, the academic researchers seldom reported using their university's library as a regular reading space (1 respondent in 2004, 2 in 2009 and none in 2014). However, specific libraries could be adopted as a regular 'roaming' location, either very occasionally (e.g. R3, a New Zealand mediaevalist reported using specific libraries in Europe on each sabbatical), or on a recurring basis (e.g. R30, a specialist in Welsh history, used the National Library of Wales at least once a month).

In the context of our library space study, there was similarly a relationship between different reading tasks and the choice of different places to read. In part this was due to library design choices: the 4th and 5th floors of the library had been set aside as quiet study areas, and were therefore rarely used by groups. However, the remainder of the library contained a variety of PC desks, in different shapes and configurations, group study rooms, informal lounge seating, regular free-standing desks, fixed booths and other types of seating and desk. The same type of desk could be found in different contexts, with variation in lighting, amount of free space, proximity of books or other resources, and, most importantly, the provision of different technology.

Across all our methods of data capture, we discovered marked patterns at both macro- and micro-scale. From the wider perspective, we observed a considerable volume of shorter, work-related reading in the library, mirroring the patterns described by the undergraduate students in their diary studies when reporting their reading activity when on campus.

The observations also hinted at some groups having established favored locations—one social group being particularly visible by their daily presence in an informal seating area. However, some areas were more used for reading than others. Even for groups, areas with a higher footfall were avoided, and groups also avoided long, thin PC benches that spread the members out in a line.

Most of the reading that could be seen in the library was digital, with a variety of supporting paper material (discussed later).

4.4 Device selection

As we have just seen, for undergraduates there was a clear pattern of association between particular devices and either leisure or work-related reading. Responses from our participants in the exit interviews underpinned both the general patterns and counter-points we have just identified.

P9 explained why they read a long PDF on their mobile: he said he was "able to quickly download wile suck on the train" —so the selection of study-focused reading on the mobile was, in this case, the product of circumstance. P8 noted that it was "easier" to read on the laptop "because of the bigger screen", and the greater ease of undertaking writing and other tasks while reading (e.g. P4 wrote in their diary that they chose a laptop for work reading as "it's much easier and faster with keyboard and mouse to multitask."). Those who used tablet PCs unanimously noted the advantage of a laptop keyboard for typing versus a tablet touchscreen, especially for taking notes or annotating the text being read.

In contrast to the task-focused selection of laptops, and the mobility-oriented use of phones, the selection of tablet PCs often was cited as being about location: e.g. P13 noted in their diary that they used a tablet "whilst sitting on the sofa … [it] has a big enough screen to view websites on", in contrast to their mobile phone; while P9 noted that tablets have "a good screen to read off from and easy to move about."—raising a recurrent theme of the relative comfort of reorienting a tablet versus a laptop.

Device choices for reading either in the early morning or evening—usually in the student's bedroom or bed—very often focused on the form factor: with choices ranging from a netbook, through tablets to larger mobile phones. Tablets proved popular "because it is easy to use whilst in bed", but those without this option did not report using anything larger than a netbook. Laptops and other devices were entirely absent from these times of day.

4.4.1 Reading Matter and Device Choices

In the undergraduate diaries, we discovered relationships between reading matter and the devices chosen. In the case of the reading of novels, all but one participant reported using an iPad or ereader device. The single exception, P15, used an iPhone for almost all their reading to avoid "using multiple devices", and she did much of her reading while commuting. The broader pattern, however, was for novel reading to be conducted at home late in the evening: a typical comment being that "I read it to relax before I went to sleep", and diary and interview data combined revealed that this reading always ended in bed.

The two users of ereaders combined both these patterns, reading during commuting and at night. Both had acquired their Kindles as dedicated book reading devices. In contrast, the iPad owners restricted their novel reading to the evenings, and used their devices for a wider range of functions across the day.

Web-page reading, for both leisure and work, was spread across the day, and across a range of devices. This material emphasized a general trend, where participants reported a strong influence of context on device choice. This contingent selection of device was reported by 4 participants in their diaries and 8 in the exit interviews. P11 noted in his diary that "I used my phone because it was already on and I had already shut my Netbook off". The immediate status of his personal devices influenced his choice, due to the startup time of the PC. As in this case, choice of device was most often a phone versus PC or tablet. The influence of context followed a few common trends, with more than half of the respondents reporting a series of factors including device status (as with P11), physical constraints and concerns about the security of larger devices. The broad pattern was to compromise effectiveness and select a smaller mobile device when a larger one was less convenient. However, there were three isolated cases of participants adjusting their context in order to make a larger device more practicable, and then switching from mobile to a tablet or laptop. Furthermore, P15 reported in her exit interview that "sometimes if I am at home and it's in the morning, as I said the battery life of the iPhone is really bad and I leave it to charge so I use the Samsung galaxy tab instead", so battery management can also result in a shift from mobile to a larger device.

The library study also casts a clear light on the use of devices at university. We noted that laptops were treated as primarily private property, even if they were regularly turned to others for short spans of shared reading. Where a shared screen was used to read together, students almost invariably used a university PC, including some PCs with large screens. In contrast, though tablets were relatively rare—perhaps because of security issues raised by our undergraduate diarists—when they were present, they were regularly used as shared devices and would be passed regularly between members of a group. Paper was also used for sharing around, but it was also commonplace to see paper being used for notetaking by group members: indeed this was almost universal amongst the twenty groups in our close observations.

As noted briefly in our consideration of reading matter, in the academic study, the changes from 2004 to 2014 have been significant, with more than half the 2014 cohort owning either a tablet or ereader. Device selection for them is not so clearly influenced by security and ownership, no doubt due to having their own office. Their reading devices sit alongside paper as part of established reading 'handapparat' toolsets. Tablet PCs are used for the convenience of portability and relatively high quality of display, while ereaders are more often credited with even greater portability and being pleasant for reading for long periods of time. These devices were frequently used alongside laptop and desktop PCs, and for referencing digital texts while working with paper documents. This compositional use of different technologies brings us to the consideration of using multiple devices at once.

4.5 Use of multiple devices

Concurrent multiple device use was seen in all studies. In our observation of the library, the use of books on their own was far behind the rate at which books were used alongside a laptop, desktop or tablet. While that pattern combined both paper and digital media, we also saw the contemporaneous use of tablets and laptop computers, and laptops being used alongside large-screen PCs. For many reading tasks, two displays, be each display paper or digital, greatly assists the user.

4.5.1 Dual Device Use

In our undergraduate diary study, three participants reported incidents of using two devices at the same time, in order to better support the reading of more than one item at a time. Revision was a common theme to all three participants where, say, a textbook would be used alongside lecture notes or even two views of the same report. P9 reported in his diary a case of reading articles on both his phone and laptop: "I was reading another article on the same topic on my laptop and wanted to cross reference between my phone and laptop for quick switching and reading".

One common format for these reading sessions was with typing being done on the reader's laptop, which was also used as the primary focus for reading. The second device—phone or tablet—then provided a supplementary view for supporting material. This echoes the comments reported earlier of the preference of users for laptops when they needed to type while reading. However, this format could also be reversed, with the laptop used for quick referencing and note-taking, while reading a textbook either on paper or in as an ebook with iPad or reader; or paper would be used for note-taking as the student worked with digital text.

Dual device use was regularly seen during the library study. On the silent floors of the library (where book use was most prevalent) 66.3% of all observed book use was in conjunction with some kind of electronic media—laptop, desktop or tablet. Tablet use overall was low, accounting for only 3.5% of all patrons of the library, making this population quite different to the one observed in the UK-based study of students. The use of ereaders was not observed at all. In close observation in the library mixed device use was seen particularly when groups were mixing the production of an artifact with reading to support their activity. In one group observation, both members of a pair were reading from a shared tablet PC while doing some other reading on a shared laptop screen. The same pattern could be seen with individual members across study groups, and as personal tasks within group reading and writing work. Furthermore, small groups and sub-groups demonstrated short-term use of two devices, often with one person turning their laptop screen for another to see, which led to the other student reciprocating with their display. In each case, the use of two devices facilitated the comparison of different material at the same time, especially where the parallel reading continued beyond a few short seconds.

The humanities interviewees who owned reading devices also reported many cases of using them alongside a PC. R24's placing of an easel by her iMac permitted her to use her iPad as a document display device while she took detailed notes on her computer. R38 regularly took his iPad to use alongside his laptop on work trips, saying that this option saved him bulk and weight, as well as allowing him to carry a large library of documents. When probed about how he used them together, he replied "not that often, because I like, often, to read and then write, rather than both at once. However, when I'm really looking at the text in detail—then it's a godsend."

As with the undergraduates in our diaries and in the library, for R38 it was the ability to place two texts opposite each other—he continued with an example "having the biography [of a poet he was researching] to hand as I pick apart the prose" simplified the work of his analysis. For his work on this task, biography and poems were interdependent sources across several months.

4.5.2 Device Choice Strategies

As noted above, there were interactions between place, task and device. The undergraduate diarists reported a number of individual approaches, but two common strategies divided "users" from "choosers". The "choosers" prioritized the use of the device that they felt was most appropriate to the reading task (e.g. in terms of display size). The two Kindle owners showed one form of this: selecting their Kindle exclusively as their book reading device. P5 had a more common example: while sitting on their sofa at home they found a useful paper—a PDF—and switched from their phone to their tablet as "my phone screen isn't that big"

In contrast, "users" simply continued with what was at hand; P11 wanted to read a longer article but continued on their phone as "If I had a choice I would have read it on my Netbook, but due to laziness I already turned my Netbook off and put it in my bag by the time...my phone was ready in my hand". Other reasons included reading starting on a device (and hence continuing on it to avoid disruption), but generally "using" was, in contrast to "choosing", seldom given an explicit justification. Eight participants showed a mixture of both strategies, while three were mostly "users", and four "choosers".

A second pairing of strategies contrasted "homers" with "movers". "Homers" kept their digital tools at home. P13, kept his tablet PC in his house, as "it's convenient... I don't like to take it out because I feel quite vulnerable...[if on] holiday then I might take it with me but only to keep in touch with the folks back home." In P13's case, the issue of security was a major concern; this caution led to most of his reading being done at home. Three further participants predominantly read at home, either in the evening or in the morning, and very rarely read elsewhere. Only two of the four "homers" reported reading even once, on their mobile phone, while away from home. In both cases, this was a quick check of content they had been made aware of when away.

The other eleven participants—the "movers" used their mobile reading devices across the day, albeit with different devices being used in different locations. Tablets were more often used in stationary positions, whereas mobile phones predominated during commuting. Early evenings most often saw laptop use at home, moving gradually to tablet PCs and ereaders as the night drew in.

The scholars showed some of these patterns, but those who regularly used digital reading devices had developed a strategy that enriched the general thrust of the undergraduate "mover" and "chooser" behavior. They had developed similarly clear associations between context and device, but had developed connections that ran between context, content, device and time. With a greater influence over their physical environments, and also higher demands on their reading work, they combine what might be dubbed 'nomadic' and 'horticultural' planning to increase their effectiveness. In 'nomadic' mode, they create sets of reading material and equipment that can travel with them and be used both on the move and at temporary 'homes'; in 'horticultural' mode, they establish alternate 'homes' that contain resident resources. These approaches are not in conflict, but rather are composed together to enable the researcher to sustain the high level of reading that is demanded of them. Furthermore, the places and spaces chosen for reading are also part of an established pattern for other reasons: they represent in the majority of cases reported to us, venues that have been nurtured and adapted to across years of repeated practice.

In the library, we examined the interaction between physical space and task effectiveness. As already noted, groups would try to avoid particular areas that poorly suited their purposes, but there were patterns of individual behavior within groups that also demonstrated an ability to adapt to and shape the current context. One common pattern, observed in groups that were studying individually, but in the same location, was to sit on alternating sides of the desk; this hid the content of one member's screen from the next. However, privacy did not appear to be the sole issue: similar behaviors were seen in groups, where screening off material would reduce distraction from other sources. Students were thus not only using space to reduce the visibility of their material to their neighbors, but also to reduce the intrusion of other's screens into their own view. The construction of effective reading places is not the preserve of experienced scholars.

4.6 Summary

In the diary study of students, we found that individual devices are often 'based' at one or more locations. Laptops move between home and university, particularly when reading is more 'serious' and is accompanied by writing. Mobile phones dominate when commuting, and for quick reference or distraction when the phone is the 'to-hand' device. Ereaders and, to a lesser extent, tablets, are chosen for longer reading. In both cases, the thin form factor make then a preferred device for longer reading, particularly at night. For both students and academics, ereaders are strongly preferred for book reading—work or leisure—while tablets cover a wider range of reading, including the web and academic PDFs.. Place, device and content all play a role when people start to read.

5. DISCUSSION

Our results demonstrate clear associations between device choice, selection of location, material being read, time management and reading task or goal. We now reflect on the significance of these insights for digital libraries, attending to the consequences for ebook use, reading devices, and library systems design in turn.

A major theme in our findings was the contrast between 'users'—using a technology for its momentary convenience—and 'choosers'—who selected the tool they considered best for the job at hand. While the undergraduates did adopt a more 'using' strategy for leisure reading, particularly when commuting, the work-oriented reading of researchers and students alike was more oriented around making optimal choices of device, location, and reading material.

We saw mobile devices being selected for reading in a number of contexts, which is notable given the data in the present literature. A significant minority of academics still print journal articles [29], many also prefer print books to ebooks [11,28]. This is also true of students, who print articles and often prefer print books [30].

Taking the case of choosing ebooks, recent DL research has investigated ebook loaning and borrowing behaviors [3] and the factors that influence ebook adoption [13]. The evidence on ebook adoption identified wealth and necessity as forces that lead to ebook use. However, in our studies, economic factors were little reported. Instead, physical factors took a central role in the choice of ebooks and PDFs. In short-term of use, this was seen in the perceived advantages of portability and in longer-term use the lower space cost of storing larger repositories of potentially useful texts was pivotal, for both students and researchers.

The students and researchers both used electronic documents because they were simple to carry, particularly in volume. In terms of storage, digital content's minimal demand on space had an influence on researchers' highly prized personal collection practices. R26 stated that "the [physical] book has to earn its keep" while digital "sits invisibly in the corner", explaining why she had a burgeoning, if hard-to-manage, digital collection in comparison to her regularly pruned print library.

Paper, however, also plays a pivotal role. Print was used when annotation was needed; when reading was at length, or when it was retained and at hand in a location. Print thus had a 'home', while digital content was chosen for nomadic use. Print was also the mark of content being valued. The more work-oriented and useful a text was seen to be, the more frequently it was kept in paper form, and the more transient or trivial a long document, the more often it was digital. The use of paper as a working medium is in sharp contrast, being the ultimate in disposable material, but it is seen, as regularly reported, as being better for annotation.

Across print and digital text, however, in working practice readers use and combine these media in sophisticated ways. From a number of perspectives then, choosing print or digital thus fits into the broader device choice context. Both can be natural choices for different types of text. Each can serve as a 'display', and a reading task is very unlikely to be restricted to one medium. However, continuity and organization of the work is most demanding on the user where the material is digital; and acknowledged weaknesses of digital texts are still restricting its use. Enhancing the experience of digital text with better user experience could still significantly improve DL design and use.

Those constructing prototype ereaders have run short-term studies of use. Chen et al [6] ran a longitudinal study with graduate students, who were each given several prototype e-Ink ereaders Multiple slates were used for concurrent reading of different texts, but as our studies show, this behavior is already well established in the wild, and is another intentional part of technology choice.

Thayer et al [30] are the most systematic study of actual reading device use. Echoing their findings, we found a reluctance to use ereaders, for tasks that involved annotation. We also shared their observation that reading was an activity that combined different media and resources. However, we extend that insight, noting that space and (chosen or made) place also plays a key role in reading.

This influence was hinted at in Colombo and Scipioni's [8] recent study of children's reading with tablet PCs. That study found that children's reading is predominantly done at home, often in their bedroom or in the living room. As with our students, the evening was the predominant time period used for reading. It may be that the patterns exhibited by young adults closely reflect the patterns they established in childhood. However, their work-related reading, and that of the academics, draws a much richer picture of place. Our data is, to the best of our knowledge, the first report of adult mobile reading and device use that is based on observation (direct and indirect), rather than logs or survey data.

Choice is thus about content, device, space and time: "choosers" paint very different pictures at different moments, and an effective DL will enable and support work across and between paper, digital and different devices.

How could DL designers enable effective bridging between the different choice-sets that DL users construct to read effectively?

Re-interpreting both reading 'place' and 'space' through the lenses provided by Harrison and Dourish [9] seems to be a potentially fruitful angle through which to understand both single- and multi-device interactions with documents: location can be understood both geographically (space) but also in a more semantic manner (place). Both these aspects interact. For the humanities researchers specific configurations of material, devices and resources are turned to a particular goal, and the tools and purpose can be understood as providing a 'place' of work. For rehearsed locations, space and place are tightly coupled. Thus, task creates an implicit connection of available resources, which is reconfigured in different moments to continue ongoing work.

This connection has repercussions for those designing reading DL tools and ereader devices: embracing and enhancing the role of space/place could lead to improved user support and experience. However, current devices were noted by both undergraduates and researchers as impeding effective practices of place. They were also criticized for being clumsier for composing working sets (or 'handapparats') of reading material. Progress has been made on supporting other aspects where digital text has fallen short of the benchmark of paper—e.g. annotation [6, 17, 24]—and so the composition of working sets, complete with an effective environment, is likely a tractable challenge for future work in digital library research.

One key problem we discovered was controlling and choosing reading material on reading devices. The difficulties that our respondents found in discriminating similar filenames from each other (often downloaded from DLs) were a consistent barrier to them choosing ereaders for journal articles. This mirrors problems with document titles in early DLs [3] and with contemporary ebook collections [22].

Building personal libraries and working sets were two other pivotal moments of choice, particularly for the academics. There is a strong tradition of research on personal digital libraries (e.g. [12,28]), and for long-term storage, such tools may work well.

However, there is a different challenge in building short-term working sets that underpin a reading task across different times and places. These sets are not held within one library, and so within-DL tools are not a solution. Neither do personal DLs, with their focus on a central repository, address the need. These sets, if in digital form, are often distributed between laptops, tablet PCs and ereaders. What appears to be required is not so much a classical centralized repository, more a digital satchel or workspace that interconnects related material. Drawing from the traditions from which DL work has developed, this suggests that effective solutions would be more informed by hypertext than databases, and come optimized for discovery and flexibility, rather than retrieval and long-term storage. In contrast to the construction of permanent collections, the support of semi-fluid personal worksets is an area where DL research has yet to mature.

6. CONCLUSIONS

This paper has provided the first concrete evidence of how users select reading devices. Two default hypotheses seem temptingly "obvious": that they use whatever is to hand, or that they choose whatever device is most suited to the material.

Using data from three separate studies we reveal a much more complex landscape: device choice sits at an intricate nexus of location, context, material choice and convenience for both students and academics. This picture is made more complex by the frequent use of multiple devices. Understanding how and when readers use specific devices could allow us to enhance DL design by adapting services and interfaces in response to context.

Within this varied landscape, we identify clear patterns: laptop based reading is almost exclusively in fixed locations; there is a distinction between those who use devices to hand and those who fit device to purpose, but the latter is more often a product of context than inherent preference. Academics use a highly selective *handapparat* or document library of current reading, and other information professionals probably have similar techniques, but digital technology erects barriers to this sort of planned use.

While this paper identifies some clear patterns, further work is needed to understand some of the more subtle questions raised: what makes a "user" or a "chooser" of available devices, for example? The changing nature of reading and emergent technology in this field will ensure it is a rich space for research for some time to come.

7. ACKNOWLEDGMENTS

Our thanks to the participants of our various studies for their generous contribution of their time. This work was supported by EPSRC Grants EP/F041217.

8. REFERENCES

[1] Adler, A., Gujar, A., Harrison, B. L., O'Hara, K. and Sellen, A. A diary study of work-related reading: design implications for digital reading devices. In *CHI '98* United States. ACM Press, 1998. 241-248.

[2] Arter, D., Buchanan, G., Jones, M., Harper, R. Incidental information and mobile search. Procs. Mobile HCI, ACM Press, 2007. 413-420.

[3] Berg, S. A., Hoffmann, K. and Dawson, D. Not on the Same Page: Undergraduates' Information Retrieval in Electronic and Print Books. *The Journal of Academic Librarianship*, 36, 6, 518-525 2010.

[4] Blandford, A., Stelmaszewska, H. and Bryan-Kinns, N. Use of multiple digital libraries: a case study. Procs. ACM/IEEE-CS joint conference on Digital libraries (JCDL '01). ACM, 2001. 179-188. DOI=10.1145/379437.379479 http://doi.acm.org/10.1145/379437.379479

[5] Buchanan, G., Cunningham, S.J. Blandford, A., Rimmer, J. and Warwick. C. Information seeking by humanities scholars. In *Procs. Europ. conf. on Digital Libraries* ECDL. Springer, 2005. 218-229. DOI=10.1007/11551362_20 http://dx.doi.org/10.1007/11551362_20

[6] Chen, N., Guimbretière, F. and Sellen, A. Graduate student use of a multi-slate reading system. In *Procs. SIGCHI Conf. on Human Factors in Computing Systems* (CHI '13). ACM, 2013. 1799-1808. DOI=10.1145/2470654.2466237 http://doi.acm.org/10.1145/2470654.2466237

[7] Church, K. and Oliver, N. 2011. Understanding mobile web and mobile search use in today's dynamic mobile landscape. In *Procs.* MobileHCI '11. ACM, New York, USA, 67-76. DOI=10.1145/2037373.2037385 http://doi.acm.org/10.1145/2037373.2037385

[8] Colombo, L., and Scipioni, M.P. Children reading ebooks on tablets: a study of the context of use. In *Procs. NordiCHI '14.* ACM, New York, NY, USA, 2014. 975-978. DOI=10.1145/2639189.2670254 http://doi.acm.org/10.1145/2639189.2670254

[9] Harrison, S. and Dourish, P. Re-place-ing space: the roles of place and space in collaborative systems. *Procs. ACM* CSCW, ACM, 1996. 67-76. DOI=10.1145/240080.240193 http://doi.acm.org/10.1145/240080.240193

[10] Hernon, P., Hopper, R., Leach, M. R., Saunders, L. L. and Zhang, J. E-book Use by Students: Undergraduates in Economics, Literature, and Nursing. *The Journal of Academic Librarianship*, 33, 1, 3-13 2007.

[11] Hinze, A., McKay, D., Vanderschantz, N., Timpany, C. and Cunningham, S. J. Book selection behavior in the physical library: implications for ebook collections. In *JCDL '12* Washington, DC, USA. ACM, 2012. 305-314.

[12] Janssen, W.C. and Popat, K. 2003. UpLib: a universal personal digital library system. In *Procs. ACM DocEng.* ACM, USA, 234-242. DOI=10.1145/958220.958262 http://doi.acm.org/10.1145/958220.958262

[13] Li, C., Poe, F., Potter, M., Quigley, B. and Wilson, J. *UC Libraries Academic e-Book Usage Survey.* Uni. of California, Springer, California Digital Libraries, USA, 2011.

[14] Loizides, F., Buchanan, G. An empirical study of user navigation during document triage, Procs. European conf. on digital libraries, Springer, 2009, 138-149.

[15] Manguel, A., The Library at Night, Yale University Press, 2009.

[16] Marshall, C. C. *Reading and Writing the Electronic Book.* Morgan & Claypool, Chapel Hill, NC USA, 2010.

[17] Marshall, C.C., Price, M.N., Golovchinsky, G. and Schilit, B.N. Introducing a digital library reading appliance into a reading group. In *Procs. ACM conf. on Digital libraries.* ACM, NY, USA, 1999. 77-84. DOI=10.1145/313238.313262 http://doi.acm.org/10.1145/313238.313262

[18] Marshall, C.C. and Ruotolo, C. Reading-in-the-small: a study of reading on small form factor devices. In *Proc JCDL 2002*, ACM Press (2002), 56-64.

[19] Marshall, C. C. and Bly, S. Turning the page on navigation. In *JCDL'05* Denver, CO, USA. ACM, 2005. 225-234.

[20] McKay, D. Gotta keep 'em separated: Why the single search box may not be right for libraries. *Procs. Conf. New Zealand Chapter of the ACM SIGCHI,* ACM, 2011. 109-112.

[21] McKay, D. A jump to the left (and then a step to the right): reading practices within academic ebooks. In *OZCHI 2011* Canberra, Australia. ACM, 2011. 202-210.

[22] McKay, D., Buchanan, G., Vanderschantz, N., Timpany, C., Cunningham, S.J. and Hinze, A. Judging a book by its cover: interface elements that affect reader selection of ebooks. In *Procs* OzCHI, ACM, NY, USA, 2012. 381-390. DOI=10.1145/2414536.2414597 http://doi.acm.org/10.1145/2414536.2414597

[23] McKay, D., Buchanan, G., On the other side from you: How library design facilitates and hinders group work, Procs. OzCHI 2014, ACM, in press.

[24] Pearson, J., Buchanan, G. Thimbleby, H., and Jones, M. The Digital Reading Desk: A lightweight approach to digital note-taking. *Interact. Comput.* 24, 5 (September), 2012. 327-338. DOI=10.1016/j.intcom.2012.03.001 http://dx.doi.org/10.1016/j.intcom.2012.03.001

[25] Petroski, H., The Book on The Bookshelf, Vintage, 2000.

[26] Rowlands, I., Nicholas, D., Jamali, H. R. and Huntington, P. What do faculty and students really think about e-books? *Aslib Proceedings*, 59, 6, 489-511 2007.

[27] Saarinen K., Vakkari, P. "A sign of a good book: readers' methods of accessing fiction in the public library", Journal of Documentation, Vol. 69 (5), 2013, 736-754.

[28] Shipman, F.M. Hsieh, H., Moore, J.M. and Zacchi, A. Supporting personal collections across digital libraries in spatial hypertext. In *Procs. ACM/IEEE-CS JCDL.* ACM, NY, USA, 2004. 358-367. DOI=10.1145/996350.996433 http://doi.acm.org/10.1145/996350.996433

[29] Tenopir, C., King, D. W., Edwards, S. and Wu, L. Electronic journals and changes in scholarly article seeking and reading patterns. *Aslib Proceedings*, 61, 1, 5-32 2009.

[30] Thayer, A., Lee, C. P., Hwang, L. H., Sales, H., Sen, P. and Dalal, N. The imposition and superimposition of digital reading technology: the academic potential of ereaders. In *CHI 2011* Vancouver, BC, Canada. ACM, 2011. 2917-2926.

[31] Walton, E.W.,Why undergraduate students choose to use e-books, Journal of Librarianship and Information Science vol. 46(4) (December 2014) 263-270.

[32] Webb, K. M., Schaller, M.A, and Hunley. S.A., Measuring library space use and preferences: Charting a path toward increased engagement., *portal: Libraries and the Academy* 8(4), 2008. 407-422.

[33] Zhang, Y., and Kudva, S., Ebooks vs. print books: readers' choices and preferences across contexts. In *Procs ASIS&T Annual Meeting: Beyond the Cloud: Rethinking Information Boundaries* (ASIST '13), American Society for Information Science, Silver Springs, MD, USA, Article 108, 2013.

Books' Interest Grading and Fiction Readers' Search Actions During Query Reformulation Intervals

Anna Mikkonen
University of Tampere
School of Information Sciences
Tel + 358-405301815
anna.mikkonen@uta.fi

Pertti Vakkari
University of Tampere
School of Information Sciences
Tel +358-505288354
pertti.vakkari@uta.fi

ABSTRACT

We compared fiction readers' search actions during various query reformulation intervals. We aimed to understand how readers' search actions differed between successful and unsuccessful QRIs and which search actions predicted the selecting of very interesting novels compared to less interesting ones. We conducted a controlled user study with 80 participants searching for interesting novels. Three types of browsing tasks and two types of catalogs were used. Our results demonstrated that browsing task type was associated to readers' document viewing behavior in terms of observed search result pages, opened book pages and dwell time on book pages. When browsing for topical novels, most effort was required to select somewhat interesting novels. When browsing for good novels, most effort was required to select very interesting ones. Logistic regression analysis yielded that the most significant predictors of higher document value were the number of observed search result pages and opened book pages.

Categories and Subject Descriptors

H.3.7 [**Information Storage and Retrieval**]: Digital Libraries – *systems issues, user issues.*

General Terms

Performance, Experimentation, Human Factors.

Keywords

Fiction retrieval; search actions; query reformulation intervals; online catalogs.

1. INTRODUCTION

In recent years research interest towards interactive information retrieval focusing on causal-leisure situations has increased [e.g. 6, 34]. Searching of fiction is an essential part of casual-leisure search: the search process is not triggered by an explicit information need to be solved [34]. Instead, it begins often with a serendipitous need to find *"just good books to read"*.

Fiction is typically accessed in public libraries [28, 29]. Fiction readers make up a large portion of the public library clientele. In addition to physical library collections, fiction is increasingly searched for and accessed in public libraries' e-collections [29]. Public libraries are actively focusing on increasing the availability of e-books both in the U.S. and in Europe. [i.e. 27, 29]. Given the growing availability of fiction books in public libraries' e-collections, a good understanding of fiction readers' search behavior in digital libraries is essential to create functioning interfaces for fiction.

In recent years public libraries' online catalogs have been actively developed and enriched to meet the needs of diverse reader groups. Previous studies [i.e. 4, 17, 20] have revealed some major search tactics applied to fiction search in public libraries. However, we have only a few studies focusing on browsing for fiction in online library catalogs. Pöntinen & Vakkari [22] have examined how readers explore the fiction metadata in a gaze tracking study. Jiang [8] has studied social library system users' information seeking modes. Tang et al. [25] have examined book-finding tools on social media.

The purpose of this study is to examine fiction readers' search behavior in browsing tasks during query reformulation intervals (QRIs). QRI refers to users' search actions that take place between two queries [11]. According to Liu et al. [11] issuing a query represents a searcher's cognitive decision to modify the current search tactic, and is likely to affect the searcher's retrieval actions. The search actions between two queries form units, which can be used e.g. for eliciting information about users' document viewing behavior. The aim is to understand how fiction readers' search actions differ between successful and unsuccessful QRIs, which search actions are emphasized when interesting novels are selected, and which search actions predict the finding of very interesting novels compared to less interesting novels.

To address these objectives, we conducted an experiment with fiction readers working on different browsing tasks to find novels. The study addresses the following research questions:

RQ 1. Do the search actions during successful and unsuccessful query reformulation interval types differ a) between an enriched catalog compared to a traditional catalog? b) between browsing tasks?

RQ 2. Are the search actions during query reformulation intervals associated to books' interest grading in browsing tasks? If yes, how?

The study provides information on fiction readers' search behavior in casual-leisure browsing situations. In addition, the study enhances understanding of the factors which are associated to search success when searching for novels.

2. RELATED RESEARCH

Document viewing and usefulness. *Search action* refers to an identifiable basic action during the search process [2, 33]. Liu et al. [11] examined users' document viewing behavior, and predicted document usefulness during QRI. Similarly to [11], in this study QRI was defined as *"an interval from the point when a*

JCDL '15, June 21–25, 2015, Knoxville, Tennessee, USA.
Copyright © 2015 ACM 978-1-4503-3594-2/15/06…$15.00.
DOI: http://dx.doi.org/10.1145/2756406.2756922

user submits a query to the point when a user starts to enter a subsequent query during the same search session" [11].

[11] noticed that QRIs with useful pages were significantly longer compared to QRIs without useful pages. Moreover, users visited more content and search result pages (SERPs) and spent more time on content and SERPs during QRIs with useful documents.

Vakkari et al. [32] observed by eye-tracking how users' inspection of metadata in book pages was associated to novels' interest grading. The authors found that most time was used to assess a somewhat interesting novel compared to a not interesting or a very interesting novel. The findings show that the association of time use and novels' interest grading was non-linear [32].

Searching for books on the web and in digital libraries. Kim et al. [9] focused on web-based book search behavior. Transaction log analysis revealed some typical patterns of users' query reformulation. Most users followed up a new query by ending their session or issuing a completely different query. Minority of users limited the original search by adding a filtering condition. Ballard & Blaine [1] showed that when limiting capabilities were automatically displayed, users were more likely to refine their search compared to not displaying the limiting options.

Koolen et al. [10] compared the usefulness of professional metadata and user-generated content in determining books' topical relevance in social book search. Findings show that professional metadata was often not enough to determine books' topical relevance. Also, user-generated content was more effective for social book search compared to professional metadata.

Mckay et al. [15] examined the influence on an e-book presentation on the length of reader interactions with e-books. Inconsistencies or errors in a cover image, a blurb and a table of contents were found to be associated to an undesirable short time-span reading: flaws encouraged the user to loan the book for a closer inspection but ended up in rejection rapidly.

Browsing for fiction in digital libraries. In fiction retrieval browsing has been a common search strategy [e.g. 8, 20, 25].

Pejtersen [20] has identified three browsing search tactics which apply to fiction searching in online catalogs and match the purpose of this study. An analytical search tactic is used when readers wish to access books about some topic. A browsing tactic is applied in situations when readers have only a vague idea of what they would like to read. Search by analogy is generated when readers want something similar to a novel they have read.

Thudt et al. [30] have introduced the concept of targeted browsing, which is equivalent to Pejtersen's [20] analytical (topical) search. In targeted browsing the reader has some idea of the book he wants to find, such as the subject of the book. Similar to Pejtersen's [20] browsing tactic, the concept of open-ended browsing [30] refers to the situation where a reader is browsing for just interesting books. The Bohemian bookshelf [30], where browsing was enabled through information visualization offering various access points to the fiction collection, was found to support especially the open-ended browsing search tactic [30].

Previous studies [e.g. 14, 31] have revealed that most search interfaces to digital libraries support topical search in the form of querying. However, when browsing for fiction in an enriched online library catalog, it was found that searching without a query was associated to higher search success [18] in an enriched library catalog. Moreover, it was found by Oksanen & Vakkari [19] that effort devoted to search results instead of querying was associated to finding interesting novels in open-ended browsing situations. This is due to the serendipitous nature of fiction searching: readers' needs for fiction are often ill-defined and best met by serendipitous discoveries when browsing [3]

Tang et al. [25] conducted a user study of aNobii, an online book sharing website that enables social browsing, which refers to the ability to re-orientate browsing by social navigational tools [21, 25]. Author browsing was found to be the most efficient in terms of number of items examined. Browsing similar and friends' bookshelves produced more novel items and serendipitous choices. Jiang [8] examined the users of a social library system and noticed that in addition to searching by using the internal search engine, catalog browsing, associative browsing and social browsing were popular search strategies applied by them. Searching was found to be the most adopted mode, while browsing appeared to be the most widespread mode.

In all, previous research has revealed that document viewing behavior seems to predict document usefulness. When searching for books in digital libraries, user-generated metadata, limiting options and interface elements are associated to user behavior. When searching for fiction in digital libraries, the adopting of browsing tactics seems to predict search success. We set out to investigate how these elements are associated to document viewing behavior during QRIs when browsing for fiction.

3. RESEARCH METHOD

3.1 Participants

80 participants with genuine fiction reading interest were recruited in public libraries, in fiction reading groups and in Finland's Open University's writing and literature classes. The Snowball sampling method and a newspaper advertisement were used. Participants were offered a movie ticket as compensation for participation.

Background variables (i.e. gender and experience in using online catalogs) did not significantly differ between control and test group. In both groups, 18 % of the participants were male and 82 % female. The age distribution of participants in the test catalog was significantly higher compared to the age distribution in the control catalog (p=.015). However, as there was no significant difference in participants' experience in using online catalogs between control and test groups, the higher age distribution in the test group is unlikely to affect the results greatly.

3.2 Fiction Search Tasks

Five search tasks were designed based on previous research [4, 20, 21, 30]. In two search tasks, the participants were given an author or a topic with which to begin the search process. The remaining three search tasks reflect the idea of individual information needs as the participants were asked to proceed according to their personal preferences. Search tasks formed reflect the following typical search tactics in fiction searching: known author/title search, topical search, open-ended browsing, search by analogy and searching without conducting a query.

The aim of this study was to examine fiction readers' search actions in *browsing situations*. Thus, the ***"known author task"*** was excluded from the analysis. Also, when conducting the user tests it was noticed that the tasks open ended browsing and searching without a query resembled each other. Thus, solely the tasks ***"topical search"***, ***"open ended browsing"*** and **"search by analogy"** were included in the analysis of this study. The browsing tasks were presented as follows: ***"Topical search"***: *"Find three novels about upper class life in the 19th century."* ***"Open ended browsing"***: *"Find three novels that interest you which you would like to read."* ***"Search by analogy"***: *"Think of* *and mention one novel that you have read and found interesting recently. Now search for three similarly interesting novels as the one you mentioned."*

3.3 The Catalogs Used

As a traditional baseline catalog, Satakirjastot -service was used (https://www.satakirjastot.fi). As an enriched test catalog the BookSampo -service was used (www.kirjasampo.fi) Satakirjastot (Sata) is the web service of the city libraries of the Satakunta region in Finland. The service consists of a library catalog and an information retrieval system from given databases. In Sata the metadata for fiction contains bibliographic information added with subject terms from the fiction thesaurus Kaunokki. Cover images and blurbs from recently published books are also available. In Sata, the search options are basic and advanced search. Figure 1 presents the advanced search option in Sata.

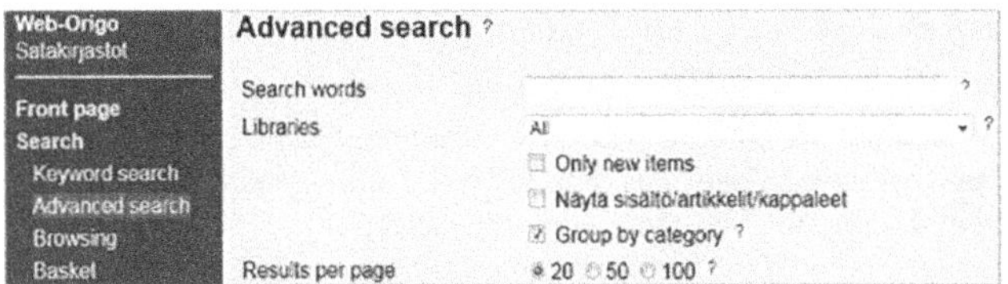

Figure 1. Advanced search in Satakirjastot.

In Sata, the search results are sorted according to format and relevance (such as book, DVD, CD). By choosing the preferred format the search results are presented in a new display according to author, title, publication year or class. Figure 2 presents the search result page in Sata.

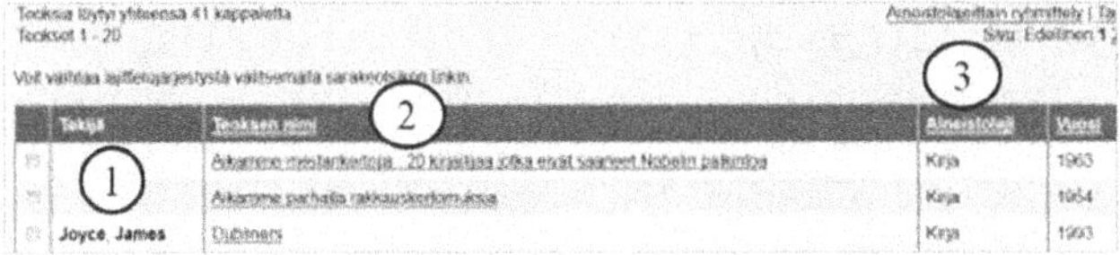

Legend: 1= Author information, 2= Title, 3= Format (book)

Figure 2. Search result page in Satakirjastot.

Sampo includes metadata on the adult fiction collection from the HelMet Library which is the web service of the city libraries of the Helsinki Metropolitan area in Finland. Compared to the baseline catalog Sata, Sampo provides fiction metadata that is more varied and accounts for different access points to literature (Table 1). In Sampo, the associations and similarities between the works of literature are realized by semantic web technologies such as the ontologization of the fiction thesaurus Kaunokki, which is used for fiction indexing in Sampo [7].

Table 1. The major characteristics of the catalogs used.

Characteristics		Sampo	Sata
Searching	Quick search	Yes	Yes
	Adv. search	No	Yes
	Image search	Yes	No
	Browsing	Yes	Yes,after querying
Book Page Info	Author, title	Yes,	Yes, always
	Keywords	Yes, often	Yes, often
	Content	Yes, often	Yes, seldom
	Cover image	Yes, often	Yes, seldom

The front page of Sampo offers a variety of access points to the collection. Users can begin the search process with a basic search (similar to baseline catalog), by browsing the images of book covers, by skimming other users' virtual bookshelves or looking at the subject term cloud. The basic search option and a search result page in Sampo are presented in Figure 3.

Legend: 1=Basic search, 2= Results by author, 3= Results by genre, 4=Snippet

Figure 3. Basic search and search result page in BookSampo.

The search results are ranked by an author and the genre of literature (novels, plays, short stories) by matching keywords to metadata. The book page represents the content of a particular novel in detail. Book descriptions, automatic recommendations and text samples are also included.

When the catalogs for the experiment were considered, the aim was to identify a traditional catalog with a fiction collection comparable to Sampo in size and content. The collection in Sata was found to be relatively similar to Sampo's collection. The fiction collection of Sata consisted of 77 000 titles and the fiction collection of Sampo of 73 000 titles, both include novels, plays and poems. Both collections included the classics and recently published titles of Finnish and foreign literature. When the data was collected, e-books were not available in the fiction collections of Sata and Sampo.

Before the experiment, the researchers conducted several test queries in both catalogs in order to compare the results. They were found to share several overlapping titles. The analysis of Sata and Sampo revealed that the size and content of these collections were comparable, and therefore they could be used in the experiment.

3.4 Experimental Procedure

Before conducting the user tests, the experimental setting was pre-tested. The experiment consisted of the following steps: 1. Pre-questionnaire (demographic questions, participant's search experience in online catalogs and their reading interest). 2. Introduction to the experiment. 3. Demo of the retrieval system. 4. Execution of five search tasks. 5. Post-task questionnaire after each completed search task. 6. Post-session questionnaire after the completion of all search tasks. 7. Brief post-task interview.

The time for completing the tasks was not limited. The participants were randomized into control and test groups. Each participant completed the tasks either on Sampo or Sata. Latin square rotation was used with the tasks. Each participant completed the tasks individually. During the experiment, the researcher was present to help in case technical problems occurred. The search logs were saved with Morae-software (http://www.techsmith.com/morae.html).

In each task, the participants were asked to search for three novels that were of interest to them. After each search task, the participants were asked to rank the novels selected according to how much they were of interest to them with an ordinal scale ranging from 1 to 3, where 1 was "a little interesting", 2 was "somewhat interesting" and 3 was "very interesting".

4. ANALYSIS

4.1 Measures

Success in search tasks was measured by the books' interest grading given by participants. Search was considered as "successful" if it resulted in a selection of a novel that was given an interest grading of "very interesting". Search was considered as "somewhat successful" if it resulted in a selection of a novel that was given an interest grading of "somewhat interesting" or "little interesting". Search was considered as "unsuccessful" if it resulted in no selections.

80 user tests were manually coded in order to identify different QRI types, and measure the search actions during the identified QRI types. In both catalogs three types of query reformulation intervals were identified: a) Successful QRI with very interesting novels selected (named as Successful QRI), b) Successful QRI with a little and somewhat interesting novels selected (named as Somewhat successful QRI) and c) Unsuccessful QRI with no interesting novels selected (named as Unsuccessful QRI). After identifying the QRI types, a coding scheme was developed for search actions. Each possible search action was identified in both catalogs by a single coder. The coding scheme was slightly different between the two catalogs used as they offer different search features (Table 2).

Table 2. The coding schemes for Sata and Sampo.

Search actions during QRI in both catalogs
Duration of QRI
Query time (total time on issuing queries in basic and advanced searching)
SERP time (total time on all search result pages)
Dwell time on book pages (total time on all book pages
Number of SERP visits
Number of opened book pages
Search actions during QRI solely in Sampo
Pivot browsing time (total time on all pivot browsing actions)
Number of pivot browsing actions

In Sata, options for submitting queries were basic and advanced search. In Sampo, solely the basic search option was provided. In Sampo, browsing the collection was possible without querying. The concept of *pivot browsing* [21] was applied to measure search actions that re-orientated browsing to follow features such as virtual bookshelves, cover images and automatic recommendations. In Sata, pivot browsing was not possible.

The search actions were measured by their frequency and duration. Each of the search tasks was coded individually. Time on issuing queries was not included in the total duration of QRI, as the aim was to investigate users' actions between two queries.

4.2 Statistical Analysis

The variables in the coding scheme (Table 2) were not normally distributed (Shapiro-Wilk=.95, $p<0.05$ in each variable). Shapiro-Wilkinson's test was used as there were fewer than 50 cases per catalog [19]. Friedman's test was used to test differences in search actions between QRI types within a task and between tasks. When comparing the search actions between catalogs, the variables were again screened for normality. Variables were not normally distributed (Kolmogorov-Smirnov=.95, $p<0.05$ in each variable). Kolmogorov-Smirnov's test was used as there were over 50 cases [24]. Mann-Whitney's non-parametric U-test was used to test differences in search actions between QRI types between catalogs.

The search actions in the open ended browsing and search by analogy tasks did not statistically differ from each other. Thus, for the economy of analysis, they were collapsed into one search task referred to here as *a browsing task*.

To analyze whether the search actions during QRIs were associated to books' interest grading, multinomial logistic regression analysis was applied. The aim was to identify the search actions that predicted the selection of very interesting novels compared to less interesting ones. Before conducting regression analysis, the data was re-coded using QRI as the unit of observation. Books' interest grading given by participants was used as a dependent variable in multinomial logistic regression analysis. The variables presented at Table 2 were used as independent variables. When constructing the regression models the method Enter was used to add independent variables into the models. Enter is a method where the researcher controls the entry of variables and the advancement of the regression process [24].

5. SEARCH ACTIONS DURING QRIs

In total, the data consisted of 1115 query reformulation intervals (Table 3). Only the valid sessions that contained at least two queries were concerned. The number of unsuccessful QRIs was significantly (p=.000) higher in Sata compared to Sampo.

Table 3. Number of successful, somewhat successful and unsuccessful QRIs in Sata and Sampo.

Measure	**Sata n=626**	**Sampo n=489**	**p**
# Successful QRIs	189	174	.974
# Somewhat successful QRIs	163	176	.752
# Unsuccessful QRIs	274	139	.000

5.1 Search Actions in Sata

In ***"topical search"***, the successful and unsuccessful QRIs differed significantly from somewhat successful QRIs (Table 4). Somewhat successful QRIs were significantly longer with more time on SERPs and book pages compared to successful and unsuccessful QRIs. Time per an individual SERP and book page visits did not significantly differ between QRI types. Interestingly, more time was used on issuing queries before unsuccessful QRIs compared to successful and somewhat successful QRIs.

More SERPs were observed and book pages opened during somewhat successful QRIs compared to successful and unsuccessful QRIs. In unsuccessful QRIs book pages were examined significantly more infrequently and significantly more time was devoted to search results examination compared to successful and somewhat successful QRIs.

Table 4. Means (standard deviations) of search actions in QRIs in *"topical search"* in Sata. (Duration in seconds.)

Measure	Mean (st.dev)			Between QRI type p-values		
	Suc. QRI n=43	**Some. Suc. QRI** n=73	**Un-suc. QRI** n=91	Suc. Some. Suc.	Suc. Un-suc.	Some. Suc. Un-suc.
QRI duration	44 (54)	118 (113)	43 (63)	**.006**	.622	**.009**
Query time	16 (24)	20 (15)	61 (72)	.206	**.004**	.105
SERP time	27 (35)	58 (57)	34 (52)	.058	.411	**.004**
BP time	17 (23)	59 (65)	9 (16)	**.004**	.083	**.000**
# SERP visits	1.6 (1.9)	3.6 (3.4)	3.0 (2.9)	**.005**	.056	.602
# BPs	1.2 (1.6)	3.3 (3.4)	0.8 (1.5)	**.009**	.117	**.000**

Legend: Suc= Successful QRI, Some. Suc= Somewhat successful QRI, Unsuc=Unsuccessful QRI, BPs=Book pages

In summary, in ***"topical search"*** the findings indicate that searchers needed most time for assessing the novel as somewhat interesting, and equally time for assessing the novel as very or not interesting. Searchers observed clearly more SERPs and book pages when assessing somewhat interesting novels compared to very interesting or not interesting ones. They tended to open several book pages before deciding the novel to be somewhat interesting. Consequently, SERP time and dwell time on book pages were the longest when somewhat interesting novels were selected. Interestingly, most time was devoted to querying before unsuccessful QRIs. This suggests, that before unsuccessful QRIs especially finding of correct query terms and conducting queries correctly was problematic to searchers. As a result, the issued queries did not produce desirable results from which to proceed to book pages and book pages were rarely opened.

In ***"browsing task"***, the successful and somewhat successful QRIs differed significantly from unsuccessful QRIs (Table 5). Searchers invested significantly more time on SERPs and book pages, and opened more book pages during successful and somewhat successful QRIs compared to unsuccessful QRIs. In unsuccessful QRIs book pages were infrequently opened. Time per an individual SERP and book page visit did not significantly differ between QRI types. Like in ***"topical search"***, most time was used on issuing queries before unsuccessful QRIs.

To summarize, in ***"browsing task"*** successful and somewhat successful QRIs resemble each other and differ from unsuccessful QRIs. In ***"browsing task"*** searchers need most time for assessing novels as very interesting, and least time for assessing novels as not interesting. Assessing somewhat interesting novels is commonly in the middle. Searchers observed clearly more SERPs and book pages when assessing interesting novels compared to not interesting ones. As a result, SERP time and dwell time on book pages were longer when interesting novels were chosen compared to not interesting ones. Similarly to ***"topical search"***, searchers devoted most time on issuing queries before unsuccessful QRIs together with very few opened book pages. Again the finding suggests that before unsuccessful QRIs, the issued queries do not produce desirable results from which to proceed to book pages. Therefore, book pages were rarely opened.

Table 5. Means (standard deviations) of search actions in QRIs in *"browsing task"* in Sata. (Duration in seconds.)

Measure	Mean (st.dev)			Between QRI type p-values		
	Suc. QRI n= 146	**Some. suc. QRI** n=90	**Un-suc. QRI** n=183	Suc. Some. suc.	Suc. Un-suc.	Some. suc. Un-suc.
QRI duration	132 (74)	81 (67)	57 (69)	.114	**.000**	**.027**
Query time	23 (20)	19 (30)	36 (40)	.150	**.000**	**.000**
SERP time	78 (44)	48 (36)	45 (59)	.114	**.000**	.206
BP time	54 (46)	38 (41)	12 (16)	.250	**.000**	**.000**
# SERP visits	3.1 (2.0)	2.6 (2.4)	3.1 (2.6)	.096	.505	.194
# BPs	2.7 (2.0)	2.2 (2.4)	0.9 (1.6)	.237	**.000**	**.002**

Legend: Suc= Successful QRI, Some. Suc= Somewhat successful QRI, Unsuc=Unsuccessful QRI, BPs=Book pages

Differences in search actions between QRI types were examined also between tasks. Compared to ***"browsing task"***, successful QRIs in ***"topical search"*** were significantly ($p<.001$) shorter. When very interesting novels were chosen significantly ($p<.01$) more SERPs were observed and more book pages were opened in browsing task compared to topical search. Therefore, SERP time and dwell time on book pages were significantly ($p<.001$) longer in ***"browsing task"*** compared to ***"topical search"***.

When assessing somewhat interesting novels, no significant differences occurred in search actions between tasks. When assessing not interesting novels in ***"topical search"***, QRIs were significantly ($p<.01$) shorter with significantly less time on SERPs compared to ***"browsing task"***.

5.2 Search Actions in Sampo

In ***"topical search"*** in Sampo, the successful and unsuccessful QRIs differed from somewhat successful QRIs (Table 6). Time devoted to SERPs and book pages was longer in somewhat successful QRIs compared to successful and unsuccessful QRIs. Time per an individual pivot browsing action, SERP and book page visits did not significantly differ between QRI types. Time devoted to issuing queries was substantially the same before each QRI type. Pivot browsing was scarce in each QRI type. Observed SERPs and opened book pages were more numerous in somewhat successful QRIs compared to successful and unsuccessful QRIs. In unsuccessful QRIs book pages were examined infrequently.

In all, in ***"topical search"*** searchers needed most time for assessing the novel as somewhat interesting and, almost equally, time for assessing the novel as very or not interesting. Searchers viewed visibly more SERPs and book pages when assessing somewhat interesting novels compared to very interesting or not interesting ones. They tended to open several book pages before deciding the novel to be somewhat interesting. Consequently, SERP time and dwell time on book pages were the longest when somewhat interesting novels were selected. Querying or pivot browsing did not differ between QRI types.

Table 6. Means (standard deviations) of search actions in QRIs in *"topical search"* in Sampo. (Duration in seconds.)

Measure	Mean (st.dev)			Between QRI type p-values		
	Suc. QRI n=40	**Some. suc. QRI** n=74	**Un-suc. QRI** n=55	Suc. Some. suc.	Suc. Un-suc.	Some. suc. Un-suc.
QRI duration	68 (84)	105 (85)	60 (92)	**.027**	.724	**.001**
Query time	17 (27)	18 (19)	28 (49)	.114	.715	.516
Pivot time	3 (10)	3 (10)	6 (15)	.969	.206	.405
SERP time	37 (51)	55 (50)	39 (60)	.058	.480	**.023**
BP time	27 (40)	47 (46)	15 (35)	**.046**	**.033**	**.000**
# pivot actions	0.4 (1.0)	0.5 (1.2)	0.5 (1.3)	.905	.527	.763
# SERP visits	1.4 (1.7)	2.6 (2.2)	1.9 (3.3)	.052	.462	**.000**
# BPs	1.2 (1.9)	2.4 (2.7)	0.9 (2.4)	**.028**	**.050**	**.000**

Legend: Suc= Successful QRI, Some. Suc= Somewhat successful QRI, Unsuc=Unsuccessful QRI, BPs=Book pages

In ***"browsing task"***, the successful and somewhat successful QRIs differed from unsuccessful QRIs (Table 7). In successful and somewhat successful QRIs pivot browsing, viewed SERPs and opened book pages were more numerous compared to unsuccessful QRIs. As a result, SERP time and dwell time on book pages were significantly longer in successful and somewhat successful QRIs compared to unsuccessful QRIs. Time per an individual pivot browsing action, SERP and book page visit did not significantly differ between QRI types. Like in topical search, in unsuccessful QRIs book pages were infrequently opened.

To sum up, in ***"browsing task"*** successful and somewhat successful QRIs resembled each other and differed from unsuccessful QRIs. In ***"browsing task"*** searchers needed most time for assessing novels as very interesting, and least time for assessing novels as not interesting. Assessing somewhat interesting novels was commonly in the middle. Searchers observed visibly more SERPs and book pages when assessing interesting novels compared to not interesting novels. As a result, SERP time and dwell time on book pages were longer when interesting novels were chosen compared to when not interesting novels were selected.

Differences in search actions between QRI types were also examined between tasks. Compared to ***"browsing task"***, successful QRIs in ***"topical search"*** were significantly ($p<.001$) shorter with less time on issuing queries and pivot browsing. Significantly ($p<.05$) more pivot browsing actions were made, SERPs were viewed and book pages were opened in ***"browsing task"*** compared to ***"topical search"*** when very interesting novels were chosen. Searchers devoted significantly ($p<.01$) more time on SERPs and book pages when assessing a very interesting novel in ***"browsing task"*** compared to ***"topical search"***.

Table 7. Means (standard deviations) of search actions in QRIs in *"browsing task"* in Sampo. (Duration in seconds.)

Measure	Mean (st.dev)			Between QRI type p-values		
	Suc. QRI n=134	**Some. Suc. QRI** n=102	**Un-suc. QRI** n=84	Suc. Some. suc.	Suc. Un-suc.	Some. Suc. Un-suc.
QRI duration	178 (140)	148 (115)	76 (89)	.118	**.000**	**.002**
Query time	21 (18)	15 (13)	27 (29)	**.002**	.806	.059
Pivot time	20 (37)	28 (41)	16 (27)	.317	.371	**.041**
SERP time	84 (71)	64 (64)	51 (64)	.071	**.008**	**.005**
BP time	74 (76)	56 (47)	9 (15)	.172	**.000**	**.000**
# pivot actions	1.1 (1.4)	1.4 (1.7)	0.5 (0.9)	.414	**.012**	.061
# SERP visits	2.8 (2.8)	2.0 (1.7)	1.7 (1.8)	**.032**	**.028**	**.050**
# BPs	2.6 (2.7)	2.1 (1.7)	0.5 (0.8)	.233	**.000**	**.001**

Legend: Suc= Successful QRI, Some. Suc= Somewhat successful QRI, Unsuc=Unsuccessful QRI, BPs=Book pages

When assessing somewhat interesting novels, significantly ($p<.001$) more time was devoted to pivot browsing and more pivot browsing actions were conducted in ***"browsing task"*** compared to ***"topical search"***. When selecting somewhat interesting novels, significantly ($p<.05$) more SERPs were viewed in ***"topical search"*** compared to ***"browsing task"***. When assessing not interesting novels, significant differences in search actions during QRIs between tasks did not occur.

Like in Sata, identifying very interesting novels required more effort in ***"browsing task"*** compared to ***"topical search"***. Moreover, when identifying interesting novels in Sampo pivot browsing was chosen as a search strategy more frequently in ***"browsing task"*** compared to ***"topical search"***.

5.3. Summary of Findings

In both catalogs the major differences between tasks occurred in the number of observed SERPs and opened book pages during the QRI types. In both catalogs, in ***"topical search"*** very interesting novels were selected by viewing only one to two SERPs and opening only one book page. When selecting somewhat interesting novels, three to four SERPs were observed and three book pages opened, while assessing not interesting novels, book pages were rarely opened. In ***"topical search"*** selecting somewhat interesting novels required more effort compared to selecting interesting or non-interesting novels, i.e. the association is curvilinear. In unsuccessful QRIs the inspecting of SERPs provided enough information to decide the results to be not interesting.

Diverging from the previous, in ***"browsing task"*** very interesting novels were selected by viewing three SERPs and opening three book pages. When assessing somewhat interesting novels, two SERPs were viewed and two book pages opened. When assessing not interesting novels, book pages were rarely opened. Thus, in ***"browsing task"*** the major differences in search actions between QRI types were linear: selecting interesting novels required most effort, while selecting not interesting ones required least effort.

6. MODELING SEARCH SUCCESS IN QRIs

The association of search actions during QRIs and books' interest grading was examined by multinomial logistic regression analysis.

Table 8. Multinomial regression models for *"topical search"*.

Indepen. variables	**Sata** n=207			**Sampo** n=169		
	VI vs NI	**SI vs NI**	**VI vs SI**	**VI vs NI**	**SI vs NI**	**VI vs SI**
	Odds ratio					
Query time	.95 *	.90 ***	.95 *	.98	.96 **	.98
Pivot time	-	-	-	.98	.90 **	.92*
SERP time	1.04 **	1.05 **	1.00	1.02	1.02*	1.00
BP time	1.05	1.10 **	1.05 **	1.06 **	1.05*	.99
# SERP visits	.11 ***	.12 ***	1.13	.37 *	.27 **	.72
# BPs	6.08 **	3.73 *	.61	1.12	2.41*	2.05 *
Model fitting	χ^2 =151.574, df=10, p=.000, Nagel. Pseudo R-square = 0.59 Overall % predicted correctly 68 %			χ^2 = 58.654, df= 10, p=.000, Nagel. Pseudo R-square = 0.33 Overall % predicted correctly 65 %		
* = p < .05 ** = p < .01 *** = p < .001 Legend: VI=Very Interesting, SI=Somewhat Interesting, NI=Not Interesting, BPs=Book pages						

In ***"topical search"***, the model for Sata suggests that when deciding between an interesting (VI and SI) and a not interesting novel (NI), the most significant predictors of the selection were the number of SERP visits and opened book pages (Table 8). An increase in the number of opened book pages produced six times greater odds to select a very interesting book compared to a non-interesting one, while a decrease in the number of viewed SERPs produced 9.1 (1/0.11) times greater odds of selecting a very interesting book compared to a non-interesting one. The association was similar in selecting between a somewhat interesting and a not interesting novel (SI and NI): the more book pages opened and the less SERPs viewed, the more likely the novel was assessed as a somewhat interesting compared to a not interesting. Interestingly, short query time and long dwell time on book pages contributed to predicting the selection of a very interesting novel instead of a somewhat interesting novel (VI and SI). The total variance explained by the model was rather high for Sata, 59 % as indicated by Nagelkerke R^2.

In ***"topical search"***, the model for Sampo suggests that when deciding whether the novel was very interesting or not interesting (VI and NI), the most significant predictor of the selection was the number of viewed SERPs. A decrease in the number of observed SERPs produced 2.7 (1/0.37) times greater odds of selecting a very interesting book compared to a non-interesting one. Like in Sata, when selecting between a somewhat interesting and a not interesting novel (SI and NI), an increase in the number of opened book pages produced two times greater odds to select a somewhat interesting book compared to a non-interesting one, while a decrease in the number of observed SERPs produced 3.7 (1/0.27) times greater odds of selecting a somewhat interesting book compared to a non-interesting one. Differing from Sata, when deciding either the novel was very interesting or somewhat interesting (VI and SI), the most significant predictor of the selection was the number of book pages opened. An increase in the number of opened book pages produced two times greater odds to select a somewhat interesting book compared to a very interesting one.

Table 9. Multinomial regression models for *"browsing task"*.

Indepen. variables	**Sata** n=419			**Sampo** n=320		
	VI vs NI	**SI vs NI**	**VI vs SI**	**VI vs NI**	**SI vs NI**	**VI vs SI**
	Odds ratio					
Query time	.94 ***	.95 **	1.01	.96 ***	.95 ***	.99
SERP time	1.04 ***	1.04 **	.99	1.00	1.00	1.00
BP time	1.04 *	1.04 *	.99	1.0 ***	1.07 **	.99
# SERP visits	.19 ***	.25 ***	1.31	.27 ***	.25 ***	.93
# BPs	3.50 **	3.27 **	.93	1.92	2.3 *	1.21
Model fitting	χ^2 =252.420, df=10, p=.000, Nagel. Pseudo R-square=0.52 Overall % predicted correctly 68 %			χ^2 = 148.036, df= 8, p=.000, Nagel. Pseudo R-square = 0.42 Overall % predicted correctly 55 %		
* = p < .05 ** = p < .01 *** = p < .001 Legend: VI=Very Interesting, SI=Somewhat Interesting, NI=Not Interesting, BPs=Book pages						

In ***"browsing task"***, the model for Sata suggests that when deciding whether the novel was interesting (VI and SI) or not interesting (NI), the most significant predictors were again the number of viewed SERPs and opened book pages (Table 9). An increase in the number of opened book pages produced almost four times greater odds to select a very interesting book compared to a non-interesting one, while a decrease in the number of viewed SERPs produced 5.3 (1/0.19) times greater odds of selecting a very interesting book compared to a non-interesting one. The trend was similar in selecting somewhat interesting books.

When selecting between very and somewhat interesting novels (VI and SI), the regression analysis yielded no significant predictors. This is in line with findings in the previous section, as it was found that successful and somewhat successful QRIs in the browsing task resemble each other, and differ from unsuccessful QRIs.

In ***"browsing task"***, the model for Sampo suggests that when selecting between very interesting and not interesting novels (VI and NI), the most significant predictor was the number of viewed SERPs. A decrease in the number of viewed SERPs produced 3.7 (1/0.27) times greater odds of selecting a very interesting book compared to a non-interesting one. The model also shows that quick queries and long dwell time on book pages predict the selection of very interesting novels compared to not interesting ones (VI and NI).

Similarly to ***"topical search"***, the most important predictors of selecting a somewhat interesting novel instead of a not interesting one (SI and NI) were the number of viewed SERPs and opened book pages. An increase in the number of opened book pages produced two times greater odds to select a somewhat interesting book compared to a non-interesting one, while a decrease in the number of explored SERPs produced four (1/0.25) times greater odds of selecting a somewhat interesting book compared to a non-interesting one. Similarly to Sata, when deciding between a very interesting or a somewhat interesting novel (VI and SI), the regression analysis yielded no significant predictors of selection.

7. DISCUSSION

As far as we know, this was the first study to examine fiction readers' search behavior during query reformulation intervals. We compared readers' search actions during successful and unsuccessful QRIs in two browsing tasks and in two catalogs.

7.1 Search Actions between Tasks

Significant differences were found in search actions between browsing tasks. Our findings demonstrated that searching for topical novels differed significantly from explorative browsing for interesting novels. Topical search for novels appeared to share characteristics with searching for topically relevant non-fiction documents. Gwizdka [5] noticed that when searching for non-fiction documents, the highest cognitive effort was required to assess partially relevant documents compared to irrelevant and relevant documents. A partially relevant document was defined as a topically relevant document not containing the answer to a particular question. Similarly to [5], we found that when searching for topically relevant novels, most effort was required to assess somewhat interesting novels compared to very or non-interesting novels. In the topical search the duration of QRI and dwell time on book pages were the longest during somewhat successful QRIs and the shortest during unsuccessful QRIs, i.e. the association was curvilinear. Similarly to [32] it seems that when browsing for topical novels, in *"selection stage most time is used for judging borderline cases compared to more valuable or valueless cases"*.

Deviating from the topical search, our results showed that in explorative browsing for novels, the duration of QRI and dwell time on book pages were linearly associated to document value. Selecting interesting novels required most effort, while non-interesting ones least effort in viewing results and book pages, but most effort in querying. The finding is in line with Liu & Belkin [12] and Liu et al. [13] who found that when selecting non-fiction documents, dwell time on document pages was linearly associated to document usefulness. Differing from the topical search, it seems that when browsing for interesting novels, in the selection stage most time is used for judging the most interesting cases. The difference could be partly explained by observing the participants: in the topical search they tended to select first a novel with high topical value and then assess its interest level. Thus, interest level was often a secondary criterion for selection in the topical search, whereas in the browsing task searcher's genuine interest was a strong motive to select a certain novel. It seems that identifying truly interesting novels in open ended browsing situations requires long dwell time on book pages, while eliminating not interesting ones requires least effort.

Finally, Liu et al. [11] found that during successful QRIs the users viewed more content pages and observed more SERPs, and spent longer time on them compared to unsuccessful QRIs. The findings of our study confirm, but also extend this result. Similarly to [11] our results demonstrated that the QRI type was associated to the duration of QRI. However, deviating from [11] our results showed that the search actions during successful and unsuccessful QRIs varied between browsing task type. In the topical search, the duration of QRI, SERP time and dwell time on book pages were the longest during somewhat successful QRIs, while shorter in both in successful QRIs. In the browsing task, the duration of QRI, SERP time and dwell time on book pages were the longest during successful QRIs and shortest during unsuccessful QRIs. To sum up, task type was clearly associated to search behavior during successful and somewhat successful QRIs.

7.2 Search Actions between Catalogs

We found that search actions during successful QRIs did not considerably differ between catalogs. Differences were found between catalogs in search actions during unsuccessful QRIs: in Sata query time and the number of viewed SERPs were significantly greater compared to Sampo. In Sata an unsuccessful search pattern was detected: particularly at the beginning of each task searchers tended to end up going in circles, where much time was devoted to selecting suitable entry terms together with a quick glance over the results before issuing a subsequent query. When glancing at the results, they were noticed unsatisfactory, and book pages were not entered. In consequence, visits in SERPs were numerous together with long query time. In Sampo a similar pattern was not discovered.

In all, it seems that in the traditional catalog more effort was invested in QRIs with no novels chosen compared to the enriched catalog. The enriched catalog result list contained rich information on novels' content such as a cover image and a snippet of a novel's blurb. Enriched result list might draw searchers into book pages for more detailed examination, and support the identification of interesting novels. Moreover, in book pages automatic recommendations are generated and searchers may proceed without entering a subsequent query. In the traditional catalog the result list provides titles and author names. If they are found not interesting, a necessity for proceeding is a re-formulated query. This may explain the difference in search actions during unsuccessful QRIs between the catalogs.

7.3 Search Actions and Search Success

We examined whether the search actions during QRIs were associated to books' interest grading in browsing tasks. We discovered that the search actions that contributed to predicting the selection of more interesting novels a) varied slightly between catalogs but b) were similar between tasks within a catalog.

Overall, our results demonstrated that in both tasks and catalogs the selection between interesting and not interesting novels was associated to few viewed SERPs and numerous opened book pages. Less viewed SERPs could be seen as a consequence of fewer queries. Thus, the first query should produce a satisfactory result list, from which to proceed to glancing at several book pages. It could be assumed that the more book pages are viewed, the higher the probability of encountering a very interesting one.

In the topical search, a difference occurred between catalogs when selecting between a somewhat interesting and a very interesting novel. In Sata, the longer the dwell time on book pages, the more likely the novel was assessed as very interesting instead of somewhat interesting. This suggests that longer dwell time on book pages was linearly associated to greater success, and is in line with Liu & Belkin's work 12]. In Sampo, the more book pages were opened, the more likely the novel was assessed as very interesting instead of somewhat interesting. This differs from Liu & Belkin's work [12] as instead of long dwell time on book pages, higher document usefulness was detected when the volume of viewed book pages was high. The difference might partly be due to differences in metadata elements between catalogs: as noted previously, in Sampo the result list and book pages contain detailed information on novels' content. In Sata, solely bibliographical and publication information together with subject terms are provided on book pages. With novels published recently, a cover image and a blurb might be available, but in a separate window. Therefore, in Sata long dwell time on book pages might be seen almost as a necessity for understanding what a novel is about, while in Sampo quick visits to book pages provide detailed information on a novel's content.

In the browsing task, when selecting between very and somewhat interesting novels, the regression analysis yielded no significant predictors of selection. This is reasonable, as we found that successful and somewhat successful QRIs in the browsing task resembled each other, and differed from unsuccessful QRIs.

7.4 Limitations and Implications

Firstly, the sample was biased towards females and the highly educated. Previous studies [i.e. 23, 26] have shown gender to be associated to different reading interests of pleasure readers. For example, women are more likely to be heavy readers than males and they tend to read a greater variety of books than men [23, 26]. In our study women's expected wider literary knowledge might have supported them to identify interesting titles better compared to men in the topical search. Then again, men's likely narrower reading preferences might have supported them to select interesting novels within a more limited range of authors and genres compared to women in the browsing task. By implication, males might have completed the browsing task quicker and with fewer search actions compared to women.

Secondly, the participants conducted search tasks in an experimental setting. Thus, it is not reasonable to generalize the findings to the population at large. Instead, the transferability of findings could be highlighted. As the search tasks reflected the major browsing tactics for fiction retrieval, it could be assumed that the search actions of fiction readers in another setting would share some characteristics with our results.

A few suggestions on system design can be made based on the findings. For the first, the high number of unsuccessful QRIs in the traditional catalog Sata hints that the searchers had a limited understanding on how to formulate effective queries [3]. Features such as Did you mean...? or semantic autocompletion could support searchers to avoid zero hit situations. For the second, as noted by McKay et al. [15] and Koolen et al. [10], content presentation and metadata are essential factors in determining books' usefulness when searching for books in digital libraries. In our study the enriched metadata in SERPs and book pages in Sampo might have supported the searchers to identify interesting topical novels more efficiently compared to Sata. In Sata, incomplete or missing metadata might have caused similar user behavior as in the work of McKay et al. [15]. Displaying solely the author and the title of a novel might have encouraged searchers to open topically relevant book pages for closer examination, and to devote much time to identifying the novel's topical relevance. If no additional metadata was provided, the novel might have been rejected or assessed as a somewhat interesting. Thus, as an implication for system design it could be acknowledged that enriched interface elements (such as a snippet, and a cover image) in SERPs might support readers to identify topical novels more quickly compared to the traditional result list that provides solely titles and author names.

For the third, in the browsing task selecting the most interesting novels required most effort. Similarly to [10], displaying the content of a novel with both professional metadata and user-generated content might support readers to assess novel's interest level more efficiently compared to providing solely professional metadata. Judging the relevance of a document with limited metadata information on a traditional catalog was found to be challenging for searchers [3]. The missing blurbs, cover images and book reviews in Sata might have affected the participants to reject novels that would have been of interest to them if enriched metadata had been available. Thus, providing a diverse range of metadata elements in title pages supports readers to judge the books. In addition, options for efficient browsing could enhance the finding of similarly interesting titles [16]. In our study identifying interesting titles by pivot browsing was often experienced as frustrating by the participants. Providing options for limited browsing, for example within a particular genre, could enhance the possibility of serendipitous discoveries.

8. CONCLUSION

We analyzed fiction readers' search actions during successful, somewhat successful and unsuccessful QRIs in browsing tasks.. Our contribution was especially in demonstrating that browsing task type was clearly associated to readers' document viewing behavior, i.e. the number of viewed SERPs, opened book pages and dwell time on book pages. In all, our study both confirmed, and extended previous findings. Browsing for topical novels resembled the retrieving of topically relevant non-fiction documents. The association of dwell time on book pages and document value was found to be non-linear: most effort was required to select somewhat interesting novels. When browsing for good books, the association of dwell time on book pages and document value was found to be linear: most effort in terms of dwell time was required to assess the most interesting cases. Therefore, if dwell time on book pages is considered as relevance feedback, it should be interpreted with understanding of the search situation, especially the task type.

9. REFERENCES

[1] Ballard, T. & Blaine, A. (2011). User search-limiting behavior in online catalogs. *New Library World*, 112, 5/6, 261-273.

[2] Bates, M. J. (1990). Where should the person stop and the information search interface start? *Inform Process Manag* 26, 5, 575-591.

[3] Blandford, A., Makri, S., Gow, J. et al. (2007). A library or just another information resource? A case study of users'

mental models of traditional and digital libraries. *J Am Soc Inf Sci Tec* 58, 3, 433-445.

[4] Goodall, D. (1989). *Browsing in the public libraries.* LISU Occasional paper No 1. Loughborough: Library and Information Statistics Unit.

[5] Gwizdka, J. (2014). Characterizing relevance with eye-tracking measures. In *Proceedings of IIiX'14.* ACM New York, NY, 58-67.

[6] Hu, X. & Kando, N. (2014) Evaluation of music search in casual-leisure situations. Presented at Searching4Fun workshop at IIiX2014. In *Proceedings of IIiX'14.* ACM New York, NY, 6.

[7] Hypén, K. & Mäkelä, E. (2011). An ideal model for an information system for fiction and its application: Kirjasampo and Semantic Web. *Library Review*, 60, 4, 279 – 292.

[8] Jiang, T. (2013). An exploratory study on social library system users' information seeking modes. *J Doc*, 69, 1, 6-26.

[9] Kim, J.Y., Feild, H. & Cartright, M. (2012). Understanding book search behavior on the web. In *Proceedings of CIKM'12.* ACM New York, NY, 744-753.

[10] Koolen, M., Kamps, J. & Kazai, G. (2012). Social book search: comparing topical relevance judgements and book suggestions for evaluation. In *Proceedings of CIKM'12.* ACM New York, NY, 185-194.

[11] Liu, C., Gwizdka, J. and Liu, J. (2010). Helping identify when users find useful documents: examination of Query Reformulation Intervals. In *Proceedings of IIiX'10.* ACM New York, NY, 215-224

[12] Liu, C. & Belkin, N.J. (2010). Personalizing information retrieval for multi-session tasks: the roles of task stage and task type. In *Proceedings of SIGIR'10.* ACM New York, NY, 26-33.

[13] Liu, C., Belkin, N.J. & Cole, M.J. (2012) Personalization of search results using interaction behaviors in search sessions. In *Proceedings of SIGIR'12.* ACM New York, NY, 205-214.

[14] Marchionini, G. (2006). Exploratory search: from finding to understanding. *Communications of the ACM* 49, 4, 41-46.

[15] McKay, D., Buchanan, G., Vanderschantz, N. et al. (2012). Judging a book by its cover: interface elements that affect reader selection of eBooks. In *Proceedings of OzCHI'12.* ACM, New York, NY, 381-390.

[16] McKay, D., Smith, W. & Chang, S. (2014) Lend me some sugar: borrowing rates of neighbouring books as evidence for browsing. In *Proceedings of JCDL 2014.* ACM, New York, NY, 145-154.

[17] Mikkonen, A. & Vakkari, P. (2012). Readers' search strategies for accessing books in public libraries. In *Proceedings of IIiX'12.* ACM, New York, NY, 214-223.

[18] Mikkonen, A. & Vakkari, P. (2014). Finding fiction: search moves and success in two online catalogs. Submitted for publication.

[19] Oksanen, S. & Vakkari, P. (2012). Emphasis on Examining Results in Fiction Searches Contributes to Finding Good Novels. In *Proceedings of JCDL 2012.* ACM, New York, NY, 199-202.

[20] Pejtersen, A. M. (1989). *The Bookhouse: modelling user's needs and search strategies as a basis for system design.* Risø report M-2794. Roskilde Risø National Laboratory.

[21] Peters, I. (2011). Folksonomies, social tagging and information retrieval. In A. Foster & P. Rafferty (Eds.), *Innovations in information retrieval. Perspectives for theory and practice* (pp 85-116). London: Facet Publishing.

[22] Pöntinen, J. & Vakkari, P. (2013). Selecting fiction in library catalogs: A gaze-tracking study. In *Proceedings of TPDL'13.* LNCS 8092. Springer, 72-83.

[23] Ross, C.S. 2001. Making choices: What readers say about choosing books to read for pleasure. *The Acquisition Librarian* 13, 25, 5-21.

[24] Tabachnick, B. G. & Fidell, L. S. (2013). *Using multivariate statistics.* 6th ed. Boston: Allyn and Bacon.

[25] Tang, M-C., Sie, Y-J. & Ting, P-H. (2014). Evaluating books finding tools on social media: a case study of aNobii. *Inform Process Manag* 50, 54-68.

[26] Tepper, S. J. 2000. Fiction reading in America: Explaining the gender gap. *Poetics* 27, 4, 255-275.

[27] The Power of Our Network. Strategic Plan 2015-2018. (2014). National Library of The Netherlands. Retrieved March 23, 2015 from: https://www.kb.nl/sites/default/files/docs/strategicplan-2015-2018.pdf

[28] The Reading Agency. (2013). *Library facts.* Retrieved October 26, 2014 from: http://readingagency.org.uk/news/library-facts004/

[29] The State of America's Libraries. (2014). A report from the American Library Association. Retrieved March 23, 2015 from:http://www.ala.org/news/sites/ala.org.news/files/content/2014-State-of-Americas-Libraries-Report.pdf

[30] Thudt, A., Hinrichs, U. & Carpendale, S. (2012). The Bohemian Bookshelf: Supporting serendipitous book discoveries through information visualization. In *Proceedings of CHI'12.* ACM, New York, NY, 1461-1470.

[31] Toms, E. 2000. Serendipitous information retrieval. In *DELOS workshop on "Information seeking, searching and querying in digital libraries"*, 17-20.

[32] Vakkari, P. & Luoma, A. & Pöntinen, J. (2014) . Book's interest grade and dwell time in metadata in selecting fiction. In *Proceedings of IIiX'14.* ACM New York, NY, 28-37.

[33] Wildemuth, B. M. (2004). The effects of domain knowledge on search tactic formulation. *J Am Soc Inf Sci Tec* 55, 3, 246-258.

[34] Wilson, M. L. & Elsweiler, D. (2010). Casual-leisure search: the exploratory search scenarios that break our current models. *HCIR'10.* New Brunswick, NJ, 28-31.

Online Person Name Disambiguation with Constraints

Madian Khabsa
Computer Science and Engineering
The Pennsylvania State Univeristy
University Park, PA, USA
madian@psu.edu

Pucktada Treeratpituk*
Science Park Promotion Agency
Ministry of Science and Technology
Bangkok, Thailand
pucktada@gmail.com

C. Lee Giles
Information Sciences and Technology
Computer Science and Engineering
The Pennsylvania State Univeristy
University Park, PA, USA
giles@ist.psu.edu

ABSTRACT

While many clustering techniques have been successfully applied to the person name disambiguation problem, most do not address two main practical issues: allowing constraints to be added to the clustering process, and allowing the data to be added incrementally without clustering the entire database. Constraints can be particularly useful especially in a system such as a digital library, where users are allowed to make corrections to the disambiguated result. For example, a user correction on a disambiguation result specifying that a record does not belong to an author could be kept as a cannot-link constraint to be used in any future disambiguation (such as when new documents are added). Besides such user corrections, constraints also allow background heuristics to be encoded into the disambiguation process. We propose a constraint-based clustering algorithm for person name disambiguation, based on DBSCAN combined with a pairwise distance based on random forests. We further propose an extension to the density-based clustering algorithm (DBSCAN) to handle online clustering so that the disambiguation process can be done iteratively as new data points are added.

Our algorithm utilizes similarity features based on both metadata information and citation similarity. We implement two types of clustering constraints to demonstrate the concept. Experiments on the CiteSeer data show that our model can achieve 0.95 pairwise F1 and 0.79 cluster F1. The presence of constraints also consistently improves the disambiguation result across different combinations of features.

Categories and Subject Descriptors

H.3.3 [[**Information Storage and Retrieval**]: Information Search and Retrieval

*Work done while at PSU

JCDL'15, June 21–25, 2015, Knoxville, Tennessee, USA.

http://dx.doi.org/10.1145/2756406.2756915.

General Terms

Algorithms, Experimentation

Keywords

Name Entity Recognition; Record Linking; Name Disambiguation; Clustering; Online Disambiguation

1. INTRODUCTION

People search is a large part of the search traffic on the internet. An old analysis of query logs from AllTheWeb and AltaVista search sites show that 11-17% of the queries were composed of a person name with additional terms and 4% were simply just person names [22, 3]. The most popular query on Google has often been a celebrity name, with other four or five names ranked in the top ten queries. Similar patterns can also be found in digital library search. Around 9% of the search requests made to the digital library CiteSeerX are queries with author names. This number goes up to almost 19% when counting search from unique IPs.

The task of searching the web for information regarding an individual person can be very challenging, especially when the name is shared by many others. According to the data from 1990 U.S. Census Bureau, 90,000 different names are shared by 100 million people [4]. As the amount of information on the web grows, more of these people are mentioned on different web pages, causing even more ambiguity in the search results. This problem is further compounded by the fact that sometimes the same person is referred to differently at various places. A person might be referred to with the full name on his/her homepage, but with just an initialized name or even just their position in some news articles. Moreover, even the information associated with one single person can be different in different sources. For instance, two web pages about the same person may provide different name spellings and different addresses.

Generally, the ambiguity of person's name comes in three varieties: (1) the aliasing problem - when a person uses multiple name variations such as "Ronald W. Williams" and "R.W. Williams", and (2) the common name problem - when there is more than one person with the same name, which is especially problematic for high frequency names such as many asian names; and (3) the typographic error problem - which often results from human input or automatic extraction systems. The goal of person name disambiguation is to resolve such ambiguities, linking and merging all the records of the same person together.

Name ambiguity is an important problem in many applications, including web search, natural language processing, information integration, and digital libraries. Name disambiguation is a specialized case of a more general database problem, called record linkage. Without name disambiguation, uses in the people search task, are often required to manually sort through search results to find the right person. In digital libraries, it hinders the accurate attribution of scholarly work, which is often used by academic institutions and funding agencies for promotion and funding consideration. In databases, name ambiguity leads to difficulty in merging multiple personal information databases, such as patient medical records from various healthcare providers. Additionally, the resulting disambiguated names can also be used to help improve other data mining results such as natural language processing, and social network analysis. While the person name disambiguation problem has long been well-studied, it has recently gained even more significance due to the increased ubiquity of names on the internet and the rise of social networking sites.

In this work we address two main practical issues found in a working name disambiguation system but generally have not been addressed by most previous person name disambiguation algorithms. First, most previous methods treat the person name disambiguation problem as a static problem, where all entities to be disambiguated are available to the algorithms. However, for working systems such as PubMed, the number of names to be disambiguated is ever increasing, for instance, when new papers are added to a digital library. Most previous methods would require the disambiguation process be periodically run on the whole data, which is time consuming and usually not scalable. Second, often the disambiguated clusters contain inconsistencies either due to insufficient information or mistakes by the similarity function. Thus, we propose an extension to the density-based clustering algorithm (DBSCAN) to handle online clustering so that the disambiguation process can be done iteratively as new data points are added. Additionally, our clustering method also imposes constraints on the clustering result, ensuring that each record in the same disambiguated cluster is consistent with each other. Our experiments show that our method not only outperforms the previous method in terms of performance, but also is capable of discovering new name clusters as new records are added.

The remainder of this paper is organized as follows. Section 2 surveys related work, while Section 3 describes the pairwise profile similarity function. In Section 4 we introduce DBSCAN with constraints and extend it to run in online fashion. The results and evaluations are reported in Section 5. Section 6 concludes the paper and discusses future work.

2. RELATED WORK

Previous work in person name disambiguation can be generally be categorized as either supervised or unsupervised approaches. Unsupervised methods harness some pre-defined likeness between people records in grouping them into clusters (e.g. similarity between topic-distribution or link-structure) [5, 21]. Supervised methods, on the other hand, explicitly learn the linking functions or rules from labeled examples [15, 16, 23, 24]. Some hybrid approaches also have been proposed. [23] and [12] use heuristics to automatically generate reference sets and use them, instead of labeled examples, as training data for the supervised methods. In [20] disambiguation is conducted using heuristics, with supervision being applied to optimize the heuristics parameters. We can also classify person name disambiguation methods based on the types of information they employ. In the digital library domain, the most often-used information is found in citations such as titles, coauthors, and venues [15, 16]. Additional information that is extracted from documents themselves, such as affiliations [16, 24] and abstract [21], have also been used. Some utilize information in the structure of the citation graph and the co-authorship graph [5]. Some explore external knowledge sources such as search engine and author homepages for disambiguation [18].

However the aspect of clustering streaming data has been ignored in most previous work on person name disambiguation. Most, if not all, assume the number of entities to be disambiguated static, and carry out the disambiguation process in a batch mode. On the other hand, many studies have been done on how to cluster streaming data in the database and data mining communities [29, 14, 13, 9, 8, 2, 1]. Ester et al. introduced an incremental version of DBSCAN [10]. While Cao et al. modify an density-based clustering method for dealing with streaming data [7]. Wagstaff and Cardie propose two types of instance-level clustering constraints, must-link and cannot-link, and show that these constraints can increase clustering accuracy and decrease runtime [27]. Whang et al. propose a general framework for entity resolution that can handle some integrity constraints, called "negative rules" [28]. Carlos Ruiz and colleagues introduced C-DBSCAN to accommodate for constraints when clustering data[19], but their work uses instance level constraints only such as must-link and cannot-link. Our work, on the other hand, introduces cluster level constraints in addition to instance level constraints. Furthermore, our work combines a streaming DBSCAN method along with constraints requirements that are not only at the instance level, but also at the cluster level.

3. PAIRWISE PROFILE SIMILARITY

Given two author profiles, p_1 and p_2 we seek to build similarity function that measures if these two profiles refer to the same author or not. In our previous work [24] we have introduced a machine learning method to learn such similarity function using random forests. Random forest is an ensemble classifier proposed by Breiman that combines a collection of decision trees [6]. Each decision tree within the forest is built with a different bootstrap sample drawn from the original data set. Each tree is then constructed to the maximum size without any pruning. The variable selection for each split in the tree is conducted on a randomly selected subset of features, instead of on the full feature set as is usually done in the traditional decision tree. Once the forest is built, the classification can be done by simply aggregating the votes of all trees. We will adapt this work to measure profile similarity with small modifications described later.

The pairwise author disambiguation service provides methods for calculating distance between a pair of author records and for retrieving the ε-neighborhood of an author record. The ε-neighborhood of a record r is a set of records with distance from r less than ε. The pairwise disambiguation service is composed of two components: the record indexes and the pairwise distance function. The indexes together with heuristic blocking function provide efficient retrieval of candidate records for ε-neighborhood generation. Currently, we simply block and index each record according to the last names and the first initials. While a more sophisticated blocking function should improve both the performance and the efficiency of the algorithm, it is beyond the scope of this work.

We extract the total of 31 features for computing the pairwise similarity. These 31 features can be grouped into six categories: name-related information (names and emails), affiliation, coauthors (names and their affiliations), venue information (venues and years), content (abstracts and titles), keyphrases and citations. Table 1 shows all the metadata used in the pairwise similarity, except citation information. Most metadata, such as author/coauthor names, affiliations, and etc, are extracted from each paper itself. These are available in all author records, albeit sometimes erroneous. The venue information (publication venue and year), on the other hand, is obtained through citation matching, and thus is less populated. Out of 3355 records of the test data set (described later), only half (~1500) contain venue names and about two-third contains years of publication. The citation information is computed from the global citation graph and thus requires access to the whole CiteSeerX database. Lastly, for the keyphrases, we use the SEERLAB algorithm [26] to extract keyphrases from each paper. The examples of keyphrases extracted by SEERLAB system are shown in Table 1.

The pairwise distance function is learned using a random forest. Since a random forest is a collection of randomized decision trees [6], the percentage of trees voting with the record pairs non-coreferent can be used as the distance measure. We use a similar feature set as proposed in [24], which includes similarities between author names, affiliations, emails, coauthors, papers titles, journals, and publication years. We also use two additional metadata types that were not in the original feature set in [24]: citations and keyphrases. For citations, we compute two features based on citation similarity: #bibliographic coupling and #co-citations. #bibliographic coupling between two author records is the number of papers that are cited by both papers, while #co-citations is the number of times that both papers appear together in the reference sections.

As for the keyphrases, we use the normalized Point-wise Mutual Information (nPMI) to measure the similarity between two keyphrases. The normalized Point-wise Mutual Information (nPMI) for two keyphrases, x and y, is defined as:

$$nPMI(x,y) = \frac{log\frac{p(x,y)}{p(x)p(y)}}{-log\,p(x,y)}$$

The $nPMI$ ranges from -1 to 1. $nPMI(x,y)$ is maximal at 1, when x and y fully co-occur and is minimal at -1 when x and y never co-occur ($p(x,y)=0$). $nPMI(x,y)$ is 0 if x and y are independent. For a record pair r_1 and r_2, with keyphrases $\{kp_{1i}\}_{i=1..n}$ and $\{kp_{2i}\}_{i=1..m}$ respectively, we compute three nPMI similarity measures: total nPMI similarity, maximum nPMI similarity and average nPMI similarity. For example, the total keyword similarity between r_1 and r_2 is

$$\sum_{i=1..n}\sum_{j=1..m} nPMI(kp_{1i}, kp_{2j})$$

Table 1: Example of metadata used for the disambiguation

Title: Tuning Memory Performance in Sequential and Parallel Programs
Abstract: Recent architecture and technology trends have led to a significant and increasing gap between processor and main memory speeds. Caches hide these latencies to some extent, but when cache misses...
Author: Anoop Gupta **Affiliation:** Department of Electrical Eng. Computer Systems Laboratory, Princeton University Stanford University
Coauthors: - Margaret Martonosi, Dept. of Electrical Eng... - Thomas E Anderson, Computer Science Division, University of California
Venue: IEEE Computer, **Year:** 1995
Keyphrases: parallel program, performance monitoring system, cache miss, performance information, program memory, memory bottleneck, program execution time, program data, technology trend

4. CLUSTERING PROFILE: ONLINE DBSCAN WITH CONSTRAINTS

To cluster author profile, we use a density-based clustering algorithm, DBSCAN [11]. DBSCAN defines a cluster as a connected region where data records are *dense*. A region is *dense*, if the number of records within ε distance from its center point (seed record) exceeds a minimum threshold, *minPts*. First, DBSCAN selects a record p that has not yet been assigned a cluster. Then, the ε-neighborhood of p is retrieved. If the ε-neighborhood is *dense*, a new cluster is created for p, otherwise p is marked as noise. If p is part of a cluster, then so is every record in p's ε-neighborhood. Thus, every record in the ε-neighborhood is added to the cluster, so are their *dense* ε-neighborhoods. With this process, the cluster is recursively expanded until it is fully discovered then a new unassigned record is selected to find a new cluster. DBSCAN does not require the number of clusters to be specified beforehand. Thus it is suitable for the author disambiguation task since different ambiguous names contain different numbers of true author clusters. This property also allows us to detect new author clusters, as new records are added. DBSCAN component relies on the pairwise similarity measure (as described in Section 3) in retrieving the ε-neighborhood of any given record p. We use $\varepsilon = 0.35$ and $minPts = 3$ in our implementation.

However, the standard DBSCAN assumes that all data points are already available at the start of the clustering process. This is not the case in the typical digital libraries setting, where new records are continuously added. In addition, the original DBSCAN does not address how to incorporate constraints in the clustering process. Thus in this section, we propose a modification to the standard DBSCAN clustering algorithm that enforce constraints on cluster-membership. We will also propose a merge subroutine to DBSCAN, that

Table 2: Examples of author records that could be mistakenly clustered without cluster-level constraints. A and B belong to the same author, while C is not.

Name
A) Execution Based Evaluation of Multistage Interconnection Networks for Cache-Coherent Multiprocessors **Name:** Akhilesh Kumar **Affil:** Intel Corporation Department of Computer Science, 2200 Mission College Blvd Texas AM University, Santa Clara College Station
B) FFT Implementations on nCUBE Multiprocessor **Name:** A Kumar **Affil:** Department of Computer Science, Texas AM University
C) Real-Time Communication in FDDI-Based Reconfigurable Networks **Name:** Amit Kumar **Affil:** Department of Computer Science, Texas AM University

allows new records to be added to the existing clustering result.

4.1 Types of Constraints and Motivation

In a real author disambiguation system, it generally is desirable to guarantee certain integrity property of each cluster. Table 2. shows an example of records that could be mistakenly clustered together by DBSCAN without an integrity check. In this case, record A and B belong to the same author, while C is of a different author. A and B are very similar on all three metadata (name, affiliation and both are multiprocessor-related). The similarity between B and C is less than the similarity between A and B; their topics are less related. So if

$$distance(A, B) < distance(B, C) < \varepsilon \ll distance(A, C)$$

Since both A and C are within ε-neighborhood of B, they will both be put in the same cluster with B, even though A and C are clearly incompatible and the $distance(A, C) \gg \varepsilon$.

Constraint enforcement can be done in two levels: at the instance-level and at the cluster-level.

Instance-level constraints are rules that check the compatibility between a record pair. With instance-level constraints, only records that are compatible with the seed record are allowed to be included in its ε-neighborhood. It restricts the local connections between a record and its neighbors.

Cluster-level constraints are rules that check the compatibility between a record and a cluster. Cluster-level constraints ensure that every record in a cluster is compatible with each other.

Instance-level constraints are relatively inexpensive and are easy to incorporate. However, it does not guarantee the integrity of the resulting cluster. For example, instance-level constraints would not address the situation shown in Table 2. Cluster-level constraints require more computation to enforce, but guarantee cluster integrity.

We now present two types of constraints currently implemented in the algorithm: the "temporal proximity" heuristic, which is a disjunctive constraint, and the "name compatibility" constraint, which is a conjunctive constraint.

4.1.1 Temporal Proximity

The intuition is that neighbors of a record r should be not only spatially close to r, but also temporally close as well. This is because two author records 10 years apart are unlikely to be coreferent if there are no records in between that time linking them. And also even if they both belong to the same author, their attributes such as coauthors and topics can be quite different because people move in and out of fields and often change collaborators. At the instance-level, temporal proximity requires that a record r can be in the ε-neighborhood of a record p only if r and p are close temporally. At the cluster-level, temporal proximity requires that a record r is a member of a cluster C, only if there exists $p \in C$, such that p is temporally close to r. Temporal proximity is a disjunctive constraint; To satisfy a cluster-level constraint of C, a record only needs to satisfy the instant-level constraint with any records in C. In our implementation, a record pair is considered to be temporally close if their publication dates are within 3 years of each other. Records missing year information are exempted from this constraint.

Table 3: Example of name variations found in CiteSeerX

Name	Found Variations	Note
Chienyu Chen	C Chen, Cy Chen, Chien Yu Chen	Chinese name Segmentation
Chun Che Fung	Lance Chun Che Fung	Extra nickname
David Johnson	Dav ID Johnson	Parsing error
James E Smith	Jim Smith, J E Smith	Nickname
Juan E. Tapiador	Juan M Estevez-Tapiador	Extra last name, confused as middle name
Jocelyn Smith	Jocelyin Smith	Misspelling

4.1.2 Name Compatibility

At the instance-level, name compatibility requires that a record r is a the ε-neighbor of a record p only if the name in r and p are compatible. At the cluster-level, it means that the name of every record in a cluster C must be compatible with each other. Unlike temporal proximity, name compatibility is a conjunctive constraint. To satisfy a cluster-level constraint of C, a record needs to satisfy the instant-level constraint with every record in C.

Table 3 shows examples of names and their variations found in CiteSeerX database. The different variations can be the results of parsing errors and misspelling like in the case of "Dav ID Johnson" and "Jocelyin Smith." Nicknames can be used in place of the first names ("Jim" instead of "James") or in addition to the full name (e.g. "Lance Chun Che Fung"). They can also be cultural dependent. Spanish names often have extra last names, which sometimes are taken as middle names (eg. "Juan M Estevez-Tapiador"), while Chinese names can be segmented and initialized in various ways. These names are all considered compatible with their variations.

Surface name matching is a very challenging problem in itself. Much research is still being devoted to the problem. Here we use the ethnicity-sensitive name matching that we introduced in [25] for enforcing the name compatibility constraint.

4.2 Clustering with Constraints

We now present our modification to the standard DBSCAN to incorporate clustering constraints, called DBSCAN$_C$. DBSCAN$_C$ maintains a data structure that keeps track of constraints for each cluster. When a record is added to a cluster, it appropriately updates the constraints for that cluster. A cluster-level constraint can be replaced if a strictly more restrictive one is added. For instance, a full middle name constraint would replace a middle name initial constraint. This allows for more efficient constraint checking. An example of constraint pairs that are compatible but one does not subsume the other are first name constraints, "James" and "Jim."

The main procedure of DBSCAN$_C$ is shown in Procedure 1, where D denotes the static collection of records to be disambiguated. The subroutine $query(D, p, \varepsilon)$ retrieves ε-neighborhood for the record p. DBSCAN$_C$ contains two main differences from the standard DBSCAN. First, each ε-neighborhood is sorted in ascending order according to the distance to the seed record p. In the standard DBSCAN, the order that records are processed is irrelevant to the final output. However, with cluster-level constraints, when a record is added to a cluster, it could introduce new constraints that would prevent some records to be added to that cluster later. Since the final result is sensitive to the order of records processed, we heuristically choose to favor the records that are closer to the seed record.

Procedure 1 DBSCAN$_C$(D)

```
Input: D - static collections of records to be disambiguated
mark all records in D as UNVISITED
for all record p in D do
    if p is UNVISITED then
        mark p as VISITED
        N ← query(D, p, ε)
        sort records in N by their distance from p
        N ← IConsFilter(p, N)
        N ← orderedIConsFilter(N)
        if |N| < minPts then
            assign p → NOISE
        else
            expandCluster(p, N)
        end if
    end if
end for
```

Second, each ε-neighborhood is first checked against instance-level constraints, before passing the density test. The call $IConsFilter(p, N)$ checks each record in the N and filters out those that do not satisfy instance-level constraints with the record p. The call $orderedIConsFilter(N)$ removes any record r in N that is not compatible with all the records that precede it in N. In other words, for every record pair $r, s \in N$, if r is closer to p than s, then s must be compatible with r. The reason behind $orderedIConsFilter(N)$ will become more clear when we describe $expandCluster(p, N)$. If the ε-neighborhood of p is sufficiently dense after both integrity checks, the function $expandCluster(p, N)$ is called to create and expand the new cluster.

$expandCluster(p, N)$, shown in Procedure 2, exhaustively expands a new cluster with a starting record p. As in the procedure $DBSCAN_C(D)$, each ε-neighborhood N' is sorted and passed through $IConsFilter$ and $orderedIConsFilter$ filters. An addition $CConsFilter$ filter is also applied to it. $CConsFilter(cid, N')$ imposes cluster-level constraints of the cluster cid to each record in N'. With $IConsFilter$, $orderedIConsFilter$, and $CConsFilter$, we can prove that $\forall$ record $q \in Q$ at all time, q can be added to the cluster cid, without violating any constraints, and that such a property is maintained throughout the clustering process. This property ensures the integrity of each cluster.

Procedure 2 expandCluster(p, N)

```
cid ← nextClusterId()
assign p → cid
Q ← N /* put records in region into a queue */
while Q ≠ ∅ do
    q ← pop a record from Q
    if q is UNVISITED then
        mark q as VISITED
        N' ← query(D, q, ε)
        sort records in N' by their distance from q
        N' ← IConsFilter(q, N')
        N' ← orderedIConsFilter (N')
        N' ← CConsFilter(cid, N')
        if |N'| ≥ minPts then
            /* append N' to the end of Q */
            Q ← Q + N'
        end if
    end if
    if q doesn't belong to any cluster then
        assign q → cid
    end if
end while
```

4.3 Online Disambiguation with Streaming Data

In the online setting, new records can be introduced to the existing clustering result. We add a *mergeRecord* procedure to the algorithm (Procedure 3). The *mergeRecord* procedure allows new records to be added to an existing cluster. The new record could also cause two or more existing clusters to merge together, if it creates a *dense* connection between those clusters. It could also cause a region of records that previously are marked as noises to become sufficiently *dense* to form a new cluster.

mergeRecord first considers the density of the ε-neighborhood of the new record. If the neighborhood is sparse, the new record is marked as noise. Otherwise, if the neighborhood contains existing clusters, the new record is added to the cluster that contains the most records in the ε-neighborhood. If more than one clusters intersect with the ε-neighborhood, they are sequentially merged according to the size of their intersections. After the new record is added to the cluster, and all appropriat clusters are merged, noise records in he neighborhood are added.

5. EVALUATION

5.1 Data & Evaluation Metrics

The CiteSeer's author disambiguation dataset is used for both training and evaluation purposes. The dataset contains author records of 10 highly ambiguous names sampled from the CiteSeer database. The names, their number of records, and their number of unique authors are shown in Table 4. This dataset and its slight variations have been used in many previous works in author disambiguation [16, 21]. The greyed out rows are used in training the random forest model (the same three names were also used in [16] as the training set). The classification accuracy is evaluated

Table 4: **CiteSeer author disambiguation collection**

	Data	#Rec	#Cluster
1	A. Gupta	498	45
2	A. Kumar	139	31
3	C. Chen	525	99
4	D. Johnson	345	40
5	J. Anderson	307	40
6	J. Robinson	111	27
7	J. Smith	729	83
8	K. Tanaka	52	19
9	M. Jones	348	51
10	M. Miller	226	35

on non-training data, while the clustering performance is evaluated on the whole data set.

We evaluate our disambiguation algorithm using three sets of standard metrics: the pairwise F1 (pF1), the cluster-level F1 (cF1) and the purity/inverse purity measures. The **pairwise F1** is defined as the harmonic mean of the **pairwise precision (pP)** and the **pairwise recall (pR)**. The pairwise precision is the percentage of record pairs placed in the same cluster that are coreferent, while the pairwise recall is the percentage of coreferent record pairs that are discovered by the algorithm (they are placed in the same cluster). Instead of counting pairs, the **cluster-level F1** counts clusters that exactly match the ground truth and is defined as the harmonic mean of the **cluster-level precision (cP)** and the **cluster-level recall (cR)**. The cluster-level precision is the fraction of generated clusters that exactly match those in the ground truth. The cluster-level recall is the fraction of the clusters in the ground truth that are exactly discovered. Lastly, the **purity** measures the purity of each of the generated clusters, while the **inverse purity** measures the fragmentation of clusters in the ground truth in the result. The formal formula of purity is

$$\sum_i \frac{|C_i|}{N} max_j Precision(C_i, L_j)$$

where C_i denotes a cluster in the result, and L_j denotes a cluster in the answer set. Similarly, the inverse purity is defined as

$$\sum_i \frac{|L_i|}{N} max_j Precision(L_i, C_j)$$

We also calculate **ratio of cluster size** *(RCS)*, which is defined as the ratio of the number of clusters retrieved over the number of true clusters.

5.2 Feature Analysis of the Clustering Results

Table 5 shows the comparison of the clustering results using each similarity feature. Two mixture models, MIX and MIX+CKP, are also evaluated. The MIX+CKP model utilizes all features, while the MIX model uses every features except keyphrases and citations. The features used in MIX are similar to those used in other previous work in author disambiguation [16, 24]. All feature sets yield over 89% pairwise-classification accuracies. As expected, the mixture models, MIX and MIX+CKP, yield the highest classification accuracies at 97%. However, other simpler feature sets also give comparable classification accuracies, with name-related features and coauthors features achieving around 95% classification accuracies.

For the clustering performance, the simplistic models do not perform well. The highest pF1 is that of the name model at only 0.65 and the highest cF1 is that of the affiliation model at just 0.54. The coauthors model produces the purest clusters (with Purity at 0.97 and pP at 0.98) but the clusters are quite fragmented (InvPurity at 0.58). This is because a highly similar coauthors connection is a good indicator of coreference, but the lack of such shared connection does not necessary mean that they do not refer to the same person. The venue model also gives a similar clustering result as the coauthors one, relatively pure clusters but very fragmented (high value of InvPurity and RCS). The content-based features such as abstract and keyphrases gave the opposite clustering results. They tend to produce less fragmented clusters but also more impure. Their InvPurity are reasonably high (0.82 and 0.78 respectively), and their Purity are relatively low.

For the mixture models, the MIX model achieves 0.86 pF1 and 0.69 cF1 while the MIX+CKP achieves 0.90 pF1 (+4%) and 0.76 cF1 (+7%), which is significantly higher. The performance of the MIX model is comparable to those of the previously reported result in [16]. The MIX+CKP performs noticeably better in cluster precision and recall (cP and cR).

It is interesting to note that while the classification accuracies of the simplistic models are comparable to those of the mixture models, their clustering performances are significantly lower. The pF1 and cF1 of the name model is just 0.65 and 0.46 respectively, compared to 0.90 and 0.76 for the MIX+CKP model. This difference is even more glaring between the two mixture models. We hypothesize that in the clustering process, misclassification errors will aggregate, thus a small difference in classification accuracy could result in a noticeable difference in the clustering result.

In random forest, one way to measure the importance of a feature in a model is by calculating the average drops in Gini index at nodes where that feature is used as the splitting criteria [6]. Table 7 shows 10 most indicative features in the MIX+CKP model according to this measurement. Middle name is the most informative feature, followed by various affiliation similarities, then keyphrase PMIs and coauthors' affiliations. We hypothesize that the high contributions of these keyphrase PMI features in the MIX+CKP model is what makes the MIX+CKP model better clustering performance over the MIX model. It is interesting to note that the number of papers cited by both records (bibliographic coupling) seems to be more indicative of linkage between authors than the number of co-citations.

5.3 Evaluating Online Disambiguation with Constraints

To evaluate the iterative disambiguation algorithm, we first randomly select 20% of the author records as the initial static records. We then run the disambiguation algorithm over these initial records, producing the initial disambiguated author clusters. The left-over 80% records are then added to the system one-by-one, simulating new incoming data. Table 6 shows the result of the iterative disambiguation algorithm with various constraint settings. Figure 1. shows the graphs of RCS, pF1, cF1, purity and inverse purity of the best configuration (MIX+CKP model with cluster-level constraints) as new records are added.

Table 5: The disambiguation result using different combination of feature sets

Similarity Model	Accuracy	RCS	pP	pR	pF1	cP	cR	cF1	Purity	InvPurity
name	94.6%	2.08	0.69	0.68	0.65	0.28	0.46	0.34	0.83	0.68
affiliation	91.3%	2.47	0.61	0.68	0.54	0.53	0.24	0.54	0.73	0.63
coauthors	93.6%	2.16	0.98	0.48	0.62	0.30	0.61	0.40	0.97	0.58
venue	89.6%	4.43	0.64	0.17	0.25	0.12	0.49	0.19	0.78	0.28
abstract	91.6%	1.07	0.45	0.86	0.52	0.41	0.43	0.40	0.61	0.82
keyphrases	92.5%	1.24	0.46	0.76	0.50	0.36	0.44	0.49	0.65	0.78
citations	92.5%	1.81	0.73	0.63	0.63	0.32	0.57	0.41	0.83	0.67
MIX	96.8%	1.03	0.81	0.94	0.86	0.69	0.69	0.69	0.89	0.87
MIX+CKP	96.9%	1.02	0.85	0.96	0.90	0.76	0.76	0.76	0.92	0.88

Table 6: The disambiguation result of the full-feature similarity and whether heuristic constraints are enforced. LASVM is the online SVM model used in Huang et al[16].

Similarity Model	Constraint	RCS	pP	pR	pF1	cP	cR	cF1	Purity	InvPurity
MIX	none	1.03	0.81	0.94	0.86	0.69	0.69	0.69	0.89	0.87
	instance	1.06	0.85	0.92	0.88	0.69	0.73	0.71	0.91	0.87
	cluster	1.08	0.89	0.94	0.91	0.70	0.74	0.72	0.93	0.87
MIX+CKP	none	1.02	0.85	0.96	0.90	0.76	0.76	0.76	0.92	0.88
	instance	1.06	0.87	0.96	0.90	0.76	0.80	0.78	0.93	0.88
	cluster	1.07	0.95	0.96	0.95	0.76	0.81	0.79	0.97	0.88
LASVM	none	0.94	0.87	0.94	0.91	-	-	0.64	-	-

Procedure 3 mergeRecord(p)

Input: p is a new record added to D, not yet processed

```
N ← query(D, p, ε)
sort records in N by their distance from p
N ← IConsFilter(p, N)
if |N| < minPts then
    assign p → NOISE
else
    C ← set of clusters C_i, such that ∀C_i, C_i ∩ N ≠ ∅
    if C ≠ ∅ then
        L ← ∅
        for all C_i ∈ C do
            if ∅ ≠ CConsFilter(i, {p}) then
                L ← L ∪ {C_i}
            end if
        end for
        sort C_i ∈ L by |C_i ∩ N| in descending order
        C_k ← the cluster ∈ L with the biggest intersection
    else
        k ← nextClusterId()
    end if
    assign p → k
    for all C_i in L \ {C_k} do
        if C_i = CConsFilter(k, C_i) then
            C_k ← C_k ∪ C_i /* merge C_i to C_k */
        end if
    end for
    noises ← {q|q ∈ N and q ∉ C_i, ∀C_i ∈ C}
    /* noises retained the sorted order of N */
    noises ← orderedIConsFilter (noises)
    noises ← CConsFilter(cid_0, noises)
    for all q in noises do
        assign q → k
    end for
end if
```

Table 7: The top 10 features (out of 31) in the MIX+CKP model according to the average Gini decrease

Rank	Features
1	middle name
2	affiliation (soft-tfidf)
3	affiliation (jaccard)
4	keyword PMI (summation)
5	coauthors' affiliations (jaccard)
6	keyword PMI (max)
7	first name (boolean rule-match)
8	first name (jaro-winkler)
9	affiliation (tfidf)
10	# of bibliographic coupling

Table 6. shows that constraints consistently improve performance across all evaluation matrices. Instance level constraints offer improvement over no constraints configuration, and the cluster level constraints offer improvement over instance level constraints. Cluster level constraints offer 5% increase in pairwise F1 and 3% increase in cluster F1 over the base model. The improvements are most noticeable in pP and cR, and purity.

MIX+CKP model with cluster level constraints achieves 0.95 pairwise F1 and 0.79 cluster F1. Its purity and inverse purity are 0.97 and 0.88. Its pairwise precision is 8% more than those with just instance level constraints, and 10% more than the no constraints setting. 0.81 cluster recall indicates that it successfully recovered 81% of the true clusters, and with 0.76 cluster precision, more than three fourths of its clusters are correct. With 0.97 purity, it rarely mixes multiple people together. While both instance constraints and cluster constraints improve purity, they, however, do not increase inverse purity. RCS is also slightly bigger in constraints conditions. So while constraints help

Table 8: Cluster-level F1 with margins of errors for the MIX+CKP with cluster-level constraints

Margin	cP*	cR*	cF1*
0	0.76	0.81	0.79
1	0.81	0.88	0.84
2	0.83	0.89	0.86

enforce cluster integrity, they do not alleviate the cluster fragmentation problem.

Compared with the previously proposed method in Huang et al [16], LASVM – online SVM, the basic MIX model performs worse in the pairwise F1, 0.86 compared to 0.91 for LASVM, but has higher cluster-level F1, 0.69 compared to 0.64 for LASVM. The basic MIX+CKP performs slightly lower in the pairwise F1, 0.91 compared to 0.91 for LASVM, but performs significantly higher in cluster-level F1, with over 0.12 improvement. With the cluster-level constraints enforced, both the MIX and the MIX+CKP perform better than LASVM model in all evaluation matrices, including both the pairwise F1 and the cluster-level F1.

As new records are introduced to the algorithm, we see the inverse purity goes up in all data sets (Figure. 1). This is because as new information becomes available, the algorithm can better join previously fragmented clusters together. The increases are most noticeable in "cchen," which is the most ambiguous case, and "ktanaka," which is one of the smaller cases. The pairwise F1 and the purity remain relatively stable as records are added. There is more fluctuation in the cluster F1. This is because when new records of a previously unseen author are introduced, it is difficult for a density-based clustering method to pick up on the new cluster. And as more records of that cluster are added, the chance that the algorithm will correctly identify that cluster increases. As new records are added, the number of the true clusters increases. But since RCS remains relatively stable over time, this means that the algorithm is able to identify previously unseen clusters.

In order to better understand the resulting clusters, we modify the definition of the cluster-level measures to include a margin factor. The standard cluster-level measures (cP, cR and cF1) only count the exact match as correct. In the modified measures (denoted cP*, cR* and cF1* respectively), near-exact clusters would also be counted as a match. More precisely, for a given margin M, a non-singleton resulting cluster C and an answer cluster L is considered a match if both $|C - L|$ and $|L - C|$ are less than M. For $M = 0$, it is equivalent to the standard definition. For $M = 1$, a cluster is still considered a match if it is off by only one record. We do not apply the margin in comparing singleton and doubleton clusters (still need a perfect match to count). Table 8 shows the modified cluster-level precision, recall and F1 for the MIX+CKP model with constraints. With the margin $M = 2$, the cluster F1 is over 0.86 with the cluster recall 0.89. This means that almost 90% of author clusters are almost perfectly identified.

Overall, precision and purity are higher than recall and inverse purity. This characteristic is actually desirable in the production system because it is generally easier to merge two (or more) pure clusters and then to split impure clusters, both from the users' and the administrator's perspective. Furthermore, two pure but fragmented clusters could be algorithmically merged if a new author record, whose its ε-neighborhood contains records from both clusters and has above-threshold density, is ingested. But if a cluster is already impure, the standard DBSCAN does not have a mechanism to re-split it.

6. CONCLUSION

Constraints can be particularly useful in a digital library or other situations where users are allowed to make corrections to disambiguated names, especially in an iterative scenario.

We describe an author disambiguation framework that incorporates both metadata information and citation information. We show that our feature set yields high pairwise disambiguation accuracy and could be used successfully in clustering author records. We also propose a novel variation of the DBSCAN-based clustering algorithm that allows external knowledge and constraints to be injected into the disambiguation processes. Two examples of constraints were implemented, one instance-level and one cluster-level constraint, namely the "temporal proximity" and "middle-name compatability." Our experiments demonstrate that our clustering with constraints approach can achieve almost 96% precision and 93% F1 measure in disambiguation accuracy. Additionally, we also propose an extension to our clustering framework, that allows an iterative disambiguation process. Our experiment shows that the iterative disambiguation process is effective. As new people profiles are added, it can use the new information to improve the existing clustering result or to discover new people clusters. Recently we have used a batch variation of this algorithm to disambiguate more than 70 million author mentions in *Medline* [17], and the proposed iterative algorithm can be used to disambiguate newly added records to *Medline*. For future work, one could explore additional types of constraints, both instance-level and cluster-level, and their effect on the disambiguation performance. It would also be interesting to study the effect on efficiency based on how the constraints are enforced.

7. ACKNOWLEDGMENTS

We gratefully acknowledge partial funding from National Science Foundation and useful comments from the referees.

8. REFERENCES

[1] C. C. Aggarwal, J. Han, J. Wang, and P. S. Yu. *A framework for clustering evolving data streams.* The 29th VLDB Conference, Sept. 2003.

[2] C. C. Aggarwal, J. Han, J. Wang, and P. S. Yu. *A framework for projected clustering of high dimensional data streams.* The 30th VLDB Conference, Aug. 2004.

[3] J. Artiles, J. Gonzalo, and S. Sekine. WePS 2 Evaluation Campaign: Overview of the Web People Search Clustering Task. *2nd Web People Search Evaluation Workshop (WePS 2009), 18th WWW Conference*, Jan. 2009.

[4] J. Artiles, J. Gonzalo, and F. Verdejo. A Testbed for People Searching Strategies in the WWW. In *Proceedings of the 28th annual international ACM SIGIR conference on Research and development in information retrieval*, page 569, New York, New York, USA, 2005. ACM Press.

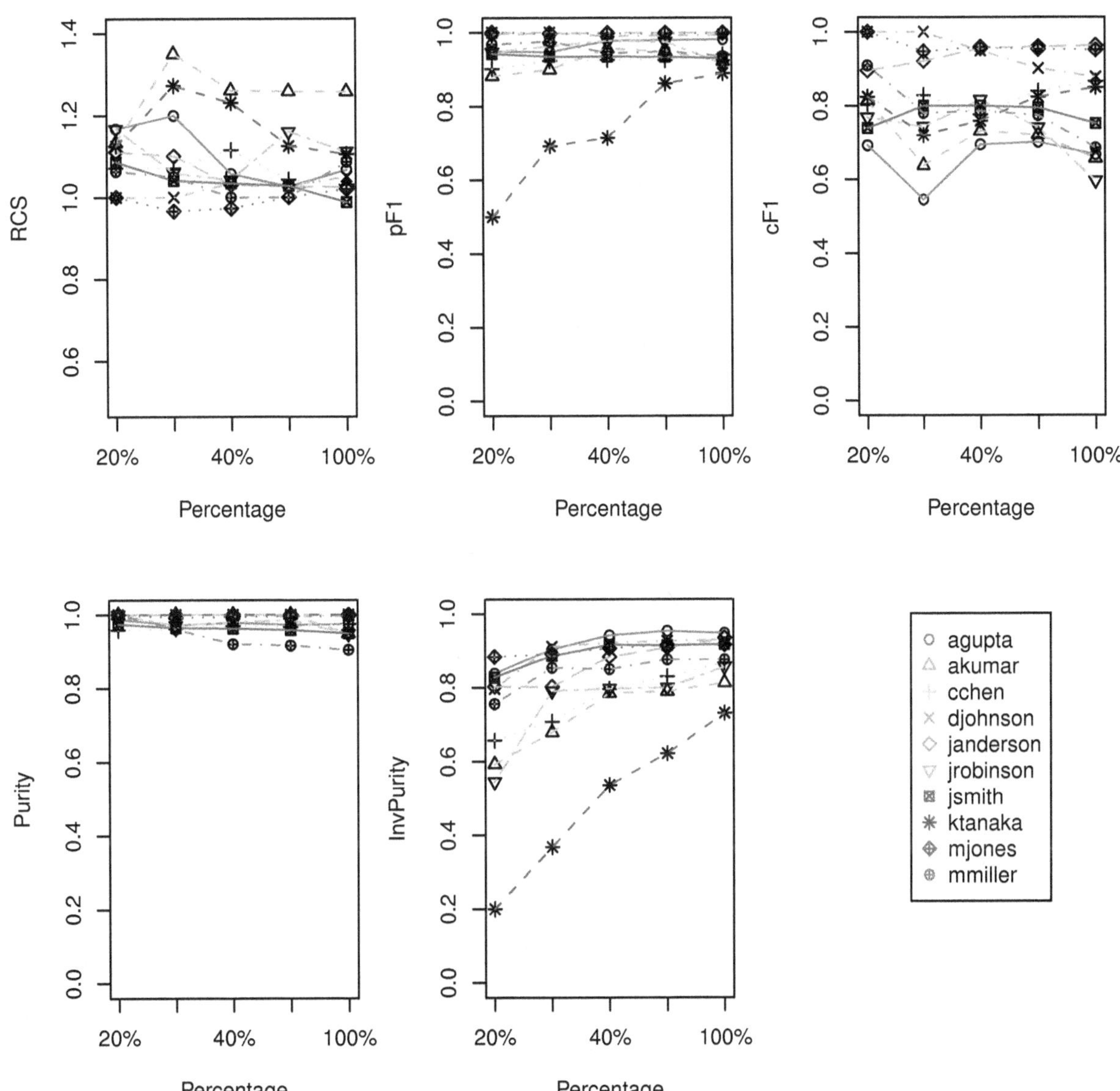

Figure 1: RCS, pF1, cF1, Purity and InvPurity of the MIX+CKP model with cluster-level constraints as new records are added.

[5] R. Bekkerman and A. McCallum. Disambiguating Web appearances of people in a social network. *In Proceedings of The 14th International Conference on World Wide Web (WWW'05)*, pages 463–470, 2005.

[6] L. Breiman. Random Forests. *Machine Learning*, 2001.

[7] F. Cao, M. Ester, W. Qian, and A. Zhou. Density-Based Clustering over an Evolving Data Stream with Noise. *the 6th SIAM International Conference on Data Mining*, May 2006.

[8] M. Charikar, L. O'Callaghan, and R. Panigrahy. Better streaming algorithms for clustering problems. *The 35th annual ACM Symposium on Theory of computing (STOC)*, May 2003.

[9] B.-R. Dai, J.-W. Huang, M.-Y. Yeh, and M.-S. Chen. Clustering on Demand for Multiple Data Streams. *The 4th IEEE International Conference on Data Mining (ICDM'04)*.

[10] M. Ester, H.-P. Kriegel, J. Sander, M. Wimmer, and X. Xu. Incremental clustering for mining in a data warehousing environment. In *VLDB*, volume 98, pages 323–333, 1998.

[11] M. Ester, H.-P. Kriegel, J. Sander, and X. Xu. A density-based algorithm for discovering clusters in large spatial databases with noise. In *Kdd*, volume 96, pages 226–231, 1996.

[12] A. Ferreira, A. Veloso, and M. Gonçalves. Effective self-training author name disambiguation in scholarly digital libraries. *In Proceedings of the ACM/IEEE Joint Conference on Digital Libraries (JCDL'10)*, 2010.

[13] S. Guha, A. Meyerson, N. Mishra, R. Motwani, and L. O'Callaghan. Clustering data streams: theory and practice. *IEEE Transactions on knowledge and data engineering*, 15(3):515–528, May 2003.

[14] S. Guha, N. Mishra, R. Motwani, and L. O'Callaghan. Clustering Data Streams. In *The 41st Annual Symposium on Foundations of Computer Science*, pages 359–366. IEEE Comput. Soc.

[15] H. Han, C. L. Giles, H. Zha, C. Li, and K. Tsioutsiouliklis. Two supervised learning approaches for name disambiguation in author citations. *In Proceedings of the ACM/IEEE Joint Conference on Digital Libraries (JCDL'04)*, 2004.

[16] J. Huang, S. Ertekin, and C. L. Giles. Efficient Name Disambiguation for Large-Scale Databases. In *The 10th European Conference on Principles and Practice of Knowledge Discovery in Databases (PKDD 2006)*, pages 536–544, 2006.

[17] M. Khabsa, P. Treeratpituk, and C. L. Giles. Large scale author name disambiguation in digital libraries. In *Big Data (Big Data), 2014 IEEE International Conference on*, pages 41–42. IEEE, 2014.

[18] D. Pereira, B. Ribeiro-Neto, and N. Ziviani. Using web information for author name disambiguation. *In Proceedings of the ACM/IEEE Joint Conference on Digital Libraries (JCDL'09)*, 2009.

[19] C. Ruiz, M. Spiliopoulou, and E. Menasalvas. C-dbscan: Density-based clustering with constraints. In *Rough Sets, Fuzzy Sets, Data Mining and Granular Computing*, pages 216–223. Springer, 2007.

[20] A. F. Santana, M. A. Goncalves, A. H. Laender, and A. Ferreira. Combining domain-specific heuristics for author name disambiguation. In *Digital Libraries (JCDL), 2014 IEEE/ACM Joint Conference on*, pages 173–182. IEEE, 2014.

[21] Y. Song, J. Huang, I. G. Councill, J. Li, and C. L. Giles. Efficient topic-based unsupervised name disambiguation. *In Proceedings of the Joint Conference on Digital Libraries (JCDL'07)*, pages 342–351, 2007.

[22] A. Spink, B. J. Jansen, and J. Pedersen. Searching for people on Web search engines. *Journal of Documentation*, 60(3):266–278, 2004.

[23] V. Torvik, M. Weeber, D. Swanson, and N. Smalheiser. A probabilistic similarity metric for Medline records: A model for author name disambiguation. *Journal of the American Society for Information Science and Technology*, 2005.

[24] P. Treeratpituk and C. L. Giles. Disambiguating Authors in Academic Publications using Random Forests. *In Proceedings of the Joint Conference on Digital Libraries (JCDL'09)*, Jan. 2009.

[25] P. Treeratpituk and C. L. Giles. Name-ethnicity classification and ethnicity-sensitive name matching. In *AAAI Conference on Artificial Intelligence*, 2012.

[26] P. Treeratpituk, P. Teregowda, J. Huang, and C. L. Giles. Seerlab: A system for extracting key phrases from scholarly documents. In *Proceedings of the 5th international workshop on semantic evaluation*, pages 182–185. Association for Computational Linguistics, 2010.

[27] K. Wagstaff and C. Cardie. Clustering with instance-level constraints. *Proceedings of the national conference on artificial intelligence*, Apr. 2000.

[28] S. E. Whang, O. Benjelloun, and H. Gracia-Molina. Generic entity resolution with negative rules. *The VLDB Journal*, 18.

[29] J. Yang. Dynamic Clustering of Evolving Streams with a Single Pass. *The 19th International Conference on Data Engineering (ICDE'03)*, Apr. 2003.

Improving Accessibility of Archived Raster Dictionaries of Complex Script Languages

Sawood Alam
Dept. of Computer Science
Old Dominion University
Norfolk, Virginia, USA
salam@cs.odu.edu

Fateh ud din B Mehmood
National University of Sciences and Technology
Islamabad, Pakistan
fatehh@gmail.com

Michael L Nelson
Dept. of Computer Science
Old Dominion University
Norfolk, Virginia, USA
mln@cs.odu.edu

ABSTRACT

We propose an approach to index raster images of dictionary pages which in turn would require very little manual effort to enable direct access to the appropriate pages of the dictionary for lookup. Accessibility is further improved by feedback and crowdsourcing that enables highlighting of the specific location on the page where the lookup word is found, annotation, digitization, and fielded searching. This approach is equally applicable on simple scripts as well as complex writing systems. Using our proposed approach, we have built a Web application called "Dictionary Explorer" which supports word indexes in various languages and every language can have multiple dictionaries associated with it. Word lookup gives direct access to appropriate pages of all the dictionaries of that language simultaneously. The application has exploration features like searching, pagination, and navigating the word index through a tree-like interface. The application also supports feedback, annotation, and digitization features. Apart from the scanned images, "Dictionary Explorer" aggregates results from various sources and user contributions in Unicode. We have evaluated the time required for indexing dictionaries of different sizes and complexities in the Urdu language and examined various trade-offs in our implementation. Using our approach, a single person can make a dictionary of 1,000 pages searchable in less than an hour.

Categories and Subject Descriptors

H.3.3 [**Information Storage and Retrieval**]: Information Search and Retrieval

General Terms

Design, Implementation, Evaluation

Keywords

Dictionary, OCR, Indexing, Digitization, Retrieval, Urdu, Scanned Image

JCDL'15, June 21–25, 2015, Knoxville, Tennessee, USA.

ACM 978-1-4503-3594-2/15/06 ...$15.00.
DOI: http://dx.doi.org/10.1145/2756406.2756926.

1. INTRODUCTION

The Internet Archive (IA) and Open Library offer over 6 million fully accessible public domain eBooks [26]. Among these eBooks there are handful of Unicode eBooks (for example, the Project Gutenberg collection [27]), but most of them are PDFs and scanned raster image based eBooks. To make these books accessible from a Web browser, IA uses an open-source application called BookReader [11]. To make the content of these raster eBooks searchable, IA uses ABBY FineReader [2] for Optical Character Recognition (OCR) [5]. For full-text searching, OCR engine returns page numbers and coordinates of the surrounding box, that is then used by the BookReader to annotate and highlight appropriate regions on corresponding pages. ABBY FineReader claims support for up to 190 languages [1]. Unfortunately several major languages such as Indian languages (Hindi, Punjabi, Telgu, Marathi, etc.) and complex script languages (Urdu, Persian, Sindhi, etc.) are not supported by this OCR engine. As a consequence, scanned books in these languages do not support full-text searching as illustrated in Figure 1(a).

Among these archived books there are a handful of dictionaries in various languages, ranging from very rare and classical to modern dictionaries. These dictionaries accumulate a treasure of ancient and obsolete as well as modern and contemporary words and phrases that are of equal interest to archivists and linguistics. In dictionaries, fielded searching is more important and desirable than full-text content searching. Generally, lookup in a dictionary involves a word or phrase, part of speech, origin language and other related metadata. Searching in the definition field is rarely desired. The type of OCR-powered full-text searching currently available in IA's BookReader makes it very difficult to lookup definitions of common words in a dictionary. For example, if we search for the term "book" in the scanned copy of [30], it returns 174 matches on various pages including pages where the term has appeared in the definitions or examples as illustrated in Figure 1(b).

To enable easy lookup, traditional dictionaries have a distinct property of being a sorted index of words that makes the interaction with them different from other books. One can easily use binary search to flip through pages while looking at the header of the pages to locate the desired page. A destination page in a dictionary may or may not have the desired word, but it ensures that if the lookup word was not found on that page then it does not exist in that dictionary. Using this property of dictionaries, we are progressively indexing pages of dictionaries manually to provide various levels of accessibility and searchability. A sparse index can make lookup in a normal size dictionary possible in matter of few hours while a complete indexing requires a few days of crowd-sourced work. Complete digitization and annotation is a long-term ongoing crowd-sourced effort.

2. BACKGROUND

Digitizing scanned book archives is an important step towards improving accessibility. Digitization can be done manually by crowdsourcing which yields good quality, but is a slow process in contrast with an OCR assisted approach which is fast and scalable but results in poor quality recognition. In complex script languages, the accuracy of the OCR is often unacceptable and sometimes there is no support at all. To understand the current state of the character recognition in Asian and complex script languages, various surveys have been published [19, 21, 44, 32]. Arabic, Persian, Urdu, and some other languages share the same script with slight variation in character sets and they are all written right-to-left (RTL). Persian and Urdu are very similar in terms of typography as they both are traditionally written in Nastaleeq (a complex cursive style) while Arabic is mostly written in Naskh (a complex but non-cursive style). Character segmentation and recognition is challenging in these scripts, hence there were OCR efforts that work with or without segmentation [13, 28, 29, 47, 58].

Urdu is a widely spoken language worldwide with a total number of 104 million speakers [61], with the majority in India and Pakistan. UrduWeb Digital Library (UWDL) [55] is an initiative of UrduWeb [38] where a designated library team manually digitizes copyright-free Urdu books and publishes them on the Web in Unicode format. UWDL has started a sub-project of digitizing dictionaries because Web-based modern dictionaries are missing historical vocabulary that are not in use. Scanned copies of various classical Urdu dictionaries are preserved in IA without any OCR processing. Digitizing these dictionaries properly with all the attributes stored separately to enable fielded searching is a time intensive task. We simplified this task by indexing images and serving appropriate scanned pages on lookup. This approach has proven successful and efficient and it is not limited to just the Urdu language.

3. RELATED WORK

There have been a lot of work in preserving books in the form of scanned images, digitizing scanned pages using OCR engines and crowdsourcing, analyzing digital data, and building archive explorers [20, 6, 16, 36, 7, 63, 43, 60, 59]. While OCR engines offer a scalable mechanism to digitize scanned images, they have limited accuracy or no support for many of the world's popular languages, hence automating digitization work-flow [51] is not feasible. Our focus is dictionaries, a very specific class of books, that are different from other general book in many ways including fielded information and some sort of ordering for easy lookup.

3.1 Major Digital Libraries

The Google Books initiative [23] is promoting the democratization of knowledge by scanning the World's books and putting them online. In 2010 Google estimated the total number of books in the world about 130 million [52] and intended to scan them all in a decade. Google Books has scanned over 30 million books by April 2013, but the process was since slowed down due to copyright issues [12].

The Open Library [25] is an initiative of the Internet Archive to facilitate access to digital books. It is a book database and digital lending library. It serves over six million digital books in various formats, but several books in the collection are in the form of scanned raster images of printed book pages also available as PDFs. Apart from downloadable books it offers online access to several scanned books with the help of a Web browser based application.

HathiTrust [45] is a collaborative repository of digital content from various research institutions and libraries to preserve cultural records and to ensure accessibility and availability of the preserved content in future.

These three libraries are good sources of scanned images of dictionaries. Mirdeghan conducted a survey to compare the interfaces of these three libraries, which shows that the majority of participants preferred Open Library followed by Google Books [34]. Our interface idea is inspired by the Open Library BookReader interface with extra features specific to dictionary exploration.

3.2 BookReader

BookReader [11] is an open-source community collaborated Web application for online reading of books which powers the Open Library as well as several other digital libraries. BookReader supports various layouts like single page, two pages, or thumbnails of multiple pages on the viewport, zooming functionality, flipping pages forward and backward, seeking direct access to a page, auto-play to flip pages automatically, highlighting matched text on the page, read aloud, and full-text searching. To facilitate full-text searching, text-to-speech, and highlighting it uses an OCR engine to process scanned pages.

3.3 ABBY FineReader

ABBY FineReader is a commercial OCR engine. IA uses it to process scanned images of books to power BookReader. It recognizes up to 190 languages that include natural, artificial, and formal languages, but unfortunately out of the world's 100 most popular languages (based on number of native speakers) [39] 63 are not supported. This proportion of unsupported languages roughly holds true for the top 50 (29 unsupported) and top 10 (4 unsupported) languages as well. Also the accuracy of the recognition for various languages is not mentioned in [1]. Figure 1(a) shows an unsuccessful search for an Urdu term in a dictionary using the Open Library BookReader due to the lack of support of OCR in the Urdu language, although the term exists on the page. In the case of a dictionary, users primarily want to search in the words not in the definitions, but this OCR engine cannot distinguish definition text from the lookup word.

3.4 Digital Dictionaries of South Asia

University of Chicago has worked on a project to digitize dictionaries of South Asian languages [54]. They have selected at least one multilingual dictionary for 26 modern literary languages of South Asia and some monolingual dictionaries for more frequently taught languages. They digitized those dictionaries manually and created an interface for fielded searching. It requires a lot of focussed manual labour to digitize books this way and the process is not scalable. Most of their work is available under a Creative Commons license [10], but some materials have further restrictions.

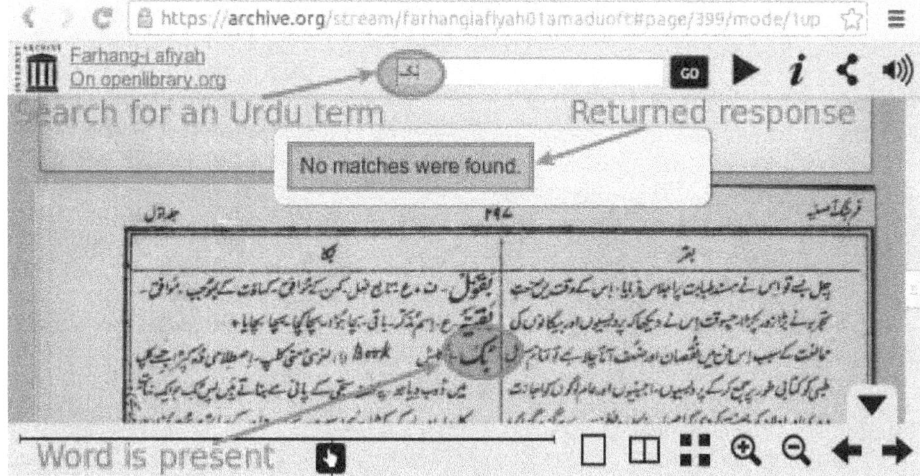

(a) Search for an Urdu term returned no matches due to lack of OCR support although the term is present in the book.

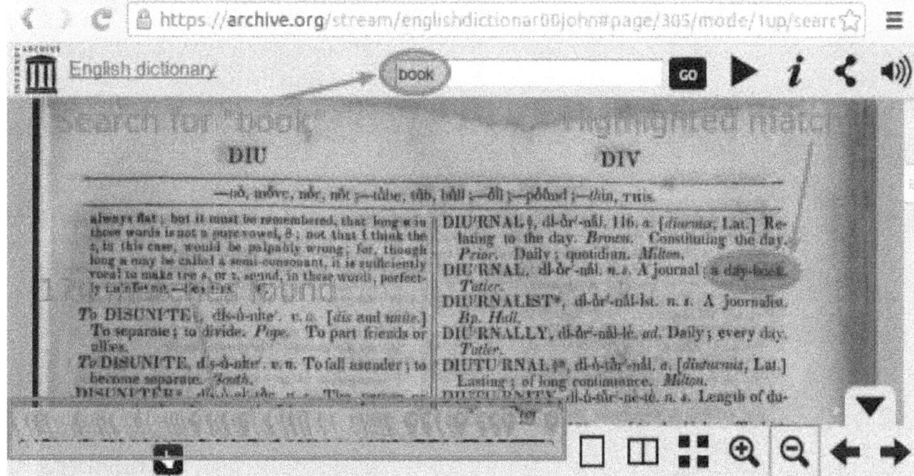

(b) Search for a common English term returned too many matches, making it difficult to find the term definition in the dictionary.

Figure 1: BookReader: Problems in searching words in raster dictionaries.

3.5 Open Annotation

Open Annotation Data Model [48, 49, 56] allows users to associate additional information with an existing Web resource or a specific part of it. It is called open because the model utilizes Linked Data [50] principles to connect open Web resources together. This technique can be used to annotate words on scanned images of dictionary pages, interlink two words across dictionaries, associate user comments about the word, or store digitized representation of the page segment related to the word.

3.6 Distributed Proofreaders

Distributed Proofreaders [40, 17] was developed in 2000 to digitize Public Domain books which is primarily used by the Project Gutenberg [22]. It is a crowdsourcing utility to allow users to collaborate on digitizing scanned books one page at a time. Users are presented with the original scanned image of the page and an editable text which is pre-populated with the OCR engine generated text if possible, which users can then edit to correct mistakes. This concept can be used in the process of annotation and digitization of dictionaries.

3.7 Urdu Encyclopedia

Urdu Encyclopedia [4] is an UrduWeb knowledge-base project with currently over 330,000 pages primarily containing digitized dictionaries of general terms in the Urdu language with some additional specialized subjects. This encyclopedia was created by accumulating licences and digital data from various publishers. We are using this as one of the sources of data in our implementation.

4. METHODOLOGY

We have adopted a progressive approach which starts with little effort and improves the accessibility as more energy is put into the system.

4.1 Indexing

To enable lookup in a dictionary, an index of words needs to be prepared that points to the corresponding page numbers in the dictionary. We have chosen a progressive approach for indexing, so that basic lookup feature can be enabled very rapidly and further improvements can be made later to increase the accessibility for the raster dictionary.

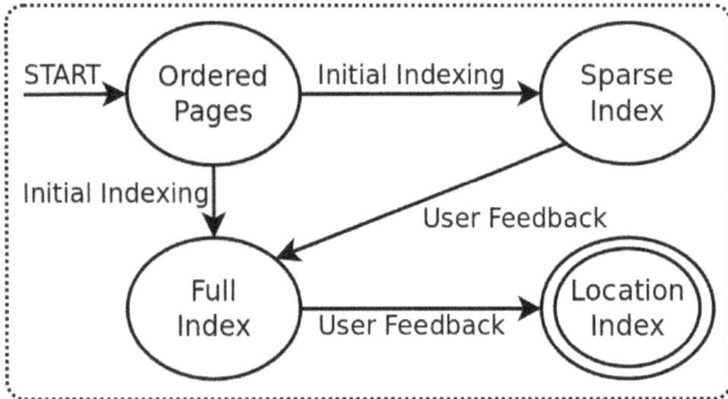

Figure 2: Index State Transition

Figure 2 illustrates the transition among various states of the indexing process that a typical dictionary may go through. Each indexing state is described in detail below.

4.1.1 *Ordered Pages*

Indexing starts with the scanned pages organized in the order they appeared in the printed book. Dictionaries in IA's BookReader are present in this "ordered pages" state. This state allows lookup of a word similar to how we interact with printed dictionaries. The user opens a page with a guess then compares the header of the page with the lookup word and decides, should it be flipped few pages forward or backward and repeats this process until reaches the destination page. On the destination page either lookup word is present or it does not exist in the entire dictionary.

Scanned books have a common issue of missing pages. If the book is rare then not much can be done about it. One strategy that we use in such cases is to add a custom page to let the users know that the page is missing, so that they can contribute if they have a copy of the book. For the sake of easy binding and portability, large books are often published in multiple volumes. In general purpose books this is not an issue, but in case of a dictionary, it is desired to have all the volumes together. In our testbed, a dictionary of four volumes was combined to form a single book. We found that those four volumes in the archive were not from the same publication and they had misaligned volume partition. As a consequence, the combined dictionary contained several duplicate and missing pages (which were later added).

4.1.2 *Sparse Index*

Sparse indexing is the quickest way to improve the lookup experience. With minimal effort, manual lookup can be turned into an automated lookup process. To prepare a sparse index, a list is created that contains the first words of every page along with the corresponding page number. This approach is only applicable if the dictionary words are already sorted, hence the list is sorted by words as well as page numbers. While this is true in most cases, section 4.4.3 describes some special cases where all the words in a dictionary are not sorted as a flat list of words. The process of lookup involves finding the appropriate place in the list where the lookup word can be inserted without breaking the sorting. In other words, finding a word in the sorted list which is either same as or prior to the lookup word, but the next word (if there is any) in the list is after the lookup word when performed string sorting. Page numbers associated with the word matching this criteria indicate where there is the possibility of existence of the lookup word. A sparse index cannot ensure the presence or absence of the lookup word in a dictionary, but it ensures that if the word exists in the dictionary, it has to be on the returned page.

A sparse index can also be made by listing only the last words of each page instead of the first words. In that case, only the matching criteria changes a little, but the overall approach remains the same. This variation does not add any value, except it might be a more expressive and readable way to write the lookup algorithm and it might also be helpful in fine-tuning an implementation for performance reasons.

Not all the pages in a dictionary have one or more words, sometimes the definition of a word and related examples span over multiple pages. This does not invalidate the working of this mechanism but at the time of implementation, this knowledge can be helpful. For example if one decides to use a plain array for storing sorted list of sparse index words and reuse array index to determine the corresponding page number implicitly, then knowing this fact is essential in order for the implementation to work properly.

A sparse index does not necessarily require indexing each page. One may decide to select a window of N pages and only add one entry per N pages in the index. This reduces the time required to index the whole dictionary, but shifts the burden to the user to scan for the word in the given window of pages. Additionally, it is not necessary to choose a window size of fixed number of pages. A practical example could be to index only the pages where a new letter of the alphabet begins. It only requires index of size equal to (or less than) the size of the alphabet in the given language. There are variable number of words starting from each letter and they span over varying number of pages. Such an index can only help the user to jump to the start of the section where first letter of the lookup term begins.

A sparse index is a sorted list hence almost any searching algorithm optimized for sorted list can be used for lookup in the list. In practice these sparse indexes are small lists, hence a linear searching algorithm may prove to be as good as a binary search.

4.1.3 *Full Index*

Full indexing involves preparing a list of all the words in the dictionary along with their corresponding page numbers. Unlike a sparse index, it does not require the list to be in any explicit sorted order. It even works on dictionaries which do not arrange their words as a flat sorted list. There are some dictionaries that arrange words based on their roots and all the variations from that root are internally sorted but there is no flat list ordering. In some dictionaries, words made of common prefixes or suffixes are accumulated together and break the overall sorting. In such cases, a sparse index is not an option. A full index has an added advantage over a sparse index in the way that it ensures either presence or absence of the lookup word in the dictionary.

Creating a full index manually takes longer as compared to a sparse index. In one of the classic dictionaries we worked on search words were not always in the beginning of the line, instead they were all over the page more like a paragraph, mixed with the definitions. To distinguish words from meaning, the dictionary used underline markers. Such situations may make the process of manually indexing dictionaries difficult and error-prone.

We propose an alternate crowd-sourced slow approach of full indexing, especially for large dictionaries. In this process initially a sparse index is made. As users search for words in the dictionary, they are asked for the feedback if they could find what they were looking for on this page. Their feedback is recorded. Given enough time, a full index will eventually be prepared. To avoid malicious feedback or unintentional error, a threshold of minimum number of agreements can be set. Alternatively, a democracy model can be used that is utilized in various crowd-sourced software localization systems, in which a translation with maximum votes wins.

Full indexes may or may not be in any sorted order as this is not a requirement for them to work. Hence a linear search is the easiest to implement. But if the list of words is large then the index can be sorted explicitly to enable binary search. Sorting or rearranging a full index does not affect the lookup functionality hence more advanced data structures like tries [57] can be built for efficient lookup.

4.1.4 Location Index

A sparse or full index can lead the user to the appropriate page, but the user has to locate the lookup word manually on the page. We can improve the accessibility here as well and point user's attention to the exact coordinates of the image where the lookup word exists. A small highlighted sticker, pin, or marker can be used as an overlay on the image to precisely locate the word on the page.

Location indexing is best suited as a crowd-sourced process in which users looking for a word in a page are asked to help position a marker on the page (if the word exists on that page). Users are allowed to move the existing markers around to correct the location. If multiple attempts are made to correct the location of a word, for simplicity, the last attempt can win. To avoid spamming a linear or quadratic mean can be utilized to determine the coordinates of the location marker. This is a finite task and given enough time, placement of markers will eventually be completed.

4.2 Annotation

Indexing is good for easily finding information that is in the scanned dictionaries. But we can improve the usefulness of a dictionary by attaching additional related information, resources, and comments in the form of annotations. Interacting with the location marker of the word reveals attached annotations in an overlay panel.

Annotation is a crowd-sourced process in which users looking for a word in a page are encouraged to annotate the word. Users are allowed to post comments and related resources in the overlay panel associated with the location marker. Unlike indexing, annotation is an ongoing process that will never reach an end, but it will mature as time passes and more people interact with the system.

4.3 Digitization

Digitization is the final stage of improving the accessibility and usefulness of a scanned raster dictionary. A dictionary in this stage is able to give users access to a fielded representation of every lookup word along with the definition, part of speech, examples, and other metadata in Unicode.

In the process of digitization, users fill a fielded form with the word and all its attributes as present in the image (if the word is not correctly digitized already). Related regions on the scanned pages are highlighted using rectangles. Often there is more than one rectangle to cover all the related text which might be in different columns on the same page or continue in the next page. This related region highlighting can be automated if the location indexing is completed. An aggregated analysis of the location marker positions over all the pages of a dictionary helps determining margins and number of columns on each page. Combining this information with the location of two consecutive words gives the coordinates of all the regions related to the first word. If the location indexing is not complete or the automatic location of related region estimates are not accurate then users are encouraged to correct it manually while digitizing.

Curation techniques can be used to check the correctness of the digitization. This information can be stored with the reference of page number and dictionary identifier. Given enough time dictionaries will be fully digitized in a way that will facilitate fielded searching. As a by-product, combining digitized data with coordinates of rectangular boxes can also be used for training OCR engines.

4.4 Sorting

Sparse indexing relies heavily on the fact that the dictionary words are arranged in a sorted order in the scanned images or PDF. Unfortunately, not every dictionary in every language follows linear sorting. Some dictionaries use different mechanisms of lookup in which the lookup key is not necessarily a prefixed substring of the desired word. Derivational prefixes and suffixes also affect the ordering.

4.4.1 Unicode Collation

Collation is ordered assembly of written information under a standard ordering scheme for easily finding an item in a list of items. In many languages, Unicode character values are not in the alphabetical order. For example Arabic script is used for many other Asian and African languages such as Arabic, Persian, Urdu, and Pashto [35]. These languages inherit the basic alphabet set from Arabic then add or remove letters. In the Unicode table Arabic script reserves values from `0600` to `06FF`. In this table, characters from the Arabic language alphabet are mostly sorted with a few exceptions. All other languages that use Arabic script as their base have their additional characters below these basic characters. This behavior changes the ordering of characters in the table from their alphabetical order. To solve this problem, the Unicode collation algorithm [14] was introduced. Unicode has also introduced a project called Common Locale Data Repository [53] to bring full support of locale related issues in the world's languages.

Sometimes dictionaries of the same language do not agree on a single ordering scheme. To deal with this issue, custom sorting functions can be written for every dictionary or a set of dictionaries that agree on the same ordering scheme.

4.4.2 Compound Letters

Some languages have compound letters where two or more characters are combined to form a single phoneme. Dictionaries often disagree on the matter of compound characters. For ordering purpose some dictionaries treat the compound character as a single letter, while others treat them as combination of multiple letters. For example in the Urdu language there is a character with Unicode value `06BE (ARABIC LETTER HEH DOACHASHMEE)` which has a place in the alphabet but it is not used independently. It can be used as a modifier to a dozen other letters to change the sound of the phoneme. Some Urdu dictionaries consider those compound letters as independent letters while others consider them as two separate characters while sorting the list of words. Accented characters and diacritic marks also affect the sorting order. A custom sorting function needs to consider these aspects to work properly.

4.4.3 Nested Ordering

In some dictionaries, lookup is not provided by words but a high-level search key is used instead. For example in some Arabic language dictionaries, root words are chosen as a key. Top level sorting is done on root words. All the derivative forms of the root words are sorted alphabetically on a secondary level. This approach keeps related words close and form a cluster that share similar meaning. This type of organization helps users understand the meaning of words in better context. This benefit comes with a cost as it requires the user to know the root of the lookup word in advance. For example a root word in Arabic of the form L_1-L_2-L_3 can have derivatives in the form of E*-L_1-E*-L_2-E*-L_3-E*, where L_1, L_2, and L_3 are three letters of the root word while E* is zero or more occurrences of extra letters in the word. Sometimes derived words change or remove root letters to simplify pronunciation (under some grammar rules) that makes identifying root of a derived word complex.

Another example of nested sorting and clustering words is found in some dictionaries where words that have same derivational prefix or suffix are grouped together. These compound words are sometimes written as a single word, but sometimes have spaces (or other word-boundary characters like a dash in other languages). Often there is no consensus about one way of writing or the other.

4.5 Retrieval

Figure 3 illustrates a response that enables the client to represent the definition of the lookup term from various sources, related resources, different dictionary images with coordinates to locate the word on the page, locations of the bounding boxes that contain the definition and other related information, and annotations for the word. Lines 4–12 have list of related resources such as descriptive images or audio. Lines 13–20 hold a list of definitions and examples of the word from external Web services or user contributions in Unicode. Lines 21–49 have data specific to scanned dictionaries. If the lookup language has multiple associated dictionaries then this block of response object will have an array of all the associated dictionaries, each dictionary internally contains related pages, and each page has source, dimensions, coordinates of the word location, coordinates of the bounding boxes, and user contributed annotations. Array blocks in the response object may have zero or more elements depending on the available data. Line 23 can have "yes" or "no" as its value for fully indexed dictionaries and in case of sparsely indexed dictionaries, the value can be "yes" or "maybe". It is helpful to return a relevant page even if the word is not found on the page, this gives the user confidence and an opportunity to provide feedback in case of an error.

```
1  {
2    "query": "SEARCH TERM",
3    "language": "LANGUAGE CODE",
4    "resources": [{
5      "type": "RESOURCE TYPE",
6      "href": "RESOURCE URL",
7      "meta": {
8        "contributor": "NAME",
9        "updated": "DATE",
10       "OTHERFIELDS": "THEIR VALUES"
11     }
12   }],
13   "definitions": [{
14     "text": "DEFINITION TEXT",
15     "meta": {
16       "contributor": "NAME",
17       "updated": "DATE",
18       "OTHERFIELDS": "THEIR VALUES"
19     }
20   }],
21   "dictionaries": [{
22     "id": "DICTIONARY ID",
23     "exists": "yes/no/maybe",
24     "pages": [{
25       "number": "PAGE NUMBER",
26       "src": "URL OF THE PAGE IMAGE",
27       "width": "WIDTH OF THE IMAGE",
28       "height": "HEIGHT OF THE IMAGE",
29       "location": {
30         "x": "X-COORDINATE",
31         "y": "Y-COORDINATE"
32       },
33       "boxes": [{
34         "top": "TOP Y-COORDINATE",
35         "bottom": "BOTTOM Y-COORDINATE",
36         "left": "LEFT X-COORDINATE",
37         "right": "RIGHT X-COORDINATE"
38       }],
39       "annotations": [{
40         "id": "ANNOTATION ID",
41         "text": "ANNOTATION TEXT",
42         "meta": {
43           "contributor": "NAME",
44           "updated": "DATE",
45           "OTHERFIELDS": "THEIR VALUES"
46         }
47       }]
48     }]
49   }]
50 }
```

Figure 3: Search API Response

5. REFERENCE IMPLEMENTATION

Using the techniques described above, we have created an application called "Dictionary Explorer" (Figure 4) for UrduWeb Dictionary project. We have added a handful of monolingual and multilingual dictionaries in various languages that are in different indexing states. Dictionary Explorer is built using open-source Web technologies like PostgreSQL [37, 62] as the database engine, Ruby on Rails [46] as Athe PI endpoint, and ExtJS [18] for its client side user interface. Our implementation respects various needs of multilingual and bidirectional interfaces [31, 3] such as flipping various components and controls horizontally for RTL languages and setting appropriate direction of the text flow for mixed (bi-directional) text.

5.1 Multilingual Multi-dictionary Lookup

Dictionary Explorer offers a way to select one of many available lookup languages and provides indexes based on the selected language. Every language is associated with a subset of all the available dictionaries. Lookup for a word in any language shows tabbed interface for associated dictionaries and loads appropriate pages in each dictionary simultaneously. If the lookup word is annotated in some dictionary pages, those annotations appear on appropriate pages. Dictionary Explorer has a dedicated tab for accumulating third party Unicode online dictionary results, related resources, audio, and user contributed materials.

5.2 Searching and Exploring

Dictionary Explorer provides various means to find words in various dictionaries including traditional manual page flipping, exploring with the help of a tree-style word index, and searching by entering the lookup word in a search box. The tree-style word index is dictionary independent presentation that is built using large corpora of words in each of the available lookup languages. It helps finding a word in

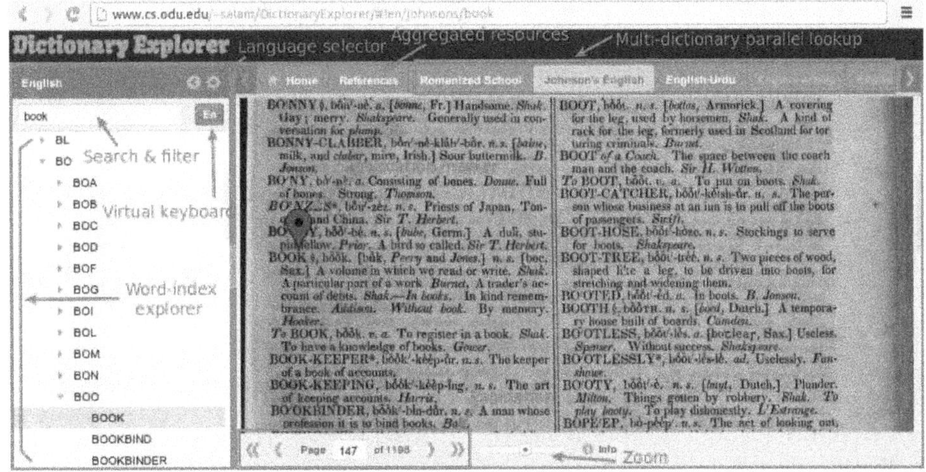

(a) Searching an English dictionary with location index.

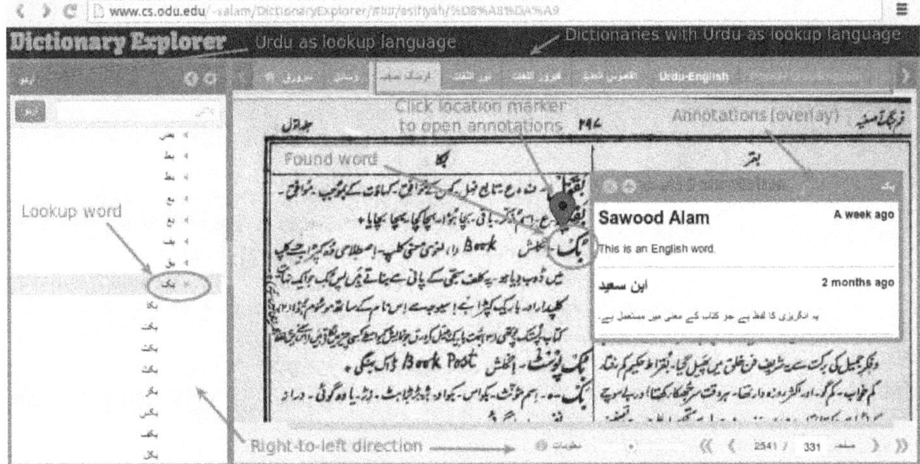

(b) Searching an Urdu dictionary with location index and annotations.

Figure 4: Dictionary Explorer: Multilingual and multi-dictionary lookup with highlighted features.

dictionaries without the need of appropriate input methods or keyboards. The search box is accompanied by a language-sensitive on-screen-keyboard to help users type the lookup words. Typing the lookup term in the search-box filters the word index in real-time.

In our experiments, we found that the depth of three letters is practically suitable for the tree to filter the list down to a manageable number of words. After that we load the actual words as leaf nodes without further nesting. This optimal depth might be different for some languages, but this is typically used by various printed dictionaries of many languages as they write three letter index on the header of each page. The explorer also comes with a full-featured paging toolbar and zooming functionalities.

5.3 User Contribution and Feedback

Context-sensitive user interface elements, appropriate notifications, and intuitive interface of Dictionary Explorer encourages users to contribute by providing feedback about presence or absence of the word on the page, locate the word on the page [24], annotate the word by adding comments and linking with other resources, and digitize the dictionary. This ongoing collaborative effort improves the accessibility of the scanned dictionaries.

6. EVALUATION

Our progressive approach of indexing involves some degree of human input at each level. A language with little or no online community may not benefit from this. For such dying languages [41, 8], Dictionary Explorer is still at least as good as IA's BookExplorer.

6.1 Indexing Time

We have started our evaluation with a small (180 pages) English-to-Urdu (Romanized) dictionary [9]. The lookup words were in English, hence associated OCR processed text format of the dictionary was also available. Using regular expressions we cleaned the text except the first lookup word appearing on each page then manually corrected some errors. This process took less than ten minutes and a sparse index for the dictionary was created.

In the next phase we have chosen an old monolingual Urdu dictionary [15] that has four volumes with over 2,500 pages combined. Since the process of creating a sparse index requires frequent page flipping, two people have decided to work together, one person was flipping pages and pronouncing the first word of each page while the other was typing it. This approach has given us a rate of indexing of over 25 pages per minute. To simplify the process of indexing, later we created a small Web-based utility that provides a text-area for typing words (one entry per line) and scanned page appearing next to it. This utility keeps track of lines and every time enter key is hit or the cursor moves up or down, it loads the appropriate scanned page. Using this utility, we were able index over 20 pages per minute per person while eliminating the need of dictation.

Finally, we chose another classical monolingual Urdu dictionary [42] that has four volumes with over 3,200 pages combined. Due to the clustering of derived words, this does not have an overall linear ordering. In such a case a sparse index would not be very helpful, hence we decided to build a full index as the initial indexing process. We distributed small subsets of pages among UWDL members and asked them to index all the lookup words appearing in each page in their free time. This process was completed in 60 days with the help of 13 volunteers, who have indexed over 75,000 words and phrases combined. We have measured an indexing speed of about 8–10 words per minute per person. This rate may vary based on complexity of the script, available input methods, readability of scanned documents, typing speed of contributors and various other factors. Distribution and tracking of pages for indexing was handled manually in this case, but utilities like Distributed Proofreaders can be used to automate the process of crowdsourcing.

6.2 Index Placement

A sparse index is usually small in size (say, a dictionary with 500 pages will have a flat list of 500 words in its index) and can be transported to the client side easily, but a full index is much larger because it depends on the number of words in the dictionary, not the number of pages. The benefit of a client side index is that it requires little communication from the server during subsequent lookup of words. In our Dictionary Explorer application, we had multiple languages and every language was associated with multiple dictionaries. If we load the index on the client side, there will be several indexes (one for each language) and the combined size will make the initialization of the application slow, hence we keep the index on the server and return a combined response (Figure 3) for each lookup with the entries of all the dictionaries associated with the lookup language.

6.3 Prefix Index

For the ease of lookup, we have added a tree-like explorer in our application which is language specific but dictionary independent. It is built using unique three letter prefixes of all the words from a spell checker word list for the language. Using prefixes reduces the data required to build the tree-like explorer to an acceptable size and splits the entire word list in manageable chunks. When a third letter is expanded in the tree, it loads a list of words from the server with that three letter prefix and appends them as leaf nodes under that third letter. For performance reasons, we cache the list on client side so that subsequent lookups under the same prefix do not load the list from the server again.

Table 1 shows standard statistical distribution of words and how the size of index changes with the size of prefix. This table was generated using 144,106 English words from the Ispell word list [33]. We found similar statistical distributions in other languages as well. If only the first letter of each word is indexed, there will be only 26 index entries, but

Table 1: Prefix analysis of 144,106 English words.

Size	Count	Min	1st Q	Med	Mean	3rd Q	Max
1	26	121	2,753	5,010	5,503.0	7,603.0	15,620
2	528	1	2	11	271.0	270.5	5,062
3	3,995	1	1	7	35.8	33.0	1,798
4	18,026	1	1	2	7.9	7.0	753
5	40,927	1	1	1	3.5	3.0	616
6	62,767	1	1	1	2.3	2.0	227

each index will point to an average of 5,000 words and the maximum number will go over 15,000. A three letter prefix is optimal, because generating prefix indexes of size four or more increases the number of entries in the index to a limit which is not suitable for transferring to the client side. There are a few outliers that increase the maximum number of words that a three letter prefix can have. These are mainly derivational prefixes like "con", "dis", "pro", "pre", and "int". A more intelligent approach of generating balanced prefix buckets is to have a tolerance limit of maximum number of words a prefix can have, then split larger buckets by increasing the prefix size for those set of words only.

Currently this prefix index only helps initiating lookup, but it can have pointers to pages of various dictionaries of that language. This will help minimise search requests while expanding the tree, but the data structure for the tree will become complex and large. It will also be coupled with the dictionaries, which will force regeneration of the data structure every time a new dictionary is added. An alternate approach to generate such an explorer is to generate all possible next level combinations based on letters of the alphabet of the language when a node is expanded. This approach requires no knowledge of any word list except the letters of the alphabet, hence it is lightweight in size, but this approach yields many branches that lead to no meaningful words.

7. FUTURE WORK

We would like to predict the pages of a dictionary in a specific language for lookup words without any explicit manual indexing for that dictionary. We would utilize the distribution of words in the corpus of the language, distribution of the popular words of the language, and the distribution of the words in other dictionaries of that language that are already indexed. This will enable lookup in a dictionary without any manual work and will improve the accuracy with the help of crowd-sourced feedback. We would also like to explore other complex languages and their specific problems to incorporate appropriate solutions for them. Our current implementation uses a local annotation mechanism, but we would like to leverage the Open Annotation standards to expand the scope of annotations, enable open sharing, and linking across various Web services. We would like to extend the functionality of Dictionary Explorer to make it a general purpose book reader that supports indexing with the help of table of contents and annotated keywords and enables user feedback mechanism to annotate and digitize scanned books. We would also like to develop a separate client or extend the interface of our current implementation that can leverage the location indexing and annotation features for various types of archived scanned documents (such as multi-column news papers, magazines, and government records etc.) to enable lookup in them. This can be helpful for languages that do not have good OCR support, but have active presence on the Web.

8. CONCLUSIONS

We have identified that general purpose online book readers are not suitable for scanned dictionaries in two ways. First, if the dictionary is in a language which is not well supported by an OCR engine used for digitizing scanned images then searching for a word yields nothing. Second, if the dictionary is well supported by an OCR engine then searching for common words returns too many results, because it cannot distinguish main words from their occurrences in the definition of other words, which is not desired for dictionary lookup. We proposed a progressive approach of indexing scanned pages of a dictionary that enables direct access to appropriate pages on lookup. Initially a sparse index is created for the dictionary that requires very little effort and makes it possible to directly jump to the page where lookup word is possibly present. In the next phase a full index is built that ensures if and where the lookup word exists in the dictionary. Finally markers are placed to precisely locate lookup words on the scanned pages. We further improve the accessibility of the dictionary by allowing annotations and fielded digitization of the dictionary words. We have implemented an application called Dictionary Explorer and utilized our technique to index various monolingual and multilingual dictionaries. We have evaluated our approach by estimating the time required for various stages of indexing and examining various trade-offs in our implementation. We have achieved a speed of over 20 pages per minute per person for sparse indexing and about 10 words per minute per person for full indexing.

9. ACKNOWLEDGEMENTS

We would like to thank Ayesha Aziz for taking responsibility of getting one of the biggest classical Urdu dictionaries fully indexed and providing missing scanned pages. Thanks to all the UrduWeb Digital Library members who have contributed in the indexing process of various dictionaries.

10. REFERENCES

[1] ABBYY. ABBYY FineReader 11: Recognition Languages. `http://finereader.abbyy.com/recognition_languages/`, 2014.

[2] ABBYY. ABBYY FineReader for Personal Use. `http://finereader.abbyy.com/`, 2014.

[3] S. Abney and S. Bird. The Human Language Project: Building a Universal Corpus of the World's Languages. In *Proceedings of the 48th Annual Meeting of the Association for Computational Linguistics*, pages 88–97, 2010.

[4] Z. Ahmad. Urdu Encyclopedia. `http://urduencyclopedia.org/`, 2011.

[5] B. Alex, C. Grover, E. Klein, and R. Tobin. Digitised Historical Text: Does it have to be mediOCRe? In *Empirical Methods in Natural Language Processing*, pages 401–409, 2012.

[6] V. Ambati, N. Balakrishnan, R. Reddy, L. Pratha, and C. Jawahar. The digital library of India project: Process, policies and architecture. In *2nd International Conference on Digital Libraries (ICDL)*, 2006.

[7] D. Bamman and D. Smith. Extracting Two Thousand Years of Latin from a Million Book Library. *J. Comput. Cult. Herit.*, 5(1):2:1–2:13, Apr. 2012.

[8] S. Bird. A Scalable Method for Preserving Oral Literature from Small Languages. In *Proceedings of the 12th International Conference on Asia-Pacific Digital Libraries*, 2010.

[9] Calcutta School Book Society. *Romanized school dictionary, English and Urdu.* 1864.

[10] C. Casserly. Creative Commons. `https://creativecommons.org/`, 2001.

[11] A. Chitipothu and mangtronix. Internet Archive BookReader. `https://openlibrary.org/dev/docs/bookreader`, 2013.

[12] R. Darnton. The National Digital Public Library Is Launched! *The New York Review of Books*, April 2013.

[13] R. Davidson and R. Hopely. Arabic and Persian OCR Training and Test Data Sets. In *Proc. of Symp. on Document Image Understanding Technology, April*, volume 30, pages 200–2. Citeseer, 1997.

[14] M. Davis, K. Whistler, and M. Scherer. Unicode Collation Algorithm. `http://www.unicode.org/reports/tr10/`, 2013.

[15] S. A. Dihlav. *Farhang-e-Asifiyah.* 1908.

[16] E. Duncker. Cross-cultural Usability of the Library Metaphor. In *Proceedings of the 2nd ACM/IEEE-CS Joint Conference on Digital Libraries*, pages 223–230, 2002.

[17] C. Franks. Distributed Proofreaders. `http://www.pgdp.net/`, 2000.

[18] J. Garcia, G. Grisogono, and J. K. Andresen. *Ext JS in Action, Second Edition.* 2014.

[19] D. Ghosh, T. Dube, and A. P. Shivaprasad. Script Recognition—A Review. *IEEE Transactions on Pattern Analysis and Machine Intelligence*, 32(12):2142–2161, 2010.

[20] A. Gotscharek, U. Reffle, C. Ringlstetter, and K. U. Schulz. On Lexical Resources for Digitization of Historical Documents. In *Proceedings of the 9th ACM Symposium on Document Engineering*, pages 193–200, 2009.

[21] V. Govindan and A. Shivaprasad. Character Recognition—A Review. *Pattern recognition*, 23(7):671–683, 1990.

[22] M. Hart. *Project Gutenberg.* 1971.

[23] M. Herwig. Google's Total Library. *Spiegel Online International*, 2007.

[24] C. Hu, A. Rose, and B. B. Bederson. Locating Text in Scanned Books. In *Proceedings of the 9th ACM/IEEE-CS Joint Conference on Digital Libraries*, pages 395–396, 2009.

[25] Internet Archive. Open Library. `https://openlibrary.org/`, 2006.

[26] Internet Archive. eBook and Texts. `https://archive.org/details/texts`, 2014.

[27] Internet Archive. Project Gutenberg. `https://archive.org/details/gutenberg`, 2014.

[28] S. T. Javed and S. Hussain. Improving Nastalique-Specific Pre-Recognition Process for Urdu OCR. In *Multitopic Conference, 2009. INMIC 2009. IEEE 13th International*, pages 1–6. IEEE, 2009.

[29] S. T. Javed, S. Hussain, A. Maqbool, S. Asloob, S. Jamil, and H. Moin. Segmentation Free Nastalique Urdu OCR. In *Proceedings of World Academy of*

Science, Engineering and Technology, volume 46, pages 456–461, 2010.

[30] S. Johnson, J. Walker, H. J. Todd, A. Chalmers, and J. E. Worcester. *English Dictionaries.* 1828.

[31] T. T. Keegan and S. J. Cunningham. Language Preference in a Bi-language Digital Library. In *Proceedings of the 5th ACM/IEEE-CS Joint Conference on Digital Libraries*, pages 174–175, 2005.

[32] M. S. Khorsheed. Off-line Arabic Character Recognition—A Review. *Pattern analysis & applications*, 5(1):31–45, 2002.

[33] G. Kuenning and G. Hills. Ispell (ver 3.1.20) Word List. `http://wordlist.sourceforge.net/`, 1993.

[34] M. Miller, G. Choi, and L. Chell. Comparison of Three Digital Library Interfaces: Open Library, Google Books, and HathiTrust. In *Proceedings of the 12th ACM/IEEE-CS Joint Conference on Digital Libraries*, pages 367–368, 2012.

[35] M. Mirdehghan. Persian, Urdu, and Pashto: A comparative orthographic analysis. *Writing Systems Research*, 2(1):9–23, 2010.

[36] L. Molwantoa. Literature Review Archive Collection Management of Cultural Artefacts: The Bleek and Lloyd Dictionaries. 2009.

[37] B. Momjian. *PostgreSQL: Introduction and Concepts*, volume 192. 2001.

[38] N. Naqvi, Z. Ajmal, and S. Alam. UrduWeb. `http://www.urduweb.org/`, 2005.

[39] Nationalencyklopedin. List of languages by number of native speakers. `http://en.wikipedia.org/wiki/List_of_languages_by_number_of_native_speakers#Nationalencyklopedin_.282007.29`, 2007.

[40] G. B. Newby and C. Franks. Distributed Proofreading. In *Proceedings of the 3rd ACM/IEEE-CS Joint Conference on Digital Libraries*, pages 361–363, 2003.

[41] D. M. Nichols, I. H. Witten, T. T. Keegan, D. Bainbridge, and M. Dewsnip. Digital Libraries and Minority Languages. *New Review of Hypermedia and Multimedia*, 11(2):139–155, 2005.

[42] Noor-ul-Hasan Nayyar. *Noor-ul-Lughaat.* 1917.

[43] D. W. Oard and J. Malionek. The Apollo Archive Explorer. In *Proceedings of the 13th ACM/IEEE-CS Joint Conference on Digital Libraries*, pages 453–454, 2013.

[44] U. Pal and B. Chaudhuri. Indian Script Character Recognition: A Survey. *Pattern Recognition*, 37(9):1887–1899, 2004.

[45] B. Plale, R. McDonald, Y. Sun, I. Kouper, R. Cobine, J. S. Downie, B. Sandore Namachchivaya, and J. Unsworth. HathiTrust Research Center: Computational Access for Digital Humanities and Beyond. In *Proceedings of the 13th ACM/IEEE-CS Joint Conference on Digital Libraries*, pages 395–396, 2013.

[46] S. Ruby, D. Thomas, and D. H. Hansson. *Agile web Development with Rails 4.* 2013.

[47] N. Sabbour and F. Shafait. A Segmentation Free Approach to Arabic and Urdu OCR. In *IS&T/SPIE Electronic Imaging*, pages 86580N–86580N. International Society for Optics and Photonics, 2013.

[48] R. Sanderson, P. Ciccarese, and H. Van de Sompel. Open Annotation Data Model. `http://www.openannotation.org/spec/core/`, 2013.

[49] R. Sanderson and H. Van de Sompel. Making Web Annotations Persistent over Time. In *Proceedings of the 10th Annual Joint Conference on Digital Libraries*, pages 1–10, 2010.

[50] B. Schandl, B. Haslhofer, T. Bürger, A. Langegger, and W. Halb. Linked Data and Multimedia: The State of Affairs. *Multimedia Tools and Applications*, 59(2):523–556, 2012.

[51] H. Schöneberg, H.-G. Schmidt, and W. Höhn. A Scalable, Distributed and Dynamic Workflow System for Digitization Processes. In *Proceedings of the 13th ACM/IEEE-CS Joint Conference on Digital Libraries*, pages 359–362, 2013.

[52] L. Taycher. Books of the world, stand up and be counted! All 129,864,880 of you. `http://booksearch.blogspot.com/2010/08/books-of-world-stand-up-and-be-counted.html`, August 2010.

[53] Unicode. Unicode CLDR Project. `http://cldr.unicode.org/`, 2013.

[54] University of Chicago. Digital Dictionaries of South Asia. `http://dsal.uchicago.edu/dictionaries/`, 2012.

[55] UrduWeb Library Team. UrduWeb Digital Library. `http://www.urdulibrary.org/`, 2005.

[56] X. Wang, L. Ye, E. Keogh, and C. Shelton. Annotating Historical Archives of Images. In *Proceedings of the 8th ACM/IEEE-CS Joint Conference on Digital Libraries*, pages 341–350, 2008.

[57] Wikipedia. Trie. `http://en.wikipedia.org/wiki/Trie`, 2001.

[58] K. Williams and H. Suleman. Using a Hidden Markov Model to Transcribe Handwritten Bushman Texts. In *Proceedings of the 11th Annual International ACM/IEEE Joint Conference on Digital Libraries*, pages 445–446, 2011.

[59] I. H. Witten and D. Bainbridge. A Retrospective Look at Greenstone: Lessons from the First Decade. In *Proceedings of the 7th ACM/IEEE-CS Joint Conference on Digital Libraries*, pages 147–156, 2007.

[60] I. H. Witten, D. Bainbridge, and S. J. Boddie. Power to the People: End-user Building of Digital Library Collections. In *Proceedings of the 1st ACM/IEEE-CS Joint Conference on Digital Libraries*, pages 94–103, 2001.

[61] WolframAlpha. Urdu. `https://www.wolframalpha.com/input/?i=urdu`, 2014.

[62] J. Worsley and J. D. Drake. *Practical PostgreSQL.* 2002.

[63] I. Z. Yalniz and R. Manmatha. Finding Translations in Scanned Book Collections. In *Proceedings of the 35th International ACM SIGIR Conference on Research and Development in Information Retrieval*, pages 465–474, 2012.

Identifying Duplicate and Contradictory Information in Wikipedia

Sarah Weissman, Samet Ayhan, Joshua Bradley, and Jimmy Lin
University of Maryland
College Park, Maryland

ABSTRACT

In this paper, we identify sentences in Wikipedia articles that are either identical or highly similar by applying techniques for near-duplicate detection of web pages. This is accomplished with a MapReduce implementation of minhash to identify sentences with high Jaccard similarity, followed by a pass to generate sentence clusters. Based on manual examination, we discovered that these clusters can be categorized into six different types: templates, identical sentences, copyediting, factual drift, references, and other. Two of these categories are particularly interesting: identical sentences quantify the extent to which content in Wikipedia is copied and pasted, and near-duplicate sentences that state contradictory facts point to quality issues in Wikipedia.

Categories and Subject Descriptors: H.3.3 [Information Storage and Retrieval]: Information Search and Retrieval—Clustering

Keywords: Hadoop; near-duplicate detection; minhash

1. INTRODUCTION

Readers of Wikipedia may notice that multiple articles contain highly-similar or even identical passages. In some cases these represent duplicate articles marked for merging, but content overlap arises in other cases as well. For example, the article about a hurricane and the article about the location where it made landfall might share the same content about the impact of the natural disaster. Identical content is most likely the result of copy and paste between articles, but interestingly, readers occasionally come across similar sentences that state contradictory facts. In a distributed environment where anyone can edit content, these observations are perhaps not surprising, but we are not aware of any formal studies. In this paper we attempt to rigorously characterize these phenomena by treating the problem as that of near-duplicate sentence detection. We adapt standard locality-sensitive hashing (LSH) techniques [8] to identify clusters of near-duplicate sentences in Wikipedia.

JCDL'15, June 21–25, 2015, Knoxville, Tennessee, USA.

ACM 978-1-4503-3594-2/15/06 ...$15.00.
DOI: http://dx.doi.org/10.1145/2756406.2756947.

We find this problem interesting in a few ways: For duplicate sentences, our analyses quantify the extent to which Wikipedia content is simply *replicated*, as opposed to *written* from scratch. In the case of *near* duplicates, some differences represent minor copyediting that does not change the substance of the content, but in other cases the differences represent contradictory facts. Quantifying these cases provides an indirect measure of the quality of Wikipedia in terms of self consistency.

This paper makes no claims about the novelty of our techniques nor our implementation in Hadoop MapReduce, which is rather straightforward. Rather, our contribution lies in the analysis and categorization of near-duplicate sentence types. We have not seen locality-sensitive hashing applied in this way before to analyze Wikipedia.

2. RELATED WORK

The problem we tackle in this paper is related to a few others that have been studied before. Near-duplicate detection of web pages [7] is important in search because web pages are often copied or mirrored with only minor differences (e.g., ads or navigation bars); it would be desirable to return only the "canonical" versions in search results. In fact, the algorithm that we use, minhash [3], was originally developed for exactly this purpose. Another closely-related problem is plagiarism detection [10], or more generally, "text reuse" [2]. In contrast to near-duplicate detection, the focus is usually on smaller segments of text as opposed to entire documents. However, similar approaches such as shingling are applicable to both.

Other formulations of the general problem are what the data mining community calls "all pairs" search [1] and what the database community calls set similarity join [13]. The task is essentially the same: given a potentially large collection of objects, identify all pairs whose similarity is above a threshold according to some similarity metric.

There are two classes of solutions to the above problems: in the *index-based* approach, an inverted index is constructed from objects in the collection and a traversal of the index allows the similar pairs to be extracted, e.g., [1, 9]; with the *hash-based* approach, the basic idea is to use locality-sensitive hashing (LSH) to identify similar pairs based on hash collisions, e.g., minhash [3]. Of course, hybrid approaches are also possible. Scaling up of these solutions has been accomplished by MapReduce [9, 13, 12].

Because of its open nature, Wikipedia has generated much controversy over its editorial quality and factual correctness. An early study found Wikipedia's accuracy to rival that of traditional encyclopedias [6], but subsequent investigations have arrived at conflicting conclusions. A thorough review is beyond the scope of this short paper, but somewhat ironically, the best summary of this ongoing debate is a Wikipedia article.[1] Since Wikipedia may be edited anonymously, information might be copied from external sources and between Wikipedia articles without verification. However, this is not to say that there are no quality assurance mechanisms in Wikipedia [11]. Although there are active communities of editors who contribute to the upkeep of various articles, much of Wikipedia is edited and expanded in an ad hoc manner. In particular, Wilkinson and Huberman [14] found the distribution of article edits on Wikipedia to have a long tail, meaning that a small number of articles accounts for most of the edits, and that the number of edits is related to article quality. Articles with few edits and low editorial attention are less likely to be updated, which is a source of contradictory information based on our analysis.

3. NEAR-DUPLICATE SENTENCES

For near-duplicate detection we use a well-known approximate algorithm called minhash [3]. We begin with a parameterized family of N hash functions F_i, $1 \leq i \leq N$. Each sentence in a Wikipedia article is broken up into n-gram "shingles" (at the character level) and for the shingle set S, a set $\{\min_{s \in S}(F_i(s)\}$ of minimum hashes over the hash family is generated. The signature of a document d is represented as a vector of K minhashes randomly selected from the set of N. To increase recall we generate M signatures for each sentence (i.e., M draws of K from N). Broder proved a straightforward relationship between minhash collisions (i.e., documents that share the same signature) and their Jaccard similarities; we refer the reader to the original paper for the relevant proofs.

3.1 MapReduce Implementation

We implemented minhash in MapReduce [5] using Hadoop for this study. Our implementation choice is primarily for convenience since we have ready access to Hadoop clusters; Wikipedia is relatively modest in size by modern standards and doesn't demand distributed processing per se. Nevertheless, having a scalable implementation lets us potentially tackle collections that are substantially larger (for example, the full edit history of Wikipedia).

The algorithm is as follows: each mapper receives a Wikipedia article identified by a unique docid. Inside the mapper we break the article into sentences using a regular expression; sentences that are shorter than 75 shingles or longer than 600 shingles are discarded. For each sentence, the M minhash signatures are then computed (per above). The family of hash functions is implemented using a "Multiply Shift" hashing scheme[2] and generated from a random seed. The hash family is parameterized by hash output key size, which is configurable. For our experiments we used a 60 bit hash and a hash family of size $N = 20$. Each signature is emitted as the key of an intermediate key–value pair with the sentence id as the value (constructed from the Wikipedia docid and the sentence number).

MapReduce guarantees that all values with the same key (minhash signatures in our case) are shuffled to the same reducer and grouped together for further processing—in effect, collecting the hash collisions for us. In a reducer we receive a signature as the key and as values all sentence ids that share the signature. If there is more than one value per key, we write out all sentence ids as a cluster. This serves as input to the final cluster generation stage (more below).

[1] http://en.wikipedia.org/wiki/Reliability_of_Wikipedia

[2] http://en.wikipedia.org/wiki/Universal_hashing

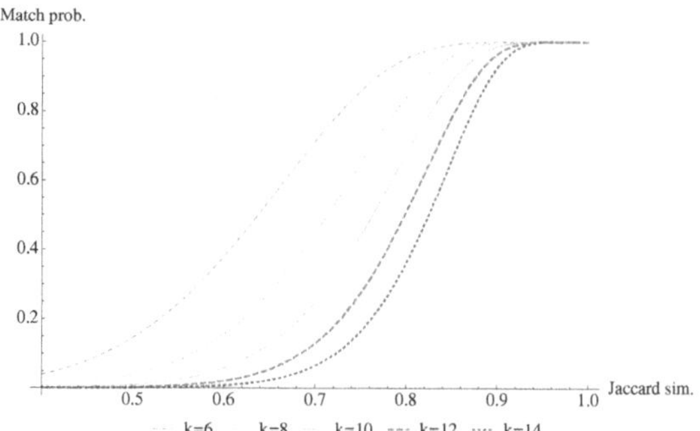

Figure 1: Minhash parameter tuning.

3.2 Parameter Tuning

One complexity of applying minhash to real-world datasets is the myriad of parameters that must be selected—each setting manifests a tradeoff between precision, recall, and computational effort. Our approach to parameter tuning relied on a combination of analytical calculations and hand-tuning based on examining the output. We began by fixing the hashing scheme and the size of the hash family ($N = 20$). We then selected 10 signatures ($M = 10$) per input sentence. Based on Broder [3], the probability of a match for sentences A and B can be expressed as $P[\text{match}(A, B)] = 1 - (1 - s^K)^M$, where $s = \text{Jaccard}(A, B)$. With the above settings, the effects of different K's are shown in Figure 1. Based on this analysis, we set $K = 10$. This means that if we choose 0.9 Jaccard similarity as our goal (90% overlap in shingle sets), then there is a 99% chance of a match (i.e., the recall). Finally, after some hand tuning, we settled on a shingle length of 12 characters. This setting means that we obtain shingles that cross word boundaries, which allows us to preserve word order in our similarity computations.

Based on the parameter settings, it is possible to estimate the amount of data that is generated by our approach, which is the product of the length of each signature, the number of signatures per sentence, and the total number of sentences. This computation is useful because the amount of intermediate data provides a rough proxy for algorithm running time, since the data shuffling phase is often the slowest component of a MapReduce algorithm.

Finally, note that it is possible to improve precision by filtering results with a second pass on the output signature clusters. In this second pass we can discard false positives or apply another similarity metric (e.g., edit distance). Compared to the computational cost of minhash, such additional processing is cheap since it is applied to much less data. However, we did not implement second-pass filtering in our experiments and leave this for future work.

3.3 Final Cluster Generation

The output of minhash is a set of clusters, where each cluster represents a signature collision. Since we generate multiple signatures per sentence, it is possible that a sentence appears in multiple clusters. We adopt the standard practice of merging all clusters that share at least one common sentence. If we were to perform secondary filtering to remove false positives, it would make sense to apply it before merging clusters.

Cluster merging is accomplished in one pass outside MapReduce with a union-find data structure [4], which represents a set as a tree where every child node maintains a pointer to its parent. Each set is represented by its root node, so taking the union of two sets A and B simply means setting the root node of set A to be a child of any node of B. In order to identify the set that a node belongs to (the "find" operation of union-find), we trace the chain of parent nodes back to the root. In practice, we can improve the efficiency of the algorithm by flattening the tree during the find operation, by pointing every node visited in the chain directly to the root. In our implementation, we maintain a lookup table from each sentence id to its node in the union-find data structure. For each input cluster, we find the corresponding set for each sentence in the cluster (or create a new set if one doesn't exist) and take their union. When this process is complete, the resulting sets form our merged clusters. We output the merged clusters as key-value pairs by iterating over every node in the lookup table and finding its set, which is assigned a numeric key. Another MapReduce job retrieves the original text of the sentences in each cluster and sorts by cluster id to group sentences by cluster.

4. EXPERIMENTAL RESULTS

Our experiments were conducted on an XML dump of English Wikipedia from July 2013. The entire corpus is around 42 GB and contains 10.2 million articles (after excluding certain non-article pages). After preprocessing, we extracted around 50 million sentences. Running our Hadoop implementation of minhash on the entire collection took approximately 25 minutes on our cluster consisting of 16 nodes, each of which has two quad core Intel Xeon E5520 processors, 24 GB RAM, and three 2 TB disks. Code for replicating these experiments have been made open source.[3]

In total, we identified 1.15 million clusters, 3.50 million article/sentence pairs over 1.09 million articles. The clusters contain 2.36 million unique sentences. Cluster sizes range from 2 to over 40k; see Figure 2 for a histogram. Most clusters are small; about 99% of the clusters have ten or fewer sentences. Of the 14,488 clusters greater than size 10, 2722 (19%) contain identical sentences; for 3890 clusters (27%), fewer than 50% of the sentences in each cluster are unique; 5725 clusters (40%) contain entirely unique sentences.

Based on manual inspection of the cluster output, we developed a taxonomy and categorized near-duplicate clusters into one of six types. Examples are shown in Figure 3 and discussed below.

Templates describe sentences that have identical structure, but with different entities, facts, or figures for *different* topics (and thus are not contradictory). They reflect conscious attempts (presumably by editors) to impose structure across groups of articles that may be related. Since several of the largest template clusters contain tens of thousands of sentences (the largest over 40k), it is likely that some template groups were automatically generated using bots. In many cases template sentences are found in stub articles.

[3]`https://github.com/seweissman/wikiduper`

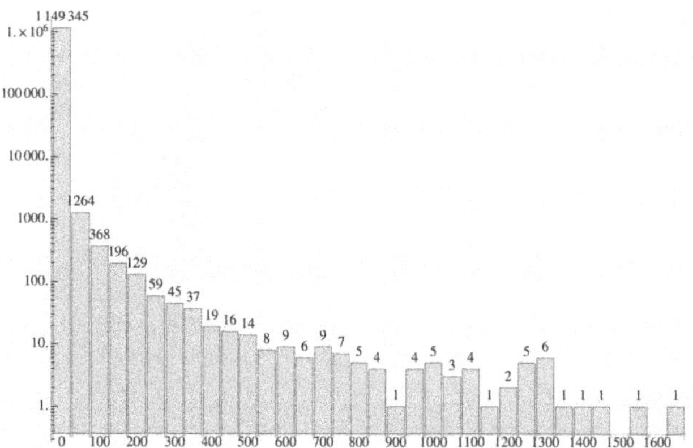

Figure 2: Histogram of cluster sizes: bars show bucketed cluster sizes and heights show number of clusters of that size (log scale). The 25 clusters of size ≥ 1700 are not shown.

Templates are interesting in that they can be viewed as a structured knowledge source for information extraction.

Identical sentences are the result of copy and paste, and are often found in articles that cover similar topics or articles that are subtopics of other topics. We find that non-identical but highly-similar sentences break down into two types: *Copyediting* refers to nearly identical sentences that differ in stylistic or otherwise non-substantive ways (based on our judgment). We believe that these arise from minor editing after a copy and paste. *Factual drift* describes sentences about the *same* topic that provide contradictory facts. Although without detailed research, there is no way to ascertain which version (if any) is correct, we can identify a common scenario. After a copy-and-paste, a fact becomes out of date (e.g., the tallest building or the death toll in a disaster) and is corrected in one instance but not the others.

References refer to citations, typically occurring at the end of articles. Since Wikipedia does not adhere to one single citation style, the same work may be cited differently, or multiple citations to the same venue may be similar.

Finally, clusters that do not fit into any of the above categories are classified as *other*. These typically represent sentences that are highly similar, but otherwise bear no semantic relationship with each other. Sentence chunking errors often contribute to these spurious results.

To quantify the distribution of these six cases, we randomly sampled 2094 clusters and performed manual classification. The distribution of the categories is shown in Table 1. If a cluster exhibited more than one type, we classified it as *other*. Overall, nearly three quarters of all clusters are either *identical* or *template*.

Finally, we manually examined a few of the large clusters and noticed that they often contain a mix of different phenomena. One common pattern is that a cluster contains distinct groups of identical sentences, where each of the groups are near duplicates. Since there are relatively few large clusters, these nuances do not have a significant impact on the figures in Table 1.

5. FUTURE WORK AND CONCLUSIONS

In this work, we applied minhash to the problem of detecting near-duplicate sentences in Wikipedia. Our MapReduce implementation is scalable and processes English Wikipedia in a short amount of time on a modest cluster. We discov-

Templates
Of the agricultural land 40.4% is used for growing crops and 26.6% is pastures while 2.2% is used for orchards or vine crops. [Gondiswil]
Of the agricultural land 26.1% is used for growing crops and 30.2% is pastures while 3.0% is used for orchards or vine crops. [Kleindietwil]

Identical
Professional organizers help redirect paradigms into more useful cross-applications that ensure properly co-sustainable futures for their clients' spaces and processes. [Professional organizing]
Professional organizers help redirect paradigms into more useful cross-applications that ensure properly co-sustainable futures for their clients' spaces and processes. [Professional organizer]

Copyediting
Scientific data on natural ball lightning are scarce, owing to its infrequency and unpredictability. [Ball lightning]
Scientific data on natural ball lightning is scarce owing to its infrequency and unpredictability. [Lightning]

Factual Drift
Bulgaria, a poor rural nation of 7 million people sought to acquire Macedonia but when it tried it was defeated in 1913 in the Second Balkan War. [History of the Balkans]
Bulgaria a poor rural nation of 4.5 million people sought to acquire Macedonia but when it tried it was defeated in 1913 in the Second Balkan War. [Home front during World War I]

References
Komjáth Péter and Vilmos Totik: Problems and Theorems in Classical Set Theory, Springer-Verlag, Berlin, 2006. [Péter Komjáth]
Péter Komjáth, Vilmos Totik: Problems and Theorems in Classical Set Theory, Springer-Verlag, Berlin, 2006. [Vilmos Totik]

Other
Army Medical Research Institute of Infectious Diseases (USAMRIID) microbiologist Bruce E. [Timeline of the 2001 anthrax attacks]
Army Medical Research Institute of Infectious Diseases (USAMRIID) which transitioned from the previous U.S. [Fort Detrick]

Figure 3: Classification of near-duplicate sentences, with examples (article titles in square brackets).

type	count	fraction
Templates	632	30.2%
Identical	948	45.3%
Copyediting	283	13.5%
Factual drift	121	5.8%
References	7	0.3%
Other	103	2.9%

Table 1: Manual classification of sample clusters.

ered that there is a substantial amount of duplicate content in Wikipedia, and that near-duplicate sentences manifest a few phenomena, the most interesting of which is contradictory facts that highlight quality issues in Wikipedia.

There are several directions in which our work can be extended. Currently, our technique only identifies *clusters* of near-duplicate sentences—missing from our analysis is the notion of information flow: Which was the source article and which was the target of copying and pasting? Are there copy "chains" where content was progressively copied from one article to the next, with possible "branches"? Our analysis of the large near-duplicate clusters suggests that there are complex edit histories that form tree-like structures. Furthermore, are there editor-specific effects? For example, is copying and pasting more likely by anonymous editors? It might also be interesting to explore topical effects: are articles on certain topics (e.g., recent events) more vulnerable to factual drift than others?

In some ways, it is not surprising that Wikipedia is internally inconsistent and contains contradictory facts—after all, it represents the collective efforts of many contributors. Nevertheless, how can we act upon this analysis constructively? We could imagine a robot that monitors Wikipedia to flag inconsistencies and requests editors to intervene and resolve. Such a service would be valuable in improving the internal consistency and quality of Wikipedia.

6. ACKNOWLEDGMENTS

This work was supported in part by the National Science Foundation under IIS-1218043. Any opinions, findings, conclusions, or recommendations expressed are those of the authors and do not necessarily reflect the views of the sponsor.

7. REFERENCES

[1] R. J. Bayardo, Y. Ma, and R. Srikant. Scaling up all pairs similarity search. *WWW*, 2007.
[2] M. Bendersky and W. B. Croft. Finding text reuse on the web. *WSDM*, 2009.
[3] A. Z. Broder. On the resemblance and containment of documents. *Compression and Complexity of Sequences*, 1997.
[4] T. H. Cormen, C. E. Leiserson, R. L. Rivest, and C. Stein. *Introduction to Algorithms*. MIT Press, 2001.
[5] J. Dean and S. Ghemawat. MapReduce: Simplified data processing on large clusters. *OSDI*, 2004.
[6] J. Giles. Internet encyclopaedias go head to head. *Nature*, 438:900–901, 2005.
[7] M. Henzinger. Finding near-duplicate web pages: A large-scale evaluation of algorithms. *SIGIR*, 2006.
[8] P. Indyk and R. Motwani. Approximate nearest neighbors: Towards removing the curse of dimensionality. *STOC*, 1998.
[9] J. Lin. Brute force and indexed approaches to pairwise document similarity comparisons with MapReduce. *SIGIR*, 2009.
[10] A. Si, H. V. Leong, and R. W. H. Lau. CHECK: A document plagiarism detection system. *SAC*, 1997.
[11] B. Stvilia, M. B. Twidale, L. C. Smith, and L. Gasser. Information quality work organization in Wikipedia. *JASIST*, 59(6):983–1001, 2008.
[12] F. Ture, T. Elsayed, and J. Lin. No free lunch: Brute force vs. locality-sensitive hashing for cross-lingual pairwise similarity. *SIGIR*, 2011.
[13] R. Vernica, M. J. Carey, and C. Li. Efficient parallel set-similarity joins using MapReduce. *SIGMOD*, 2010.
[14] D. M. Wilkinson and B. A. Huberman. Assessing the value of cooperation in Wikipedia. *First Monday*, 12(4), 2007.

Scholarly Document Information Extraction using Extensible Features for Efficient Higher Order Semi-CRFs

Nguyen Viet Cuong, Muthu Kumar Chandrasekaran, Min-Yen Kan, Wee Sun Lee*
Department of Computer Science, National University of Singapore
{nvcuong,muthu.chandra,kanmy,leews}@comp.nus.edu.sg

ABSTRACT

We address the tasks of recovering bibliographic and document structure metadata from scholarly documents. We leverage higher order semi-Markov conditional random fields to model long-distance label sequences, improving upon the performance of the linear-chain conditional random field model. We introduce the notion of extensible features, which allows the expensive inference process to be simplified through memoization, resulting in lower computational complexity. Our method significantly betters the state-of-the-art on three related scholarly document extraction tasks.

Categories and Subject Descriptors

H.3.7 [**Information Storage and Retrieval**]: Digital Libraries

Keywords

Metadata Extraction; Logical Structure Discovery; Conditional Random Fields

1. INTRODUCTION

The publication metadata of a scholarly work and those of its referenced publications form the foundation of citation indices, which enable a variety of digital library services. Accurate extraction, parsing and matching of bibliographic reference strings is needed to properly attribute a work and its components: author, institution and publication venue. The full text also enables extraction of citation context and document structure used in literature review generation, citation function and keyphrase extraction. However, a work's metadata and those of its cited works – along with its logical document structure – remain largely machine-inaccessible as the ubiquitous PDF document format often does not expose this information. Automated extraction is needed to address this class of scholarly document information extraction needs.

Extraction from PDF typically employs optical character recognition to first recover the text and its formatting and layout characteristics. In digital libraries, this input is passed to other systems, such as a conditional random field (CRF), to extract or infer the document metadata. CRF-based systems for such tasks are common in the literature, and fielded in both academic and industrial circles. Mendeley[1], Citeseerχ [1] and ParsCit [2] are notable systems that address reference string parsing using standard linear-chain CRFs. Similar works have also applied them to the logical document extraction task [3, 4, 5]. While it works well, a linear model is limited: it cannot capture non-adjacent dependencies common in such tasks. Stacked linear-chain CRF models have been proposed for the task of reference string parsing [6], in response to this shortcoming. This solution has a cheaper inference cost, but still lacks the expressiveness needed to model long-range dependencies.

To address this shortcoming, we focus on two improvements to CRFs that have been proposed to increase their modeling sophistication and performance. Higher order CRFs capture long-range label patterns, while semi-Markov CRFs (semi-CRFs) model successive labels of the same type as cohesive segments. Both methods individually improve model fidelity, and hence prediction accuracy, but are often computationally expensive, increasing running time (both training and testing) and memory requirements. Our work applies both advances to document information extraction tasks. With such higher order semi-Markov CRFs (HO-SCRFs), we capture long-range dependencies between segments of labels which often occur in scholarly data: *e.g.*, patterns such as *author+ date+ title+*[2] in reference string parsing and *abstract+ introduction+ method+* in document structure labeling.

Our key contribution is to make HO-SCRFs more tractable for practical use. By introducing the notion of *extensible features*, we can distinguish features that can benefit from reusing prior computations (memoization) in the calculation of the potential functions Ψ. Using our technique, we demonstrate overall inference improvements HO-SCRFs make over the standard, state-of-the-art linear-chain CRFs on three public scholarly document information extraction tasks.

*This research is supported by the Singapore National Research Foundation under its International Research Centre @ Singapore Funding Initiative and administered by the IDM Programme Office.

JCDL'15, June 21–25, 2015, Knoxville, Tennessee, USA.

ACM 978-1-4503-3594-2/15/06 ...$15.00.
DOI: http://dx.doi.org/10.1145/2756406.2756946.

[1] http://www.mendeley.com/

[2] The symbol '+' denotes a segment with one or more consecutive labels of the same class.

Definitions: Let $\mathbf{x} = (x_1, \ldots, x_{|\mathbf{x}|})$ be an input sequence and $\mathcal{Y}$ be a set of labels.
· A *segment* of $\mathbf{x}$ is a triplet (u, v, y) where $1 \le u \le v \le |\mathbf{x}|$ and $y \in \mathcal{Y}$ is the common label of the subsequence $\mathbf{x}_{u:v} = (x_u, \ldots, x_v)$.
· A *segmentation* for $\mathbf{x}$ is a sequence of consecutive segments $\mathbf{s} = (s_1, \ldots, s_p)$, where $s_t = (u_t, v_t, y_t)$ with $u_1 = 1$, $v_p = |\mathbf{x}|$, and $u_{t+1} = v_t + 1$ for all t (i.e., the segments are juxtaposed and cover the whole input).

Figure 1: Segment and segmentation definitions drawn from the semi-CRF literature.

2. METHOD

We describe the higher order semi-CRFs (HO-SCRFs) with extensible features that are used in our paper. A linear-chain CRF (L-CRF) models the probability of a label sequence for an input sequence. Semi-CRFs [7] extend the L-CRF to model the probability of a sequence of variable-length segments, each of which consists of consecutive tokens with the same label, for an input sequence. This model additionally allows features over segments (as opposed to just tokens), such as aggregate properties of segments like length of fields. For example, in reference string parsing, transitions between two fields such as *author* → *title* can be explicitly specified. HO-SCRFs allow features to be specified over more than two consecutive segments. For example, a 2nd-order semi-CRF can model the transition between three consecutive fields such as *author* → *date* → *title.*

Formally, a semi-CRF [7] models the conditional distribution over all segmentations $\mathbf{s}$ of an input sequence $\mathbf{x}$ by:

$$P(\mathbf{s}|\mathbf{x}) = \frac{1}{Z_{\mathbf{x}}} \exp\left(\sum_{i=1}^{m}\sum_{t=1}^{|\mathbf{s}|} \lambda_i f_i(\mathbf{x}, \mathbf{s}, t)\right),$$

where $\mathcal{F} = \{f_i(\mathbf{x}, \mathbf{s}, t) : 1 \le i \le m\}$ is a set of semi-Markov features, each of which has a corresponding weight λ_i, and $Z_{\mathbf{x}}$ is the partition function to normalize $P(\mathbf{s}|\mathbf{x})$ to a proper probability. An HO-SCRF [8] allows the semi-Markov features to have the following form:

$$f_i(\mathbf{x}, \mathbf{s}, t) = \begin{cases} g_i(\mathbf{x}, u_t, v_t) & \text{if } y_{t-|\mathbf{z}^i|+1} \cdots y_t = \mathbf{z}^i \\ 0 & \text{otherwise} \end{cases},$$

where $\mathbf{z}^i$ is the segment label pattern associated with feature f_i, and $\mathbf{s}$ is a segmentation of $\mathbf{x}$. *I.e.*, at segment t, if the label pattern of the segmentation $\mathbf{s}$ matches the segment label pattern $\mathbf{z}^i$, then f_i has the value g_i that depends only on the observation sequence. The feature f_i is said to be a kth-order semi-Markov feature, if the length of the label pattern $\mathbf{z}^i$ is $k+1$.

We use an example drawn from our digital library datasets to explain the modeling power of such features. In the task of reference string parsing, we can specify a 2nd-order semi-Markov feature which returns the number of times a specific word *Scholarly* appears in a *title* field, when the previous two fields are *author* and *date*, respectively. The segment label pattern $\mathbf{z}^i$ associated with this feature is *author+ date+ title+*. Such *bag-of-words* features can be further generalized as *bag* features that count the number of times a certain property appears in a field rather than simply counting specific word occurrences.

2.1 Extensible Semi-Markov Features

To enable faster inference, we make the key observation that certain higher order features can be incrementally computed – such features can reuse computations made previously for inferring the label of a previous token. We thus partition the feature set into two disjoint sets: the *extensible* features and the *non-extensible* ones. Extensible features are such features; those whose values can be aggregated over tokens within a segment, e.g. the bag features above.

Formally, a feature $f_i \in \mathcal{F}$ is called *extensible* if for any $1 \le u < v \le |\mathbf{x}|$, we have:

$$g_i(\mathbf{x}, u, v) = g_i(\mathbf{x}, u, v-1) + h_i(\mathbf{x}, v) = h_i(\mathbf{x}, u) + g_i(\mathbf{x}, u+1, v),$$

where $h_i(\mathbf{x}, u) := g_i(\mathbf{x}, u, u)$ for all u. In other words, a feature is extensible if its value on a segment can be computed from the value at either of the segment's boundary plus the value on the remaining segment. In many cases, h_i is an easy-to-compute function.

Unigram L-CRF features (those depending only on the label of the current token) can often be encoded as bag features in semi-CRFs. Thus, we can include many L-CRF features into HO-SCRFs as extensible features. Examples of extensible features include word counts within segments and lengths of segments.

2.2 Inference Algorithms

Inference algorithms for HO-SCRFs with extensible features are essentially similar to the original algorithms for HO-SCRFs in [8], except for modifications to re-use the computations for extensible features which we detail next.

Recall that inferences for HO-SCRFs require the computation of both forward and backward variables. These variables will be used to compute the partition function $Z_{\mathbf{x}}$, the expected feature sum, and the marginal probabilities. During testing, the most likely segmentation for a given input sequence is computed using the Viterbi algorithm.

A key step in the inferences is to compute the factor $\Psi_{\mathbf{x}}(u, v, \mathbf{p}) = \exp(\sum_{i:\mathbf{z}^i \le^s \mathbf{p}} \lambda_i g_i(\mathbf{x}, u, v))$, where $\mathbf{p}$ is a sequence of segment labels and $\le^s$ is the suffix relation. This factor gives the total contribution within the subsequence $\mathbf{x}_{u:v}$ of all the activated features that match the segment label sequence $\mathbf{p}$. We can factorize $\Psi_{\mathbf{x}}(u, v, \mathbf{p})$ into $\Psi^e_{\mathbf{x}}(u, v, \mathbf{p}) \times \Psi^n_{\mathbf{x}}(u, v, \mathbf{p})$ such that:

$$\Psi^e_{\mathbf{x}}(u, v, \mathbf{p}) = \exp(\textstyle\sum_{i:f_i \in \mathcal{F}_e \wedge \mathbf{z}^i \le^s \mathbf{p}} \lambda_i g_i(\mathbf{x}, u, v)), \text{ and}$$
$$\Psi^n_{\mathbf{x}}(u, v, \mathbf{p}) = \exp(\textstyle\sum_{i:f_i \in \mathcal{F}_n \wedge \mathbf{z}^i \le^s \mathbf{p}} \lambda_i g_i(\mathbf{x}, u, v)),$$

where $\Psi^e_{\mathbf{x}}$ only aggregates over extensible features while $\Psi^n_{\mathbf{x}}$ aggregates over non-extensible features.

If f_i is an extensible feature, we can decompose g_i into $g_i(\mathbf{x}, u, v) = h_i(\mathbf{x}, u) + g_i(\mathbf{x}, u+1, v)$. With such decomposition and the above factorization, we can write:

$$\Psi_{\mathbf{x}}(u, v, \mathbf{p}) = \exp(\sum_{\substack{i:f_i \in \mathcal{F}_e \\ \mathbf{z}^i \le^s \mathbf{p}}} \lambda_i h_i(\mathbf{x}, u)) \Psi^e_{\mathbf{x}}(u+1, v, \mathbf{p}) \Psi^n_{\mathbf{x}}(u, v, \mathbf{p}).$$

Here, $\Psi^e_{\mathbf{x}}(u+1, v, \mathbf{p})$ is the computation that is memoized previously. We then only need to calculate the incremental value of $\Psi^n_{\mathbf{x}}(u, v, \mathbf{p})$ and the exponential factor to get the new value of $\Psi_{\mathbf{x}}(u, v, \mathbf{p})$. Hence, using this formula and a simple rearrangement for the recurrence to compute the forward variable (in Section 2.3.1 of [8]), we can achieve a speedup in the forward inference as the value of $\Psi^e_{\mathbf{x}}(u+1, v, \mathbf{p})$ is memoized when we compute $\Psi_{\mathbf{x}}(u, v, \mathbf{p})$ (i.e., dynamic programming can be used to compute the values of $\Psi_{\mathbf{x}}$).

This memoization based speed-up is applicable to many parts of the inference pipeline. Aside from the forward variable computation, the speedup also applies to the backward variables (by decomposing g_i similarly into $g_i(\mathbf{x}, u, v) = h_i(\mathbf{x}, v) + g_i(\mathbf{x}, u, v-1)$), computation of marginal probabilities, and for the Viterbi algorithm during testing. To be clear, this computational shortcut applies to both HO-SCRFs and normal semi-CRFs.

2.3 Computational Complexity

The complexity analysis for the original inferences in [8] assumed that the features $g_i(\mathbf{x}, u, v)$ can be computed in $O(1)$, an unrealistic assumption since the computation of such segment features depends on the length of the segment. In this paper, we assume the computation of $h_i(\mathbf{x}, v)$ is $O(1)$ instead, thus making the computation of g_i linear in the segment length, which we feel is more realistic.

For simplicity, we also assume that all the values of $\Psi_{\mathbf{x}}$ (equivalently, $\Psi^e_{\mathbf{x}}$ and $\Psi^n_{\mathbf{x}}$) are pre-computed before we compute the forward and backward variables. In practice, $\Psi_{\mathbf{x}}$ is computed on-the-fly using memoization. Note that computing $\Psi_{\mathbf{x}}$'s is the computational bottleneck in CRF inference, and that our strategy directly decreases its computational complexity.

Indeed, if we do not leverage extensibility, the worst-case time complexity to pre-compute $\Psi_{\mathbf{x}}$'s is $O(T^3|\mathcal{F}||\mathcal{P}||\mathcal{Y}|^2) = O(T^3(|\mathcal{F}_e| + |\mathcal{F}_n|)|\mathcal{P}||\mathcal{Y}|^2)$, where T is the maximal input sequence length and $\mathcal{P}$ is the forward-state set [8]. In contrast, when we use extensibility, this worst-case complexity is $O((|\mathcal{F}_n|T^3 + |\mathcal{F}_e|T^2)|\mathcal{P}||\mathcal{Y}|^2)$. Since most ordinary features are extensible, the bulk of the inference changes from cubic to quadratic complexity in T, a large savings. Once we have all the values of $\Psi_{\mathbf{x}}$, the time complexity for other inference steps remain identical.

3. EVALUATION

To validate the performance of HO-SCRFs, we re-use three scholarly extraction tasks which have previously been formally defined and which have freely-available datasets.[3]

· **Reference String Parsing** is the task of tokenizing and labeling individuals fields of reference strings (i.e., the bibiography) of a scholarly work. Given a reference string as input, the models should appropriately label its tokens. The set of labels are listed in Column 1 of Table 2. We re-use the exact features and values described in [2] for direct comparison.

· **Generic Section Labeling** seeks to recover the logical structure of the main sections of a scholarly work. Models are tasked to label the section sequence of an input work, picking labels from Column 1 of Table 3. We re-use the exact features and their values as described in [4].

[3]We note that the reference string parsing dataset is a compendium of Cora, FLUX-CiM, ICONIP and humanities datasets. Section labeling is evaluated on the generic section labeling dataset used in [4]. Author and Affiliation extraction is evaluated on the compendium of works published by the ACL and from a cross-domain dataset reported in [5]. All datasets are publicly available at `https://github.com/knmnyn/ParsCit/tree/master/crfpp/traindata`.

Table 1: Statistics of the datasets used.

Task [Citation]	Train	Validation	Test
Reference string parsing [2]	883	–	501
Generic section labeling [4]	102	44	65
Author extraction [5]	13	10	144
Affiliation extraction [5]	6	10	145

Table 2: F_1 (%) for HO-SCRFs on the reference string parsing task.

Label (Size)	L-CRF	1SCRF	2SCRF	3SCRF
author (2085)	99.00	98.97	99.02	98.78
booktitle (3116)	93.60	93.67	94.15	93.71
date (671)	93.61	92.98	93.26	93.11
editor (207)	75.33	71.54	75.60	75.60
institution (27)	79.17	79.17	79.17	96.43
journal (451)	89.31	89.60	90.12	88.22
location (408)	89.20	89.18	89.91	90.68
note (69)	57.14	57.14	57.53	60.00
pages (580)	95.91	95.59	94.56	95.49
publisher (125)	83.33	83.68	83.33	84.39
tech (5)	46.15	46.15	46.15	62.50
title (4086)	94.53	94.74	95.35	95.22
volume (154)	91.28	92.20	87.74	90.00
Micro-average	**94.01**	**94.01**	**94.35****	**94.26****

· **Author and Affiliation Extraction** is to extract author (affiliation) occurrences from the author (affiliation) lines in the header section of a paper [5]. These lines also contain other markers (symbols) and other separators to delimit multiple authors (affiliations). Models are to assign labels from the inventory of *author* (*affiliation*), *symbol*, and *separator*.

For ease of reference, we restate the demographics of the public datasets we used in Table 1. Except for reference string parsing, we use a validation set to select the best regularization parameter σ among the values 0.1, 1, 10, 100. The models with the best parameter settings are then trained on the union of the train and validation sets, and then tested on the test set. For reference string parsing, we only use the default $\sigma = 1$ without applying validation, due to the long training time.

Results. In what follows, L-CRF, 1SCRF, 2SCRF and 3SCRF denote the linear-chain CRF (our baseline), 1st-, 2nd- and 3rd-order semi-CRF models, respectively. In the prior literature, only L-CRFs were used to address these tasks. As input for 1SCRF, we use all the features of the L-CRF together with all 1st-order semi-Markov transition features. For both the 2SCRF and 3SCRF models, we re-use all features for the $k-1^{th}$ model and in addition incorporate the kth-order semi-Markov transition features.

For the reference string parsing task, from Table 2, 2SCRF and 3SCRF perform significantly better than L-CRF ($p < 0.01$) in aggregate. Overall, 2SCRF achieves the best score (94.35%), and it performs equally or better than L-CRF on 10 out of 13 labels, including some dominant labels such as *title*, *booktitle*, and *author*. Many errors for this task come from the humanities datasets, which contain non-English references. Other errors come from the ambiguity of the labels, some of which even confused human annotators. For instance, the token *16(3):52-55* was labeled as *volume* by 2SCRF but its true label is *pages* (the token contains both the volume and page information).

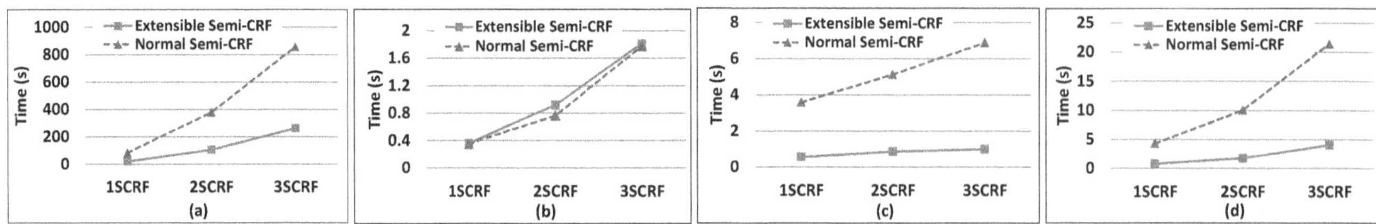

Figure 2: Elapsed running time of the standard and our extensible higher order semi-CRFs for the (a) reference string parsing, (b) generic section labeling, (c) affiliation extraction, and (d) author extraction tasks on their respective test sets (or 25% of the test set for reference string parsing).

Table 3: F_1 (%) for HO-SCRFs on the generic section labeling task.

Label (Size)	L-CRF	1SCRF	2SCRF	3SCRF
abstract (65)	100	100	100	100
acknowledgement (29)	100	94.92	94.92	93.10
background (8)	80.00	85.71	94.12	100
categories (50)	99.01	99.01	99.01	99.01
conclusions (55)	92.98	92.31	94.74	92.17
discussions (15)	72.00	50.00	80.00	50.00
evaluation (42)	89.74	81.08	92.31	83.95
general terms (46)	100	100	100	100
introduction (64)	97.67	97.67	97.67	97.67
methodology (183)	96.24	93.96	97.56	95.70
references (65)	100	100	100	100
related works (30)	100	94.74	100	100
Micro-average	**96.63**	**94.79**	**97.39***	**95.71**

Table 4: F_1 (%) for HO-SCRFs on the author and affiliation extraction tasks.

Problem	L-CRF	1SCRF	2SCRF	3SCRF
Author	93.64	93.53	94.06*	93.21
Affiliation	98.33	98.50	98.50	98.50

For generic section labeling, Table 3 shows that 2SCRF performs significantly better than L-CRF ($p < 0.05$) in aggregate. 2SCRF achieves the best score overall (97.39%), performing equally or better than L-CRF on 11 of 12 categories, inclusive of dominant categories such as *methodology* and *conclusions*. Errors for this task include confusion between the *conclusions* section and the *evaluation* or *discussion* sections in the data. For example, 2SCRF may predict that there is a conclusions section before the references section in a paper, while the correct label is *discussion*.

On the author extraction task, Table 4 shows that 2SCRF performs significantly better than L-CRF in aggregate ($p < 0.05$) and achieves the best F_1 score (94.06%). For the affiliation extraction task, all of the semi-CRF configurations perform better than L-CRF with $p < 0.057$. Many errors for these tasks, especially the author extraction task, come from the *separator* class.

Running Time. For all tasks, we measured the testing time on the test data sets[4] using a 24-core machine (800 MHz per core; Figure 2). Similar trends also occurred in training times. For the reference string parsing and author–affiliation extraction tasks, Figure 2a,c,d shows that leveraging the extensible property of the semi-Markov features improves the running time significantly. Generic section labeling task is the exception (Figure 2b). One possible explanation is that the test set for this task is small (65 instances), and the running time is dominated by the parallel communication between the threads (which is non-deterministic).

[4]We used 25% of the test set for reference string parsing.

4. CONCLUSION

We have demonstrated the feasibility of using higher order semi-CRFs (here, HO-SCRFs) to improve performance on scholarly document extraction tasks. By noting that many semi-CRF features are extensible (amenable to incremental calculation and hence memoization), we can also efficiently train and test such models.

We note that learning solutions are not the only solution to scholarly document information extraction tasks. For reference string parsing, sourcing scholarly metadata through external sources (*i.e.*, the Web) is a promising avenue [9, 10]. In future work, we plan to integrate both learning and Web lookup (when appropriate) to solve such tasks.

5. REFERENCES

[1] C. Lee Giles, Kurt D. Bollacker, and Steve Lawrence. Citeseer: An automatic citation indexing system. In *DL*, pages 89–98, 1998.

[2] Isaac G. Councill, C. Lee Giles, and Min-Yen Kan. ParsCit: An open-source CRF reference string parsing package. In *LREC*, 2008.

[3] Alan Souza, Viviane Moreira, and Carlos Heuser. ARCTIC: metadata extraction from scientific papers in pdf using two-layer CRF. In *DocEng*, 2014.

[4] Minh-Thang Luong, Thuy Dung Nguyen, and Min-Yen Kan. Logical structure recovery in scholarly articles with rich document features. *IJDLS*, 1(4):1–23, 2010.

[5] Huy Hoang Nhat Do, Muthu Kumar Chandrasekaran, Philip S. Cho, and Min Yen Kan. Extracting and matching authors and affiliations in scholarly documents. In *JCDL*, pages 219–228, 2013.

[6] Peter Kluegl, Martin Toepfer, Florian Lemmerich, Andreas Hotho, and Frank Puppe. Stacked conditional random fields exploiting structural consistencies. In *ICPRAM*, 2012.

[7] Sunita Sarawagi and William W. Cohen. Semi-Markov conditional random fields for information extraction. In *NIPS*, pages 1185–1192, 2004.

[8] Nguyen Viet Cuong, Nan Ye, Wee Sun Lee, and Hai Leong Chieu. Conditional random field with high-order dependencies for sequence labeling and segmentation. *JLMR*, 15:981–1009, 2014.

[9] Liangcai Gao, Xixi Qi, Zhi Tang, Xiaofan Lin, and Ying Liu. Web-based citation parsing, correction and augmentation. In *JCDL*, pages 295–304, 2012.

[10] Dat T. Huynh and Wen Hua. Self-supervised learning approach for extracting citation information on the web. In *Web Technologies and Applications*. 2012.

Towards Use and Reuse Driven Big Data Management

Zhiwu Xie[1], Yinlin Chen[1], Julie Speer[1], Tyler Walters[1], Pablo A Tarazaga[2], and Mary Kasarda[2]
[1]University Libraries and [2]Department of Mechanical Engineering
Virginia Polytechnic Institute and State University
Blacksburg, USA
{zhiwuxie, ylchen, jspeer, tyler.walters, ptarazag, maryk}@vt.edu

ABSTRACT

We propose a use and reuse driven big data management approach that fuses the data repository and data processing capabilities in a co-located, public cloud. It answers to the urgent data management needs from the growing number of researchers who don't fit in the big science/small science dichotomy. This approach will allow researchers to more easily use, manage, and collaborate around big data sets, as well as give librarians the opportunity to work alongside the researchers to preserve and curate data while it is still fresh and being actively used. This also provides the technological foundation to foster a sharing culture more aligned with the open source software development paradigm than the lone-wolf, gift-exchanging small science sharing or the top-down, highly structured big science sharing. To materialize this vision, we provide a system architecture consisting of a scalable digital repository system coupled with the co-located cloud storage and cloud computing, as well as a job scheduler and a deployment management system. Motivated by Virginia Tech's Goodwin Hall instrumentation project, we implemented and evaluated a prototype. The results show not only sufficient capacities for this particular case, but also near perfect linear storage and data processing scalabilities under moderately high workload.

Categories and Subject Descriptors

H.3.7 [**Information Storage and Retrieval**]: Digital libraries – *collection, dissemination, systems issues.*

H.3.4 [**Information Storage and Retrieval**]: Systems and Software – *Distributed systems, performance evaluation.*

Keywords

Big data; digital library; cloud computing; digital repository; smart infrastructure; sensor data

JCDL'15, June 21–25, 2015, Knoxville, Tennessee, USA.

ACM 978-1-4503-3594-2/15/06 $15.00
DOI: http://dx.doi.org/10.1145/2756406.2756924

1. INTRODUCTION

What can the digital libraries community contribute to tame the data deluge? In terms of the conceptual framework, infrastructure, and implementation, the answers vary from the optimistic "just read and implement the OAIS specification" [6] [13], the less encouraging "can't do" at the institutional level [23] because it "takes big organization" [26], to the cautious "knowledge infrastructures are not yet in place" [7]. We resonate more with the cautious note, especially its assessment that focusing on archiving inactive data "limits the application of digital libraries for scientific data management" [7].

Indeed, the OAIS Reference Model [17] may form a tunnel vision for data repositories and reduce them to a niche far less relevant to researchers than self-serving librarians and archivists. No matter how thorough we document and how detailed we describe the data and their usage context [34] [24], mummifying live data out of their natural habitats of analysis to be preserved in an isolated vault can significantly diminish their value. This is particularly evident in the big data management scenario, where making sense of data requires extensive technology maneuvers and infrastructure support. If an archival repository does not include appropriate capabilities to perform analytics tasks and directly answer data-intensive science questions, the researchers will find the repository impractical, giving data producers less incentive to hand over fresh and hot data therefore making the repository even less useful. To break away from this paradox, we need to adopt a use and reuse driven approach, in which the digital library is a pluggable component of the research infrastructure. It then follows that the data preservation and curation will result as a by-product of the research process, not its ultimate goal or end product.

In this paper we focus on the high volume and high velocity aspects of big data, which pose different challenges from those caused by high variety and high veracity. As of this writing, typical institutional repository implicitly or explicitly limits the unit data deposit to an arbitrarily low size, e.g., 10GB [23] or 20GB [18]. This certainly is far below the volume now churned out from the laboratories and observatories. The "big" aspect should therefore be gauged against the data capacity currently handled by a typical digital library.

It is easy to dismiss the capacity concern as purely technical therefore trivial. After all, given sufficient funding, any existing repository can build up its storage capacity and raise the bar. But it will soon become clear that simply expanding the storage capacity does not solve the problem. The use and reuse pattern starts to change when the data volume reaches a threshold. Beyond that, researchers cannot easily move the data from the storage to a remote analytics environment therefore need sufficient computing capacity close to where the data are stored. If provisioned with new technologies such as virtualization, big data analytics, and cloud computing, this new usage pattern will then open up opportunities for organizational, cultural, and social changes surrounding big data sharing and reuse. Unfortunately, existing archive-centric repositories are not well prepared for these changes.

Prior work [15], [6], [7], [13] tend to associate big data with big science, which is also characterized with big organization and big budget. We intentionally avoid the big/small science dichotomy for two reasons. First, the data volume separating the big and small science is shifting up very fast that many big science data management challenges are now also confronting small research teams. For example, the much-revered 1000 Genomes project [43] produced 200 TB of data from 2008 to 2012. The Sloan Digital Sky Survey [46] produced about 130TB of raw and derivative data over 8 years in phase I and II [38]. In contrast, the sensors installed in Virginia Tech's Goodwin Hall alone can collect as much data in shorter period of time, and we expect the data acquisition lasts much longer. While motivating this research, the Goodwin Hall project was started by two faculty members, a small lab, and until now is mostly internally funded.

Second, managing big data does not have to begin with a big organization and a big budget. Ramping up big data management with limited budget and in small team settings can transcend both big and small science. Organization structure wise, starting from a bottom-up approach will be more appropriate, where user communities naturally form and self-organize around the data out of their own needs, use cases, and perspectives. It is also important to build systems that allow diverse communities to contribute human, technology, and financial resources in a self-motivated, ad hoc, and on-demand manner. The approach proposed in this paper will foster collaborations significantly different from both the top-down, tightly managed big science model and the lone-wolf, gift-exchanging small science model [44].

Motivated by the Goodwin Hall project, we propose a big data management approach driven primarily by data use and reuse. We then build an implementation prototype in the cloud and evaluate its performance. The results show perfectly linear scalability under moderately high workload, indicating that the public cloud can be a viable big data sharing and management platform.

This paper is structured as follows. After describing the Goodwin Hall project, we analyze its requirements and show why OAIS reference model is insufficient for its data management needs. We then make the case for building a use and reuse driven big data management infrastructure in the public cloud and describe its system model. The next few sections address its implementation prototype and evaluation, discuss the "soft" impacts of this approach, and conclude the paper with reviewing and comparing related work.

2. BACKGROUND

The main motivation of this research is the need for a big data management system primarily intended for, but not limited to, the Virginia Tech Goodwin Hall sensor data.

Virginia Tech's Smart Infrastructure Laboratory (VT-SIL) is building a full-scale living laboratory in the newly opened 160,000-square-foot Goodwin Hall. VT-SIL is finishing mounting over 240 vibration-monitoring accelerometers in more than 130 strategic locations throughout the building, as well as planned for hundreds of temperature, flow, and other sensors to be installed in the near future. Upon completion, Goodwin Hall will be the world's most instrumented building for vibrations and will generate more than 60TB of sensor data per year.

The Goodwin Hall instrumentation differs from similar projects [41] [22] in that from the very beginning it was designed as a multi-purpose living laboratory instead of just for seismology and structural monitoring. Higher density of sensor mounts were directly wielded to the structural beams during the building construction instead of that as an afterthought, and the multi-dimensional accelerometers are strategically positioned and are sufficiently sensitive to detect human movements in the building [14] [39]. This opens up opportunities for multi- and cross-disciplinary exploration and discovery.

VT-SIL will utilize the collected data to improve the design, monitoring, and daily operation of civil and mechanical infrastructure as well as to investigate how humans interact with the built environment. In collaboration with Virginia Tech Libraries, VT-SIL also intends to open up much of the data to the public through both live streaming and a data repository, the latter being the main motivation of this research. The objective is to encourage exploratory researches and foster an open and inclusive community of researchers and educators in a myriad of disciplines. As of this writing, VT-SIL has engaged researchers from many universities, covering a broad range of disciplines including civil, construction, mechanical, electrical, environmental, industrial, safety, systems engineering and mathematics, computer science, and even visual and performing arts, all interested to explore how to use the Goodwin Hall sensor data.

The research reported in this paper intends to apply digital libraries methods and techniques, assist researchers in data management, and foster sustainable user communities around them. Although seismology data repositories exist, they usually mandate data access methods, processing tools, and have very limited search options that mostly gear towards seismology researches. In contrast, we purposefully avoid prescribing and limiting what the data shall be used for and how they are used. In the next section we will examine our goals against OAIS, a popular data management model, to identify gaps.

3. OAIS CONSIDERED INADEQUATE

The OAIS Reference Model [17] is widely recognized to have provided a conceptual framework and common vocabulary to digital preservation problems. Many document-centric digital repository software claim to be OAIS-compliant, indicating its usefulness as an abstraction for archival functions, workflows, and organizations. Some would even suggest that implementing the OAIS model is sufficient for managing scientific data [6][13]. However, after examining the Goodwin Hall project use cases, we find the OAIS model inadequate for this purpose.

3.1 OAIS Environment

The OAIS environment divides the organizational and functional roles of the information producer, the archive, and the information consumer in an overly specific and sequential manner. This artificially elevates the archive from a facilitating infrastructural piece that should have been hidden in the background to an autonomous, potentially self-serving, and even intrusive middleware.

In reality, typical researchers don't produce data solely for others to consume, therefore the first and foremost information consumers are usually the information producers themselves. These users already understand the data, don't necessarily have an immediate need for long-term preservation, but may need infrastructural help to store, process data, and make sense of them. Studies have shown that these researchers are highly sensitive to the first-use right when considering sharing [42][44]. This is particularly true for big data sets since they are both more costly to collect and potentially more valuable to science. But an archive in the OAIS sense does not have much to contribute to the first-use cycle therefore is unlikely to be engaged.

If we are to follow the OAIS model, in order for the data ingestion to happen, the archive needs to negotiate a binding submission agreement with the producers outlining the legal responsibilities between the two parties, implying once the data are out of their hands, the producers will have little control. The obvious consequence of this zero-sum strategy is that, even if the producers are still willing to share their data through the archive, the sharing would not happen until the producers have exploited the data to the maximum, which is usually fairly late in the research cycle. Because moving large data sets from where they originally reside to an archiving environment is understandably more difficult [38], it may take even longer for the archive to begin sharing the data. Extrapolating to research data the findings linking the paper recency to citation rate [35][28], we reasonably expect lower reuse rate for older data sets. Moreover, since researchers collaborate outside of the archive anyways while data are still fresh and active, such sharing would not be captured, improved, and augmented by the archive; further diminishing its potential value.

The model is also problematic on the consumer side, in that it needs to predict the unpredictable designated communities in the future. Besides the original data producers and their collaborators, unconventional, cross-disciplinary, and explorative researchers constitute important sources as data consumers. Indeed, one of the most exciting aspects of the data-intensive science is to break the artificial disciplinary boundaries, ask unconventional questions, and shed new light on old data. Enforcing disciplinary consensuses as well as biases in the archive, as many disciplinary data repositories currently do, may serve to build up the unwanted boundary.

3.2 OAIS Information Model

The OAIS information model is based on the assumption that the archive should primarily act as a storage facility that receives from the producer and disseminates to the consumer variably packaged information in discrete transmissions. The actual information consumption happens outside of the archive; therefore it is of little concern to it. This assumption starts to break down in big data management scenarios.

First, making sense of big data depends heavily on technologies and infrastructure. Big data sets cannot be easily analyzed with personal computers. No matter how complete and detailed the Representation Information is, without access to big data analytics infrastructure such as appropriately configured computer clusters, the Dissemination Information Package (DIP) is of little help to consumers.

Second, OAIS archives typically disseminate information through download links, but moving big data sets in and out of data centers is error-prone and time-consuming. It is not a secret that shipping hard drives is still the preferred option to move data when the size reaches a certain threshold. Disseminating information through user downloads is not likely to scale well.

These technology obstacles can easily paralyze an OAIS archive for big data management. Moreover, the OAIS information model overemphasizes describing and understanding information than putting the information into actual use. After all, we learn about fire by getting burnt, not by reading manuals and documentations describing its chemical compounds and temperature measure. The OAIS approach puts unnecessary burdens on both the producers and the consumers to produce and consume Representation Information. For example, how can a well-documented, but hardly actionable, big data DIP help an explorative researcher who needs to filter 60TB of vibration data against a specific wave pattern?

The above pattern filtering use case also brings out an important big data usage pattern not sufficiently addressed by the OAIS model. A document-centric archive can easily perform full-text indexing against all the content then use the resulting indexes as Access Aids to Information Packages. The assumption is that the indexing only needs to be performed once as long as the content has not changed. However this assumption does not hold for research data sets made up of digits instead of natural language vocabularies [12]. There is no good way to pre-index them for filtering queries yet to be invented in the future. Different from the specified OAIS data flow, such access queries need to be routed back to Archival Storage and trigger heavy data analytics computing jobs. A preservation and storage focused archive is not typically equipped with such capabilities.

3.3 The Use and Reuse Driven Approach

Now it should be clear that we are proposing a different data management approach than the OAIS model. This approach is more aligned with the DCC Curation Lifecycle Model [16], with the focus that the use and reuse should be the driving force. Metaphorically speaking, a data management system should not function like an antique store where people offload their attic findings and scavengers dig for hidden treasure. Instead, it should be a lively workshop equipped with powerful tools to handle big data sets as the raw materials. The workers then collaboratively build more sophisticated and specialized tools to cut, polish, and assemble the raw materials and various intermediate products in ways that make sense to their own needs, and along the way trade both their products and tools. In this workshop, data preservation and curation is like the stocking crew who cleans up the spaces and puts various materials and tools back to clearly labeled and easily accessible shelves. The purpose is to facilitate more efficient production, not to compete for the best-stocked shelves. A similar metaphor is "treating data like software" [40].

4. CORE REQUIREMENTS

The use and reuse driven data management approach described in section 3 gravitates towards a digital repository coupled with big data storage and processing capabilities. It should serve as both a data archive and a low-barrier big data analytics platform. In this section we extract its core capacity, performance and functional requirements and provide justifications.

4.1 Data Storage

Large, affordable, high-performance, highly available, and easily accessible long-term storage is the foremost core requirement to manage big data. We estimate the raw sensor data from Goodwin Hall alone will be accumulated at the rate of about 60 TB per year. The data acquisition system runs continuously with no pause in between. To detect long-term structural changes, we must compare data spanning long enough periods, e.g., more than 5 years. When running analytics, we will need to access large amounts of data but prefer not to wait for very long. We will also need to open some of the data for public access therefore the storage system must not be constrained behind a security perimeter. These form the minimum storage requirements that must be met by any viable data management system. Since intermediate data will need temporary and in many occasions also long-term storage, the volume requirement will surely far exceed the minimum estimate.

Although the storage pricing keeps dropping, building mass storage systems still goes beyond the budget of most academic libraries. Before we receive sufficient funding to build our own storage system, we should consider renting from commercial storage vendors or applying for storage grants from institutional or even national computing infrastructure. However, we must carefully evaluate their pricing, performance, availability, and accessibility. Many storage grants are not meant for long-term use and must be cleared out in a few years.

4.2 Data Processing

Servers running archival repositories do not usually require high CPU or memory because once ingested the content does not need to be constantly and heavily processed. This may change for our system because it also serves as the data analytics platform for users. Depending on the analysis, some may even require extremely powerful servers. We differentiate these scenarios into horizontally and vertically scalable analysis tasks. Clustering many lower-end computing nodes can solve the former, but the latter must use high-end computers. Most shallow analytics tasks belong to the former and many even fall into the so-called "embarrassingly parallelizable" category. We should fully support horizontal scaling, but may choose to limit the support for vertical scaling, mainly because high-end machines are much harder to come by and would otherwise limit our infrastructure options and flexibility.

4.3 Links Between Storage and Processing

The links between the data storage and data processing must be fast, reliable, and scalable enough to sustain large amount of data movements. To understand the link scalability, consider moving n equally sized files from the storage to n different computing nodes. If the time required to complete this move is about the same as that to move a single file from the storage to the computing node, then the links scale very well. Such scalability is usually achieved by replicating and/or sharding the data among different storage nodes. Moreover, the physical bandwidth between the storage and processing nodes becomes a significant bottleneck when the size of the data reaches a threshold. Co-locating both type of nodes to the same data center can effectively break the blockage.

4.4 Data Repository

The repository may not need to physically store data, but can link to external data storage. Nevertheless it should be very fast, flexible, and scalable. Traditional repositories make the assumption that their workloads are largely READ dominant, but this may differ in our case, because ingesting large datasets and their derivatives may cause very high WRITE workload. The repository will need to scale well for both workloads. Preferably it would also support flexible metadata schemas or even linked data to accommodate multi-disciplinary data use and reuse.

4.5 Data Analytics

Although data curation may need some data analysis capability, the main purpose to build data analysis into our system is to empower researchers to directly answer science questions from the data. The barrier to perform analysis should be as low as possible. We must not make assumptions on how researchers ask questions and perform analysis, including what tools they'll be using. Although a few VT-SIL graduate students use MATLAB to filter data, we must not extrapolate this to all users and make MATLAB a mandatory tool to access and analyze the data. We should not even assume the computing platform, the operating system and its distribution, the programming language, the compiled libraries and their version numbers.

4.6 Reusable Data Analytics Deployment

Achieving 4.5 used to be very difficult. But with the advancement of virtualization techniques, analysis tools can now be developed and deployed through virtual machines without losing much usability and performance. As a result, analysis tools and processes built by one researcher may be easily replicated, replayed, and improved by another researcher. Our system should be able to support reuses of this type.

4.7 Data Reuse

Beside the tools built to analyze the data, the results of the analysis may also be deposited back to the repository as derivatives, and linked to both the tools and deployment used to perform the analysis as well as the researcher who developed them.

4.8 On-Demand Scalability

Much of the data analysis workload may not persist over time but occur in an ad hoc and on-demand manner. If we build the system based on the maximum possible load then most of the system resources may be wasted during the idle time. Ideally our system should be built on a shared infrastructure such that we can scale system resources up and down based on the workload.

4.9 Sustainability

Making use of large scale IT infrastructure certainly is expensive. We must consider how the system can sustain itself both technically and financially. What if the technologies used to build the system becomes obsolete? Is it possible to share the financial burden with the data users?

5. THE CASE FOR PUBLIC CLOUD

We have proposed a rather ambitious vision that depends heavily on IT infrastructure. Libraries do not usually consider themselves as being in the business of building infrastructure, especially at the individual institution level. However this does not prevent us from leveraging the existing infrastructure to architect data management systems. In this section we discuss the options we have and make the case for building the system in the public cloud.

5.1 Proprietary or Local Infrastructure

A small number of research projects may be fortunate enough to have sufficient funding to build proprietary big data management infrastructure. Assuming such an infrastructure satisfies the capacity and performance requirements, what are downsides? Cost/benefits balance can be the most significant one. If built by the peak load capacity, by not sharing infrastructure these projects will waste a lot of resources during low tides. Sustainability will also become problematic because IT infrastructure ages rather fast therefore needs sustained funding.

Many research institutions also have campus-wide high-performance computing (HPC) infrastructure, typically consisting of clusters with hundreds of nodes plus some scratch storage space. Massive, long-term storage has not been incorporated in most such infrastructure, and the institutional boundary may pose a major obstacle for sharing and collaboration. Most such HPC infrastructure also suffers similar weaknesses described in the next section.

5.2 National HPC Infrastructure

Many big science projects have taken advantage of regional or even national HPC infrastructure to build their data management solutions. Why can't projects like the Goodwin Hall instrumentation do the same? Although we indeed intend to apply for such grants, we also notice a number of potential problems.

First, although new capacities are continuously added, in general the national HPC infrastructure is fairly crowded. It has been reported that some supercomputers have reached extremely high usage rate that even high-profile existing projects had to limit usage and look for external computing resources such as Amazon cloud [27]. Long-term storage is far from sufficient to support large numbers of big data projects. As of this writing, within XSEDE only the Texas Advanced Computing Center (TACC) is capable of allocating sufficient long-term storage space for the Goodwin Hall sensor data from its RANCH long-term storage system [46]. Even with more advanced data transfer tools [11], moving data across XSEDE still presents a major challenge [3]. If we are to avoid moving data far from the storage, TACC's Lonestar and Stampede become the only viable resources for the associated data processing and reuse. Furthermore, HPC services may experience frequent interruptions and overall do not match the quality of service promised by their commercial counterparts [3].

Second, the HPC resources tend to be allocated and used in a very rigid way. Very few supercomputers run virtualizations and allow users to customize operating systems and software. In order to take advantage of the computing resources, users have to adapt existing analysis code and software to different supercomputer environments. Deployments also differ from one environment to another therefore are generally not portable.

The HPC resources funding model is also rather apathetic to small teams and explorative researches. To gain access to national HPC resources the users must write grant proposal to gatekeeping committees to justify the request. But big data projects from small team, at infancy and researchers at the exploratory stage can hardly present well-defined use cases to compete with well-organized grand challenges. The situation is so severe that some would even allege, "there is an increasing divide" [9] between the Haves and the Have-Nots. Researchers in the latter group, while the majority in numbers, are more and more distanced from participating in the data intensive science due to the lack of access to big data resources and the required computing infrastructure.

5.3 Public Cloud

In contrast to the HPC infrastructure, public clouds have already provided a much larger pool of storage and computing resources, with much lower barriers for entry, and affordable pricing. Google, Microsoft, and Amazon are each running cloud services with about 1 million computing nodes located in a handful of mega data centers. Amazon EC2 spot prices remain low, indicating a low usage rate. Amazon S3 and Glacier were both estimated to have long surpassed exabyte order of storage. With large amount of co-located storage and computing nodes, moving big data sets out of the data center is no longer necessary.

Virtualization enables the users to run a wide range of software and code in the cloud without modification. Automated deployments may be shared between users like sharing code, and data can be acted upon without understanding every bit of details about the context. The cloud elasticity makes it possible to only pay for the resources consumed and return the excesses back to the shared pool. More importantly, a valid credit card is the only requirement to gain access. Combined with a nimble usage model, large public clouds are becoming more and more attractive to researchers with big data management needs. Recognizing this trend, even NSF has recommended in its CIFS21 Vision and Strategic Plan to balance traditional HPC services with "the growing number and capabilities of cloud systems and services" [31].

What about the handful of smaller, research oriented cloud providers such as the Open Science Data Cloud and CloudLab? Although these providers retain all the technical benefits of the cloud computing, for our purpose they have two serious limitations. First, the total size of the cloud is too small for us to benefit from economies of scale. While the Goodwin Hall sensor data set seems large for these smaller clouds, it is rather tiny in big ponds such as Google, Amazon, or Microsoft cloud. Second, these cloud providers retain the HPC funding model that allocates resources via grant application and review, therefore discriminates against open-ended, collaborative projects like ours.

Balancing the above options, it seems that large, openly shared public cloud such as Amazon, Google, or Microsoft becomes the most viable infrastructure candidate for our project. We therefore choose Amazon cloud as a starting point and build an implementation prototype, as described in the next few sections.

6. SYSTEM ARCHITECTURE AND WORKFLOWS

In this section we describe the cloud-based system architecture and its typical workflows of the proposed data management system.

6.1 Architecture

As illustrated in Figure 1, the system consists of 4 modules: data acquisition, cloud storage, digital library, and data processing.

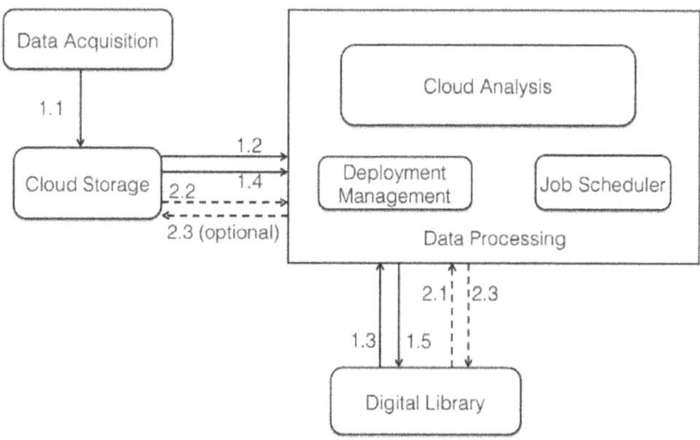

Figure 1. System Architecture and workflows

The data acquisition module collects data from distributed sensors, then calibrates, preprocesses, formats, and stores them in a local storage server. The Goodwin Hall accelerometer measurements are currently formatted in HDF5. The acquisition system also uploads the data to the cloud storage module in parallel. In case of any network interruption or upload error, the locally stored copy will be used to rectify the problem.

The cloud storage module provides the space to store both the raw sensor data uploaded from the data acquisition module and the derivative data resulting from various analysis and curation actions. Its reliability should be comparable to regular hard disc based file systems. The storage module should also be capable of triggering messages upon successful completion of typical file creation operations. We make the assumption that the storage and data processing modules are connected with reliable, high bandwidth, and highly scalable network links. This assumption will be evaluated in the next section.

The data analysis module is in turn made up of cloud analysis, deployment management, and job scheduler modules. The cloud analysis module holds the elastic virtual computing resources also called workers. It performs the user-defined data analysis tasks as well as system-defined data curation tasks. These tasks usually involve querying the digital library, finding out the cloud storage locations of various bitstreams, moving them via the scalable links to workers in the cloud analysis module, performing analysis, and if appropriate, depositing the results back to the digital library and the cloud storage. In order for this to happen, we need the deployment management module to deploy the workers and scale them depending on the size of the job. In many occasions we also need the job scheduler module to allocate computing jobs to workers. We will also evaluate in the next section how scalable the data processing module is.

The digital library module is a typical repository system with the exception it does not directly store all bitstreams in itself. Many bitstreams, especially those that constitute large data sets, are stored in the cloud storage with only the access links stored in the library. The library also holds the metadata, the software codes used for analysis and those to deploy analysis in the cloud analysis module. Relations between the data, the analysis and deployment codes, and users are also recorded in the library in forms of metadata. The library also provides web interfaces for user management and various user interactions with the data management system, such as performing data analyses and downloads.

In this architecture, the cloud storage and the cloud analysis modules must be co-located in the same data center.

6.2 Workflows

We now describe two typical workflows: data ingestion and data analysis.

6.2.1 Ingestion

The ingestion workflow starts from the data acquisition module. As shown in Figure 1 in solid lines, once 1.1) a data file is uploaded to the cloud storage, 1.2) the storage sends a message to the deployment management module notifying the upload completion. The deployment management module then initiates a data ingestion deployment, which 1.3) takes stock deployment script from the library to deploy workers, and schedules an ingestion job. When this job is popped from the job queue, either a new worker is created for this job or an existing free worker is assigned to this job. The worker starts to run the ingestion code, and 1.4) copies the file from the cloud storage to the worker and extracts the necessary metadata, then 1.5) creates a suitable container object in the library, attaches the corresponding bitstream link and extracted metadata. If many files are uploaded to the cloud storage in parallel, the job queue may grow longer, at which point more workers will be created to ingest files until the job queue shortens and workers become idle. Then the idle workers will be shut down one after another until the job queue is empty.

6.2.2 Analysis

The analysis workflow starts from the user triggered digital library action, as shown in Figure 1 in dotted lines. The library 2.1) initiates a data processing request, the deployment management module takes analysis deployment script from the library to deploy workers and schedules analysis jobs. When an analysis job is popped from the job queue, the assigned worker 2.2) copies corresponding file from the cloud storage to the worker to run the analysis job. Upon completion, 2.3) the worker returns the results back to the library. Optionally, if the user chooses to deposit the analysis results back to the repository, the worker moves the derivative bitstreams to the cloud storage and creates in the library an object container, the associated bitstream link, and metadata.

7. PROTOTYPE AND EVALUATION

The proposed system and its architecture would immediately collapse if the following two assumptions, even if reasonable in theory, do not hold up in reality. First, moving data between co-located storage and computing nodes should be fast and scale well. Second, embarrassingly parallelizable data analysis workload should scale well even if it involves previously assumed data movements. In order to gain high confidence before advancing to the next development phase, we build an evaluation prototype in the Amazon cloud based on the Goodwin Hall sensor data.

7.1 Prototype

As shown in Figure 2, the implemented prototype is largely based on the system architecture described in section 6.

We choose the newly released Fedora Repository version 4.0.0 [10] as the digital library, hoping its new features including improved performance, linked data platform support, clustering capability, and embedded fixity check etc. will form a solid foundation for future developments. We assume the typical digital library and archival functions can be successfully implemented in this prototype, given that a subset of this prototype is almost identical to what APTrust has already implemented, based on Fedora 3, Hydra, and Amazon S3 [1], as one of the five primary preservation nodes in the Digital Preservation Network (DPN).

We use Amazon S3 as the cloud storage module and Amazon EC2 as the cloud analysis module. We manually deploy EC2 instances as both workers and the library, and use Amazon SQS as the job scheduler. All Amazon services are deployed in the Amazon US East region.

We wrote Python codes that extract metadata from HDF5 files, perform simple mathematical operations such as calculating the maximum, minimum, mean, and median values from the data file, split and merge files, and draw wave charts from them, as well as call Fedora 4 APIs to create containers and attach bitstreams and metadata to them. We then deploy these code to 1-16 EC2 instances as workers to perform the evaluation tests. Figure 3 shows a small segment of a wave chart drawn from the accelerometer measurements from one signal channel.

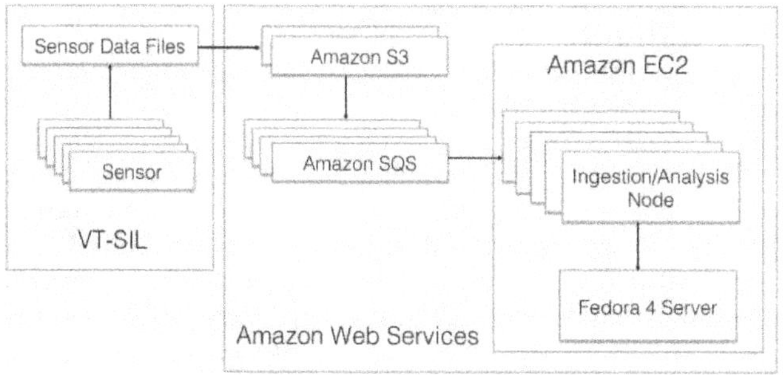

Figure 2. Evaluation prototype

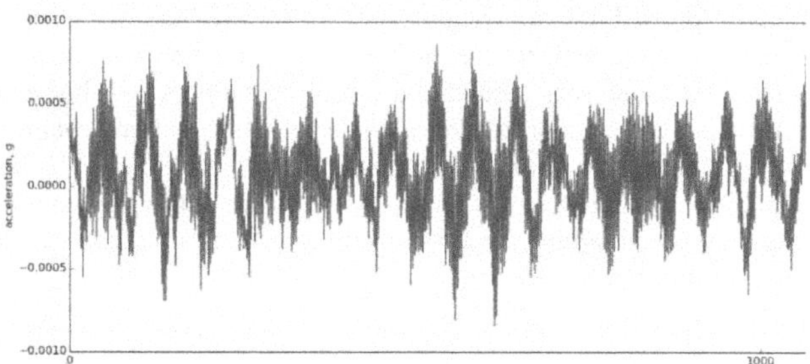

Figure 3. Accelerometer measurements

7.2 Evaluation

We evaluate the prototype using 24 hours of accelerometer measurements from 12 signal channels, with a total data size of about 130 GB. The actual data volume will be much higher than this because there are many more channels and other sensor types. We then evaluate the system against three different test cases: 1) simple data ingestion without data copying into the library, 2) simple data analysis with additional metadata write back to the library, and 3) a more CPU, I/O, and network intensive job. The third job first splits the data file into 6-second segments, then creates visualization from each segment, and finally deposits all created images, 172,800 in total, back to the library as a derivative data set and creates relations between them and the measurement data set. We run these three cases under the same system settings and the number of ingestion/analysis computing nodes, or workers, increases from 1 to 2, 4, 8, and finally 16.

For the sake of simplicity, our implementation took the following shortcuts without affecting the validity and the accuracy of the evaluation.

First, instead of fully developing the deployment module, we manually deploy the workers. We have not developed any web interfaces for these tests and other user interactions. All tests are completed with command line.

Second, we combine the data analysis test cases 2 and 3 with the simple ingestion test case 1 to create three similar test cases so that we can compare them on the same footing. In test case 1, we move the data from S3 to the workers, extract metadata, then create a container in Fedora 4 and insert the data items and metadata we extracted. In test case 2, we do all the above plus calculate the minimum, maximum, mean, and median values for each file then write them back to the library as the data item metadata. In test case 3, we do everything in test case 1 plus splitting the data, drawing 172800 image files, and depositing them back to the library.

Third, we bypass the upload stage of the workflow to save time. This is acceptable because we are not testing the Amazon upload bandwidth for external users. Instead, we copy the sensor data from one S3 bucket to another to emulate the upload completion.

Fourth, to ensure the library does not constitute a performance bottleneck in the evaluation, we tested and chose a rather powerful EC2 instance type, r3.8xlarge, for the Fedora 4 server. We choose m3.large for the worker nodes.

7.3 Results

The experimental results are presented in this section. The experiments were repeated for multiple times to ensure the results are reproducible. It takes about 2 weeks in total to complete all the experiments.

Table 1 lists the average time used to copy one single file from the cloud storage to a worker. A full day's vibration data collected from 12 channels are split into 972 files in more or less equal size. When multiple workers are deployed, they can process these sensor data files in parallel. Because the average time spent to move each file from S3 to EC2 does not change significantly with the job complexity or the number of workers, we can reasonably expect data movement speeds up linearly with the number of workers. The first assumption has been shown to hold up well.

Table 1. Average time in second spent to copy a file from Amazon S3 to Amazon EC2, both in the US East Region

	Number of Workers				
	1	2	4	8	16
1	0.2150	0.2525	0.2665	0.2045	0.2077
2	0.2186	0.2134	0.2675	0.2192	0.2073
3	0.2257	0.2412	0.2233	0.2086	0.2063

Table 2 lists the time spent to complete three different test cases using different number of workers. The results clearly show that in all three test cases, if we double the number of workers, the job gets done in approximately half the time previously required. The data processing scales linearly, therefore the second assumption is also shown to be satisfactory.

Table 2. Time in second spent to complete the test case

	Number of Workers				
	1	2	4	8	16
1	213.77	105.54	52.74	25.80	12.93
2	625.92	320.71	157.03	77.13	38.27
3	81564.42	40619.44	20284.53	10113.05	5059.34

8. DISCUSSIONS

Although much still needs to be done to fully realize the vision of use and reuse driven data management, the evaluations presented in section 7 have clearly demonstrated the technical feasibility to manage big data in the cloud. Since technology changes inevitably carry organizational, cultural, and social consequences, in this section we briefly discuss what potential "soft" impact this approach may bring out.

8.1 Finance

The elephant in the room is how to fund the cloud operation in the long run [5]. The underlying concern is that the cloud may not be the most economic option.

If only considering the storage cost, a prior comparison argues the cloud preservation costs more than buying own servers [37], which is further corroborated by a few anecdotal reports from university IT departments who built their own mass storage facilities. These, however, have not taken into consideration the need for elastic computing capabilities co-located with the storage facility. We leave the more detailed cost analysis as important work in the near future, particularly when more realistic data reuse scenarios are implemented.

In addition to the monetary cost, we must also consider the opportunistic cost not included in these calculations. As explained before, time is of the essence for many research data management projects. If fresh data are not properly managed and sufficiently use and reused to answer science questions, they will age quickly, and their value will dilute and vanish. In most cases we do not have the budget, time, and expertise to build massive data centers, without which big data management cannot be done. The opportunistic cost is indeed what drives many small start-ups as well as large and mature IT organizations to the public clouds.

The flexible cloud billing approach also carries its own challenges and opportunities. Universities, especially the land grant, public accountable institutions, often frown upon novel billing methods. Unless the recurring charge is on a grant or kept to a rather small minimum, we are repeatedly advised by our controller's office to get an annual contract with Amazon for our pay-as-you-go cloud expenses.

The positive side of the flexible billing and deployment is that now we do not have to run a data management system fully funded by ourselves. At least we have the option not to cover the user-generated data usage and analytics costs, which is only fair. We may also adjust the operational costs on demand. For example, if very few people are using a certain data set for an extended period of time, we may move it to a cheaper, but less accessible storage tier, spin it off to user communities who strongly believe its long-term value, or eventually remove it altogether.

8.2 Organization

The use and reuse driven data management approach calls for a slightly different organizational structure from what is currently in place. We need to put the researchers' needs in higher priority and even adjust job responsibilities to reflect this change of mindset. Virginia Tech Libraries has created and filled data consultant positions co-funded with the academic colleges and departments.

The library IT department also adjusted with the technology changes. More system administrators are learning virtualization and cloud deployment, and one system administrator was converted to a systems engineer position created to support the cloud operation.

8.3 Culture

Researches have identified two distinctive data sharing culture among researchers: the top-down, highly organized sharing culture mandated by big science projects, and the lone-wolf, gift-exchanging culture predominating the small science projects. It is curious to us why the ad hoc sharing culture commonly seen in the open source software developments has not seeped into research data sharing. After all many influential software projects flourish in this culture and many developers are themselves researchers. We speculate the reward mechanism currently in place for data sharing may need some more tweaking.

Many researchers worry their data may be used for publications without properly acknowledgments. This rarely bothers the open source development, where each line of published code can be traced back and attributed to individual developers. For big data sets, it is hard enough to take the data to a different environment to be useful, therefore our approach of providing analytics capabilities with a library alongside with the data may actually create the overarching environment where every tiny bit of contribution can be recorded.

The "viral" open source license has also contributed to the success of the open source movement. It may be worth trying to enforce similar licenses in our system that demands the data user not only acknowledge the data producer, but also open up their own derivative work under the same terms and conditions.

8.4 Society

As the poor man's data center, the computing cloud has been attributed to the democratization of science [4][11]. By adding the digital library piece, we hope the increasing number of data-intensive researchers not fitting in the big science/small science dichotomy can also find their niche and flourish.

9. RELATED WORK

Equipping digital libraries with superior processing capabilities is not a new idea. Simulation libraries like HUBZero [30] and SimDL [25] would be futile if without powerful computing resources to run the models. HUBZero can tap into national HPC centers through the grid. SimDL is backed by a local cluster and co-located mass storage facility. Similarly, the SCAPE project outfits a large image repository with a local cluster running Hadoop in order to quickly validate and extract features from large number of archived JP2 images [19].

However, as we point out in section 5, these infrastructure choices may not be the best fit for big data management. A recent study clearly illustrates the limitations of using HPC for data management. It reports the experience running file format identification tool DROID on TACC's Stampede to extract metadata from a 4.3 TB dataset. A single Stampede node can reduce the processing time from 2 days to 6 hours, but moving data from where they are stored to Stampede, both of which are on the University of Texas Austin campus, took 28 hours [3]. In contrast, if using our 16-worker test results as a reference, we may be able to copy the same amount of data from S3 to EC2 in 7 minutes or even shorter if we use more workers. Moreover, in order to run DROID on Stampede, the researcher has to modify and rebuild DROID software.

HPC centers around the world are routinely occupied by big science teams, especially high-energy physicists. Their take on long-term data preservation [20][21] is worth comparing with the librarians' view. To these physicists, data is not just a package that can be stashed away. Instead, "data analysis capabilities must be preserved"[2], e.g., in the form of deployable virtual machines or even better, recipes to recreate these machines [20] [21]. [2] gives an example on preserving 4PB of CDF data from Fermilab to INFN-CNAF in Italy. Besides replicating data, CNAF also offers grid-computing resources to run replicated Fermilab analysis tools on CERN supercomputers. Running virtual machines in private clouds is proposed as the key preservation strategy [20] [21] [36]. The approach proposed in this paper is more aligned with these scientists' view.

Cloud computing slowly gains traction in digital libraries. Duracloud [8] and APTrust [1] are two examples in which cloud storage is used for as long-term preservation. [45] describes migrating CiteSeerX to a private cloud, although the system shares crawled data in very specific, limited ways and does not allow users to perform customized analysis against the data.

If paring with Amazon cloud services, Amazon's own public data sets [33] may be used in very flexible ways. But except for a searchable catalog page and links to each data set, no other digital library function appears to exist. Data submission is a manual process via a contact email. Data sets are made available in various ways. Some stored in S3, some must be mounted as EBS blocks or EC2 images. Without a digital library, users lack an integrated environment to collaborate and share tools as well as derivative data.

10. CONCLUSIONS

Motivated by big data management needs arising from a small team, we work towards integrating digital libraries and big data analytics in the cloud. We developed a prototype that has been shown to largely satisfy our requirements. It scales linearly therefore warrants more extensive use in the future. We also discuss the "soft" impact of this approach.

Despite the cloud's vast popularity among researchers and the industry, its full recognition and adoption by the digital libraries community is surprisingly long and strenuous. The community has raised many legitimate concerns, ranging from the cost, the vendor lock-in, and some unacceptable terms of use. Balancing these concerns with the cloud's obvious advantages and values should be beneficial.

11. REFERENCES

[1] Academic Preservation Trust: *http://aptrust.org/*. Accessed: 2015-01-23.

[2] Amerio, S., Chiarelli, L., dell' Agnello, L., Girolamo, D.D., Gregori, D., Pezzi, M., Prosperini, A., Ricci, P., Rosso, F. and Zani, S. 2014. Long Term Data Preservation for CDF at INFN-CNAF. *Journal of Physics: Conference Series*. 513, 4 (Jun. 2014), 042011.

[3] Arora, R., Esteva, M. and Trelogan, J. 2014. Leveraging High Performance Computing for Managing Large and Evolving Data Collections. *International Journal of Digital Curation*. 9, 2 (Oct. 2014), 17–27.

[4] Barga, R., Gannon, D. and Reed, D. 2011. The Client and the Cloud: Democratizing Research Computing. *IEEE Internet Computing*. 15, 1 (Jan. 2011), 72–75.

[5] Berman, F. and Cerf, V. 2013. Who Will Pay for Public Access to Research Data? *Science*. 341, 6146 (Aug. 2013), 616–617.

[6] Bicarregui, J., Gray, N., Henderson, R., Jones, R., Lambert, S. and Matthews, B. 2013. Data Management and Preservation Planning for Big Science. *International Journal of Digital Curation*

[7] Borgman, C.L., Darch, P.T., Sands, A.E., Wallis, J.C. and Traweek, S. 2014. The ups and downs of knowledge infrastructures in science: Implications for data management. *2014 IEEE/ACM Joint Conference on Digital Libraries (JCDL)* (Sep. 2014), 257–266.

[8] DuraCloud: http://www.duracloud.org/. Accessed: 2015-01-23.

[9] Farcas, C., Balac, N. and Ohno-Machado, L. 2013. Biomedical CyberInfrastructure Challenges. *Proceedings of the Conference on Extreme Science and Engineering Discovery Environment: Gateway to Discovery* (New York, NY, USA, 2013), 6:1–6:4.

[10] Fedora Repository: http://fedorarepository.org/. Accessed: 2015-01-23.

[11] Foster, I. 2011. Globus Online: Accelerating and Democratizing Science through Cloud-Based Services. *IEEE Internet Computing*. 15, 3 (May 2011), 70–73.

[12] Friedrich, T. and Kempf, A.O. 2014. Making research data findable in digital libraries: A layered model for user-oriented indexing of survey data. (Sep. 2014), 53–56.

[13] Gray, N., Carozzi, T. and Woan, G. 2012. Managing Research Data in Big Science. University of Glasgow. arXiv:1207.3923. (Jul. 2012).

[14] Hamilton, J.M., Joyce, B.S., Kasarda, M.E. and Tarazaga, P.A. 2014. Characterization of Human Motion Through Floor Vibration. *Dynamics of Civil Structures*, Volume 4. F.N. Catbas, ed. Springer International Publishing. 163–170.

[15] Heidorn, P.B. 2008. Shedding Light on the Dark Data in the Long Tail of Science. *Library Trends*. 57, 2 (2008), 280–299.

[16] Higgins, S. 2008. The DCC curation lifecycle model. *International Journal of Digital Curation*. 3, 1 (2008), 134–140.

[17] ISO 14721:2003 2003. Open Archival Information System - Reference Model.

[18] Johns Hopkins University Data Management Services. 2014. Archiving Services We Offer: *http://dmp.data.jhu.edu/preserve-share-research-data/archiving-services-we-offer/*. Accessed: 2015-01-09.

[19] Jurik, B.A., Blekinge, A.A., Ferneke-Nielsen, R.B. and Moldrup-Dalum, P. 2014. Bridging the gap between real world repositories and Scalable Preservation Environments. *IEEE/ACM Joint Conference on Digital Libraries (JCDL)* (Sep. 2014), 127–136.

[20] Kemp, Y. and Ozerov, D. 2012. Preparing experiments' software for long term analysis and data preservation. *Journal of Physics: Conference Series*. 396, 6 (Dec. 2012), 062011.

[21] Kemp, Y., Strutz, M. and Hessling, H. 2012. A validation system for data preservation in HEP. *Journal of Physics: Conference Series*. 368, 1 (Jun. 2012), 012027.

[22] Kohler, M.D., Heaton, T.H. and Bradford, S.C. 2007. Propagating waves in the steel, moment-frame factor building recorded during earthquakes. *Bulletin of the Seismological Society of America*. 97, 4 (2007), 1334–1345.

[23] Krafft, D.B. 2014. The National Data Service: A Library Perspective. http://www.youtube.com/watch?v=_C2UIgRrcB4

[24] Lee, A.C. 2011. A framework for contextual information in digital collections. *Journal of Documentation*. 67, 1 (2011), 95–143.

[25] Leidig, J., Fox, E.A., Hall, K., Marathe, M. and Mortveit, H. 2011. SimDL: A Model Ontology Driven Digital Library for Simulation Systems. *Proceedings of the 11th Annual International ACM/IEEE Joint Conference on Digital Libraries* (New York, NY, USA, 2011), 81–84.

[26] Lynch, C. 2008. Big data: How do your data grow? *Nature*. 455, 7209 (Sep. 2008), 28–29.

[27] Madduri, R.K., Dave, P., Sulakhe, D., Lacinski, L., Liu, B. and Foster, I.T. 2013. Experiences in Building a Next-generation Sequencing Analysis Service Using Galaxy, Globus Online and Amazon Web Service. *Proceedings of the Conference on Extreme Science and Engineering Discovery Environment: Gateway to Discovery* (New York, NY, USA, 2013), 34:1–34:3.

[28] Martin, T., Ball, B., Karrer, B. and Newman, M.E.J. 2013. Coauthorship and citation patterns in the Physical Review. *Physical Review E*. 88, 1 (Jul. 2013).

[29] McKay, D. 2014. Bend me, shape me: A practical experience of repurposing research data. *2014 IEEE/ACM Joint Conference on Digital Libraries (JCDL)* (Sep. 2014), 399–402.

[30] McLennan, M. and Kennell, R. 2010. HUBzero: A Platform for Dissemination and Collaboration in Computational Science and Engineering. *Computing in Science Engineering*. 12, 2 (Mar. 2010), 48–53.

[31] NSF. 2012. *Cyberinfrastructure for 21st Century Science and Engineering (CIF21) Advanced Computing Infrastructure: Vision and Strategic Plan*. [Online]. Available: http://www.nsf.gov/pubs/2012/nsf12051/nsf12051.pdf. [Accessed: 05-Dec-2014]"

[32] Palmer, C.L., Weber, N.M. and Cragin, M.H. 2011. The analytic potential of scientific data: Understanding re-use value. *Proceedings of the American Society for Information Science and Technology*. 48, 1 (2011), 1–10.

[33] Public Data Sets on AWS: http://aws.amazon.com/public-data-sets/. Accessed: 2015-01-23.

[34] PREMIS Editorial Committee. 2008. *PREMIS data dictionary for preservation metadata*, version 2.0.

[35] Redner, S. 2005. Citation statistics from 110 years of physical review. *Physics Today*. 58, 6 (Jun. 2005), 49–54.

[36] Resines, M.Z., Heikkila, S.S., Duellmann, D., Adde, G., Toebbicke, R., Hughes, J. and Wang, L. 2014. Evaluation of the Huawei UDS cloud storage system for CERN specific data. *Journal of Physics: Conference Series*. 513, 4 (Jun. 2014), 042024.

[37] Rosenthal, D.S.H. and Vargas, D.L. 2013. Distributed Digital Preservation in the Cloud. *International Journal of Digital Curation*. 8, 1 (Jun. 2013), 107–119.

[38] Sands, A.E., Borgman, C.L., Traweek, S. and Wynholds, L.A. 2014. We're Working On It: Transferring the Sloan Digital Sky Survey from Laboratory to Library. *International Journal of Digital Curation*. 9, 2 (Oct. 2014), 98–110.

[39] Schloemann, J., Malladi, S., Woolard, M., Hamilton, J. M., Buehrer, M., Tarazaga, P.A. 2015. Vibration Event Localization in an Instrumented Building, *IMAC XXXIII A Conference and Exposition on Structural Dynamics*, (Orlando, FL, 2015).

[40] Schopf, J.M. 2012. Treating Data Like Software: A Case for Production Quality Data. *Proceedings of the 12th ACM/IEEE-CS Joint Conference on Digital Libraries* (New York, NY, USA, 2012), 153–156.

[41] Snieder, R. and Şafak, E. 2006. Extracting the building response using seismic interferometry: Theory and application to the Millikan Library in Pasadena, California. *Bulletin of the Seismological Society of America*. 96, 2 (2006), 586–598.

[42] Tenopir, C., Allard, S., Douglass, K., Aydinoglu, A.U., Wu, L., Read, E., Manoff, M. and Frame, M. 2011. Data Sharing by Scientists: Practices and Perceptions. *PLoS ONE*. 6, 6 (Jun. 2011), e21101.

[43] The 1000 Genomes Project Consortium 2010. A map of human genome variation from population-scale sequencing. *Nature*. 467, 7319 (Oct. 2010), 1061–1073.

[44] Wallis, J.C., Rolando, E. and Borgman, C.L. 2013. If We Share Data, Will Anyone Use Them? Data Sharing and Reuse in the Long Tail of Science and Technology. *PLoS ONE*. 8, 7 (Jul. 2013), e67332.

[45] Wu, Z., Wu, J., Khabsa, M., Williams, K., Chen, H.-H., Huang, W., Tuarob, S., Choudhury, S.R., Ororbia, A., Mitra, P. and Giles, C.L. 2014. Towards building a scholarly big data platform: Challenges, lessons and opportunities. (Sep. 2014), 117–126.

[46] XSEDE Storage: https://www.xsede.org/storage. Accessed: 2015-01-22.

[47] York, D.G., Adelman, J., Anderson Jr, J.E., Anderson, S.F., Annis, J., Bahcall, N.A., Bakken, J.A., Barkhouser, R., Bastian, S., Berman, E. and others 2000. The sloan digital sky survey: Technical summary. *The Astronomical Journal*. 120, 3 (2000), 1579

iCrawl: Improving the Freshness of Web Collections by Integrating Social Web and Focused Web Crawling

Gerhard Gossen, Elena Demidova, Thomas Risse
L3S Research Center, Hannover, Germany
{gossen, demidova, risse}@L3S.de

ABSTRACT

Researchers in the Digital Humanities and journalists need to monitor, collect and analyze fresh online content regarding current events such as the Ebola outbreak or the Ukraine crisis on demand. However, existing focused crawling approaches only consider topical aspects while ignoring temporal aspects and therefore cannot achieve thematically coherent and fresh Web collections. Especially Social Media provide a rich source of fresh content, which is not used by state-of-the-art focused crawlers. In this paper we address the issues of enabling the collection of fresh and relevant Web and Social Web content for a topic of interest through seamless integration of Web and Social Media in a novel integrated focused crawler. The crawler collects Web and Social Media content in a single system and exploits the stream of fresh Social Media content for guiding the crawler.

Categories and Subject Descriptors

H.3.7 [**Information Systems**]: Digital Libraries

Keywords

web crawling; focused crawling; social media; web archives

1. INTRODUCTION

With the advancement of analysis and mining technologies, a growing interest in collecting and analyzing Web content can be observed in various scientific disciplines. Our user requirements study [23] revealed that more and more disciplines are interested in mining and analyzing the Web. User-generated content and especially the Social Web is attractive for many humanities disciplines. Journalists are also interested in the content as it provides a direct access to the people's views about politics, events, persons and popular topics shared on Social Media platforms. These users require a comprehensive on-demand documentation of the activities on the Web around global events (e.g. Ebola outbreak, Ukraine crisis) and local events (e.g. Blockupy, squatting). A comprehensive documentation consists of official communications, news articles, blogs, and Social Media content.

Both the Web and Social Media can provide a wealth of information and opinions about emerging events and topics. Often these media are used complementary, in that discussions about documents on the Web occur on Social Media or that Social Media users publish longer posts as articles on Web sites. Organizations generating fresh Web content, e.g. news agencies, often offer entry points to this content via Social Media such as Twitter. These are taken up by other Twitter and Facebook users for recommendation and discussion with other users. During the discourse further links are recommended. Especially Twitter turns out to be one of the most popular media to spread new information.

Large scale analysis and mining of Web and Social Media content requires that the relevant content is stored in easily accessible collections (as opposed to being distributed across the Web). The user requirements posed on such collections include most importantly topical relevance, freshness, and context [23]. As the Web and Social Web are ephemeral and under constant evolution, Web pages can quickly change or become unreachable even within hours. Content linked from Social Media content typically has a very short life span [24], which increases the risk of missing Web content linked from Social Media unless it is collected immediately. Timely collection of the embedded information (like embedded Twitter feeds) plays a crucial role in building comprehensive collections that cover all important media on the Web. On the other hand, tweets containing embedded links should be accompanied by the linked pages to understand their context.

In order to create Web collections on demand, Web crawlers are gaining interest in the community. Web crawlers are automatic programs that follow the links in the Web graph to gather documents. Unfocused Web crawlers (e.g. Heritrix [16] and Apache Nutch [1]) are typically used to create collections for Web archives or Web search engines, respectively. These crawlers collect all documents on their way through the Web graph and produce vast document collections on a variety of topics. In contrast, focused Web crawlers [e.g. 3, 8] take topical or temporal [19] dimensions of the collected pages into consideration.

Existing focused crawling approaches consider topical and temporal aspects in isolation, and thus failing to create collections of Web documents that are not only thematically coherent, but also up-to-date. Furthermore, most crawlers are dedicated to collect either Web [e.g. 3, 8] or Social Web content [e.g. 6, 20]. Even in crawlers that make use of both Web and Social Web content like the ARCOMEM crawler

JCDL 2015, June 21–25, 2015, Knoxville, Tennessee, USA.
ACM 978-1-4503-3594-2/15/06 ...$15.00.
DOI: http://dx.doi.org/10.1145/2756406.2756925.

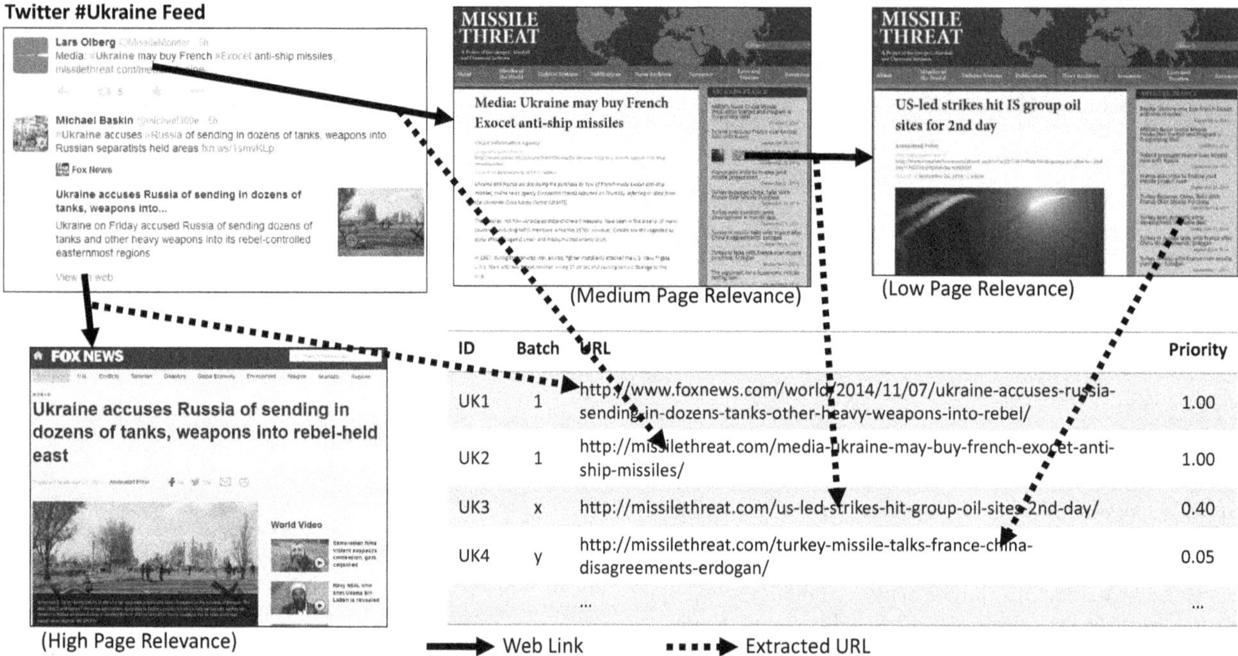

Figure 1: Interlinking of Twitter and Web and resulting Crawler Queue

[22], the connection is rather loose as Social Web content is collected independently of Web content. The usage of loosely coupled crawlers can easily lead to a big time gap between the collection of the content and linked or embedded content.

By reducing this time gap the freshness of the content can greatly be improved. Finding recent and relevant Web pages automatically is a difficult task for the Web crawler. In order to initiate the crawling process, existing Web crawlers require seed URLs, i.e. a set of pages to start the crawling. Typically, these seed URLs are provided by the researcher manually, such that crawl setup requires expert knowledge and lacks flexibility. Especially as recently created Web content may not (yet) be well interlinked on the Web, static crawl specifications can miss important entry points to collect fresh content appearing on the Web during the crawl. Therefore, it is important to provide means to automatically identify relevant and fresh content in a continuous way [26].

In contrast to Web crawling, Social Media sites like Twitter or Flickr provide access to their selected content through custom APIs. For example, the Twitter streaming API allows the collection of fresh and topically relevant tweets using standing queries making it possible to focus the requested stream on the topic of interest.

In this paper we address the problem of enabling on demand snapshot collections of fresh and relevant Web content for a topic of interest. To this goal we combine the advantages of focused Web crawling and Social Media API queries in the novel paradigm of integrated crawling. In this paradigm we use recent tweets to continuously guide a focused crawler towards fresh Web documents on the topic of interest and to jointly collect recent and relevant documents from different sources.

The contributions of this paper are as follows:

- We present the novel paradigm of integrated crawling that enables the continuous guidance of a focused crawler towards fresh and relevant content. In order to directly provide the Web crawler with entry points to fresh Web content, we exploit the idea of integrating Social Media with focused Web crawling.
- We present iCrawl[1], an open source integrated crawler to perform focused crawls on current events and topics on demand. The extensible iCrawl architecture seamlessly integrates Twitter API query and Web crawling. To achieve scalability, our architecture extends the Apache Nutch crawler [1].
- We demonstrate the efficiency and effectiveness of our approach in a number of experiments with real-world datasets collected by iCrawl. Specifically, we create and analyze collections about the Ebola epidemic and the Ukraine crisis.

2. INTEGRATING WEB CRAWLING AND SOCIAL MEDIA

Whereas Web content is typically collected through Web crawlers that follow outgoing links from Web pages, Social Media platforms such as Twitter supply fresh content via streaming APIs. Combining the two paradigms would allow us to follow recent events and discussions in both media in a seamless way.

In the example shown in Figure 1, a researcher or a journalist is interested in creating a specific Web snapshot regarding reports that Russia was sending tanks to the East Ukraine on November 7, 2014. Fresh information around this event can be received from Twitter. Since it is early in the event and the impact is unclear, no specific hashtag exists. Therefore the more generic topic of #Ukraine

[1]Available at `http://icrawl.l3s.uni-hannover.de`. The system is unrelated to other similarly named projects.

can be followed. From the #Ukraine Twitter stream many links can be extracted around the Ukraine crisis, but not all of them are related to the topic of Russian tanks. For example, the posted link to the Fox News article is of high relevance as it describes the event itself. The relevance of the posted link from Missile Threat is on a medium level since it talks about Ukraine and missiles, but not about this specific event. Furthermore links from this unrelated page point to other unrelated pages, which have overall low relevance as they only talk about weapons in some form. The task of the crawler is to prioritize the extracted links for fetching according to their relevance as we discuss in Section 2.3.

Since the aim of our integrated crawler is the creation of collections with fresh and relevant content we first need to define freshness in the context of Web collections. Afterwards we present the architectural challenges for an integration of focused Web crawling with Social Media streams.

2.1 Estimating Freshness of Web Content

Along with the topical relevance, freshness of the collected pages is one of the crucial requirements of journalists and researchers, who are interested in irregular crawls on current events and topics performed on demand. In this context, it is important to automatically guide the crawler towards relevant and fresh content and to estimate freshness of the crawled pages efficiently and accurately. Intuitively, freshness of a page can be determined using the length of the time interval between the fetch time of this page and the (estimated) creation time.

DEFINITION 2.1. ***Page Freshness:*** *If the page P was fetched at time t_f and the (estimated) time of the creation of this page is t_c, then the freshness F_P of P is proportional to the length of the time interval between the fetch time and the (estimated) creation time:* $F_P \approx t_f - t_c$.

The creation time of collected pages can be easily estimated if a crawl history is available. This history is typically obtained by regular unfocused large-scale crawls and can show the changes in the Web graph as well as provide the date the document has first been discovered by the crawler (*inception date*) [10]. This approach is used by many of the larger organizations in the field of Web crawling, e.g. Web search engines and Web archiving institutions. In case of irregular on-demand crawls on current events and topics such crawl history may not be available. In this case the crawler can rely on the content-based creation date estimates.

Content-based estimation of Web page creation time faces technical challenges as such information is highly syntactically heterogeneous and not always explicitly available. Moreover, Web pages do not offer reliable metadata concerning their creation date [25]. In order to allow an efficient freshness evaluation, in this paper we combine several features including page metadata and page content. Other possibilities include the usage of tools such as DCTFinder [25] that combine rule-based approaches with probabilistic models and achieve high precision.

2.2 Crawler Architecture

Web and Social Media crawling follow two different paradigms and are therefore handled separately in current systems. Standard Web crawling is a *pull* process: The crawler fetches pending URLs from its queue while taking into account the expected utility of the URLs, politeness requirements and other factors. In turn, the outlinks from the fetched documents are added to the queue to continue the crawling process. These steps are continuously repeated until the crawler is stopped. The pull characteristic of the process enables the crawler to control its strategy during the entire process, for example with regard to the crawl rate and the scope of the created collection.

In contrast, Social Media streaming APIs are based on a *push* mechanism meaning that the crawler has to submit a fixed standing query to the API. The platform returns fresh content matching the query asynchronously. This access mechanism does not give the crawler sufficient control over the input, as the rate and time intervals of the input from the Social Media API are not known in advance.

These differences together with the dynamic nature of Social Media platforms present several major challenges with respect to the seamless integration of the Web and Social Media crawling. Due to these differences, Social Media access cannot occur as part of the Web crawler loop, but has to be handled separately. However, the results of both processes are highly interdependent and impact each other in several ways. First, Social Media is a valuable source of relevant links to the Web (as well as to related streams in the Social Web). Therefore, the filtered stream of relevant Social Media messages containing outgoing Web links need to be placed into the Web crawler queue. Second, one flavor of Social Media integration is the embedding of message feeds into Web pages. Since it can be assumed that the embedded feed is relevant to the page content, the feed content should also be collected. Therefore, the Web crawler needs to communicate such embedded feeds to the Social Media crawler so that it can collect relevant posts by adjusting its queries. Third, the highly dynamic nature of platforms like Twitter requires that the interaction between Web and Social Media crawlers is efficient and has a low latency to ensure that content can be captured effectively.

2.3 Prioritization for Focus and Freshness

The Web crawler needs to decide at each step, which of the queued URLs it will crawl next. This is typically based on a **relevance score** for the URL based, for example, on the relevance of pages linking to that page, the importance of the web site host or (if the URL has been crawled before) the estimated change probability. Focused crawlers primarily use the content of the linking pages to estimate the relevance of the URL to the crawl focus, based on the assumption that Web pages typically link to other pages on the same topic.

In contrast, Social Media often only provide a limited amount of content that can be used for the relevance assessment. For example, Twitter only allows 140 characters for each post. However, Social Media platforms offer more expressive queries. For example, it is possible to retrieve posts matching certain keywords, posts written by specified users or posts from a given geographical region. This can allow the crawler to directly query the posts relevant to the crawl focus. Additionally, the crawler can make use of the Social Media specific measures of relevance, such as the popularity of a post or the profile of the posting user.

Existing focused Web crawlers typically aim to collect topically coherent Web content for a topic of interest [8]. Only few works have considered time as the focusing target [19]. Neither of these works have however considered the aspect of **freshness** (see Section 2.1) of the collected documents in

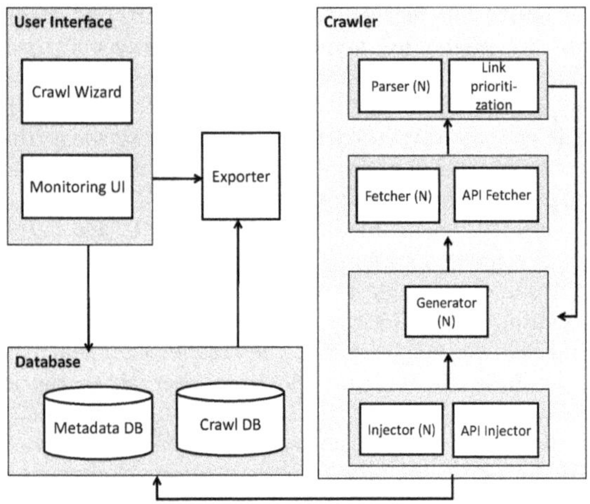

Figure 2: Architecture of the iCrawl system. Components marked with (N) are provided by Apache Nutch.

the context of crawler prioritization. As we will show in this work, the use of Social Media makes it possible to create fresh and focused Web document collections.

3. CRAWLER ARCHITECTURE

The iCrawl architecture (see Figure 2) is based on Apache Nutch [1], an established Web crawler that is designed to run as a distributed system on the Hadoop map/reduce platform. Nutch provides the general functionality of a Web crawler, such as crawl queue management, fetching and link extraction. Nutch is highly extensible through a plugin system that provides extension points for all phases of the crawl. As Nutch is run as a series of map/reduce jobs, it can also be customized by replacing or inserting custom jobs into the crawling cycle. In order to implement an integrated and focused crawler, we modified the Nutch crawler and complemented it with additional modules. Additionally, we created several components such as a graphical user interface that make the system more useful for our target users. In the following we will describe the facets of our system relevant to integrated and focused crawling.

3.1 Web Crawler

Nutch implements the basic Web crawler through collaborating map/reduce jobs (see Figure 2). First, the seed URLs of a crawl are added to the queue by the *Injector* job. Then the crawl is executed as a series of batches. Each batch starts with the *Generator* job that picks n URLs from the queue that have the highest priority and can be fetched right now. The *Fetcher* job downloads the Web pages for these URLs and stores them locally. The *Parse* job extracts links and metadata from the pages, calculates the priority for the outlinks and updates the crawler queue with the new values. The *Generator*, *Fetcher* and *Parse* jobs are repeated until the crawl is stopped.

3.2 Integrated Crawling

As described above, Nutch only adds seed URLs to the queue at the beginning of the crawl through the *Injector* job. However, Social media streams provide us constantly with new potential seed URLs. We therefore implemented custom *API Injectors* for URLs from Social Media streams to enable integrated crawling. Currently, we provide support for the Twitter streaming API and RSS feeds; other sources can be added. The crawler user can specify for each API the queries they want to monitor when starting the crawl. Furthermore, additional queries can be added during the crawl manually or automatically and the current queries can be modified to reflect a shifting topic.

The API Injectors cannot run inside Nutch, as each Nutch job runs only for a short amount of time, whereas the *push* nature of the APIs (see Section 2.2) requires a continuously running process. Our system automatically starts the API Injectors for the requested sources and also shuts them down when the crawl is stopped. When an API Injector is started, it receives the specified queries and is then responsible for creating and maintaining the API connection. The API Injector inject URLs into the crawler queue, store received posts and add information about resolved redirects (e.g. from URL shorteners) through a simple interface modeled on Hadoop[2].

An URL is only added to the crawler queue when it is first discovered. If an URL was already discovered by crawler, its relevance is unchanged as the content in social media posts is typically to short to estimate relevance.

Social Media APIs are also used during the regular crawl to augment the Web crawler. Through the APIs information about for example posts is available in formats such as JSON. These are easier to process automatically and sometimes even contain additional information. When we encounter links to known Social Media websites, we rewrite the links to point directly to the APIs and enqueue those links in addition to the Web URLs. The crawler then calls the *API Fetcher* module for the appropriate Social Media site when the URL needs to be fetched to retrieve the document through the API and store it in the crawl database.

The described process is illustrated in Figure 1 where the Twitter stream is filtered for "#Ukraine". The extracted links from the filtered stream (Fox News [UK1] and Missile Threat [UK2]) are added to the queue with a high priority of 1 and crawled in the first batch. After UK2 is crawled, its outgoing links are analyzed. This analysis results in a relevance score of 0.4 for the extracted link UK3 to be crawled in a later batch x. After the crawling of UK3 the analysis results in a low relevance of 0.05 for the outlink UK4 to be crawled at a later point in time (if at all).

The combination of Web crawler, API Injectors and API Fetchers allows us to seamlessly cross the boundaries between Web and Social Media in a single system.

3.3 Focused Crawling

As our goal is to create a topical Web collection, we need to ensure that only Web pages relevant to that topic are crawled. However, Nutch only uses a relevance measure based on the link graph (Adaptive On-line Page Importance Computation [2]). This measure does not take the topic into account at all. Furthermore, it requires multiple crawls of the same pages until the relevance predictions converge. Therefore we replace the priority computation of Nutch with our own module (*Link prioritization*). It implements the prioritization by determining the relevance of each downloaded

[2]The library to communicate with Nutch is available separately as open source at `https://github.com/L3S/nutch-injector`

page to the crawl topic and computing a priority score for each of its outlinks. These scores are returned to Nutch, which in a separate step combines them with scores from other pages and updates the crawler queue accordingly. In this way URLs linked to from pages of high topical relevance are moved to the front of the queue, especially if they are linked to repeatedly, whereas the outlinks of low relevance pages are moved to the back of the queue. When the relevance of pages at the front of the queue sinks below a threshold, we stop the crawl and ensure in this way that the collected pages are of overall high relevance.

3.4 Data Storage

During the *Parse* job we extract and store entities and keywords from the crawled documents. This metadata is used to provide an improved monitoring interface for the crawl and can be used for semantic indexing of the crawled data. We also collect extensive metrics about the crawl itself to provide a good documentation. This means that our crawl generates two different types of data with varying characteristics and access patterns, namely crawled content and metadata. The crawled content is typically larger (several kilobytes or megabytes per record) and is frequently accessed in sequence, e.g. by analysis or export processes. This data is stored in the *Crawl DB* backed by the distributed Apache HBase datastore which can easily store gigabytes or terabytes in a fault-tolerant manner. On the other hand, metadata is smaller in size (less than a kilobyte per record), but needs to be accessed and queried in many different ways. Standard relational databases work better for this data than HBase, therefore we store it in a separate *metadata DB*. By having these two data stores we can ensure a good performance of all components of our platform.

3.5 WARC Exporter

There are already many systems to provide index and analyze Web collection. Rather than duplicate this effort, we provide a way to export the final collection in the standard WARC format. The exported files also contain the extracted metadata. This metadata can be used for exploration of the collection or can be indexed to provide richer search interfaces for the content.

3.6 Crawl Specification and User Interface

The crawling process starts with the manual definition of the *crawl specification*: a list of seeds (URLs and Social Media queries) and keywords that best describe the topical focus of the crawl from the user's point of view. The *crawl specification* is used in two ways: (1) to support the focusing and prioritization of the crawl and (2) to provide an initial seed list for the crawler. The setup and scoping of a crawl is supported through a 'Wizard' interface that allows the user to find and select relevant Web and Social Media seeds through simple keyword queries. More details about the user interface can be found in [13].

4. EVALUATION

The goal of the evaluation is to measure the impact of the Social Media integration on the freshness and the relevance of the resulting collections with respect to the topical focus of the crawl as well as to better understand the domains of the content covered using the different crawler configurations. To achieve this goal, in our evaluation we compare several crawler configurations that vary with respect to the focusing and integration:

Unfocused (UN): Our first baseline is a typical unfocused state-of-the-art Web crawler. For this configuration we use an unmodified version of Apache Nutch. We expect this configuration to collect less relevant documents than the other configurations.

Focused (FO): As a second baseline we incorporate state-of-the-art focusing features into Apache Nutch to get a focused crawler. This configuration is expected to find more relevant documents than the unfocused crawler, but still does not take their freshness into account.

Twitter-based (TB): To better understand the role of Social Media API input in the integrated crawler, we use a simple crawler that monitors the Twitter streaming API for a given query and downloads all documents linked from the returned tweets (without following further outlinks of those pages). We expect that the tweeted links are typically very fresh.

Integrated (INT): This configuration uses our proposed system and combines the focused Web crawler and the Twitter API input as described in Section 3. This configuration combines the advantages of the focused crawler and the Twitter API and is expected to deliver fresh and relevant results.

For each of these configurations, we measure the relevance and freshness of the collected documents during the runtime of the crawl. An ideal system would have a constantly good relevance and freshness until all relevant documents have been crawled, after which the relevance has to drop. However, in contrast to previous work on focused crawlers we target ongoing events, where new relevant documents can be created during the crawl. This means that the crawler can have a continuous supply of relevant and fresh documents to collect. We also analyze the most frequent web sites of the gathered document collection to see if the different configurations prefer different types of Web sites.

Relevance evaluation: In iCrawl, the topical focus of the crawl is represented by the crawl specification, a list of seeds (URLs and Social Media queries) and keywords specified by the user. To evaluate the relevance of the crawled documents to the topical focus of the crawl, we build a *reference vector* representing the crawl specification and *document vectors* representing each crawled document. Then the relevance of a crawled document is measured as its cosine similarity to the reference vector. Such automatic evaluation is scalable and provides a fair comparison of the different crawler configurations.

As the reference vector is composed of multiple seed documents, the absolute similarity scores of any specific document to this vector is always lower than 1. In fact, the relevance scores of the seed pages are in our evaluation in the interval $[0.5, 0.85]$.

Freshness evaluation: We measure the freshness as the time interval between fetch time of the page and the date of the page creation (see Definition 2.1). In practice, the creation date of a page is often hard to estimate because Web pages often provide misleading metadata. For example, the HTTP `Last-Modified` header is often equal to the fetch time because the page was dynamically generated. We therefore

#	ID	Feature Description	Docs
1	url	date is contained in URL path	3%
2	time	HTML5 `<time/>` element	9%
3	meta	HTML `<meta/>` elements for e.g. `Last-Modified`	8%
4	trigger	next to trigger word such as "updated on"	5%
5	content	occurrence in text	42%

Table 1: Features used to estimate the page creation date in the order of application and the percentage of documents.

	Ebola Epidemic				Ukraine Tensions			
	TB	UN	FO	INT	TB	UN	FO	INT
en	83	69	85	72	43	92	83	71
ru					29	1	3	17
fr	2	6	3	4				
de	1	5	7	1	10	3	1	2
zh	1	6	2	1	3	1	1	1
es	3	1	1	9				

Table 2: Language distribution (in %) of the Ebola Epidemic and Ukraine Tensions crawls. Values less than 1% are omitted.

estimate the creation date based on several content-based features. The features are applied sequentially until one of them finds a date. We filter out dates before 1990 and future dates as false positives. Table 1 shows the features in the order of application and the percentage of documents each feature has been successfully applied to during the evaluation. Using these features we could determine the date for approximately 67% documents. Pages for which no valid creation date could be found were excluded from the evaluation.

4.1 Crawled Datasets

We perform our evaluation using two crawls on current topics: The *Ebola Epidemic* crawl about the recent developments in the Ebola epidemy and the *Ukraine Tensions* crawl about the tensions between Russia and Ukraine at the beginning of November 2014. The crawler ran for 5 (Ebola Epidemic) resp. 2 days (Ukraine Tensions) in November 2014, with all configurations presented above running in parallel on separate machines.

The crawl specification for the Ebola Epidemic crawl included five relevant seed URLs from health organizations (`cdc.gov`, `who.int`, `healthmap.org`, `ebolacommunication-network.org` and `ecdc.europa.eu`). Twitter was queried for tweets from the users *@WHO* and *@Eboladeeply* and tweets containing one of the hashtags *#ebola* or *#StopEbola* or the term *ebola*. We added the keywords *ebola*, *liberia* and *UN* for the prioritization.

For the Ukraine Tensions crawl, we used eight seed URLs from the international news sites including articles on the specific event (reports of tanks crossing the border on November 7th) as well as on the Ukraine crisis in general (`bbc.com`, `rt.com`, `kyivpost.com`, `theguardian.com`, `dw.de`, `reuters.com`, `nytimes.com` and `time.com`). In this crawl, Twitter was queried with the user names *@KyivPost* and *@EuromaidanPR*, the hashtag *#ukraine* and the query term *ukraine*. The keywords *ukraine* and *russia* were added to the crawl specification for prioritization.

The crawl process was executed in batches of 1000 URLs, i.e. in each batch the first 1000 URLs from the crawler queue are selected and fetched. This batch size is a compromise between the goals of efficiency (large batch size for higher parallelism) and efficiency (small batch size for short batch processing times). Note that this may lead to the inclusion of less relevant URLs in the beginning of the crawl when the queue contains less relevant URLs than the batch size, leading to lower precision values.

The number of pages collected for the Ebola Epidemic and the Ukraine Tensions crawls was 16,000 and 13,800 per configuration on average, respectively.

Although the crawler started from the seed pages in English, it collected varying proportions of non-English content (see Table 2). In the configurations that used Twitter, we also obtained some content from multimedia sites such as `instagram.com`. Although our manual investigation shows that the collected non-English and multimedia content is in many cases highly relevant to the crawl intent, automatic relevance evaluation of such content appears difficult for two reasons. First, the reference vector is built using English terms. Second, multimedia sites like `instagram.com` do not provide sufficient textual descriptions. Therefore, in this paper we exclude the content of non-English and multimedia sites from further evaluation. We would like to investigate the issues related to the multilingual and multimedia collections as part of our future work.

4.2 Web Site Distribution

The distribution of the most frequent Web sites for each crawl is presented in Table 3. For the Ebola Epidemic crawl the Social Media influenced crawlers (Twitter based and Integrated) collected content most often from Social Media oriented sites like `instagram.com`, `linkis.com`, or `vine.co`. Also links to news aggregators like `newslocker.com`, `news0.tk`, `allnews24h.com`, and `weeder.org` were often tweeted and collected by the crawler. The Twitter-based crawl includes also renown addresses like `nytimes.com` or `huffingtonpost.com`.

The focused and unfocused crawls include most often the WHO web site (`who.int`) since it was part of the initial seed list. The focused crawler collected also content from CDC (`cdc.gov`) and a Liberian news network (`gnnliberia.com`), the Russian news agency RIA Novosti (`ria.ru`) and from "Doctors Without Borders" in Austria (`aerzte-ohne-grenzen.at`). The unfocused crawler collected instead a large number of content from Twitter and Google and the Irish news Web site "The Journal.ie".

For the Ukraine Tensions case the Twitter-based crawl behaves similar as in the Ebola Epidemic case. Not surprisingly, Social Media sites are most often mentioned but only one news site is among the most frequent Web sites. Also subdomains of the Web hoster (`hosting-test.net`) are often included as it hosts a large number of Ukrainian and Russian Web pages.

All other crawlers have a high coverage of news sites like `reuters.com`, `rt.com`, `ria.ru` (both are Russian news sites), `kyivpost.com` (a Kiev newspaper) and `theguardian.com`. Furthermore, the focused and integrated crawler collected

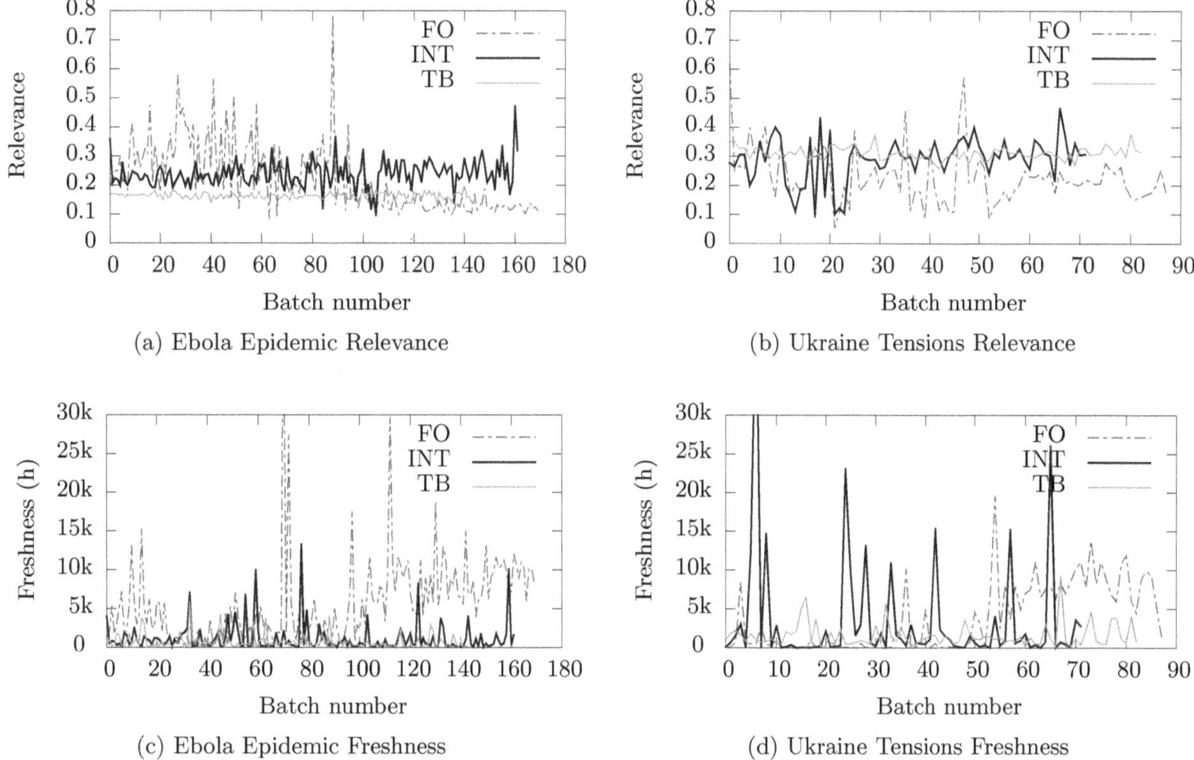

Figure 3: Relevance and freshness of the documents during the Ebola Epidemic and Ukraine Tensions crawls. The X-axis represents the batches processed by the crawler in the chronological order. The Y-axis represents the average relevance and freshness (in hours) of the documents in a batch, respectively. Each curve corresponds to a crawler configuration (Focused (FO), Twitter-based (TB), and Integrated (INT)). The unfocused crawler performed worse than the other baselines and was therefore omitted for readability. Higher relevance values and lower freshness values are better.

blogs posts from `wordpress.com` most frequently.

4.3 Relevance Evaluation

Figure 3a and Figure 3b present the relevance of the documents collected during the Ebola Epidemic crawl and the Ukraine Tensions crawl, respectively. The X-axis reflects the batches downloaded by the crawler in chronological order. The Y-axis represents the average relevance of the documents in a batch (higher values correspond to more relevant documents).

Relevance of the Ebola Epidemic Crawl: For the Ebola Epidemic crawl shown in Figure 3a we can observe at the beginning of the crawling process that the average relevance of the focused crawler is higher than for the other configurations. This can be attributed to the high relevance of the seed pages and the high effectiveness of the focusing strategy. In some batches the focused crawler downloaded a large number of highly relevant pages at once, e.g. from the WHO website, which are visible as spikes in the average relevance (e.g. in batch 92).

However, Figure 3a also indicates that the average relevance of the content collected by the focused crawler drops over time. This can be explained by the limited number of relevant web resources connected to the initial seed URLs.

In contrast, the average relevance of the Twitter-based crawl remains at a lower but more stable level over time. The reason for the on average lower relevance scores of the Twitter-based crawl can be explained by the source of the collected documents: This crawler collects more 'popular' documents, e.g. from Social Media sites (see Table 3), which use a different vocabulary than the seed documents that were used to create the reference vector.

The Twitter input enables the integrated crawler to find relevant content independently of the original seed URLs and thus to remain more stable over time with respect to the relevance compared to the focused crawler. The focusing of the integrated crawler can handle the noisy input from Twitter which can be observed when it starts to outperform the baseline focused crawler after around 100 batches in the Ebola Epidemic crawl.

Relevance of the Ukraine Tensions Crawl: In case of the Ukraine Tensions crawl the general observations remain similar as shown in Figure 3b. The focused crawler begins with highly relevant content due to the impact of the seed list. Afterwards it drops rapidly and continues with quite high variance until batch 50. Finally, the variance decreases and the content relevance remains on a lower level.

In contrast, the Twitter-based Ukraine Tensions crawl shows similar to the Ebola Epidemic case a stable relevance over the entire crawl duration. Due to the closeness of the crawl to the ongoing event, the crawled content is of higher relevance compared to the Ebola Epidemic case.

The integrated crawler shows in the early stages a similar

Ebola Epidemic				Ukraine Tensions			
TB	UN	FO	INT	TB	UN	FO	INT
instagram.com	who.int	who.int	instagram.com	youtube.com	reuters.com	rt.com	rt.com
linkis.com	reuters.com	cdc.gov	vine.co	hosting-test.net	rt.com	wikipedia.org	ria.ru
newslocker.com	twitter.com	gnnliberia.com	news0.tk	nvua.net	kyivpost.com	wordpress.com	wordpress.com
nytimes.com	thejournal.ie	ria.ru	allnews24h.com	instagram.com	pehub.com	ria.ru	kyivpost.com
huffingtonpost.com	google.com	aerzte-ohne-grenzen.at	weeder.org	facebook.com	theguardian.com	theguardian.com	theguardian.com

Table 3: Most frequent Web sites in each crawl configuration for the Ebola Epidemic and the Ukraine Tensions crawl.

high variance as the focused crawler. The reason is again the influence of the original seeds at the beginning of the crawl. Later it drops but stabilizes after 20 batches due to the increasing impact of the extracted links from Twitter. Over time the integrated crawler demonstrates a similar relevance as the Twitter-based crawler but with a higher variance.

Relevance Summary: In summary, in both use cases we can observe the positive influence of the Twitter integration on the relevance distribution over time. Although the baseline focused crawler can obtain relevant pages at the beginning, its ability to identify such pages highly depends on the seeds and reduces over time. In contrast, continuous Twitter input enables the integrated crawler to outperform the baseline focused crawler as the crawl progresses.

The high variance of the focused and integrated crawlers can be explained by the number of links e.g. from site menus even of relevant pages. Those still need to be fetched to realize that they are irrelevant. The number of those links varies and therefore causes a wider spread of the average relevance per crawler batch. In case of the Twitter-based crawl, the variance is significantly lower. This is because in this crawl we just follow the already filtered links from the Tweets, but do not collect the pages from the Web graph around them. However, the cost of the lower variance is the lower coverage of the related pages on the Web.

We also performed an evaluation of relevance and freshness with the unfocused crawler baseline. As expected, this configuration was outperformed by the focused crawler baseline with respect to both relevance and freshness. We omit this configuration from the graphs in Figure 3 for readability.

4.4 Document Freshness Evaluation

Figure 3c and Figure 3d show the freshness of the documents collected during the Ebola Epidemic and Ukraine Tensions crawls, respectively. The X-axis reflects the batches downloaded by the crawler over time. The Y-axis show the average freshness of the documents in a batch in hours (lower freshness values correspond to the more recent documents).

Freshness of the Ebola Epidemic Crawl: As we can observe in Figure 3c, the average freshness of the Twitter-based crawler is the best throughout the crawling process, followed by the integrated crawler. The focused crawler fetches more older pages after about 100 batches. This is similar to the trend we observed for relevance, where the focused crawler collected less relevant content after a certain number of pages.

Figure 4 shows the distribution of the freshness obtained by different crawler configurations on the topic of Ebola Epidemic. The Y-axis represents the freshness of the crawled content (in hours). The box boundaries correspond to the upper and lower quartile of the data points, such that 50% of the data points lay inside the boxes.

The Twitter-driven settings achieve a significantly better freshness than the other crawl configurations, as shown in Figure 4a For example, the Twitter-based crawl has the best freshness values with a median of 24 hours, second is the integrated crawler with a median freshness of 65 hours. The focused crawler collects pages with the median freshness of 980 hours, which is 15 times longer than the integrated crawl, while the median of the unfocused crawler is even 2300 hours (i.e. approximately 3 months).

Freshness of the Ukraine Tensions Crawl: Figure 3d shows the freshness of the collected pages in the Ukraine Tensions crawl. The Twitter-based crawl shows again the highest freshness.

For the focused crawl we see the same behavior as for the Ebola Epidemic crawl: The freshness is high at the beginning, but starts decreasing after 50 batches. Again this is accompanied by a drop in relevance: the crawler seems to have collected all reachable relevant content here as well.

The content crawled by the integrated crawler is in general of similar and sometimes higher freshness as that of the Twitter-based crawler. However, it has some outlier batches where more old content is crawled. As discussed in the relevance of the Ukraine Tensions crawl this can be another indicator that old and unrelated content has been collected before the crawler was able to follow related and fresh links.

These observations are confirmed by the distribution of the freshness shown in Figure 4b. Again the values differ significantly across the crawler configurations. The Twitter-based crawl provides content with the highest freshness at a median of 20 hours. The freshness values of the unfocused and focused crawler are rather low with a median of 1920 and 1415 hours, respectively. Finally, the integrated crawler results in a mixture of fresh and old content with the median of 120 hours and therefore with higher degree of fresh content compared to both of the unfocused and focused baselines.

Freshness Summary: Overall, we can conclude that the integrated crawler significantly outperforms both unfocused and focused baseline crawlers in terms of freshness, especially as the crawler moves away from the (fresh) seed URLs. The Twitter-based crawls demonstrate the highest freshness, which shows that the Twitter input clearly contributes to the improved freshness of the integrated crawler.

4.5 Evaluation Results Discussion

As our evaluation results indicate, the most effective crawler configuration depends on the distribution of the relevant

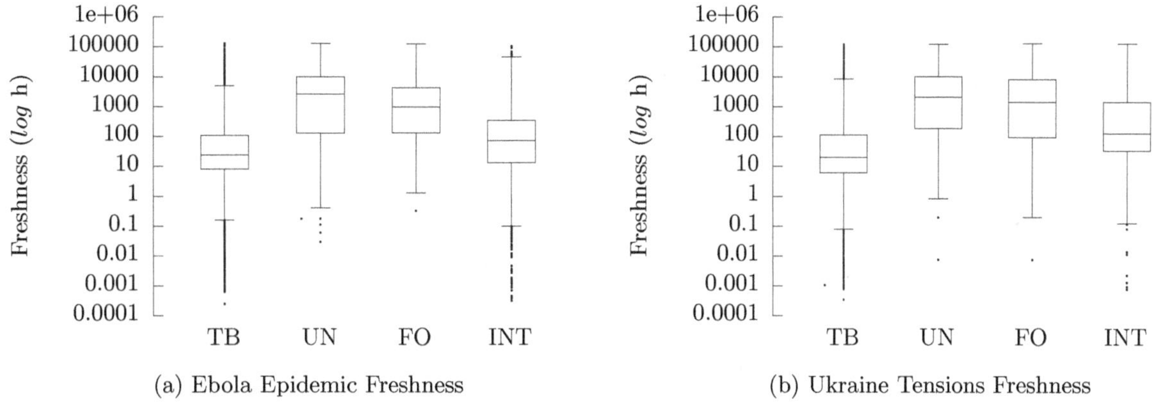

(a) Ebola Epidemic Freshness

(b) Ukraine Tensions Freshness

Figure 4: The boxplot representing the distribution of the freshness in the Ebola Epidemic and Ukraine Tensions crawls obtained with different crawler configurations. The Y-axis (log scale) presents the freshness of the content (in hours). The box boundaries correspond to the upper and lower quartile of the data points.

data across the media. For example, the Ebola Epidemic topic is more generic and is covered widely in news sites. However, Tweets containing keywords related to Ebola address a variety of aspects and are often off-topic for the crawl intent (e.g. "Things worse than ebola"). In contrast, the Ukraine Tensions topic targeted a very recent and specific event. For this topic we observe higher relevance of the Tweets and lower coverage in the news sites.

Our experiments show that the Ebola Epidemic topic profits most from focused Web crawling, but the baseline focused crawler still exhaust its seed URLs very quickly. On the other hand, the Ukraine Tensions topic profits most from the relevant Tweets, here Twitter alone however provides only the limited view of what Twitter users decide to share. The integrated crawler takes advantage of both precise focused crawling and continuous input of fresh Twitter stream and automatically adapts its behavior towards the most promising information source.

5. RELATED WORK

Web crawlers are typically developed in the context of Web search applications. General considerations for these crawlers are described by [15, chap. 20], with more recent developments summarized in [17]. For Web archiving, the web crawler Heritrix by the Internet Archive [16] is commonly used. Standard crawling methods aim to capture as much of the Web as possible. In contrast, *focused crawling* [8] aims to only crawl pages that are related to a specific topic. Focused crawlers [e.g. 3, 18] learn a representation of the topic from the set of initial pages (*seed URLs*) and follow links only if the containing page matches that representation. Extensions of this model use ontologies to incorporate semantic knowledge into the matching process [12, 11], 'tunnel' between disjoint page clusters [5, 21] or learn navigation structures necessary to find relevant pages [9, 14]. In the recently proposed time-aware focused crawling [19] time is used as a primary focusing criteria. Here the crawler is guided to follow links that are related to a target time, but the topical relevance is not considered. In summary, existing solutions to focused Web crawling consider relevance and time dimensions in isolation and do not address the problem of jointly finding relevant as well as fresh content.

The Social Web provides an important source of data for Web Science researchers. Many services such as Twitter, Youtube or Flickr provide access to structured information about users, user networks and created content through their APIs and are therefore attractive to researchers. Data collection from these services is not supported by standard Web crawlers. Usually it is conducted in an ad-hoc manner, although some structured approaches targeting specific aspects exist [6, 20]. For example, [6] collects Twitter data from particular user communities, [20] proposes a cross Social Media crawler, whereas [4] addresses topic detection in Twitter streams. These studies typically focus on crawling and analyzing data from specific Social Networks, whereas our work addresses the problem of integrated collection of interlinked Web and Social Web data.

The potential relevance of Tweets for Web archive creation has been explored [26]. In the ARCOMEM project [22] first approaches have been investigated to implement a social and semantic driven selection model for Web and Social Web content. The results show that combination of social and semantic information can lead to focused Web archives. However, their system has separate Web and Social Media crawlers which causes a drift of focus between the subsystems. In contrast, iCrawl is a fully integrated crawler to seamlessly collect interlinked Web and Social Web content and guide the focused Web crawler using Social Media.

Data freshness is a data quality dimension that has various application-dependent definitions and metrics [7]. The aspects of freshness include e.g. *currency*, i.e. the time interval between the data extraction and its delivery to the user, and *timeliness*, i.e. the actual age of the data. Current search engines use the freshness of documents as part of their scoring algorithms. Here freshness is estimated based on the crawling history associated with the documents (such as the inception date, i.e. the date the document has been discovered and indexed by the search engine or the date it first appeared in the search results) [10]. Even though content freshness is one of the most important requirements of the iCrawl users, they cannot always rely on the crawl history to estimate freshness of pages. Instead, iCrawl relies on Social Media to provide entry points to the fresh content and uses content-based freshness estimates for evaluation.

6. CONCLUSION

In this paper we addressed the problem of collection of fresh and relevant Web and Social Web content for current events and topics of interest. To achieve thematically coherent and fresh Web collections, we proposed the novel paradigm of integrated crawling that exploits Social Media streams and interlinking between the Web and Social Web content to continuously guide a focused crawler towards fresh and relevant content. We presented iCrawl (available online at `http://icrawl.l3s.uni-hannover.de`), an open source integrated focused crawler that seamlessly connects focused Web crawling and Twitter API query in one system and enables scalable and efficient collection of interlinked fresh Web and Social Web content on a topic of interest. We confirmed, that Twitter can be effectively used as a source of fresh content. Our experiments with real-world datasets collected by iCrawl demonstrate that the integrated crawler takes the advantage of both precise focused crawling and continuous input of fresh Social Media streams and automatically adapts its behaviour towards the most promising information source.

Acknowledgements

This work was partially funded by the ERC under ALEXANDRIA (ERC 339233) and BMBF (Project "GlycoRec").

References

[1] Apache Nutch: Highly extensible, highly scalable Web crawler. Available online: `http://nutch.apache.org/` (accessed on 23 October 2014).

[2] S. Abiteboul, M. Preda, and G. Cobena. Adaptive on-line page importance computation. In *World Wide Web Conference*, WWW '03, 2003. doi: 10.1145/775152.775192.

[3] C. Aggarwal, F. Al-Garawi, and P. S. Yu. Intelligent crawling on the world wide web with arbitrary predicates. In *World Wide Web Conference*, pages 96–105, 2001. doi: 10.1145/371920.371955.

[4] L. Aiello, G. Petkos, C. Martin, D. Corney, S. Papadopoulos, R. Skraba, A. Goker, I. Kompatsiaris, and A. Jaimes. Sensing trending topics in twitter. *IEEE Transactions on Multimedia*, 15(6):1268–1282, Oct 2013. doi: 10.1109/TMM.2013.2265080.

[5] D. Bergmark, C. Lagoze, and A. Sbityakov. Focused crawls, tunneling, and digital libraries. In *Research and Advanced Technology for Digital Libraries*. Springer, 2002.

[6] M. Boanjak, E. Oliveira, J. Martins, E. Mendes Rodrigues, and L. Sarmento. Twitterecho: A distributed focused crawler to support open research with twitter data. In *World Wide Web Conference Companion*, pages 1233–1240, 2012. doi: 10.1145/2187980.2188266.

[7] M. Bouzeghoub. A framework for analysis of data freshness. In *Proceedings of the Workshop on Information Quality in Information Systems*, IQIS '04, pages 59–67, 2004. doi: 10.1145/1012453.1012464.

[8] S. Chakrabarti, M. van den Berg, and B. Dom. Focused crawling: a new approach to topic-specific web resource discovery. *Computer Networks*, 31(11-16):1623–1640, 1999. doi: 10.1016/S1389-1286(99)00052-3.

[9] M. Diligenti, F. Coetzee, S. Lawrence, C. L. Giles, and M. Gori. Focused crawling using context graphs. In *Conference on Very Large Data Bases*, pages 527–534, 2000.

[10] A. Dong, Y. Chang, R. Zhang, Z. Zheng, G. Mishne, J. Bai, K. Buchner, C. Liao, S. Ji, G. Leung, et al. Incorporating recency in network search using machine learning, Apr. 21 2011. US Patent App. 12/579,855.

[11] H. Dong and F. K. Hussain. SOF: a semi-supervised ontology-learning-based focused crawler. *Concurrency and Computation: Practice and Experience*, 25(12):1755–1770, 2013.

[12] M. Ehrig and A. Maedche. Ontology-focused crawling of web documents. In *ACM Symposium on Applied Computing*, pages 1174–1178, 2003. doi: 10.1145/952532.952761.

[13] G. Gossen, E. Demidova, and T. Risse. The iCrawl Wizard – supporting interactive focused crawl specification. In *Proceedings of the European Conference on Information Retrieval (ECIR) 2015*, 2015.

[14] J. Jiang, X. Song, N. Yu, and C.-Y. Lin. Focus: Learning to crawl web forums. *IEEE Transactions on Knowledge and Data Engineering*, 25(6):1293–1306, June 2013. doi: 10.1109/TKDE.2012.56.

[15] C. D. Manning, P. Raghavan, and H. Schütze. *Introduction to Information Retrieval*. Cambridge University Press, New York, NY, USA, 2008. ISBN 0521865719.

[16] G. Mohr, M. Kimpton, M. Stack, and I. Ranitovic. Introduction to Heritrix, an archival quality web crawler. In *4th International Web Archiving Workshop (IWAW04)*, 2004.

[17] C. Olston and M. Najork. Web crawling. *Foundations and Trends in Information Retrieval*, 4(3):175–246, 2010. doi: 10.1561/1500000017.

[18] G. Pant and P. Srinivasan. Learning to crawl: Comparing classification schemes. *ACM Transactions on Information Systems*, 23(4):430–462, Oct. 2005. doi: 10.1145/1095872.1095875.

[19] P. Pereira, J. Macedo, O. Craveiro, and H. Madeira. Time-aware focused web crawling. In *European Conference on IR Research, ECIR 2014*, pages 534–539, 2014. doi: 10.1007/978-3-319-06028-6_53.

[20] F. Psallidas, A. Ntoulas, and A. Delis. Soc web: Efficient monitoring of social network activities. In *Web Information Systems Engineering 2013*, pages 118–136. Springer, 2013. doi: 10.1007/978-3-642-41154-0_9.

[21] J. Qin, Y. Zhou, and M. Chau. Building domain-specific web collections for scientific digital libraries. In *Joint ACM/IEEE Conference on Digital Libraries, 2004*, pages 135–141, June 2004. doi: 10.1109/JCDL.2004.1336110.

[22] T. Risse, E. Demidova, S. Dietze, W. Peters, N. Papailiou, K. Doka, Y. Stavrakas, V. Plachouras, P. Senellart, F. Carpentier, A. Mantrach, B. Cautis, P. Siehndel, and D. Spiliotopoulos. The ARCOMEM architecture for social- and semantic-driven web archiving. *Future Internet*, 6(4):688–716, 2014. ISSN 1999-5903.

[23] T. Risse, E. Demidova, and G. Gossen. What do you want to collect from the web? In *Proc. of the Building Web Observatories Workshop (BWOW) 2014*, 2014.

[24] H. M. SalahEldeen and M. L. Nelson. Losing my revolution: How many resources shared on social media have been lost? In *Theory and Practice of Digital Libraries*, pages 125–137. Springer, 2012. doi: 10.1007/978-3-642-33290-6_14.

[25] X. Tannier. Extracting news web page creation time with DCTFinder. In *Conference on Language Resources and Evaluation (LREC-2014)*, pages 2037–2042, 2014.

[26] S. Yang, K. Chitturi, G. Wilson, M. Magdy, and E. A. Fox. A study of automation from seed URL generation to focused web archive development: The CTRnet context. In *Proceedings of the 12th ACM/IEEE-CS Joint Conference on Digital Libraries*, JCDL '12, pages 341–342, 2012. doi: 10.1145/2232817.2232881.

The Sum of All Human Knowledge in Your Pocket: Full-Text Searchable Wikipedia on a Raspberry Pi

Jimmy Lin
The iSchool — College of Information Studies
University of Maryland, College Park
jimmylin@umd.edu

ABSTRACT

We demonstrate a prototype that takes advantage of open-source software to put a full-text searchable copy of Wikipedia on a Raspberry Pi, providing nearby devices access to content via wifi or bluetooth *without requiring internet connectivity*. This short paper articulates the advantages of such a form factor and provides an evaluation of browsing and search capabilities. We believe that personal digital libraries on lightweight mobile computing devices represent an interesting research direction to pursue.

Categories and Subject Descriptors: H.3.7 [Information Storage and Retrieval]: Digital Libraries

Keywords: low-power devices; mobile computing

1. INTRODUCTION

Wikipedia aspires to provide every single person on the planet free access to the sum of all human knowledge.[1] According to Alexa, it is the 7th-most visited website in the world, with approximately 40% of its traffic coming from search engines (as of December 2014). Today, accessing Wikipedia requires internet connectivity for most users, but what if this weren't the case? We have assembled a prototype that takes advantage of existing open-source software to provide a full-text searchable copy of Wikipedia on a Raspberry Pi, an inexpensive computer the size of a deck of playing cards. This provides any nearby device access to Wikipedia either via wifi or bluetooth *without requiring internet connectivity*. Before describing our prototype, we first address two obvious questions:

Why is this better than using a web search engine? Today, internet connectivity is ubiquitous and Wikipedia is easily accessible from a web browser. What's compelling about Wikipedia on a Raspberry Pi?

First, ubiquitous connectivity is an illusion frequently disrupted by dead zones, data limits, and network congestion. This is especially true in the developing world, where many users do not have access to (or cannot afford) the internet. Second, full-text search on Wikipedia via a web search engine lacks the flexibility of open software running on a device under one's control. Our prototype runs a completely open software stack, which provides a platform for arbitrary customization. With full control over both the hardware and software, users are no longer beholden to external services.

Finally, having a local resource eliminates the possibility of third parties collecting access statistics, interaction data, and query logs. Users could issue sensitive queries without privacy concerns, e.g., targeted ads that start appearing in a cloud-based email service. A self-contained search engine also opens the door to new search personalization strategies based on personal data that users might not feel comfortable sharing with a third party.

Why is this better than using a mobile phone? Why couldn't the functionalities described here be implemented on a mobile phone, e.g., as an Android or iOS app? We see a few advantages of the Raspberry Pi, the biggest of which is flexibility. The machine runs a full-featured operating system, which provides much greater control over the hardware. It is also significantly more expandable via numerous USB ports and other custom connector ports. The storage requirements of Wikipedia and the full-text index still represent a substantial fraction of mobile devices' total capacity today: on a storage per unit cost basis, the Raspberry Pi is cheaper, and so it makes sense to offload Wikipedia onto a separate device. Finally, users today have multiple devices, e.g., mobile phones and tablets, and may desire access from all of them. Rather than duplicating content, it makes sense to hold a single copy of the data on a stand-alone device.

2. SYSTEM DESIGN

The Raspberry Pi (Figure 1) is an inexpensive, single-board computer the size of a deck of playing cards originally developed to promote computer science education, but has gained popularity in the maker community. The machine is based on the Broadcom BCM2835 system on a chip, which runs a 700 MHz processor from the ARM11 family. The B+ model used in our experiments has 512 MB RAM, and storage is provided via a microSD card.

The starting point of our demonstration is the open-source Kiwix package, which is an offline reader for web content that supports the ZIM format. The "Kiwix plug" project began in 2012 to provide offline Wikipedia access in a small form factor, specifically for developing countries in Africa.[2]

[1] `http://en.wikiquote.org/wiki/Jimmy_Wales`

[2] `https://blog.wikimedia.org/2012/06/28/`

JCDL'15, June 21–25, 2015, Knoxville, Tennessee, USA.

ACM 978-1-4503-3594-2/15/06 ...$15.00.
DOI: http://dx.doi.org/10.1145/2756406.2756938.

Figure 1: Raspberry Pi B+ Model; peripherals connect via USB ports (right) and HDMI (bottom).

The software has since been ported to the ARM architecture, and specifically, to the Raspberry Pi.

Kiwix comes with a stand-alone HTTP server that allows any connected device to access Wikipedia content; it also provides built-in full-text search. We evaluated the performance of both capabilities under two different connectivity options: wifi and bluetooth. Note that wifi is needed only to connect to the Raspberry Pi; external connectivity to the internet is not required. We also compared the performance of Kiwix's full-text search to ATIRE [3], a state-of-the-art search engine written in C.

3. EVALUATION

Our hardware configuration is as follows: a Raspberry Pi B+ model overclocked to "turbo" at 1 GHz, a 64 GB microSD card, and external USB dongles for wifi and bluetooth. To avoid idle power draw, in the wifi configuration the bluetooth dongle was removed, and vice versa. We used Kiwix 0.9 with the pre-built version of English Wikipedia from January 2014 (containing all text but no images). The article content occupies 12 GB and the full-text index another 11 GB. We used the latest version of ATIRE; its index is substantially more compact at 2.0 GB (Wikipedia articles were first cleaned to remove wiki markup; terms were stemmed but no stopwords were removed). In addition to measuring performance in terms of latency, we also measured power usage with an electricity usage monitor. The cost of our setup is as follows (as of Dec. 2014, in USD): the Raspberry Pi costs $35 and the 64 GB microSD card costs $25 (a 32 GB microSD card costs $13 and provides sufficient space). The AC power supply costs $9, or alternatively, one can purchase battery packs of varying capacities. These costs do not include the display and peripherals.

Our first experiment evaluated the performance of the device for serving Wikipedia article content. We sampled 600 "popular" Wikipedia articles as a query set using the following procedure: from Wikipedia page view statistics,[3] we downloaded all hourly logs for December 1, 2014; for each hour, we retained the top 1000 articles, and from the union, we sampled 600 articles total. We then accessed these articles from a client laptop connected to the Raspberry Pi (either wifi or bluetooth). Results averaged over three runs are shown in Figure 1, which lists article access latency (in seconds) as well as the power consumption during the experiments (in Watts). For reference, while idle, the Raspberry Pi draws 2.1 W using wifi and 1.6 W using bluetooth.

[3]`https://dumps.wikimedia.org/other/`

	latency (s)	power (W)
Wifi	0.88	2.7
Bluetooth	3.57	1.8

Table 1: Latency and power consumption of Wikipedia article access using Kiwix.

	Kiwix	ATIRE
Wifi	1.94	1.04
Bluetooth	2.46	1.08

Table 2: Query latency (seconds) for full-text search, comparing Kiwix and ATIRE.

Results show that while bluetooth consumes less power than wifi (which is consistent with previous work [1]), page access is substantially slower. Using wifi, the device is reasonably responsive and appears sufficient to support interactive browsing. The data transfer rate over bluetooth is substantially lower than over wifi, which explains slower page accesses. Whether the tradeoff of speed for lower power is worthwhile depends on user preferences.

Our second experiment compared full-text search provided by Kiwix internally and the ATIRE search engine. This evaluation focused only on efficiency (query latency) and left aside the issue of effectiveness (result quality), since we did not have relevance judgments to assess search output. We used 300 queries from the web track of the Text Retrieval Conferences (TRECs) from 2009 to 2014 [2]. As with before, queries were issued from a laptop connected to the Raspberry Pi. Results averaged over three runs are presented in Table 2, showing query latencies for both Kiwix and ATIRE using wifi and bluetooth.

We see that ATIRE is substantially faster than Kiwix's built-in search (and takes less space in terms of index size), although both are slower than what users have come to expect today (query latencies of a couple hundred milliseconds). The performance of Kiwix degrades substantially when switching from wifi to bluetooth, whereas ATIRE performance is about the same. Using wifi, the Raspberry Pi draws 2.7 W during the search experiments with both systems, and 2.2 W using bluetooth. These results show that there is a substantial performance difference between a "black box" search engine and a state-of-the-art system. Nevertheless, more improvements are still needed to provide a truly responsive, interactive search experience.

In conclusion, our experiments show that low-power computing devices today are affordable and achieve sufficient performance to warrant more exploration of personal mobile digital libraries. This represents an interesting future research direction.

Acknowledgments: This work was supported by NSF under IIS-1218043 and Verisign. Any opinions, findings, conclusions, or recommendations expressed are those of the author and do not necessarily reflect the views of the sponsors.

4. REFERENCES

[1] R. Balani. Energy consumption analysis for bluetooth, wifi and cellular networks, 2007.

[2] C. Clarke, N. Craswell, and I. Soboroff. Overview of the TREC 2009 web track. *TREC*, 2009.

[3] A. Trotman, X.-F. Jia, and M. Crane. Towards an efficient and effective search engine. *SIGIR 2012 Workshop on Open Source Information Retrieval*, 2012.

Big Data Text Summarization for Events: A Problem Based Learning Course

Tarek Kanan
Dept. of Computer Science
Virginia Tech, USA
tarekk@vt.edu

Xuan Zhang
Dept. of Computer Science
Virginia Tech, USA
xuancs@vt.edu

Mohamed Magdy
Dept. of Computer Science
Virginia Tech, USA
mmagdy@vt.edu

Edward Fox
Dept. of Computer science
Virginia Tech, USA
fox@vt.edu

ABSTRACT

Problem/project Based Learning (PBL) is a highly effective student-centered teaching method, where student teams learn by solving problems. This paper describes an instance of PBL applied to digital library education. We show the design, implementation, results, and partial evaluation of a Computational Linguistics course that provides students an opportunity to engage in active learning about adding value to digital libraries with large collections of text, i.e., one aspect of "big data." Students are engaging in PBL with the semester long challenge of generating good English summaries of an event, given a large collection from our webpage archives. Six teams, each working with a different type of event, and applying three different summarization methods, learned how to generate good summaries; these have fair precision relative to the Wikipedia page that describes their event.

Categories and Subject Descriptors

K.3.2 [**Computers and Education**]: Computer and Information Science Education; H.3.7 [**Digital Libraries**]: Collection

General Terms

Experimentation, Measurement, Design

Keywords

Problem based learning; Digital libraries; Computational linguistics; Text summarization; Big data

1. INTRODUCTION

As a student-centered teaching approach, Problem/project Based Learning (PBL) encourages students to learn by solving problems [1]. To test our hypothesis that PBL is valuable as part of digital library education, we applied PBL to a new Computational Linguistics course, closely connected to a large digital library effort. We hope our findings will encourage other institutions to teach similar courses. The course problem is to produce a good summary of an event, given a text collection from the Integrated Digital Event Archiving and Library (IDEAL) project. Started in 2013, IDEAL aims to integrate archiving with digital library [2] concepts, along with appropriate technologies and applications [3]. There is a wide range of services required to build a suitable information infrastructure, and to provide helpful methods of analysis, access, and visualization [4] for stakeholders [5]. Our contributions described in this paper include: 1) a pedagogical approach that worked well last semester in helping students learn about big data text summarization using computational linguistics methods as they engage in problem based learning, 2) good results from applying these methods to corpora about events. This paper is organized as follows. Section 2 explains the preparations for the course, including the organization, the learning target, and the datasets. Section 3 shows some summarization results for three main computational linguistics methods with the big collections, along with a partial evaluation for these methods. The last section draws conclusions and proposes future work.

JCDL'15, June 21–25, 2015, Knoxville, Tennessee, USA.
© 2015 ACM. ISBN 978-1-4503-3594-2/15/06...$15.00
DOI: http://dx.doi.org/10.1145/2756406.2756943

2. PBL COURSE PREPAERATIONS

2.1 Computer Science Capstone Course

An undergraduate course about Computational Linguistics, focused on supporting digital libraries, was taught in the 2014 fall semester at the Department of Computer Science, Virginia Tech. It is a new course planned to be taught each fall. This course gives students the opportunity to engage in active learning about how to work with large collections of text, one aspect of "big data".

Using methods employed in search engines, linguistic analysis, NLP, digital libraries, and statistical techniques, students are engaging in problem based learning [1], with the semester long challenge of analyzing content collections automatically, extracting key information, and generating easily readable summaries of important events in English. Just-in-time learning will allow development of an understanding of concepts, techniques, and toolkits, so students will master the key methods related to computational linguistics and digital libraries.

2.2 Course Learning Targets

The learning target is how to summarize a big text collection regarding an event. Events are important to people/ organizations, and are remembered based on time (when), location (where), person (who), and the subject or topic of interest (what). Given a set of text documents relevant to an event, students are asked to extract frequent/important words, topics, key sentences, and frequent named entities, for summarization. To help students learn summarization techniques in a PBL approach, we designed a course structure with nine units. Ultimately, though, student teams are charged with coming up with their own method for getting best results.

2.3 Dataset

We selected six types of disasters, and one community event, from the IDEAL archives. The community event differs from the others since it covers multiple topical areas. Though, for each category, both a small and big collection was analyzed, for our evaluation purposes we chose to show the results and information for the six big collections. Table 1 describes those events and the corresponding collection information.

Table 1. Characteristics of the Seven Corpora

Event collection type	Event location	Event date	Collection size	Event collection name
Disease Outbreak	World Wide	2014	15,000	Ebola
Earthquake	Virginia USA	2011	8,765	Virginia earthquake
Fire	Brazil	2013	690,281	Brazil club fire
Flood	Pakistan	2011	20,416	Pakistan flood
Hurricane	East Coast USA	2012	75,929	Hurricane Sandy
Shooting	Tucson,AZ USA	2011	37,829	Tucson shooting
Community	Blacksburg USA	2011 2012	16,024	Blacksburg events

2.4 Computational Resources

A tailored Cloudera virtual machine (VM), and an 11-node Hadoop [6] cluster, along with other supporting computing resources (shown in Table 2), aid the handling of over 11 terabytes of webpages.

Table 2. Hadoop Cluster Specification

Nodes	11 cluster nodes + 1 manager node
CPU	Intel Xeon, Intel i5
RAM	208 GB = 2 * 32 + 9 * 16
HDD	51.3 TB =1* 12TB + 1* 6TB + 7* 3TB + 2* 2TB + 8.3TB NAS backup

3. SUMMARIZATION METHODS, RESULTS, AND EVALUATION

3.1 Methods

The class has engaged 30 students, assembled into seven teams, in active learning, through its adoption of problem based learning [1]. Students have one goal during the course, i.e., to create good summaries of a large corpus of webpages. They are obliged to do that in a way that would be applicable to other corpora about events of the same kind. To provide scaffolding that will aid their solving of this challenging problem, the course materials provide content related to a set of units, Table 3 shows the 9 units that served as scaffolding for the course.

The course started by introducing; a) PBL [1], b) course goals, c) units overview, d) supporting facilities, and e) applicable resources such as the Python NLTK [8]. Below we introduce the 9 units in more detail.

In Unit 1, students find the frequency of words (single words and collocations) and pick the most frequent words in their collection. They should discuss the advantages/disadvantages of the approach they used; this is required in all the units.

Unit 2 asks students to propose a list of indicative words for their event. Students improve their summary by calculating the

Table 3. Summarization Goals

Unit	Desired Results
1	A set of frequent words
2	A set of WordNet synsets that cover all entries in the set of frequent words
3	A set of words constrained to POS tagging
4	A set of features, and classifiers to classify the documents in the collection
5	A set of N most frequent & important named entities
6	A set of the most important topics, by using LDA [7]
7	A set of indicative sentences, identified by clustering
8	A set of values for each of a template's slots
9	A generated English readable summary based on the filled-in template from Unit 8

word length distribution and readability (ARI). After that, students learn how to extend their indicative words with WordNet synsets. Parallel processing methods (MapReduce and Hadoop) are introduced in this unit, and used in subsequent units as well.

Part-Of-Speech (POS) helps with the selection of appropriate words. Unit 3 introduces the POS tagger of NLTK. Students are asked to extract nouns (and verbs if they feel them useful) that can best reflect the characteristics of their events.

Classification is used for eliminating noise and categorizing documents. In Unit 4, students label (i.e., as relevant or not) a small set of text files out of each collection, select appropriate lexical features, build training sets, and experiment with multiple classifiers (Naive Bayes, Decision Tree, Maximum Entropy, and Support Vector Machine) to categorize text files.

Named entities often carry important information about documents. In Unit 5, students learn to extract named entities by NER, e.g., the Stanford NER [9] and the NLTK chunking utility. Then, they use high frequency named entities to improve their summaries.

Topic modeling can extract the main topics from a text through the Latent Dirichlet Allocation algorithm, which helps users identify the key themes appearing in corpora. In Unit 6, students learn how to extract topics from their collections with two LDA tools: the gensim Python, and Mahout LDA [7] for Hadoop.

Unit 7 focuses on clustering, which helps group similar content. The instances to be clustered may include sentences, paragraphs, and documents. Students learn how to cluster content units and select the best representative instances with Mahout K-Means [10], e.g., the best sentence in each cluster.

Unit 8 requires students to work with templates carefully crafted for each type of event. The students need to design grammars or other methods for finding values appropriate for each template slot. Then, they use tools such as regular expressions to extract candidate values for the slots; the candidate values are sorted by frequency. Finally, to fill a slot, the best of the candidates is selected.

Unit 9 requires students to explore automatic methods for English text generation based on their filled-in templates. They are to devise automatic methods for ensuring broad coverage, cohesion, and coherence in the generated text.

Table 4. The Representative Sentence for Three Clusters

Cluster (Event)	A Sample Sentence
Police-Crime	Michael Edwards and Johnny Worrell were arrested on scene and charged with manufacturing less than 227 grams of mixture containing a detectable amount of meth conspiracy to possess meth and possession of precursors to manufacture meth.
Weather	The National Weather Service in Blacksburg placed most of Southwest Virginia under a winter storm warning today and tonight with snow accumulations of 4 to 8 inches.
Virginia Tech	At the Aspirations in Computing ceremony the honorees heard from two speakers: Letitia Long director of the National Geospatial-Intelligence Agency and a 1982 graduate of Virginia Techs electrical engineering and Diane Reineke vice president of business.
Local Festival	The Christiansburg High School music department will be hosting Night on Broadway March 30 and 31 in the Christiansburg High School auditorium.

3.2 Sample Results

3.2.1 The Community Collection

Since the Blacksburg community collection covers multiple small events and news, rather than focusing on a single event as in the other collections, summarization was difficult. Clustering the content was found to yield the best results. First, contents were filtered based on the frequent words and named entities. Next, the collection was clustered to produce 4 main clusters; for each of those, the sentence closest to the centroid was selected as the cluster summary. Thus, Table 4 shows three cluster names along with their summary sentence.

3.2.2 Disaster Collections

Due to the limitation of space, we show results for the other six collections, for only three methods, i.e., those used in Units 5, 6, and 9. Table 5 gives sample student results. As results show, for their collection, the students were able to extract important and representative named entities and topics, and to generate a meaningful English text summary.

Table 5. Example Results for each Collection and for 3 Main Methods Extracted from Students Submissions

Collection / Method	Unit 5, Named Entities	Unit 6, LDA	Unit 9, Summary
Ebola	*Organizations*: Doctors Without Borders, National Centre for Disease, UN Security Council, World Health Organization, Infectious Disease Research. Locations: Africa, India, Kenya, Gorakhpur, Mumbai, USA *Person*: Modi, Desai, Patrick Sawyer, Anna Hazare, Sri Sene.	ebola, news, health, India, encephalitis, new, us, virus, world, people, news, health, people, disease	There has been an outbreak of Ebola reported in the following locations: Liberia, West Africa, Nigeria, Guinea, and Sierra Leone. In January 2014, there were between 425 and 3052 cases of Ebola in Liberia, with between 2296 and 2917 deaths. Additionally, In January 2014, there were between 425 and 4500 cases of Ebola in West Africa. In January 2014, there were between 425 and 3052 cases of Ebola in Guinea, with between 2296 and 2917 deaths.
Virginia earthquake	*Organization*: Sports, Health, News, Business *Location*: Virginia, East, Washington, U.S, NY, *Person*: Alexander, Kearney, Vervaeck, Armand, Paulm	Voting, Virginia, print election, god, rabbi, global, Washington, power, market	On 23 August, 2011 at 1:51, a 5.8 magnitude earthquake struck Virginia, The epicenter of the quake was located at Louisa. There were aftershocks that followed the earthquake and no tsunami was caused by the earthquake. There are no reports of landslides due of this earthquake. A total of 140 deaths occurred.
Brazil club fire	Organization: Post, North, Americas, News, People, World, News, Europe *Location*: East, India, Pakistan, Central, Brazil *Person*: Mark, Clinton, Hollande	Fire, brazil, people, Santa, club, news, Maria, sign, nightclub, news, youtube, Maria	In January 2013 there was a fire started by indoor fireworks in Santa Maria. This fire, fueled by ignited foam, grew to the size of the building, engulfed the club and ended up killing 309. One exit was made unavailable for a period of time. Compared to previous fires in the city was a fast-moving fire.
Pakistan flood	*Organization*: Time, Gwal, Sahiwal, Chagai, Jalapur, Shaikh, Ahmadpur, Bazar, Daulat, Nawan, Mithrau, Shah, *Location*: Islamabad, Khairpur, Pakistan *Person*: Khan, Chauki, Tando, Tangi,Toba, Shahpur, Ziarat, Fort, Kalat, Dera, Garhi, Haji	Flood, destroyed, damaged, Pakistan, shahdadkot, water, Indus, jaffarabad, sindh, Hyderabad, international, disaster, relief	In August 2010 a flood spanning 600 miles caused by heavy monsoon affected the Indus river in Pakistan, The total rainfall was 200 millimeters and the total cost of damage was 250 million dollars. The flood killed 3000 people, left 809 injured, and approximately 15 million people were affected. The cities of Nasirabad Badheen and Irvine were affected most by flooding, in the province of Sindh Mandalay and Punjab, finally nearly all of the flood damage occurred in the state of Pakistan.
Hurricane Sandy	N/A	Nicolas, sea, supplies, central, evacuation, grave, forecast, power, nation, food, typhoon	The storm, Hurricane Sandy, hits in New York on October 2012. The hurricane was a Category 1. Furthermore, the hurricane had a wind speed of 75 mph. hurricane Sandy formed in the Atlantic. Also, Hurricane Sandy had a size of 1000 miles wide. Hurricane Sandy caused 10 inches of rain. For more information. Search for hurricane sandy.
Tucson shooting	*Organization*: news, Inc., Abc, cnn, supermarket *Location*: Tuscan, Arizona, Casas, *Person*: Giffords, Chief, John, Tylor, Loughner	Tuscan, shooting, news, gabrielle, killed, police, loighner, public, January, business,	On the night of Sunday, January 9, Jared lee opened fire in Tucson. The suspect fired 5 rounds out of his rifle. 6 people lost their lives. 32 of the people were hurt, and are being treated for their injuries. The victims were between the ages of 40 and 50

More details about the students' summarization results can be found at https://vtechworks.lib.vt.edu/handle/10919/50956

3.3 Evaluation

An evaluation is underway using two surveys of student ratings of aspects of the course, along with free-form comments; students reported learning much, and liking both the course and the PBL approach. Students clearly were engaged when other teams presented approaches and outputs; a good deal of sharing and adoption of software and methods resulted. Evaluating results of the student work is much harder. There are no "gold standards" for our data, since the class engaged in authentic activities to aid IDEAL. Our first analysis, for each of the six groups, compared Named Entities, LDA Topics, and Summaries, as reported, with related Wikipedia pages for 6 events. Table 6 shows *Precision (Words in both summary and Wikipedia entry / Words in summary),* for the 3 methods, for each collection. Though a lengthy explanation of this table is needed, and other comparisons are required, it is clear students were on the right track.

Table 6. Precision Results for 6 Collections Using 3 Methods

Collection / Method Names	Unit 5, Named Entities	Unit 6, LDA	Unit 9, Summary
Ebola	0.209	0.571	0.159
Virginia Earthquake	0.173	0.117	0.541
Brazil club fire	0.0465	0.545	0.297
Pakistan flood	0.022	0.289	0.283
Hurricane Sandy	N/A	0.190	0.393
Tucson shooting	0.421	0.388	0.26

4. CONCLUSION

Project based learning was applied in a computational linguistics class to help students learn how to build automatic text summaries for big collections. Different methods were applied to produce multiple types of summaries. Results demonstrate that the 30 students, in 7 teams, were able to learn and apply big data and computational linguistics methods to produce reasonable corpus summaries. Through active learning and PBL, students generally unfamiliar with computational linguistics or using a Hadoop cluster to handle large digital library collections, mastered a broad range of valuable skills. Feedback from students, and review of student deliverables by the teaching assistants, has all been very positive. Accordingly, we offer our approach, corpora, and course details to others interested in working with big data summarization. More evaluation is needed to better understand the role and impact of PBL in such courses. Meanwhile, PBL is being used this semester in a graduate Information Retrieval class. Further, one of the graduate teaching assistants who helped with the course is extending the approach and methods to aid with Arabic summarization research on news corpora in a related project.

5. ACKNOWLEDGEMENTS

This publication was made possible by NPRP grant # 4-029-1-007 from the Qatar National Research Fund (a member of Qatar Foundation). Thanks also go to NSF for support, especially through grants DUE-1141209, IIS-0736055, IIS-0916733, and IIS - 1319578. The statements made herein are solely the responsibility of the authors. Thanks also go to the Digital Library Research Lab and CS Department. Special thanks go to the 30 students enrolled in the computational linguistics class in the fall of 2014. Finally, we are grateful for Mary English's guidance regarding PBL.

6. REFERENCES

[1] Buck Institute for Education. *Why Project Based Learning (PBL)?* Retrieved January, 2015, from http://bie.org/

[2] Fox, E. A., Akbar, M., Abdelhamid, S. H. E. M., Elsherbiny, N. I., Farag, M. M. G., Jin, F., Leidig, J. P. and Neppali, S. T. *Digital Libraries*. In *Computing Handbook*, Third ed., vol. 2, Chapman & Hall/CRC Press, Taylor and Francis Group, 2014.

[3] Fox, E. A. and Leidig, J. P. *Digital Library Applications: CBIR, Education, Social Networks, eScience/Simulation, and GIS.* Morgan & Claypool Publishers, San Francisco, 2014.

[4] Yang, S., Chung, H., Lin, X., Lee, S., Chen, L., Andrew Wood, Kavanaugh, A. L., Sheetz, S. D., Shoemaker, D. J. and Fox, E. A. *PhaseVis: What, When, Where, and Who in Visualizing the Four Phases of Emergency Management Through the Lens of Social Media.* Proceedings of the 10th International ISCRAM Conference. Baden-Baden, Germany, May 12-15, 2013.

[5] Goncalves, M. A., Fox, E. A. and Watson, L. T. Towards a Digital Library Theory: A Formal Digital Library Ontology. *International Journal Digital Libraries. 8*(2): 91-114. doi: 10.1007/s00799-008-0033-1.

[6] Apache Hadoop. *Welcome to Apache Hadoop!* Retrieved January, 2015, from http://hadoop.apache.org/

[7] Apache Mahout. Latent Dirichlet Allocation. Retrieved January, 2015, from https://mahout.apache.org/users/clustering/latent-dirichlet-allocation.html

[8] Bird, S., Klein, E. and Loper, E. *Natural Language Processing with Python: Analyzing Text with the Natural Language Toolkit.* O'Reilly, 2009.

[9] Stanford Natural Language Processing Group. *Stanford Named Entity Recognizer (NER).* Retrieved January, 2015, from http://nlp.stanford.edu/software/CRF-NER.shtml

[10] Apache Mahout *k-Means clustering - basics.* Retrieved January, 2015, from https://mahout.apache.org/users/clustering/k-means-clustering.html.

Multi-Emotion Estimation in Narratives from Crowdsourced Annotations

Lei Duan
Graduate School of Information Science and Technology
Hokkaido University
Sapporo 060-0814, Japan
duan@eis.hokudai.ac.jp

Satoshi Oyama
Graduate School of Information Science and Technology
Hokkaido University
Sapporo 060-0814, Japan
oyama@ist.hokudai.ac.jp

Haruhiko Sato
Graduate School of Information Science and Technology
Hokkaido University
Sapporo 060-0814, Japan
haru@complex.ist.hokudai.ac.jp

Masahito Kurihara
Graduate School of Information Science and Technology
Hokkaido University
Sapporo 060-0814, Japan
kurihara@ist.hokudai.ac.jp

ABSTRACT

Emotion annotations are important metadata for narrative texts in digital libraries. Such annotations are necessary for automatic text-to-speech conversion of narratives and affective education support and can be used as training data for machine learning algorithms to train automatic emotion detectors. However, obtaining high-quality emotion annotations is a challenging problem because it is usually expensive and time-consuming due to the subjectivity of emotion. Moreover, due to the multiplicity of "emotion", emotion annotations more naturally fit the paradigm of multi-label classification than that of multi-class classification since one instance (such as a sentence) may evoke a combination of multiple emotion categories. We thus investigated ways to obtain a set of high-quality emotion annotations ({instance, multi-emotion} paired data) from variable-quality crowdsourced annotations. A common quality control strategy for crowdsourced labeling tasks is to aggregate the responses provided by multiple annotators to produce a reliable annotation. Given that the categories of "emotion" have characteristics different from those of other kinds of labels, we propose incorporating domain-specific information of *emotional consistencies* across instances and *contextual cues* among emotion categories into the aggregation process. Experimental results demonstrate that, from a limited number of crowdsourced annotations, the proposed models enable gold standards to be more effectively estimated than the majority vote and the original domain-independent model.

JCDL'15, June 21–25, 2015, Knoxville, Tennessee, USA.

DOI: http://dx.doi.org/10.1145/2756406.2756910.

Categories and Subject Descriptors

H.3.1 [**Information Storage and Retrieval**]: Content Analysis and Indexing—*indexing methods, linguistic processing*; J.5 [**Arts and Humanities**]: *literature*

General Terms

Algorithm, Experimentation, Human Factors, Measurement, Reliability

Keywords

Multi-emotion annotation; Emotional Consistency; Contextual cue; Crowdsourcing; Human computation

1. INTRODUCTION

Humans, by nature, can be emotionally affected by literature, music, fine art, etc., so "emotion" (also referred to as affect, feeling, sentiment, mood, etc.) conveyed in digital contents is essential for enjoying such content. Such information is usually provided as emotion annotations provided by human annotators. The paradigms used for emotion annotation depend on the application. For simple applications, it is sufficient to annotate whether an instance (such as a narrative line, a movie clip, or a music piece) is emotive or the instance's emotional valence (positive or negative). Such annotations obviously simplify the complexity of human emotion and are thus not effective for more complicated applications such as expressive text-to-speech synthesis [25] and affective education support [8]. Some researchers in this area [2, 15] have considered human emotion as a single category, with only one particular emotion (e.g., *happiness* or *sadness*) appearing at a time. However, this assumption has been undermined by the results of psychology studies. It has been demonstrated that a single emotion category is unable to represent all possible emotional manifestations [24] and that some emotional manifestations are a combination of several emotion categories [33]. For example, Alm

[1] observed that the following sentence from H. C. Andersen's fairy tale "The Ugly Duckling[1]" refers to *happiness* and *sadness* simultaneously:

> He now felt glad at having suffered sorrow and trouble, because it enabled him to enjoy so much better all the pleasure and happiness around him; for the great swans swam round the new-comer, and stroked his neck with their beaks, as a welcome.

A single emotion category would fail to represent this multiplicity.

Consequently, much of the recent emotion-oriented research [18, 23, 29] has concentrated on exploiting the multifaceted nature of emotion so that an instance can be associated with a combination of multiple emotion categories. An enormous number of emotion annotations ({instance, multi-emotion} paired data) is generally necessary for such research to be used as input for expressive text-to-speech synthesis, reference material for affective education support, training data for machine learning algorithms supporting automatic emotion detection, etc. Moreover, the annotation quality directly affects the quality of the research.

One way to obtain an enormous number of emotion annotations is to use online crowdsourcing services, which are being used more frequently in the labeling community. The state-of-the-art is for each instance to be annotated by one crowdsourcing annotator. However, the emotion labeling is more subjective than most other labeling tasks. There are different tendencies and substantial variations among individuals when detecting emotions, so high-quality emotion annotations should be in accordance with the general consensus of large crowds. This means that the annotation quality greatly depends on the judgment of an annotator, and is actually problematic in most cases. It is thus necessary to develop quality control strategies.

A promising quality control strategy is to introduce redundancy by asking several annotators (a sub-set of the crowd) to work on an instance and then aggregating their responses (crowdsourced annotations) to produce a reliable annotation (crowd's opinion). This is also called "approximating the crowd" [12]. The simplest aggregation strategy, *majority vote*, is valid only if the number of annotators is large enough. It is based on the implicit assumption that all annotators have the same probability of making an error. If the number of annotators is less than a certain unknown number, the detrimental effect of the noisy responses is significant, so treating responses given by different annotators equally would produce poor results. However, collecting responses from a large number of annotators is impractical due to the high cost (time and expense). To alleviate this problem, a number of state-of-the-art statistical techniques [7, 10, 22, 31, 32] have been proposed for producing a reliable annotation from a limited number of annotator responses used for crowdsourced labeling[2].

A crowdsourced labeling task is a form of semantic interpretation in which the instances are signs, the labels are referents, and the annotators are interpreters, as illustrated by the triangle of reference [21] (Figure 1). The interpreter perceives the sign (e.g., a word, a sound, an image, a sentence) and through some cognitive process attempts to find the referent of that sign (e.g., an object, an idea, a class of things). As discussed further in section 6.2, most state-of-the-art quality control techniques include latent factors related to these three components, such as annotator bias [7], annotator expertise [32], and instance difficulty [31, 32]. However, they ignore the internal relationships among instances and among labels.[3] In other words, for each repeatedly annotated instance, the reliable annotation is produced separately.

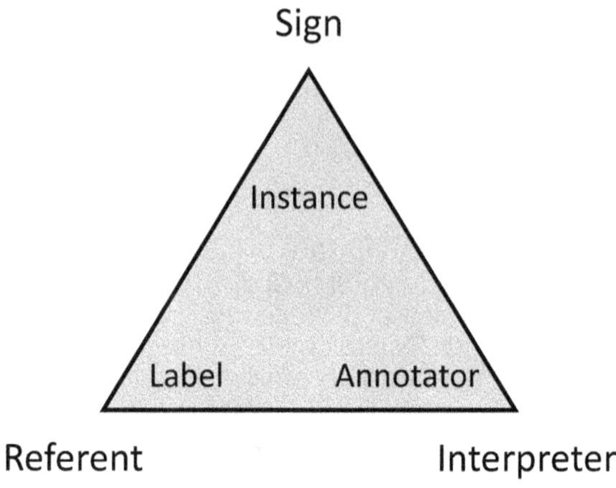

Figure 1: Triangle of Reference

In addition to the subjectivity characteristic as discussed above, "emotion" has its unique characteristics in comparison with other kinds of labels:

- **Internal relationships among instances**

Emotive expressions can not be divorced from their context [3]. The media used to convey emotion include (but are not limited to) narrative, music, cinema, facial expression, and body language. Take narrative, the main focus of this paper, as an example. As the genre of literature characterized by description, narrative usually subjects to certain emotional tendency, and characters in a narrative typically have distinct personalities. Both narrative emotional tendency and character personality tend to remain consistent across instances (sentences) in the same context. If they did not, the emotive expression of the utterances of expressive text-to-speech synthesis, a potential application, would result in unnatural pronunciation.

- **Internal relationships among labels**

Emotions (labels) expressed by a sentence likely relate to the emotions expressed by the subsequent sentences. For example, a boy scolded by his mother for some mistake would more likely feel sad and disgusted while the mother would more likely feel angry. It is thus beneficial to know the contextual cues among emotions.

In this work, we explore the domain-specific viability of crowdsourced emotion annotations in narratives. We asked crowdsourcing annotators to read narrative lines such as those shown in Figure 2 and spontaneously indicate the

[1]http://www.surlalunefairytales.com/uglyduckling/index.html

[2]For a detailed discussion, see Section 6.2

[3]The relationship among annotators in a collaborative crowdsourcing task should normally be taken into account, but this is not relevant here since the annotators made their decisions independently in our experiments.

Jiro: "Come here, Makoto! Here are some little kittens!"
happiness fondness relief anger sadness fear
shame disgust excitement surprise *neutral*

Jiro is shouting in the yard at the front of the dyehouse.

Two or three children are running behind Makoto to see what happened.
There are two kittens hiding in a carton.

Makoto: "Who put them here?"
happiness fondness relief anger sadness fear
shame disgust excitement surprise *neutral*

Shyo: "John has already killed three on the bridge."
happiness fondness relief anger sadness fear
shame disgust excitement surprise *neutral*

Figure 2: Example task input screen (translated from Japanese). Annotators were native Japanese language speakers. Both candidate emotions and lines were presented to annotators in their original Japanese form.

character's emotions expressed in each line. The true (gold standard) emotions for each line were then estimated by aggregating the obtained multi-emotion responses. As an extension to our previous work [10] on domain-independent multi-label estimation, we propose incorporating the internal relationships among lines (instances) and among emotions (labels) into the estimation process. The two relationships are respectively specified as the domain-specific information of *emotional consistencies* across lines and *contextual cues* among emotions. An expectation maximization (EM) based incremental algorithm is used to estimate the gold standard emotion annotations together with the parameters of the proposed models. The experimental results demonstrate that incorporating the domain-specific information into the estimation process makes the accuracy rates of the proposed models higher than those of the majority vote and the original domain-independent model for the same number of annotations.

The remainder of this paper is organized as follows. Section 2 briefly describes the sources of annotated narratives and candidate emotions. Section 3 reviews the original domain-independent multi-label estimation model, the foundation of our study, and introduces the two proposed domain-specific multi-emotion estimation models. Section 4 describes the use of the EM algorithm to estimate the gold standard emotion annotations together with the model parameters. Section 5 describes the experimental design and discusses the results obtained by applying the proposed models to real-world data. Section 6 provides background material by introducing related research. Section 7 summarizes the main points and suggests several future research directions.

2. DATASET DESCRIPTIONS

2.1 Aozora Library

The Aozora (Blue Sky) Library[4] is a Japanese online repository containing freely available books. It contains over 10,000 books of various genres (philosophy, history, art, etc.) published in Japanese for which copyrights have expired (50 years after the death of the copyright holder). The children's book genre in Aozora Library includes sub-categories such as *history books*, *beautiful arts and crafts books*, and *literature*. Children's narratives are included in the *literature* category, which contained 1217 books in December 2014. From this category we chose two narratives at random for our experiments, which are discussed in Section 5.

[4]http://www.aozora.gr.jp

Table 1: Distribution of separate expressions across emotions in Nakamura's dictionary, ordered by number of expressions per emotion.

Emotion	No. of expressions	Emotion	No. of expressions
Disgust	532	Fondness	197
Excitement	269	Fear	147
Sadness	232	Surprise	129
Happiness	224	Relief	106
Anger	199	Shame	65
		Total	2100

2.2 Emotive Expression Dictionary

Since the chosen narratives were in Japanese, we had to use a candidate emotion category set proven to be appropriate for the Japanese language. The Emotive Expression Dictionary [19] is a dictionary developed by Akira Nakamura over a period exceeding 20 years. It is a collection of over 2000 expressions describing emotional states that were collected manually from a wide range of literature. It is not a tool for emotion analysis *per se* but was converted into an emotive expression database by Ptaszynski *et al.* [23] in their research on emotion analysis of utterances in Japanese. This dictionary is a state-of-the-art example of a hand-crafted lexicon of emotive expressions. In particular, it uses ten emotion categories that appropriately reflect the Japanese language and culture. This classification is also applied in the lexicon itself. Each expression is classified as representing one specific emotion category, or more if applicable. The distribution of separate expressions across all emotion categories is represented in Table 1.

3. STATISTICAL MODELS

Multi-emotion estimation from crowdsourced annotations can be seen as an unsupervised multi-label classification problem. Two widely used methods for multi-label classification are the binary relevance (*BR*) method and the label combination or label power-set (*LP*) method [30].

The *BR* method decomposes the multi-label classification problem into several independent binary-label classification problems, one for each label in the set of candidate labels. The final labels for each instance are determined by aggregating the predictions from all binary estimators. In other words, the *BR* method does not consider dependency among candidate labels. This is reasonable only in the extreme case that labels are mutually independent. However, it is obvious that emotions are interrelated. Some emotions may reveal clues about others. For example, a line expressing *fear* may also express a certain degree of *anger* and/or *surprise*.

To take into account the dependency relationship among candidate emotions, we use the *LP* method. It treats each unique subset of labels in the set of candidate labels as an atomic "label" and defines a new single-label estimation problem, i.e., estimating each member of the power-set of the candidate label set. We use the concept of "conjoint-emotion" to represent a subset of the candidate emotion set. For example, the two conjoint-emotions {*happiness*, *relief*} and {*happiness*, *excitement*} express two different kinds of "happiness": one is comparatively mild while the other is strong.

Problem Formulation:

Let I be the set of lines, J be the set of candidate emotions, and K be the set of annotators. The number of times that annotator k annotated line i with conjoint-emotion $\mathcal{L}$ is given by $n_{i\mathcal{L}}^{(k)} \in \mathbb{N}$ $(k \in K, i \in I, \mathcal{L} \subseteq J)$. The true conjoint-emotion, namely the multiple true emotions, for line i is denoted by $\mathcal{T}_i \subseteq J$ $(i \in I)$. The objective is to aggregate the set of annotations $\left\{n_{i\mathcal{L}}^{(k)} : k \in K, i \in I, \mathcal{L} \subseteq J\right\}$ to estimate the set of true conjoint-emotions $\{\mathcal{T}_i : i \in I\}$.

We first introduce the original model aimed at handling domain-independent multi-label estimation in Section 3.1, and then discuss how we extended it to handle domain-specific multi-emotion estimation by considering *emotional consistencies* and *contextual cues* in Sections 3.2 and 3.3.

3.1 Original Domain-independent Multi-label Estimation

The original domain-independent model was proposed in our previous work [10]. The graphical representation of the model is illustrated in Figure 3(a). The true conjoint-emotion for line i is determined by the maximum a posteriori (MAP) principal:

$$\mathcal{T}_i = \underset{\mathcal{J} \subseteq J}{\arg\max}\, \mathrm{E}\left[\mathcal{T}_i = \mathcal{J}\right], \tag{1}$$

where the expectation of the true conjoint-emotion for line i is estimated as the conditional distribution given the annotations for line i:

$$\mathrm{E}\left[\mathcal{T}_i = \mathcal{J}\right] = \Pr\left[\mathcal{T}_i = \mathcal{J} \mid \left\{n_{i\mathcal{L}}^{(k)} : k \in K, \mathcal{L} \subseteq J\right\}\right]. \tag{2}$$

The bias for annotator k is defined as the probability that she annotated a line with conjoint-emotion $\mathcal{L}$ when the true conjoint-emotion of the line is $\mathcal{J}$:

$$\pi_{\mathcal{J}\mathcal{L}}^{(k)} := \frac{\sum_{i \in I} \gamma_{i\mathcal{J}} \cdot n_{i\mathcal{L}}^{(k)}}{\sum_{\mathcal{L} \in J} \sum_{i \in I} \gamma_{i\mathcal{J}} \cdot n_{i\mathcal{L}}^{(k)}},$$

where $\gamma_{i\mathcal{J}}$ is defined as the prior probability that $\mathcal{J}$ is the true conjoint-emotion for line i:

$$\gamma_{i\mathcal{J}} := \Pr[\mathcal{T}_i = \mathcal{J}].$$

Since the annotators make their decisions independently, the numbers of times that an annotator annotated instance i with different conjoint-emotions when $\mathcal{J}$ is the true conjoint-emotion are distributed according to a multinomial distribution. Using Bayes' Theorem, we obtain the expectation in Equation (2):

$$\mathrm{E}\left[\mathcal{T}_i = \mathcal{J}\right] = \frac{\gamma_{i\mathcal{J}}}{z_i} \prod_{k \in K} \prod_{\mathcal{L} \subseteq J} \left(\pi_{\mathcal{J}\mathcal{L}}^{(k)}\right)^{n_{i\mathcal{L}}^{(k)}}, \tag{3}$$

where z_i is defined as the normalization constant:

$$z_i := \sum_{\mathcal{J} \subseteq J} \left(\gamma_{i\mathcal{J}} \cdot \prod_{k \in K} \prod_{\mathcal{L} \subseteq J} \left(\pi_{\mathcal{J}\mathcal{L}}^{(k)}\right)^{n_{i\mathcal{L}}^{(k)}}\right),$$

which ensures that the posterior distribution in Equation (2) is a valid probability density and can be integrated to one. The detailed derivation is given elsewhere [10].

3.2 Multi-emotion Estimation Considering Emotional Consistencies

Multi-emotion estimation is a domain-specific aspect of multi-label estimation. To improve the accuracy of the domain-independent estimation model described in Section 3.1, we first propose incorporating *emotional consistencies* into the estimation process. As discussed in Section 1, there are *emotional consistencies* across lines (as well as *contextual cues* among emotions) in narrative emotional tendency and in character personality. We thus define narrative emotional tendency as the distribution of separate expressions over conjoint-emotions:

$$\alpha_{\mathcal{J}} := \frac{\sum_{i \in I} \gamma_{i\mathcal{J}}}{|I|}.$$

It is obtained by maximum-likelihood estimation (MLE) of the proportion of lines expressing conjoint-emotion $\mathcal{J}$ over all lines.

Let $c(i)$ $(i \in I)$ denote the character speaking in line i and $I_{c(i)}$ $(i \in I)$ denote the lines spoken by character $c(i)$. Similar to the narrative emotional tendency, the character personality is also defined as the distribution over conjoint-emotions:

$$\beta_{c(i)\mathcal{J}} := \frac{\sum_{\imath \in I_{c(i)}} \gamma_{\imath\mathcal{J}}}{\left|I_{c(i)}\right|}.$$

It is obtained by MLE of the proportion of the lines expressing conjoint-emotion $\mathcal{J}$ over all the lines spoken by character $c(i)$.

As a domain-specific extension of Equation (2), the expectation of the true conjoint-emotion for line i is then estimated considering *emotional consistencies* in the narrative emotional tendency and in the character personality:

$$\mathrm{E}\left[\mathcal{T}_i = \mathcal{J}\right] = \Pr\left[\mathcal{T}_i = \mathcal{J} \mid \left\{n_{i\mathcal{L}}^{(k)} : k \in K, \mathcal{L} \subseteq J\right\}; \alpha_{\mathcal{J}}, \beta_{c(i)\mathcal{J}}\right]. \tag{4}$$

This means that the true conjoint-emotion of each line is determined not only by the annotations but also by the narrative emotional tendency and the character personality. The graphical representation of the model is illustrated in Figure 3(b). In a manner similar to that for Equation (3), using Bayes' Theorem, we obtain the expectation in Equation (4):

$$\mathrm{E}\left[\mathcal{T}_i = \mathcal{J}\right] = \frac{\alpha_{\mathcal{J}} \cdot \beta_{c(i)\mathcal{J}} \cdot \gamma_{i\mathcal{J}}}{z_i} \prod_{k \in K} \prod_{\mathcal{L} \subseteq J} \left(\pi_{\mathcal{J}\mathcal{L}}^{(k)}\right)^{n_{i\mathcal{L}}^{(k)}}, \tag{5}$$

where z_i is the normalization constant:

$$z_i = \sum_{\mathcal{J} \subseteq J} \left(\alpha_{\mathcal{J}} \cdot \beta_{c(i)\mathcal{J}} \cdot \gamma_{i\mathcal{J}} \cdot \prod_{k \in K} \prod_{\mathcal{L} \subseteq J} \left(\pi_{\mathcal{J}\mathcal{L}}^{(k)}\right)^{n_{i\mathcal{L}}^{(k)}}\right).$$

Equation (5) demonstrates that the domain-specific model considering *emotional consistencies* automatically assigns higher weights to the conjoint-emotions that are more consistent with the narrative emotional tendency and with the character personality, and assigns lower weights to those that are less consistent.

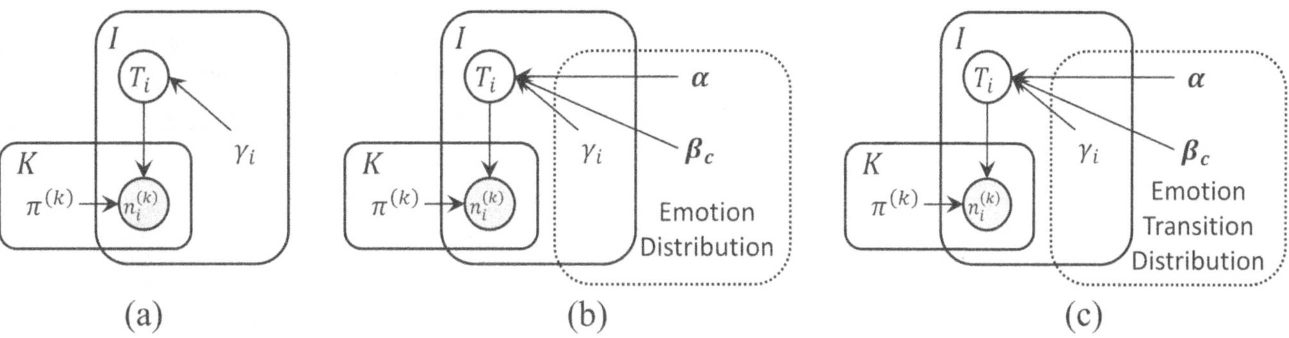

Figure 3: Graphical model representation for multi-emotion estimation: (a) original domain-independent model, (b) model considering *emotional consistencies*, and (c) model considering *emotional consistencies* with *contextual cues*.

3.3 Multi-emotion Estimation Considering Emotional Consistencies with Contextual Cues

As mentioned in Section 1, the emotions expressed by a sentence likely relate to the emotions expressed by the subsequent sentences, so it is beneficial to know the *contextual cues* among emotions. As a statistical measure of those "cues" we use the possibility of a conjoint-emotion following another conjoint-emotion. For example, the conjoint-emotion $\{anger, disgust\}$ is more likely followed by $\{sad, fear\}$ than $\{happiness, fondness\}$. This means that $\{anger, disgust\}$ has a closer relationship with $\{sad, fear\}$ than with $\{happiness, fondness\}$.

As an extension to the model proposed in Section 3.2, we propose estimating *emotional consistencies* across instances by using *contextual cues* among emotions. We use the idea of *bi-gram* to learn the transition distribution over conjoint-emotions. This means that the conjoint-emotion expressed by a line is conditional on the conjoint-emotion expressed by the previous line. Let $i-1$ be the line before line i and $\bar{\mathcal{J}}$ be the true conjoint-emotion of line $i-1$, which means

$$\bar{\mathcal{J}} = \arg\max_{\mathcal{J} \subseteq J} \mathrm{E}[\mathcal{T}_{i-1} = \mathcal{J}] .$$

The *contextual cues* are extracted using parameters $\{\alpha\}$, $\{\beta\}$, and $\{\gamma\}$, which are the counterparts of the parameters defined in Sections 3.1 and 3.2. They are estimated considering the true conjoint-emotions for two consecutive lines:

$$\alpha_{\mathcal{J}} = \frac{\sum_{i \in I} \Pr\left[\mathcal{T}_{i-1} = \bar{\mathcal{J}}, \mathcal{T}_i = \mathcal{J}\right]}{\sum_{i \in I} \Pr\left[\mathcal{T}_i = \bar{\mathcal{J}}\right]} ,$$

$$\beta_{c(i)\mathcal{J}} = \frac{\sum_{i \in I_{c(i)}} \Pr\left[\mathcal{T}_{i-1} = \bar{\mathcal{J}}, \mathcal{T}_i = \mathcal{J}\right]}{\sum_{i \in I_{c(i-1)}} \Pr\left[\mathcal{T}_i = \bar{\mathcal{J}}\right]} ,$$

$$\gamma_{i\mathcal{J}} = \frac{\Pr\left[\mathcal{T}_{i-1} = \bar{\mathcal{J}}, \mathcal{T}_i = \mathcal{J}\right]}{\Pr\left[\mathcal{T}_{i-1} = \bar{\mathcal{J}}\right]} .$$

The annotations for each line are provided by arbitrary annotators, but we need to obtain cases in which one conjoint-emotion followed by another as complete as possible. Therefore, we use a *cross-strategy* among annotators to compute the joint distribution for two consecutive lines:

$$\Pr[\mathcal{T}_{i-1} = \bar{\mathcal{J}}, \mathcal{T}_i = \mathcal{J}] = \frac{\sum_{k \in K} n^{(k)}_{(i-1)\bar{\mathcal{J}}} \cdot \sum_{k \in K} n^{(k)}_{i\mathcal{J}}}{\sum_{k \in K} \sum_{\jmath \subseteq J} n^{(k)}_{(i-1)\jmath} \cdot \sum_{k \in K} \sum_{\jmath \subseteq J} n^{(k)}_{i\jmath}} .$$

The differences among the original domain-independent model, the model considering *emotional consistencies*, and the model considering *emotional consistencies* with *contextual cues* are illustrated in Figure 3. The proposed domain-specific multi-emotion estimation models, (b) and (c), extend the original domain-independent model (a) by statistically analyzing *emotional consistencies* in narrative emotional tendency and character personality, which are estimated as probabilistic variables following different distributions.

4. INFERENCE ALGORITHM

Inference of the gold standard emotion annotations and the parameters can be greatly simplified if we use the EM algorithm. The EM algorithm is an efficient iterative procedure for computing the maximum-likelihood solution in presence of hidden/missing data. It is widely used in crowd-sourcing related research [7, 32, 22, 10]. We treat the MLEs of the parameters

$$\{\alpha_{\mathcal{J}} : \mathcal{J} \subseteq J\}\,(\text{narrative emotional tendency}),$$
$$\{\beta_{c(i)\mathcal{J}} : i \in I, \mathcal{J} \subseteq J\}\,(\text{character personality}),$$
$$\{\gamma_{i\mathcal{J}} : i \in I, \mathcal{J} \subseteq J\}\,(\text{prior distribution}),$$
$$\left\{\pi^{(k)}_{\mathcal{J}\mathcal{L}} : k \in K, \mathcal{J} \subseteq J, \mathcal{L} \subseteq J\right\}\,(\text{annotator bias}),$$
$$\{z_i : i \in I\}\,(\text{normalization constant}),$$

as the hidden data, with the expectations of the true conjoint-emotions for each line

$$\{\mathrm{E}\left[\mathcal{T}_i = \mathcal{J}\right] : i \in I, \mathcal{J} \subseteq J\}$$

as unobserved variables (missing data). The observed variables

$$\left\{n^{(k)}_{i\mathcal{L}} : i \in I, k \in K, \mathcal{L} \subseteq J\right\}$$

can be directly calculated from the obtained crowdsourced annotations.

We therefore proceed as follows.

(1) Initialization

Obtain the initial estimates of unobserved variables {E}:

$$\mathrm{E}\left[\mathcal{T}_i = \mathcal{J}\right] = \frac{\sum_{k \in K} n_{i\mathcal{J}}^{(k)}}{\sum_{k \in K} \sum_{\jmath \subseteq J} n_{i\jmath}^{(k)}} ,$$

which is an intuitive way to assign the MLEs. This approach can be computationally demanding because it is equivalent to estimating a $|J|$-dimensional joint distribution for each instance over the candidate emotions. Because the emotion states are binary-valued, the joint distribution requires the probabilities of $2^{|J|}$ different assignments of values. For all but the smallest $|J|$, the explicit representation of the joint distribution is unmanageable from every perspective. Therefore, at the practical level, it is too expensive and nearly impossible to acquire a sufficient number of samples from annotators to robustly estimate the high-dimensional joint distribution. An effective strategy to overcome the adverse effect of data sparsity is to represent the underlying joint distribution more compactly. By using the conditional independence properties, we can approximate the joint distribution from a finite number of annotations. Several methods are available for such approximation [6]. We used a Bayesian network as it was previously shown to be effective for multi-label estimation [10].

(2) Maximization

Estimate the MLEs of hidden parameters $\{\alpha\}$, $\{\beta\}$, $\{\gamma\}$, $\{\pi\}$, and $\{z\}$ using the equations in Section 3 with the current estimates of {E}, which means

$$\Pr\left[\mathcal{T}_i = \mathcal{J}\right] = \mathrm{E}\left[\mathcal{T}_i = \mathcal{J}\right] .$$

(3) Expectation

Estimate the expected values of the unobserved variables, {E}, using Equation (5) with the current estimates of the parameters calculated in step (2).

(4) Alternation

Alternately perform steps (2) and (3) until the likelihood for all annotations $\Pr\left[\left\{n_{i\mathcal{L}}^{(k)} : k \in K, i \in I, \mathcal{L} \subseteq J\right\}\right]$ converges. Since all lines are independently annotated, we have

$$\Pr\left[\left\{n_{i\mathcal{L}}^{(k)} : k \in K, i \in I, \mathcal{L} \subseteq J\right\}\right] = \prod_{i \in I} z_i .$$

At this point, the $\mathcal{J}$ with the maximum $\mathrm{E}[\mathcal{T}_i = \mathcal{J}]$ is the true conjoint-emotion for line i, as specified in Equation (1).

One of the characteristics of the EM algorithm is that, after alternately performing steps (2) and (3), only one of the unobserved variables for a line has a probability converging towards 1 while the other unobserved variables for the line have a probability converging towards 0. In other words, it is unlikely that any of the expectations {E} is between 0.1 and 0.9.

5. EMPIRICAL STUDY

To evaluate the effectiveness of the proposed models, we needed narratives in which the lines express clear emotions. Since children typically have an elementary level of psychological development, narratives written for them usually have vibrant affection tints and distinct character personalities as the aim is to better attract the attention of children.

Table 2: Annotation frequencies of emotions and *neutral*, ordered by total frequency

Emotion	"Love"	"Apple"	Total
Relief	516	362	878
Anger	242	623	865
Sadness	522	298	820
Happiness	458	306	764
Fondness	467	226	693
Excitement	379	270	649
Disgust	279	265	544
Neutral	*120*	*352*	*472*
Surprise	190	243	433
Fear	164	107	271
Shame	84	68	152
Total (except *Neutral*)	3301	2768	6069

Table 3: Statistics for the experiments

	"Love"	"Apple"	Total
No. of lines	63	78	141
No. of characters	12	9	21
No. of annotators	30	57	84
No. of annotations	1890	2340	4230
Avg. no. of checked labels per annotation	1.75	1.18	1.43
Avg. no. of annotations per line	30	30	30

The proportion of speaking lines in children's narratives is also higher than that in other narrative genres. Therefore, children's narratives are commonly used in emotion-oriented research [2, 8]. These characteristics of children's narratives are also the focal points of our research. We thus chose two Japanese children's narratives, "Although we are in love"[5] ("Love" for short) and "Little Masa and a red apple"[6] ("Apple" for short), from the Aozora Library[7] as the annotated texts. We conducted the experiments using the Lancers crowdsourcing service[8].

Due to different aspects that emotion-oriented research looks to capture, the candidate emotion category set used differs among research efforts. While the six basic emotions (*happiness*, *fear*, *anger*, *surprise*, *disgust*, and *sadness*) [11] are typically used [1, 2, 29], we used ten candidate emotions in order to provide more choices to the annotators and thereby enable us to perform an in-depth study on multi-emotion estimation. They were taken from the "Emotive Expression Dictionary"[9], which contains emotions proven to be appropriate for the Japanese language and culture [23]. An example task input screen is shown in Figure 2. If none of the candidate emotions was felt, the annotator would check *neutral*. The candidate emotions are shown in Table 2 with their annotation frequencies. Other statistics for the experiments are shown in Table 3.

[5]http://www.aozora.gr.jp/cards/001475/files/52111_47798.html
[6]http://www.aozora.gr.jp/cards/001475/files/52113_46622.html
[7]For a detailed description, see Section 2.1
[8]http://www.lancers.jp
[9]For a detailed description, see Section 2.2

For the emotion annotations to be reliable, they should be in accordance with the general consensus of large crowds. The majority vote strategy most objectively reflects the general consensus if the number of annotators is large enough. Therefore, we obtained gold standards by having each line annotated 30 times and then taking the majority vote. That is, the most often annotated conjoint-emotion for a line was used as the gold standard for that line. For the "Love" narrative, we asked each of the 30 annotators to annotate each line one time, which ensured that each annotator annotated the complete set of the lines. For the "Apple" narrative, the annotation task was divided into small parts and distributed to the annotators in a nonspecific manner, so the 30 annotations for every line were provided by arbitrary annotators, and few, if any, of them annotated the complete set of the lines. This is a more realistic situation since it is not a good idea to submit a very large task to a crowdsourcing service because a big task tends to diminish annotator enthusiasm or even cause annotators to avoid the task. We conducted the "Apple" task in this way simply to examine the effects of "arbitrary annotator interference" on the model results.

Although our proposed models can handle a line being annotated more than once by an annotator, to collect opinions as widely as possible at a fixed cost, it is still best to avoid this situation even though an annotator may interpret a line differently at different times. Therefore, in our experiments, all the annotations for a line were obtained from different annotators. This means that the values of the observed variable $n_{i\mathcal{L}}^{(k)}$ ($k \in K, i \in I, \mathcal{L} \subseteq J$) was either 0 or 1.

To determine the effect of the number of annotators per line on accuracy, we randomly split the 30 annotators who annotated a particular line into various numbers of groups of equal size. We used five different group sizes: 3 (ten groups), 5 (six groups), 10 (three groups), 15 (two groups), and 30 (one group). The true conjoint-emotion for each line was estimated given the annotations within each group using the following four models:

- *MV*: **M**ajority **V**ote;
- *OL*: **O**riginal domain-independent multi-**L**abel estimation model;
- *EC*: domain-specific multi-**E**motion estimation model considering *emotional* ***C****onsistency*;
- *EC+*: domain-specific multi-**E**motion estimation model considering *emotional* ***C****onsistency* with *contextual cues*.

MV and *OL* are the baselines to which we compare the results for *EC* and *EC+*.

Both the estimation result and the gold standard for a line can be regarded as a binary vector. It is unreasonable to check whether the two binary vectors match exactly. For example, {*happiness, fondness*} is closer to {*happiness, relief*} than {*anger, disgust*}. Therefore, the average *Simple Matching Coefficient* is used to evaluate the performance of the proposed models, i.e., the average proportion of correct emotions between the estimation results and the gold standards for all lines within a group.

The MV results for 30 annotators in Figure 4 represent the accuracy (1.00) of the gold standard group. For both narratives, when the group size was 3, 5, 10, or 15, all three statistical models achieved better average accuracies than the MV model. Although the accuracies of the statistical

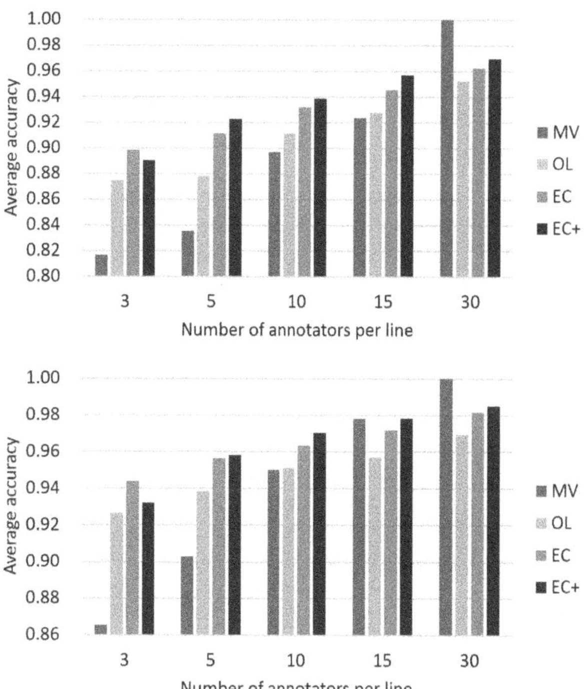

Figure 4: Average accuracy for "Although we are in love" narrative (upper) and "Little Masa and a red apple" narrative (lower).

models increased with the group size, the *EC* and *EC+* models consistently outperformed the *OL* model and had accuracies greater than 90 % for five or more annotators per line. This means that considering *emotional consistencies* in narrative emotional tendency and in character personality is effective for multi-emotion estimation, and five would be a reasonable number of annotators for each line to achieve satisfactory performance. Moreover, the average accuracy of the *EC+* model increased fastest and exceeded that of the *EC* model when the group size was five or more. The reason for this phenomenon is that, when the group size was 3, the adverse effect of data sparsity was dominant, and the quantity of annotations was insufficient to well learn the transition distribution over conjoint-emotions. However, once the quantity was sufficient, the superiority of the *EC+* model, which considers *emotional consistencies* with *contextual cues*, became evident. Finally, none of the models was particularly sensitive to the effect of "arbitrary annotator interference" in the "apple" narrative.

All the models were run on a workstation with an Intel Core i7-3770 3.40-GHz 4-core processor, 8-GB RAM, and the Windows 7 64-bit operating system. We found that even the most complicated model, the *EC+* model, converged in less than 10 seconds when using the annotations of 30 annotators as the input. There are two reasons for this performance. One is that the computational complexity of the proposed models is linear in the number of lines, the number of annotators, and the number of candidate emotions and the dataset used was not so large. The other is that we did not estimate the expectations {E} over all possible conjoint-emotions ($2^{|J|}$) for all the sentences (I). In fact, we only estimated those of conjoint-emotions that have been annotated in a sentence by at least one annotator.

6. BACKGROUND AND RELATED WORK

6.1 Emotion-oriented Research

Emotion is an important access point in digital libraries and online repositories. Analyzing how we are affected is a vital research direction in digital media processing as it is potentially applicable to many further emotion-related applications, including expressive text-to-speech synthesis [25] and therapeutic education of children with communication disorders [8]. Many researchers have thus concentrated on this area. Alm *et al.* [2] investigated the importance of various features for emotion analysis and classified the emotional affinity of sentences in the narrative domain of children's fairy tales. Kim *et al.* [15] modeled emotion as a continuous *manifold* and constructed a statistical model connecting it to documents and to a discrete set of emotions. A number of machine learning algorithms have been proposed for classifying music by mood in the music digital library domain [4, 14].

Several researchers concentrated on exploiting the multifaceted nature of emotion. Trohidis *et al.* [29] modeled emotion detection in music pieces as a multi-label classification task. Liu *et al.* [18] proposed an implicit video multi-emotion tagging method. Ptaszynski *et al.* [23] did an experiment on multi-emotion analysis of certain characters in narratives. A complete discussion of emotion-oriented research is beyond the scope of this paper but can be found in Calvo *et al.* [5].

Traditional emotion classification research is aimed at detecting single or multiple emotion(s) from an instance using a trained detector. Our work is aimed at estimating multiple emotions directly from crowdsourced annotations. The goal is to prepare high-quality emotion annotations at low cost for use with emotion-related applications and training data for emotion detectors. To the best of our knowledge, there is no work comparable to our proposed models, except our previous work [10] (the *OL* model in Section 5, introduced in Section 3.1).

6.2 Crowdsourcing and Quality Control

For the term *crowdsourcing*, Howe [13] offers the following definition:

> Crowdsourcing represents the act of a company or institution taking a function once performed by employees and outsourcing it to an undefined (and generally large) network of people in the form of an open call. This can take the form of peer-production (when the job is performed collaboratively), but is also often undertaken by sole individuals. The crucial prerequisite is the use of the open call format and the large network of potential laborers.

Simply put, crowdsourcing is an economical and efficient approach to performing tasks that are difficult for computers but relatively easy for humans. With the recent expansion of crowdsourcing platforms such as Amazon Mechanical Turk[10] (MTurk) and CrowdFlower[11], the concept of crowdsourcing has been successfully leveraged in various areas of computer science research, including natural language processing [27] and computer vision [28]. There have also been several attempts in the emotion detection domain. Alm [1] analyzed the characteristics of sentences with high-agreement crowdsourced emotion annotations. He tentatively hypothesized that some characteristics of high-agreement annotations may show particular affinity with certain emotions. Lee *et al.* [16] compared the music emotion annotations collected from music experts with annotations collected using MTurk. They showed that the overall distribution of emotions and agreement rates from music experts and MTurk were comparable.

Although annotations can be obtained from a crowdsourcing service at very low cost (time and expense), there is no guarantee that all annotators are sufficiently competent to complete the offered tasks. In fact, crowdsourcing annotators are rarely trained and generally do not have the abilities needed to accurately perform the offered task. Some annotators may even simply submit random responses as a means to earn easy money. Therefore, ensuring the annotation quality from noisy responses is one of the biggest challenges in crowdsourcing.

A simple strategy would be to offer incentive programs for the annotators, such as giving monetary bonuses to high-performance ones and denying payments to low-performance ones. In addition, several approaches geared toward efficient quality control have been applied. For example, MTurk provides a pre-qualification system to assess the skill level of a prospective annotator, and CrowdFlower enables requesters to inject a collection of tasks with known correct answers into their tasks to automatically measure an annotator's performance.

Meanwhile, various statistical schemes have been proposed to aggregate multiple variable-quality annotations from non-expert annotators to yield results that rival gold standards. Dawid *et al.* [7] presented a method for inferring the unknown health state of a patient given diagnostic tests by several clinicians, where the biases of the annotators (clinicians) were modeled by a confusion matrix. Whitehill *et al.* [32] presented a model for simultaneously estimating the true label of each repeatedly labeled instance, the expertise of each annotator, and the difficulty of each question. Welinder *et al.* [31] incorporated into their bird image classification model all the above factors, along with a normalized weight vector for each worker, where each weight indicates relevance to the worker. Snow *et al.* [27] demonstrated that by using an automatic bias correction algorithm, MTurk can be used effectively for a variety of natural language annotation tasks. Lin *et al.* [17] took a decision-theoretic approach to estimating the correct answer for a task that can have a countably infinite number of possible answers. Ertekin *et al.* [12] presented an algorithm that works in an online fashion to produce a weighted combination of a subset's votes that approximates the crowd's opinion. Oyama *et al.* [22] investigated the use of not only crowdsourced annotations, but also annotators' self-reported confidence scores. These works focused on single-label estimation.

In the multi-label domain, Duan *et al.* [10] proposed a method for estimating multiple true labels for each repeatedly multi-labeled instance, with flexible incorporation of label dependency into the label-generation process. Nowak *et al.* [20] studied inter-annotator agreement for multi-label

[10]http://www.mturk.com
[11]http://crowdflower.com

image annotation. They found that using the majority vote strategy to generate one annotation set from several responses can filter out noisy responses of non-experts to some extent.

Some research in the machine learning community addressed the problem of supervised learning directly from crowdsourced annotations. Sheng *et al.* [26] explored several methods for choosing which instances should get more labels and how to include label uncertainty information when training classifiers. Donmez *et al.* [9] proposed simultaneously estimating annotator accuracies and training a classifier using annotator responses to actively select the next instance for annotating.

7. CONCLUSION

We investigated multi-emotion estimation from crowdsourced annotations, where an instance (such as a narrative line, a movie clip, or a music piece) can be associated with a combination of multiple emotion categories. The original domain-independent multi-label estimation model ignored the internal relationships among instances and among labels. To improve the accuracy, we extended it to specify those two relationships as the domain-specific information by making use of the characteristics of emotion, the *emotional consistencies* across instances, and the *contextual cues* among emotions. An EM-based incremental algorithm was devised for estimating the gold standard emotion annotation for each narrative line together with the model parameters. The objective was to determine how many crowdsourcing annotators have to provide annotations in the emotion labeling task in order for the aggregated annotation to be accurate. The experimental results demonstrate that incorporating *emotional consistencies* across instances enables the gold standard, i.e., the general consensus of large crowds, to be effectively estimated from the responses of a limited number (about five) of annotators. They also demonstrate that incorporating *contextual cues* among emotions improves the accuracy.

Emotion annotations are important metadata for narrative texts in digital libraries and emotion-oriented research. The annotation quality directly affects the quality of the research. Collecting high-quality annotations from both experts and large crowds can be expensive and time-consuming. The proposed models enable the cost of preparing high-quality annotations for emotion-oriented research to be reduced, with minimal degradation in the quality of the results.

Our exploration of this human computation issue produced promising results that encourage us to overcome the limitations of our present work and continue our study in this area. We plan to enhance our research efforts in several ways. First, our experiments were conducted on a small dataset, two children's narratives. We plan to explore whether the proposed models are also accurate for larger datasets. Second, *bi-grams* were used to learn the transition distribution over conjoint-emotions. It would be worth investigating whether *tri-grams* or higher *n-grams* yield better results, especially when dealing with larger contexts. Third, every instance was annotated by an equal number of annotators. However, for simple instances, few (one or two) annotators may be sufficient. This means that taking into account instance difficulty could further reduce preparation cost. We thus plan to design an effective mechanism for automatically identifying the difficulties of instances, such as using the annotators' annotation histories and the time needed for annotating an instance.

Our proposed models are for estimating the gold standard for crowdsourcing tasks that implicitly contain information for "consistency" and "context". This general idea may also be applicable to tasks such as art style annotation (music composers and movie directors generally have distinctive styles, which generally remains consistent in their works), *parts of speech* tagging (a word's tag may depend on the tags of neighboring words), and social network analysis (a text message and the replies often have consistent emotional tendency, and the feelings of a poster and repliers may have contextual cues). We plan to perform more experiments to test the feasibility and validity of the proposed models across different domains.

Acknowledgements

This work was supported in part by JSPS KAKENHI 24650061.

8. REFERENCES

[1] C. O. Alm. Characteristics of high agreement affect annotation in text. In *Proceedings of the Fourth Linguistic Annotation Workshop (LAW)*, pages 118–122. Association for Computational Linguistics, 2010.

[2] C. O. Alm, D. Roth, and R. Sproat. Emotions from text: Machine learning for text-based emotion prediction. In *Proceedings of the Conference on Human Language Technology and Empirical Methods in Natural Language Processing (HLT/EMNLP)*, pages 579–586. Association for Computational Linguistics, 2005.

[3] L. F. Barrett, B. Mesquita, K. N. Ochsner, and J. J. Gross. The experience of emotion. *Annual Review of Psychology*, 58:373, 2007.

[4] K. Bischoff, C. S. Firan, W. Nejdl, and R. Paiu. How do you feel about dancing queen?: deriving mood & theme annotations from user tags. In *Proceedings of the 9th ACM/IEEE-CS Joint Conference on Digital libraries*, pages 285–294. ACM, 2009.

[5] R. A. Calvo and S. D'Mello. Affect detection: An interdisciplinary review of models, methods, and their applications. *Affective Computing, IEEE Transactions on*, 1(1):18–37, 2010.

[6] C. Chow and C. Liu. Approximating discrete probability distributions with dependence trees. *Information Theory, IEEE Transactions on*, 14(3):462–467, 1968.

[7] A. P. Dawid and A. M. Skene. Maximum likelihood estimation of observer error-rates using the em algorithm. *Applied Statistics*, pages 20–28, 1979.

[8] M. d. R. D. Dias, S. d. S. B. L. d. Faria, S. C. M. Ibrahim, et al. I'm like a river: a health education instrument for stuttering. *Revista de Psicologia da IMED*, 5(2), 2013.

[9] P. Donmez, J. G. Carbonell, and J. Schneider. Efficiently learning the accuracy of labeling sources for selective sampling. In *Proceedings of the 15th ACM SIGKDD International Conference on Knowledge Discovery and Data Mining*, pages 259–268. ACM, 2009.

[10] L. Duan, S. Oyama, H. Sato, and M. Kurihara. Separate or joint? estimation of multiple labels from crowdsourced annotations. *Expert Systems with Applications*, 41(13):5723–5732, 2014.

[11] P. Ekman. An argument for basic emotions. *Cognition & Emotion*, 6(3-4):169–200, 1992.

[12] S. Ertekin, C. Rudin, and H. Hirsh. Approximating the crowd.

[13] J. Howe. Crowdsourcing: A definition. *Crowdsourcing: Tracking the Rise of the Mmateur*, 2006.

[14] X. Hu and J. S. Downie. Improving mood classification in music digital libraries by combining lyrics and audio. In *Proceedings of the 10th annual Joint Conference on Digital libraries*, pages 159–168. ACM, 2010.

[15] S. Kim, F. Li, G. Lebanon, and I. Essa. Beyond sentiment: The manifold of human emotions. *International Conference on Artificial Intelligence and Statistics (AISTATS)*, pages 360–369, 2013.

[16] J. H. Lee and X. Hu. Generating ground truth for music mood classification using mechanical turk. In *Proceedings of the 12th ACM/IEEE-CS Joint Conference on Digital Libraries*, pages 129–138. ACM, 2012.

[17] C. H. Lin, Mausam, and D. S. Weld. Crowdsourcing control: Moving beyond multiple choice. In *Proceedings of the 28th Conference on Uncertainty in Artificial Intelligence (UAI). Catalina Island, CA, USA. August 2012*, pages 491–500, 2012.

[18] Z. Liu, S. Wang, Z. Wang, and Q. Ji. Implicit video multi-emotion tagging by exploiting multi-expression relations. In *Automatic Face and Gesture Recognition (FG), 2013 10th IEEE International Conference and Workshops on*, pages 1–6. IEEE, 2013.

[19] A. Nakamura. Kanjo hyogen jiten [dictionary of emotive expressions]. *Tokyodo*, 1993.

[20] S. Nowak and S. Rüger. How reliable are annotations via crowdsourcing: a study about inter-annotator agreement for multi-label image annotation. In *Proceedings of the International Conference on Multimedia Information Retrieval*, pages 557–566. ACM, 2010.

[21] C. K. Ogden and I. A. Richards. The meaning of meaning. *New York*, 1923.

[22] S. Oyama, Y. Baba, Y. Sakurai, and H. Kashima. Accurate integration of crowdsourced labels using workers' self-reported confidence scores. In *Proceedings of the Twenty-Third International Joint Conference on Artificial Intelligence (IJCAI)*, pages 2554–2560. AAAI Press, 2013.

[23] M. Ptaszynski, H. Dokoshi, S. Oyama, R. Rzepka, M. Kurihara, K. Araki, and Y. Momouchi. Affect analysis in context of characters in narratives. *Expert Systems with Applications*, 40(1):168–176, 2013.

[24] J. A. Russell and J. M. Fernández-Dols. *The Psychology of Facial Expression*. Cambridge university press, 1997.

[25] M. A. M. Shaikh, A. R. F. Rebordao, and K. Hirose. Improving tts synthesis for emotional expressivity by a prosodic parameterization of affect based on linguistic analysis. In *Proceedings of the 5th International Conference on Speech Prosody (SP5)*, 2010.

[26] V. S. Sheng, F. Provost, and P. G. Ipeirotis. Get another label? improving data quality and data mining using multiple, noisy labelers. In *Proceedings of the 14th ACM SIGKDD International Conference on Knowledge Discovery and Data Mining*, pages 614–622. ACM, 2008.

[27] R. Snow, B. O'Connor, D. Jurafsky, and A. Y. Ng. Cheap and fast—but is it good? evaluating non-expert annotations for natural language tasks. In *Proceedings of the Conference on Empirical Methods in Natural Language Processing*, pages 254–263. Association for Computational Linguistics, 2008.

[28] A. Sorokin and D. Forsyth. Utility data annotation with amazon mechanical turk. *Urbana*, 51(61):820, 2008.

[29] K. Trohidis, G. Tsoumakas, G. Kalliris, and I. P. Vlahavas. Multi-label classification of music into emotions. In *International Society for Music Information Retrieval (ISMIR)*, volume 8, pages 325–330, 2008.

[30] G. Tsoumakas, I. Katakis, and I. Vlahavas. Mining multi-label data. In *Data Mining and Knowledge Discovery Handbook*, pages 667–685. Springer, 2010.

[31] P. Wellnder, S. Branson, P. Perona, and S. J. Belongie. The multidimensional wisdom of crowds. In *Advances in Neural Information Processing Systems (NIPS)*, pages 2424–2432, 2010.

[32] J. Whitehill, T.-f. Wu, J. Bergsma, J. R. Movellan, and P. L. Ruvolo. Whose vote should count more: Optimal integration of labels from labelers of unknown expertise. In *Advances in Neural Information Processing Systems (NIPS)*, pages 2035–2043, 2009.

[33] S. C. Widen, J. A. Russell, and A. Brooks. Anger and disgust: Discrete or overlapping categories? In *2004 APS Annual Convention, Boston College, Chicago, IL*, 2004.

Debugging a Crowdsourced Task with Low Inter-Rater Agreement

Omar Alonso
Microsoft Corporation
omalonso@microsoft.com

Catherine C. Marshall
Texas A&M University
ccmarshall@cse.tamu.edu

Marc Najork*
Microsoft Corporation
najork@acm.org

ABSTRACT

In this paper, we describe the process we used to debug a crowdsourced labeling task with low inter-rater agreement. In the labeling task, the workers' subjective judgment was used to detect high-quality social media content—interesting tweets—with the ultimate aim of building a classifier that would automatically curate Twitter content. We describe the effects of varying the genre and recency of the dataset, of testing the reliability of the workers, and of recruiting workers from different crowdsourcing platforms. We also examined the effect of redesigning the work itself, both to make it easier and to potentially improve inter-rater agreement. As a result of the debugging process, we have developed a framework for diagnosing similar efforts and a technique to evaluate worker reliability. The technique for evaluating worker reliability, Human Intelligence Data-Driven Enquiries (HIDDENs), differs from other such schemes, in that it has the potential to produce useful secondary results and enhance performance on the main task. HIDDEN subtasks pivot around the same data as the main task, but ask workers questions with greater expected inter-rater agreement. Both the framework and the HIDDENs are currently in use in a production environment.

Categories and Subject Descriptors

H.1.2 [Models and Principles]: User/Machine Systems—*Human information processing*

General Terms

Design, Experimentation, Human Factors

Keywords

Crowdsourcing; labeling; inter-rater agreement; relevance judgment; debugging; Captchas; worker reliability

1. INTRODUCTION

Researchers and practitioners often rely on crowdsourcing as a quick and inexpensive means to produce labeled data sets. Labeled corpora may serve a range of functions: they may be used to train and evaluate machine learning algorithms; they may be used as reference datasets for implementing and evaluating information retrieval techniques; and they can aid in the curation of large information resources. In essence, labels are important metadata for systematically classifying and describing heterogeneous items. Thus care must be taken to ensure the crowdsourced labels are as high-quality as the metadata assigned by experts [1].

Assigning a label is usually considered a judgment task, where the judgments may be more or less subjective. A judgment on the objective end of the spectrum may suggest a single right answer, so we can rely on a single worker or a small number of workers to accurately label an item. If the judgment is more subjective, we might ask more workers the question, and use consensus or some other method of aggregation to determine a best-choice label.

We are focusing on labeling tasks in which the judgment is at the subjective end of the spectrum. These tasks can be thought of more like polling: although inter-rater agreement may not be high, the label choice should be replicable across groups of workers as long as the workers are diverse, reliable, and consistent in their judgments and the datasets can be adequately characterized to show their similarities and differences. In other words, if the same type of crowd labels the same type of data, the outcome will be predictable. Yet tasks with low inter-rater agreement are problematic to debug. If the judgments are more subjective, it may be difficult to tell whether the workers are indeed reliable (e.g. there is no gold set or consensus answer with which to vet their performance) or whether problems have been properly diagnosed and eliminated before the labeling process is scaled and put into a production environment.

In this paper, we'll address two research questions intrinsic to crowdsourced labeling tasks with low inter-rater agreement:

- Can we develop an effective way of debugging such a crowdsourced labeling task?
- How can we determine that the workers are performing this type of labeling task in good faith?

The example labeling application that has driven the investigation we describe in this paper is identifying high-quality content in a socially-produced feed. Specifically, we are asking workers to identify interesting tweets from a dataset that represents the contents of the high volume Twitter feed. Once a set of tweets can be reliably labeled as interesting (or not interesting), it can be used to train and evaluate a classifier that works on the entirety of the feed.

Naturally, what constitutes an interesting tweet is variable and relies on the judges' perceptions; we can think of it as a question at the subjective end of the range. Yet the ability to identify and label high-quality socially produced content has practical value.

JCDL'15, June 21–25, 2015, Knoxville, Tennessee, USA.

DOI: http://dx.doi.org/10.1145/2756406.2757741

---

* Author is now at Google.

For example, consider the use case of identifying and covering a news story via selection of interesting tweets. Predictive features have already been used to identify tweets at the other end of the value spectrum (uninteresting tweets) with similar applications in mind [2]. The next challenge is to extract sufficient signal to label interesting tweets. Alonso, Marshall, and Najork began that process by testing aspects of the data and workers, and by building a classifier whose performance may be improved [3].

Figure 1 shows our two-phase model. In the figure, information is represented as boxes and functions as labeled arcs. In Phase 1, the focus of this paper, the dataset we start with consists of a representative portion of the data that will eventually be processed via Phase 2. One or more judges assigns a label (usually from a constrained set of possibilities) to each item from the dataset. Since judge characteristics (e.g. expertise, interests) and item characteristics (e.g. topic, provenance) may influence label production, the degree to which the judgments vary depends on both. This variability (i.e. differences in judges' assessment of which label is appropriate for an item) may be addressed by developing an aggregation method that resolves the differences. For example, some aggregation methods rely on worker consensus. Others might use the labels assigned by the most reliable workers. In Phase 2 of the process, a portion of the labeled items are reserved to form a *holdout set*. The rest, the labeled training set, are used by a machine learning algorithm to produce a model that predicts labels based on item characteristics. The holdout set can thus be compared with the predictions to evaluate how well the model captures the judges' assessments.

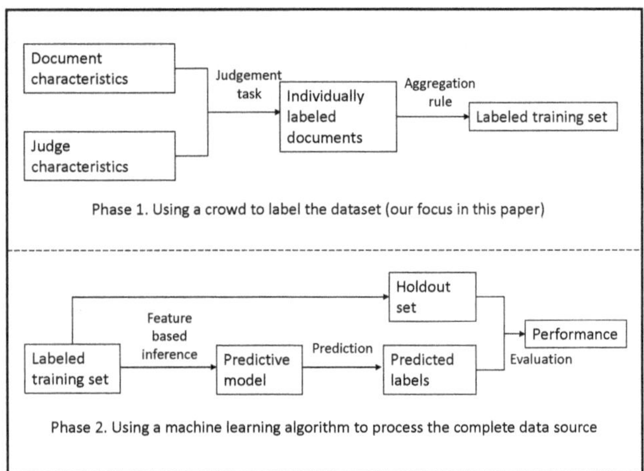

Figure 1. A two-phase model of labeling documents and assessing the performance of a classifier that uses the labels.

This paper will first consider related work. Then we will present a series of investigations designed to debug our labeling task. The debugging process accounts for the workers, the datasets they are labeling, and the design of the template they use to perform the work. We will also describe a promising technique to vet the workers' reliability and improve their task performance. We will conclude by discussing some avenues for future work, especially the evaluation of the techniques we developed during the course of the research presented in this paper.

2. RELATED WORK

Three types of related work informed our effort: (1) using crowdsourcing to evaluate content quality, including such efforts in the TREC community; (2) improving the crowdsourcing process by applying techniques for crowdsourcing at scale and for validating worker reliability; and (3) developing techniques to address low inter-rater agreement. We discuss each in turn.

Evaluating content quality. This work aims to identify high-quality content in very short documents, especially tweets and comments. André, Bernstein, and Luther [4] rely on self-selected volunteers to rate tweets from accounts that they follow to characterize worthwhile tweets. We are similarly trying to identify interesting tweets; however, we are ultimately concerned with identifying predictive features so that the process can be scaled to evaluate tweets in near real-time. Momeni et al. use a crowdsourcing approach to label a set of useful comments against which to build a classifier [14]. Although TREC ranking algorithms estimate a tweet's relevance to a query, some of the features identified by Metzler and Cai [13] are similar to interestingness features used by Alonso, Marshall, and Najork [3], work that is the basis for ours. Alonso et al. have taken a related subtractive approach by identifying tweets that are not interesting [2]. Like Lin, Etzioni, and Fogarty [11], we began by looking for consensus on what is interesting, although our crowd has a more diverse view on what constitutes interestingness; we are building on these results to understand if we can harness this diversity and work with the reduced level of inter-rater agreement in labeling.

Crowdsourcing techniques. Crowdsourcing at scale has been the focus of recent workshops and conversations [8]. Because we are planning to use our technique in production, we have paid particular attention to work that considers experimentation as the first step to scaling up [3]. Worker reliability has been a focus of von Ahn, Blum, and Langford's Captcha research [17]. Captcha-like techniques were introduced to crowdsourced user studies by Kittur, Chi, and Suh [9]. Because user studies tend to involve more effort per Human Intelligence Task (HIT) than labeling tasks, we have taken a variant approach to ensuring worker reliability; this approach is described in Section 4.2.

Addressing low inter-rater agreement. Much of the related work uses inter-rater agreement to label content. What is an acceptable minimum signal upon which to base a binary classifier? Alonso, Marshall, and Najork were only able to achieve moderate agreement (Fleiss's $\kappa = 0.51$) between crowd-labeled tweets and a classifier [3]. Our work ultimately strives to increase classification accuracy by improving label quality; the first step in this process is to productively use low inter-rater agreement. Aroyo and Welty have investigated a technique for productively using disagreement among judges [5]; like them, we are exploring a crowdsourcing task in which we do not expect consensus labels. Others cope with low inter-rater agreement in the data cleaning process, for example, by removing items that cannot be labeled through consensus [16]; we are attempting to develop a process that will allow us to retain the entire signal.

3. APPROACH

Our overall approach involves rapid iteration of labeling tasks using small datasets, from 100 to 2,500 tweets, each judged by 5 workers; because we are focused on debugging the labeling process, we have decreased the dataset size to make it practical to test different aspects of the dataset, the workers, and the task itself. Most trends we are interested in are observable by comparing these results; otherwise it would be costly and slow to test combinations of multiple factors to pinpoint the source(s) of low inter-rater agreement (e.g. dataset recency or the question we are asking the workers). Once this technique is refined, we can begin testing it at scale. Figure 2 shows our general approach to structuring the investigation. The circles in the top part of the diagram identify the portion of the work we are varying; the boxes along the bottom specify individual debugging exercises. Each debugging exercise may involve multiple datasets.

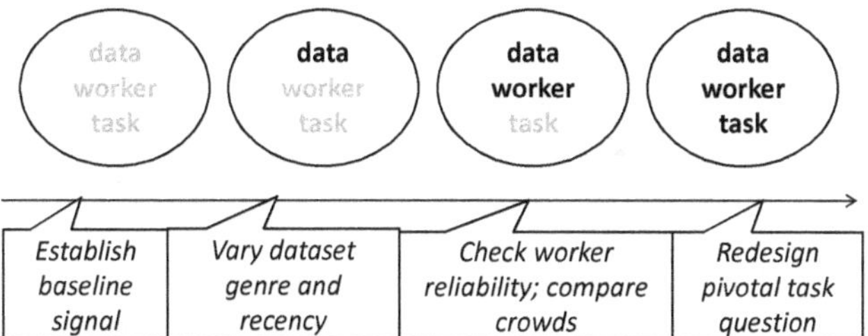

Figure 2. Structure, strategy, and flow for debugging a crowdsourced task with low inter-rater agreement.

For each investigation, we circulated and discussed a report summarizing the cumulative results, including the performance of individual judges, the outcome of subtasks, significant or surprising results, the level of inter-rater agreement using the measure described above, and other variations in the experiment. Examining the cumulative results each time allowed us to compare the factors we varied between individual runs.

We go on to describe specific aspects of our approach to debugging, including preparing the many datasets we used, discussing the difference in the crowdsourcing platforms, how we measured agreement, and how we established a baseline that represents our real task, judging the interestingness of tweets.

Preparing the datasets. Fourteen datasets were used to test each aspect of the flow described in Figure 2, and two additional datasets were used to set baseline worker agreement values and interest level. All datasets were sampled from the Twitter firehose, and filtered according to the needs of the investigation. For example, news tweets were filtered from random tweets according to the account issuing the tweet and the tweet's date.

Necessarily this process suggests we use a large number of small datasets to compare the effects of different factors on inter-rater agreement, and to identify the sources that might be influencing the outcome. As we progressed through the process described in Figure 2, we sometimes increased the number of factors that we compared to resolve their individual effects. After we became confident we understood a particular effect, we could once again eliminate a particular factor from the process and return to our original goal of identifying interesting tweets from a dataset of random tweets. Table 1 describes the sixteen datasets used in the debugging process. We will remind the reader of what the datasets contain when we present individual results; Table 1 just shows the lay of the land. Datasets B1-B2 were drawn to set a baseline; G1-G3 were drawn to test changes in the dataset contents; W1-W7 were drawn to test worker reliability and expertise; and T1-T4 were drawn to test the task design.

dataset IDs	tweets	genre	date (relative to task)
B1	2,000	random	Two months prior to task
B2	2,000	random	Recent
G1	2,500	news	Two years prior to task
G2	2,500	news	One year prior to task
G3	2,500	news	Recent
W1, W2, W5, T1	100	news	Recent
W3, W6, T2	100	news	One year prior to task
W4, W7,T3	100	news	Two years prior to task
T4	100	random	Two years prior to task

Table 1. Datasets used in the debugging process. In all cases, each tweet was judged by 5 workers, so 100 tweets yields 500 labels. The dataset IDs correspond to each debugging phase.

Datasets B1 and B2, each containing 2,000 random tweets, were used to establish a 10,000 judgment baseline. Datasets G1, G2, and G3, each containing 2,500 tweets, were used to test effects of both genre (specifically news) and recency. After we noticed recency effects from the baseline set, we drew subsequent datasets that were either contemporaneous with the task, or one or two years old. Datasets W1 through W7, each containing 100 tweets, were used to test the effects of worker reliability and expertise. Finally, datasets T1 through T4, each containing 100 tweets, were used to test the effects of a new task design.

Crowdsourcing platforms. To test the influence of platform during our debugging process, we recruited workers from two different platforms: a Microsoft-internal crowdsourcing platform which specializes in relevance judgments (UHRS) and Amazon Mechanical Turk (AMT). Workers were paid according to the market rate on each; workers are paid relatively more on UHRS than they are on AMT because of the presumed expertise of UHRS workers. On AMT, we used recognized best practices, and required that workers had 97% past success and had completed at least 50 past tasks; this tends to eliminate most spammers. UHRS has no equivalent ability to set worker qualifications; thus we vetted the workers by blocking spammers as they appeared. Tasks were monitored when they were underway to ensure that workers understood the instructions and were able to use the templates to label the collections. Unless we otherwise specify, the tasks were done by UHRS workers.

Measuring agreement. Obtaining trusted data is vital to our approach. Because we expect to run crowdsourcing jobs continuously, it is important to show that the data produced by each step is reliable. We rely on a standard measure of inter-rater agreement, Krippendorff's α, which produces values between 1 and -1. A value of 1 indicates perfect agreement among workers, a value of 0 suggests that workers may be assigning labels randomly. A negative value further indicates that disagreements are systematic. The literature on inter-rater reliability provides recommendations on cutoffs for data to be considered reliable. Values above 0.8 suggest that the judges are in almost perfect agreement whereas values between 0.61 and 0.8 suggest substantial agreement. Lower values indicate progressively less agreement and hence lower reliability. In Section 4, we report values for the disaggregation of interest at the ends of the spectrum ("worthless" and "important"; see Table 7, T1) that fall under the rubric of fair agreement. Many of the values for inter-rater agreement in this paper suggest only slight agreement. It is this problem—how to pinpoint the source of low agreement values—that we address in this paper. Krippendorff's α is capable of handling datasets where the number of raters per item varies, which is the case for some of the label sets we produced. Generally, inter-rater agreement will be higher when there are fewer categories to choose from; in our investigations, we are asking workers to make binary judgments.

Establishing a baseline. Before we started running debugging probes, we needed to set a baseline for worker performance. This baseline used datasets B1 and B2, each containing 2,000 random tweets (drawn from the Twitter firehose, as we explain above). Each dataset was used to establish a 10,000 judgment baseline. Recall that B2's tweets were recent and B1's were older. As we discovered earlier [3], random tweets vary in quality and topic. However, a tweet that looks obviously worthless to us might match an individual judge's interests in a completely subjective way. For example, in earlier investigations, when asked about brief cryptic tweet, a judge who labeled it as *Interesting* explained that it was recent gossip about Kim Kardashian (who was referred to in the tweet by a nickname none of us were aware of), and that he or she loved Kim Kardashian. It is easy to see why inter-rater agreement on random tweets might be low.

Figure 3 shows an annotated version of our baseline task for judging tweets. The judges were given brief instructions about the judgment, but no further definition of interesting. They were asked if the tweet—as it was shown—was interesting to a broad audience.

Paul Allen offers up $8M for artificial intelligence researchers to uncover 'world-changing breakthroughs': geekwire.com/2014/paul-alle...

Q1. Do you think the tweet is interesting to a broad audience?

○ Yes
○ No

Figure 3. Sample baseline task for judging tweets. A tweet is displayed and the main judgment question is posed.

Table 2 shows the results from our two baseline tasks. The percentages have been averaged over all 10,000 judgments. Krippendorff's α expresses inter-rater agreement. We compute % interesting by using majority vote.

	B1 (older, random)	B2 (recent, random)
% interesting	16.7%	14.3%
Krippendorff's α	0.013	0.052

Table 2. Baseline values for 5 workers labeling random tweets.

In our baseline case, the age of the tweets appears to have little influence on the overall level of interest that the judges express.

4. RESULTS

In this section, we will discuss the results of each set of explorations, with the ultimate aim of both debugging this particular tweet labeling task before we scale it, as well as developing a reliable debugging process in general. The general debugging process is an important research outcome for us.

As Figure 2 suggests, our first variations were aimed at discovering whether we could elicit higher agreement by narrowing the data genre to news. In other words, was it the nature of the task that elicited such low agreement, or was it the type of data we were using?

We then turned our attention to the workers: because the judgment task is subjective, a gold set or agreement can't be used to validate the workers' labels. So we needed to develop a different type of method to evaluate the quality of their work. Because regular quality checks produce so much drag (they are creating more work for the workers), we were also interested in using this method to not just evaluate their work, but also to improve the quality of their work.

Finally, we scrutinized the task design: would a user-centered process of label assignment, one that considered different emotional components of what made something interesting, reduce the task's cognitive load as well as improve inter-rater agreement?

4.1 Effects of changing the dataset

Our first area to debug was the effects of dataset genre: would limiting the dataset to recent news tweets improve inter-rater agreement? Knowing this effect helps set our expectations for the results of our interestingness question. In other words, is our low inter-rater agreement the result of the subjectivity of the question, or does it stem from the quality of the data?

Although people have differing levels of interest in some types of news stories, we thought it likely that the workers would agree that some stories were of more universal importance. Thus for our first investigation, we extracted tweets from ten recognized top US newspapers, news services, and broadcast news: the *Los Angeles Times* (*@latimes*), Reuters newswire (*@reuters*), the *New York Times* (*@nytimes*), the *Wall Street Journal* (*@WSJ*), *USA Today* (*@USATODAY*), the *Washington Post* (*@washingtonpost*), the *Christian Science Monitor* (*@csmonitor*), ABC News (*@ABC*), Bloomberg News (*@BloombergNews*), and BBC News (*@BBCNews*). Because our baseline measurements suggested that the age of the tweets may influence workers' assessment, we drew 2,500 random news tweets for a date contemporaneous with the task, and dates one and two years older.

Genre. Table 3 compares the results of judging a recent news dataset with the agreement and interestingness of the recent baseline dataset of random tweets. Again, each tweet was judged by 5 workers. Although there are more than twice as many tweets judged to be interesting in the recent tweets, the inter-rater agreement shows relatively little improvement. Genre thus may have less effect than we had thought it might.

	B2 (recent, random)	G3 (recent news)
% interesting	14.3%	29.3%
Krippendorff's α	0.052	0.068

Table 3. Comparison of inter-rater agreement for baseline (recent random tweets) and news tweets.

Recency. We might think recency would have a more profound effect on news tweets than it did on our baseline random tweets, since the interestingness of news stories decays quickly. Table 4 compares three datasets of news tweets, G1, G2, and G3. G1 is the oldest of the news datasets (the tweets are two years old relative to when the task was put out for judgment). G2 contains one year old tweets and G3 contains tweets contemporaneous with the task. B1 is the non-recent baseline random tweets. We can see that the old news tweets become less interesting over time, but that there's still slightly better inter-rater agreement on which ones are interesting. There is also a decrease in inter-rater agreement, but it is not as profound as we expected it to be.

The genre constraint did not improve inter-rater agreement as much as we had expected. Thus we have to believe the fault lies with either the workers or the question itself.

	B1	G1 (oldest)	G2	G3 (recent)
% interesting	16.7%	21.3%	27.8%	29.3%
Krippendorff's α	0.013	0.037	0.074	0.068

Table 4. Effect of dataset age on interestingness and on inter-rater agreement.

4.2 Checking worker reliability and expertise

Our debugging efforts next shifted to the workers: were they continuing to pay attention as they judged tweet after tweet? Would we see better performance on one crowdsourcing platform than another? The crowdsourcing literature urges us to focus on the quality of worker output as a likely culprit when the results don't meet expectations. Unreliable performance, either as a result of fatigue, frustration, carelessness, lack of requisite expertise, or out-and-out fraud needs to be ruled out as part of our debugging process. But how could we eliminate poor quality work without a gold set to spot-check workers' performance or high inter-rater agreement to identify normative answers?

Worker reliability. To assess workers' reliability, we drew on two existing forms of worker checks, attention checks and memory checks. Attention checks ensure crowdsourced user studies are completed in good faith [9]. Workers are periodically asked unrelated questions to test whether they are still paying attention. Clever attention checks may also engender good will between worker and requestor [12]. Unlike attention checks, which are not task-related, memory checks evaluate reading comprehension. Although both checks address worker reliability, adaptation was necessary to make them suitable to our needs, since our HIT content varied, and our microtasks were much smaller than a conventional user study that employs memory checks.

Thus we supplemented the checks with the notion of reCaptchas [18], in which spam detection relies on the results of a useful microtask, such as OCR correction [17]. Successful completion of a reCaptcha makes it likely that a real human is at the keyboard and has the beneficial side effect of completing useful work for some ancillary task. We also added a third goal, improving data quality, since we were adding drag to the process by significantly increasing the size of the task. Thus, instead of being unrelated to the HIT content, the additional microtasks were designed to focus the workers' attention on the tweets they were about to judge. We call these specialized within-task reCaptchas Human Intelligence Data-Driven Enquiries (HIDDENs). HIDDENs allowed us to assess task performance in the absence of a gold set and achieved two quality-related goals:

1. To complete the judgment task, workers had to read the tweet three times, attending to different aspects of the short post for each microtask (first, its topic; second, whether it was about a specific person; and finally the original judgment task). The design goal was to avoid distracting the worker from the primary task; instead the each part built up to assigning the label.
2. Each of the embedded questions was designed to represent increasing levels of subjectivity. The first question we asked was objective and computable; the second was less objective, relying on worker agreement to determine an acceptable answer; and the third was our original more subjective judgment task.

Specifically in our initial implementation of HIDDENs, the first embedded microtask asked workers to count the tweet's hashtags. Although this is computable, it required workers to read the tweet a first time (albeit superficially). The second embedded microtask, assessing whether a tweet was about a specific person (i.e. contained a proper noun that was a person's name), required additional thought. Instructions specified that the name could neither be an account name (@name), nor a hashtag (#name). Figure 4 shows the resulting task template.

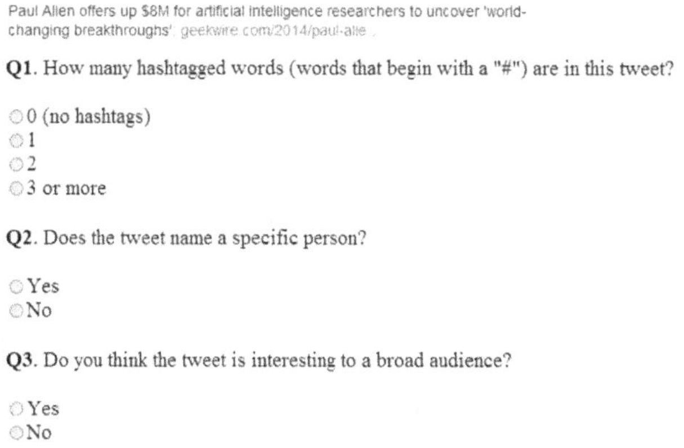

Paul Allen offers up $8M for artificial intelligence researchers to uncover 'world-changing breakthroughs' geekwire.com/2014/paul-alle...

Q1. How many hashtagged words (words that begin with a "#") are in this tweet?

○ 0 (no hashtags)
○ 1
○ 2
○ 3 or more

Q2. Does the tweet name a specific person?

○ Yes
○ No

Q3. Do you think the tweet is interesting to a broad audience?

○ Yes
○ No

Figure 4. Task template with HIDDENs (Q1 and Q2). Q3 is the original judgment question shown in Figure 3.

Q1 relies only on characteristics of the tweet; Q2 relies on the worker's knowledge (e.g., being aware that Mubarak is a person, not a place); and Q3 is our original judgment question. We anticipated high agreement on the first subtask (otherwise the worker was suspect, either because he or she wasn't paying close attention to the task or because he or she wasn't consulting the tweet). We expected good agreement on the second, depending on the breadth of a worker's awareness. The HIDDENs allowed us to evaluate worker reliability in the absence of a gold set and gave a way to assess the individual worker's attentiveness and skill. Repeated anomalies in Q1's answer across workers may reveal problems in the dataset (e.g. a hashtag that's part of an emoticon) or can inform dataset analytics. Because Q2 relies on some expertise, its results can be useful to a colleague, or may be used to perform a related task (this way work can be interlocked, so spam detection on one task can provide useful results for another). By design, Q1, Q2, and Q3 are tied together by the single piece of content being judged.

Table 5 shows the results of the first investigations that used the HIDDENs. Both W1 and W2 contained 100 current news tweets. The rows labeled ***all*** contain the results of all the judgments; the rows labeled ***cleaned*** use the performance on Q1 to remove workers with accuracy of under 0.9. Agreement on Q1 (counting hashtags) was high across both labeling investigations. Q2 (finding names) elicited expectedly less agreement, but higher than the main task (judging tweet interestingness). Most importantly, removing the work of the judges whose accuracy on Q1 was below 0.9 did not improve agreement on Q2 and Q3. In other words, performance on the HIDDENs revealed that the workers were doing the task in good faith.

	W1 (news, recent)	W2 (news, recent)
Q1 α (all)	0.779	0.775
Q1 α (cleaned)	0.824	0.888
Q2 α (all)	0.722	0.734
Q2 α (cleaned)	0.731	0.708
Q3 α (all)	0.050	0.157
Q3 α (cleaned)	0.045	0.160

Table 5. Check of worker reliability using HIDDENs (Q1 and Q2). The rows labeled *cleaned* use the performance on Q1 to remove workers with accuracy of under 0.9.

There are several other phenomena of interest shown in Table 5. Removing the work of the judges who perform poorly on Q1 does not necessarily result in comparable performance improvements on Q2 (e.g. compare the ***all*** and ***cleaned*** columns for W2). Furthermore, the inter-rater agreement on Q1 and Q2 was roughly comparable (and high) for both datasets, but the performance on Q3 continued to show low inter-rater agreement and variability.

Comparing platforms to check expertise. Performance on Q2 suggests that it requires some expertise to do it correctly (in addition to attentiveness). In diagnosing the worker portion of our task, it seems wise to check the performance across platforms too. What would happen if we tried our task template plus HIDDENs (i.e. the template shown in Figure 4) on the AMT crowdsourcing platform? We would expect UHRS workers to perform better on Q2 (their specialty in relevance judgment would suggest they have the broad knowledge Q2 requires). Using different crowdsourcing platforms also allowed us to further explore the efficacy of the HIDDEN technique.

Table 6 documents this cross-platform comparison. All datasets consist of news tweets, drawn from different periods. As in the other tasks, each tweet has been judged by 5 workers. The table does not exclude any workers based on their performance on the HIDDEN subtasks, so we can compare worst-case workers. The data from W1 and W2 in Table 5 has been carried forward to Table 6 for the sake of easy comparison.

The performance on the first two questions (Q1 and Q2) should tell us something about worker reliability (Q1) and expertise (Q2). Table 6 shows that inter-rater agreement is similar for Q1 on both platforms, ranging from 0.800 to 0.876 on AMT and from 0.775 to 0.882 on UHRS. The difference on Q1 is negligible; workers on both platforms must care about appearing reliable. Because Q2 requires more specialized knowledge—workers must not only follow instructions, they also had to be familiar with a range of world leaders, celebrities, and other newsmakers—we expected UHRS workers to perform better on Q2 (especially since they are routinely exposed to similar tasks). Table 6 shows this was by and large not the case. AMT workers mostly did as well or better.

The results on Q3 tell us more about worker diversity than about worker reliability; if the platform attracts more diverse workers, we might expect lower inter-rater agreement. Our expectations are borne out by the Krippendorff's α scores for Q3: AMT workers are likely to be more diverse (inter-rater agreement is lower for comparable datasets). Thus, for our purposes, we might evaluate specific trade-offs between the platforms depending on a project's goals; worker reliability on both platforms appears good.

	platform	Q1 α	Q2 α	% int	Q3 α
W1 (news, recent)	UHRS	0.779	0.772	43.8%	0.050
W2 (news, recent)	UHRS	0.775	0.734	57.0%	0.157
W3 (news, older)	UHRS	0.882	0.752	48.8%	0.157
W4 (news, oldest)	UHRS	0.819	0.774	53.4%	0.190
W5 (news, recent)	AMT	0.850	0.843	55.0%	0.105
W6 (news, older)	AMT	0.800	0.840	51.0%	0.030
W7 (news, oldest)	AMT	0.876	0.734	40.2%	0.085

Table 6. Comparison of workers from UHRS and AMT platforms. Krippendorff's α is used to assess inter-rater agreement. Percent judged interesting is also shown for Q3.

4.3 Redesigning the task

Now that we have established that inter-rater agreement is not significantly improved by changes in the dataset or by worker reliability or expertise, we turn our attention to the work itself: Is there a way of formulating the task and redesigning the template such that we can improve inter-rater agreement?

In our earliest efforts, we assumed that workers would reach consensus that a small subset of tweets were inherently interesting because they referred to global events, major celebrities, or culturally pervasive memes. But it proved to be difficult to judge tweets' interestingness out of context.

Could we render the task more accessible by breaking down this disembodied notion of interestingness? The psychology literature considers interestingness to be a complex human emotion [6]. Colton and Bundy tie interestingness to plausibility, novelty, surprisingness, comprehensibility, and complexity [6]; Silvia adds curiosity-provoking to that list, and suggests that reverse measures of these properties are useful for triangulation [15]. Although it was impractical to use this literature to fully disaggregate interestingness into its component parts, specific characteristics could be used to evaluate the efficacy of this approach in redesigning the task.

The trade-off was thus to ask six simpler questions in the place of one complex judgment (interesting or not?) with the hope that greater specificity would make the work easier to do and would improve inter-rater agreement. Workers were asked to make the six decisions independently (although in practice several were mutually exclusive and could be used for triangulation).

Using our interpretation of the interestingness literature, we gave workers the ability to specify whether each tweet is some combination of: (a) worthless, (b) trivial, (c) funny, (d) piquing my curiosity, (e) useful information; or (f) important news. Although these characteristics are not comprehensive, they may be ordered along a spectrum from negative (worthless) to positive (important news). They were incorporated in our existing template with the HIDDEN questions (Q1 and Q2) to vet the workers. Figure 5 shows the redesigned template. The new template design was tested against workers from AMT, since they performed well in our previous tests of worker reliability and expertise.

Paul Allen offers up $8M for artificial intelligence researchers to uncover 'world-changing breakthroughs': geekwire.com/2014/paul-alle...

Q1. How many hashtagged words (words that begin with a "#") are in this tweet?

○ 0 (no hashtags)
○ 1
○ 2
○ 3 or more

Q2. Does the tweet name a specific person?

○ Yes
○ No

Q3. Please check all the boxes that apply to this tweet

☐ Worthless
☐ Trivial
☐ Funny
☐ Makes me curious
☐ Contains useful information
☐ Important news

Figure 5. Redesigned task template showing HIDDENs (Q1 and Q2) and disaggregated interest characteristics (Q3).

Table 7 summarizes the results of testing the interestingness characteristics against four different datasets. T1 was the pilot for four investigations using the new task design; so we could compare it with other results, we began with a dataset of recent news tweets. T2 and T3 showed the workers older news tweets (comparable to W3 and W4 in Table 6); T4 returned to our original goal of having the workers judge random tweets; these again were old tweets. Aggregate values are computed by assigning each of the six Q3 characteristics a positive or negative value (worthless and trivial are -1; funny, curious, useful, and important are 1) and adding them together. If the value is greater than 0, the tweet is considered to be interesting. If the value is less than or equal to 0, the tweet is considered uninteresting. Krippendorff's α is calculated as it was in previous tables.

Question	T1 (news, recent)	T2 (news, older)	T3 (news, oldest)	T4 (random, oldest)
Q1	0.910	0.907	0.954	0.974
Q2	0.758	0.728	0.618	0.843
Q3 (aggregate)	0.137	0.063	0.014	0.088
Q3, worthless	0.384	0.033	0.045	-0.023
Q3, trivial	0.097	0.043	-0.061	0.025
Q3, funny	0.134	-0.016	0.169	0.049
Q3, curious	0.056	0.026	0.130	0.061
Q3, useful	0.079	0.048	0.014	0.160
Q3, important	0.314	0.207	0.000	0.170

Table 7. Krippendorff's α for four datasets after a task redesign based on a decomposition of interestingness (using concepts from [6] and [15]).

Workers performed well on the first HIDDEN subtask (counting hashtags) and acceptably on the second (identifying whether a person appeared in the tweet by name); inter-rater agreement for both HIDDEN subtasks was high. As we found in the last series of tests (see Table 5), eliminating the judgments of workers who performed poorly on the HIDDEN subtasks had minimal effect on inter-rater agreement, although this could mean that the HIDDENs had the desired effect of slowing the workers down and causing them to reflect on the tweets. We still believe this technique to be a useful addition to our arsenal of crowdsourcing tactics, especially since the HIDDEN subtasks are designed to produce useful secondary results.

Inter-rater agreement for the new decomposition of interestingness varied, depending on the age and genre of the tweets. For example, for T1 (fresh news tweets), both ends of the spectrum (worthless and important) elicited relatively high agreement. In between, agreement was lower. As the tweets aged, consistent with our other results, agreement also dropped. Interestingly, for very old news tweets (dataset T3), agreement was higher for those tweets that were *evergreen* (a journalistic term for stories that can be published at any time): funny tweets and those that provoked reader curiosity. On the other hand, the weakest signal appeared at the positive end of the spectrum, which tweets were useful or important. For random tweets (T4) inter-rater agreement was highest when workers were picking out important or useful tweets.

In other words, workers seemed to agree on the tweet characteristics that were in high contrast to the rest of the dataset. For current news, these would be the tweets that were most important and most worthless. For old news, this would be the tweets that were evergreen. Finally, the positive characteristics of old random tweets (tweets that were useful or important) stuck out against a sea of undistinguished content.

4.4 Effects of changing the task

To debug the crowdsourced labeling task, we made significant changes to three elements: the data, the workers, and the task design (see Figure 2). These adjustments all had effects on the task template, the work we asked the crowd to do. Our initial task template was simple; it displayed a tweet and posed the central question, "Do you think the tweet is interesting to a broad audience?" (see Figure 3). The next set of changes involved only the type of tweet the workers had to judge, in this case, tweets pulled from news sources. A subsequent change to the task template, the addition of HIDDENs, had a more profound effect on the work (see Figure 4). Finally, the disaggregation of interestingness characteristics into the task template shown in Figure 5 changed the work once again: for better or for worse, one judgment turned into six semi-independent judgments. (A tweet could be both trivial and worthless, or both important news and curiosity-provoking, for example).

We might expect this series of changes to the task template and the data characteristics to influence how long workers spent on an individual HIT. The aim of switching from random tweets to news was to improve the quality of the material the judges were working with (with the ultimate goal of improving inter-rater agreement). Thus we might expect the judges to spend more time pondering the relative merit of an individual tweet.

The HIDDENs implemented deliberate speed bumps. They were designed to slow the workers down and to cause them to read each tweet three times, each time with a different perspective. Although the HIDDENs were not difficult, we might expect them to add time to a worker's task performance.

The final change, the disaggregation of "interesting" into six characteristics might add a bit of drag to the work. But how much? The worker has more decisions to make (six times as many), but they should be easier decisions. We did not expect a significant change in the time spent on the task.

Table 8 compares the workers' times to perform the judgement task using the three task templates (the basic interestingness question, the template with the added HIDDENs, and the template with the disaggregated central judgment). We present a sensible progression of judgment tasks to illustrate the effects of the changes. Because the two crowdsourcing platforms may have minor differences in basic overhead (e.g. time to fetch and submit the HIT), we pivot on this change too. We use both average and median times (in seconds) to characterize task performance, specifically to compensate for some known variations in working style. Some workers are working as fast as they can; others are working against a backdrop of deliberate distractions like TV. We have chosen to use only the datasets of recent tweets in each case, just to eliminate one more factor that might influence judgment time. We refer to the judgment-only template shown in Figure 3 as "judgment only"; the template with the HIDDENs shown in Figure 4 is called "judgment+HIDDENs"; and the complete template shown in Figure 5 with disaggregated judgment and HIDDENs is called "HIDDENS+disagg". Although a few workers judging tweets in datasets B2 and G3 allowed the task to time out, there were sufficiently few who employed this strategy that it had minimal effect on the average or median times. Interestingly, once the judgments involved HIDDENS, no workers allowed the task to time out.

dataset	description: genre, platform, template	Avg. time/ tweet (sec.)	median time per tweet (sec.)
B2	random; UHRS; judgment only	2	1
G3	news; UHRS; judgment only	3	2
W1	news; UHRS; judgment+HIDDENS	14	11
W5	news, AMT, judgment+HIDDENS	18	13
T2	news, AMT, HIDDENS+dlsagg	26	18

Table 8. Comparison of time (in seconds) to perform judgment tasks using the three templates.

The values in Table 8 reveal several important differences. First, as we expected, it takes longer to judge higher quality content. A comparison of the values in rows B2 and G3 illustrates this difference: it might take almost twice as long to work with higher quality content. Once we shifted the focus to news tweets, it was no longer easy for workers to quickly discard tweets as uninteresting.

A comparison of the values in rows G3 and W1 gives us a sense of the magnitude of the speed bump we have introduced through the HIDDENs. Answering the two extra questions they pose more than triples the average time a worker spends on each HIT. Rather than seeming inefficient, this difference demonstrates that workers must read each tweet a little more carefully to complete the work. If the HIDDENs are well-designed—that is, they contribute to the overall data-related processing we want to do—they are worth the extra time they take. Workers should simply be paid somewhat more to undertake the redesigned task with the expectation that the quality of the work is improving.

The values in rows W1 and W5 represents the same work completed using different crowdsourcing platforms. Evidently it takes slightly (but not significantly) longer to complete the HIT using Amazon Mechanical Turk (AMT) than it does on Microsoft's internal crowdsourcing platform (UHRS). This difference could reflect simple bookkeeping differences (e.g. When does timing start? When does it end?) or network speed. In any event, the values look comparable using the two platforms.

How much does the expanded template—the version of the task that mandates six simple judgments in place of one complex subjective judgment—increase the time to perform the task? The values in row W5 and T2 help us sort out the answer to this question. To our surprise, while the final version of the template adds a bit of drag to the task, it does not increase it to an unworkably large extent. Again, considerations like this should be factored in to calculating a fair payment for the work.

Overall, the largest and most important difference is added by the introduction of the HIDDENs, which we hope will result in useful secondary data curation and produce higher-quality labels.

5. DISCUSSION

We set out to identify high quality tweets as an instance of an important problem: how to use the tremendous volume of socially produced content, much of it in the form of non-traditional documents. Tweets are very short and often cryptic; sometimes they make sense only to their immediate audience (the author's followers), and sometimes they can be presented to a much broader audience because they are perceived as interesting and important. Although there are social mechanisms for surfacing content in individual services, we are investigating a more general crowdsourced judgment process that is both timely and thorough. Initially we hoped to use a standard relevance judgment crowdsourcing process (which identifies the desired content through inter-rater agreement, and vets the workers by the degree to which their judgment aligns with their peers), but our experience demonstrated the need for a new way of handling this type of problem. Subjective assessment is key to working with socially produced data.

We have investigated a "data-workers-task design" process by varying each of these three crucial elements in turn to evaluate their influence. Our goal was to develop an effective way of debugging this type of crowdsourced labeling task, one with low inter-rater agreement. We also sought to develop a cost-effective and respectful way of vetting workers, since agreement with a norm was not going to be an effective way of assessing worker reliability and expertise.

5.1 A process for debugging

The key to our diagnostic process is to adjust each element in turn using small datasets. This allows us to try multiple combinations without worrying about whether to keep or discard the data; production runs are costly, and this technique enables us to debug the process beforehand.

Our first step was to pick detectable genres that are apt to yield a greater density of interesting content. If the interesting content is sparse and its overall utility is ambiguous, the task may begin to seem meaningless to the workers [3]. Although we ultimately intended to return to random tweets (since that is what the real data source consists of), switching to news tweets revealed that the low inter-rater agreement could not be attributed to the dataset.

Next we combined the news genre with worker-oriented changes: Were the workers working in good faith? We were aware that we were asking a subjective question, but it was the type of question that we needed to ask. Many questions about social media have to do with value, and labels associated with content value or relevance can be subjective. Furthermore, we were interested in finding out if it was necessary to use the expertise-rich UHRS crowdsourcing platform, or determining whether AMT's worker diversity was advantageous for our task. Answering this question about platforms enabled us to experiment without further burdening the more costly (and slower turn-around) resource.

Finally, we discovered that it was useful to redesign the task itself. In our example task, teasing apart what we meant by "interesting" can reduce the task's complexity (workers were asked to judge qualities that are psychological components of the higher-level emotional concept). It may be easier for a worker to say whether a tweet is funny or potentially useful, than it is to assess the content's overall interestingness. The interestingness literature suggests two other variations we have yet to try. The first is to ask the questions as a negative rather than a positive. Research in this area tells us it may be more straightforward to detect the absence of a characteristic rather than its presence [15]. In other words, it may be easier for workers to tell us that content is useless, than to say that it is useful, or that it is not funny, rather than funny. The characteristics worthless and trivial are examples of a negative approach, although aggregating these two qualities may prove to be more effective. Economics literature also suggests that we ask the question in a way to distance it from the individual's own judgment. In other words, it might be better to ask, "Will others find this content useful?" rather than asking, "Do you find this content useful?"

Although we focused on tweets as an example of a socially-produced data source and on interestingness as the judgment characteristic, we believe that other complex judgement concepts (e.g. value) can be similarly disaggregated.

5.2 HIDDENs

Our second goal was to develop a method for assessing worker reliability that:

(1) incorporates worker-independent judgments to achieve inter-rater agreement on a per-microtask basis;

(2) contributes to the main question we were asking (in other words, doing this extra work can improve label quality and will provide a single point of focus, the content under judgment);

(3) does not seem like a meaningless attention check to the workers (although the workers expect checks like this, they appreciate work that is more meaningful or is designed to recognize their humanness [12]); and

(4) produces useful results, possibly for a colleague, for follow-up research.

Recent crowdsourcing work has found that workers also like being given a HIT that's essentially a break in the action, a task that's just fun (e.g. read this cartoon), which gives them a chance to catch their breath and go back to the central work refreshed [7]. Although our current task design is not particularly entertaining, because workers do a lot of these judgment tasks, working quickly, this second type of break may prove to be useful.

To fully evaluate the HIDDENs, we need to establish whether the order that we ask the questions has any unanticipated effects: Would we get the same results if we asked the more difficult named entity detection task first? Are workers put off by the computability of the first task (counting a tweet's hashtags)? It would also be useful to develop other types of subtasks along a spectrum of subjective judgment and future utility.

6. CONCLUSION AND FUTURE WORK

Our data-workers-task design process has proven effective in rapid-turnaround debugging of a difficult labeling task. The HIDDEN technique also shows promise as an avenue for measuring worker reliability and potentially improving label quality. Finally, we are beginning to understand how to work within the confines of a more subjective question that depends on the judges' preferences and backgrounds.

In addition to the research we identified in the Discussion section, we are pursuing a more sophisticated incentive structure that will allow us to reward workers who are adept at predicting how their peers will label data. We are also investigating how the HIDDENs can draw reliability questions from a library of pre-categorized subtasks (that is, the subtasks must address the same data sources, and must either be somewhat objective, or subjective only to the extent that the answer can be readily determined by inter-rater agreement). Finally, we are drawing on multi-disciplinary literature to learn how to test the reliability of the data (labels) we are gathering. Taken together, advances in all of these areas will be an important step in improving access to social data, and in using subjective judgments in a variety of data-driven applications.

7. REFERENCES

[1] Alonso, O. Implementing Crowdsourcing-based Relevance Experimentation: An Industrial Perspective. *Information Retrieval*, 16(2), 2013, 101-120.

[2] Alonso, O., Carson, C., Gerster, D., Ji, X., and Nabar, S. Detecting Uninteresting Content in Text Streams. *Proceedings of CSE 2010*, 39-42.

[3] Alonso, O., Marshall, C. and Najork, M. Are Some Tweets More Interesting Than Others? #HardQuestion. *Proceedings of HCIR 2013*, pp. 2:1--2:10.

[4] André, P., Bernstein, M., and Luther, K. Who Gives a Tweet?: Evaluating Microblog Content Value. *Proceedings of CSCW 2012*, 471-474.

[5] Aroyo, L. and Welty, C. Harnessing Disagreement in Crowdsourcing a Relation Extraction Gold Standard. Tech. Rep. RC25371, IBM Research, 2013.

[6] Colton, S., Bundy, A., and Walsh, T. On the Notion of Interestingness in Automated Mathematical Discovery. *International Journal of Human-Computer Studies*, 53(3), 2000, 351-375.

[7] Dai, P., Rzeszotarski, J., Paritosh, P., and Chi, E. And Now for Something Completely Different: Improving Crowdsourcing Workflows with Micro-Diversions. *Proceedings of CSCW 2015*, 628-638.

[8] Josephy, T., Lease, M., and Paritosh, P. (Eds.). Crowdsourcing at Scale Workshop. *Proceedings of HCOMP 2013*.

[9] Kittur, A., Chi, E., Suh, B. Crowdsourcing user studies with Mechanical Turk. *Proceedings of CHI 2008*, 453-456.

[10] Krippendorff, K. *Content Analysis*. Sage, 2004.

[11] Lin, T., Etzioni, O., and Fogarty, J. Identifying Interesting Assertions from the Web. *Proceedings of CIKM 2008*, 1787-1790.

[12] Marshall, C.C. and Shipman, F.M. Experiences Surveying the Crowd: Reflections on Methods, Participation, and Reliability, *Proceedings of WebSci 2013*, 234-243.

[13] Metzler D. and Cai, C. USC/ISI at TREC 2011: Microblog track. *Proceedings of TREC 2011*.

[14] Momeni, E., Tao, K., Haslhofer, B., and Houben, G. Identification of Useful User Comments in Social Media: A Case Study on Flickr Commons. *Proceedings of JCDL 2013*, 1-10.

[15] Silvia, P. What is Interesting? Exploring the Appraisal Structure of Interest. *Emotion*, 5, 2005, 89-102.

[16] Sultan, M.A., Bethard, S., Sumner, T. Towards automatic identification of core concepts in educational resources. *Proceedings of JCDL 2014*, ACM, 379-388.

[17] von Ahn, L., Blum, M., and Langford, J. Telling Humans and Computers Apart Automatically. *CACM*, 47(2), 2004, 57-60.

[18] von Ahn, L., Maurer, B., McMillen, C., Abraham, D., and Blum, M. reCaptcha: Human-Based Character Recognition via Web Security Measures. *Science*, 321(5895), 2008, 1465-1468.

Why Do Social Media Users Share Misinformation?

Xinran Chen Sei-Ching Joanna Sin Yin-Leng Theng Chei Sian Lee
Wee Kim Wee School of Communication and Information
Nanyang Technological University, 31 Nanyang Link, Singapore 637718
(65) 6790 5966
{chen0872, joanna.sin, tyltheng, leecs}@ntu.edu.sg

ABSTRACT
Widespread misinformation on social media is a cause of concern. Currently, it is unclear what factors prompt regular social media users with no malicious intent to forward misinformation to their online networks. Using a questionnaire informed by the Uses and Gratifications theory and the literature on rumor research, this study asked university students in Singapore why they shared misinformation on social media. Gender differences were also tested. The study found that perceived information characteristics such as its ability to spark conversations and its catchiness were top factors. Self-expression and socializing motivations were also among the top reasons. Women reported a higher prevalence of misinformation sharing. The implications for the design of social media applications and information literacy training were discussed.

Categories and Subject Descriptors
J.4 [Computer Applications]: Social and Behavioral Sciences; H.3.5 [Online Information Services]: Data sharing.

General Terms
Human Factors, Theory, Measurement

Keywords
Social media, sharing of misinformation, Uses & Gratifications, perceived information characteristics

1. INTRODUCTION
The popularity of social media platforms such as social networking sites (SNS) and microblogs contribute to a large and ever-growing online collection of user-generated digital content. In this collaborative information environment, users are no longer simple consumers of digital content. They also serve the roles of information creators, curators, promoters, and sharers. While the potential of social media for collaborative information seeking and event detection is well-recognized [1], widespread misinformation on social media is a cause of concern [2]. Multi-pronged interventions are needed to reduce misinformation on social media. On one hand, algorithms and systems are being developed to detect inaccurate social media messages. On the other hand, active strategies are needed to curb users from sharing misinformation in the first place. Researchers have observed that misinformation would not become so viral if malevolent users were the only ones sending it. Rather, regular social media users (i.e., those who do not have malicious intent) often perpetuate the spread of misinformation by inattentively forwarding misinformation to their own networks [3].

Currently, it is unclear what factors, such as individual motivations or perceived information characteristics, prompt regular users to share misinformation. Understanding these factors would inform the design of social media applications so that system features can be included to deter users from sharing misinformation. Such findings will also inform the development of suitable information literacy interventions. Building from the Uses and Gratification (U&G) theory and the literature of credibility assessment and rumor research, this study examines two research questions: (1) How prevalent is social media misinformation sharing among the respondents, and are there gender difference in prevalence? (2) What individual motivations and perceived information characteristics prompt regular users to share misinformation on social media, and are there gender differences in their reasons?

2. LITERATURE REVIEW

2.1 Misinformation sharing on social media
Notable incidents of crisis-related misinformation sharing have occurred on social media, such as misinformation related to Ebola. Other misinformation can take the form of "factoids", which is more likely to be related to everyday life. Because such misinformation is less likely to be event-specific, it can persistently circulate on SNSs and emerge repeatedly whenever the conditions are right, thereby continuously creating misunderstandings. Misinformation on social media can cause confusion and anxiety among the public [4]. Notably, inaccurate messages often continue to go viral even after being debunked, whereas the correct information does not receive as much attention [5]. Researchers have observed that catchiness rather than truthfulness often drives information (and misinformation) diffusion on social media [3].

2.2 Motivation: Uses & Gratifications
The motivation of regular users to share misinformation on social media is not well-understood. However, a number of significant studies have explored what motivates social media usage in general. Previous studies have investigated the reasons behind the use of social media platforms such as SNS and photo sharing sites, news sharing on social media, and information sharing on mobile gaming sites [6-10]. These studies on individual

JCDL'15, June 21 - 25, 2015, Knoxville, TN, USA

ACM 978-1-4503-3594-2/15/06...$15.00
DOI: http://dx.doi.org/10.1145/2756406.2756941

motivations often drew from the Uses and Gratifications (U&G) theory [11]. They often find individual motivations to be salient.

Social media literature informed by the U&G theory identifies four main motivational categories: entertainment, socializing, information seeking, and self-expression and status seeking [9; 12]. "Entertainment" refers to the use of social media for personal enjoyment. "Socializing" focuses on developing and maintaining relationships with friends and family. "Information seeking" refers to using social media to meet informational needs. "Self-expression and status seeking" refers to expressing oneself and gaining reputation. This study will test if these motivations are also pertinent to misinformation sharing on social media.

2.3 Perceived information characteristics

Beyond the U&G theory which focuses on individual motivations, this study introduces another factor for testing. We posit that the perceived characteristics of information may also play a role in users' decisions to share social media postings. Some evidence shows that authoritativeness might not be a high priority when it comes to information sharing on social media [2]. Rumor research suggests that people tend to spread rumors that are consistent with their beliefs and that involve a high level of threat [13]. Some individuals also use rumors as conversational topics [14]. The role of these characteristics on social media misinformation sharing will be tested in this study.

2.4 Gender differences

Gender differences in computer and Internet usage have generally become less notable over the years [15]. Interestingly, gender differences are often observed in the use of social media, particularly on SNS. More women use SNS in general, and for information seeking in particular [16, 17]. They tend to post more status updates and make more comments on others' postings [18]. In contrast, some evidence shows that female students use wikis, blogs, and Internet forums less than male students [19]. Women also tend to be more cautious when it comes to the perceived quality of online platforms such as Wikipedia [20].

3. METHOD

Data were collected using a survey method, which is suitable for collecting self-reported data on individual attitudes and motivations. Several examples of misinformation related to everyday life that were common on social media were included in the questionnaire as references. To illustrate, one of the misinformation examples was that a man was infested with tapeworms after eating sushi. Respondents answered questions about their reasons for sharing misinformation on social media using a 7-point Likert-like scale. This questionnaire included 29 items (see Figure 1). Of these, 16 covered individual motivations developed to represent the four main U&G motivation categories discussed above (i.e., entertainment, socializing, information seeking, and self-expression and status seeking) [6, 9, 12]. The other 13 factors were related to perceived information characteristics. They were drawn from the literature on information quality and rumor research [2, 13, 21]. Demographic information was collected.

The study sample included students from two public universities in Singapore; these students were (i) social media users and (ii) between 18 and 29 years of age. Social media is popular in Singapore [22]. In a comparative study of 15 countries including the U.K. and the U.S., Singapore respondents were found to spend the most time on social media [23]. A comparative study of U.S. and Singapore college students' social media use found their usage behavior to be similar [24]. The respondents' age range for this study was set at 18–29 years old, which is comparable to other social media studies that sampled college students [25]. The questionnaire was pilot tested and revised before distribution.

The questionnaires were distributed to students around the two universities' campuses. Convenience sampling was used. As such, the sample may not be representative of all students. Rather than aiming for population generalization, this study serves as a first step in identifying potential salient factors and individual differences in social media misinformation sharing. Future studies can test these relationships with larger sample sizes and different population groups. In this study, descriptive and inferential statistics (independent sample t-tests) were used. These analyses were conducted with SPSS.

4. FINDINGS

4.1 Respondent characteristics

Of a total of 200 questionnaires that were distributed, 171 questionnaires were completed and included in the data analysis. This yielded a response rate of 85.5%. There were more female (n = 98, 57.3%) than male (n = 73, 42.7%) respondents. The average age was 24 (SD = 2.1). About 81.3% of the respondents used social media every day.

4.2 RQ1: Misinformation sharing behavior

About two-thirds of the respondents (n = 116, 67.8%) reported that they had shared misinformation on social media. The independent sample t-tests showed that female respondents were statistically significant more likely to have shared misinformation than male respondents, $t(169)$, $p = .029$ ($M_{Men} = 2.95$, $SD = 1.58$; $M_{Women} = 3.49$, $SD = 1.62$).

4.3 RQ2: Reasons of misinformation sharing

Respondents rated 29 items on a scale of 1 ("completely disagree") to 7 ("completely agree") to indicate the extent to which the items matched their reasons for sharing misinformation on social media. The top three reasons were all related to information characteristics. They were: "The information can be a good topic of conversation," "the information is interesting," and, "the information is new and eye catching." "Sharing helps me get other people's opinions regarding the information/event," an item based on the U&G information seeking category, ranked fourth overall. The reason "I can express my opinion by sharing that information," an item in the U&G self-expression category, ranked fifth.

Accuracy—often taught as an important factor in information credibility assessment—was not a prominent factor; it ranked 24th. The authoritativeness of the information source—another important factor for information credibility assessment—ranked even lower at 26th.

The independent sample t-tests showed significant gender differences in 10 of the 29 factors. Nine of them were related to U&G motivations; one was related to information characteristics. Women scored higher than men in all 10 factors. These factors, in descending order of mean gender difference, were: (1) Sharing helps me bookmark useful information; (2) Sharing helps me enhance interpersonal relations; (3) Sharing helps me keep updated on the latest happenings; (4) Sharing helps me keep in touch with friends; (5) Sharing helps me get other related information; (6) Sharing is a good way to relax; (7) The information is fun; (8) Sharing is a culture, and I share like others do; (9) I feel enjoyment while sharing; and (10) Sharing helps me interact with people.

5. DISCUSSION

The reasons given for misinformation sharing provide insight into the possible avenues of intervention. First, many of the top-ranked reasons were non-informational. Only one of the top-five reasons was related to information seeking. The other top reasons suggest a tendency towards sharing information they considered as fun and interesting as well as motivations that are social in nature. Factors that are pertinent to general discussions of IL and to the topics of information retrieval and use (e.g., accuracy, authority of sources, perceived usefulness, and importance of information) ranked rather low.

These findings suggest that the considerations behind sharing misinformation on social media are quite different from those behind other forms of information seeking, retrieval, and information credibility assessment. The findings agree with recent discussions in human-computer interaction and information behavior literature that affective and motivational factors (e.g., self-expression and socialization) are often at play. To deter misinformation sharing, system designers and educators may target these social motivations. They may highlight, for example, how misinformation sharing might hurt a user's reputation and socialization (e.g., friends may view the misinformation sharer as being undiscerning and untrustworthy).

This study found that women were more likely to indicate having shared misinformation on social network. This finding is interesting, as prior studies suggest that women are more cautious online [20]. Further research is needed to investigate if this is common. For further testing, we hypothesized that women may view their social media usage (including misinformation sharing) as more of a social activity—and less of an informational activity—than men did. Studies on general Internet usage suggest that women's Internet use has stronger social and communicative intentions than men's [26]. In this study, women cited all four social factors in the 29 items ("sharing helps me interact with people," "sharing helps me keep in touch with friends," "sharing is a culture, and I share like others do," and "sharing helps me enhance interpersonal relations") significantly more than men did. We posit that while women have been shown to be more cautious in their online information seeking (e.g., when evaluating the quality of Wikipedia information) [20], they might not apply the same level of caution when it comes to activities they perceive as being primarily social (e.g., sharing information/misinformation with friends).

System designers can help provide interfaces that facilitate such critical analysis and collective sense-making. For example, it would be beneficial for a system to introduce features that allow users to flag officially debunked messages and prominently display accurate information alongside misinformation. The findings also show that some respondents share misinformation as a way to bookmark a posting (the 14th-ranked reason). This behavior can be tackled by features that encourage users to curate and store postings in a private collection.

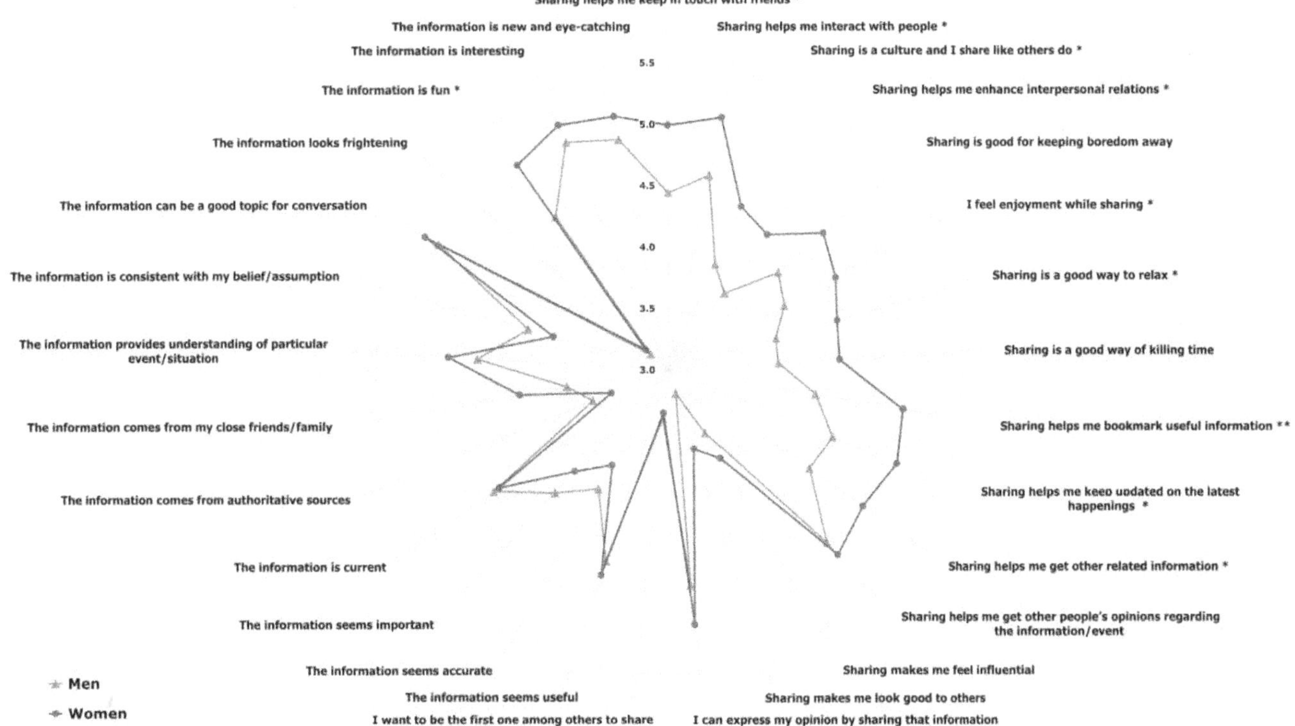

Figure 1. Reasons behind misinformation sharing on social media

Note: Items with statistically significant gender differences are denoted with asterisks (* $p < .05$; ** $p < .01$).

6. CONCLUSION

The study shows that respondents share misinformation often for non-informational reasons. The reasons cited significant gender differences. The findings suggest that concerted efforts are needed in the design of social media applications and in information literacy training to not only help reduce misinformation sharing, but also to encourage users to flag and constructively rebut misinformation. Given the popularity and reach of social media, efforts in correcting users' misinformation sharing will be worthwhile.

7. ACKNOWLEDGEMENTS

This work was in part supported by the Academic Research Fund (RG58/14) of Nanyang Technological University.

8. REFERENCES

[1] Shah, C. 2012. *Collaborative information seeking: The art and science of making the whole greater than the sum of all.* Springer, Berlin.

[2] Anne P. Mintz ed. 2012. Web of deceit: Misinformation and manipulation in the age of social media. Information Today, Medford, NJ.

[3] Ratkiewicz, J., Conover, M., Meiss, M., Gonçalves, B., Patil, S., Flammini, A., and Menczer, F. 2010. *Detecting and tracking the spread of astroturf memes in microblog streams.* Technical Report. arXiv:1011.3768 [cs.SI], CoRR. Retrieved 27 Janurary, 2015 from http://arxiv.org/abs/1011.3768

[4] Budak, C., Agrawal, D., and Abbadi, A. E. 2011. Limiting the spread of misinformation in social networks. In *Proceedings of the 20th International World Wide Web Conference Committee (IW3C2)* (Hyderabad, India, March 28–April 1 2011), ACM, New York, NY, pp. 665-674

[5] Friggeri, A., Adamic, L. A., Eckles, D., and Cheng, J. 2014. Rumor cascades. In *Proceedings of the Eighth International AAAI Conference on Weblogs and Social Media* (Ann Arbor, Michigan, USA, June 1–4 2014), The AAAI Press, Palo Alto, CA, pp. 101-110.

[6] Kim, J. H., Kim, M.-S., and Nam, Y. 2010. An analysis of self-construals, motivations, Facebook use, and user satisfaction. *Int. J. Hum.-Comput. Int. 26*, 11-12, 1077-1099.

[7] Dunne, Á., Lawlor, M.-A., and Rowley, J. 2010. Young people's use of online social networking sites – A uses and gratifications perspective. *J. Res. Interact. Mark. 4*, 1, 46-58.

[8] Nov, O., Naaman, M., and Ye, C. 2009. Analysis of participation in an online photo-sharing community: A multidimensional perspective. *J. Am. Soc. Inf. Sci. Tec. 61*, 3, 555-566.

[9] Lee, C. S. and Ma, L. 2012. News sharing in social media: The effect of gratifications and prior experience. *Comput. Hum. Behav. 28*, 2, 331-339.

[10] Lee, C. S., Goh, D. H.-L., Chua, A. Y. K., and Ang, R. P. 2010. Indagator: Investigating perceived gratifications of an application that blends mobile content sharing with gameplay. *J. Am. Soc. Inf. Sci. Tec. 61*, 6, 1244-1257.

[11] Ruggiero, T. E. 2000. Uses and gratifications theory in the 21st century. *Mass Commun. Soc. 3*, 1, 3-37.

[12] Park, N., Kee, K. F., and Valenzuela, S. 2009. Being Immersed in social networking environment: Facebook groups, uses and gratifications, and social outcomes. *CyberPsychol. Behav. 12*, 6, 729-733.

[13] DiFonzo, N. and Bordia, P. 2007. *Rumor psychology: Social and organizational approaches*. American Psychological Association, Washington, DC.

[14] Guerin, B. and Miyazaki, Y. 2006. Analyzing rumors, gossip, and urban legends through their conversational properties. *Psychol. Rec. 56*, 1, 23.

[15] Weiser, E. B. 2000. Gender differences in Internet use patterns and Internet application preferences: A two-sample comparison. *CyberPsychol. Behav. 3*, 2, 167-178.

[16] Duggan, M. and Smith, A. January 2014. *Social media update 2013.* Pew Research Center. Retrieved 27 Janurary, 2015, from http://pewinternet.org/Reports/2013/Social-Media-Update.aspx

[17] Sin, S.-C. J. and Kim, K.-S. 2013. International students' everyday life information seeking: The informational value of social networking sites. *Libr. Inform. Sci. Res. 35*, 2, 107-116.

[18] Hampton, K., Goulet, L. S., Rainie, L., and Purcell, K. June 2011. *Social networking sites and our lives.* Pew Research Center. Retrieved 27 Janurary, 2015, from http://pewinternet.org/~/media//Files/Reports/2011/PIP - Social networking sites and our lives.pdf

[19] Kim, K. S., Sin, S.-C. J., and Tsai, T. I. 2014. Individual differences in social media use for information seeking. *J. Acad. Libr. 40*, 2, 171-178.

[20] Lim, S. and Kwon, N. 2010. Gender differences in information behavior concerning Wikipedia, an unorthodox information source? *Libr. Inform. Sci. Res. 32*, 3, 212-220.

[21] Rieh, S. Y. 2002. Judgment of information quality and cognitive authority in the Web. *J. Am. Soc. Inf. Sci. Tec. 53*, 2, 145-161.

[22] Koh, D. 2011. *Study: Singapore most "evolved" in social media.* Retrieved from http://asia.cnet.com/study-singapore-most-evolved-in-social-media-62113936.htm

[23] Firefly Millward Brown 2010. *The language of love in social media - New rules for brand engagement.* Retrieved 27 Janurary, 2015, from http://bit.ly/18x5URZ

[24] Kim, K.-S. and Sin, S.-C. J. 2014. *Social media as information sources: Use and evaluation of information from social media.* 2013 OCLC/ALISE research grant report published electronically by OCLC Research. Retrieved 27 January, 2015 from http://www.oclc.org/content/dam/research/grants/reports/2013/kim2013.pdf

[25] Correa, T., Hinsley, A. W., and de Zúñiga, H. G. 2010. Who interacts on the Web?: The intersection of users' personality and social media use. *Comput. Hum. Behav. 26*, 2, 247-253.

[26] Rodgers, S. and Harris, M. A. 2003. Gender and E-commerce: An exploratory study. *J. Advertising. Res. 43*, 03, 322-329.

Improving Consistency of Crowdsourced Multimedia Similarity for Evaluation

Peter Organisciak
University of Illinois at Urbana-Champaign
organis2@illinois.edu

J. Stephen Downie
University of Illinois at Urbana-Champaign
jdownie@illinois.edu

ABSTRACT

Building evaluation datasets for information retrieval is a time-consuming and exhausting activity. To evaluate research over novel corpora, researchers are increasingly turning to crowdsourcing to efficiently distribute the evaluation dataset creation among many workers. However, there has been little investigation into the effect of instrument design on data quality in crowdsourced evaluation datasets. We pursue this question through a case study, music similarity judgments in a music digital library evaluation, where we find that even with trusted graders song pairs are not consistently rated the same. We find that much of this low intra-coder consistency can be attributed to the task design and judge effects, concluding with recommendations for achieving reliable evaluation judgments for music similarity and other normative judgment tasks.

Categories and Subject Descriptors: [Collaborative and social computing]: *Collaborative and social computing design and evaluation methods*; [Information Retrieval]: *Evaluation of retrieval results, Music Retrieval*

Keywords: crowdsourcing; similarity judgments

1. INTRODUCTION

Judging the similarity of audio is a difficult and time-consuming task. Since 2006, the Music Information Retrieval Evaluation eXchange (MIREX) has been using volunteer human graders for evaluating the performance of music systems submitted to the Audio Music Similarity and Retrieval (AMS) task. We analyze four years of judgments from AMS, finding that the consistency across different raters and years is remarkably poor. This paper looks at the role of crowdsourcing design and modeling choices in this data error, pursuing user normalization, collection instrument design changes, and multiple independent judgments.

The primary contribution of this paper is an understanding of data issues that stem from crowdsourced evaluation datasets, and methods to avoid data quality pitfalls. Particularly, our case study of music information retrieval judgments generalizes to a class of evaluation tasks that are subjective-biased. Music similarity is desired by music digital library users [10], and other digital libraries deal with a comparable form of *normative* task where there is no absolutely correct ground truth but a desire to reach a consensus or a generally agreeable classification; e.g. item similarity ratings, information quality judgments, and information retrieval relevance judgments. Our findings are also important to understanding the reliability of Audio Music Similarity evaluation, and we provide recommendations to improve future tasks.

JCDL'15, June 21–25, 2015, Knoxville, Tennessee, USA.

ACM 978-1-4503-3594-2/15/06 ...$15.00.
http://dx.doi.org/10.1145/2756406.2756942.

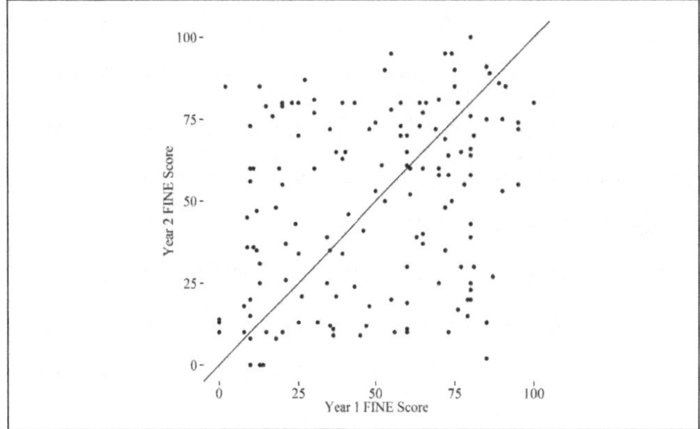

Figure 1: Audio similarity judgments for (S_x, S_y) pairs judged in multiple years. Note that the query is S_y in year 1 and S_x for year 2.

2. BACKGROUND

MIREX is an annual evaluation event where techniques tailored to a variety of Music Digital Library (MDL) and Music Information Retrieval (MIR) tasks are submitted by research laboratories from all over the world. The Audio Music Similarity and Retrieval (AMS) task was started in 2006. AMS resembles a classic information retrieval scenario, whereby the systems being evaluated are expected to return a ranked list of audio items that are considered similar to a given query [2]. It is also desired by digital library users: in a survey of MDL users, 54% said they were likely to use music similarity functions [10].

AMS relies on human judgments for evaluation, recruiting volunteers each year to judge the similarity of song "candidates" to randomly selected queries. For each query song, each retrieval system under evaluation gives MIREX a list

Table 1: Relationship of categorical judgments for pairs of songs when judged again.

		Judge 2		
		NS	SS	VS
Judge 1	Not Similar (NS)	5	—	—
	Somewhat Similar (SS)	20	14	—
	Very Similar (VS)	10	21	8

of candidate similar songs. These query–candidate' sets are presented randomly to evaluators in a judging system called "Evalutron 6000" (E6K) [1, 4]. To avoid exhaustion, E6K saves judgments continuously, so that graders can step away and return without losing data.

3. DATA

We compiled 26024 human judgments of audio similarity across four years of MIREX's AMS judgments. Candidates were selected for judgment by 8 submitted systems in 2010, 18 in 2011, 10 in 2012, and 8 in 2013. Until 2011, 100 queries were evaluated each year, after which MIREX shifted to 50 queries per year.

All the candidates for a query were graded on two scales of similarity. The BROAD scale is a categorical ranking from three choices: "not similar", "somewhat similar", and "very similar." The FINE scale is a 101-point numerical rating. The graders were generally trusted volunteers from the MIR community, and multiple keying was not done.

To understand the consistency of judgments across years of MIREX, we need to look at song pairs that have recurred in judging. Since AMS evaluation queries are randomly selected each year, there are only two instances where a query has recurred. However, 80% of queries have also occurred as candidates for other songs. As a result, there are 156 judgments of the same song pairs across the years, with the caveat that the query-candidate relationship is inverted.

4. PROBLEM

There is a concerning lack of agreement between judges in the set of reciprocal song pairs, shown in Figure 1. The slope shows the expected relationship if similarity was an agreeable metric independent of "which song is listened to first" order effects – an assumption implicitly made in treating similarity as something that can be evaluated.

The noise presented here suggests a great deal of circumstance and randomness in evaluating music similarity algorithms for MIREX. Since our best prediction for the true similarity of two songs is the mean of both judgments, we can measure the deviation from the expected value as Root Mean Squared Error.

In our case, $RMSE = 16.58$ against a prediction assuming symmetric similarity. Comparing the BROAD category of reciprocal pairs tells a similar story (Table 1): only 35% of graders agreed on the category and nearly half was agreement on "somewhat similar" items. While some of this is to be expected, it also suggests that SS functions as a catch-all category where graders hedge their bets. This is supported by its much wider range (Figure 2).

The weak correlation in re-judging makes it difficult to assess the extent to which the evaluation is actually reflecting the 'truth' of what songs are similar. What are the reasons for this weak correlation? We evaluate this question in the context of crowdsourcing choices, looking at collection format and data treatment as possible sources for the variance. First, let's consider some possible explanations.

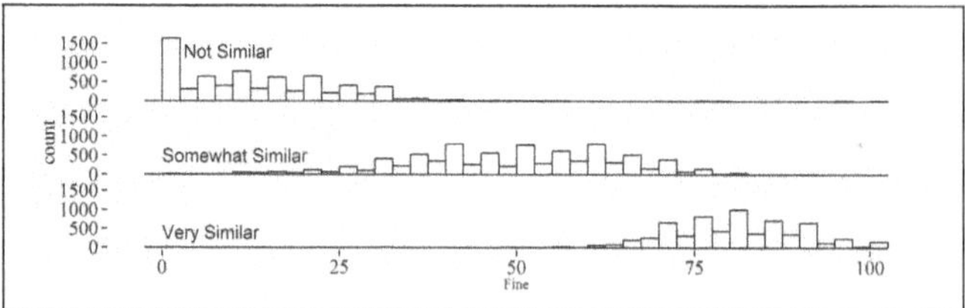

Figure 2: Distribution of FINE scores relative to BROAD categories.

Order and priming effects. Perhaps there is an order effect based on either which song a judge listens to first, or a priming effect caused by a judge listening consecutively to a set of song pairs with the same query. Research in other contexts has noted the possibility of asymmetrical effects [14, 13, 5].

Different interpretations of the scale. Do different people treat the rating scale differently? This would be a user bias, but a predictable one.

Bad intercoder reliability due to task design. Perhaps the E6K system does a poor job controlling for consistency?

Bad graders. Much crowd research looks at malicious or unreliable contributors. This is possible, but unlikely to happen systematically since the volunteers are trusted members of the MIR community.

An inherently subjective task: Does this task present challenges to agreement?

It is likely that the noisy, high-variance MIREX music similarity judgments stem from multiple sources. We focus on measuring how much of that is recoverable: what can be improved by changes to practice. Particularly, we apply corrections for user-specific biases, we collect multiple-keyed judgments, and we redesign the collection task. While we do not focus on order effects, our results showing improved judgment consistency provide a better sense of the magnitude at which such effects might exist.

5. RELATED WORK

The feasibility of scoring melodic similarity has been challenged by [11], who noted high variation in MIREX 2005 similarity judgments. Though on different MIREX data, our study is able to identify collection instrument design as one such factor source of variance.

An alternative to the form of graded similarity judgment that MIREX uses is partially ordered lists, introduced by Typke et al. [15]. This form of judgment has been shown to be effective for judging the relative similarity of candidates to a query. However, it is more time-consuming to create, a factor in the decision to use a graded scale for MIREX. Also, it suffers from similar inconsistency problems to what we observe in this paper [17].

Despite the inconsistency that we observe, a study into the power of AMS evaluation, for an year not overlapping with our study, concluded that the relative rankings of AMS systems in MIREX are sound, with contention on about 4% of pairwise system comparisons [16].

This study turns to paid crowdsourcing on Mechanical

Turk for additional judgments, an option shown as a viable approach to music similarity judgments in multiple studies [17, 9]. [17] looked to paid crowdsourcing for lowering the difficulty of finding human labor for *ranked* similarity judgments. They use an approach similar to ordered lists, inferring an order through pairwise preference judgments, whereby graders choose the more similar option between two candidates. Additional research has also looked at *graded* similarity judgments in the context of the AMS task [9], finding that the MIREX style of evaluation does not suffer significant drops in quality with paid workers.

6. APPROACH

To address possible sources of the error in MIREX's crowd-sourced relevance judgments, we evaluate *1.* whether the weak correlation still exists when asking new graders for judgments, *2.* compare the error when adding additional workers, *3.* normalize workers by their personal habits, and *4.* test an alternate interface that gives graders more guidance on what rating is appropriate.

6.1 Normalizing for Grader-Specific Effects

RQ1: Are intra-grader inconsistencies responsible for the lack of reciprocation in AMS similarity judgments?

The human graders are given a large amount of leeway regarding how they perform a task. We set out to see if this contributes to superficial variance, and whether correcting for it can address the poor reciprocation in AMS. While the BROAD categories are fairly clear, the FINE scale does not constrain graders to follow a specific codebook. This is appears to be done by design: workers are told, "You have the freedom to make whatever associations you desire ... we expect to see variations across evaluators as this is a normal part of human subjectivity."

Differences in graders' interpretations of a task can contribute to different internal scales. This type of error is commonly seen in collaborative filtering for recommendation, where users' opinions are often treated as a mixture of their nominal rating, adjusted by user-specific and item-specific biases [8].

To normalize graders against their specific biases, FINE judgments were translated to z-score values, represented as standard deviations from the judge's mean rating habit. This approach was previously seen in [6]; in our case, adjusted ratings were blocked by a judge's BROAD score, resulting in three values for each judge: deviation from their typical FINE score for "not similar"', "somewhat similar", and "very similar" candidates.

The adjusted rating $r'_{u,b}$ for judge u and BROAD category b was calculated in the following way:

$$r'_{u,b} = \sqrt{\frac{1}{N} * \sum_{i=1}^{N} r_{u,b} - \mu_{u,b}} \qquad (1)$$

where $b \in B$ and $B = \{``NS", ``SS", ``VS"\}$.

Since this normalization provides ratings against three different scales, we mapped it back into a new FINE score by assuming a normal distribution for each category. With this mapping, 95% of not similar ratings occur between $FINE = 0 - 27.63$; somewhat similar ratings between $30.21 - 67.80$; and very similar ratings between $68.74 - 92.17$.

6.1.1 Results

Normalizing user FINE judgments weighted against their BROAD judgments resulted in variance of $RMSE = 16.15$, a non-significant change. Thus, we did *not* find evidence that greatly different internal scales by graders were the reason for the low consistency. In other words, the notion that graders were internally consistent in a way that can be normalized globally is not tractable.

6.2 Verifying Judgments with New Graders

RQ2: Are problem graders responsible for inconsistent reciprocal ratings?

RQ3: Is subjectivity or disagreement of the grading task responsible for inconsistent reciprocal ratings?

Would we see the same effect in our data if we asked new graders? Getting a second opinion addresses two possibilities: expected error (good graders, biased task) and unexpected error (agreeable task, bad graders).

To answer these two research questions, we posted the 156 tasks on Mechanical Turk. Turk is an online crowd marketplace, where small tasks can be posted and completed for correspondingly small payments. Asking paid workers *individually* provides an insight into MIREX grader quality, while asking *multiple* workers helps to see if it is simply a task that is not easily agreed upon, regardless of how well-intentioned a grader is.

In parameterizing the task for this study, worker graders were presented with a query and a single candidate. The audio files were the same clips used in MIREX. We did not apply restrictions on how fully they were listened to, and found that the average task time was lower than the length of the clips. We were also careful to mimic the question phrasing and level of guidance from the original task.

The primary way that the new task differs from grading for MIREX is that tasks were split into smaller parts. As a result, Turk workers are potentially less fatigued [9], but may also be less experienced. This was done both due to the conventions of Mechanical Turk and because our MIREX data was not rich enough to emulate the order or continuity of task sets. Thus, any priming effects from the series of songs would not translate here.

6.2.1 Results

Asking individual paid amateur graders to provide judgments yielded an average $RMSE = 15.53$, a comparable level of inconsistency. With regards to *RQ2*, the low consistency when asking a new group of graders for judgments suggests that the MIREX volunteers are not unreliable compared to other workers.

In contrast, aggregating multiple worker judgments toward a normative opinion results in drastic improvements: aggregating two workers by mean judgment improved the RMSE to 9.72 (41.4% improvement), while three grader judgments improved the RMSE to 7.45 (55.1% improvement). This means that, as asked in *RQ3*, the task is too subjective to trust a single judge and has a high natural variance in judgment.

6.3 Improving task guidance

RQ4: Does the task design affect the quality of judgments? One of the threats to grading reliability is a hard to understand or poorly defined coding scheme [12]. For this reason, as a final evaluation we briefly looked at the effect of a task's

Table 2: Deviation (in RMSE) of similarity judgments from expectation.

Approach	RMSE
Baseline (AMS Graders)	16.58
Normalizing Graders	16.15 (-0.03%)
Second-opinion (Individual turk workers)	15.53 (-6.3%)
Aggregating workers: 2 votes/judgment	9.72 (-41.4%)
Aggregating workers: 3 votes/judgment	7.45 (-55.1%)
Alternate design (individual judgments)	11.44 (-31.0%)
Alternate design (2 votes/judgments)	7.55 (-54.5%)
Alternate design (3 votes/judgments)	5.40 (-66.1%)

design on the consistency of judgments, by evaluating a different collection interface.

In contrast to the previous evaluation's fidelity to the original collection interface, here we changed the task design to more carefully guide graders. Previous literature notes that the similarity ratings can be biased because the perceived distance between points in a rating scale is not linear, and word choice can affect interpretation of the task [7, 3]. This motivated us to measure some changes to the rating scale: BROAD scores were no longer collected, and FINE scores gave textual descriptions for ranges of the 0-100 scale, serving as anchors. We also tested this interface with colloquial language to make the instructions more broadly accessible.

6.3.1 Results

When workers were provided our modified FINE rating scale, they averaged an RMSE of 11.44. In light of the gains observed earlier with multi-worker aggregation, this interface was also looked at in conjunction with 2- and 3-worker judgments (RMSE=7.55 and 5.40, respectively). As seen in Table 2, this means that the alternate design offered consistent per-worker improvement without increasing cost.

7. DISCUSSION

The poor consistency in crowdsourced similarity judgments in MIREX results can be greatly attributed to difficulties inherent to the task of grading music. We show that MIREX does not have a problem with poor or misguided judges. However, notable improvements to the evaluation data quality can be made by changes to the collection and treatment of judgments. We recommend two primary changes to improve the judging for AMS, and for other uses of human-based evaluation over partially subjective tasks:

Collecting multiple judgments. Despite the added complexity or cost of collecting multiple judgments for each query-candidate pair, it is an important step toward collecting consistent results. While finding enough volunteer judges in the MIR community is a restricting factor, amateur paid crowds offer similar performance [9, 17] and may be one way to augment the volunteer judgments.

Providing a more specific codebook. While it is important to acknowledge the subjectivity of similarity judging, providing structure for graders to anchor their interpretations into a score improves the reliability of their contributions. Unlike multiple judgments, these sorts of task design changes do not add to the cost of evaluation.

For the benefit of further study, it would be also beneficial for MIREX to retain information about judgment order and time taken for each judgment. While the poor consistency is improved through multiple judgments and stronger instructions, an outstanding question is whether a grader's approach to a task evolves over time.

Normalizing for systematic user-specific biases did not improve the consistency of the data. However, when graders were provided a rating scale that gave them more guidance, they performed better. Why did the former not improve consistency, while the latter did? One possibility is that, in addition to intra-grader differences in interpreting the FINE scale, graders were also internally less strict, something that the task design might have corrected.

8. CONCLUSIONS

Finding human graders for a time-consuming task is difficult. However, since music similarity tries to derive a consensus for a quality that people do not always agree on, it is imperative to collect multiple judgments for reliable evaluation. Judging music similarity is normative: it does not have a clear truth but it is possible to strive for a rough consensus that strives to satisfy most opinions. This type of task is important to building better information systems: it can apply to certain contexts of information retrieval relevance, or ratings of item quality in online collections, or even in crowd-curated lists, but as we found with audio similarity, it is important to treat it as such.

9. REFERENCES

[1] J. S. Downie. The music information retrieval evaluation eXchange (MIREX). *D-Lib Magazine*, 12(12):795–825, 2006.

[2] J. S. Downie. The music information retrieval evaluation exchange: Some observations and insights. In *Advances in music information retrieval*. Springer Berlin/Heidelberg, 2010.

[3] M. B. Eisenberg. Measuring relevance judgments. *Information Processing & Management*, 24(4):373–389, 1988.

[4] A. A. Gruzd, J. S. Downie, M. C. Jones, and J. H. Lee. Evalutron 6000: Collecting music relevance judgments. In *Proc. of the 7th Joint Conference on Digital Libraries*, 2007.

[5] L. Hiatt and J. Trafton. The role of familiarity, priming and perception in similarity judgments, 2013.

[6] T. Hofmann. Latent semantic models for collaborative filtering. *ACM Trans. Inf. Syst.*, 22(1), Jan. 2004.

[7] R. V. Katter. The influence of scale form on relevance judgments. *Information Storage and Retrieval*, 4(1):1–11, Mar. 1968.

[8] Y. Koren. The bellkor solution to the netflix grand prize. *Netflix prize documentation*, 2009.

[9] J. H. Lee. Crowdsourcing music similarity judgments using mechanical turk. In *ISMIR*, page 183–188, 2010.

[10] J. H. Lee and J. S. Downie. Survey of music information needs, uses, and seeking behaviours. In *ISMIR*, volume 2004. Citeseer, 2004.

[11] A. Marsden. Interrogating melodic similarity: A definitive phenomenon or the product of interpretation? *Journal of New Music Research*, 41(4):323–335, Dec. 2012.

[12] K. A. Neuendorf. *The Content Analysis Guidebook*. Sage Publications, Thousand Oaks, CA, USA, 2002.

[13] T. A. Polk, C. Behensky, R. Gonzalez, and E. E. Smith. Rating the similarity of simple perceptual stimuli. *Cognition*, 82(3), Jan. 2002.

[14] A. Tversky. Features of similarity. *Psychological Review*, 84(4):327–352, 1977.

[15] R. Typke, M. den Hoed, J. de Nooijer, F. Wiering, and R. C. Veltkamp. A ground truth for half a million musical incipits. *JDIM*, 3(1), 2005.

[16] J. Urbano, D. Martín, M. Marrero, and J. Morato. Audio music similarity and retrieval: Evaluation power and stability. In *ISMIR*, 2011.

[17] J. Urbano, J. Morato, M. Marrero, and D. Martín. Crowdsourcing preference judgments for evaluation of music similarity tasks. In *ACM SIGIR workshop on crowdsourcing for search evaluation*, 2010.

What does Twitter Measure? Influence of Diverse User Groups in Altmetrics

Simon Barthel, Sascha Tönnies, Benjamin Köhncke, Patrick Siehndel, Wolf-Tilo Balke
L3S Research Center
Hannover, Germany
{barthel, toennies, koehncke, siehndel, balke}@l3s.de

ABSTRACT

The most important goal for digital libraries is to ensure high quality search experience for all kinds of users. To attain this goal, it is necessary to have as much relevant metadata as possible at hand to assess the quality of publications. Recently, a new group of metrics appeared, that has the potential to raise the quality of publication metadata to the next level – the altmetrics. These metrics try to reflect the impact of publications within the social web. However, currently it is still unclear if and how altmetrics should be used to assess the quality of a publication and how altmetrics are related to classical bibliographical metrics (like e.g. citations). To gain more insights about what kind of concepts are reflected by altmetrics, we conducted an in-depth analysis on a real world dataset crawled from the Public Library of Science (PLOS). Especially, we analyzed if the common approach to regard the users in the social web as one homogeneous group is sensible or if users need to be divided into diverse groups in order to receive meaningful results.

Categories and Subject Descriptors

H.3.7 [**Information Systems**]: Digital Libraries—*Standards*; H.3.3 [**Information Systems**]: Information Search and Retrieval

Keywords

Altmetrics; Twitter; Correlation Analysis; Social Media; Expert Mining

1 INTRODUCTION

The most important goal for digital libraries is to ensure a high quality search experience for the user. One central aspect to reach this goal is the assessment of the impact and quality of scientific publications, which is of course far from being trivial. In the scientific field this judgment is mostly performed with respect to the reputation of the publication venue and the number of citations the publication has. The reputation of a researcher is analogously assessed by scanning publication venues and number of citations in the researcher's publication list.

Since the 1960s with the release of the science citation index [1] several metrics were introduced to measure the success of publications, researchers or even whole journals in a deterministic way. Famous examples that are based on this index are e.g. the impact factor [2] and the h-index [3]. However, nowadays, the practicability of such metrics seems more and more questionable due to increasing agility in scientific progresses and communication. When relying on citation based metrics, this agility is impossible to provide since citation counts take several years to become stable [4].

When on the other hand observing the impact of an article within the social Web like bookmarking services, micro blogging platforms or social networks, reactions can be detected immediately after the date of publication [5], [6], [7]. Also this reaction originates from a much more diverse set of users in contrast to the science citation index, where only citations by peers can be regarded. The general meaningfulness and the basic ideas of altmetrics [8], [9], [10], [11] has been confirmed by empirical studies [12], [13] and therefore the usage of these measures is continuously increasing. This is demonstrated by the progression of first Web 2.0 tools, e.g. PlumX[1] and Altmetric[2] and the implementation by several information providers, e.g. PLOS[3] and Nature[4].

The main problem regarding altmetrics is however that it is still not clear what general conclusions can be drawn when an article is frequently mentioned within the social web. It is also not clear how altmetrics are related to classical bibliographical metrics like e.g. citations. It is certain however, that this relationship is not trivial like e.g. more tweets mean more citations. This becomes clear when comparing the tweeting behavior within different communities. For example, the average social science article in our corpus is mentioned 16 times on twitter while the average chemistry article is only mentioned 2.5 times. To judge, whether a certain number of tweets is "high" therefore always depends on the context.

The problem to associate altmetrics to citation counts has been studied a lot recently. This is an interesting problem since citation counts are currently the best naive estimate of scientific quality. If a connection between citation counts and altmetrics existed, this connection could be used to judge the scientific quality of an article much faster as it were possible with citation counts. Of course, before such concepts were introduced in practice several problems have

[1]http://www.plumanalytics.com
[2]http://www.altmetric.com
[3]http://article-level-metrics.plos.org/
[4]http://www.nature.com/

JCDL'15, June 21–25, 2015, Knoxville, Tennessee, USA.

DOI: http://dx.doi.org/10.1145/2756406.2756913.

to be solved. Possible negative indications are e.g. the appearance of spam in the social web to boost the reputation of bad articles or on the other hand good articles suffering from false predictions. Previous experiments investing the relation between altmetrics and citation metrics are however very diverse in their conclusions, which can be explained by the diverse communities and journals the experiments were performed on.

In this paper we therefore attempt to examine the effect of diverse user groups within the social web. For this purpose we proposed several methods to separate users by their field of interest, by their expertise or by other statistical properties. Our experiments are based on a real world dataset (PLOS) with more than 70,000 articles. In the first part of the experiments, we analyze and introduce the used corpus. In this part we illustrate typical progressions of different article metrics and the correlations between different metrics. In the second part we will take a deeper look into the available twitter data to identify different groups of users and we will analyze if these groups behave differently.

The contributions of our paper are:

- An in-depth correlation analysis between Web 2.0 metrics, view metrics and bibliographic metrics with respect to different scientific domains
- The identification of diverse user groups in the social media and an analysis of their impact on correlations to article metrics
- The introduction of a method for finding and characterizing a user group that maximizes the correlation between tweets and citations counts

The rest of the paper is organized as follows: In chapter 2 we introduce important related work introducing basic fundamentals of altmetrics and recent works searching for correlations between bibliographic metrics and altmetrics. In chapter 3 we describe our corpus and the conducted experiments. Afterwards, in chapter 4 the results obtained in chapter 3 are discussed and conclusions are drawn.

2 RELATED WORK

Recently, data from social media services has been frequently used to provide a new way of measuring the early impact of scholarly publications. This approach gets more and more popular under the term of altmetrics [5], [6], [7]. These metrics try to reflect activity in social media services with the purpose of gathering scholarly impact besides the traditional citation based metrics. By tracking these activities, it is possible to monitor the manner in which scholarly documents are disseminated and discussed in almost real-time [6], [17], [18]. The role of social media in scholarly communication has been investigated in several studies including their use in dissemination [19], conference chatter [20], science popularization [21], and promotion of scholarly products [22]. In addition, several tools have been introduced to facilitate the use of Altmetrics, e.g. PlumX, ImpactStory, Altmetrics and Scholarometer [23]. Finally, the authors of [24] conclude that the potential of altmetrics is nothing short of a complete map of scholarly activity and influence.

Twitter, as one of the most popular social media services which claims more than 200 million active users in March 2013 creating 400 million Tweets each day [32], is a very interesting source for altmetrics, because in addition to the links, contextual information is also available, which can be further used for content analysis. There are already many studies analyzing Twitter, for example in the area of expert finding. The authors of [27] analyzed different indicators for expertise and interest in an enterprise social software suite. Their results show that micro blogs produced good results in terms of recall and precision for expert mining. In [28] it was shown that the use of the Wisdom of the Crowds provided by the list information in twitter is a very effective way for mining expertise in Twitter. The authors showed that their system which relies on list information can compete with the proprietary who-to-follow system provided by Twitter.

Also, studies investigating the prediction of citations based on published tweets are available. However, the results of these papers are sometimes contradictory. In [29] the authors discovered that tweets correlate with citations. The evaluations shown in [29] are however based on very low numbers of articles (ranging from 8 to 55 articles). Also in [30] the authors concluded that tweets and citations are correlated. The authors also analyzed progression patterns of several metrics and found out that download patterns and response patterns in the social web differ significantly. The number of regarded articles in that study were however also very low (70 articles) and the selection of articles to calculate the correlations with was biased, since only the 70 top tweeted articles in their corpus were regarded. While we can support the findings considering progression patterns of different metrics, in our dataset we could not find a direct correlation between tweets and citations.

There are also other papers supporting our findings. In [31] the authors worked with 134,000 articles from the PubMed corpus ranging across different scientific fields. The articles were annotated with altmetrics provided by Altmetric.com. Their results show that the presence and density of altmetric counts are still very low for scientific publications. Only 15%-24% of the publications presenting some altmetrics activity. However, this depends on the domain of the publication: publications from social science, humanities and the social and life sciences showed the highest percentage of alt-metrics. The correlations between tweets and citations (ranging from 0.104 to 0.183) can be considered as very low. Also in [32] only weak or no correlations between tweets and citations were found. The goal of their research was to provide an overview about how often Twitter is used to disseminate information about journal articles in the biomedical sciences. Only 10% of the articles were mentioned in Twitter. The experiments regarding the correlation between these tweets and citations show almost no correlations.

Nevertheless, large-scale studies of altmetrics are still too rare to provide systematic evidence about the reliability, validity, and expressiveness of these measures [15], [16]. One study investigated the spread of scientific information by their Web usage statistics [25]. This study, as well as our study, is based on the statistics obtained from the PLOS Article Level Metrics dataset compiled by PLOS. The authors have shown that the cumulative number of HTML views follows a long tail distribution. In addition, they have shown that the spread of information displays two distinct decay regimes: a rapid downfall in the first month after publication, and a gradual power law decay afterwards.

3 EXPERIMENTS

For our experiments, we used a corpus that we have crawled from the PLOS journal consisting of 74,130 articles that have been published between October 2008 and August 2013. The distribution of articles over time is shown in Figure 1.

For each document the corpus contains a collection of metadata fields, like the DOI, the title and the publication date. Additionally, the corpus contains log summaries for different sources (like Twitter or Facebook). The log summaries consist of a list of "events", where each event is an entity crawled by the respective crawler of a source (e.g. a tweet, a citation or a comment). Furthermore, the log contains several aggregated values to summarize the list of events (like the *current number* of tweets, or citations). Finally, the progression of this aggregations are logged in a history. The history is updated irregularly every time the respective source has been crawled. The crawler then appends the current timestamp and the current aggregated value for the respective source to the history of that source. Unlike the current aggregated values, the values for the history only consist of a single value at a certain time per source. For example, the Facebook event log contains the current number of shares, comments and likes for a document separately, but the Facebook event history only contains the *sum* of shares, comments and likes at different points in time.

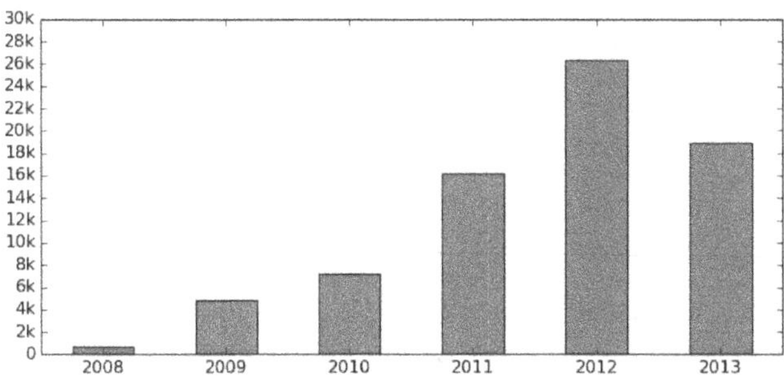

Figure 1: Distribution of articles over time

The sources contained in our corpus cover several Web 2.0 metrics like Twitter, different Facebook measures and CiteULike. From Twitter tweets referencing articles in our corpus with a link are available. For Facebook the corpus distinguishes between likes, comments and shares (a mechanism to share a link on Facebook). CiteULike is a social bookmarking service, allowing users to save and share citations to academic papers. Here, the number of shares for an articles is of interest. The Mendeley data covers the amount of readers for an article and groups working with that article. In addition, the corpus contains various citation metrics. These metrics count the number of references to an article within the respective data source. The sources taken into account for citation metrics are CrossRef, PubMed, Scopus, Nature and Postgenomic. Finally, the corpus contains multiple view metrics from PLOS and PubMed Central (PMC).

PLOS is a nonprofit open access project for publishing peer reviewed journals with a strong focus on biology and medicine. Nevertheless, PLOS also contains articles in other domains published in the PLOS ONE journal. Table 3 shows the proportion of disciplines represented in the PLOS corpus for the most frequent disciplines. The disciplines were derived from the Mendeley metadata contained in the PLOS corpus. Since multiple disciplines can be assigned to one article the sum of the percentages is larger than 100%. PMC is an open access branch of PubMed with a strong focus on medicine. From PLOS and PMC both HTML views and PDF views are available.

To provide an initial overview of the data, Table 1 summarizes the most important statistical values for each metric. The since-field corresponds to the first occurrence of a non-zero entry logged in any history for that metric in the whole corpus. The min-value for each metric is not listed, since the min value is zero or close to zero for each metric and therefore not meaningful. The maximum, average and standard deviation fields were determined by using all documents published after the metric was crawled (after the respective since-date).

Table 1: Summary of available metrics

Metric	Max	Avg	Std	Since
Tweets	1,179	2.82	16.4	05/12
Facebook shares	2,325	2.56	24.0	12/11
Facebook comments	4,979	1.89	24.2	12/11
Facebook likes	4,068	3.86	30.4	12/11
Mendeley readers	627	6.5	9.90	01/12
Mendeley groups	1	0.19	0.39	01/12
CiteULike shares	138	0.45	1.97	03/09
PLOS HTML views	274k	1,637	3,529	09/09
PLOS PDF views	24k	330	382	09/09
PMC HTML views	59k	239	346	06/11
PMC PDF views	3,689	118	130	06/11
CrossRef citations	842	3.71	8.32	03/09
PubMed citations	392	2.34	5.80	03/09
Scopus citations	1,069	4.85	11.4	03/09
Nature citations	8	0.005	0.09	03/09
Postgenomic citations	8	0.004	0.09	03/09

For several metrics the statistical overview indicates that further investigations are not very promising. For example, for the Nature and Postgenomic citations the number of citations is zero for almost all articles. Also the Mendeley groups are not suitable for further investigations, since for this field only a Boolean value (is contained in a group or not) is available. Therefore, these metrics were left out of further experiments.

To provide an impression of the progression of the regarded metrics, the aggregation of histories of each source was plotted in Figure 2. The plots were created by selecting every history from the corpus that belongs to the corresponding metric, starting after the metric was crawled (after the since-date) and lasting at least for the period of time that the plot shows. The value for the n'th day was then determined by fetching from each history the record that was closest to the n'th days after the corresponding article was published. The average of these values is the y-value for day n.

The graphs show typical behavior for the respective metrics. The citation metrics from Scopus, PubMed and CrossRef show a typical long term progression pattern indicating that the number of references to an article continues to grow after 500 days and more. The Web 2.0 metrics from Facebook, CiteULike and Twitter grow very quickly immediately after an article was published and very slowly afterwards. The view metrics from PLOS and PMC grow almost linearly and the progression of Mendeley readers are in between citation progressions and view count progressions.

3.1 Correlations of different metrics

To detect possible interplay between different metrics, we analyzed the correlation between each pair of metrics. Known methods for measuring correlations are the Pearson correlation, Kendall's τ rank correlation coefficient and Spearman's rank correlation coefficient. The Pearson correlation is however not suitable for this task, since the data must be normal distributed. In our corpus this prerequisite

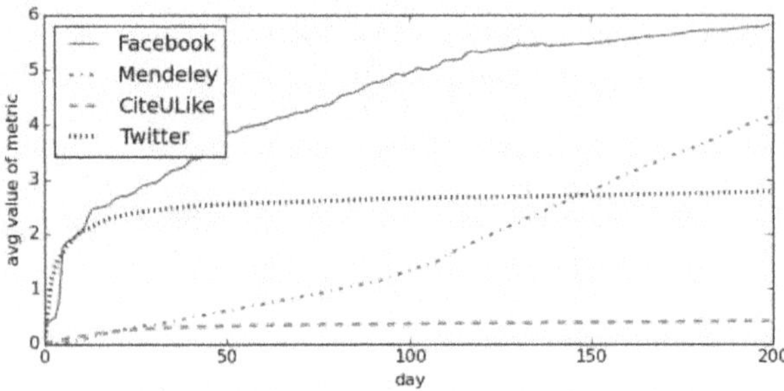

(a) Facebook, Mendeley, CiteULike and Tweets

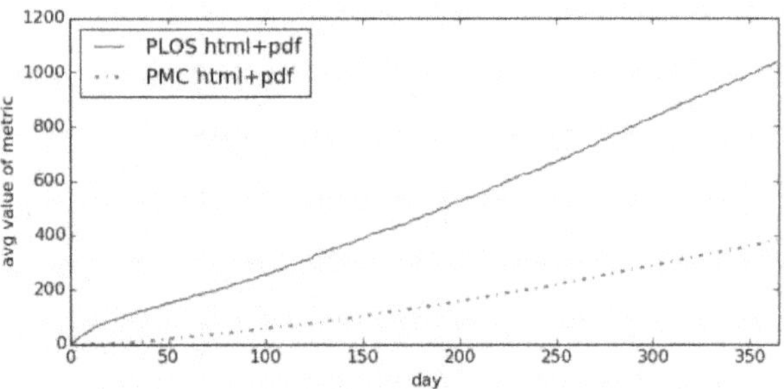

(b) PLOS views+pdf and PMC views+pdf

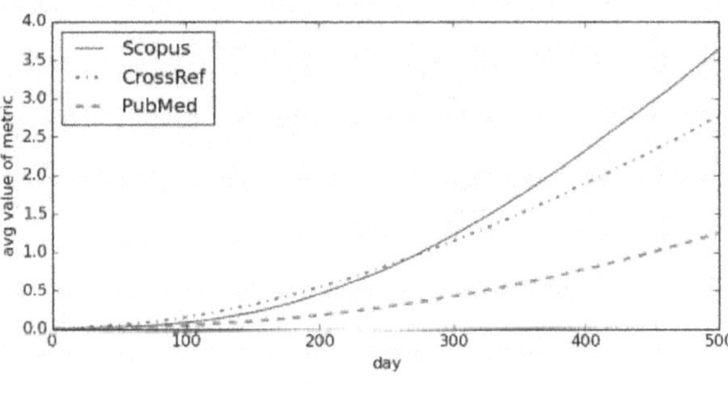

(c) Scopus, CrossRef, PubMed

Figure 2: Progression of different metrics over time

does not comply. Kendall's τ or Spearman's rank correlation coefficient are both applicable for this task but since former work mainly used Spearman's method, we also used Spearman's rank correlation to deliver comparable results. We also calculated the p-values for statistical significance testing which was below 0.01 for each correlation. This suggests that the resulting correlations are statistically significant.

For our correlation analysis, we only used articles from a certain time window, since articles from different time windows are hardly comparable. Take for instance the progression of Tweets in Figure 2a and the CrossRef citations in Figure 2c. The figures show that for most articles the number of tweets is stable after the first few weeks, while the number of citations continues to grow even after 500 days. Hence, the proportion of tweets and citations is highly dependent on the age of the article. For our correlation analysis, we chose all documents between June 2012 and August 2012 (6,731 articles). We performed the last update of the article metrics for these articles in July 2014. The article metrics for this analysis were therefore sampled roughly two years after the articles' publication.

Table 2 shows the pairwise correlation between all examined metrics using Spearman's rank correlation coefficient. Most of the strong correlations are rather obvious like Facebook Comments being correlated to Facebook Likes or HTML views being correlated PDF views. It is interesting however that the correlation between PDF and HTML views on PubMed Central is much higher than on PLOS. It is also interesting that correlations between Facebook and the remaining metrics only seem to rely on Facebook shares since correlations between Facebook shares and other metrics are consistently higher than to any other Facebook metric. It is also noticeable that strong correlations between citation metrics and other metrics are very rare. There are some connections to the view metrics and also to Mendeley but these correlations are rather weak.

Additionally to the analysis on the whole corpus we also analyzed different subsets of the corpus by regarding only document from certain scientific disciplines. Since another set of matrixes would however be far too verbose, we visualized the correlations of these metrics as graphs shown in Figure 3. To build these graphs, we had to choose a threshold defining whether two nodes should be connected by an edge or not. We set this threshold to a correlation of 0.5 which can be considered as a decent correlation. The weight and the color of the edges indicate the strength of the correlation. The size of the nodes indicate the number of non-zero entries for that metric.

The graphs for computer science and medicine show in general much more correlations passing the threshold of 0.5. Especially the view metrics and citation metrics are much more connected to each other. The computer science graph is also the only graph containing correlations to CiteULike, while the social sciences graph is the only graph that has a connection to Twitter. It is also noticeable that the social science graph has no connection to any PubMed Central metric. One commonality of all graphs is however that no correlation between Web 2.0 metrics and citation metrics exist but only between citation metrics and view metrics and between view metrics and Web 2.0 metrics.

This high variance in the correlation of different metrics when observing different communities can be an explanation to the high discordance in the experiments mentioned in the related work. Table 3 further shows a high discordance in the average number of tweets for articles in different domains. Having in mind that the main focus of PLOS is biology and medicine, it is also likely that this effect is even stronger in corpora of domain specific journals in other domains than biology. Another factor that characterises PLOS the open access to its content. Therefore not only scientists have access to the documents in our corpus, but everyone. This influence will also be analyzed.

In the following chapter we therefore plan to analyze the influence of diverse user groups in the social web. For our experiments we mainly used Twitter as one of the most popular social media services, claiming more than 200 million active users in March 2013 creating 400 million Tweets each day [33]. Additionally, Twitter provides very useful metadata for each tweet like the author of the tweet, the actual tweet text, the exact date etc. Besides that, the Twitter API provides detailed profile information for every user.

In the experiments we will first verify if scientist contribute more to the correlation between Web 2.0 metrics and citation metrics. Then we partition the twitter users into diverse groups to verify if different groups of users show different behavior with respect to correlations between the

Table 2: Pairwise correlation between each regarded metric

	Tweets	Facebook shares	Facebook comments	Facebook likes	Mendeley readers	CiteULike shares	PLOS HTML views	PLOS PDF views	PMC HTML views	PMC PDF views	CrossRef citations	PubMed citations	Scopus citations
Tweets	1.000	**0.406**	0.254	0.280	0.313	0.221	**0.425**	0.286	0.060	0.021	0.140	0.110	0.118
Facebook shares	**0.406**	1.000	**0.592**	**0.671**	0.263	0.159	**0.412**	0.294	0.053	0.001	0.125	0.095	0.110
Facebook comments	0.254	**0.592**	1.000	**0.800**	0.193	0.128	0.279	0.216	0.030	-0.005	0.092	0.058	0.097
Facebook likes	0.280	**0.671**	**0.800**	1.000	0.208	0.143	0.301	0.228	0.029	-0.017	0.087	0.072	0.096
Mendeley readers	0.313	0.263	0.193	0.208	1.000	0.309	**0.527**	**0.564**	0.106	0.082	0.276	0.229	0.270
CiteULike shares	0.221	0.159	0.128	0.143	0.309	1.000	0.276	0.249	0.015	-0.017	0.112	0.124	0.108
PLOS HTML views	**0.425**	**0.412**	0.279	0.301	**0.527**	0.276	1.000	**0.797**	**0.406**	0.338	0.383	0.312	0.392
PLOS PDF views	0.286	0.294	0.216	0.228	**0.564**	0.249	**0.797**	1.000	**0.520**	**0.492**	**0.436**	0.341	**0.452**
PMC HTML views	0.060	0.053	0.030	0.029	0.106	0.015	**0.406**	**0.520**	1.000	**0.926**	0.348	0.272	0.347
PMC PDF views	0.021	0.001	-0.005	-0.017	0.082	-0.017	0.338	**0.492**	**0.926**	1.000	0.338	0.263	0.338
CrossRef citations	0.140	0.125	0.092	0.087	0.276	0.112	0.383	**0.436**	0.348	0.338	1.000	0.388	**0.710**
PubMed citations	0.110	0.095	0.058	0.072	0.229	0.124	0.312	0.341	0.272	0.263	0.388	1.000	**0.621**
Scopus citations	0.118	0.110	0.097	0.096	0.270	0.108	0.392	**0.452**	0.347	0.338	**0.710**	**0.621**	1.000

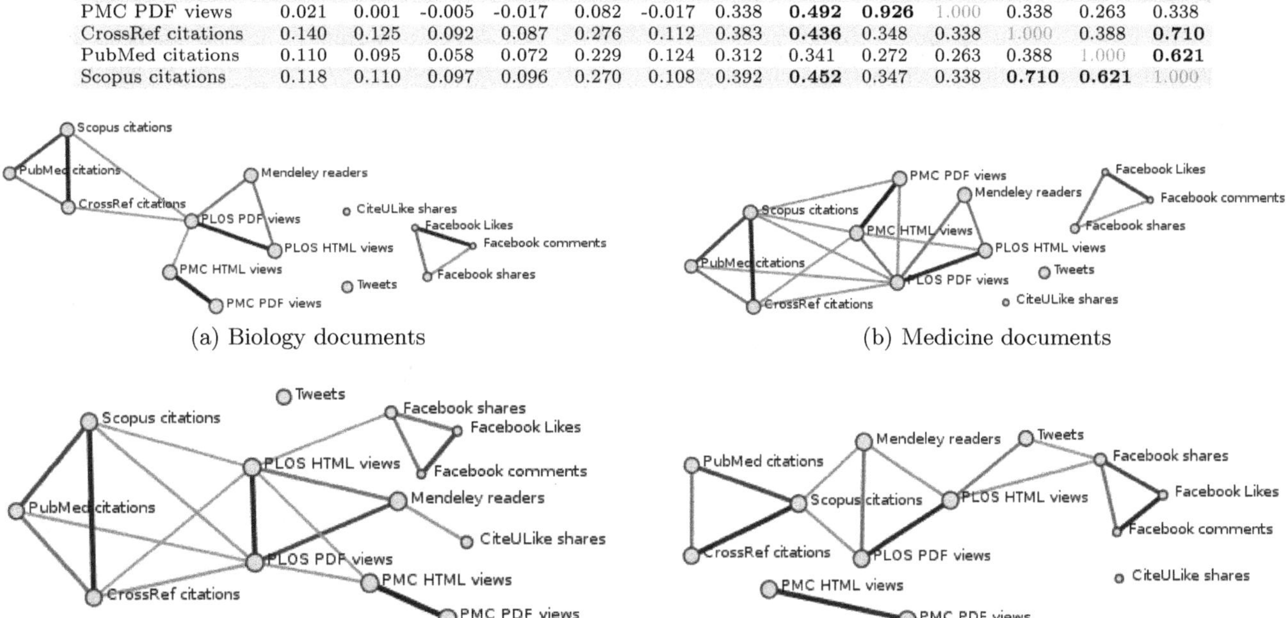

Figure 3: Correlations between metrics as graph

Table 3: Proportion of documents in scientific domains with the average number of tweets referencing papers the domain

Discipline	% Docs	⌀ Tweets
Biological Science	73.48%	3.19
Medicine	32.53%	4.07
Environm. Science	7.82%	7.32
Psychology	7.41%	10.82
Computer Science	5.87%	7.51
Chemistry	5.08%	2.64
Engineering	4.91%	2.92
Physics	3.68%	3.35
Social Science	3.44%	15.98
Earth Science	2.71%	8.28

article metrics. In the end we will present an approach to identify and characterize users that correlate most to the regarded citation metrics.

3.2 Identifying diverse user groups in Twitter

In our corpus twitter related data is available since the middle of March 2012. There is a total amount of 115,892 tweets referencing articles in the PLOS corpus where 10,811 of these tweets reference articles published before the twitter data was available. These tweets were disregarded for the following experiments since otherwise incomplete tweet progressions would interfere with complete tweet progressions. Overall, 53% of all articles was referenced by at least one tweet that were posted by 10,858 distinct users.

In the following experiments we will introduce several methods to identify special user groups. For this user groups we analyzed if the tweets posted by that user group correlate more or less to the remaining article metrics. This is done by ignoring all tweets in the corpus that were not posted by a user in the regarded user group. Afterwards the correlations to all other metrics are recalculated and compared to a baseline.

Used baseline for the following experiments. It is worth mentioning that in order to receive a perfect rank correlation of 1.0 e.g. between tweets and citations there is a minimum amount of tweets needed, since all best cited papers also must have the most tweets, all second best cited papers must have at least one tweet less, and so on. For our corpus, this minimum amount of tweets would be 29,716. Thus, when regarding all tweets in our corpus, it would in theory be possible to reach a rank correlation of 1.0. But if we for instance only regard tweets posted by a very specialized group of domain experts who only composed 5% of all tweets, a rank correlation of 1.0 would even in theory not be achievable anymore. In fact, removing random tweets reduces the correlation between tweets and the remaining metrics significantly. Therefore, when we want to assess the correlations resulting from a certain user group we need a baseline that aware of this condition. In order to build this baseline we picked a random sample of tweets with the same size as the number of tweets that the analyzed user group has tweeted. Additionally, to ensure that this random sample has no undesired properties, we repeated this random sampling 100 times and averaged the correlations gained from the individual runs. This also ensures reproducible results to a satisfying degree.

3.2.1 Detect scientists by exploring user descriptions

In our first experiment we plan to find out if tweets posted by scientists correlate more to citation metrics than tweets posted by other users. To identify scientists we analyzed the twitter descriptions given by the users in their twitter profile. This description is a short text that twitter users can provide to describe themselves and their interests in a short text. In this experiment we assume that scientists mention some characteristic words in their profile descriptions. These words include e.g. "university", "Ph.D." (in different ways of spelling), "professor", "doctor" or "institute". By searching for user descriptions containing at least one of the words in our word list, we found 1232 users.

To ensure that the returned user descriptions really belong to scientists, we manually examined a random sample of 100 user descriptions. In our random sample we had a precision rate of 88%. False positives included for instance twitter accounts directly associated to certain institutes or universities as well as non-researchers hired in a university (e.g. technical staff). A recall could not be determined as for this we must know the true identity of each twitter user (even of those who didn't provide a description). In average the returned users posted 2 tweets referencing articles in the PLOS corpus. Table 4 shows the changes in correlation when only tweets by the identified scientists were used.

Table 4: Differences in correlations when only regarding scientists compared to the baseline described in section 3.2.1

Metric	Δ_{baseline}	Metric	Δ_{baseline}
Crossref	+0.020	PubMed	+0.025
Scopus	+0.020	PLOS pdf	+0.049
PLOS HTML	+0.043	PMC pdf	-0.045
PMC HTML	-0.042	Facebook Shares	+0.027
Facebook Comments	+0.028	Facebook Likes	+0.033
Mendeley Readers	+0.066	CiteULike	+0.073

The results show that the tweets posted by the identified scientists have a slightly higher correlation to citation metrics than average users. Bigger impacts can be found when observing the metrics for scientific document management i.e. Mendeley and CiteULike. Here the increase lies at 7 percent points. It is also noticeable that the identified scientists seam to prefer PLOS over PMC since the increase in correlation to the PLOS view metrics is almost identical to the loss in correlation to the PMC metrics.

3.2.2 Detect experts by annotation of user tweets

One problem with the previous experiment was that not only scientists in the field of biology (which is the main focus of the corpus) were regarded, but scientists in arbitrary domains. The expertise of a user in a certain domain would however be of great interest, since a domain experts recommendation to an article is certainly more valuable. Since another word filtering approach for different domains would however be very prone to errors and would further reduce the number of analyzable users, we instead analyzed the users tweets as an aditional data source for each user. The basic idea is, that if users tweet very often in a certain domain, they certainly have some expertise in that domain. In the following we will use this assumption to identify experts in diverse domains and analyze how the correlations change if only one group of experts is regarded.

Annotating user tweets with Wikipedia categories. The domains that we assign to the twitter users should be as diverse as possible and universally applicable. A good candidate for this purpose are the 24 top categories provided by Wikipedia's category graph. These are Medicine, Sports, Culture, Technology, Education, Health, Business, Belief, Humanities, Society, Life, Arts, Language, Law, History, Geography, Agriculture, Politics, Mathematics, Science, Nature, Environment, People and Chronology. To assign one of this top categories to a tweet, we used the Wikipedia Miner framework [34]. The Wikipedia Miner provides for each tweet a set of concepts (articles in the Wikipedia) that are related to the tweet. By using the Wikipedia category graph, the category of this concept could then be generalized to identify the respective top category. An expert of a top category was then defined as a user who posts more tweets than in that category than an average user. A more detailed description of the method is given in [35]. In this experiment we only used the 200 most recent tweets posted by a user. This both increases the feasibility of the approach due to restrictions from the Twitter API and this also functioned as a normalization since users with a low tweet frequency had an equal chance of being identified as expert as users with high tweet frequency.

Since biology is the main focus in our corpus, we had to ensure that this category is well represented by the used categories. Unfortunately, in the Wikipedia category hierarchy biology firstly occurs in the third level (Nature $\rightarrow$ Natural Science $\rightarrow$ Biology) and is therefore not very well represented. Thus, we introduced an exception and added the biology category to the list of regarded categories. If the category of a tweet can be generalized to biology, the tweet is then annotated both with Biology and Nature. Table 5 shows the number of users considered as experts in the respective discipline.

Table 5: Number of experts w.r.t. Wikipedia's top categories

Category	#users	Category	#users	Category	#users
Biology	1466	Medicine	2986	Sports	2506
Culture	5094	Technology	3861	Education	4349
Health	3158	Business	4367	Belief	4929
Humanities	4391	Society	4775	Life	4236
Arts	4292	Language	4340	Law	2967
History	4131	Geography	3691	Agriculture	3020
Politics	3838	Mathematics	4354	Science	3918
Nature	4463	Environment	2785	People	3598
Chronology	3920				

It is striking that the number of users is significantly higher than the number of identified scientists in our previous experiment. Fortunately, the distribution of experts is also very uniform with the exception of Biology experts. This can however be explained by the fact that Biology is a much more specific category in the Wikipedia category graph. In the following we will analyze the differences in correlations when only tweets posted by those experts are regarded.

Analyze correlations for diverse user groups. In our experiments we first analyzed every category independently and considered only the tweets posted by the experts of a certain category and analyzed the differences in correlations compared to the baseline (as explained in section 3.2). As a whole list of all differences in correlation would be far to verbose, we instead listed for each metric the 3 categories that yielded the most positive impact to that metric and the 3 categories that yielded the most negative impact (see Table 6).

The experiment shows that different user groups can have a significant influence on the metrics in a positive as well as in negative way. For instance when selecting Health and/or Medicine experts, the view correlations to PMC increased significantly while the view correlation to PLOS decreased significantly. Also, most negative correlations considering Facebook occurred when Medicine and/or Health experts were regarded. Some improvements to the Facebook correlations could be observed when People, Arts or Culture experts were regarded.

Our next experiment is inspired by two findings that are observable in the previous experiment. The first observation is that the negative influences in Table 6 is significantly higher than the positive influences. For instance the correlation to Facebook metrics decreases by 10 percent points when only Health experts were regarded. This raises the question if *excluding* certain domain experts from the set of all users would also increase the correlation to certain metrics.

The other finding refers to Table 5, showing the number of experts for each category. Having in mind that the total amount of users in the considered time window is 10,858 and each of the 25 categories contain about 3,000-4,000 users, it is easy to see that the overlap of these expert groups must be very high. To decrease this overlap, it is necessary to increase the threshold that defines a user as expert. E.g. users could be identified as experts if they tweeted more than the average user plus a multiple of the standard deviation in that category. A method to normalize values with respect to their average value and standard deviation is the z-score, where z is the multiple of a standard deviation in the equation $x = \mu + z\sigma$. To give an impression of the selectivity of different z-scores, Table 8 shows the number of users for some categories for different z-scores.

Table 7 shows the results of this improved method. For this results we determined expert groups for each category for different z-scores between -1 and 3 and either included or excluded the tweets of these users from the set of regarded tweets. The results are shown in a similar manner as in the previous experiment: For each metric we show the three sets of users that resulted in the biggest increase in correlation and the three sets of users that resulted in the biggest decrease in correlation. The number in index shows the z-score used to define the experts and the leading sign shows, whether the respective expert group was excluded or included from the set of regarded users ("–": excluded, "+": included). E.g. "+$\text{Life}_{3.0}$: -0.22" in the row "Facebook Likes" means that when only regarding users with a z-score of 3.0 or higher in the Life category, the correlation to Facebook Likes decreases by 22 percent points. And "–$\text{Sports}_{-1.0}$: 0.03" in the CrossRef row means that when *disregarding* users with a z-score of -1.0 or higher in Sports, the correlation to CrossRef citations increases by 3 percent points.

The results show that the effect of the previous experiment were significantly increased by changing the selectivity of the regarded expert groups and by allowing expert groups to be excluded from the set of regarded users. E.g. if only the expert group $\text{Life}_{3.0}$ is regarded, the correlation to all Facebook metrics fall by more than 20 percent points. Also the increase in citation metrics is slightly higher. The best increase for PubMed citations could for instance be achieved by selecting a very focused group in Biology ($\text{Bio}_{2.0}$). And the biggest increase for CrossRef and Scopus citations results when disregarding every user that occasionally talk about topics that are rather unrelated to science like Sports, Law, Arts or Nature. Also the category Mathematics seem to have a negative impact on Scopus citations, which can be seen in both directions: When excluding the user group $\text{Math}_{0.5}$, the correlation to Scopus citations increases and when *only* regarding the user group $\text{Math}_{2.0}$, the correlation to Scopus citations decreases. This tendency accords with the distribution of indexed articles in Scopus which has a clear focus on life science, social science and medicine.

Table 8: Number of experts w.r.t. some exemplarily categories for different z-scores

Category	z=-1	z=0	z=1	z=2	z=3
Biology	2967	1466	728	363	189
Medicine	9054	2986	1623	1030	653
Arts	9267	4292	599	120	44
History	9362	4131	608	136	55
Mathematics	9354	4354	987	288	111
Sports	8801	2506	839	421	235
Life	9387	4236	1487	523	175

3.2.3 Identify users that maximize the correlation to citations

Even though the previous experiments provided some interesting insights on different kinds of user groups, it is noticeable that no experiment had a significant positive impact on the correlation to citation metrics. Therefore, in this experiment we will perform a bottom up approach and first find a user group that positively influences the correlation to citation metrics and will then analyze this set of users to find communalities.

Sort users by impact to citation metrics. In this experiment we will order the users with an insertion sort like algorithm with respect to their impact to citation metrics. An insertion sort algorithm is one of the simplest ordering algorithms where in each step the "smallest" element is appended to a new list of elements and is removed from the original list. This procedure is repeated until the original list of elements is empty.

In our case, the definition of "small" for users is their negative impact on citation metrics. To determine the negative impact of a user in each iteration step, the correlations between tweets and citations are recalculated, ignoring tweets posted by that user. The "smallest" user is then defined as the user where the removal of tweets resulted to the biggest positive impact on the correlation between tweets and citations.

Aggregate citation metrics. One last problem that needs to be addressed is that we do not have a metric, to determine a correlation to *the citation metrics*, but only to every citation metric *independently*. We therefore aggregated the

Table 6: Differences in correlations when only regarding experts of certain categories

Metric	Best cat.		2nd best cat.		3rd best cat.			3rd worst cat.		2nd worst cat.		Worst cat.	
Crossref	Biology	0.01,	Agriculture	0.00,	Sports	-0.00,	...,	Language	-0.03,	Law	-0.03,	Humanities	-0.04
PubMed	Health	0.03,	Biology	0.02,	Medicine	0.02,	...,	Humanities	-0.03,	Language	-0.03,	Arts	-0.03
Scopus	Biology	0.01,	Agriculture	0.00,	Environm.	0.00,	...,	Culture	-0.03,	Language	-0.03,	Humanities	-0.04
PLOS pdf	People	0.02,	Agriculture	0.00,	Chronology	-0.00,	...,	Society	-0.05,	Health	-0.05,	Medicine	-0.05
PLOS HTML	People	0.02,	Chronology	0.02,	Environm.	0.01,	...,	Science	-0.03,	Health	-0.05,	Medicine	-0.05
PMC pdf	Health	0.11,	Medicine	0.10,	Biology	0.05,	...,	Humanities	-0.09,	Geography	-0.09,	Language	-0.09
PMC HTML	Health	0.09,	Medicine	0.08,	Biology	0.03,	...,	Humanities	-0.08,	Language	-0.09,	Geography	-0.09
Facebook Shares	People	0.05,	Culture	0.03,	Sports	0.02,	...,	Biology	-0.08,	Medicine	-0.10,	Health	-0.11
Facebook Comments	People	0.04,	Arts	0.03,	Culture	0.02,	...,	Biology	-0.06,	Medicine	-0.08,	Health	-0.09
Facebook Likes	People	0.05,	Arts	0.03,	History	0.02,	...,	Biology	-0.07,	Medicine	-0.09,	Health	-0.10
Mendeley Readers	Humanities	0.04,	Language	0.03,	Arts	0.03,	...,	Business	-0.04,	Medicine	-0.08,	Health	-0.08
CiteULike	Language	0.05,	Humanities	0.04,	Arts	0.03,	...,	Agriculture	-0.04,	Health	-0.05,	Medicine	-0.06

Table 7: Maximal differences in correlations when including or excluding experts of certain categories. The leading sign indicates whether the respective expert group was excluded or included ("–": excluded, "+": included). The number in the index shows the z-score used to define the selectivity of the expert group (See section 3.2.2 for explanation)

Metric	Best cat.		2nd best cat.		3rd best cat.			3rd worst cat.		2nd worst cat.		Worst cat.	
Crossref	$-$Sports$_{-1.0}$:	0.03,	$-$Law$_{-1.0}$:	0.03,	$-$Human$_{-1.0}$:	0.03,	...,	+Math$_{2.0}$:	-0.05,	+Society$_{1.5}$:	-0.05,	+Politics$_{1.0}$:	-0.06
PubMed	+Bio$_{2.0}$:	0.04,	+Bio$_{1.5}$:	0.03,	+Life$_{1.5}$:	0.03,	...,	+Human$_{1.0}$:	-0.04,	+Nature$_{2.0}$:	-0.04,	+Nature$_{1.5}$:	-0.05
Scopus	$-$Nature$_{-0.5}$:	0.03,	$-$Arts$_{-0.5}$:	0.03,	$-$Math$_{0.5}$:	0.03,	...,	+Math$_{2.0}$:	-0.04,	+Politics$_{1.0}$:	-0.05,	+Belief$_{0.5}$:	-0.05
PLOS pdf	$-$Society$_{0.0}$:	0.03,	$-$Society$_{0.5}$:	0.03,	$-$Health$_{3.0}$:	0.03,	...,	+Health$_{2.5}$:	-0.12,	+Health$_{3.0}$:	-0.14,	+Life$_{3.0}$:	-0.14
PLOS HTML	$-$Med$_{2.5}$:	0.03,	+Arts$_{1.0}$:	0.03,	$-$Health$_{2.5}$:	0.03,	...,	+Health$_{2.5}$:	-0.15,	+Nature$_{2.0}$:	-0.16,	+Life$_{3.0}$:	-0.19
PMC pdf	+Health$_{2.0}$:	0.15,	+Health$_{2.5}$:	0.15,	+Med$_{3.0}$:	0.15,	...,	+Geo$_{1.0}$:	-0.11,	+Geo$_{1.5}$:	-0.12,	+Env$_{1.0}$:	-0.12
PMC HTML	+Health$_{1.5}$:	0.12,	+Health$_{2.0}$:	0.12,	+Health$_{2.5}$:	0.11,	...,	+Geo$_{1.0}$:	-0.11,	+Geo$_{1.5}$:	-0.12,	+Env$_{1.0}$:	-0.13
Facebook Shares	$-$Med$_{0.5}$:	0.06,	$-$Med$_{0.0}$:	0.06,	$-$Health$_{0.5}$:	0.06,	...,	+Bio$_{2.5}$:	-0.20,	+Bio$_{3.0}$:	-0.22,	+Life$_{3.0}$:	-0.23
Facebook Comments	$-$Health$_{-0.5}$:	0.06,	$-$Med$_{0.0}$:	0.05,	$-$Health$_{0.0}$:	0.05,	...,	+Life$_{2.5}$:	-0.16,	+Bio$_{3.0}$:	-0.17,	+Life$_{3.0}$:	-0.20
Facebook Likes	$-$Health$_{0.0}$:	0.06,	$-$Med$_{0.0}$:	0.06,	$-$Health$_{0.5}$:	0.06,	...,	+Bio$_{3.0}$:	-0.18,	+Life$_{2.5}$:	-0.19,	+Life$_{3.0}$:	-0.22
Mendeley Readers	+Env$_{2.0}$:	0.05,	$-$Health$_{0.5}$:	0.05,	$-$Health$_{0.0}$:	0.05,	...,	+Med$_{3.0}$:	-0.15,	+Health$_{2.5}$:	-0.17,	+Life$_{3.0}$:	-0.18
CiteULike	+Belief$_{1.0}$:	0.06,	+Math$_{1.5}$:	0.05,	+Lang$_{0.0}$:	0.05,	...,	+Med$_{3.0}$:	-0.13,	+Health$_{2.5}$:	-0.14,	+Life$_{3.0}$:	-0.16

citation metrics known for an article as described in the following section.

The citation metrics given by the available sources Scopus, PubMed and CrossRef correspond to the amount of times an article was cited *within the respective corpus*. Thus, the provided number of citations is not necessary the "real" number of citations to an article, since the article can also be cited by articles not contained in the respective corpus. Therefore, the number of citations for an article given by a source can only be an estimate of the real number of citations to an article which is always smaller or equal to the real number of citations. To get the best estimate of citations to an article, the best approach would be to compose the union of the citations found by each source, but unfortunately the exact articles citing the article in focus are only provided by CrossRef, while Scopus and PubMed only provide the *number* of citations. Therefore, we can either assume that the citations found in each corpus are mostly distinct or mostly the same. In the first case, a good measure to the aggregate citation based metrics would be the *sum* of the respective metrics and in the latter case the *maximum value* would be more suitable. As we can assume that the overlap of the regarded sources is quite high, we will in the following use the maximum value of Scopus citations, CrossRef citations and PubMed citations as an estimate for the real number of citations for an article.

Characterize users with high impact to citation metrics. For the suggested sorting of users by their impact to citation metrics we only regarded users who posted at least 5 tweets, as for users who posted less than 5 tweets no significant changes in correlations is expected when ignoring their tweets. The pure removal of all users with less than 5 tweets did not influence the correlation between tweets and citations significantly (-0.009).

After the removal of all users who posted less than 5 tweets, 534 users remained to perform the proposed sorting method. Figure 4 shows the differences in the correlation to citations when only the first n users with respect to our sorting are regarded. When only the tweets posted by the first 180 users are regarded, the correlation increases by 18.1 percent points to 27.4%, which can be considered as a weak correlation. The users contained in that set of 180 users will in the following be referenced as the *positive users* (the remaining users as negative users respectively). In our last experiment we will analyze the positive users to find characteristics featuring these users.

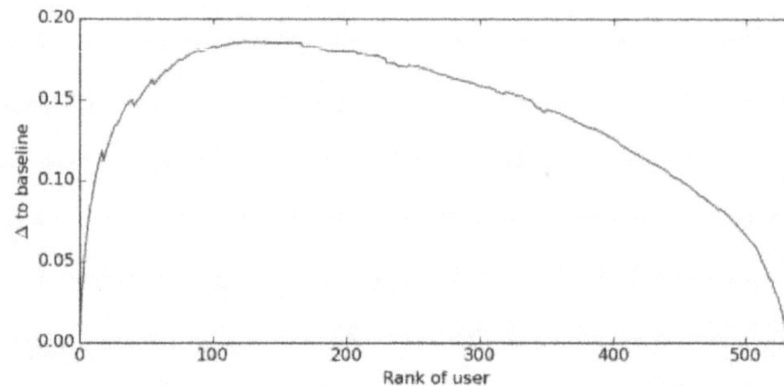

Figure 4: Correlation of first n users to citations metrics w.r.t. the introduced sorting method

In our experiments we identified features that occur more often for positive users than for negative users. The first feature examined were the descriptions given by the users.

Each description was translated into a set of words whereupon frequent words for positive and negative users were determined. To determine frequent words we identified the odds ratio between every word and the positive users, so that the unequal amount of positive and negative user descriptions is of no importance.

The second feature regarded in this experiment are the Twitter lists the users are in. Again, we find for each user the lists they are listed in and determine for each list the odds ratio to positive users.

Finally, as the last feature we analyzed the tweets of a user to find concepts annotated by the Wikipedia miner. The process is analogous to the previous features: The tweets of each user were annotated with Wikipedia concepts (Article titles) to get a set of concepts for each user. Afterwards, the odds ratio between every concept and positive users was calculated.

To ensure that only representative features were selected, we additionally introduced an occurrence threshold that has to be passed before a feature is considered as representative. This step is necessary since the number of distinct features is very high and many inexpressive features with low occurrence can have a high odds ratio just by chance. Table 9 shows for each type of feature a list of the most positive and most negative features.

The list of the most positive features contained in the table are very significant. The positive concepts include the biomedical research foundation Wellcome Trust and several biology related articles. The negative concepts on the other hand seem to be more or less random and unrelated. The most positive lists are also very relevant to biology and science. The positive words are a little bit harder to interpret. There are some biology/medicine relevant words like NCDs (Non-communicable deseases), microbiology or globalhealth. Also some words occur that indicate that our first description filtering approach heads into the right direction. This words include e.g. study, school, education and MD (Doctor of Medicine).

However, this features can currently only to be used to estimate if the returned group of users is reasonable (which seems to be the case). If it is sensible to use this features to actively search for users with high correlation with citations has to be evaluated in future work.

4 CONCLUSION AND FUTURE WORK

In our experiments we identified several diverse user groups and showed the difference in correlation that occur when only one group of users is regarded. We identified these diverse groups by their field of interest, by their expertise and by their influence on the resulting correlations. Our experiments showed that the identified user groups show significant differences in the character of article level metrics. Even though the main focus of the PLOS corpus is biology and medicine, the differences in correlations and average metric values in different domains were significant. The proposed methods are general enough to be applied to arbitrary corpora and provide the chance to view article-level-metrics on a corpus on various different ways.

The high variance in correlations when regarding several diverse user groups also indicates that universal statements regarding altmetrics (e.g. under what conditions tweets might correlate to citations) cannot be made by analyzing just one corpus. Before such universal statements can be proposed, it is necessary to have a large variety of studies conducted on a diverse set corpora. Based on this studies it would be possible to conduct a large meta-study where the experience and knowledge of previous work is aggregated. Unfortunately, the diversity and amount of such studies is currently still insufficient. The correlation analysis conducted on the PLOS corpus in the first part of our experiment section can therefore be seen as a contribution to attain this goal in the future.

The correlation analysis on the PLOS corpus showed that there are three separated classes of metrics that have strong correlations within the same class, but low correlations between different classes. On the one hand there are classic bibliographic measures, like citations, and on the other hand there are Web 2.0 metrics, like tweets or Facebook likes. These two groups have no correlations with each other. However, they are connected by the view metrics (HTML and PDF page views). Although we were able to show that these correlations show significant discordance among different scientific domains, this property still holds for all regarded domains.

In a second series of experiments we identified several diverse groups of users on Twitter and compared their impact on the correlations to the article metrics. First we identified a set of scientists with a simple keyword search approach on profile descriptions. Even though the rate of scientists found with this approach was quite high, we could not confirm that scientists contribute significantly more to citations than other users. This either means that the assumption that scientists contribute more to citation metrics is wrong or that the profession of the scientists was not taken into account appropriately, since also scientists with other research professions than biology or medicine were returned in this experiment.

In subsequent experiments we partitioned the users by their fields of interest that were designed to be as diverse as possible. We did this by identifying users as experts with respect to the Wikipedia's top-level categories. By including and excluding user groups defined by that approach, we could show that significant changes to several metrics could be achieved. For content provider this approach can be interesting, since it can be used as tool to identify particularities and preferences of their community. If a large change in correlation can be observed when a certain group of users is regarded, this indicates that this group is a predominant group within the regarded corpus. E.g. using this approach it was very clear that medicine and health experts are an important user group to PubMed Central, which is certainly true.

In our last experiment we used a bottom up approach to first find a set of users that enhances the correlation between tweets and citations significantly and afterward analyzed and characterized that set of users. In our experiment we used this method to identify a group of users that raises the correlation between tweets and citation metrics from about 10% to about 30%. Afterwards we characterized that set of users by analyzing their profile descriptions on twitter, the Twitter lists the users are listed on and the concepts the Wikipedia miner annotated to their tweets. The features found for the group of users were related to biology, medicine or science in general.

Currently, these identified features are only to be used to estimate if the returned group of users is reasonable. In future work we plan to find out if these features can also be used to actively search users that are more appropriate for an early estimate of scientific quality for articles. Of course this approach can also be used to find and characterize users

Table 9: List of positive and negative features characterizing users with high correlation to citation metrics

Words	pos: ncds, people, microbiology, general, conservation, study, school, practice, evidence, globalhealth, md, education, tropical, ... neg: global, working, neuroscientist, technology, leading, cell, work, founder, into, media, daily, psychologist, dad, math, ...
Lists	pos: pharma, computational biology, genetics, genomics, bioinfo, genome, medicina, top scientists, twitter science, ... neg: blinded me with science, cognitive, my feed, neuro/psych, social media, colleagues, journals, mental health, technology, ...
Concepts	pos: Commentary (magazine), Wellcome Trust, Whole genome sequencing, Long non-coding RNA, Biome, Omics, Humanos, ... neg: Hypertext Transfer Protocol, Spacetime, Tears, Point and click, Wall Street, Synchronization, Matrix (mathematics), ...

that have a high correlation to other metrics like e.g. view counts. This could be used to measure an effective hubness of a user i.e. find users whose tweets really result in more views. For future work it will be interesting to find out if this effective hubness differs conceptually from the number of followers.

The proposed methods can also be considered as fundamentals to distinguish more important and less important tweets. This will be a very relevant problem in the moment when altmetrics are used as a means to judge scientific quality in a large scale. In this case, it is a matter of time until services that publish tweets for money (REF) also specialize on boosting the reputation of scientists for money. In this scenario the proposed methods can be good fundamentals to detect and ignore spam tweets, as they will probably not correlate to any metric that is interesting for an information provider.

5 References

[1] A. Pritchard, Statistical Bibliography or Bibliometrics, Journal of Documentation, vol. 25, pp. 348–349, 1969

[2] E. Garfield, The Thomson Reuters Impact Institute, Technical Report, Factor for Scientific Information, 1994

[3] J. E. Hirsch, An index to quantify an individual's scientific research output, Proc. Natl. Acad. Sci. U. S. A., vol. 102, pp. 16569–16572, 2005

[4] T. Brody and S. Harnad, Earlier Web Usage Statistics as Predictors of Later Citation Impact, Journal of the American Society for Information Science and Technology, vol. 57, no. 8, pp. 1060–1072, 2006

[5] J. Priem, K. Costello and T. Dzuba, Prevalence and use of Twitter among scholars, figshare, DOI: http://dx.doi.org/10.6084/m9.figshare.104629, 2012

[6] J. Priem and K. L. Costello, How and why scholars cite on Twitter, Proc. Am. Soc. Inf. Sci. Technol., vol. 47, no. 1, pp. 1–4, 2010

[7] J. Bar-Ilan, S. Haustein, I. Peters, J. Priem, H. Shema, and J. Terliesner, Beyond citations: Scholars' visibility on the social web, in Proceedings of 17th International Conference on Science and Technology Indicators, vol. 52900, pp. 98–109, 2012

[8] J. Priem and B. M. Hemminger, Scientometrics 2.0: Toward new metrics of scholarly impact on the social Web, First Monday, vol. 15, no. 7, 2010

[9] C. Neylon and S. Wu, Article-level metrics and the evolution of scientific impact, PLoS Biol'09, vol. 7, no. 11, 2009

[10] D. Taraborelli, Soft peer review: Social Software and Distributed Scientific Evaluation, in International Conference on the Design of Cooperative Systems, 2008

[11] M. Fenner, What can article-level metrics do for you?, PLoS Biol., vol. 11, no. 10, p. e1001687, 2013

[12] P. Groth and T. Gurney, Studying Scientific Discourse on the Web using Bibliometrics: A Chemistry Blogging Case Study, WebSci'10, 2010

[13] M. Thelwall, S. Haustein, V. Larivíére, and C. R. Sugimoto, Do altmetrics work? Twitter and ten other social web services, PLoS One, vol. 8, no. 5, 2013

[14] R. C. Roemer and R. Borchardt, Institutional Altmetrics and Academic Libraries, Inf. Stand. Q., vol. 25, no. 2, pp. 14–19, 2013

[15] J. Liu and E. Adie, Five challenges in altmetrics: A toolmaker's perspective, Bull. Am. Soc. Inf. Sci. Technol., vol. 39, pp. 31–34, 2013

[16] P. Wouters and R. Costas, Users' narcissism and control – tracking the impact of scholarly publications in the 21 st century, Image Rochester NY, p. 50 pages, 2012

[17] H. A. Piwowar, Altmetrics: Value all research products, Nature, vol. 493, p. 159, 2013

[18] X. Li, M. Thelwall, and D. Giustini, Validating online reference managers for scholarly impact measurement, Scientometrics, vol. 91. pp. 461–471, 2012

[19] E. S. Darling, D. Shiffman, I. M. Côté, and J. a. Drew, The role of Twitter in the life cycle of a scientific publication, PeerJ Prepr., vol. 1, p. 16, 2013

[20] K. Weller, E. Dröge, and C. Puschmann, Citation Analysis in Twitter: Approaches for Defining and Measuring Information Flows within Tweets during Scientific Conferences, Proc. ESWC'11, pp. 1–12, 2011

[21] C. R. Sugimoto and M. Thelwall, Scholars on Soap Boxes: Science Communication and Dissemination via TED Videos, J. Am. Soc. Inf. Sci. Technol., 2012

[22] B. Cronin, Metrics á la mode, J. Am. Soc. Inf. Sci. Technol., vol. 64, no. 6, pp. 1091–1091, 2013

[23] J. Kaur, D. T. Hoang, X. Sun, L. Possamai, M. JafariAsbagh, S. Patil, and F. Menczer, Scholarometer: A Social Framework for Analyzing Impact across Disciplines, PLoS One, vol. 7, 2012

[24] M. Taylor, Exploring the Boundaries: How Altmetrics Can Expand Our Vision of Scholarly Communication and Social Impact, Inf. Stand. Q., vol. 25, no. 2, p. 27, 2013

[25] K.-K. Yan and M. Gerstein, The spread of scientific information: insights from the web usage statistics in PLoS article-level metrics, PLoS One, vol. 6, no. 5, 2011

[26] W. Gunn, Social signals reflect academic impact: What it means when a scholar adds a paper to Mendeley, Inf. Stand. Q., vol. 25, no. 2, pp. 33–39, 2013

[27] I. Guy, U. Avraham, D. Carmel, S. Ur, M. Jacovi, and I. Ronen, Mining expertise and interests from social media, WWW'13, pp. 515–526, 2013

[28] S. Ghosh, N. Sharma, and F. Benevenuto, Cognos: crowdsourcing search for topic experts in microblogs, SIGIR'12, no. 1, pp. 575–584, 2012

[29] G. Eysenbach, Correction: Can Tweets Predict Citations? Metrics of Social Impact Based on Twitter and Correlation with Traditional Metrics of Scientific Impact, Journal of Medical Internet Research, 2012

[30] X. Shuai, A. Pepe, and J. Bollen, How the Scientific Community Reacts to Newly Submitted Preprints: Article Downloads, Twitter Mentions, and Citations, PLoS One, vol. 7, 2012

[31] R. Costas, Z. Zahedi, and P. Wouters, Do altmetrics correlate with citations? Extensive comparison of altmetric indicators with citations from a multidisciplinary perspective, CoRR'14, 2014

[32] S. Haustein, I. Peters, C. R. Sugimoto, M. Thelwall, and V. Larivíere, Tweeting biomedicine: An analysis of tweets and citations in the biomedical literature, J. Assoc. Inf. Sci. Technol., 2013

[33] K. Wickre, Celebrating #Twitter7, [Accessed: 10-Mar-2014]. https://blog.twitter.com/2013/celebrating-twitter7, 2013

[34] D. Milne and I. H. Witten, An open-source toolkit for mining Wikipedia, Artif. Intell., vol. 194, pp. 222–239, 2013

[35] P. Siehndel and R. Kawase, Twikime! User profiles that make sense, In Proceedings of the 11th International Semantic Web Conference (Posters and Demos), 2012

Unified Relevance Feedback for Multi-Application User Interest Modeling

Sampath Jayarathna, Atish Patra, and Frank Shipman
Computer Science & Engineering, Texas A&M University
College Station, TX 77843-3112
(Sampath, apatra, shipman)@cse.tamu.edu

ABSTRACT

A user often interacts with multiple applications while working on a task. User models can be developed individually at each of the individual applications, but there is no easy way to come up with a more complete user model based on the distributed activity of the user. To address this issue, this research studies the importance of combining various implicit and explicit relevance feedback indicators in a multi-application environment. It allows different applications used for different purposes by the user to contribute user activity and its context to mutually support users with unified relevance feedback. Using the data collected by the web browser, Microsoft Word and Microsoft PowerPoint, combinations of implicit relevance feedback with semi-explicit relevance feedback were analyzed and compared with explicit user ratings. Our results are two-fold: first we demonstrate the aggregation of implicit and semi-explicit user interest data across multiple everyday applications using our Interest Profile Manager (IPM) framework. Second, our experimental results show that incorporating implicit feedback with semi-explicit feedback for page-level user interest estimation resulted in a significant improvement over the content-based models.

Categories and Subject Descriptors

H.3.3 [**Information Storage and Retrieval**]: Information Search and Retrieval – *Information filtering, Retrieval models*

Keywords

User interest modeling, implicit and explicit feedback, personalized information delivery

1. INTRODUCTION

Perhaps due to the difficulty in expressing a more precise query, many queries consist of only a few keywords to model the real information need. These short queries often contain only marginally informative content about user's actual intention and therefore may have difficulty returning content relevant to the user's desired topic. Such query term mismatch is compounded by synonymy and polysemy [10], resulting in user confusion.

In order to mitigate the inherent ambiguity of queries, web search engines employ search personalization to customize search results based on the inferred interests of the user. The belief is that detailed knowledge about a user's interests, i.e. the *user interest model*, can improve the support of searching and browsing activities as every user has a particular goal and a distinct combination of context and background knowledge [35].

JCDL'15, June 21–25, 2015, Knoxville, Tennessee, USA.

ISBN 978-1-4503-3594-2/15/06…$15.00
DOI: http://dx.doi.org/10.1145/2756406.2756914

Even though personalized information delivery has the potential to provide users accurate results relevant to search intentions, personalization is particularly challenging due to two key issues. First, it requires identifying the interests of users in semi-persistent user profiles. Estimating user preferences in a real user interaction with a web search engine is a challenging problem, since the interactions tend to be more noisy than a controlled setting [2]. Second, given the user preferences recorded in a user profile, personalized information delivery requires a way to alter the presentation of search results to reflect those preferences. This paper is focused on the first of these problems. The particular approach being explored here looks to broaden current techniques by including a variety of direct and indirect evidence of interest across multiple applications.

Real-world personalization is often dynamic in nature and information delivered to the user can be automatically personalized and catered to individual user's information needs [25]. However, people interact with different applications, and have extra information about the content they are interacting with. These interactions results in implicit feedback (e.g., click-through data, reading time) and semi-explicit feedbacks (e.g., annotations) data that varies depending on their task and the type of information being explored. For example, a user may examine a list of search results in a web browser; or PDF Reader to examine the contents of individual documents; she may use a note-taking tool to keep track of interesting snippets; and she may use word processing applications or a presentation tool to author her own interpretation of what she has found. Therefore, a user model from a single application is unlikely to be as effective as a user model based on the aggregate activity across applications [4].

1.1 Contributions

We have previously reported [5] on the aggregation of semi-explicit feedback across a web browser and customized organization tool and its use. Here, we present a software framework and server for using both semi-explicit and implicit relevance feedback affects resulting user models in the context of multiple everyday applications. One objective of the research is to collect, measure and evaluate the predictive power of implicit and semi-explicit relevance indicators in a multi-application environment.

The rest of this paper is as follows: Section 2 describes related work in multi-application interest modeling and relevance feedback; Section 3 describes the system architecture; Section 4 explains how the activity data is turned into user models; Section 5 describes the collection of the corpus; Section 6 analyzes the results from evaluating alternative user modeling approaches with the corpus data; and Section 7 presents discussion, conclusions and some possible future work.

2. RELATED WORK

Our work is informed by related and prior work in the areas of multi-application user modeling and relevance feedback.

2.1 Multi-Application User Modeling

User models can be developed by adapting the content consumed or produced by the user, and their specific task, background, history and information needs [31]. These models can bring users' attention to valuable content via personalized presentations. Recognizing the user interest based on observed user activity is confounded by idiosyncratic work practices. As a result, systems that aggregate evidence of user interest from a wide variety of sources are more likely to build a robust user interest model.

There are two main approaches to user modeling in a component-based architecture. These vary based on the degree of centralization of the user models. Decentralized (or distributed) user modeling had its roots in agent-based architectures; here fragments of user model are kept and maintained by each independent application. In a centralized approach, the integrated user model is stored in a central server and the model is then shared across several user-adaptive applications. These include user modeling servers such as IPM [5], CUMULATE [9], UMS[21] and PersonisAD [3]. Another important distinction among user modeling approaches is whether the model is represented via features or content (see Table 1). Feature-based user models define a set of feature-value pairs representing various aspects of the user, such as interest in a specific category or a level of knowledge in a specific area. Content-based approaches take into account the user's area of interest, as an example, the textual content of documents the user has previously indicated as relevant. These systems generate recommendations by learning user needs with the analysis of available rated content.

Table 1: Related work in multi-application user modeling architectures and software frameworks

	Centralized	Distributed
Feature-based	PersonisAD [3], UMS [21]	Mypes [1], Life-log sharing [15]
Content-based	IPM [5], CUMULATE [9]	G-profile [6]

PersonisAD is a framework for building ubiquitous computing applications. It defines a user model based on data gathered from different sensors and combines their preferences using resolvers to provide a tailored experience. CUMULATE is a generic modeling server developed for a distributed E-Learning architecture to help students select the most relevant self-assessment quizzes by inferring their knowledge of a predefined set of topics based on authored relationships among activities in the educational applications and topics. UMS is a user modeling server based on the LDAP protocol which allows for the representation of user interests using a predefined taxonomy for the application domain. External clients can submit and retrieve information about users using the arbitrary components that perform user modeling tasks on these models.

In Mypes [1], the authors introduce a cross-system user modeling on the social web based on interoperable distributed model where a single vector-based user model is built using hand crafted alignment rules to map between different social web applications (e.g. Flickr, Twitter, and Delicious). In [15] authors present a distributed, decentralized architecture for sharing and re-using logged data from different systems using standalone agents with the help of broker for a successful exchange. G-profile [6] provides a general-purpose, flexible user model system based on abstract protocol to interact with and concept mapping between user data among applications. In [29], the authors present a vision of a P2P architecture to generate and maintain a distributed user model based on pre-defined information exchange templates. Each peer acts as a stand-alone user model agent which only handles information from a single source. In [11] , the authors present a model for achieving user model interoperability by means of semantic dialogues in a P2P manner.

A number of the related approaches for multi-application interest modeling require a predefined set of potential interests/taxonomy or require pair-wise alignment rules to be developed that map interests between applications. In our approach the set of user interests and the distinctions between them are constructed based on the content encountered rather than pre-agreed upon by the contributing applications. In comparison, our system extends prior work on IPM [4, 5, 18] and enables the comparison of the effectiveness of user models via unified relevance feedback

2.2 Relevance Feedback

User modeling can be viewed as a form of relevance feedback. Relevance feedback has a history in information retrieval systems that dates back well over thirty years and has been used for query expansion during short-term modeling of a users' immediate information need [20]

Implicit interest indicators are based on user actions rather than on explicit value assessments. During a search task, readers indicate their interest in documents by how they interact with them: by how much of the document they examine (e.g. how far into a document they scroll); and through other behaviors and events that are specific to the tools they are using. For example, the Curious Browser [13] records various types of implicit feedback include aspects of mouse usage, keyboard usage and the time spent viewing documents.

Explicit feedback requires users to assess the relevance of documents or to indicate their interest in certain aspects of the content. Explicit feedback has the advantages that it can be easily understood, is fairly precise and requires no further interpretation [13]. Explicit feedback can be recorded in the form of user ratings of documents' "relevance score", "readability score" and "topic familiar before" ratings [37]. WebMate [12], InfoFinder [22], and contextual relevance feedback [14, 23] learn and keep track of user interests incrementally as users provide explicit assessments of pages they examine. Some user actions, particularly annotations, and bookmarking, can be interpreted as semi-explicit feedback in that the user's action is clear evidence of their desire

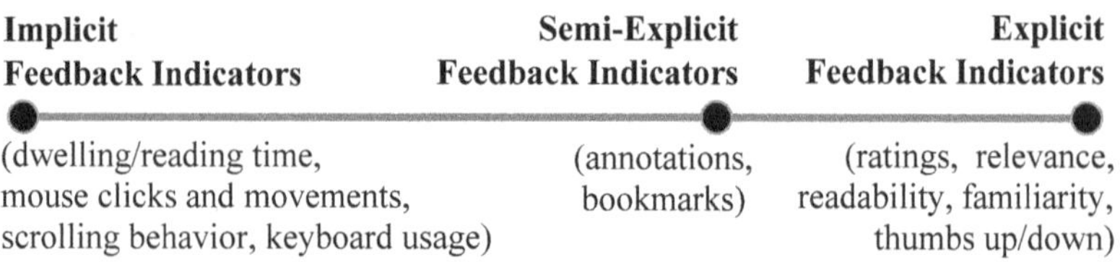

Figure 1: Types of relevance feedback indicators

to re-access this content. A user can mark-up a portion of a document by highlighting a paragraph or attaching an electronic sticky note. Not all reading results in annotations. Annotations are most likely when people read materials crucial to a particular task at hand and are infrequent when reading for fun [34].

Figure 1 shows how user actions form a continuum from implicit to explicit feedback. There is a clear tradeoff between the quantity and quality when comparing implicit feedback with explicit feedback. Explicit feedback indicators are higher in quality but lower in quantity because it is rather burdensome to enter a rating for every item a user liked or disliked [24]. On the other hand, implicit feedback indicators are abundant in quantity but lower in quality because they must be interpreted by heuristic algorithms that make assumptions about the relationships between the observable low-level actions and the high level goals of users. In [28], authors evaluated the costs and benefits of using implicit feedback indicators over explicit feedback indicators. The results suggested that the implicit ratings can be combined with existing explicit ratings to form a hybrid system to predict user satisfaction. In [16], authors showed that implicit and explicit positive feedback complement each other with similar performances despite their different characteristics. This implies that systems can be designed to use the correlation between implicit and explicit feedback to tune the interest modeling algorithms based on implicit feedback.

In this research, we combine semi-explicit and implicit feedback together in a multi-application environment to infer users' information preferences.

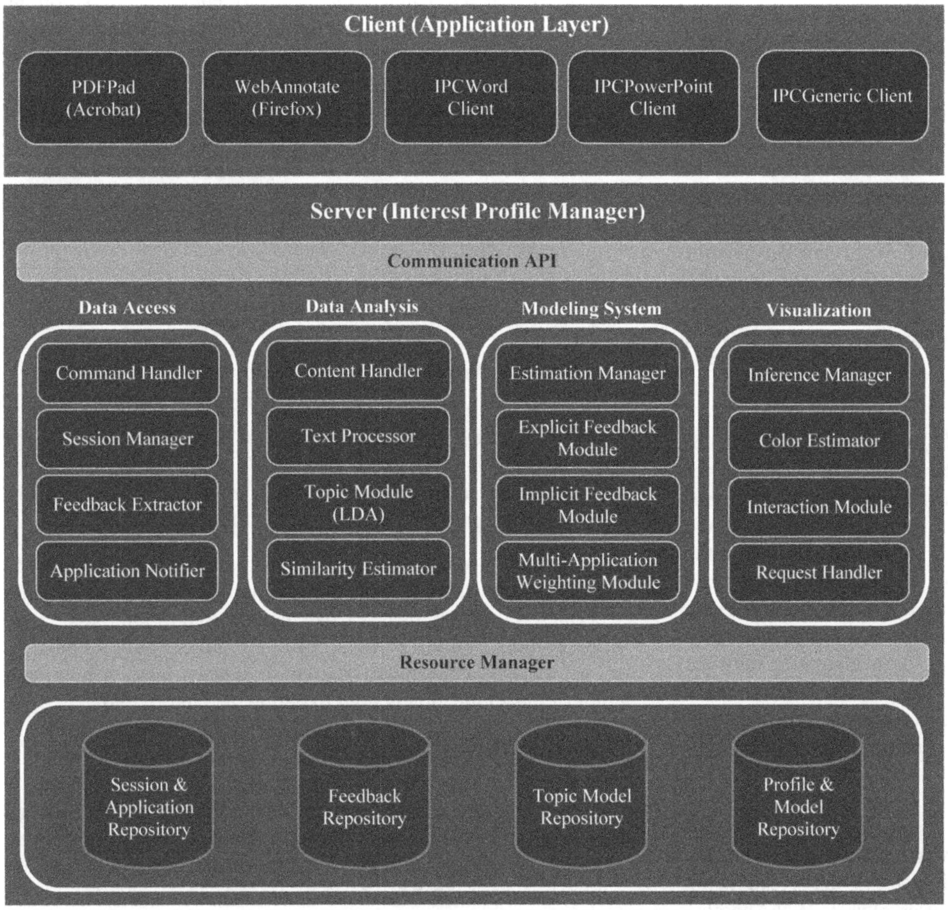

3. System Architecture

The Interest Profile Manager (IPM) is a multi-application environment based personal profile server (see Figure 2) to support search personalization. The IPM collects user activity across many applications and infers user interests using this collected implicit and semi-explicit interest information. It also shares the inferred user interests with registered applications that ask for it. We also presents a generic client stub to show that any application that can be modified to include the interest profile client software and communicate with the IPM enabling user interest modeling capability.

We have used Mozilla-Firefox as the application to present search results and also to visualize recommendations and three other applications: PDFPad which is an acrobat add-on; IPCWord which is a Microsoft Word add-on; IPCPowerPoint which is a Microsoft PowerPoint add-on. Records of user activity in PDFPad, Mozilla, MS Word and MS PowerPoint are stored in the IPM and drive the visualizations that the IPM generates for each of the application registered for relevant notification request. An interest profile is made up of the aggregated heterogeneous interest evidence collected from these different IPM clients.

The IPM defines the XML communication interface so that other application clients can interact with IPM over TCP/IP. The IPM framework includes two modules involved in estimating the user interest, the Estimation Manager and the Estimation module which is again decomposed to 3 sub-modules: Multi-Application Weighting module, implicit feedback module and explicit feedback module. The Estimation Manger provides a generic high level interface to the other modules within the IPM and also enables multiple modules to estimate the user's interests using different algorithms. In the Multi-Application Weighting module (see section 4.2 for further discussion), each application is assigned a weight based on the particular user's activities in the various applications. These learned weights are used to merge the estimated interests from the different applications when modeling the overall user interest. The implicit and explicit relevance modules handle the implicit and explicit feedback indicators respectively. The combined outputs from these two modules are used to estimate the final unified user interests for a search task.

The Resource Manager communicates with data repository to update the user interests according to the user activity data sent from application clients. The Data Repository also saves session data both in terms of contextual and temporal features so that the user activity can be defined as a group of search tasks related to each other in order to make inferences about evolving information needs. This is

Figure 2: Interest Profile Manager architecture and software components

particularly important because if we are able to accurately identify changes to the users' information seeking intent, then we will be in a better position to limit the application of particular inferences about user interests [19]. The Data Repository also saves both feedback data and application data received from application clients for further processing at the estimation modules.

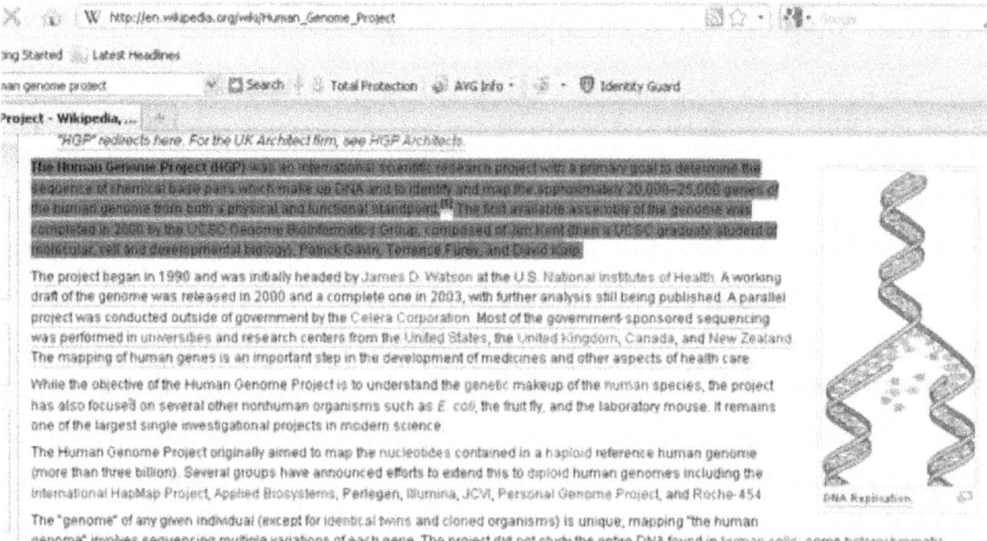

Figure 3: User highlights and system generated recommendations underlined

3.1 Interest Representation

Although each application has unique information that may be used to gauge human interest, this interest assessment needs to be sharable among the different applications to be useful in building the complete interest model of a user. The IPM depends on an abstract XML representation for receiving interest-related information from applications and for broadcasting inferred interest to client applications. Because we realize that we cannot foresee all of the ways different applications will allow users to interact with documents, the representation is extremely general and extensible. Thus an interest profile consists of a document identifier, an application identifier, and a list of application-specific attribute/value pairs. In this way, new applications only have to inform the IPM of the attributes and how they demonstrate user interest when registering.

While some of these applications support two-way communication, this is not required; an application could merely provide information to the IPM or only receive interest information from the IPM. PDFPad and WebAnnotate support two-way communications while Microsoft Word and PowerPoint support one-way communication. Applications also can be categorized into (i) *Consumption Applications*, for examining existing content; and (ii) *Production Applications*, for creating content.

3.2 Interest Extraction

Whenever a document is opened in Microsoft Word or PowerPoint, event handlers are registered for user events. Event handlers save each interaction and their values locally and send them in XML format to IPM. Additionally, the content of the document and document characteristics are sent to the IPM at the time of closing the document. Similarly, WebAnnotate parses raw text to identify every paragraph when a new web page is opened. It also appends mouse and keyboard events in a buffer and saves the color and relevance score assigned to each annotation until the browser is moved to the background. All the raw information is sent to IPM in an XML format at focus out event or at the web page close event. The buffer is reset once the focus is brought back to the web page.

3.3 Explicit Feedback

During an information gathering activity, useful documents may be long and cover multiple subtopics; users may read some segments and ignore others. The browser plug-in WebAnnotate [5] enables basic annotation capabilities so that users can make persistent annotations on web pages and passages and get suggestions within these documents based on estimated user interests. The interest classes can be defined based on annotations' color, type and content in WebAnnotate. To identify segments of new or unread documents to bring to the user's attention, these classes are then compared against the segments of the document currently displayed in WebAnnotate generated by the text-tiling algorithm. When a match is identified, an underline (based on the intensity of the inferred interest value) of the appropriate color for the class is used to signal the similarity. In Figure 3 the user has opened the Wikipedia page for the Human Genome Project and highlighted text related to the history of the project. It can be seen that other paragraphs are underlined with the same color indicating that they are similar to the passage highlighted.

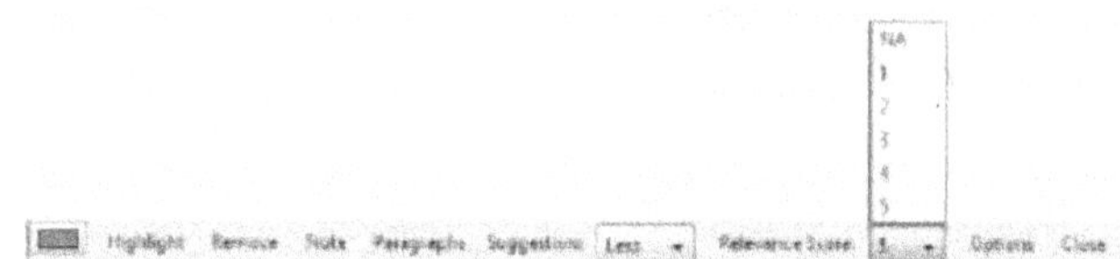

Figure 4: WebAnnotate toolbar for rating paragraphs

In the current study, WebAnnotate was extended to include three types of explicit ratings for content: "page relevance", "page familiarity", and "paragraph relevance" on a 5-point scale after each paragraph annotation, WebAnnotate allows the user to mark individual paragraphs as relevant to their task (see Figure 4).

A user might also use Microsoft Word or PowerPoint applications to open, read or modify some documents. The user's actions while working on these applications can also be used to infer some type of user's interests. MS Word and PowerPoint consider all the data in one document to belong to a single interest class. The default color of the application is used to define the interest class.

3.4 Implicit Feedback

We utilize a set of the implicit feedback indicators during a document reading activity to characterize the interactions between the user and documents. These document reading activities include user actions during a passive reading in a consumption application (web browser or PDF reader). This consists of time spent in a document, number of mouse clicks, number of text selections, number of document accesses and characteristics of user scrolling behaviors such as number of scrolls, scrolling direction changes, time spent scrolling, scroll offset, total number of scroll groups. Furthermore, we collect time spent on a production application (MS Word or PowerPoint), focus in/out and other formatting activities. Table 2 summarizes the user events and document attributes collected from both production and consumption applications during this research study.

Table 2: Interest indicators from applications

Interest Category/ Application	Microsoft Word/PowerPoint	Browser (Firefox)
User characteristics	Click, double click, right click, focus in/out, total Time, edit time, idle time, away time	Click, double click, right click, focus out, total Time, reading time, away time, number of scrolls, number of scrolling direction changes
Document characteristics	Size, number of characters, images, links, last access time, number of slides, text boxes	Images, links, document relevance and familiarity score (explicit)
Textual characteristics	Text edited (semi-explicit)	Text annotated (semi-explicit)

The interest profile broadly contains three types of interest indicators, characteristics of the user, the document as a whole, and the textual content of the document. The user features are derived from implicit feedback data. All these features vary from one user to another as they heavily depend on the individual practices. Document features are high level features of the documents that are the same across users. Finally, document text features are generated from the user's annotations in consumption applications and from the user's produced content from production applications. Document text content provides evidence of more focused interest than the general document features. Such evidence is important when identifying the specific parts of documents that are expected to be relevant.

Another type of feature important in this work is content similarity. Content similarity metrics are used to measure the overlap between the textual content of the user's previous interactions and any future text content. These similarities are computed between text considered valuable to the user (user authored or annotated text) and all other paragraphs displayed in the browser. The similarity score represents the user's interest expressed through the textual content. In this work, Latent Dirichlet Allocation (LDA) is used to compute the content similarity using Hellinger Distance measure (see section 4.1 and 6.1 for further discussion) and are then normalized to be between [0-1] using max-min normalization.

4. MODELS OF USER INTEREST

The IPM uses the document attributes (e.g. metadata, term vectors, user-assigned color) to determine classes of user interest. Attributes of the document as a whole and textual characteristic of document segments are selected based on evidence of interest in individual documents. To aid in the creation of descriptions of document classes, the IPM includes term vector and metadata analysis capabilities as well as text tiling capabilities to allow clients and the IPM to analyze text at the sub-document level. Currently, user-assigned annotation color is used to identify the known members of an interest class while the identification of documents and document components similar to that class is based on the other document attributes and user characteristics.

The next subsections describe the use of topic modeling for similarity assessments of textual content in the user model or of potential value to the user, the weighting of features across the different applications, and the development of semi-explicit and unified feedback models.

4.1 Topic Modeling of Textual Content

Before introducing our topic modeling approach for inferring user interests, we first give a brief review of the statistical model LDA and its parameters used in this research study. LDA [8] is a hierarchical Bayesian model that assumes each document is a finite mixture of a set of topics K and each topic is an infinite mixture over a set of topic probabilities. Unlike clustering methods, LDA does not assume that each document can only be assigned to one topic. Given a document collection, we use LDA to find a set of topics discussed in the document collection. Each topic is represented as a set of words that have a higher probability than others to appear in the text unit related to the topic. Based on the probability distribution of words in each topic, we can calculate the probability that each document may contain a topic and obtain a document-topic assignment.

We set LDA parameters; a number of topics $K = 5$ to match the number of topic clusters anticipated (see section 6.1 and Figure 5 for a detailed discussion on topic selection), two smoothing parameters $\alpha = 0.01$ and $\beta = 0.01$ [27]. As words are the only observable variables in an LDA model, conditional independence holds true for the outputs of LDA model which are document-topic and topic-words distributions Φ and Θ.

For a corpus containing D documents, the parameters, the $D \times K$ matrix of document-topic probability distribution per each document and the $K \times W$ matrix of topic-words probability distribution per each topic must be learned from the data. Parameter fitting is performed using collapsed Gibbs sampling [30] with sampling and burn-in iterations set to 1 and 5 respectively. We look at the difference in the content from two text units by first computing the LDA document-topic distributions Φ_i and Φ_j $(i, j = 1..K, i \neq j)$ and then by calculating the divergence between these two document-topic distributions. The smaller the divergence is, the stronger the associated similarity is.

We performed an evaluation to determine the feasibility of topic modeling divergence methods in our context and to select among alternative topic modeling approaches (this is described in detail in section 6.1). Based on those results, we use Hellinger distance [7] to compare the similarity between document-topic distributions.

$$D_{LDA+H}(\Phi_i || \Phi_j) = \sqrt{\frac{1}{2} \sum_{i,j=1}^{K} \left(\sqrt{\Phi_i} - \sqrt{\Phi_j}\right)^2} \quad (1)$$

4.2 Multi-Application Weighting

Once we have user, document, and textual characteristics as well as textual similarity measures, we need to weight the various features to predict the likelihood of interest in the target. Rather than using one set of weights for all users, we train the interest model using weighted K nearest neighbor (WKNN). This enables weights to adapt to the user-specific patterns present in the feature space. The weights for the features result in a classifier algorithm that tries to predict relevance score for each paragraph on a 5-point scale. From here onwards, we denote C as the relevance label.

In this work, we have combined two variants of KNN, i.e., attribute-weighted and distance-weighted KNN to a build our weighted KNN classifier. By introducing a feature weight component in the distance metric (Equation 2), the quality of the feature is also considered in addition to the difference in value of the feature. Thus, more useful features are given more weight while the less useful features have less weight in the ultimate distance measurement. As a result, useful features have greater impact on the distance function compared to irrelevant features.

$$d(x,y)_w = \sqrt{\sum_{j=1}^{d} w_{cj}^2 (y^j - x^j)^2} \quad (2)$$

Where c = class(x), x ∈ F, w_{cj} = weight of feature j belonging to class c

Since we intend to learn the individual importance of each feature corresponding to each class, we have implemented a normalized version of the class dependent RELIEF algorithm, NCW-R [26]. All the feature weight vector values are initialized to zero and updated iteratively by processing each data point x in X as per Equation 3.

$$w_c = \sum_{x \in X_c} \left\{ \sum_{z \in WKNN(x,c)} -|x-z| + \sum_{\substack{z \in WKNN(x,\acute{c}) \\ \acute{c} \notin c}} |x-z| \right\} / N_c \quad (3)$$

4.3 Semi-Explicit Feedback Model

In this section, we first focus on the user interest model based on semi-explicit and implicit relevance feedback. For the semi-explicit model, we use baseline-LDA to infer content similarity and use it in the user interest estimation to determine how likely a page or a segment is of interests to a user.

Suppose at time t, the user has annotated a segment from document d_{ti} whose previous annotations (from same user) are $a_1, \ldots, a_n$. We update our baseline-LDA model by modified Rocchio algorithm [32, 33] computing the centroid vector of all annotations created by the user for the given task and interpolates it with the previous source document vector to obtain an updated term vector (Equation 4). In this context we define the set of annotations as the combination of the relevant user annotations from the browser and the produced text from content producer applications (MS Word or PowerPoint).

$$\vec{Q}_t = \lambda \vec{Q}_{t-1} + (1-\lambda)\frac{1}{n}\sum_{i=1}^{n} \vec{a}_i \quad (4)$$

Where $\vec{Q}_{t-1}$ is the previous source vector, n is the number of annotations the user created immediately following the current annotation, and λ is the parameter that controls the influence of the annotations on the inferred user model. In our experiments, λ is set to 0.5.

4.4 Unified Relevance Feedback Model

Previous work shows that implicit relevance feedback alone is not adequate to estimate the interest of a user during document interactions in some situations [24, 36]. The results suggested that the implicit ratings can be combined with existing explicit relevance data to form a hybrid system to predict user interest.

For a target document d_{ti}, we define a scalar valued interest prediction from the observations of user behavior as

$$r_i = \mu R_E(i) + (1-\mu)R_I(i), \quad 0 \le R_E(i) \le 1, \quad 0 \le R_I(i) \le 1 \quad (5)$$

Where $R_E(i)$ is the similarity score estimated from semi-explicit feedback model, $R_I(i)$ is an implicit feedback estimated from the following equation, and $\mu = 0.8$ is a heuristically tuned scaling factor representing the relative importance of the implicit feedback. We calculate $R_I(i)$ from,

$$R_I(i) = \sum_{j \in F} w_j f_j(i) \quad (6)$$

Where w_j is the weight for each feature j of the implicit feedback generated from WKNN. All the features were normalized to zero mean and unit variance.

5. MULTI-APPLICATION ACTIVITY AND CONTENT RELEVANCE COLLECTION

31 undergraduate and graduate students (ages 21 to 40) were recruited to perform a set of four tasks requiring the use of the Firefox web browser with the WebAnnotate extension, Microsoft Word and Microsoft PowerPoint. All participants reported spending at least 1-3 hours daily browsing the Internet. None of the participants had any prior experience with WebAnnotate.

Participants were given the task of writing summaries and generating short slide presentations on topics in four different domains (technology, science, finance, and sports; shown in Table 3) based on a set of eight web resources per domain. The instructions suggested that each task would take about 30 minutes, but that they could continue working as long as they needed to.

The resources provided were selected from the top documents returned from a Google query on the topic and were chosen to include pages with varying degrees of relevance to each task. Table 3 includes the average and variance of post-task relevance scores assigned by participants for the documents per task. It shows that each task contained both relevant and non-relevant web pages in similar proportions.

Table 3: Task topics with mean and variance of post-task document relevance assessments

Task No	Task Name	Relevance Score Mean and Variance
1	How does Google Glass work?	3.55 ± 0.96
2	What is mars one project?	3.23 ± 1.11
3	How to improve your credit score?	3.53 ± 0.98
4	What are the rules of American football?	3.52 ± 1.01

User activity data in the three applications and post-task relevance assessments of each document were collected. Activity data collected during the tasks included all the features originally described (in Table 2). Due to experimental setup, this data required preprocessing. For example, as it is expected due to the data collection process, document features such as last access time, creation time, and last write time features are not informative because each individual task lasted approximately 30 minutes. Thus, these features are not considered during the evaluation process. In total, the data captured includes 34 potentially useful features out of 48 features.

In addition to the post-task page level assessments of relevance, each participant was requested to annotate and rate individual segments of documents, so that each segment in a page could be considered as a unique piece of content with the goal of the interest model learning to identify relevant segments in web pages. Pre-processing of the data assumes any segment that was not explicitly annotated and rated by a participant was irrelevant ($C = 1$). At the end of the tasks we conducted a survey about participant's prior knowledge of the applications involved, understanding of tasks and other details. The average score for the question "How comfortable were you doing the tasks" is 4.35 on a scale from 1 to 5 (1 being Lowest & 5 being Highest). This indicates that participants did not have many issues comprehending the topics.

Small segments were also removed from consideration; any segments with less than 10 words are ignored from the data set to avoid noise. We ignored data collected for tasks when participants did not generate the requested document or slides and for participants that did not annotate at least fifty paragraphs across the four tasks. Finally, since the web pages shown to the participants are real web pages and there may be some unwanted segments (comments, page headers) in the content. We removed 6247 such data instances during data filtering stage. Final dataset includes 33212 data instances across 108 tasks available for model evaluation

5.1 Evaluation Metrics

We evaluate our models by examining their performance in interest prediction in both page-level and paragraph-level interest modeling. We use Root Mean Square Error (RMSE) to measure the rating prediction quality where a smaller RMSE value indicates better performance.

Given that our primary goal is to learn the user's preference from her relevance feedback and use these to identify relevant document content, we consider the standard information retrieval domain evaluation metrics such as precision, recall, harmonic mean (F1), and mean average precision (MAP) to compare the performance of alternative user modeling techniques. MAP gives us an overall sense of how well we identify relevant estimations to recommend from sent of annotation content.

6. RESULTS

A number of subcomponents of our approach to unified relevance feedback for multi-application user interest modeling were evaluated. We used data from an earlier data collection activity that included annotations and post-task relevance assessments to test the feasibility of alternative topic modeling techniques.

6.1 Topic Modeling Approach Selection

We evaluated alternative topic modeling approaches within our context to determine how well they would work with the type of data available (a small collection of small and large segments of annotated or authored text). We applied LDA to compute the probability distributions of topics for two or more selections of textual content. We then used three distance measures of the divergence between these probability distributions and compared those assessments to the user-provided assessments. The three distance measures are: the Hellinger Distance (H), the Kullback-Leibler divergence (KL), and the Jensen-Shannon divergence (JSD). The algorithmic details of these similarity measures are beyond the scope of this paper. Additional information about these similarity measures are available in our previous work [18]. In addition, we also evaluated the performance of a Non-negative Matrix Factorization (NMF) model to the three LDA-based techniques. Additional information about the NMF and its parameters used in this research study are available at [17].

To compare these approaches and before the data collection effort described in Section 5, we collected a set of text selections from web documents that indicated relevance to given search tasks. The data was based on 17 participants selecting the relevant paragraphs (text segments) from a set of 20 pre-selected web documents for each of five different information gathering tasks. This resulted in a total of 1267 text segments being selected across the 100 documents.

To assess the quality of the topic modeling alternatives, we used each of the user-selected text segments to predict the remainder of that user's selections based on the similarity metrics. When the user-selected paragraph reached a similarity value of 0.5 (experimentally chosen to have reasonable performance) it was assumed to be recommended by the system. When a system-generated recommended by the system was indeed one of that user's other selections, it was counted as a true positive. When a paragraph in the text did not reach that threshold it was counted as a true negative. Table 4 presents the resulting average precision, recall, F-measure and accuracy across the 5 search tasks.

Table 4: Performance comparison of 4 similarity measures

	Precision	Recall	F1	Accuracy
LDA+H	0.944	0.367	0.499	**0.722**
LDA+KL	**0.954**	0.350	0.485	0.719
LDA+JSD	0.736	**0.548**	**0.576**	0.713
NMF	0.814	0.418	0.500	0.692

We also examined the effect of varying the number of latent topics in the LDA model on performance. Figure 5 shows the overall accuracy of the different distance measure for 5, 10, 15, 20, 25 topics across the 5 information selection tasks. From these results, we first observe that the effect on the final performance is consistent for all three LDA models.

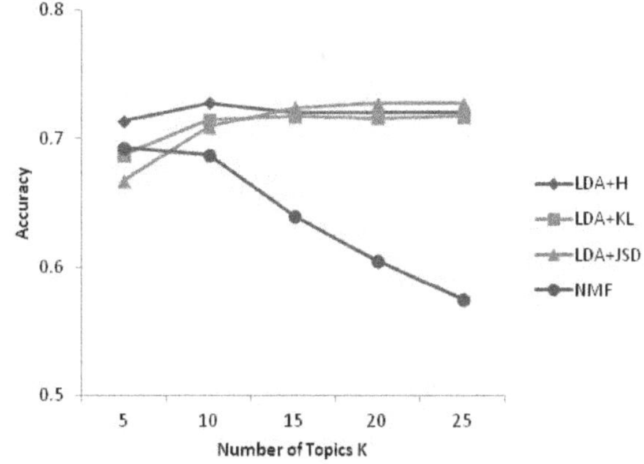

Figure 5: Impact of varying the number of latent topics

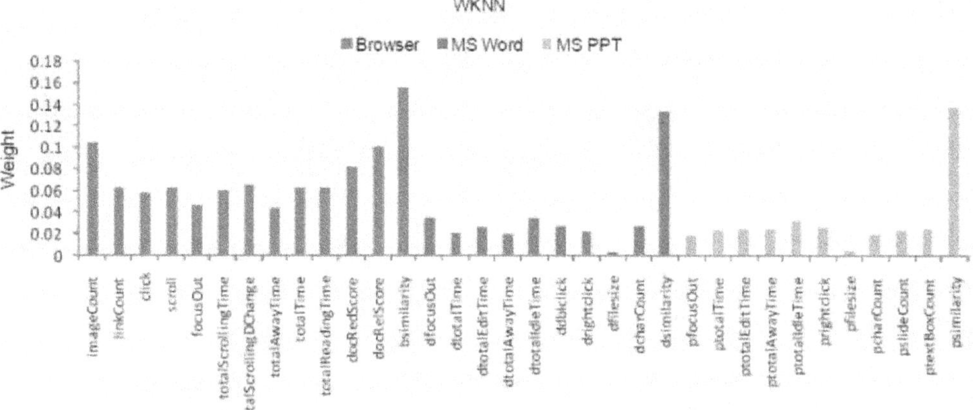

Figure 6: Comparison of feature weights computed from WKNN

The Hellinger distance measure offers the best overall accuracy among the similarity measures. Therefore, the Hellinger distance was used for the remainder of our experiments involving further analysis of our unified relevance model.

6.2 Multi-Application Feature Weights

We explored the use of WKNN to assign weights to the various features in our unified model to predict the likelihood of interest.

The feature weight values are obtained after averaging 200 iterations of the WKNN classifier. The training data set is generated by randomly selecting 70% data points from the entire data set and the remaining 30% is treated as test data for each iteration. The optimal parameter K=5 for the WKNN is selected based on performance after a 5-fold cross validation.

In WKNN, features computed (see Figure 6) from the content-consumer application have higher weights than the features from the content-producer applications except for content similarity. One interpretation of this is that similarity to content being produced by the user is such a strong signal that other features from content-production applications are not needed to help interpret that assessment.

The same cannot be said of content consumption applications. While content similarity is also the strongest feature for the browser, many other features also (including measures of clicks, scrolling, and reading) have strong weights. As opposed to the results from the content production applications, this shows that when assessing activity in the browser, it is important to gauge just how much interest the user has in the content, not just that the content was visited. Each of the three applications contributed one of the three highest strength features. This reinforces the potential for multi-application interest models to improve personalized information delivery via visualizations or recommendations. Feature weight comparison results indicated that WKNN performed well in understanding the importance of individual features of user activity. It also indicated that while content similarity is important across all applications, content consumption applications benefit considerably from additional features in order to interpret the perceived value of that content.

6.3 Unified User Model Performance

Once the particular topic modeling and evidence weighting schemes were determined based on the results in Sections 6.1 and 6.2, the overall user modeling approach could be examined. The central question being how the unified user model would perform relative to simpler models. To compare the performance of semi-explicit and unified feedback we compared the performance of classifiers provided with the different sets of features and report on the resulting classifications.

We performed our evaluation on page-level user interest estimation by running each user data through the three levels of interest models from baseline-LDA (text edited from production applications), semi-explicit (data from previous model + text annotated from consumption application), and unified (data from previous two + implicit relevance feedback through equation (5)). Each evaluator provided RMSE on the relevance of each page. The RMSE results (see Table 5) for the 4 tasks were computed by averaging the values obtained per each task performance. Although baseline-LDA (M=1.31, SD=0.14) and semi-explicit models (M=1.29, SD=0.05) are quite close; t(3)=0.9459, p=0.414, there was a significant difference in the RMSE for baseline and unified (M=1.21, SD=0.12); t(3)= 8.2641, p=0.0037, and semi-explicit and unified; t(3)= 3.9641, p=0.0287. In all cases the unified relevance model improvement over the semi-explicit relevance models is statistically significant. This demonstrates the importance of implicit relevance feedback indicators in interest predictions.

Table 5: Page-level performance of interest models

	Page-Level RMSE			
	Task-1	**Task-2**	**Task-3**	**Task-4**
Baseline-LDA	1.180	1.315	1.239	1.515
Semi-Explicit	1.126	1.326	1.258	1.463
Unified	**1.097**	**1.198**	**1.162**	**1.388**

Clearly the unified approach was of value when locating whole resources of interest. But being able to identify relevant segments within the pages is also important for personalized information delivery. We were thus particularly interested in these models performance in this respect.

To examine this segment-level performance we compared the ordering of the segments' similarity to the user models for each task performed by each user to that user's ordered rating of those segments. We calculate MAP and F1 for each task, judging a segment as relevant when it was annotated by the user. Results are shown in Figure 7 and Table 6. Unfortunately, the implicit data captured is limited to page-level analysis (we do not know what particular content was being presented when users performed each recorded event). Therefore we only compare the baseline model and the model including semi-explicit content. Table 6 points out the benefit of exploiting paragraph-level user interest via user annotations. MAP improvement of semi-explicit model is both substantial and significant over the baseline-LDA.

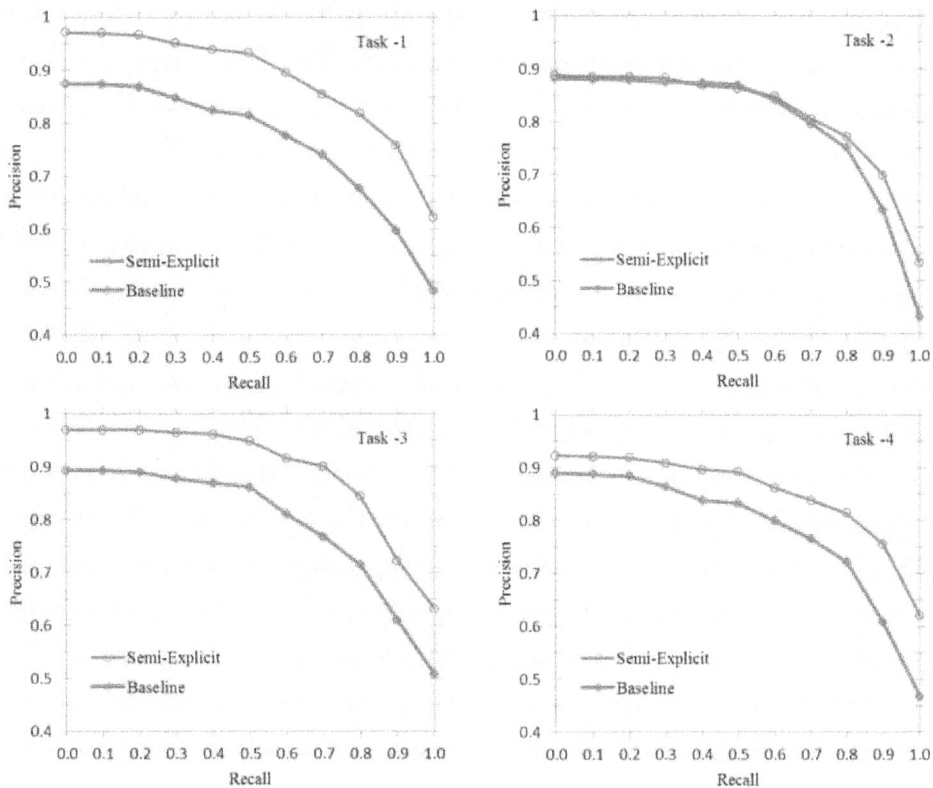

Figure 7: Precision-recall curves. Segment-level performance comparison

Table 6: Segment-level performance of semi-explicit interest models

	Segment-Level							
	Task-1		Task-2		Task-3		Task-4	
	MAP	F1	MAP	F1	MAP	F1	MAP	F1
Baseline-LDA	0.6276	0.5308	0.6371	0.5486	0.6586	0.5739	0.6293	0.5376
Semi-explicit	**0.7827**	**0.6208**	**0.6943**	**0.5568**	**0.7912**	**0.6391**	**0.7488**	**0.5804**

7. DISCUSSION AND CONCLUSION

The work presented in this paper addresses a rarely investigated topic: the potential of aggregating activity across multiple applications for user interest modeling. While there are theoretical or software frameworks for distributed user modeling, assessments of modeling techniques are almost always reported in terms of single applications. In this work, we present and evaluate a multi-application modeling technique that combines implicit and semi-explicit feedback across multiple everyday applications.

Our system and tool set supports a wide range of potential applications communicating with the user interest server. To affect the contents of the user interest model an application must be augmented to capture some information about content and its usage. The features described are occasionally specific to the applications (e.g. MS Word and PowerPoint, Firefox) but similar features would be available in most content producer and consumer applications involving text. Thus, the overall architecture and approach will generalize across a wide range of software applications. To the best of our knowledge, this is the first software framework designed to share explicit and implicit relevance feedback among applications.

The evaluation of the alternative modeling techniques involved collecting activity data and post-task relevance assessments for a common type of activity: rapidly browsing/reading content and writing a report or presentation based on that content. While other types of information tasks exist, this is a frequent and broad enough category of task to warrant investigation.

The experimental results show that incorporating implicit feedback in page-level user interest estimation resulted in significant improvements over the original models, using both baseline and semi-explicit data. Furthermore, incorporating semi-explicit content (e.g. annotated text) with the authored text is effective in identifying segment-level relevant content. Our results open up many possibilities for using unified feedback in predictive tasks, especially in the context of search personalization. Since we have a model that relates this unified feedback to ratings, we can use methods used for explicit feedbacks on unified data. In the future, we plan to study how semi-explicit feedback can be combined with implicit feedback for segment-level assessment and in additional personalized information delivery contexts.

8. ACKNOWLEDGMENTS

This work was supported in part by National Science Foundation grant DUE–0938074.

REFERENCES

[1] Abel, F., et al., *Cross-system user modeling and personalization on the social web.* User Modeling and User-Adapted Interaction, 2013. 23(2-3): p. 169-209.

[2] Agichtein, E., E. Brill, and S. Dumais. *Improving web search ranking by incorporating user behavior information.* in *ACM SIGIR*. 2006. p. 19-26.

[3] Assad, M., et al., *PersonisAD: Distributed, active, scrutable model framework for context-aware services*, in *Pervasive Computing*. 2007, Springer. p. 55-72.

[4] Badi, R., et al. *Recognizing user interest and document value from reading and organizing activities in document triage.* in *IUI*. 2006. ACM: p. 218-225.

[5] Bae, S., et al. *Supporting document triage via annotation-based multi-application visualizations.* in *JCDL*. 2010. p. 177-186.

[6] Bennani, N., et al. *Multi-application profile updates propagation: a semantic layer to improve mapping between applications.* in *WWW*. 2012. p. 949-958.

[7] Bishop, C.M., *Pattern recognition and machine learning.* Vol. 1. 2006: springer New York.

[8] Blei, D.M., A.Y. Ng, and M.I. Jordan, *Latent dirichlet allocation.* the Journal of machine Learning research, 2003. 3: p. 993-1022.

[9] Brusilovsky, P., S. Sosnovsky, and O. Shcherbinina, *User modeling in a distributed e-learning architecture*, in *User Modeling 2005*. 2005, Springer. p. 387-391.

[10] Carpineto, C. and G. Romano, *A survey of automatic query expansion in information retrieval.* ACM Computing Surveys (CSUR), 2012. 44(1): p. 1.

[11] Cena, F. and R. Furnari, *A model for feature-based user model interoperability on the web*, in *Advances in Ubiquitous User Modelling*. 2009, Springer. p. 37-54.

[12] Chen, L. and K. Sycara. *WebMate: a personal agent for browsing and searching.* in *AGENTS*. 1998. p. 132-139.

[13] Claypool, M., et al. *Implicit interest indicators.* in *IUI*. 2001. p. 33-40.

[14] Harper, D.J. and D. Kelly. *Contextual relevance feedback.* in *Information interaction in context*. 2006. p. 129-137.

[15] Iyilade, J. and J. Vassileva. *A Decentralized Architecture for Sharing and Reusing Lifelogs.* in *UMAP Workshops*. 2013. Citeseer.

[16] Jawaheer, G., M. Szomszor, and P. Kostkova. *Comparison of implicit and explicit feedback from an online music recommendation service.* in *proceedings of the 1st international workshop on information heterogeneity and fusion in recommender systems*. 2010. p. 47-51.

[17] Jayarathna, S., A. Patra, and F. Shipman, *Learning Topic Models for Multi-Application User Interest Modeling*, 2014, Texas A&M University.

[18] Jayarathna, S., A. Patra, and F. Shipman. *Mining user interest from search tasks and annotations.* in *CIKM*. 2013. p. 1849-1852.

[19] Jones, R. and K.L. Klinkner. *Beyond the session timeout: automatic hierarchical segmentation of search topics in query logs.* in *CIKM*. 2008. p. 699-708.

[20] Kelly, D. and J. Teevan. *Implicit feedback for inferring user preference: a bibliography.* in *ACM SIGIR Forum*. 2003. p. 18-28.

[21] Kobsa, A. and J. Fink, *An LDAP-based user modeling server and its evaluation.* User Modeling and User-Adapted Interaction, 2006. 16(2): p. 129-169.

[22] Krulwich, B. and C. Burkey, *The InfoFinder agent: Learning user interests through heuristic phrase extraction.* IEEE Expert, 1997. 12(5): p. 22-27.

[23] Limbu, D.K., et al. *Contextual relevance feedback in web information retrieval.* in *Proceedings of the 1st International Conference on Information interaction in Context*. 2006. p. 138-143.

[24] Liu, N.N., et al. *Unifying explicit and implicit feedback for collaborative filtering.* in *CIKM*. 2010. p. 1445-1448.

[25] Lu, Z., D. Agarwal, and I.S. Dhillon. *A spatio-temporal approach to collaborative filtering.* in *RecSys*. 2009. p. 13-20.

[26] Marchiori, E., *Class dependent feature weighting and k-nearest neighbor classification*, in *Pattern Recognition in Bioinformatics*. 2013, Springer. p. 69-78.

[27] McCallum, A.K., *Mallet: A machine learning for language toolkit.* 2002.

[28] Nichols, D., *Implicit Rating and Filtering*, in *The fifth delos workshop on filtering and collaborative filtering*1997.

[29] Paraskevopoulos, F. and G. Mentzas. *A Peer to Peer Architecture for a Distributed User Model.* in *UMAP*. 2014.

[30] Porteous, I., et al. *Fast collapsed gibbs sampling for latent dirichlet allocation.* in *KDD*. 2008. p. 569-577.

[31] Renda, M.E. and U. Straccia, *A personalized collaborative digital library environment: a model and an application.* Information processing & management, 2005. 41(1): p. 5-21.

[32] Rocchio, J.J., *Relevance feedback in information retrieval.* 1971.

[33] Shen, X., B. Tan, and C. Zhai. *Implicit user modeling for personalized search.* in *CIKM*. 2005. p. 824-831.

[34] Shipman, F., et al., *Identifying useful passages in documents based on annotation patterns*, in *Research and Advanced Technology for Digital Libraries*. 2003, Springer. p. 101-112.

[35] Sieg, A., B. Mobasher, and R. Burke. *Web search personalization with ontological user profiles.* in *CIKM*. 2007. p. 525-534.

[36] Wang, B., et al., *Expectation-Maximization collaborative filtering with explicit and implicit feedback*, in *Advances in Knowledge Discovery and Data Mining*. 2012, Springer. p. 604-616.

[37] Zigoris, P. and Y. Zhang. *Bayesian adaptive user profiling with explicit & implicit feedback.* in *CIKM*. 2006.p. 397-404.

PivotViz: Interactive Visual Analysis of Multidimensional Library Transaction Data

Matthias Nielsen
Department of Computer Science
Aarhus University
Denmark
matthiasnielsen@cs.au.dk

Kaj Grønbæk
Department of Computer Science
Aarhus University
Denmark
kgronbak@cs.au.dk

ABSTRACT

As public libraries become increasingly digitalized they become producers of Big Data. Furthermore, public libraries are often obliged to make their data openly available as part of national open data policies, which have gained momentum in many countries including USA, UK, and Denmark. However, in order to utilize such data and make it intelligible for citizens, decision makers, or other stakeholders, raw data APIs are insufficient. Therefore, we have developed PivotViz that is a comprehensible visualization technique, which combines parallel coordinates and pivot tables. It provides, a multidimensional visual interactive pivot table for analysis of library transactions – loans, renewals, and returns of books and other materials across location and time. The paper presents the PivotViz technique and discusses its prospects based on implementations in two publicly available versions using open data from the two largest municipalities in Denmark. Examples of analysis results from these data illustrate the power of PivotViz.

ACM Classification Keywords

H.5.2 User Interfaces (D.2.2, H.1.2, I.3.6)

Author Keywords

Library Data; Information Visualization; Visual Analytics; Big Data; Open Data

1. INTRODUCTION

Libraries of today are hybrid libraries, where both physical and digital material can be loaned. But a common feature of physical or digital material loans is that the administration of loans is fully digitized and thus generate huge amounts of data, which due to its sheer volume, velocity, and variety bears the characteristics of Big Data [3]. This provides new opportunities for making this data useful for a wide range of stakeholders, such as users of libraries, librarians, managers, politicians etc. Concurrently, many countries have launched Open Data initiatives aiming at making all sorts of governmental data publicly available for anybody to use, such as the UK's open data initiative [4]. This makes public libraries a special case because they, like other libraries, will generate large amounts of data, and additionally they can be obliged to make such data publicly available if they fall within their governments open data policy. However, making data available is very different from making it discernable especially for public libraries, because their stakeholders range from politicians and decision makers to the common citizen, who are not per se trained in business intelligence type data analysis.

We have developed a visualization technique called PivotViz to support efficient and comprehensible analysis of big open data sets, here open loan transaction data from public libraries. In our work with PivotViz, we have taken offset in publicly available data describing transactions of materials at libraries in the two largest municipalities Denmark, Aarhus and Copenhagen, both maintaining around 20 physical branches respectively. We have developed a novel visualization technique, based on parallel coordinates and pivot tables, to facilitate interactive visual analysis of loaner transactions. Furthermore, we have implemented two publicly available versions, available at URLs [1, 2], which, although targeted for managers or decision makers, allows anyone interested to analyze library transactions across location (library branch), time (weekday and hour of day), and transaction type (loan, renewal, or return).

In the remainder of this paper we first cover related work in data mining and interactive visualization of library data. Second, we elaborate and discuss the PivotViz visualization technique developed by combining parallel coordinates and pivot tables. Third, we present use cases of two PivotViz visualizations of library transaction data in Aarhus and Copenhagen. Fourth, we discuss future work for evolving the PivotViz visualization technique into generally applicable tool for visualizing and interactively analyzing multidimensional data.

2. RELATED WORK

In this section, we cover a selection of previous research addressing mining, analyzing and visualizing data in the context of libraries. Furthermore, we cover specific related work from the field of information visualization.

Bibliomining combines bibliometrics and data mining [5, 6] for the purpose of mining data collected by libraries for knowledge that can help users, librarians, managers, or other relevant parties. It is a multifaceted approach covering a wide scope from data handling to communication, and related to our work because we visualize large datasets of library transaction data to enable interactive analysis and hence knowledge generation.

Research in visualization of data from libraries has taken many forms. Strategies and tools for visual querying or exploring (digital and/or physical) library collections have been investigated in [7, 8], and Gelernter [9] present a selection of information

JCDL'15, June 21 - 25, 2015, Knoxville, Tennessee, USA.

ACM 978-1-4503-3594-2/15/06...$15.00
DOI: http://dx.doi.org/10.1145/2756406.2756937

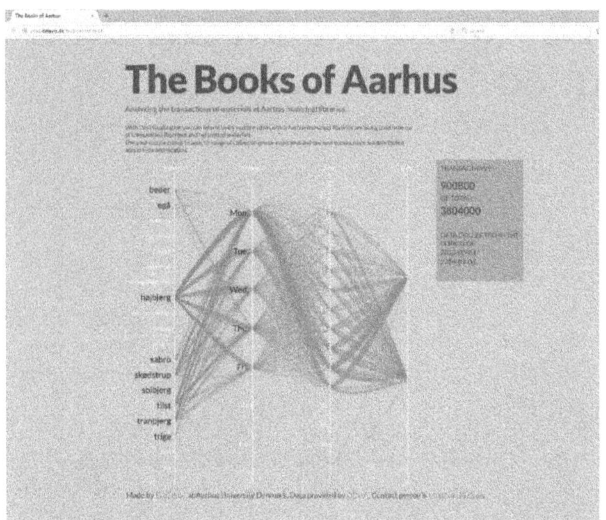

Figure 1: PivotViz: The Books of Aarhus, see URL in [1]

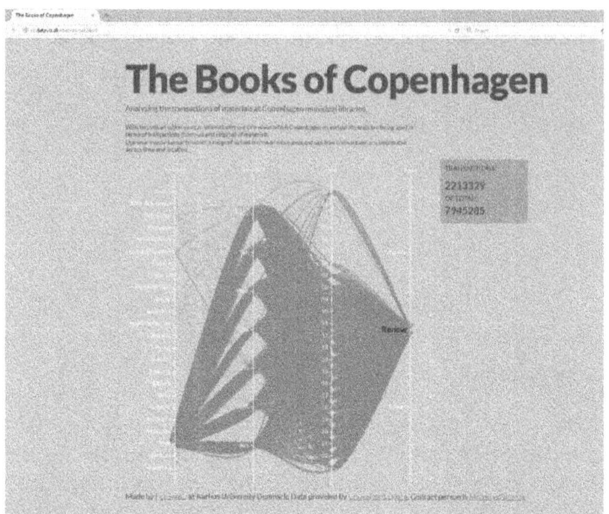

Figure 2: PivotViz: The Books of Copenhagen, see URL in [2]

visualization interfaces to collections of digital libraries and propose the foundation for a classification of information visualization for digital libraries. Furthermore, Radburn et. al. [10, 11] have researched how visualizations of library records can assist local authorities in Leicestershire in understanding the needs of its citizens and providing better services for them. These researchers all tackle challenges of how to handle digital aspects of libraries by visualization, and therefore relates to our work.

In relation to the field of information visualization, our work relates specifically to the exhaustive work with the parallel coordinates visualization technique by Inselberg [12] and Dasgupta et. al. [13] among others, as well interaction techniques with parallel coordinates as explored in [14, 15]. Furthermore, our work relates specifically to the pivot table functionality, which is common in spreadsheet software applications [16].

3. PIVOTVIZ

The core principle in the PivotViz visualization technique is the combination of the structural layout of the parallel coordinates with the summated, but easily comprehensible, numbers of pivot tables, to create an interactive visualization of large datasets. The visualization technique was originally developed to enable municipal decision makers analyze transaction data from public libraries, because the millions of material transactions being collected had become too extensive for them to analyze using conventional methods.

3.1 Multidimensional Visual Pivot Table

PivotVis borrows the structural layout of parallel coordinates [12, 13], which represents data dimensions as parallel axes and plots data entries as individual lines according to coordinates on these axes. Instead of plotting data tuples as individual lines, as conventionally done in a parallel coordinates visualization, PivotViz plots a line, represents the summated number of all transactions that have identical values. I.e. each line in the visualizations in Figure 1 and Figure 2, available online at URLs [1] and [2], represents all transactions of the same type that have taken place at a specific location, weekday, and hour of day, with the summated number represented as thickness and opacity of the line. The strategy of summing all identical tuples and only representing aggregated numbers is similar to the functionality of pivot tables [16], which represents precise summated numbers of a dataset across select dimensions.

This combination of parallel coordinates and pivot can best be described as an interactive multidimensional visual pivot table. PivotViz is illustrated in use in Figure 1 and Figure 2.

Incorporating the summarized numbers of pivot tables [16], means that, for the same layout, the maximum number of lines will stay same (the number of properties on each dimension multiplied). Even if the underlying dataset keeps growing each line will just represent an increasingly larger number - like a cell in a pivot table. This means that the visualization technique scales well as data grows in size and therefore it is highly suitable for visualizing Big Data. Like a pivot table, however, this is limited to datasets with entries that can be treated as discrete data and be mapped onto ordinal or nominal scales. Visualizing datasets with continuous data dimensions would mean that the number of lines needed in the visualization would equal the number of entries in the dataset. That is, unless the continuous data dimension can be converted to a non-continuous scale, as is exemplified in the usage of time in the online versions at URLs [1, 2], which has been reduced to two ordinal dimension (weekday and hour of day) although it is continuous in the underlying dataset. Making a pivot table visual means that outliers and patterns becomes easier to detect because graphical structures are effectively processed by human vision [17]. On the other hand, overlapping lines can clutter the visual representation, making interactive selection and filtering a necessity rather than just a useful feature.

PivotViz incorporates the multiple dimensions of parallel coordinates visualization technique [12, 13], which means that it is suitable for visualizing complex multidimensional datasets and still maintaining an overview of the data. This is a significant improvement over the tabular layout of pivot tables because pivot tables on the other hand loses interpretability if more than two data dimensions are included. However, the scalability of PivotViz only extends to a certain limit as hundreds or even tenths of concurrently visualized dimensions would counter overview of the visualization both in terms of scattering of axes as well as in terms of increase in the number of individual lines.

3.2 Interactive Visual Analysis

Interaction is crucial in PivotViz because the visual representation does not yield comparatively precise visual queries as e.g. a conventional bar chart does (i.e. bar A is approximately 2/3 the height of bar B). However, with interaction, it traverses large scales from municipality wide transactions to a single library's transactions in a narrow timeframe for specific types of transactions. Furthermore, cluttering of lines reveals clusters in the data, but dominant lines can hide subtle clusters, making interactive filtering important. PivotViz supports flexible filtering in the form range selection and selection of single elements on one or more axes, as shown in Figure 1 (deselection is implemented as inverted selection and is equally supported). Range selections are performed by means of temporary brushing over a range of ticks on an axis and single elements are selected by clicking on a tick. The selection functionality facilitates flexible filtering meaning that PivotViz follows Shneiderman's overview first, zoom and filter, then details-on-demand mantra [18]. Although the details available on-demand is only an increasingly precise number and not contextual information on actual materials that were objects of transactions.

Even though PivotViz combines properties of parallel coordinates and pivot tables it does not, however, substitute either as some of strengths normally associated with the two is not carried over. For instance, the immediately available high detailed numbers of the pivot table can only be reproduced in PivotViz through interaction. Likewise, advanced visual queries supported in conventional parallel coordinates, like correlation analysis between axes if a select set of lines have a similar slope, is not supported either.

3.3 Architecture and Implementation

PivotViz is developed as web-browser based visualization using JavaScript, including D3 [19], to create SVG elements in the browser DOM, making the web-browser render the visualization without the need for third party plugins, thus making it easily accessible for interested parties.

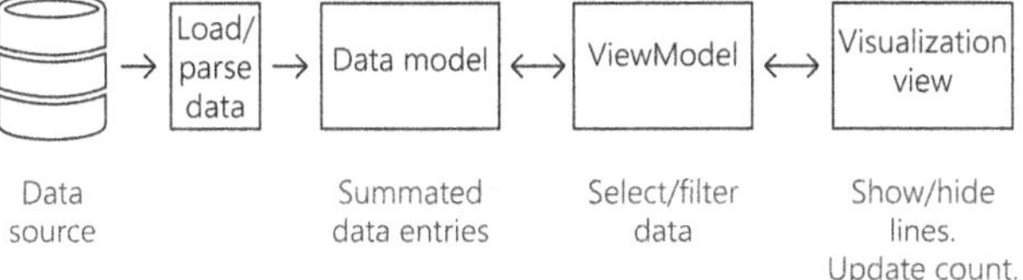

Figure 3: Architecture in PivotViz.

The current implementation visualizes batch-processed static datasets that are loaded by a single-page web application, which creates the visualization following a Model View ViewModel pattern. Albeit with a simple model in the current implementation because the data in the model is static and the bindings between the ViewModel and the View are not updated. However, it is trivial to either update the model or replace with a new data source, making it a flexible architecture, shown in Figure 3. Furthermore, no persistence of performed analyses or functionality for sharing or cooperation is currently built-in (needed for process and provenance in Heer and Shneiderman's taxonomy [20]), meaning that currently the only way to persist, share, or corporate analysis results is conventional screenshots. However, making deep links to make persistent analysis results is possible to implement, by e.g. implementing server based save functionality or by creating custom URLs using a hashtag fragment identifier that contains information of a specific state of the visualization, which should be created on load.

The visualizations in [1, 2] have been tested, and they render and work interactively, in the four major desktop browser – Mozilla Firefox, Google Chrome, Internet Explorer, and Apple Safari. However, due to the implementations' heavy use of CSS selections of large sets of elements (for interaction) it performs best in Mozilla Firefox with Google Chrome a close second best.

4. TWO MUNICIPALITY USE CASES

The two versions of PivotViz have been publicly available for approximately 1½ year for Aarhus municipal libraries, and for approximately ½ year in Copenhagen municipal libraries. Both versions have been used by library management in their respective municipalities. In this section, we present the two use cases and examples of types of analysis results.

4.1 Analysis: Usage of Self-Service Libraries

In response to comparatively little usage, some of the smaller public libraries residential areas or suburbs in Aarhus have had their opening hours extended into the evening while not being staffed. The intention with this initiative was to keep libraries open when users are not at work and have time to loan or return books, while at the same time not increasing the cost of running these libraries by staffing them in the afternoon and evening. This initiative has resulted in that almost 6 % of the total transactions of materials in public libraries in Aarhus municipality takes in unstaffed libraries. A screenshot of this analysis is available Figure 4 and can be recreated via the URL in [1].

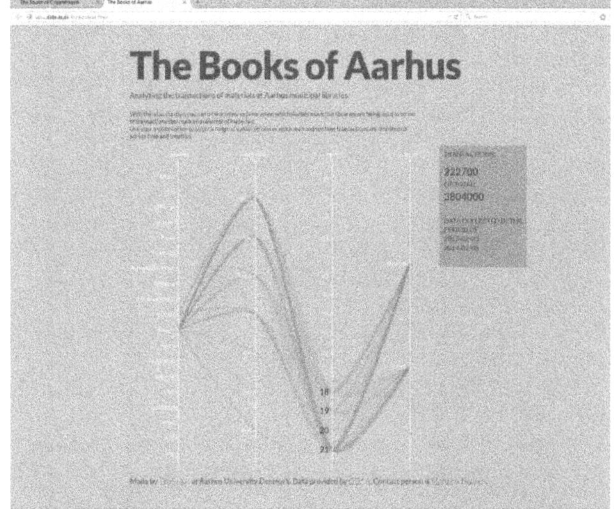

Figure 4: Usage of unstaffed public libraries in Aarhus

4.2 Analysis: Online Renewal of Materials

Besides loans and returns, the data from Copenhagen municipal libraries also includes renewals. Furthermore, the data also includes transactions that have taken place through the municipal libraries' common web-portal. A screenshot showing the distribution of all renewals is shown in Figure 2, which shows a distinctive clustering at a specific location on the first axis, which, admittedly intelligible in Figure 2, is the Web. The number of renewals performed through the municipal web-portal equates to almost 82 % of the total number of renewals across all libraries. This indicates that the users of the municipal libraries in Copenhagen also use the web-portal extensively, meaning that it is a highly integrated part of the service that the municipal libraries provide.

5. FUTURE WORK

In our efforts to develop the PivotViz visualization technique, used in The Books of Aarhus (Figure 1), available at URL [1], and The Books of Copenhagen (Figure 2), available at [2], a generally applicable visualization technique has emerged that we intend to expand upon in terms of modularity and flexibility.

The current implementations at URLs [1, 2] only allows end-users, i.e. non-programmers, to interact with a predefined static dataset, as discussed in section 3.3. According to the reference model for visualization [17], this means that human interaction is currently limited to view transformations and visual mappings and data transformations requires programmers to perform. We plan to demonstrate the general applicability of the PivotViz visualization technique by developing a tool that allows end-users to perform both visual mappings and view transformations. As discussed in section 3.1, the visualization technique applies to certain types of data and, generally, we do not consider it feasible to implement functionality for end-users to perform data transformations. However, for data commonly collected at libraries, such as electronic visitor counts, ILS data, etc., data parsers or connectors could also be implemented to allow end-users to import data.

Creating such a tool means increasing modularity in terms of allowing end-users to change, update, remove, and add data sources. Furthermore, because data sources increasingly are providing dynamic data (e.g. streams) [21], timed or event-based updates of data should also be supported. Besides modularity, flexibility should also be increased, meaning that end-users should be able to specify what parts of datasets should be visualized and to some extent how – related to Heer and Shneiderman's Data & View Specification [20].

Increasing modularity and flexibility of a visualization is also highly relevant for the data visualized at URLs [1, 2]. In the presented visualizations, time, location, and type of transaction is included, but it could also be desirable to correlate transaction patterns with other data commonly collected at libraries, e.g. visitor numbers, events, ILS data, etc.

For the future version of PivotViz, we plan to conduct evaluations of the visualization technique and its applicability for visual analysis by end-users. Because we envision the future version of PivotViz as a generally applicable tool, evaluations will be conducted with both extended datasets of library transactions, as described above, as well as datasets from other domains.

6. CONCLUSION

This paper has introduced the PivotViz visualization technique for library transaction data. The main contributions of the paper are 1) PivotViz, a generalizable visualization technique for visual analysis of library transaction data, and potentially other data. 2) Two publicly available interactive visualizations – The Books of Aarhus and The Books of Copenhagen – exhibiting the PivotViz visualization technique for analyzing library transaction data in practice. 3) Discussion of prospects for the PivotViz visualization technique and how to evolve it into a modular and flexible visualization tool.

Based on the successful implementations of PivotViz in the library domain, we see promise for PivotViz in other domains where big data on location and time tagged events needs to be analyzed. We are already looking into evaluating PivotViz in such new domains.

7. ACKNOWLEDGEMENTS

The work was supported by Danish DSF grant no. 11-115331.

8. REFERENCES

[1] http://odaa.datavis.dk/thebooksof.html.

[2] http://kk.datavis.dk/thebooksof.html.

[3] Zikopoulos, P. and Eaton, C. Understanding big data: Analytics for enterprise class hadoop and streaming data. McGraw-Hill Osborne Media, 2011.

[4] Maude, F. Open Data White Paper-Unleashing the potential. The Stationary Office Limited on behalf of HM Government, Cabinet Office, London, United Kingdom2012.

[5] Nicholson, S. The basis for bibliomining: Frameworks for bringing together usage-based data mining and bibliometrics through data warehousing in digital library services. *Inf. Process. Manage.*, 42, 3 2006, 785-804.

[6] Nicholson, S. and Stanton, J. M. Gaining strategic advantage through bibliomining: Data mining for management decisions in corporate, special, digital, and traditional libraries. *Organizational data mining: Leveraging enterprise data resources for optimal performance*2003.

[7] Shiri, A. Metadata-enhanced visual interfaces to digital libraries. *Journal of Information Science*2008.

[8] Smits, J. Libraries mapped: a question of research! *Journal of Map & Geography Libraries*, 7, 2 2011, 220-244.

[9] Gelernter, J. Visual classification with information visualization (infoviz) for digital library collections. *Knowledge Organization*, 34, 3 2007, 128-143.

[10] Radburn, R., Dykes, J. and Wood, J. vizLib: developing capacity for exploratory data analysis in local government–visualization of library customer behaviour. Citeseer, City, 2009.

[11] Radburn, R., Dykes, J. and Wood, J. vizLib: Using the seven stages of visualization to explore population trends and processes in local authority research. *Proc. GIS Research UK*2010, 409-416.

[12] Inselberg, A. and Dimsdale, B. *Parallel coordinates*. Springer, City, 1991.

[13] Dasgupta, A. and Kosara, R. Pargnostics: Screen-space metrics for parallel coordinates. *Visualization and Computer Graphics, IEEE Transactions on*, 16, 6 2010, 1017-1026.

[14] Kosara, R. *Indirect multi-touch interaction for brushing in parallel coordinates*. International Society for Optics and Photonics, City, 2011.

[15] Nielsen, M., Kjærgaard, M. B. and Grønbæk, K. Exploring Interaction Techniques and Task Types for Direct-Touch as Input Modality. *IEEE VIS Proceedings*2013.

[16] Alexander, M. and Jelen, B. *Pivot Table Data Crunching*. Pearson Education, 2001.

[17] Card, S. K., Mackinlay, J. D. and Shneiderman, B. *Readings in information visualization: using vision to think*. Morgan Kaufmann, 1999.

[18] Shneiderman, B. The eyes have it: A task by data type taxonomy for information visualizations. IEEE, City, 1996.

[19] Bostock, M., Ogievetsky, V. and Heer, J. D³ data-driven documents. *Visualization and Computer Graphics, IEEE Transactions on*, 17, 12 2011, 2301-2309.

[20] Heer, J. and Shneiderman, B. Interactive dynamics for visual analysis. *Queue*, 10, 2 2012, 30.

[21] Cottam, J. A., Lumsdaine, A. and Weaver, C. *Watch this: A taxonomy for dynamic data visualization*. City, 2012.

User and Topical Factors in Perceived Self-Efficacy of Video Digital Libraries

Dan Albertson
University of Alabama
School of Library and Information Studies
Tuscaloosa, AL 35487
+1 205 348 4610
dea@ua.edu

Boryung Ju
Louisiana State University
School of Library and Information Science
Baton Rouge, LA 70803
+1 225 578 3158
bju1@lsu.edu

ABSTRACT
A survey measured users' perceived self-efficacy about interactively retrieving digital video, both overall and according to different factors potentially related to user confidence preceding an actual video search session. A total of 270 surveys, with quantifiable responses, were collected and analyzed. *T*-tests and correlation tests produced significant findings about users' levels of perceived self-efficacy, including associations with topic familiarly, type or nature of the information need, and system context. Findings give researchers a better understanding of users' confidence and preconceptions prior to interactive information retrieval (IIR) sessions for video, providing valuable insight about users' attitudes which can be used to promote initial and continued use of interactive tools like digital libraries.

Categories and Subject Descriptors
H.5.1 [**Information Interfaces and Presentation**]: Multimedia Information Systems – *video.*

H.5.2 [**Information Interfaces and Presentation**]: User Interfaces – *user-centered design.*

General Terms
Design, Human Factors.

Keywords
Video digital libraries; self-efficacy; interactive video retrieval.

1. INTRODUCTION
Self-efficacy is a feeling about one's ability to perform and complete certain tasks, while perceived self-efficacy extends the concept to include self rated levels of abilities, or confidence, which in turn can influence actions and resulting emotions [9]. Interactive information retrieval (IIR) involves users' interactions, judgments, and performance while "in the loop" with user interfaces of retrieval systems being employed to satisfy information needs. Self-efficacy and IIR have been examined in conjunction with one another for understanding how users rate their abilities and/or confidence levels for completing information tasks and fulfilling needs. Prior research has been conducted from different contexts spanning basic technology use [6,7,8,12] to IIR within certain academic or professional domains, such as health, education, business, and others [10,12,13].

JCDL'15, June 21 - 25, 2015, Knoxville, Tennessee, USA
 ISBN 978-1-4503-3594-2/15/06…$15.00
DOI: http://dx.doi.org/10.1145/2756406.2756950

Interactive video retrieval is an IIR process for seeking, finding, assessing, selecting, and using video to satisfy video information needs. The makeup and structure of video information inevitably results in additional considerations and criteria for both users and interface developers alike. More specifically, users in the interactive video retrieval process will view, contemplate, and assess visual, audio, and semantic (e.g. storyline) information (among others) as part of one search session for video, which can be influential to use and thus user interface design [1].

Therefore, it is warranted to individually assess users' initial perceptions and confidence, i.e. perceived self-efficacy, preceding a video IIR process or session. The present study measured overall levels of users' perceived self-efficacy for fulfilling certain information needs or requests for video which also enabled comparisons of such levels across different factors pertaining to search topics and user experience.

2. RESEARCH QUESTIONS
Different factors, including users' confidence, can influence attitudes about employing technologies to conduct information-based tasks. Influences on users' perceptions and ultimate use of interactive video retrieval systems, such as digital libraries, are no different. Further, there can be different considerations and factors potentially influential to users' confidence and use of systems for performing video-related tasks that warrant assessment, including characteristics of the information needs, the retrieval system or tools, and individual characteristics of the users. Furthermore, the influence of perceived self-efficacy in the IIR process in conjunction with the unique characteristics of video and video retrieval systems (i.e. user interface features) motivate the examination of the following research questions:

RQ1. Do users' levels of perceived self-efficacy for successfully finding video information vary according to aspects or considerations of the video information need statement or search topic, including:

a. its type or nature, such as a collocation (recall) versus known-item (precision) search?

b. a user's knowledge or level of familiarity with the topic of the video content being requested in an information need?

RQ2. Do users' perceived self-efficacy for successfully fulfilling a video information need vary according to their level of exposure or use (i.e. regularity of use) of a video retrieval system or digital library?

Examining these research questions enable targeted evaluations of individual factors in regards to their influence on users' perceived self-efficacy for interactively retrieving needed video to complete information tasks.

3. RELATED RESEARCH

HCI and user-centered research can be found throughout the video retrieval literature. Further, prior research has examined what users perceive to be important as part of their experiences along with certain influences comprising video search sessions.

Users' criteria for interactive video retrieval systems, like digital libraries, and their user interfaces have been reported. [2] employed an open-ended survey to directly collect and assess the design criteria for video digital libraries from users. Responses were coded and categorized, and the emerging criteria (i.e. categories of system/interface features) were ranked according to both frequency and weighted frequency. Results of the primary categories showed that retrieval features were specified most often by users, followed by criteria pertaining to the user interface, video collection (qualities), and user support features [2]. Such findings are significant to perceived self-efficacy, as the needs and/or criteria of users can be associated with initial attitudes and thus levels of confidence.

Researchers from the Open Video (OV) Project developed a framework for video digital library evaluation. Their framework provides considerations and justification for assessing different interrelated factors as part of video digital library evaluations including those involving information tasks and individual characteristics of the user(s) (among others). Such factors are related to those examined here as they correspond to the expended efforts of the user, final outcomes (success or failure), and overall levels of satisfaction [11]. Further, evaluations of different types or designs of video surrogate were also central to the framework based on individual effectiveness and preferences of users [14]. Prior user-centered and evaluation research is significant to the present study considering the influences leading up to an actual interactive session between a user and system, particularly, those deriving from the individual characteristics of users, e.g. experience and expertise, search tasks, and system/interface designs. Further, self-efficacy can be influenced by deliberate design decisions, including video surrogates, as users' criteria and preferences about video display and representation (for assessment purposes) should be considered in order to improve user attitudes and, in turn, encourage both initial and sustained use.

Influences within actual interactive sessions or situations with video digital libraries, which involve users with different individual characteristics and information needs, have been examined to assess and observe variations among user interactions, performances, and satisfaction. Prior research showed that users' knowledge of information needs, the level of difficulty of a given search, and video search topic structure were all significantly related to these measures in interactive video search experiments [1].

4. METHODOLOGY

A survey method was employed to examine the research questions of the present study. Data were collected, for the most part, using paper surveys; however, a small set of surveys was sent and received through direct email. No particular group of participants was targeted for inclusion; the goal was to assemble an evenly distributed group of participants from any background. Recruiting took place both on and off campus at a major university. The present study did not conduct any formal IIR experiments, but assessed users' (i.e. survey participants) perceived self-efficacy through a survey-based scenario, which described an information need situation, comprising topic and system context, and asked participants to rate their confidence level for successfully finding the requested video using a particular video retrieval system. The survey itself was piloted before formal data collection to examine where potential points of clarity may be needed.

Two versions of a survey were created. The different versions were distinguished by the system (i.e. system context) presented in each. One survey assessed participants' self-efficacy for finding video if asked to use YouTube, deemed to be a system context more representative of general video searching. The other survey posed the same topic, video information needs, and (scaled) questions, but instead used the CSPAN Digital Video Library (not YouTube) as the system context. The CSPAN Digital Video Library was selected as a system context for the survey because it was a commercial video digital library, with a large collection of content of interest to many (i.e. public affairs), yet still specialized in its coverage. These factors would help garner a variability among the participants in terms of their exposure, interest on the content coverage, and level of use.

A screengrab of the homepage – with displayed search features – of the system context being used in each respective survey was embedded. This approach enabled the collection of initial reactions or perceptions from potential users. All individual participants completed one (and only one) version of the survey; no participant was given both. The result was two groups, each completing different versions of the survey.

On both versions of the survey, participants were first asked about their current level of use with the video system context of the survey, i.e. either YouTube or CSPAN Digital Video Library, on a scale of 1 (never used before) to 5 (daily use).

Beyond the varying system contexts presented in the different survey versions, the survey itself was the same. Furthermore, the survey presented:

1) The same general information topic, "How the Chief Justice of the Supreme Court ruled on 'Obama Care.'" Participants rated familiarity with this information topic on a scale of 1 (absolutely no familiarity) to 5 (expert on topic).
2) The same two video information need statements including:
    a. "An unedited video of the Chief Justice of the Supreme Court discussing his ruling on Obama Care during a college campus interview," coded for the present study as a known-item (or precision) video search.
    b. "Many video clips of political analysts critiquing the Chief Justice's ruling on Obama Care," designed as a collocation (or recall) search.

Participants rated their level of confidence, i.e. perceived self-efficacy, for fulfilling these video information needs using the system context of their respective survey, i.e. either YouTube or CSPAN Digital Video Library. The survey design and data collection method would enable comparison across different factors, spanning users and video needs and search topics, as potentially significant to self-efficacy [3].

Quantitative analyses were conducted on the scaled survey responses. Descriptive statistics of the participants' self-rated confidence levels for completing the information needs using the system context within their survey, i.e. perceived self-efficacy, were computed. Means were compared between groups of participants presented with the different system contexts, the different topic types, and those with varying levels of topic familiarity.

In total, 270 surveys were collected across both versions of the survey, which included an equal number of 135 of each of the YouTube and CSPAN Digital Video Library surveys. The overall sample, across both groups of participants, is shown according to frequencies among age and gender in Figure 1 and Figure 2.

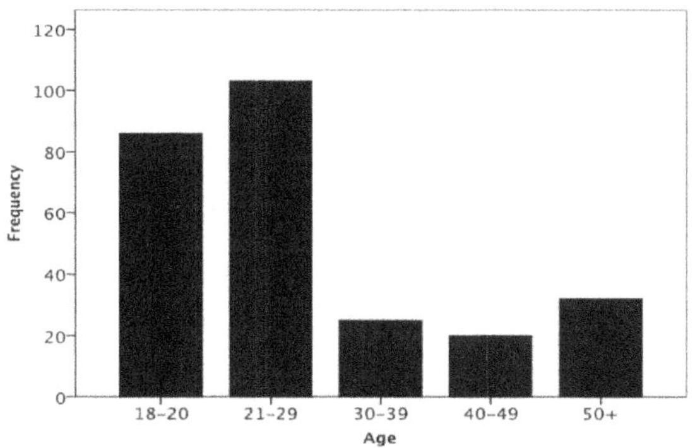

Figure 1: Overall number of participants by age group.

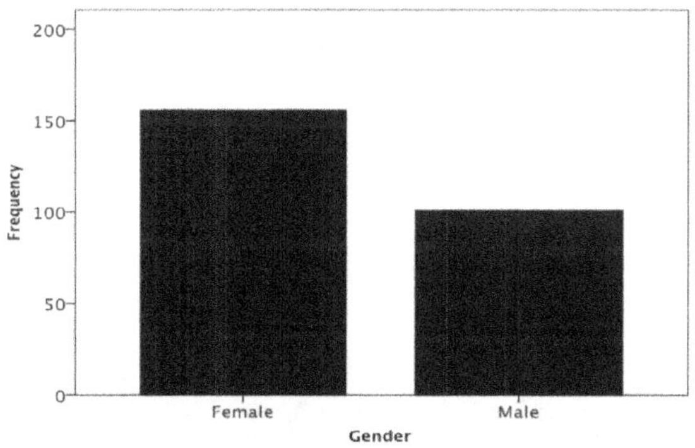

Figure 2: Overall number of participants by gender.

5. RESULTS

The collected surveys provided understanding about perceived self-efficacy in an interactive video retrieval context. Further, current findings begin to show significant relationships among the variables examined as being associated with users' perceived self-efficacy, which provide further validation for the present study and motivation for additional analyses to follow. A summary of the current results include:

RQ1. The overall combined mean (average) of users' perceived self-efficacy for successfully finding video that fulfills the different video information needs across both system contexts was 3.22 (out of 5), with a range of 4 (1-5) and a standard deviation (SD) of 1.11.

RQ1a. Results of users' self-reported levels of perceived self-efficacy between the different types of video search topics produced a mean score of M=3.15 for the known-item (or precision) need, with a SD of 1.18, and M=3.30 and SD=1.15 for the collocation need. A paired sample *t*-test produced a significant difference between these levels of perceived self-efficacy at $t(268)=-3.26$, $p<0.01$. There was also a positive correlation between the two types of video information needs, $r=.795$, $n=269$, $p<0.01$.

RQ1b. The overall mean familiarity with the general information topic was 2.30, including a range of 3 (1-4) and SD of 0.92. Out of all 270 responses, no participant self identified as a 5 "expert of the topic"; therefore, levels of perceived self-efficacy between the groups of participants identifying at the low end of topic familiarity, 156 of the 270, were compared to that of the participants at the higher end (3-4), i.e. the other 114 participants. An independent samples *t*-test showed significantly higher levels of perceived self-efficacy among the participants who were more familiar ($t(154)=-3.33$, $p<0.01$) with the information topic, at a mean of 3.48 (SD=0.99), compared to the overall mean of 3.03 (SD=1.16) for those less familiar with the general topic.

The association between users' self-rated levels of topic familiarity and perceived self-efficacy was also examined across the entire sample using a correlation analysis. This analysis produced a positive correlation between users' familiarity with the general information topic and their levels of perceived self-efficacy at $r=.178$, $n=270$, $p<0.01$.

RQ2. The overall level of use or experience with YouTube was measured at M=3.53 with a range of 4 (1-5) and SD of 1.27, compared to the mean for the CSPAN Digital Video Library at 1.18 with a range of 4 (1-4) and SD of 0.61.

Considering the stark contrasts between the levels of use or experience with the different system contexts, the first analysis for RQ2 examined mean comparisons between the different groups of participants, i.e. those completing the YouTube survey versus those taking the CSPAN version. Variations among the perceived self-efficacy of both groups were tested using an independent samples *t*-test, which produced a significant difference ($t(268)=4.58$, $p < 0.01$). YouTube participants rated significantly higher levels of perceived self-efficacy (M=3.52; SD=1.02) compared to those completing the CSPAN survey (M=2.92; SD=1.11).

Further, to draw comparisons across the entire sample, despite the contrast between the two groups of participants, correlation statistics were computed to further test the associations between the prior system use (or levels thereof) and averaged self-efficacy for fulfilling both video needs. This produced a significant positive correlation between these variables at $r=.389$, $n=270$, $p<0.01$.

6. DISCUSSION

Perceived self-efficacy is significant for video digital library design, development, and evaluation, as user confidence can ultimately be a factor that is influential to initial and sustained use of information retrieval tools. Furthermore, if users are not certain a given tool can help satisfy information needs and/or that its design can be accommodating to individual situations, inclinations to use such a tool may decline. User uncertainty (among other variables) is an attitude about technology use and ultimate acceptance, with self-efficacy being influenced by users' perceptions of usefulness and ease of use [5].

This first examination of an ongoing study demonstrated that factors corresponding to both users and topics in an interactive video retrieval context were significant to perceived self-efficacy. Furthermore, results of the present study derived from the first application or examination of self-efficacy within the context of video, which was warranted considering digital video, a multi-dimensional and time-based resource, can inevitably cause variations among users' needs, actions, and assessment of information, and, subsequently, approaches to the design and development of retrieval tools.

Significant associations between participants' self-rated levels of current system use and self-efficacy were reasonable. Similar relationships have been identified in other contexts, including as part of the image information seeking process, where prior experiences of users were found to be influential to preconceptions about retrieval tools and, in turn, tool selection [4]. Therefore, it was significant to thoroughly examine different factors potentially contributing to users' perceptions within an interactive video retrieval context which may ultimately affect potential and subsequent actions.

Discovering a relationship between perceived self-efficacy and factors pertaining to video information needs specifically, including both the nature of individual video search topics and user familiarity of the general topic being searched, can be applicable across other contexts of IIR research. Knowledge or familiarity with search topics has been examined in terms of its influence within actual video search sessions where it was found to be related to the interactions, performance, and satisfaction of users [1]. Therefore, significant associations between topic familiarity and users' levels of perceived self-efficacy, even though a phenomenon preceding actual search sessions, were also reasonable. The nature (or type) of the individual requests for video, e.g. known-item versus collocation video search topics, and its associations with self-efficacy was, again, the first such examination or application within IIR research; self-efficacy, while examined across various technologies and IIR processes, has not been examined specifically according to the type or nature of individual information needs.

Future analyses will more closely examine survey data to draw finer-level comparisons between more-specific groupings of factors in order to more thoroughly understand current findings and provide a holistic user-centered depiction of perceived self-efficacy in interactive video retrieval. Also, results of the present study can be rigorously examined in conjunction with users' criteria for video digital libraries, such as measured in [2], to make progress toward a framework capable of generalizing use and inclinations to use video retrieval tools like digital libraries.

In conclusion, findings of the present study can indicate immediate practical implications and recommendations for video digital libraries, including some that may help promote or encourage initial and continued use of collections by users. Such suggestions could include: 1) collection integration into larger and more universally-known platforms, 2) ample opportunities for topical learning, beyond the boundaries of the collection, as part of exploratory search interfaces, and 3) attention to precision with emphasis on curated content centered on the needs of users. These could provide users additional confidence and will be further expanded upon in subsequent future studies.

7. REFERENCES

[1] Albertson, D. 2013. An interaction and interface design framework for video digital libraries. *J. Doc.* 69 (5), 667-692.

[2] Albertson, D. & Ju, B. 2015. Design criteria for video digital libraries: Categories of important features emerging from users' responses. *Online Info. Rev.*, 39(2), 214-22.

[3] Bandura, A. 1986. *Social foundations of thought and action: A social cognitive theory*. Prentice-Hall, Englewood Cliffs, NJ.

[4] Conniss, L. R., Ashford, A. J., & Graham, M. E. (2000). *Information Seeking Behaviour in Image Retrieval: Visor I Final Report*. University of Northumbria at Newcastle, Trading Services, Newcastle, UK.

[5] Davis, F.D. 1989. Perceived usefulness, perceived ease of use, and user acceptance of information technology. *MISQ*, 13 (3): 319–340.

[6] Delcourt, M. and Kinzie, M. 1993. Computer technologies in teacher education: The measurement of attitudes and self-efficacy. *J. Res. and Dev. in Ed.*, 27(1), 35–41.

[7] Hill, T., Smith, N.D., and Mann, M.F. 1987. Role of efficacy expectations in predicting the decision to use advanced technologies: The case of computers. *J. Applied Psyc.*, 72(2), 307-13.

[8] Karsten, R. and Roth, M.R. 1998. The relationship of computer experience and computer self-efficacy to performance in introductory computer literacy courses. *J. Res. on Tech. Ed.*, 31(1), 14-24.

[9] Kurbanoglu, S.S. 2003. Self-efficacy: A concept closely linked to information literacy and lifelong learning. *J. Doc.*, 59(6), 635-46.

[10] Mansourian, Y. and Ford, N. 2007. Web searchers' attributions of success and failure: An empirical study. *J. Doc.*, 63(5), 659–679.

[11] Marchionini, G., Wildemuth, B.M., and Geisler, G. 2006. The open video digital library: A möbius strip of research and practice. *JASIS&T*, 57 (12), 1629-1643.

[12] Nahl, D. 1996. Affective monitoring of Internet learners: Perceived self-efficacy and success. In S. Hardin (Ed.) *Proceedings of the 59th Annual Meeting of the American Society for Information Science* (Baltimore, MD, October 21-24, 1996. Information Today, Medford, NJ. pp. 100-9.

[13] Ren, W.H. 1999. Self-efficacy and the search for government information: A study of small-business executives. *RUSQ*, 38(3), 283-91.

[14] Wildemuth, B. M., Marchionini, G., Yang, M., Geisler, G., Wilkens, T., Hughes, A., and Gruss, R. 2003. How fast is too fast?: Evaluating fast forward surrogates for digital video In *Proceedings of the 3rd ACM/IEEE-CS Joint Conference on Digital Libraries* (Houston, TX, May 27-31, 2003) ACM, New York, pp. 221-230.

Improving Access to Large-scale Digital Libraries Through Semantic-enhanced Search and Disambiguation

Annika Hinze
Computer Science
University of Waikato
Hamilton, New Zealand
hinze@waikato.ac.nz

Craig Taube-Schock
Computer Science
University of Waikato
Hamilton, New Zealand
schock@waikato.ac.nz

David Bainbridge
Computer Science
University of Waikato
Hamilton, New Zealand
davidb@waikato.ac.nz

Rangi Matamua
Māori & Pacific Development
University of Waikato
Hamilton, New Zealand
rmatamua@waikato.ac.nz

J. Stephen Downie
Library and Information Science
University of Illinois
jdownie@illinois.edu

ABSTRACT

With 13,000,000 volumes comprising 4.5 billion pages of text, it is currently very difficult for scholars to locate relevant sets of documents that are useful in their research from the HathiTrust Digital Libary (HTDL) using traditional lexically-based retrieval techniques. Existing document search tools and document clustering approaches use purely lexical analysis, which cannot address the inherent ambiguity of natural language. A semantic search approach offers the potential to overcome the shortcoming of lexical search, but—even if an appropriate network of ontologies could be decided upon—it would require a full semantic markup of each document. In this paper, we present a conceptual design and report on the initial implementation of a new framework that affords the benefits of semantic search while minimizing the problems associated with applying existing semantic analysis at scale. Our approach avoids the need for complete semantic document markup using pre-existing ontologies by developing an automatically generated Concept-in-Context (*CiC*) network seeded by *a priori* analysis of Wikipedia texts and identification of semantic metadata. Our Capisco system analyzes documents by the semantics and context of their content. The disambiguation of search queries is done interactively, to fully utilize the domain knowledge of the scholar. Our method achieves a form of semantic-*enhanced* search that simultaneously exploits the proven scale benefits provided by lexical indexing.

1. INTRODUCTION

A few decades ago, scholars of humanities would have had to travel to the Library of Congress and national archives to visually examine many of the documents of interest to their research. Digitized archives such as the one made available in the HathiTrust Digital Library allow scholars to perform these kinds of explorations online, and scholars now regularly analyze large sets of digitized documents. Access to the digitized document collections is available primarily by string-based search, through inverted indexes of both document full-texts and metadata. Within the HathiTrust corpus, the document full-texts have been obtained through optical character recognition (OCR), and the metadata drawn from library catalogues. Such text-based searching identifies documents purely according to lexicographical analysis.

Most research questions and areas of scholarly interest, however, can rarely be described by simple textual keywords; rather they are conceptually-based, such as searching for content on "Māori Astronomy", "Niuean / European encounters" and "mythology in Shakespeare". Taking the first example, a simple text search for the terms "Māori" and "astronomy" obviously cannot identify all documents that may be pertinent to the scholar. Current practice is for the scholar to identify marker terms that might occur in a document set, such as "tohunga ko-ko-rangi" (astronomers), as well as English or Māori names of star constellations. This approach is restrictive and of limited use because large sets of unrelated documents may be included in search results, *i.e.*, where the names of Māori stars are used in a different context with no connection to astronomy. For instance "Matariki" can refer to both the Pleiades star cluster and the Māori New Year. Relevant sources may remain undetected unless the right keyword is found.

Easy identification of appropriate keywords is further hindered when different languages are involved (English and Māori in our example) and when an area contains sources from diverse fields that do not share a common vocabulary. Further problems are introduced through the inherent ambiguity of natural language, *e.g.*, synonyms and homonyms. In all these cases, false negatives (*i.e.*, missed documents) and false positives (*i.e.*, unrelated documents that have to be manually identified and eliminated) have significant adverse effects on the scholar's research.

Focus of this paper. We propose to automatically analyze documents not purely by their text but rather by the semantics of their content and metadata. Our work differs from the concept of semantic search, which we discuss in detail in Section 3. In a first step, the semantic analysis entails text analysis of the whole corpus to generate a specific knowledge structure we have termed a Concept-in-Context (CiC) network. Starting from a network of known concepts, we analyze which of these concepts appear in the document

JCDL'15, June 21–25, 2015, Knoxville, Tennessee, USA.

DOI: http://dx.doi.org/10.1145/2756406.2756920

No	Maori name	English name	Constellation	Cross ref	Prim. source	Ty pe	Quote
003	Kōpū	Venus		Ngā Ihiihi o Kōpū. Matariki.	Andersen, J. (1962). Māori String Figures. Steele Roberts Limites. Wellington. P.5	2	"There are several figures with star names – Kōpū, Nga ihiihi o Kōpū, Matariki. In Polynesia too there are many figures representing stars."
171	Matariki	Pleiades	Taurus	Tohunga Rongoā Toutouwai Tāwera	Tregear, E. (1904). The Māori Race. A. D. Willis Printer and Publisher: Wanganui. P 22	6	"...the wizard doctor could revive a man if there were certain favourable conjunctions at the time; thus if the robin (toutouwai) was to sing for the first time just as the morning star (Tawera) was seen, if also the Pleiades (Matariki) were high in the sky, and the dying man had a shivering fit, then with all these auspicious signs occurring a certain invocation would bring back the departing soul."
274	Puanga	Rigel	Orion	Atutahi, Puanga Maruaonui, Matariki, Whakaahu Rangiāio	Te Tiupiri 1898-1900: Volume 1, No. 43: 4	1	"Waihoki i roto i tenei ra, ko Puanga kua ngaro ki roto o Te Maruaonui, ko tona kai whakahaere ko Matariki; ko Whakaahu kua ngaro ki roto o Te Rangiaio, tona kai whakahaere ko Tautoru; [...]."
Selection of further names : Rēhua (Antares), Takurua (Sirius), Whānui (Vega), Atutahi (Canopus), Maruaonui, Whakaahu (Castor/Pollux), Rangiāio, Mangaroa (Milky Way), Ranginui (Rigel Kentaurus), Tautoru (Orions Belt)							

Figure 1: Word list aiding repeated searches in Māori Astronomy

set, thus assigning meaning to each document. In a second step, the documents can be clustered set into proto work-sets based on the assigned concepts. In the final step, the scholar uses semantic-enhanced search on the data collection using concepts instead of text keywords.

The challenges encountered in this project span technical issues and those of interaction design. The technical challenges lie in the implementation of searching semantically in a text-based environment (*i.e.*, the available information is not encoded using semantic web markup) and in the development of a suitable Context-in-Context network. The challenges in interaction design relate to the development of work-flows and interfaces that are suitable for humanities scholars, who are assumed to be without extensive expertise in semantic querying (technical non-experts). In comparison, traditional interfaces for semantic search and knowledge manipulation are highly complex, and require prior experience and expertise in semantic query languages.

Contributions. This paper provides the new search and interaction concept of *semantic-enhanced search*. We introduce the conceptual design and implementation of our Capisco (Italian for "I understand") system, detail our process of manual disambiguation, and illustrate the effectiveness of our approach by two use cases (a complex one of Māori Astronomy, and a simpler one on that allows a detailed comparison between the different search approaches). We also discuss the insights gained from this project so far, and identify future challenges. Our approach is designed to scale well and has the benefits of semantic capabilities without complex query languages that are unsuitable for technical non-experts.

The remainder of the paper is structured as follows: Section 2 introduces our use case of scholarly search in Māori Astronomy, Section 3 discusses the background of our research, while Section 4 analyses related research. Sections 5 and 6 introduce our semantic-enhanced search and query disambiguation. Section 7 discuses a detailed example and two use cases to highlight the effectiveness of our approach. We conclude with a summary and discussion of future work.

2. USE CASE: Māori ASTRONOMY

Traditionally, Māori held great knowledge of astronomy and their studies of the night sky played an important role in everyday life. Much of this knowledge remains recorded in *Te Reo* (Māori: "the language") and sits within songs, prayers, proverbs and place names. The scholarly field Māori Astronomy is concerned with exploring traditional Māori Astronomy and understanding its practise, application and position within traditional Māori society. It is further concerned with understanding the language of traditional Māori Astronomy, its terms and use. As such, potentially relevant documents are not restricted to the scholarly publications but also other Māori document.

In a current project, scholars are exploring the significance of Māori Astronomy seeking to better understand its importance in traditional Māori society. An additional component to this study is the creation of tools to re-introduce Māori Astronomy into a modern world. One of the problematic issues has been the collection of relevant data. The current process is pain-staking and error-prone. The scholars have to take single Māori words or names related to astronomy, and search through various document collections for each. For example, the term *Matariki* may be first entered into Google search. The scholar then explores each link to judge how related it is to the study. Then the same term is entered into various databases such as the online Māori Newspaper collection *Niupepa*[1] or the Journal of Polynesian Society databases. Again the scholar analyzes each link. Finally, they check the books and papers from the library looking for references to the various star names and terms they have collected. The process is repetitive and tedious. Over the years the scholar has compiled a dataset of several hundred terms referring to star constellations and related concepts, often in both Māori and English language. This expedites the process and serves as a memory aid. The dataset has been extended with references to a primary literature source for each term and a quote linking the term and Māori Astronomy. Figure 1 shows a selection of the terms and their related information. The type information refers to the source of the reference quote (*e.g.*, journal, book, manuscript, online). For an exhaustive search on a new source potentially all terms would need to be checked.

From this simple example it is apparent that this process is very slow and more often than not produces information that is not relevant to their work. As described in an interview by the scholar, the current approach is experienced as being "extremely restrictive".

3. BACKGROUND

Before presenting our semantic-enhanced search, we first need to distinguish between different search approaches, which are often confused due to unclear nomenclature. We briefly introduce our text corpus of the HathiTrust Digital Library (HTDL). We then discuss existing methods for search enhancement in Section 4.

3.1 Search approaches

Our approach is concerned with the search for (mainly text-based) documents, not knowledge searches that aim to infer answers to a question. Document search approaches can be distinguished by the types of documents and queries (text-based vs SPARQL/RDF), and indexing (see Figure 2).

Text-based (lexicographic) search. Classic text-based search uses keywords (*literals*) as query terms and the target documents are also (predominantly) text-based (*i.e.*, *literals*, see Figure 2, top). In the first phase (indexing), the documents are analyzed for keywords, which are then built into an index. During search, the index of keywords is used to identify matching documents (identified by *docID* in Figure 2).

Semantic search. Traditional semantic search uses a semantic query language (*e.g.*, SPARQL), while the target items are semantic web documents encoded, *e.g.*, using RDF. Each RDF document contains references to its concepts defined in one or more ontologies, and a number of literals. In the first phase (indexing), the documents are analyzed for concepts (as defined in the ontologies), which are then built into an index. Additionally, the ontologies used will be indexed according to the concepts they contain (*e.g.*, via a database). These details are shown in Figure 2, middle. During search, the SPARQL query (also containing concepts and literals) is executed on the ontology index (to identify relevant concepts) and document index (to identify documents referring to these concepts).

Semantic-enhanced search. Semantic-enhanced search as proposed in this paper uses text keywords and the target documents are also (predominantly) text-based (*i.e.*, literals in both queries and documents, see Figure 2, bottom). In this respect, semantic-enhanced search is similar to lexicographic search and can be used in the same settings. Internally an ontology or concept network is used to translate between keywords and concepts (disambiguation). In the first phase (indexing), the documents are analyzed for keywords indicating concepts (using the ontology or concept network), which are then build into an index of concepts. During the search phase, the user's keywords are also first translated into concepts, which are then used to lookup the index for matching documents.

Semantic-enhanced search as proposed here allows technical non-experts to use semantic technology when querying document corpora that do not provide semantic mark-up.

3.2 HathiTrust Digital Library

The HTDL is one such document corpus without semantic markup. It stores over 13,000,000 volumes comprising some 4,500,000,000 pages. Of these volumes, approximately one third are in the public domain [5]. The remainder is under copyright restrictions, which inhibits open access by scholars and researchers. The *non-consumptive research model* developed by the HathiTrust Research Center[1] aims to overcome these limitations by integrating analytic software into the data collection to allow for analysis of large collections while adhering to the restrictions of the copyright environment. The HTDL has great potential as source and platform for scholarly research. Researchers using digital libraries must be able to find, access and organize collections of materials. However, assisting scholars in building such collection subsets that they can then analyse for their research is challenging due to the scale and diversity of the corpus [10]. The documents in more than 100 languages are represented in the corpus, some of them are in multiple languages. Our research feeds into the project on Workset Creation for Scholarly Analysis, one of those goals is to enrich the available metadata for documents in the HTDL. A full-scale semantic analysis of each document, such as [2], is not feasible for reasons of scale and copyright.

[1] http://www.hathitrust.org/htrc

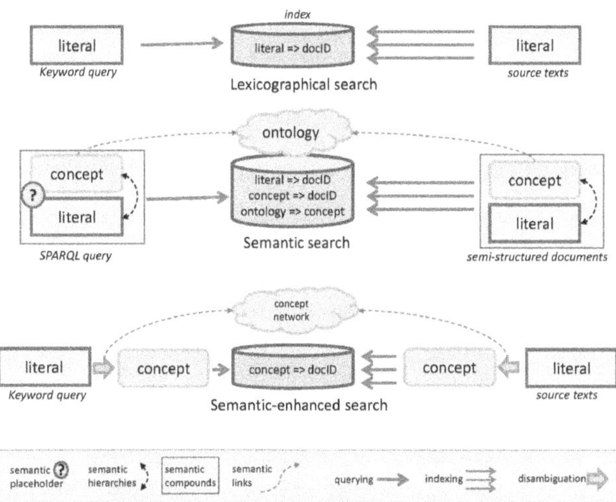

Figure 2: Comparison of search approaches

4. TERMINOLOGY AND RELATED WORK

This section introduces the terminology used in this article. It also places our project in the context of related work.

4.1 Lexicographic search enhancement

Semantic-enhanced search requires a translation between text keywords and their respective concepts. A similar need for term clarification is typically encountered in *lexicographic search*, known as the vocabulary problem [12], because users often do not phrase their query in the language and terms of the documents they aim to retrieve [34]. The vocabulary problem is compounded by synonymity (different words, similar meaning) and polysemy (same word, different but related meaning), leading to decreased recall (missed relevant documents) and precision (inclusion of irrelevant documents), respectively [4].

The problem has been addressed by a number of approaches, including automatic query expansion (AQE), interactive query refinement, relevance feedback, word sense disambiguation and search results clustering, each of which we briefly describe now.

4.1.1 *Automatic query expansion*

Because large corpora may contain different expressions of the same concept, the vocabulary problem may be addressed by expanding the user query with terms that are related to the keywords provided by the user. Automatic query expansion has long been used in Information Retrieval to improve search results [4]. The words used for query expansion may be selected using probabilistic methods based on term co-occurrence (*i.e.*, based on their statistic co-occurrence) or based on controlled vocabularies (*i.e.*, thesauri or ontologies). We will refer to these methods as *probabilistic* and *ontological* methods, respectively.

Probabilistic methods can be distinguished into global and local methods depending on the basis on which they calculate the co-occupance of terms (top-n or all documents in the collection). Local methods are executed ad-hoc at query time. It has been shown that a simple approach of using statistical relations has little effect [25]. Vorhees in 1994 used Wordnet[2] as a simplified ontology to expand user queries. In her study, Voorhees manually identified the appropriate concepts—automatic methods still had to be developed. She observed that detailed user queries benefit little from query expansion, but that most users typically enter relatively short queries [34]. She concluded that expanded queries generally are unlikely to outperform well-formulated user-supplied queries. However, it has been observed that search engine users tend to begin by entering short queries, which are gradually modified [28].

4.1.2 Query refinement

The reasons for short search queries might be that users are unfamiliar with the content of a document repository (thus avoiding too specific or narrow queries that might be unsuccessful) [21], or that the user has poorly-defined information needs (redefining their information need as they go along) [3]. This iterative process is called *query refinement* or interactive query expansion [32]. It aims at supporting the user in their decision making process. Efthimiadis found that only about one third of the terms suggested to the user for query expansion was considered useful [7]. In this study, interactive query expansion achieved on average an improvement from originally three highly relevant documents to the inclusion of further nine highly relevant documents. Typically query refinement is done on a syntactic basis.

Query refinement can also be used for semantic queries. Automatic semantic refinement of ontology-based queries aims to incrementally tailor a query to a given ontology and the user's needs [32]. Stojanovic follows an approach related to that of a personal assistant [32, 31]. They analyze the user behaviour during the search process. They refer to the gap between the information need and the current query as *query ambiguity*. Their approach navigates through a neighborhood of similar queries with the aim to decrease the query ambiguity.

4.1.3 Word Sense Disambiguation

None of the approaches described above address the problem faced in our situation. Semantic-enhanced search needs to identify relevant concepts for a given keyword or phrase. Rarely does a keyword belong to exactly one concept alone; the process of identifying the correct concept is called *disambiguation*. The correct concept in a query refers to the intention and query need of the users, while correct concepts for source documents refer to the context and semantics of the document content. Word Sense Disambiguation (WSD) is the task of determining the meaning of a word in a given context [24].

Automatic disambiguation attempts to derive word senses automatically, either as targeted WSD and all-word WSD. Targeted disambiguation aims to identify a selected set of words, whereas all-words disambiguation aims to identify all words in a text. We are interested in targeted disambiguation of keywords. WSD typically uses some kind of knowledge base, which may be ontologies, dictionaries, annotated text corpora, or thesauri. A widely used source is Wordnet [9], which encodes more than 100,000 synonym sets of English words. Kohamban and Lee built a WSD system using a classifier using Wordnet [20]. Most knowledge organization systems like thesauri, classification systems, or DBpedia do not carry information about context and are therefore not suitable for our purpose.

Another approach is using Wikipedia as the originating data collection. WikipediaMiner [23] analyses Wikipedia articles, and based on the results of mining this large text corpus, it exploits word usage statistics to achieve disambiguation. It relies on Wikipedia's prior link probability (likelihood of a link between a word and a concept based on statistical analysis) to determine concepts that match given words. WikipediaMiner uses data mining techniques to disambiguate the semantics of a word. WikipediaMiner therefore does not provide the facility for end-users to influence the disambiguation process, nor does it allow for the manual introduction or modification of concepts.

4.2 Markup for Semantic Search

In order to enable semantic search on existing full-text documents *a-posteriori* semantic mark-up is needed. This is predominantly done with automatic tools, and occasionally manually. Here, semantic search, like lexicographic search, encounters the challenge of disambiguation.

4.2.1 Semantic annotation

Automatic annotation tools, such as OpenCalais,[3] Zemanta,[4] DBpedia Spotlight,[5] and Cohse [35] are services for the semantic web community to increase the volume of interconnected data. Most of these these tools use named entity extraction, also called named entity recognition (NER) and natural language processing. Named entities are " information units such as the name of a person or a location found in a sentence"[13]. Typically the entities are organized in a knowledge base or ontology. The tools use different algorithms and training data, and few comparative evaluations have been conducted to identify the conditions under which each tool is the most appropriate [27, 29, 17]. However, due to the algorithms used, the tools work best on full-text documents but not on a user's search keywords. Furthermore, because the systems use machine learning techniques, the end user cannot explore why these annotations were given or take direct influence.

4.2.2 Semantic keyphrase extraction

Keyphrase extraction aims to identify the most relevant keyphrases of a document, while semantic keyphrase extraction aims to identify the most relevant concepts of a document. Two prominent system for keyphrase extraction have been evaluated and tested in comparison to semantic annotation: KP-miner [8] and Maui [22]. The comparison found that both KP-miner and Maui outperform semantic annotation tools [17]. Maui integrally relies on WikipediaMiner [23] for computing semantic relatedness between phrases and for disambiguation. Our preliminary tests have shown that Capisco outperforms WikipediaMiner's disambiguation.

[2]from `http://wordnet.princeton.edu`

[3]`http://opencalais.com`

[4]`http://www.zemanta.com`

[5]`http://dbpedia.org/spotlight`

4.2.3 *Manual semantic mark-up*

Some argue that automatic annotation is not always of sufficient quality to enable focused search and retrieval: either too many or too few terms are semantically annotated. User-defined semantic enrichment allows for a more targeted approach than automatic semantic enrichment. Manual systems may be distinguished into commenting tools, web-annotation tools, wiki-based systems, content composition systems, digital library tools, and linguistic text analysis. We here discuss as an example system the semantic content authoring tool Loomp, which supports manual markup of text with semantic concepts. A one-click annotator interface is provided for non-expert users to bridge the gap between objective knowledge (as encoded in an RDF data model and ontology) and subjective knowledge of human cognition. The annotator supports this process by presenting labels and contextual information about named entities for identification of semantic identity [15, 16].

Loomp and other manual annotations tools cannot provide semantic markup for large corpora such as the one used in this project. The Loomp authors identified as the most promising annotation approaches those that are semi-automatic, providing automatic suggestions that are manually refined. The resulting documents can be searched using semantic query languages. However, the complexity of such languages still pose a serious impediment for technical non-experts. However, their approach is interesting for the disambiguation of search terms.

5. SEMANTIC-ENHANCED SEARCH

This section introduces our approach of semantically-enhanced search. One of the central components of Capisco is a Concept-in-Context network, whose principles we explain in Section 5.1. We then introduce the system architecture and data flow in Section 5.2. Our search interfaces including the user-guided disambiguation is introduced in detail in Section 6.

5.1 Concept-in-Context network

Instead of an ontology or knowledge base, we use our Concept-in-Context (CiC) network to capture the semantic concepts and the relationships between them. Typically the development of both knowledge bases or ontologies faces similar challenges to that of the semantic annotation of texts: it is a complex task that often consumes considerable human effort [11]. However, ontology and knowledge base engineering is typically executed by experts in semantic technologies and is not necessarily suitable for end-users. Moreover, often the bottleneck in building lies in the social process rather than in the technology [6].

We follow a different approach here creating a Concept-in-Context network that has been seeded with concepts derived from Wikipedia that was inspired by WikipediaMiner (see top-part of Figure 4). Relationships between symbols and their meaning are extracted from Wikipedia links. Representing the semantics with our CiC approach has several advantages. The representation base has a less-strictly formalized structure compared to an ontology. Instead of classes and relationships defined in RDF/Schema and OWL structures that tightly define the semantics and relationships for each concept, our representation structure encapsulates only two types of relationships: synonyms and contexts. This is expressed through words, concepts and context.

We here follow Sowa's understanding of knowledge representation in which word meaning has two aspects: the intension of a word (or *symbol*) refers to its general principles (*i.e.*, the *concept*) while the extension of a word refers to the existing *expressions* of the concept [30]. For the purpose of writing about symbols and concepts, we introduce the following notation: symbols (words, literals) are marked with "quotes" and concepts (both intensions and extensions) are indicated through [brackets]. For example, the symbol "Matariki" refers to the concept [Matariki star cluster]; the symbol "Pleiades" also refers to [Matariki star cluster]. Internally, the concepts are predominantly identified by concept IDs, but within the paper we will use human readable references ([Matariki star cluster] instead of [id:96471]).

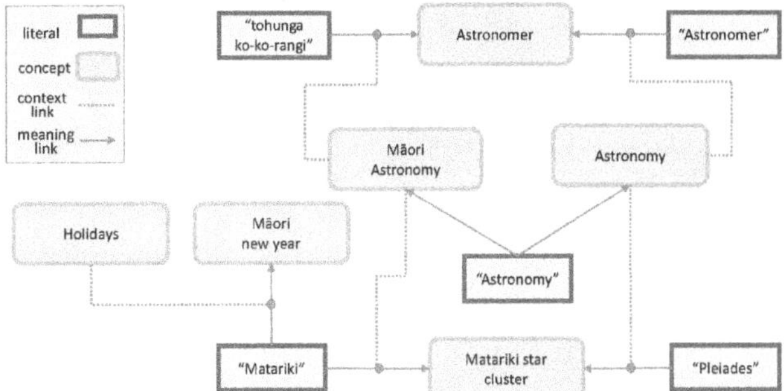

Figure 3: CiC network example

Although Sowa provides a basis for semantic conceptual understanding, he does not cover, or resolve, the problem of ambiguity. Ambiguity is created through the same symbol referring to different concepts. For example, the symbol "Matariki" may also refer to the concept [Māori new year] The way to distinguish between these concepts is by examining their context. Figure 3 shows a small example of the modeling of the relationships between words and concepts and also shows how concepts can serve as context for words.

It can easily be seen that our approach to encoding synonyms as concepts and contexts allows multi-linguality to be treated as a special case of ambiguity because words and phrases of differing languages are synonyms of the underlying concept.

Due to its seeding from Wikipedia, the CiC network may contain noisy data. Because Wikipedia entries are developed through crowd-sourcing, not all entries are of the desired high quality. Furthermore, although the Wikipedia process aims to create a network of information resources, it does not necessarily aim to produce a viable network of semantic concepts.

5.2 Conceptual Architecture

Figure 4 shows the conceptual architecture of the system. Components indicated in dashed lines have been conceptualized but not implemented yet. We now describe each of the components.

CiC Network Seeding. As described above, our knowledge representation is initially seeded through the Capisco system; the relationships between concepts and literals are derived from the links between Wikipedia articles and the anchor terms used in these links (see Figure 5). The location of the link (*i.e.*, information about the originating article) is retained as contextual information. Capisco assigned each concept with an internal concept id (cID). These are stored as triples of the form <*literal,cID,cID*>, which expresses a word or phrase (literal) a meaning in a given context (*i.e.*, <*phrase, context, meaning*>).

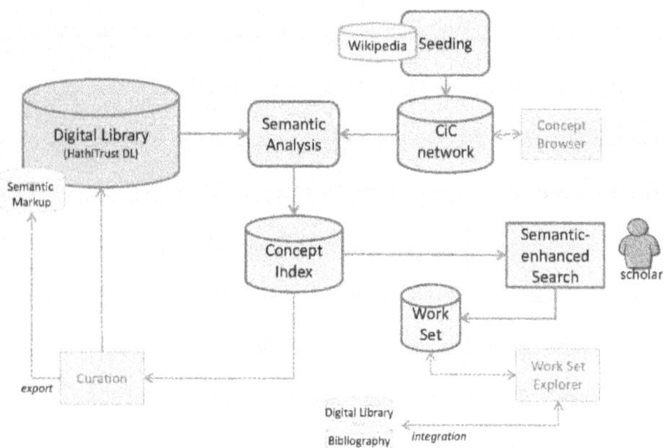

Figure 4: System architecture

Note that both meaning and context are concepts (identified by cID). For example, "Matariki" refers to [Māori New Year] in the context of New Zealand [Holidays]. Additionally we store a short description for each concept. The triples are stored in a MongoDB[6].

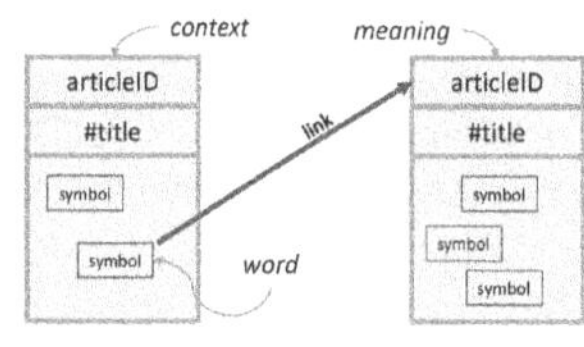

Figure 5: *CiC* triple structure

Adaptation of the network to reflect current scholarly research and specialized domain knowledge will be done via a concept browser.

Semantic analysis and indexing. The documents in the text corpus or digital library are semantically analyzed using the concepts contained in the CiC network. Our disambiguation works on the assumption that it is very likely that terms that appear together in a document will have related meanings. For example, if a sentence mentions "tennis" and the term "set", this most likely refers to the concept [tennis set] not mathematical [set theory]. Thus disambiguation of terms appearing in a document is done through analysing the presence of other terms in the context of the text, which may in turn also be ambiguous. An ambiguous term (*i.e.*, one that refers to a number of concepts in the CC network) may, however, be unambiguous in a given context (that is, it may have only one meaning in a given context). We use those terms that are not ambiguous as anchor points for disambiguation. Conceptually, our disambiguation identifies clusters of all directed graphs between the text of a document and every possible concept in order to identify the most likely semantics. The result of this semantic analysis is a concept index that maintains links between the documents in the corpus and the concepts in CiC network. The semantic information contained in the concept index can be manually refined or exported into semantic markup for the text corpus. The concept index is implemented as Lucene[7] index, for the creation of which auxiliary documents containing the concepts identified for each document in the corpus are used. The document links in the index are redirected from the auxiliary concept documents to the actual text documents.

Semantic-enhanced search. To simplify access to the digital library, Capisco provides a text-based search interface that scholars would find familiar. Search terms entered, however, are processed quite differently to lexicographic search. First, terms are automatically mapped to a list of concepts by Capisco, that are returned to the scholar for inspection. This is the point where manual disambiguation can occur (described in more detail in Section 6). By selectively clicking on the terms returned, a traditional lexicographic search is constructed and – once the scholar is satisfied with their selection – executed against our Lucene index. Returned by this step is a traditional result set with links to matching documents. The resulting set of documents can be saved as a workset to be explored and annotated. Worksets can also integrate documents and references from other sources (digital libraries, corpora or reference systems), or be exported in full or as metadata into other formats suitable for integration into the workflow of the scholar (*e.g.*, endnote or zotero).

Test corpus. The HathiTrust test corpus we are using for our current tests contains over 2 million OCR pages (2,348,172) that are each indexed separately. The pages refer to 8,489 volumes. The corpus' size is 14GB. Metadata about the pages is held in pair tree format,; metdadata about the volumes is available from the HathiTrust. Capisco's CiC network as seeded from Wikipedia contains 4,562,497 concepts that are involved in 101,115,481 triples. The index between HathiTrust test corpus and the CiC network is 256MB (2,942,698 terms link to 2,331,194 documents — missing documents due to unindexable OCR results). We observe that when ranked by frequency in the index, only the top 1115 concepts appear more than 10,000 times. For example, rank 1 is the concept [Shilling] with 268,914 document links, and rank 10 is the concept [water], which appears in 144,916 links. Most terms, however, appear only a few times, such as [St. Stephen's day] with 21 times (rank 100,000).

6. INTERACTIVE DISAMBIGUATION

Manual semantic disambiguation is known to be a challenging task for users that are not familiar with the intricacies of semantic web or ontology concepts [15, 16]. The vocabulary needs to be kept simple and as close as possible to terms with which users are familiar [18, 19]. Our semantic-enhanced search has two main interfaces for scholars without technical knowledge in semantic web technology: one for inserting the query keywords and disambiguation, and one for display of the result list.

Query interface and disambiguation. Figure 6 shows the initial query interface (all screen-shots have been cropped, but retain high resolution for detailed digital reading). The scholar is prompted to insert their search keywords (literals), divided by "|". Note that for simplicity in the Capisco interface we refer to our semantic-enhanced search as 'semantic search'. Figure 7 shows the inserted query containing the two literals "Fox River" and "Public Lands".

Figure 8 shows the list of candidate concepts returned in response to the query entered in Figure 7. The black dot next to the literals indicated that they have not yet been disambiguated. The user is prompted to select a concept for the first literal "Fox River" (top part of screen). Again, for simplicity the term 'concept' is not used but instead the user is prompted for the "sense of 'Fox Rover'". The list of concepts shows all those that are connected with the literal "Fox River" in the CiC network.

Figure 9 shows the screen after the scholar has disambiguated the concept [Fox River (Illinois River tributary)] as the relevant semantics of the literal "Fox River". The concept has been inserted into

[6]http://www.mongodb.org

[7]http://lucene.apache.org

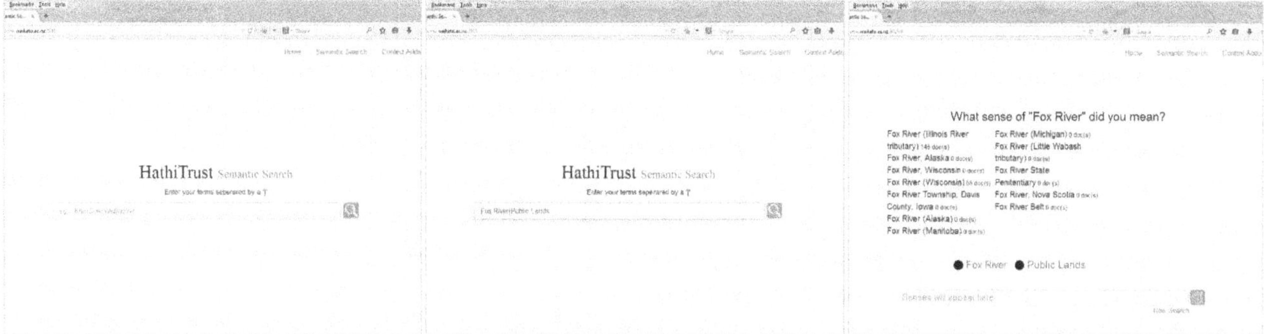

Figure 6: Query interface (start) Figure 7: Inserted query of literals Figure 8: Disambiguation of first term

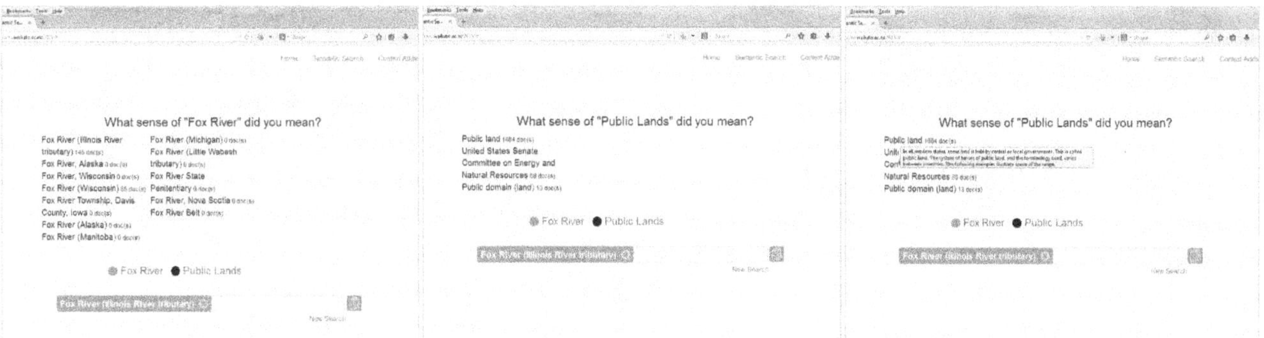

Figure 9: Concept has been identified Figure 10: Disambiguation of second term Figure 11: Pop-up for information

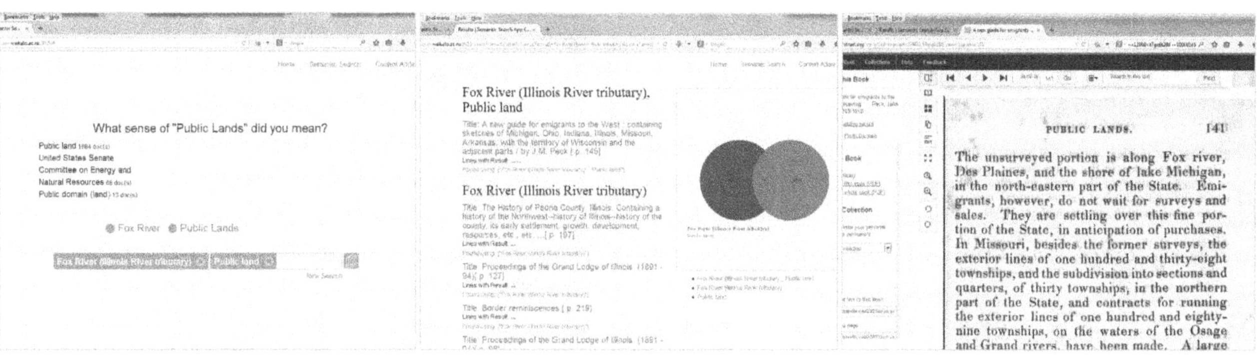

Figure 12: Final query Figure 13: Result listing Figure 14: Document view in HTDL

the list of query concepts (in orange), and the orange dot at the literal indicates that this term has been disambiguated. The second literal that needs disambiguating is “Public Lands" (see Figure 10). The scholar switched to this term by selecting the literal next to the black dot. Again, an array of concepts are offered for disambiguation. As the scholar hovers the mouse over each concept, a pop-up window provides the context to the concept through scope notes (see Figure 11). The scholar selected the concept [Public Land], which is inserted into the concept query as shown in Figure 12. The query is now ready to be submitted.

Result list and Document view. The result list shows the documents found and also a Venn Diagram of how many documents were found for each of the concepts, and their overlap. Figure 13 shows the results for our query using the two concepts [Fox River (Illinois River tributary] and [Public Land]. The list of resulting documents is ordered by the number of query concepts that are found in the document. We are currently exploring a secondary ranking by strength of connection between document and concept. The document titles are pulled from the HTDL metadata (via document ID) and are not held in Capisco’s index.

By selecting a link in the result list shown in Figure 13 takes the scholar directly to the HTRC resource as held at the HTDL. Figure 14 shows an example page from the returned result in the HTDL.

7. USE CASES AND DISCUSSION

We show two use cases, one running on the original Wikipedia-seeded CiC network and HathiTrust corpus subset, and a second one running off a subject-specific CiC network and test set, seeded from scholar submitted information.

7.1 “Puck" on the original CiC network

We executed a search for Puck, for which our system offered 14 concepts for disambiguation, among them the concepts [Puck (Mythology)] and [Hockey Puck]. Because we were interested in the mythological figure Puck, we selected this concept. The current subset of HathiTrust documents contained in our corpus returned a list of 116 documents. One of the documents returned is "Sylvia", by Adeline Adams (1859-1948) notwithstanding that the term "Puck" appears nowhere in its 120 pages. However, as shown in Figure 15, it contains two references to "Robin Goodfellow". Analysing our Wikipedia-seeded CiC network (see Figure 16), we find that "Robin Goodfellow" is one of the labels for the concept [Puck (Mythology)]. It is, in fact, one of Puck's euphemistically disguised names.

We also entered the same query "Puck" into the online HTDL interface that uses lexicographic search. 281,407 results are returned. Within the first 100 documents (4 Spanish, 1 Swedish, 1 Polish, 1 Latvian, 1 Italian, 1 German), 44 referred to the concept of Ice Hockey. Explicitly excluding the term "Hockey" (i.e, by inserting -Hockey) results in an appropriately reduced result set. However, documents that refer only to Robin Goodfellow (such as the above cited "Sylvia") were not included.

Entering the same query into Google yields also a mixture of results. Prominently displayed is "Puck, also known as Robin Goodfellow, is a character in William Shakespeare's play". However of the first 100 hits provided results referring to a mix of the mythological Puck, Hockey, a game, a comic, a pub, and a programmer. All 5 images shown were of Hockey pucks and the News section was about the Yahoo Sports' NHL blog "Puck Daddy" and "Puck Headlines". Excluding the term "Hockey" removed the results referring to Ice Hockey but not the images of Hockey pucks. Most importantly, Adeline Adams' "Sylvia" was not included and could only be found by explicitly asking for "Robin Goodfellow".

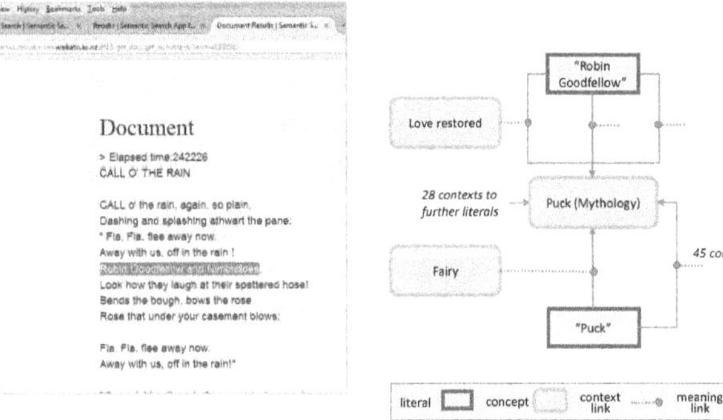

Figure 15: Document view of "Sylvia" (cropped)

Figure 16: *CiC* sub-network

7.2 "Māori Astronomy" on subject-specific CiC network

There are certain subjects where Wikipedia does not contain sufficient content to generate a useful CiC network that adequately represents those subjects. One such example is Maori Astronomy. For our second use case, we therefore took the tabulated content on Astronomy (see Figure 1) compiled by an internationally recognized scholar on Maori Astronomy—and co-researcher—and developed Content-in-Context triples that were ingested into Capisco to provide the necessary coverage.

Similarly we created a test corpus composed of documents deliberately chosen to confound the meanings of terms that could be associated with Maori Astronomy. We selected documents from three different groups: (Set I) Māori documents that mention the phrase "Māori astronomy, (Set II) documents about the Matariki star cluster without the phrase "Māori Astronomy", and (Set III) documents about Matariki, the Māori New Year.

We use some simple queries here to illustrate the effect of the system. When one searches for:

1) "Māori Astronomy" and disambiguates to [Māori Astronomy] the result set contains the documents from both Set I and Set II.

2) "Matariki" and disambiguates to [Matariki star cluster] the result set contains the documents from Set II and Set I.

3) "Matariki" and disambiguates to [Māori New Year] the result set contains the documents from Set III.

These examples illustrate that on this small test set and the subject-specific CiC network, the system addresses our use case as introduced in Section 2. Documents in Set II are about Māori Astronomy but never mention the term explicitly. However, this meaning is inferred from the words and phrases for which Māori Astronomy defines the context. 5 We illustrate this for a document from Set II: the document contains Chapter 17 ("Heavenly Bodies") from Edward Tregear's 1904 book titled "The Māori Race"[33]. This is one of the historic books referenced in the word list mentioned in Section 2 and in Figure 14. The document contains the word "Astronomical" once, which may disambiguate to both [Astronomy] and [Māori Astronomy]. It further contains terms such as "Matariki", "Tautoru", "te Kakau", "Pou-ta-te-rangi", "Makahea", "stars", all of which use the context of [Māori Astronomy] for disambiguation. Finally, the text also refers to [Māori people], which provides the contextual support for the link between "Astronomical" and [Māori Astronomy]. We could say that all these star names form the *context support set* of [Māori Astronomy], *i.e.*, the presence of these terms indicates that the concept [Maori Astronomy] acts as a context for this document.

A further example illustrates the result of the disambiguation of this example document corpus. The document is one from Set I, an article titled "A review of Māori Astronomy in Aotearoa-New Zealand" [14]. Figure 17 illustrates the disambiguation decisions taken, and also possible future improvements. We here show the concepts identified in the disambiguation step (and encoded in the index) as a concept map for the document. The number next to each literal indicates how often this phrase appeared in the document. The literal "Māori Astronomy" is unambiguous and can serve as an anchor point for the disambiguation. For example, the term "Atutahi" appears four times in the document (see Figure 17, bottom right). It might refer to the [Atutahi Island], but since there is no context of [Cook Island] in the document to support this disambiguation, this link cannot be established. Rather the context [Māori Astronomy] supports a disambiguation of "Atutahi" to the star [Canopus]. A number of other star names appear, for most of which [Māori Astronomy] provides context. The document also contains "Matariki" 17 times, and additionally the phrase "New Year" seven times. Both readings of [Matariki star cluster] and [Māori New Year] are included. The granularity of our current contextual analysis can be set to whole documents or single pages. The case of "Matariki" is a good motivation for a more fine-grained analysis, which is planned for the future. In this case it would allow us to identify that "Matariki" should only once be disambiguated to [Māori New Year] when the terms appear within the same paragraph. This information can then be used for result ranking.

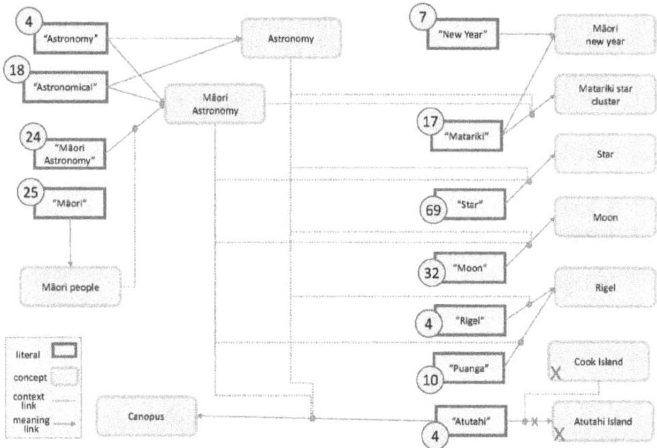

Figure 17: Concept map for document after disambiguation

As a last example, we show how our method can also be used to analyze parts of documents (or to cluster semantically similar documents). Due to human error we used the complete proceedings of the 2008 conference on Traditional Knowledge [26]. We had intended to index one of the articles, which contains a discussion of the phrase "tohunga tātai arorangi" for [Māori Astronomer] and the context of [Māori Astronomy]. The resulting network of concepts for the book shows only a small cluster of terms connected with [Māori Astronomy] (each appearing up to four times), and an overwhelming number of occurrences of Māori (1077), "New Zealand" (334) and "world" (171). Also many of the occurring concepts to not link together well, and the document seems to fall into a number of clusters. It is clear from analysing the concept map for the document that only a fraction of the full document refers to [Māori Astronomy], and that the planned extension to more fine-grained context capturing is appropriate.

7.3 Quality of disambiguation

For in-depth manual analysis, we also built a small corpus of 23 documents. The documents were short articles or introductions into topics (*e.g.*, honey, twitter, family, microbrews), collected from online archives of newspaper articles and the Encyclopedia Britannica; each article was between 1 and 2 pages long. We processed this test corpus in three ways: (1) using WikipediaMiner for identification of concepts, (2) semantic annotation using Capisco, and (3) manual semantic mark-up of concepts. For the manual mark-up each article was independently read by two researchers, using the same concept set seeded by Wikipedia, and the resulting mark-up was checked and by a third researcher and aligned into a single set of concepts. As both WikipediaMiner ad Capisco are seeded by Wikipedia, the set of concepts that can potentially be identified is the same in all three cases.

The first observation is that Capisco did not miss any concepts that the human annotators wished to include. WikipediaMiner had few miss-identified concepts, for example the Africa article contained the phrase "world's land mass", which was wrongly disambiguated by WikipediaMiner to [Mass] and correctly identified by Capisco as [Land Mass].

Overall, the agreement between human annotators and WikipediaMiner per article ranged between 71% and 92% for the 23 articles (avg. of 82%). Out of overall 1531 identified concepts, 1215 were confirmed by the human annotators (78.9%). Out of 1232 concepts identified by Capisco, 98.62% were confirmed by human annotators. The agreement between human annotators and Capisco was 100% for nine of the 23 documents. For 14 documents, Capisco included between one and three additional concepts that the human annotators did not include (agreement on terms 88.8% and above). For example, Capisco identified the concept [Canning] for the article about beer brewing and canned beer. The human annotators excluded this term as the article did not focus on the process of canning beer. None of the additionally identified concepts were wrong, but the human annotators felt that they did not describe well the main focus of the article.

However, we noticed that concepts for which no Wikipedia page had yet been created, could not be included in any of our three methods. This particularly applied to concepts describing recent events ("Ebola virus epidemic") and names of people or organisations. For example, Wikipedia Miner wrongly disambiguated the aid group SIM, which is not contained in Wikipedia, to the concept [Subscriber Identity module]; Capisco omitted this concept. The concept sets in both WikipediaMiner and Capisco could be updated once Wikipedia has been updated. In Capisco, these cases would additionally be able to be addressed through manual extension of the CiC network.

When comparing the number of concepts the three methods produced, we found that the human annotators included the fewest and WikipediaMiner the most concepts. The concepts that WikipediaMiner suggested, which were not included by Capisco, were almost only those concepts that the human annotators did not wish to include. The reason is that often WikipediaMiner's analysis is too literal. For example, "General Information About Africa" was disambiguated by WikipediaMiner into [General officer]. It was disambiguated by Capisco into [General Knowledge]. Similarly WikipediaMiner identified the concept [Run (baseball)] from "Nile River, which runs through ..."; Capisco found no context for baseball in the text and discarded this concept. The same article about Africa also contained information about the hight of Mt. Kilimanjaro (19,340 feet). Both WikipediaMiner and Capisco correctly identified the concept [Foot (unit)], but Capisco (correctly) did not include the concept because no further context supported the notion that the article could be *about* this concept. Capisco correctly identified the Seinfeld episode [Comedians in Cars Getting Coffee], while WikipediaMiner here identified the concept [Coffee]. Overall, Capisco excluded 123 concepts that Wikipedia had identified (*e.g.*, as in the [Coffee] example). A further 186 concepts were excluded because no supporting context was found. Capisco's strength is thus in the indexing of concepts in context, which led to the correct exclusion of 12.15% of WikipediaMiner's concepts.

8. CONCLUSION

Summary. This paper introduced our method of *semantic-enhanced search*, which provides a bridge between lexicographic and semantic search. Our Capisco system implements this multi-lingual approach, which was also used for initial evaluations. We used a Concepts-in-Context network of over 4 million concepts sourced from Wikipedia, combined with the largest scholarly DL to enable scholarly access to OCR'ed documents.

Different to other systems providing disambiguation, Capisco stores context information to ensure quality disambiguation. Our approach thus extends and improves the effective, low-cost measure of semantic relatedness from Wikipedia. On the Digital Library side, this is a simpler and faster approach than building dedicated ontologies. On the scholars' side, it avoids complex semantic queries while addressing scholars' needs.

We explored two use cases and explored an extended example. The example showed how our semantic-enhanced search uses keyword queries and text documents but provides the quality of semantic search. The first use case showed the improvements of searches for scholars in the area of Māori Astronomy. We discussed in detail how our search worked for three different document sets. The second study compared the disambiguation of human annotators, WikipediaMiner and Capisco. We found that Capisco further improved the already excellent results of WikipediaMiner through the use of concepts.

Future work. Although Capisco supports multiple languages, the current CiC network uses English anchor terms for concepts (based on English Wikipedia). We plan for the next version of Capisco to become fully language-transparent. The component interfaces for CiC network manipulation, workset exploration and curation are currently under development. Once these are completed, we plan to perform large-scale tests for usability and integration into scholarly workflows, as well as detailed scalability and performance tests.

9. REFERENCES

[1] M. Apperley, S. J. Cunningham, T. T. Keegan, and I. H. Witten. Niupepa: a historical newspaper collection. *Communications of the ACM*, 44(5):86–87, 2001.

[2] V. Basile, J. Bos, K. Evang, and N. Venhuizen. Developing a large semantically annotated corpus. In *LREC*, volume 12, pages 3196–3200, 2012.

[3] I. Campbell. *The Ostensive Model of Developing Information-Needs*. PhD thesis, University of Glasgow, 2000.

[4] C. Carpineto and G. Romano. A survey of automatic query expansion in information retrieval. *ACM Comput. Surv.*, 44(1):1:1–1:50, 2012.

[5] J. S. Downie, T. Cole, B. Plale, K. Fenlon, K. Wickett, and M. Senseney. The workset creation for scholarly analysis (wcsa) prototyping project: Background and goals. In *Proceedings of the Chicago Colloquium on Digital Humanities and Computer Science*, Chicago, IL, December 5–7 2013.

[6] A. Duineveld, R. Stoter, M. Weiden, B. Kenepa, and V. Benjamins. Wondertools? a comparative study of ontological engineering tools. *International Journal of Human-Computer Studies*, 52(6):1111–1133, 2000.

[7] E. N. Efthimiadis. Interactive query expansion: A user-based evaluation in a relevance feedback environment. *J. Am. Soc. Inf. Sci.*, 51(11):989–1003, Sept. 2000.

[8] S. R. El-Beltagy and A. Rafea. Kp-miner: A keyphrase extraction system for english and arabic documents. *Information Systems*, 34(1):132–144, 2009.

[9] C. Fellbaum. *WordNet*. Wiley Online Library, 1998.

[10] K. Fenlon, M. Senseney, H. Green, S. Bhattacharyya, C. Willis, and J. Downie. Scholar-built collections: A study of user requirements for research in large-scale digital libraries. In *Proc. of the Association for Information Science and Technology*, 2014.

[11] G. Flouris, D. Manakanatas, H. Kondylakis, D. Plexousakis, and G. Antoniou. Ontology change: Classification and survey. *The Knowledge Engineering Review*, 23(02):117–152, 2008.

[12] G. W. Furnas, T. K. Landauer, L. M. Gomez, and S. T. Dumais. The vocabulary problem in human-system communication. *Commun. ACM*, 30(11):964–971, Nov. 1987.

[13] R. Grishman and B. Sundheim. Message understanding conference-6: A brief history. In *Proceedings of the 16th Conference on Computational Linguistics - Volume 1*, COLING '96, pages 466–471, Stroudsburg, PA, USA, 1996. Association for Computational Linguistics.

[14] P. Harris, R. Matamua, T. Smith, H. Kerr, and T. Waaka. A review of Māori Astronomy in Aotaora-New Zealand. *Journal of Astronomical History and Heritage*, 16(3):325–336, 2013.

[15] A. Hinze, R. Heese, M. Luczak-Rösch, and A. Paschke. Semantic enrichment by non-experts: usability of manual annotation tools. In *The Semantic Web–ISWC 2012*, pages 165–181. Springer, 2012.

[16] A. Hinze, R. Heese, A. Schlegel, and M. Luczak-Rösch. User-defined semantic enrichment of full-text documents: Experiences and lessons learned. In *Theory and Practice of Digital Libraries*, pages 209–214. Springer, 2012.

[17] L. Jean-Louis, A. Zouaq, M. Gagnon, and F. Ensan. An assessment of online semantic annotators for the keyword extraction task. In *PRICAI 2014: Trends in Artificial Intelligence*, pages 548–560. Springer, 2014.

[18] D. Karger. Unference: Ui (not ai) as key to the semantic web. Panel on Interaction Design Grand Challenges and the Semantic Web, at the 3rd International Semantic Web User Interaction Workshop, 2006.

[19] D. Karger and mc Schraefel. The pathetic fallacy of rdf. In *The 3rd International Semantic Web User Interaction*, September 2006.

[20] U. S. Kohomban and W. S. Lee. Learning semantic classes for word sense disambiguation. In *Proceedings of the 43rd Annual Meeting on Association for Computational Linguistics*, pages 34–41. Association for Computational Linguistics, 2005.

[21] M. Lytras, M. Sicilia, J. Davies, V. Kashyap, and N. Stojanovic. On the conceptualisation of the query refinement task. *Library Management*, 26(4/5):281–294, 2005.

[22] O. Medelyan, E. Frank, and I. H. Witten. Human-competitive tagging using automatic keyphrase extraction. In *Proceedings of the 2009 Conference on Empirical Methods in Natural Language Processing: Volume 3-Volume 3*, pages 1318–1327. Association for Computational Linguistics, 2009.

[23] D. Milne and I. H. Witten. An open-source toolkit for mining wikipedia. *Artificial Intelligence*, 194:222–239, 2013.

[24] R. Navigli. Word sense disambiguation: A survey. *ACM Computing Surveys (CSUR)*, 41(2):10, 2009.

[25] H. J. Peat and P. Willett. The limitations of term co-occurrence data for query expansion in document retrieval systems. *Journal of the American Society for Information Science*, 42:378–383, 1991.

[26] J. S. T. Rito and S. M. Healy, editors. *Proceedings of the Traditional Knowledge Conference 2008: Traditional Knowledge and Gateways to Balanced Relationships*. New ZealandŠs Māori Centre of Research Excellence, 2008.

[27] G. Rizzo and R. Troncy. Nerd: evaluating named entity recognition tools in the web of data. In *ISWC'11, Workshop on Web Scale Knowledge Extraction (WEKEX'11)*, 2011.

[28] C. Silverstein, M. Henzinger, H. Marais, and M. Moricz. Analysis of a very large altavista query log. *ACM SIGIR Forum*, 33, 1998.

[29] R. Sinkkilä, O. Suominen, and E. Hyvönen. Automatic semantic subject indexing of web documents in highly inflected languages. In *The Semantic Web: Research and Applications*, pages 215–229. Springer, 2011.

[30] J. F. Sowa. *Conceptual structures: information processing in mind and machine*. Addison-Wesley Longman Publishing Co., Inc., 1984.

[31] N. Stojanovic. Information-need driven query refinement. *Web Intelli. and Agent Sys.*, 3(3):155–169, July 2005.

[32] N. Stojanovic, R. Studer, and L. Stojanovic. An approach for step-by-step query refinement in the ontology-based information retrieval. In *Proceedings of the 2004 IEEE/WIC/ACM International Conference on Web Intelligence*, WI '04, pages 36–43, Washington, DC, USA, 2004. IEEE Computer Society.

[33] E. Tregear. *The Maori Race*. AD Willis, 1904.

[34] E. M. Voorhees. Query expansion using lexical-semantic relations. In *Proceedings of the 17th Annual International ACM SIGIR Conference on Research and Development in Information Retrieval*, SIGIR '94, pages 61–69, New York, NY, USA, 1994. Springer-Verlag New York, Inc.

[35] Y. Yesilada, S. Bechhofer, and B. Horan. Cohse: dynamic linking of web resources. Technical report, Sun Microsystems, Inc., 2007.

Demystifying the Semantics of Relevant Objects in Scholarly Collections: A Probabilistic Approach

José María González Pinto
IFIS TU Braunschweig
Mühlenpfordstrasse 23
38106 Braunschweig, Germany
+49 (531) 391 2232
pinto@ifis.cs.tu-bs.de

Wolf-Tilo Balke
IFIS TU Braunschweig
Mühlenpfordstrasse 23
38106 Braunschweig, Germany
+49 (531) 391 3271
balke@ifis.cs.tu-bs.de

ABSTRACT

Efforts to make highly specialized knowledge accessible through scientific digital libraries need to go beyond mere bibliographic metadata, since here information search is mostly entity-centric. Previous work has realized this trend and developed different methods to recognize and (to some degree even automatically) annotate several important types of entities: genes and proteins, chemical structures and molecules, or drug names to name but a few. Moreover, such entities are often crossreferenced with entries in curated databases. However, several questions still remain to be answered: Given a scientific discipline what are the important entities? How can they be automatically identified? Are really all of them relevant, i.e. do all of them carry deeper semantics for assessing a publication? How can they be represented, described, and subsequently annotated? How can they be used for search tasks? In this work we focus on answering some of these questions. We claim that to bring the use of scientific digital libraries to the next level we must find treat topic-specific entities as first class citizens and deeply integrate their semantics into the search process. To support this we propose a novel probabilistic approach that not only successfully provides a solution to the integration problem, but also demonstrates how to leverage the knowledge encoded in entities and provide insights to explore the use of our approach in different scenarios. Finally, we show how our results can benefit information providers.

Categories and Subject Descriptors

H.3.7 [INFORMATION STORAGE AND RETRIEVAL]: Digital Libraries

General Terms

Experimentation, Algorithms, Reliability.

Keywords

Scientific Digital Libraries, hidden knowledge, semantics entities, probabilistic topic models.

JCDL'15, June 21 - 25, 2015, Knoxville, TN, USA
 ISBN 978-1-4503-3594-2/15/06...$15.00
DOI: http://dx.doi.org/10.1145/2756406.2756923

1. INTRODUCTION

A lot of effort in the Digital Library community is put on assuring high quality metadata, because it is considered vital for search tasks. Yet most of this metadata is merely of bibliographic nature like title, author, or year of publication. In contrast, search tasks often are *entity-centric* as has been shown especially in scientific digital libraries: For instance, in the biomedical domain special tools for identifying and extracting genes, proteins, and drug names [4, 5] have been developed. In chemistry relevant entities, e.g., chemical substances, mulecules, and reactions, have yielded commercial tools for automatic recognition such as CliDE[1] together with focused research efforts such as [6–8] and of course as a human effort-based provider: the Chemical Abstract Service (CAS[2]). In physics the manually curated portal ScienceWISE[3] offers entity-based access to information, including also a variety of mathematical expressions, too. And also for such formulae we find lots of tools such as Symbolab[4], Springer LATEX[5] and research efforts [9–11] in the information retrieval community.

Indeed, the relevance of entities for scientists is paramount. But the challenge for indexing entities in a meaningful way is to really capture their semantics, including the role of the entities [11–13] in each document. Certainly this is a major problem still needing attention from the research community: *How to semantically represent or at least annotate those entities found in documents that cannot be indexed by current state of the art indexing mechanisms?* After all, considering chemical molecules, gene sequences, mathematical formulae, etc. What are these entities? How to describe them? What do they mean? How can we validate the relevance of these entities regarding a document?

To make our point clear, consider the classic representation of the well-known Pythagorean theorem: $a^2 + b^2 = c^2$ and imagine a student looking for papers in a Scientific Digital Library where this theorem is actually used. First our student might type in the equation to find a set of relevant documents. Now, to what degree could e.g., a document containing the equation $x^2 + y^2 = z^2$ be considered to fulfill the student's information need? Currently there are several research projects underway trying to figure out

---

[1] http://www.simbiosys.ca/clide/

[2] http://www.cas.org/

[3] http://www.sciencewise.info/

[4] http://www.symbolab.com/

[5] http://www.latexsearch.com/

structural similarities between mathematical expressions, some go down to trying to fully understand mathematical equivalence of even complex expressions. But is such a degree of effort really the only solution to sufficiently capture entity semantics?

A viable alternative to answer the question might be to only look at the *surrounding context* of the equation and then try to index the entity in a conventional fashion. While this often proves to work well, we are still facing two challenges:

- Among the variety of instances of the same class of entities we need to determine a criterion to identify those, which are suitable in terms of relevance and useful for a given task;
- We need to find a suitable representation of each entity found according to the above criterion, aiming at uncovering its semantics.

In this paper we tackle the problem of capturing relevant entity semantics for publications and implement a practical model to meet both challenges: to discover the set of relevant entities from some collection, and to encode these entities' semantics. We also validate the indexed entities' usefulness in a real world use case.

To discover the set of relevant entities we propose a probabilistic approach to perform an analysis of the collection and deal effectively with the uncertainty of the selection of relevant entities. In our setting, each document –after removing non-entity elements is seen as a bag of entities. On this representation we apply a probabilistic topic model over the entities. Once we have selected all relevant entities from the probabilistic model, we proceed to discover their semantics. We propose an innovative application of a probabilistic topic model to capture the different intended meanings of each of the entities. Our intuition in this second model is based on the assumption that "You shall know a word by the company it keeps . . ." [18]. In our work we argue that by capturing the companionship of each entity, we can generate a highly effective approximation of the entities' meaning and hence their semantics. Finally, we use an application oriented approach to validate the relevance of the entity semantics. In summary, our contributions are as follows:

- We design and implement a model to find relevant entities and represent and its semantics in a collection.
- We validate our model with a case study from mathematics:
    - We harness a highly specialized collection to find relevant entities (formulae).
    - We discover through several experiments how to model the semantics of the entities.
    - We provide a sample application case to validate our model in a very difficult but interesting task: given a document predict its corresponding taxonomy main class.
- We yield evidence of the validity of our approach to apply it in other domains.

The rest of the paper is organized as follows: in section 2 we will give an overview of related work. Section 3 introduces the model and the problem formulation. In section 4 we present our case study and results. And in section 5 we conclude with a summary and future work.

2. BACKGROUND AND RELATED WORK

Our approach builds on ideas from the Natural Language Processing (NLP) community. In particular, from the task of word sense induction. The idea is the following: any representative object –as words can have different meanings depending on its surrounded context. In NLP the intuition is that it is possible to infer the sense of a word automatically using unsupervised learning methods. Previous work in machine translation [14, 15] gave evidence that supports the idea and inspire us to design a model base on the results found in the literature. Furthermore, the work of [16, 17] explores the use of topic models for a very similar challenge but here we are dealing with a entirely different scenario –entities. Indeed, here instead of looking at words, where exists belief of the number of senses, we look at entities with the similar underlying assumptions.

For instance, given any entity of interest, we can imagine that it can have different meanings depending on its use. How do we know the intended meaning? The answer is straightforward: by its context. Therefore, identifying and modeling properly the context is the key aspect to consider to solve the problem. But finding the correct context is not trivial and it depends on the data. Relying on experts is not an option because data grows exponentially and it would be not only too expensive but also too much time consuming to solve the problem. Thus, we explore the use of Latent Dirichlet Allocation (LDA)[1] as our main data driven approach for this challenge. Probabilistic topic models have been used and adapted in different kinds of data and applications: to find patterns in genetic data, social networks, word sense induction and disambiguation, etc. These algorithms have also the advantage that they can be applied to massive collections of documents [3].

In the interest of generating useful context we implement several models to capture the intended meaning of an entity. Our hypothesis is that once we can find the proper context, we cannot only use these objects as features for different types of applications: metadata annotation, classification, cluster analysis, etc. but also validates their use and relevance for a given task.

3. MODEL AND PROBLEM FORMULATION

Here, we argue that we can find and represent any type of objects with its semantics from a collection. Concretely:
Given a set of documents $C = \{d_1, \dots, d_n\}$ and a definition of a class of representative entities –gene sequences, chemical molecules, mathematical, etc., the task can be summarized in the following steps:

1. Select a relevant set of objects from the collection.
2. Find the semantics of the set of relevant objects.

In order to apply these two steps, the collection C has to be preprocessed and transformed. For the first step, the document collection is modeled as a "bag of entities". So we do as sketched in Algorithm 1. Once we have performed this process –depicted in Figure 1, we have our collection $C_{entities}$ which contains the same number of documents of the original collection but only with the entities as content. In section 3.1 we will refer to this collection for the process of objects' selection. For our second step, we describe in section 3.2 our pre-processing of the collection C, given the output of our selection step.

Algorithm 1 Generate collection of entities

Input: the collection C
Ouput: the collection $C_{entities}$

for each document d in the collection C **do**
  create a new empty document $d_{entities}$
  extract from d all the entities
  assign extracted entities to $d_{entities}$
end for

We use LDA in the two steps. Here we give the intuition behind our approach. Basically, LDA captures the idea of learning from data without the need of coercing a document to be only about one single topic. Instead, the intuition is to talk about a hidden variable model of documents. In LDA, what we observed are the words of each document and the hidden variables represent the latent topical structure: the topics and the way each document exhibits them [2]. Figure 2 illustrates the latent Dirichlet allocation model.

More formally what we have in a typical LDA is the following:

1. For each topic,
   a. Draw a distribution over words β_k
2. For each document,
   a. Draw a vector of topic proportions θ_d
   b. For each word,
      (a) Draw a topic assignment $Z_{d,n}$

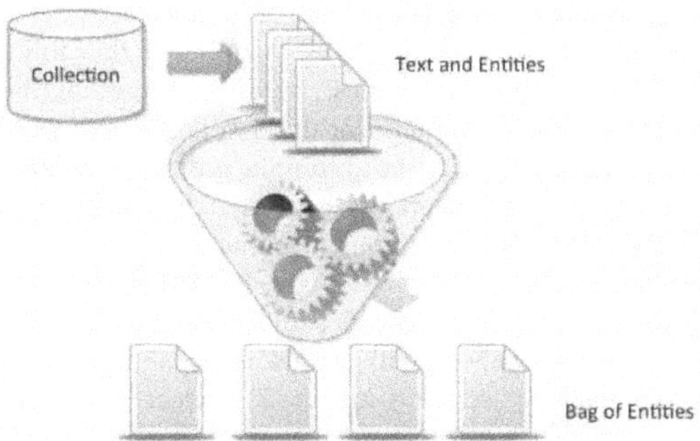

Figure 1. From a collection of text and entities to a collection of entities.

The distribution over the words given the number of k topics is assumed to be a Dirichlet as well as the distribution over the topic proportions. In the first step of our model the observed variable is the entity and it is what we called the LDA over instances.
Certainly, in our first step the assumption is the notion of the "bag of entities" instead of the traditional view of the "bag of words" in text processing scenarios in which probabilistic topic models have been extensively used.

And for our second step our observed variable are the context window words which captures the semantics of each entity. Indeed in this second step we put the model in a situation in which each of the documents to use in the process is rather small. In this second step therefore, the number of topics gives the number of senses for each entity. In the following subsections we give the details of each of these two steps and we use object and instance

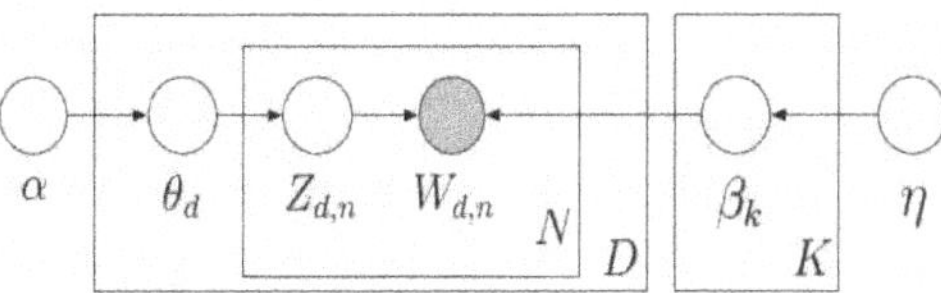

Figure 2. Graphical model representation of LDA.

interchangeable to refer to a specific example of the class of entities we are interested.

3.1 Object selection

First of all, our model assumes that exists a way to find and extract from each document in the collection every instance of an entity. Thus, this information is available to us by some preprocessing step over the collection –a named entity recognition tool. Our problema reduces to extract a relevant set of entities from these objects. Our approach relies on LDA to find the set of relevant instances, which can be seen as extracting the most probable instances from the most probable topics from the collection. To perform this step, we use the collection $C_{entities}$ described in the heading of this section. This is what we call the LDA over instances. After some empirical investigation we set the number of topics t and the parameters α and β to obtain the set of representative objects. For our sample case, we show in section 4 the dataset and the heuristics used for selection. Notice that it is possible to go to the second step of our model if we already have the set of objects to work with. However, we provide a full solution to the problem in cases where there is no such a set and hence has to be infer from data.

3.2 Semantics of the set of relevant objects

Given the set of relevant objects, we proceed with the next step of our approach: find the semantics of each of the instances. The intuition of our approach considers the following: every object that occurs t times in the collection has s senses –semantic meaning. The semantic meaning of an object is given by its context, in our case the words around the instance. The challenge for us is to find the correct number of senses and the correct number of words as context. First, we perform over the collection lower case transformation, we remove punctuation and stop words. We keep the instances of interest in its original form in the document. The modified collection with this preprocessing steps is what we call C_{trans}. Once we have created this new curated collection, we proceed as follows:

Given a set of objects $O = \{o_1, \dots, o_n\}$ obtained from section 3.1 and a collection of documents $C_{trans} = \{d_1, \dots, d_n\}$:

1. For each document d:
   (a) For each o found in d
   i. Extract context sizes s window from d and generate a new document d'_{od}
   ii. Add the d'_{od} to the collection of $Context_{objects}$
2. Save the new collection $Context_{objects}$which has context size s.

With this new collection we investigate the derived number of likely senses –semantics for each entity from the set of relevant

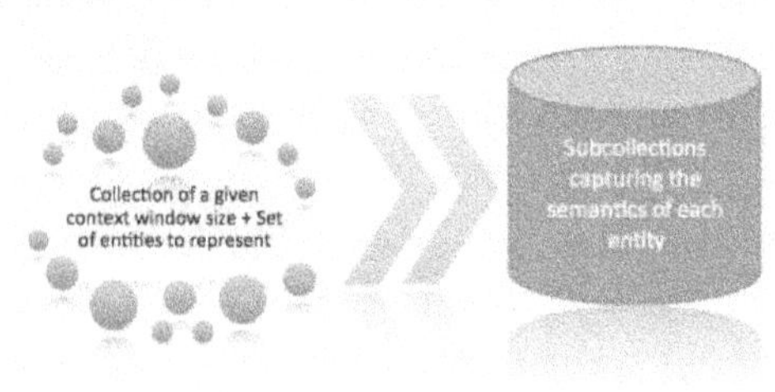

Figure 3. Process to find the semantics of the relevant entities.

entities as outlined below:

1. For each object in $O = \{o_1, \ldots, o_n\}$
   (a) Select from collection $Context_{objects}$ the documents which correspond to object o
   (b) Apply LDA in this sub-collection to infer the semantics of object o

Figure 3 shows the idea behind this step. We will be generating n LDA models for each context window size collection, where n is the number of entities selected in the first step. Our model for this step then has two additional parameters: s –the size window and n–number of senses. Since we have neither any previous knowledge of the correct number of senses nor of the correct number for the size context parameter we will perform step 2 with different values of n and s.

Notice that in the $Context_{objects}$ collection each document is small and contains the words-context window of a particular object appearing in a particular document. In other words, in each d'_{od} the subindex stands for an object o found in document d of the collection $C_{entities}$. This representation allow us to find the semantics of each of the objects given that we know which files in the collection $C_{objects}$ accounts for each object o.

In section 4 we present a use case to show how to deal with the parameters s and n.

4. EXPERIMENTS

For our approach to work, there must have a predefined annotated entities in a given collection. One can for instance use a Named Entity Recognition tool and apply it to the collection or use a collection with this preprocessing step already performed by such tools. The second thing that we need is a way to extract the text from the document collection. This can be done with a tool such as Apache Tika[6] or a similar framework. Once these two prerequisites have been satisfied we can start with the model.

We selected mathematical expressions as our case study due to the ease of identifying them in an open collection that was provided to us. Formulae have received attention from the information retrieval community but from the perspective of encoding its structure using different approaches and heuristics. The main idea behind these attempts is to index formulae using traditional methods of the information retrieval community with some variants splitting formulae into tokens. In our case study, we turn our interest in the analysis of the semantics of the formulae. Therefore, instead of decomposing the formulae in tokens we take a formula as an entity –a relevant object of a document and discover a way to represent its semantics. Our case study thus complements math information retrieval's previous attempts by providing plausible ways to attach keywords to a formula capturing its use and, therefore, its intended meaning.

4.1 Data set description

We use a dataset of 101,120 XHTML5 files from the collection of the NTCIR-11 Math Retrieval Task. The collection contains documents from Mathematical Physics, High Energy Physics, Computer Science, Nonlinear Sciences and Statistics. However, for our application guided approach –the classfication task, we needed for each document in the collection its corresponding Mathematics Subject Classification (MSC[7]). The MSC is a taxonomy used by several mathematical journals to help users find the documents of potential interest to them. And since the collection does not contain the MSC classes of the documents we had to do some pre-processing to gather them from the source Cornell University Library[8]. After harvesting the collection to account for the MSC classes of each document of the collection we end up with 56,051 files. This accounts for a total of 37,075,959 mathematical expressions, including monomial expressions.

4.2 Model and set of relevant objects selection

In our first step we need to find the number of relevant object by applying LDA over the collection $C_{entities}$. Remember that in this model we use the notion of a bag of entities, mathematical expressions in out case study. The model has the following parameters: the number of topics, α, β and the number of iterations for the Gibbs sampler. For the first challenge –selecting the number of topics, we first need to reduce the vocabulary size. Usually one has at least two options to reduce the vocabulary size: selecting only terms –entities in our case that occur in a minimum number of documents [19] or using the highest term-frequency inverse document frequency (tf-idf) scores such as in [2] We use these successful experiences with words as our guidance for our first step. We opted to use the tf-idf score to select the vocabulary only, but we use the frequencies of the remaining entities to feed the LDA. Because we are dealing with entities, we could not use any other preprocessing over our collection such as lower case conversion, stemming and omitting terms below a certain minimum length.

Indeed, we are considering each entity as a black box; in other words, we do not perform any modification of the manner the entities were written in the collection. We did remove punctuation characters and through empirical exploration we create our stop entities list –similar to the notion of stop words list using the tf-idf score. For our second challenge, selecting the number of topics, we started by using the number of different MSC top clases represented in our collection and fixing α and β to investigate the effect of varying the number of topics from the initial number and up to 400 which seems to work in practice given the size of the collection. We measure this effect by selecting from each model

[6] http://tika.apache.org/

[7] http://www.ams.org/msc/msc2010.html

[8] http://arXiv.org

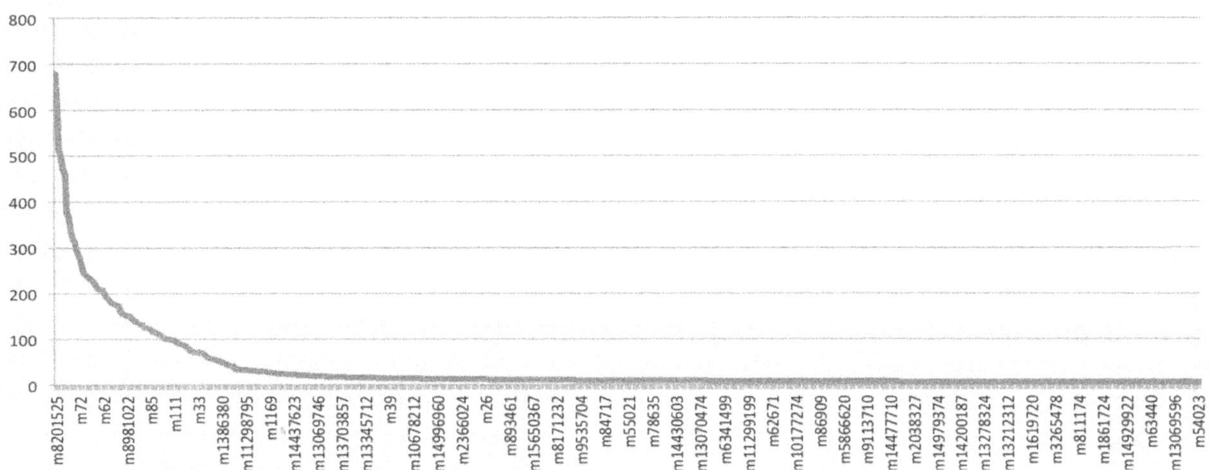

Figure 4. Distribution of entities in the collection.

the top 10 topics and from each topic the top 5 most probable mathematical expressions to select the final set of entities for the second step of our model. In all the experiments the Gibbs sampler was run 1,000 iterations. In Figure 4 we show the distribution of the frequencies of the top 3000 entities. This figure is similar to a word distribution over corpora and motivates the use of tf-idf for the selection of the vocabulary. After pruning the entities found in the collection we proceeded to use LDA over the entities.

4.3 Semantic representation

Once we have the set of relevant objects our next task is to find the semantics of these objects by using another probabilistic model. In our approach outlined in section 3.2 we mentioned that for finding the semantics given the set of objects to use, we need to account for two parameters: the size of the context window and the number of senses that each object can have in the collection.

We argue that to find satisfactory values of these parameters we need to advocate for an iterative application and data driven approach. Therefore, following successful results from the natural language community for nouns and verbs inductions, we run several models and choose the one that best fits our task. Indeed, the selection of these two parameters will vary depending on the task. In our case study, we want to see if we can help to predict the primary MSC class for our collection. In the following section we describe the models used for the prediction task. Since our interest is to investigate the effect of the context window size and the number of senses, we fixed the parameters of the LDA model α to .01, β to 0.1, and the number of iterations for the Gibbs sampler was set to 2,000 in all the experiments.

4.4 Evaluation and results

We generated 12 models with different combinations of the two parameters of our interest: the number of senses and the context size window. For the number of senses we use: 3, 5 and 7. And for each one we generate four window size corpora: 7, 9, 13 and 17 from the collection $\mathbf{C}_{\text{trans}}$. With this setting and given the number of entities selected from Section 3.1 –500, we proceed to compute LDA as mentioned in step 2 section 3.2. And after that we carry on to the task of predicting the top MSC class of our original collection $\mathbf{C}_{\text{entities}}$.

We used Support Vector Machines [20] as our machine learning algorithm and applied ten-fold cross-validation for model selection. Results for this classification task are shown for each sense-context combination in Tables 1, 2 and 3 and in Figure 5.

Table 1. F1 scores for 3 senses

Context size	F1 Score
Window length of 7 words	.3307
Window length of 9 words	.3180
Window length of 13 words	.3203
Window length of 17 words	.3320

The results might look displeasing since ideally one would like to have nearly human performance in this type of classifications task. Information providers are eager when solutions do seem to accomplish nearly perfect results automatically. However, if we abstract for a moment and reflect about the results, lets remember the fact that this is just one entity –relevant from a document, a scientific document, in which the language is far more difficult to model than simpler scenarios such as a news. And yet another important matter to keep in mind is that people perform this task today –experts trained for the task. Therefore, to interpret the results we need to inspect how the model captures the semantics of the mathematical expressions. We show five mathematical monomial expressions with their most likely keywords in tables 4, 5, 6 and 7. For each case we selected the dominant sense of each context size window from the probability distribution of the topic model.

Table 2. F1 scores for 5 senses

Context size	F1 Score
Window length of 7 words	.2867
Window length of 9 words	.2730
Window length of 13 words	.4440
Window length of 17 words	.2740

Table 3. F1 scores for 7 senses

Context size	F1 Score
Window length of 7 words	.2443
Window length of 9 words	.2500
Window length of 13 words	.2483
Window length of 17 words	.2543

The model has been able to capture the use of the mathematical expressions even though as features to predict the taxonomy class of a document they have failed. Interesting to notice is that most of the entities selected by the probabilistic model are short mathematical expressions. And in a way it makes sense since these are the building blocks for more complex but yet very specific mathematical equations very often described by these simple expressions. It is remarkable that even this intuition has been been assimilated by the probabilistic model. Now, to continue in our journey we tackle two questions: first, how good are the semantics encoded in the mathematical expressions in this particular classification task? should we continue and generate more models?

Table 4. Keywords for mathematical expression k

Context sense	Top keywords
Three senses	function, theorem, model
Five senses	algebra, function, equation
Seven senses	function, algebra, equation

Table 5. Keywords for mathematical expression A

Context sense	Top keywords
Three senses	equation, set, lemma
Five senses	theorem, set, lemma
Seven senses	nahm, assume, lemma

Table 6. Keywords for mathematical expression g

Context sense	Top keywords
Three senses	ideal, model, algebra
Five senses	space, function, graded
Seven senses	prime, finite, model

To investigate these issues, we need to depend on statistics analysis. Therefore, the question we need to answer is the following: how good are these semantics to help in the classification process? To gain an intuition about it, we implemented another model based on the title and abstract of each document in the collection as a baseline. We implemented a simple model, so no deep learning for words or phrases in this first approximation. Thus, we use the "bag of words" assumption as our document model; and formulae found in abstracts were ignored –treated as stop-words. Moreover we joined the text of the title and the abstract and therefore the model knows nothing about these two metadata elements, only its content as one single element: plain bag of words. We then perform some basic

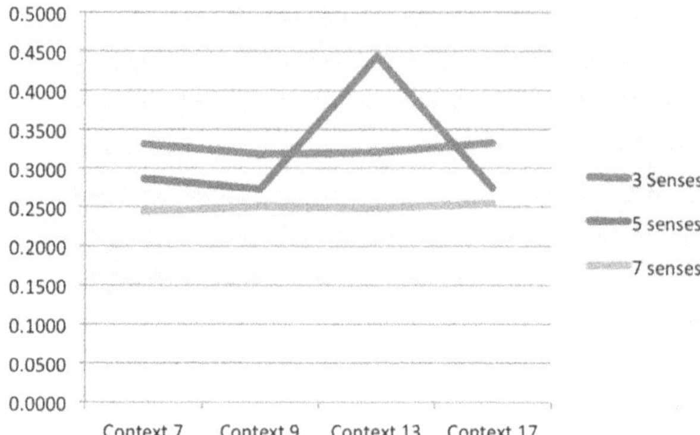

Figure 5. Summary of SVM Classification.

preprocessing: lower case conversion, stemming and omitting terms below length four to prune the vocabulary size, and terms that occur less than five times in the corpus. Finally, we use the tf-idf scores to further select our final vocabulary size and proceed with the classification task. Again, we use SVM with ten-fold crossvalidation for model selection. The results on the classification task were .42. This result is slightly less than our best model. To conclude whether this difference is significative we performed a Wilcoxon signed rank test over the F1 scores per class between the two models. With a p-value of 1.597e-05 we conclude that statistically speaking the difference is significative. These findings are encouraging. We can argue about at least two conclusions from our classification task: one, mathematical expressions can help in a classification task such as predicting the MSC classes from a document collection. Two, even though they are relevant as entities, in order to improve in the task one can imagine applying our model but looking at another type of entities, perhaps theorems. In fact, the results help to understand the role of mathematical expressions for this particular task. We can argue that they are not the first class citizens but they do represent valuable assets. To further determine what other entities are worth modeling to solve more accurate this particular task, one can gain insight probably through a user study. This user study can be helpful to discover what other entities are relevant in this domain and use our model to investigate if the findings for such a user study correlates to what the model can perform for this particular task.

5. CONCLUSIONS AND FUTURE WORK

In recent years the efforts to provide quality of metadata in the growing number of scientific digital library collections has heightened the need to exploit first class citizens: entities. Indeed, work has increased in the area of entity recognition. And the idea is to find both through manual work or automatic procedures different types of entities. Today we can find evidence in domains such as in chemistry, biomedicine, physics, and mathematics and definitely seeking is entity centric and it is here to persist. But when one makes a pause to think about this issue we can imagine a point in which we ask ourselves: what are these entities? How can we represent them? How can we find them? And how can use them? Surely, one central piece of work missing in the literature is the analysis of the semantics of these entities. And our work presented in this paper has provided new insights to bridge this profound gap.

The idea behind of our solution is to understand how to represent the semantics of these entities and –equally important how to find them in a given collection. Since there is uncertainty in both tasks we have chosen a probabilistic data driven approach. We use a probabilistic topic model that even though is simple, has positively helped us to bring valuable findings to the community. Furthermore, our findings confirm that data driven approaches should be considered as a valid framework to deal with the challenge of making sense of current trends –such as entity search to infer and represent this explosion of knowledge generation.

Nevertheless there is still some room for improvement. In particular, for the first step of our model –finding relevant objects, some empirical tests need to be performed to account for cases in which there is no knowledge to use when trying to initiate the model with a plausible number of topics. Even though experimenting with this parameter can yield to a solution, using a nonparametric Bayesian method could be time saving and perhaps obtain a better solution. For instance, one can use [21]. Therefore, in the near future we will investigate the effect of using such methods.

Another direction of work relates to the selection of the number of senses for each entity. In this work we have used the same for all the entities of interest, however, further work remains to be done to find for each entity a number of senses that yields an optimal solution. We anticipate to work on a solution for this problem that can be general enough to consider a data driven approach, perhaps with some sort of network analysis and/or user feedback provided by query logs.

Finally, another course we would like to explore is to combine more than one observed entity in the probabilistic model to investigate if such a model complexity can provide us with better results for a particular application.

6. ACKNOWLEDGMENTS

The German Research Foundation supported this work (DFG) within the Qualimeta Project.

7. REFERENCES

[1] D. M. Blei, A. Y. NG, and M. I. Jordan. Latent dirichlet allocation. Journal of Machine Learning Research. 2003

[2] Blei, D. M., & Lafferty, J. D. (2009). Topic Models. In Text Mining: Classification, Clustering, and Applications (pp. 71–89). Chapman & Hall/CRC Data Mining and Knowledge Discovery Series. doi:10.1145/1143844.1143859

[3] Blei, D. M. (2012). Introduction to Probabilistic Topic Modeling. Communications of the ACM, 55, 77–84. doi:10.1145/2133806.2133826.

[4] Goulart, R. R. V., Strube de Lima, V. L., & Xavier, C. C. (2011). A systematic review of named entity recognition in biomedical texts. Journal of the Brazilian Computer Society. doi:10.1007/s13173-011-0031-9.

[5] Settles, B. (2005). ABNER: An open source tool for automatically tagging genes, proteins and other entity names in text. Bioinformatics, 21, 3191–3192. doi:10.1093/bioinformatics/bti475

[6] Filippov, I. V., & Nicklaus, M. C. (2009). Optical structure recognition software to recover chemical information: OSRA, an open source solution. Journal of Chemical Information and Modeling, 49, 740–743. doi:10.1021/ci800067r

[7] Lowe, D. M., Corbett, P. T., Murray-Rust, P., & Glen, R. C. 2011. Journal of Chemical Information and Modeling, 51, 739–753. doi:10.1021/ci100384d

[8] Park, J., Rosania, G. R., Shedden, K. A., Nguyen, M., Lyu, N., & Saitou, K. (2009). Automated extraction of chemical structure information from digital raster images. Chemistry Central Journal, 3, 4. doi:10.1186/1752-153X-3-4

[9] P. Sojka and M. Lška. The Art of Mathematics Retrieval. Proceedings of the ACM Conference on Document Engineering. 2011

[10] Michael Kohlhase, Bogdan A. Matican, and Corneliu C. Prodescu. MathWebSearch 0.5 -Scaling an open Formula Sarch Engine. Conferences on Intelligent Computer Mathematics (CICM). 2012

[11] Kamali, S., & Tompa, F. W. (2013). Retrieving documents with mathematicalcontent. In Proceedings of the 36th international ACM SIGIRconference on Research and development in information retrieval – SIGIR '13 (p. 353). doi:10.1145/2484028.2484083

[12] Sun, B., Mitra, P., & Giles, C. L. (2008). Mining, indexing, and searching for textual chemical molecule information on the web. In Proceeding of the international conference on World Wide Web (pp. 735–744). doi:10.1145/1367497.1367597

[13] Tönnies, S., Köhncke, B., Koepler, O., & Balke, W.-T. (2010). Exposing the Hidden Web for Chemical Digital Libraries. In Int.l Joint Conference on Digital Libraries (pp. 234–244). doi:10.1145/1816123.1816159

[14] Vickrey, D., Biewald, L., Teyssier, M., & Koller, D. (2005). Word-Sense Disambiguation for Machine Translation. In Proceedings of the conference on Human Language Technology and Empirical Methods in Natural Language Processing (HLT '05) (pp. 771–778). doi:10.3115/1220575.1220672

[15] Carpuat, M., & Wu, D. (2007). Improving statistical machine translation using word sense disambiguation. Proceedings of the 2007 Joint Conference on Empirical Methods in Natural Language Processing and Computational Natural Language Learning (EMNLP-CoNLL), 61–72. Retrieved from papers2://publication/uuid/CA8E0BC3-96B6-4123-8674-4E4BD98AACA9

[16] Brody, S., & Lapata, M. (2009). Bayesian Word Sense Induction. Computational Linguistics, 103–111. doi:10.3115/1609067.1609078

[17] Lau, J. H., Cook, P., McCarthy, D., Newman, D., Baldwin, T., & Computing, L. (2012). Word sense induction for novel sense detection. In Proceedings of the 13th Conference of the European Chapter of the Association for computational Linguistics (EACL 2012) (pp. 591–601).

[18] Firth, J. R. (1957). A synopsis of linguistic theory 1930-55. Studies in Linguistic Analysis (special Volume of the Philological Society), 1952-59, 1–32.

[19] Griffith TL, Steyvers M (2004). Finding Scientic Topics. Proceedings of the National Academy of Sciences of the United States of America, 101, 5228-5235

[20] Burges, C. J. C. (1998). A Tutorial on Support Vector Machines for Pattern Recognition. Knowledge Discovery and Data Mining, 2, 121–167. Retrieved from /papers/Burges98.ps.gz

[21] Teh, Y. W., Jordan, M. I., Beal, M. J., & Blei, D. M. (2006). Hierarchical Dirichlet Processes. Journal of the American Statistical Association. doi:10.1198/016214506000000302

An Ontological Framework for Describing Games

David Dubin and Jacob Jett
Center for Informatics Research in Science and Scholarship
University of Illinois
Champaign, IL USA
{ddubin, jjett2}@illinois.edu

ABSTRACT

This paper describes an ontological framework for game description. Games are a multi-billion dollar industry and are cultural heritage objects studied by a growing number of scholars. The conceptual model described here supports the description of both individual games and relationships among games, their versions and variants for more effective discovery, more reliable provenance, and detailed scoping of copyright, patent, and trademark claims.

Categories and Subject Descriptors

H.1.m [**Models and Principles**]: Miscellaneous

General Terms

Design; Standardization; Theory;

Keywords

conceptual modeling; data representation; game scholarship; game studies; ontologies; RDF

1. BACKGROUND AND MOTIVATION

In 2014 the Entertainment Software Association (ESA) reported that 59% of Americans play video games [3]. ESA's 2014 report also notes that more than one half of all households in America own at least one dedicated video game platform (e.g., a PlayStation, an XBox, a Wii, or similar dedicated console). World-wide, the video game industry commands a huge market whose revenue exceeds $76 billion and is projected to exceed $86 billion by 2016 [4]. The board game industry is also experiencing a new golden age as their market has grown an average of 15% annually for the past 10 years—a pattern of growth that shows no signs of abating in the near future [2].

Increasing use, collection scope, and size of game description databases have been consequences of these trends over the past decade and a half. Not only do consumers obtain digital games for consoles and hand held devices online, large databases of tabletop games and digital game modifications have emerged from social networking in the gaming hobbies. Tabletop gamers purchase print-on-demand cards, boards, rules, and playing pieces for games that often evolve in distributed online design communities. Advances in 3D printing and digital display technologies promise a future of hybrid tabletop and electronic designs for the game industry, with a consequent need for richer, more detailed game descriptions in digital collections.

The potential for games as learning and literacy tools is being increasingly recognized in traditional library settings [5], creating a need for more nuanced understandings of games both as cultural heritage objects worthy of academic study and also as bibliographic objects in need of more accurate bibliographic description. The latter activity has been pursued in three ways with respect to video games: describing aspects of video game design [17], describing attributes and properties of video games that support archival provenance modeling [13], and describing entities, attributes, and relationships that support rich bibliographic description of video games [10, 8, 7]. All of these efforts are responding to a burgeoning need to preserve and examine video games, and games in general, as rich cultural heritage objects. While each of them have specific roles that they can play with regards to specific communities, e.g., game development communities, digital archives, and digital libraries respectively, none of them directly address descriptive challenges that we discuss below.

This paper introduces an ontology to support the description of both individual games and relationships among games, their versions and variants. In order to facilitate the broadest, most flexible account of games as cultural heritage objects, our ontology considers games in general, and is not specific to video games, board games, mental games, or similar kinds of games. Such distinctions are becoming less meaningful: many board games are finding expanded lives as video games, and tabletop games such as *Settlers of Catan*, *Carcasonne*, and *Small World* are available as digital versions for computers, tablets, and smart phones.

2. DESCRIPTIVE CHALLENGES

As games become more deeply entwined with our day-to-day lives, there is an increasing need to understand and remark on them as a familiar form of human communications phenomenon (much as novels, plays, art, poetry, and film are remarked upon). As McDonough, et al. [12] and Lee, et al. [10] have noted, the majority of existing bibliographic models fall far short of being adequate for de-

JCDL'15, June 21–25, 2015, Knoxville, Tennessee, USA.

DOI: http://dx.doi.org/10.1145/2756406.2756939 .

Table 1: Classes in the model

Class	Superclass	Remarks
GameSession	Event	A specific episode of game play.
GameRule	Description	A rule governing a game session, constraining player behavior.
GameRuleSet	Set	Any set of game rules.
GameElement	Concept	Concepts referenced in game rules, and defining game states.
AbstractGameState	Relation	A relation among game elements representing circumstances relevant to a game session.
GameStateDescription	Description	A partial or complete description of a game state.

scribing video games (or games in general, in our view). Particularly lacking are models that describe the relationships among game constituents. Lee, et al. [9] propose a number of relationships such as derivation, whole/part, and thematic connections. Their relationship predicates such as 'inspiredBy', 'spin-offOf', 'hasPrequel', and 'hasSequel', and grouping entities such as 'Franchise', 'Series', and 'Universe' address some descriptive problems. But these relationships do not capture the modular structure of many games, i.e., that precisely *what* game is being played in any particular session often depends on what house rules, errata, or published expansions are in use (in the case of tabletop games) or what downloadable content is active (for video games).

Our ontology is directed at this problem, and other related issues, as described below. But since these do not exhaust all use cases we intend the model to be used in combination with other general purpose and application specific ontologies. For example, Espen Aarseth recommends that formal definitions in game ontologies serve specific purposes, such as game criticism, game design theory, and psychological research on the effects of playing games [1]. Such approaches should (according to Aarseth) help to model properties or dimensions that highlight differences among particular games or game genres. However, our work is intended for a different set of use cases. In particular, our interest is to support precise accounts of:

1. how it is that a game played on a physical surface and another mediated by a computer are two versions of the same game;
2. what exactly is preserved in the derivation of one game design from another;
3. the relationships among game variants created by house rules, errata, published scenarios, and player-contributed modifications;
4. different levels of abstraction at which the creative contributions of game designers are realized and expressed.

As one among many bases for game description and classification in digital libraries, this ontology is intended to enable more effective discovery, more reliable provenance, and more detailed scoping of copyright, patent, and trademark claims.

3. ONTOLOGY DESCRIPTION

The *GameOn* Ontology is a conceptual model defining unary predicates (classes) and binary predicates (relational properties). It is a not a single RDF vocabulary, but intended to serve as a basis for general and special-purpose vocabularies at different levels of expressive power. The core of our ontology consists of four classes: game *sessions*, *rules*, *elements*, and *states*. The key relations among these classes are *governance* (rule to session), *definition*, (rule to description), *allusion* (rule to element), and *role* (endurant to element).

3.1 Game Sessions

In 1978 the philosopher Bernard Suits proposed an answer to Ludwig Wittgenstein's 1953 challenge to define the word "game" [16]. Being a game, on this account, is a contingent property of an event or gaming episode, not an activity (e.g., ball rolling) or a creative work (such as Scrabble®). For Suits, a game is an "attempt to achieve a specific state of affairs, using only means permitted by rules, where the rules prohibit use of more efficient [means] in favor of less efficient means, and where such rules are accepted just because they make possible such activity" [16]. In other words, almost any rule-governed activity could be a game, if players engage in it with an appropriate "lusory attitude." This definition of gaming is more inclusive than we need, since it covers game episodes that have no public *institution* linking them to other sessions of "the same game." But the Suits definition offers some attractive advantages: by including separate constructs for different senses of the word "game" (e.g., session vs. publication) we avoid the problem of assigning a single definition to what is, after all, a word not a concept.

Listing 1 shows an example of how a game session might be described using an RDF vocabulary based on our model. The resource `bgsession11671345` inherits place, time, and agent properties as a subclass of Event (using, in this example, the Centre for Digital Music's Event Vocabulary[1]).

3.2 Game Rules and Rule Sets

By the Suits definition we have adopted, game sessions are governed by sets of constitutive rules. Describing rules as governing particular sessions provides a solution to the modularity problem described above: rules from different sources (errata, downloadable content, etc.) can be in effect

[1]http://motools.sf.net/event/event.html

Table 2: Properties in the model

Property	Domain	Codomain
governedByRule	GameSesion	GameRule
gameRuleDefinedIn	GameRule	Description
gameRuleConcernsElement	GameRule	GameElement
gameElementRole	Endurant	GameElement
gameStateValidSequent	AbstractGameState	AbstractGameState
gameStateIsStartState	AbstractGameState	Truth Value
gameStateIsEndState	AbstractGameState	Truth Value
describesGameState	GameStateDescription	AbstractGameState

at the same time. Similarity relations on sessions can then serve as a basis for (or an alternative to) levels of institutional equivalence, such as the family of chess variants.

We view rules as a subclass of *description*, which is to say that they are language-specific expressions, not language-independent constraints on human or machine behavior. Tabletop or field games are, by our view, governed by particular written or orally expressed rules. Where the execution of a video game enforces particular game rules, we understand those to be part of the software's source or object code.

How one represents sets of rules will be constrained by the level of expressive power chosen for vocabularies based on our model. Listing 1 shows an example using OWL restrictions to represent the assertion that the set of rules governing a particular game session are exactly those defined in a particular published work.

3.3 Game States and State Descriptions

Representing games as graphs of abstract states or positions has been a common practice in combinatorial game theory and computer science for decades [15, 14]. It is consistent with both this tradition and with the Suits gaming definition to identify these states with the general class, *state of affairs*, or with the narrower subclass of physical object configurations in space. A game's constitutive rules may indeed connect changes of state to spatial relationships or physical properties, such as chess piece locations on the same file or a ball of certain dimensions having crossed a goal line. But one of our aims is accounting for the medium independence of those game institutions based in discrete symbol systems [6]. In our model the relationship between, for example, a chess king and a checking rook is an abstract relationship between conceptual objects that can be represented either by spatial arrangements of physical pieces, or via written or spoken expressions using chess notation. A soccer game on a field would involve not only a physical ball and goal lines, but conceptual counterparts for each of those. That additional level of abstraction would account for what an actual soccer game has in common with a paper or electronic soccer simulation.

A game state, then, is by our account a fully abstract relation among *every* conceptual game element alluded to in the rules governing a game session. In practice, however, game states are rarely expressed or represented in complete detail. Listing 2 illustrates this with an RDF description of a start state for a game of Gin Rummy[2]. The description provides enough information to discriminate this starting state from any other, but leaves out, for example, that the six of hearts and the King of clubs are face down in the deck. The RDF class `gin:GinRummyState` would be, in our model, a subclass of *game state description*, and diverse instances of that subclass could describe a single *game state* (reified as an opaque resource, if at all).

[2]An RDF vocabulary for the standard 52-card french suit deck, and game ontology similar to ours in scope can be found at http://data.totl.net/ .

3.4 Game Elements

As stated, the constituents of our game states are conceptual objects, and these stand in relationships that are abstracted from relations among physical endurants that fill game element roles in a session. For example, the starting state described by Listing 2 might be realized with paper cards in human hands, or that *very same state* might be represented by a sequence of binary digits in computer memory. That is because by our account "the Ace of clubs," "the deck," and "the dealer's hand" are social objects, and a relationship like "the up card" is an abstract relationship between concepts. Discriminating these social objects in natural language discourse requires analysis, since noun phrases in game rules may pick out particular concepts (e.g., "white queen's rook,"), abstract concept classes ("trump card,") or an endurant filling a role ("the perimeter of the board"). Our view of concepts is, in most respects, consistent with the 2004 proposal by Masolo, et al. [11]. However, we do not insist that concept identity depends on particular semantic descriptions.

4. CONCLUSIONS AND FUTURE WORK

The *GameOn* ontology targets a limited number of game dimensions, specifically the relationships among episodes of play, expressed constitutive rules, conceptual game elements, and the physical matter or energy that temporarily represent/denote those social objects. The model is directed at particular descriptive challenges, and is intended to complement both general and application-specific ontologies that capture games at other levels of abstraction and granularity.

Our current work on this project includes the refinement and publication of reference vocabularies at different levels of expressive power (e.g., OWL DL and OWL Full) that take this model as a basis. In addition, we are compiling a concept repertoire of common game elements (e.g., "marker," "card suit," "goal") that are broadly applicable across a variety of different game institutions.

Listing 1: A game session description

```
bgsession:11671345 a gameOn:GameSession ;
  owl:sameAs bgsession:11671346 ;
  event:place <http://sws.geonames.org/4887158/>;
  event:time [ a tl:Interval;
    tl:at "2014-04-24T18:30:00-5:00"^^xsd:dateTime ;
    tl:duration "PT4H"^^xsd:duration] ;
  event:agent bggamer:ddubin ;
  event:agent bggamer:Vandal\+Thorne ;
  event:agent bggamer:jtgorman ;
  event:agent [ a foaf:Person;
           foaf:givenName "James" ;
           foaf:familyName "Kim"] .

bggame:40765 a frbr:Work ;
  dcterms:title "Clash of Cultures"@en ;
  dcterms:created "2012"^^xsd:gYear ;
  dc:creator "Christian Marcussen" .

_:rulesEx1 a gameOn:GameRuleSet ;
  owl:equivalentClass [a owl:Restriction ;
    owl:onProperty gameOn:gameRuleGovernsSession ;
    owl:hasValue bgsession:11671345].

_:rulesEx2 a gameOn:GameRuleSet ;
  owl:equivalentClass [a owl:Restriction ;
    owl:onProperty gameOn:gameRuleDefinedIn ;
    owl:hasValue bggame:40765] ;
  owl:sameAs _:rulesEx1 .
```

Listing 2: A Gin Rummy starting state

```
ex:handEx1 a games:CardHand ;
  rdf:_1 card:AceOfClubs ;
  rdf:_2 card:JackOfClubs ;
  rdf:_3 card:AceOfSpades ;
  rdf:_4 card:TwoOfDiamonds ;
  rdf:_5 card:JackOfDiamonds ;
  rdf:_6 card:QueenOfDiamonds ;
  rdf:_7 card:TenOfHearts ;
  rdf:_8 card:SevenOfSpades ;
  rdf:_9 card:TenOfSpades ;
  rdf:_10 card:QueenOfSpades .

ex:handEx2 a games:CardHand ;
  rdf:_1 card:FourOfClubs ;
  rdf:_2 card:ThreeOfSpades ;
  rdf:_3 card:JackOfSpades ;
  rdf:_4 card:KingOfSpades ;
  rdf:_5 card:SevenOfDiamonds ;
  rdf:_6 card:EightOfDiamonds ;
  rdf:_7 card:NineOfDiamonds ;
  rdf:_8 card:FiveOfHearts ;
  rdf:_9 card:NineOfHearts ;
  rdf:_10 card:JackOfHearts .

ex:ginStartEx a gin:GinRummyState ;
  gin:upCard card:ThreeOfClubs ;
  gin:dealerHand ex:HandEx1 ;
  gin:opponentHand ex:HandEx2 ;
```

5. REFERENCES

[1] AARSETH, E. "Define real, moron!" some remarks on game ontologies. In *DIGAREC Keynote-Lectures* (Potsdam, 2009), vol. 10, Potsdam University Press, pp. 50–69.

[2] CARLSON, C. We are living in a board game renaissance. *Deseret News* (Aug. 2013).

[3] ENTERTAINMENT SOFTWARE ASSOCIATION. Essential facts about the computer and video game industry: 2014 sales, demographic, and usage data. Tech. rep., ESA, Washington, DC, Apr. 2014.

[4] GALARNEAU, L. 2014 global gaming stats: Who's playing what, and why?, Jan. 2014.

[5] GEE, J. P. *What video games have to teach use about learning and literacy.* Palgrave Macmillan, New York, 2007.

[6] HAUGELAND, J. *Artificial Intelligence: The Very Idea.* MIT Press, Cambridge, MA, 1989.

[7] JETT, J., SACCHI, S., LEE, J. H., AND CLARKE, R. I. A conceptual model for video games and interactive media. *Journal of the American Society for Information Science and Technology* (2015). Accepted. Publication pending.

[8] LEE, J. H., CHO, H., FOX, V., AND PERTI, A. User-centered approach in creating a metadata schema for video games and interactive media. In *Proceedings of the 13th ACM/IEEE-CS Joint Conference on Digital Libraries* (Indianapolis, Indiana, USA, 2013), ACM, pp. 229–238.

[9] LEE, J. H., CLARKE, R. I., SACCHI, S., AND JETT, J. Relationships among video games: Existing standards and new definitions. *Proceedings of the American Society for Information Science and Technology 51* (2014).

[10] LEE, J. H., TENNIS, J. T., CLARKE, R. I., AND CARPENTER, M. Developing a video game metadata schema for the seattle interactive media museum. *International Journal on Digital Libraries 13*, 2 (2013), 105–117.

[11] MASOLO, C., VIEU, L., BOTTAZZI, E., CATENACCI, C., FERRARIO, R., GANGEMI, A., AND GUARINO, N. Social roles and their descriptions. In *Principles of Knowledge Representation and Reasoning: Proceedings of the Ninth International Conference (KR2004)* (Menlo Park, Calif., 2004), D. Dubois, C. Welty, and M.-A. Williams, Eds., AAAI Press, pp. 267–277.

[12] MCDONOUGH, J., KIRSCHENBAUM, M., RESIDE, D., FRAISTAT, N., AND JERZ, D. Twisty little passages almost all alike: Applying the FRBR model to a classic computer game. *Digital Humanities Quarterly 4*, 2 (2010).

[13] MCDONOUGH, J. P., OLENDORF, R., KIRSCHENBAUM, M., KRAUS, K., RESIDE, D., DONAHUE, R., PHELPS, A., EGERT, C., LOWOOD, H., AND ROJO, S. Preserving virtual worlds final report. Tech. rep., Champaign, IL, Aug. 2010.

[14] SHANNON, C. E. XXII. programming a computer for playing chess. *Philosophical magazine 41*, 314 (1950), 256–275.

[15] SPRAGUE, R. Über mathematische kampfspiele. *Tôhoku Mathematical Journal 41* (1935), 438–444.

[16] SUITS, B. *The Grasshopper: Games, life and utopia.* University of Toronto Press, Toronto, 1978.

[17] WOLF, M. J. *The medium of the video game.* University of Texas Press, Austin, TX, 2001.

Building Complex Research Collections in Digital Libraries: A Survey of Ontology Implications

Terhi Nurmikko-Fuller*, Kevin R. Page*, Pip Willcox#
* Oxford e-Research Centre, University of Oxford
# Bodleian Libraries, University of Oxford
terhi.nurmikko-fuller@oerc.ox.ac.uk
kevin.page@oerc.ox.ac.uk
pip.willcox@bodleian.ox.ac.uk

Jacob Jett, Chris Maden, Timothy Cole, Colleen Fallaw, Megan Senseney, J. Stephen Downie
Graduate School of Library and Information Science
University of Illinois at Urbana-Champaign
{jjett2, crism, t-cole3, mfall3, mfsense2, jdownie}@illinois.edu

ABSTRACT
Bibliographic metadata standards are a longstanding mechanism for Digital Libraries to manage records and express relationships between them. As digital scholarship, particularly in the humanities, incorporates and manipulates these records in an increasingly direct manner, existing systems are proving insufficient for providing the underlying addressability and relational expressivity required to construct and interact with complex research collections. In this paper we describe motivations for these "worksets" and the technical requirements they raise. We survey the coverage of existing bibliographic ontologies in the context of meeting these scholarly needs, and finally provide an illustrated discussion of potential extensions that might fully realize a solution.

Categories and Subject Descriptors
H.3.7 [**Information Storage and Retrieval**]: Digital Libraries – *systems issues, user issues.*

General Terms
Design, Human Factors, Languages, Theory.

Keywords
Digital libraries; bibliographic metadata; Linked Data; RDF; ontologies; worksets.

1. INTRODUCTION AND USE CASES
The HathiTrust Digital Library (HT) is a repository of over 13 million volumes, comprised of some 4.5 billion pages, complete with bibliographic metadata for the entirety of its holdings, and full-text access to approximately 4.8 million volumes released into the public domain. The HathiTrust Research Center[1] (HTRC) is the research branch of the HT, offering scholars tools and services that enable computational access to HT content.

Scholars use bibliographic records from the HT Digital Library to select subsets of texts according to their particular research objectives. We refer to these subsets, along with associated external data sources, as "worksets." Worksets are machine-actionable, referential research collections that allow researchers to define formal sub-collections with definite and finite parameters and content, run computational analyses across them, reference them persistently, and accurately describe them in dissemination of results.

JCDL '15, June 21–25, 2015, Knoxville, Tennessee, USA.

http://dx.doi.org/10.1145/2756406.275694

Metadata records, such as those conforming to the MARC standard[2], are traditionally used in libraries and information science to manage relationships, versioning, addressability, and curation of bibliographic resources. Identification is constrained by the granularity of the metadata standard, itself derived from the bibliographic requirements for which it was specified, e.g. metadata records describing an edition or a particular printing [8].

In developing workset tools that meet the needs of today's digital humanists, HTRC has found the descriptive power of basic bibliographic metadata insufficient and problematic [2, 7]. The different and at times disparate requirements of various use cases have led to the proposal of inherently flexible RDF-based technologies as an extensible mechanism for more expressive and intricate linking. In this paper we assess the requirements of advanced scholarly investigation over a large scale collection, survey the state of semantic bibliographic metadata standards, analyze their shortcomings, and provide an initial discussion of ontological extensions to meet the requirements. We begin by describing three short illustrative use cases.

1.1 UC1: Workset refinement
In large digital library systems that support (sub-)collection building, faceting helps scholars to create worksets, e.g. for all items associated with works by a given author. However, creating a workset based solely on these criteria frequently imports multiple items representing the same work, potentially skewing workset analysis. Identifying one particular item from among multiple copies is therefore crucial, but any selection criteria must both represent the scholar's interests and preference, and be expressible through the underlying metadata.

A scholar may, for example, rely on publication date to select the earliest text, discarding other copies; but analyses have shown that identification of specific editions within HT can be unreliable. Instances of the same edition of a work digitized from multiple collections may be associated with metadata records that do not match: instances may falsely appear distinct. The same work may have been printed twice in the same year, and variations in title and name strings introduced by differences in cataloging practice are not uncommon. Titles of works may change across editions, or from serialization in periodicals.

---

[1] http://www.hathitrust.org/htrc
[2] http://www.loc.gov/marc/bibliographic/

R. L. Stevenson's *Weir of Hermiston* illustrates this problem. HT metadata returns 13 distinct catalog records, six dating from 1896. Of these, four have New York as place of publication; one has London and one, Leipzig, with minor differences in page count and title. To identify the earliest text, which bibliographic entity should be selected? Were there four distinct New York printings or editions of this in 1896? Do scan quality or completeness vary, unrecorded in the metadata?

1.2 UC2: Complex physical and historical relationships

The previous use case highlights how a scholar might wish to revise a workset by removing items that are considered duplicated in that academic context. When creating worksets that span multiple digital libraries, or in large digital libraries that are an aggregation of earlier collections, doing so can expose a complex web of manifestation and item copies compounded by inconsistent metadata and incomplete provenance. These subtleties must be made available by a digital library both for the management of the workset and so that the scholar can investigate the provenance of the source material being studies. An example is the text by Jacobus de Cessolis found in the EEBO-TCP collection[3], via the British Library; a copy of this text also exists in HathiTrust[4] via the University of California. One scholarly interpretation is that this is the same manifestation but which has previously been microfilmed, printed and bound from film, and then scanned as part of the Google Books effort (none of this provenance is reflected in the metadata).

1.3 UC3: Granularity of reference

Scholars must be able to reference and cite supporting source text into differently sized granules, as evidenced by Fenlon, et al. [3]:

> "So we need to slice it by page. That's pretty natural. We need to slice it by poem, which doesn't conveniently overlap or match the page boundaries. We potentially need to slice it by sections within a poem...We actually need to slice these works in fairly fine grained ways, depending on what particular analytical approach we're looking for".

This extends to accurately referencing specific versions (e.g. copies, editions) of texts that are distinguished through complex relationships such as those in the previous two use cases.

2. TECHNICAL REQUIREMENTS

Addressing the exemplified needs of digital humanities scholars elicits technical requirements for the metadata and identifier schemes implemented by digital libraries. Broadly we consider these as issues of: (i) **addressability**, that is the ability to create and resolve identifiers that unambiguously anchor to, allow reference, and potentially retrieval of, digital resources and metadata; and (ii) **relational expressivity**, such that it is possible to overlay complex and possibly indirect relationships between identifiers, often going beyond the scope of traditional bibliographic records.

Common to all use cases is the need for persistent resource addressability (identifiers) at multiple levels of granularity - a segment of OCR, a scanned page, a digitized volume, a TEI-encoded derivative, an editorial correction, a bibliographically distinct manifestation. This requirement is supported directly from a scholarly viewpoint in UC3.

Granularity often extends beyond digital parallels of physical objects, and can make use of existing identifiers to connect HTRC resources to external resources and entities, e.g. to connect a digitized manifestation in HTRC with an abstract work. The deduplication in UC1 can only occur once some sufficient notion of equivalence has been ascertained, which must be evaluated against a chain of previously expressed relationships. This chain will almost certainly include identifiable and addressable (abstract) items, not (and not needing to be) digitally retrievable.

UC2 requires a chain of identifiable items and provides a strong example of the relational expressivity required to link the resources at each extremity. As noted above, it is not the case that the relationship between any two items in the chain is particularly uncommon, rather the cumulative effect of the chain of items in turn requires those items to be addressable. Possible solutions for expressing UC2 are explored in Section 5. Relationships need to be expressed both between resources wholly within the 'home' digital library (here, HT) and to or from external resources.

In addition to expressing relationships about the contextual history of a work, scholars' needs include identifying the provenance and curation of versions and changes and how these relate addressable items. These can be artifacts of the digital process, e.g. an improved OCR process producing text that supersedes a previously referenced earlier version. They need clear and persistent means of identifying specific text resources at specific times so that text objects used in their work remain citable and their research methods remain reproducible. In order to support such interoperability over time, identifiers for both concrete file objects (e.g. scanned page images or OCR text files) and abstract chunks of text (e.g. a chapter, page or poem) need to be both persistent across time and portable across web-based tool environments [4].

3. SURVEY AND ANALYSIS OF BIBLIOGRAPHIC ONTOLOGIES

An approach building upon Linked Open Data (LOD)[5] principles and based on RDF[6] provides a good foundation for satisfying these requirements: ontologies support descriptions that are extensible, composable, and precise; tools and models exist for evaluating and comparing RDF graphs. Libraries, physical and digital, are actively developing methods that apply LOD principles through initiatives such as LODLAM[7]. In this section we evaluate several evolving RDF-based vocabularies for bibliographic metadata.

The schemas considered here – MODS RDF[8], Bibframe (BF) [6], Schema.org[9] and FRBRoo [1] – support a diversity of typed relationships useful for describing elements of the use cases above. We surveyed all bibliographic terms contained within these ontologies and provide a representative summary in Table 1, where selected rows illustrate found equivalences and differences between the four.

---

3 http://eebo.chadwyck.com/search/full_rec?SOURCE=config.cfg &ACTION=ByID&ID=99842193

4 http://babel.hathitrust.org/cgi/pt?id=uc1.31158011066163

5 http://linkeddata.org/

6 http://www.w3.org/RDF

7 http://lodlam.net

8 http://www.loc.gov/standards/mods/modsrdf

9 https://schema.org/docs/documents.html

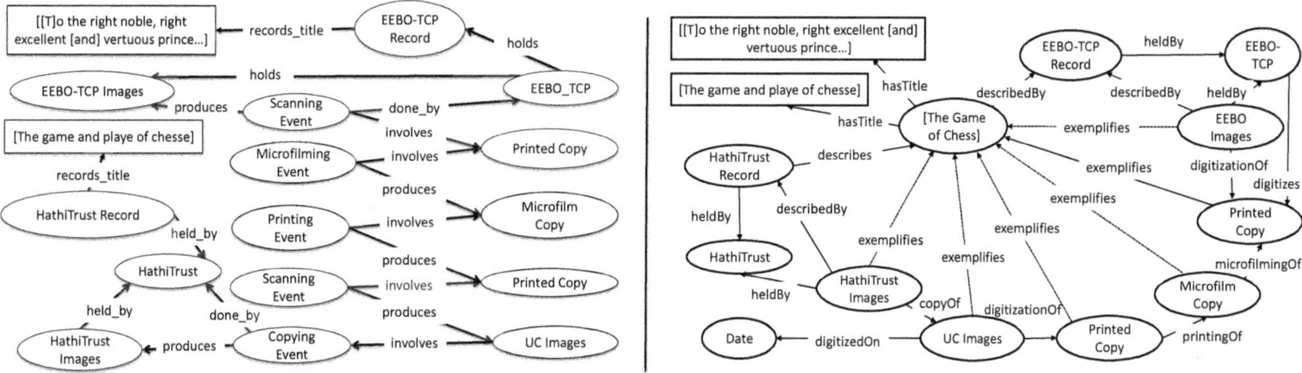

Figure 1. Partial illustrative encodings of UC2 using (a, on the left) event-based and (b, on the right) description-based approaches

Table 1. Excerpts from the bibliographic ontology survey

	MODS RDF	Bibframe	Schema.org	FRBRoo
1	Mods Resource	Resource	Creative Work	CRM Entity
2	edition	edition	bookEdition/ version	
3		Work		Work
4	Issuance		<rdf:type>	has issuing rule
5	Title	Title	Thing:name	Title
6	Geographic	Place	Place	Place
7	subjectTopic/ Complex Subject	Topic/subject	Creative Work:about	E89 P129 E1
8	statementOf Responsibility	Responsibility Statement		F4 P128 F2 P148 E33 P2 E55
9		Manuscript		Manifestation Singleton
10	hasIdentifier	22 classes		Identifier
11				Work Conception
12	Temporal	Temporal		Event

Equivalence was determined by the possibility of assertion against the same instance data, regardless of whether via class or property term, and was found across all ontologies: each, for example, include the notion of *Resource* (row 1). *Title* and *Place* (rows 5 and 6) illustrate a direct equivalence; we also consider row 7 equivalent, where *modsrdf:subjectTopic* is a property, *bf:Topic* a class, and the FRBRoo entry a combination of both. The limitations of Schema.org and FRBRoo are also illustrated: they do not cater for the nuanced differences between topics and subjects (these are amply supported by MODS RDF and BF).

MODS RDF and FRBRoo demonstrate the spectrum between description and event-based approaches; BF bridges these styles, combining elements from both, adhering to traditional notions of bibliographic metadata at the same level of granularity as MODS RDF (e.g. *Edition* (row 2)), yet simultaneously modelling the conceptual content of a text independently of the physical carrier (*Work* in FRBRoo and BF, row 3). Neither BF nor MODS RDF explicitly differentiate between an edition and a version, unlike Schema.org, but both contain a number of assertions about a particular expression or manifestation level entity, and record links to item-level entities that serve as exemplars, preserving the sensibilities of the ISBD and MARC standards. BF occasionally differs from all of the other ontologies, as illustrated by the absence of an equivalence for Issuance (row 4).

In most cases, the representation of information required a more complex encoding in FRBRoo. A statement of responsibility (row 8) whilst straightforward in MODS RDF and BF, is expressed via: *F4 Manifestation Singleton P128 carries F2 Expression P148 has component E33 Linguistic Object P2 has type E55 Type {"Statement of responsibility"}.*

Only BF and FRBRoo specify a singular manifestation of a unique physical object (row 9). Other specialist features of the reviewed ontologies include the separate classes for identifiers (row 10) in BF (cf. a single equivalent in others), and the use of *Elements* as subclasses in MODS RDF in a property-like capacity. FRBRoo alone is event-based, and an upper-level ontology, the only one to include moments of conceptual creation (*F27 Work Conception*, see row 11) and to incorporate cultural heritage elements (via the CIDOC CRM [5]). The representation of a *Temporal* element is possible in all other ontologies, except Schema.org (row 12).

4. ONTOLOGICAL EXTENSIONS

As Table 1 illustrates, and the full survey confirms, none of the existing ontologies can singularly provide the requisite addressability or relational expressivity to satisfy the use cases, and thereby the wider requirements for scholarly worksets they represent. This suggests that workset tooling will require additional ontological elements that bridge, combine, and extend the schemas surveyed. In this section we explore how description-based or event-based approaches might provide such extensions.

Since both approaches can represent much of the most desirable metadata (e.g. title, author) we highlight the *differences* when applying the two approaches, building upon the core concepts surveyed in Section 3. Figure 1 partially encodes the object biography, as described in UC2, between the original text in the British Library and the digitized text held in the HT.

The event-based model is centered on the narrative of the object's biography as a sequence of distinct events, five of which are represented in Figure 1(a). Properties specify information regarding the agents enacting the event, its date and location. The model captures information regarding the heritage of the resulting digital records as they relate to each other, such that information retrieval need not be limited to matching explicit pre-existing terms as often found in traditional metadata records; on the other hand this makes it harder to segment and reduce the model since the context of each event is dependent on the relationship to its neighbors (that is to say, if there is no Printing Event, we cannot assert truths about the resulting printed copy).

Unlike event-based ontologies, the descriptive ontology (Figure 1(b)) directly links metadata about a bibliographic entity using predicates to capture the semantic relationships, delineating the nature of attributes and context of associations – but necessitating a greater number of specialized (pre-)defined predicates. Without the need for an intervening event entity this provides a more efficient path for information retrieval at the expense of explicit context. The description-based model also includes typed relationships which play no role in lifecycle events but which uniquely identify blocks of content such as chapters, pages, paragraphs, or sentences, that are of interest to scholars.

Both models differentiate between the work – an intangible but recognizable cohesive whole – and the physical and digital representations (although this illustrative event-based model does not aim for upper-level universal applicability, unlike e.g. FRBRoo). The two models share entities (title, printed copy, images) and some relationship types (the record and the holding institution), but there is little overlap in the graph pattern through which these are expressed. Both are exemplars of provenance graphs, and are inherently similar conceptually. The event-based model, however, is more linear – the descriptive model, centered more firmly on the represented item, has a central node with a fanning out of additional information.

The difference, then, between the two modelling approaches is primarily one of perspective, rather than expressiveness. For example, an event-based model might assert a *Writing Event E* by *Author X* of *Document Y* on *Date D*, while a description-based model would say that *Document Y* was written by *Author X* and written on *Date D*. A deeper model of either perspective might assert multiple writing events, or a period of writing. Any comparison assessing the suitability of either model to capture specific metadata ought therefore to focus on features other than the inherent nature of either approach.

5. CONCLUSIONS AND FUTURE WORK

The three use cases illustrate different types of challenges and opportunities for scholarly investigation. The flexibility provided by ontologies enables the delivery of suitable structured metadata for each separate case, although none of the four surveyed were found to be completely sufficient on their own for capturing all aspects of a bibliographic entity's nature and lifecycle. Our examination of approaches, comparing event-based and description-based models, has highlighted the potential benefits of both types to address the information capture requirements derived from the use cases.

We consider the description-based model better suited for the domain-specific data structures of library and information sciences as it adheres closely to their traditional formats of data capture and directly supports in-depth analyses such as text-mining. The event-based model, although no less expressive, has flexibility which opens up possibilities of information dissemination in other domains such as the cultural heritage sector and some fields of historical and library research, which are likely to have complementary data including curatorial and custodial information but in structures which differ from those based on the MARC standards.

The main consideration, then, is one of focus and user expectations rather than expressiveness. If one model is "native" to a system, and it has ideally been thoroughly populated with data, then the other can be generated dynamically, potentially on demand. Given the requirements arising from scholarly use cases it is apparent that HTRC will most likely need to present interfaces supporting both modelling viewpoints in this way.

Our next steps are to study scholarly interactions using prototype ontologies exposed via a user tool, allowing us to evaluate which will be of greater utility and demand for sub-populations of HTRC users. This will determine the model(s) used to "mint" the URIs necessary to identify entities according to the ontologies, and provision services and APIs that make these web resources available to users and tools.

6. ACKNOWLEDGMENTS

We gratefully acknowledge the Andrew W. Mellon Foundation for generously funding Workset Creation for Scholarly Analysis: Prototyping Project; the HathiTrust Research Center; and colleagues from the Early English Print in the HathiTrust (ElEPHãT) project.

7. REFERENCES

[1] Bekiari, C., Doerr, M., et al., 2013. *FRBR object-orientated definition and mapping from FRBRER, FRAD and FRSAD (version 2)*. International Working Group on FRBR and CIDOC CRM Harmonisation.

[2] Fenlon, K., Fallaw, C., et al., 2014. A Preliminary Evaluation of HathiTrust Metadata: Assessing the Sufficiency of Legacy Records. *Digital Libraries 2014*, (London, Sept. 8 – 12, 2014), 317 – 320.

[3] Fenlon, K., Senseney, M., et al., 2014. Scholar-built collections: A study of user requirements for research in large-scale digital libraries. *The 77th ASIS&T Annual Meeting* (Seattle, WA, Oct. 31 – Nov. 5, 2014).

[4] Henry, C., and Smith, K. 2010. Ghostlier demarcations: large-scale text digitization projects and their utility for contemporary humanities scholarship. In *The idea of order: transforming research collections for 21st century scholarship* . Council on Library and Information Resources, 106 – 115.

[5] Le Boeuf, P., Doerr, M. et al., 2014. *Definition of the CIDOC Conceptual Reference Model (version 5.1.2)*. ICOM/CIDOC CRM Specialist Interest Group.

[6] Miller, E., Ogbuji, U., Mueller, V., et al. 2012. *Bibliographic Framework as a Web of Data: Linked Data Model and Supporting Services*. Report. Library of Congress.

[7] Smith-Yoshimura, K., Argus, et al., 2010. *Implications of MARC Tag Usage on Library Metadata Practices*. Report. OCLC Research in support of the RLG Partnership, 27 – 35.

[8] Tennant, R. 2004. A bibliographic metadata infrastructure for the twenty-first century. *Library Hi Tech*, 22, 2 (2004).

WikiMirs 3.0: a Hybrid MIR System Based on the Context, Structure and Importance of Formulae in a Document

Yuehan Wang, Liangcai Gao*, Simeng Wang, Zhi Tang
ICST, Peking University
Beijing, China
{wangyuehan, glc, wangsimeng, tangzhi}@pku.edu.cn

Xiaozhong Liu
Department of Information and Library Science
Indiana University
Bloomington, IN, USA
liu237@indiana.edu

Ke Yuan
Department of Software Engineering
Sichuan University
Chengdu, China
yuanke@stu.scu.edu.cn

ABSTRACT

Nowadays, mathematical information is increasingly available in websites and repositories, such like ArXiv, Wikipedia and growing numbers of digital libraries. Mathematical formulae are highly structured and usually presented in layout presentations, such as PDF, LaTeX and Presentation MathML. The differences of presentation between text and formulae challenge traditional text-based index and retrieval methods. To address the challenge, this paper proposes an upgraded Mathematical Information Retrieval (MIR) system, namely *WikiMirs 3.0*, based on the context, structure and importance of formulae in a document. In *WikiMirs 3.0*, users can easily "cut" formulae and contexts from PDF documents as well as type in queries. Furthermore, a novel hybrid indexing and matching model is proposed to support both exact and fuzzy matching. In the hybrid model, both context and structure information of formulae are taken into consideration. In addition, the concept of formula importance within a document is introduced into the model for more reasonable ranking. Experimental results, compared with two classical MIR systems, demonstrate that the proposed system along with the novel model provides higher accuracy and better ranking results over Wikipedia.

Categories and Subject Descriptors

H.3 [**Information Storage and Retrieval**]: Information Search and Retrieval

Keywords

Mathematical Information Retrieval; Structure Matching; Context Information; Importance of Formulae

*Liangcai Gao is the corresponding author.

JCDL'15, June 21–25, 2015, Knoxville, Tennessee, USA.

DOI: http://dx.doi.org/10.1145/2756406.2756918

1. INTRODUCTION

Mathematical information exists widely in a lot of areas, such as Science, Technology, Engineering and Mathematics (STEM). It also plays an essential role for dissemination and communication of science. A growing number of resources containing mathematical information are available online. For example, many traditional courses or Massive Open Online Courses (MOOCs) release accessible resources (books, lecture notes, exercises, etc.) in PDF or HTML. As a consequence, Mathematical Information Retrieval (MIR), namely searching for a particular mathematical formulae, concept or object, has drawn increasing attention from researchers.

The most common form of mathematical information is formula, which is also the most challenging part of MIR [13]. Different from text information in most cases, formulae are presented in special formats, such as LaTeX, MathML or PDF. Meanwhile, formulae are highly structured. For instance, $a+b+c$ is a sub-structure of $\frac{1}{a+b+c}$. Besides, some formulae are ambiguous, in other words, one formula may have two or more possible meanings in different situations. For example, the formula $\bar{x} = \frac{1}{\sum_{i=1}^{n} \frac{1}{x_i}} \times a$ is the harmonic mean equation in mathematics ($a = n$), while it also can be used for calculating parallel resists in physics ($a = 1$). Due to the particular characteristics of formulae, the methods of traditional search engines which mainly consider about plain text retrieval are usually inapplicable for MIR. Moreover, MIR systems have the special requirements on query interface, tokenization, indexing and ranking, which are illustrated as follows.

Interface. For mathematical information retrieval systems, formulae are usually taken as queries. Most current engines require users to encode a formula in a predefined format [15, 16] or use a formula editor [9, 18] as input. Besides formulae, keywords of mathematical information are also utilized for MIR. For example, a few of MIR systems support searching mathematical information by inputting the names of formulae [17].

Table 1: Comparison of MIR Systems/Methods

Method System \ Module	Interface	Tokenizer	Index	Ranker
FSE [24]	CMML[1]	Tree-based	Inverted Index	*tf-idf*
ICST [3]	PMML[2]	Tree-based	Inverted Index	*tf-idf*, Weights
IFISB [21]	CMML	Feature	Inverted Index	/
KWARC [5]	CMML	Text-based	Inverted Index	/
MCAR [4]	PMML	Tree-based	Inverted Index	*tf-idf*, Weights
MIRMU [22]	PMML, CMML	Tree-based	/	Custom
RIT [20]	PMML, LaTeX	Tree-based	Inverted Index	*tf-idf*
TUW-IMP [12]	CMML	Text-based	Inverted Index	/

[1] Content MathML [2] Presentation MathML

Tokenization. For MIR, one of the main challenges should be tokenization, namely how to convert formulae into terms which are utilized to build the index. The same with text tokenizer, a text-based category of tokenizers is employed for formula [15, 16, 17]. However, different from plain text, formulae are highly structured. They can be expressed and parsed as tree structures. Thus, tree-based methods are the most common tokenization approach in recently proposed MIR systems [6, 9, 23, 26].

Indexing. In the field of information retrieval, *indexer* is utilized to construct index files so as to improve searching efficiency. In traditional information retrieval systems [25], inverted index is widely employed to reduce the time consumption for searching. Likewise, based upon novel tokenization methods, MIR systems with the aid of inverted index technique can provide real-time mathematical searching [6, 11].

Ranking. The purpose of ranking is to sort the retrieved documents which are collected from index files according to the query. Nevertheless, how to rank the retrieved documents is still an open problem for MIR. Weighted *tf-idf* models are employed by some MIR systems [16, 19, 26]. In the models, each candidate document has a ranking score, which is calculated on the basis of both the frequency properties of the query terms and the weighted algorithms. The scores of the documents determine their order in the final retrieval results.

To address the special requirements and characteristics of mathematical information retrieval, several MIR methods and systems have been proposed since 2003 [15]. The core algorithms of them are quite different from each other. However, the main modules or components of the systems are similar, including *interface*, *tokenizer*, *indexer* and *ranker*. Most of the open MIR systems have been discussed in our previous papers [6, 11]. As an update, the newly proposed methods and systems on MIR would be further introduced and analyzed in this paper, which are listed in Table 1.

Last year, the NTCIR-11 Math-2 Task[1] developed an evaluation collection for mathematical formula search with the aim of facilitating and encouraging research in MIR and its related fields [1]. The methods or systems of NTCIR-11 Math-2 Task participants are summarized in Table 1. In the task, the team of IFISB extracted features of formulae as terms [21]. Nevertheless, only few kinds of features were considered. TUW-IMP team utilized the XML parser as *tokenizer* for formulae [12]. Whereas, their approach missed the semantic and structured information of formulae. RIT team used the tree-based methods for tokenization [20]. However, their system had limited function for wildcards, therefore fuzzy matching was not supported.

In *WikiMirs 2.0*, hierarchical generalization of substructures is proposed to generate index terms in order to support substructure matching and fuzzy matching. *WikiMirs 2.0* only takes formula information into consideration, while most formulae do not occur alone, but with context. The context is usually the description or explanation of formulae, which could be helpful for MIR. Moreover, in *WikiMirs 2.0*, all of the formulae from the same document are equally treated. Actually, the importance or role of different formulae for a document may be different. The significant formulae deserve much attention.

Aiming at overcoming the limitations of *WikiMirs 2.0*, this paper upgrades the system and proposes *WikiMirs 3.0*[2], a publicly available hybrid MIR system, based on the context, structure and importance of formulae in a document. First of all the progresses of the system, a new interface is implemented, by which users can obtain mathematical information including formulae and their context paragraphs directly from PDF documents. Secondly, a hybrid index consisting of a formula index and a context index is introduced to leverage more comprehensive mathematical information. Finally, the importance of formulae in a document is calculated to distinguish the roles of the target formulae in the documents.

The rest of this paper is organized as follows. In Section 2, the proposed *WikiMirs 3.0* is described in detail based on workflows and modules. The design and analysis of

[1]http://ntcir-math.nii.ac.jp/

[2]http://www.icst.pku.edu.cn/cpdp/wikimirs3/

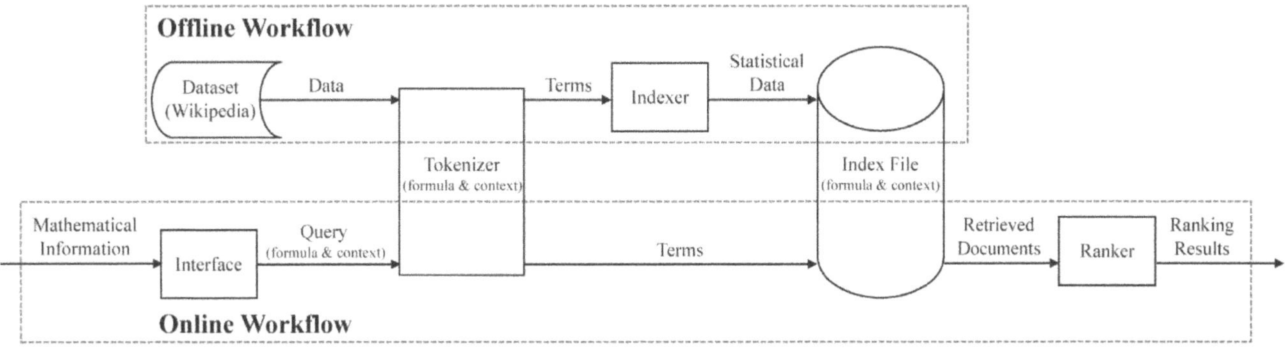

Figure 1: Framework of *WikiMirs 3.0*

experiments are presented in Section 3. Section 4 is the conclusion of this paper and the future work of *WikiMirs*.

2. WIKIMIRS 3.0

2.1 Overview

The proposed MIR system in this paper, *WikiMirs 3.0*, is based upon *WikiMirs 1.0* [6] and *WikiMirs 2.0* [11]. Compared with the last two versions of *WikiMirs*, the most distinct feature of *WikiMirs 3.0* is that it takes not only the structure but also the context and importance of formulae in a document into consideration. The framework of *WikiMirs-3.0* is illustrated in Figure 1. It contains two workflows, i.e. the *offline* workflow to construct the index and the *online* workflow to search based on a query. *WikiMirs 3.0* also consists of four modules: *interface*, *tokenizer*, *indexer* and *ranker*, as detailed as follows.

2.2 Workflows

2.2.1 *offline workflow*

In Figure 1, the components in the upper red box represent the *offline* workflow to build the indexes. In the workflow, mathematical information is obtained from the dataset at first, which is Wikipedia in *WikiMirs 3.0*. Meanwhile, the importance values of each formula in each document are calculated according to the roles of formulae in the documents and they will be utilized in the *online* workflow to rank the retrieved documents. Afterwards, both the formula and context terms are extracted by *tokenizer* from the mathematical information of Wikipedia. Finally, *indexer* stores statistical data of formulae (e.g., *tf-idf*) in the index files. The statistical data is mainly about the context terms, formula terms and importance values of formulae, corresponding to the context, structure and importance of formulae.

2.2.2 *online workflow*

In Figure 1, the components in the lower blue box denote the *online* workflow, namely the searching process. In the workflow, users can "cut" the query, a formula with context, directly from PDF documents as well as type in or paste the query. Next, the query is parsed into terms including formula terms and context terms by *tokenizer*. Then, documents containing the terms of the query are collected from the indexes which are built in the *offline* workflow. Lastly, the retrieved documents are sorted by *ranker* according to the frequency properties of matching terms and the weighting factors, such as the importance value of formulae in a document.

2.3 Modules

2.3.1 *Interface*

The *interface* module is used to input queries in the *online* workflow. For human-machine interaction of information retrieval systems, interface is a critical part. Different modes of interfaces offer users distinct experiences, especially for the MIR systems due to the complicated forms of formulae.

In *WikiMirs 3.0*, two modes of interfaces are supported to facilitate inputting queries for users. In the first mode, users can input queries via manually typing or pasting into *WikiMirs 3.0*, which supports both LaTeX and Presentation MathML markups. Nevertheless, this mode is inconvenient because it costs users extra time and effort to learn how to encode formulae in special formats. The other mode is to "cut" queries directly from PDF documents with the aid of a supplementary plugin tool as shown in Figure 2. In more details, users can input queries by the steps as follows: op en a PDF document by Apabi Reader, choose the "*WikiMirs* Search" mode and select the formula region, like the red solid box in Figure 2(a). After the series of actions, the formula is recognized by the refined method proposed in [28]. The method is designed to extract the semantic structure of formulae based on the image information of pages. And it is modified and improved on the base of the precise character information contained in PDF documents in *WikiMirs 3.0*. The context paragraphs, like the paragraphs in the blue dotted box in Figure 2(a), are obtained by the approach of [2]. It is employed to analyze the underlying layout structures and logical structures of PDF documents. Then the selected formula and its context are input into *WikiMirs-3.0*, as shown in Figure 2(b). Finally, the system returns the searching results to users, as shown in Figure 2(c). The Apabi Reader with the search plugin has been released as a publicly available tool in *WikiMirs 3.0*.

2.3.2 *Tokenizer*

The *tsokenizer* module is utilized in both the *online* workflow and the *offline* workflow. The searched dataset and queries are extracted into terms by *tokenizer*. The method of *tokenizer* greatly influences the precision, recall and

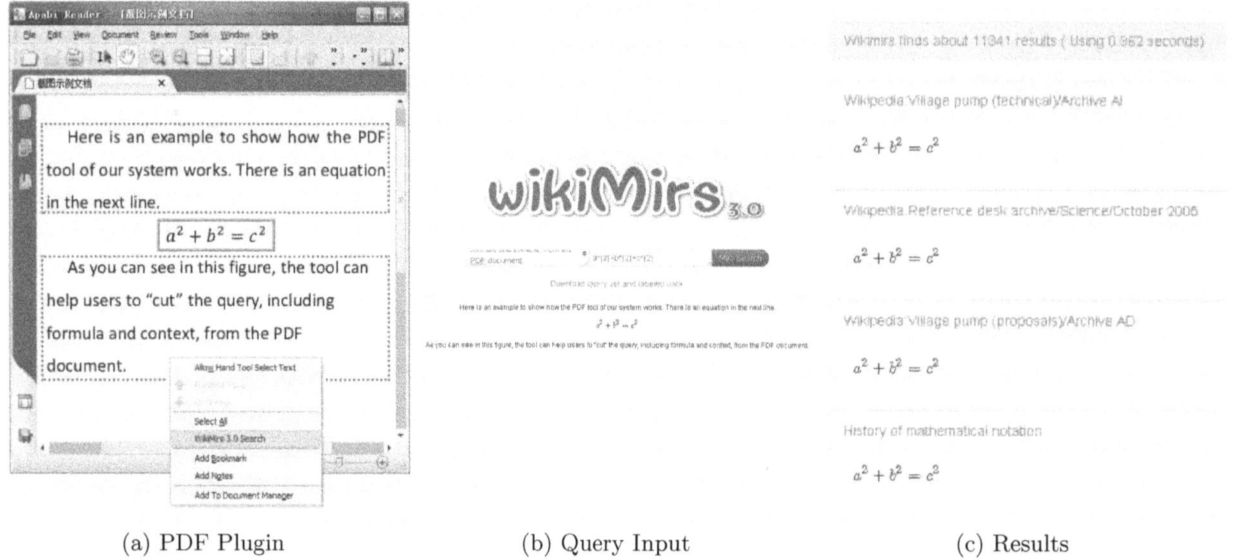

(a) PDF Plugin (b) Query Input (c) Results

Figure 2: Interface of *WikiMirs 3.0*

generalization ability of MIR systems. As for *WikiMirs-3.0*, the query is comprised of a formula and its context. Therefore, there are two tokenizers in the system, the formula tokenizer and context tokenizer.

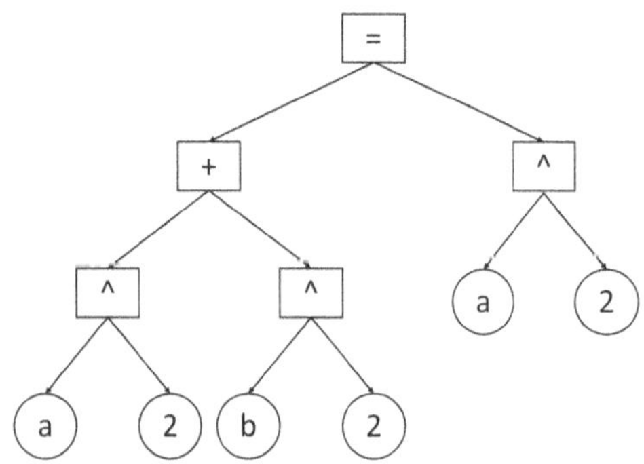

Figure 3: Semantic Tree Presentation of $a^2 + b^2 = c^2$

Formula Tokenizer. Formula tokenizer consists of two parts, normalization and term extraction. In the normalization process, different formulae with a same meaning are converted into a uniform formula so as to ensure the high recall of relevant formulae. Variables, constants and the order of operands are all taken into account in the process. The description of the term extraction algorithm is shown in Algorithm 1.

At the beginning, formulae are converted into semantic tree presentation. For instance, the semantic tree presentation of $a^2 + b^2 = c^2$ is shown in Figure 3. After that, formula index terms are extracted from the tree hierarchically. In *WikiMirs 3.0*, there are two kinds of terms, original terms and generalized terms. As the structure of a formula is an important cue to understand it, the original terms are defined as the substructures of the semantic tree presentation of the formula. For the sake of fuzzy matching, the generalized terms are proposed by changing the variables and constants of the original terms into wildcards. Variables are replaced by "$*_v$" and "$*_c$" is regarded as a substitution for constants. For example, the generalized term of "$a^2 + b^2 = c^2$" is "$*_v^{*c} + *_v^{*c} = *_v^{*c}$". All the sub-tree levels and terms of formula, $a^2 + b^2 = c^2$, is shown in Table 2. More details about the formula tokenizer including how to construct the semantic tree of a formula could be found in the paper of *WikiMirs 2.0* [11].

Algorithm 1 Term Extraction

Convert formula into semantic tree(ST)
Let $O(ST)$ is the original of the semantic tree
Let GST is the generalization of the semantic tree
Let $L(ST)$ is the level of the semantic tree
Let T is the set of formula terms
procedure EXTRACTOR(ST, $L(ST)$)
    if ST is not just a leaf **then**
        $T += (O(ST), L(ST))$ ▷ original term
        $T += (G(ST), L(ST))$ ▷ generalized term
        for $ST_i \leftarrow$ each child of ST **do**
            EXTRACTOR($ST_i, L(ST) + 1$)
        end for
    end if
end procedure

Table 2: Terms of $a^2 + b^2 = c^2$

Level	Original	Generalized
1	$a^2 + b^2 = c^2$	$*_v^{*c} + *_v^{*c} = *_v^{*c}$
2	$a^2 + b^2$	$*_v^{*c} + *_v^{*c}$
2	c^2	$*_v^{*c}$
3	a^2	$*_v^{*c}$
3	b^2	$*_v^{*c}$

Context Tokenizer. Most of existing MIR systems, including last version of WikiMirs [11], only take formula information into consideration. This may lead to a situation: when users searches a query, the top returned formulae could be exact the same with the query formula. However, the retrieved documents corresponding to the formulae may be not really related to the query. In other words, the ranking of the searching results is not reasonable enough only relying on the matched formulae.

For this issue, this paper utilizes the observation that most formulae do not appear independently, but with context. The context which may be application scenario or explanation of the formula is also helpful for MIR systems.

The context tokenizer is introduced to extract the terms of formula context. In *WikiMirs 3.0*, the preceding paragraph and the following paragraph of a formula are regarded as the context of the formula. The terms of a paragraph are extracted similarly with the traditional text searching engines [14].

2.3.3 Indexer

In order to support real-time online searching, the index files are built in the *offline* workflow by *indexer*, in which the inverted index data structure is employed. Different from the previous versions of *WikiMirs*, two index files are built to calculate a composite similarity score of a query and a document. One index file is built for formula terms. In this index, the importance value of each formula in a document which will be utilized in *ranker* is recorded. The other index file is constructed for context terms.

Formula Indexer. In *WikiMirs 3.0*, formulae and contexts are tokenized into terms as described in Section 2.3.2. As shown in Table 3, the index of formula terms is constructed and it is referred to as $index_{tf-f}$ hereafter. For each term, a list of formulae which contain this term is recorded. A formula (f) contains a formula term (ft) denotes that one of the terms extracted from f is exactly the same as ft.

Table 3: Index of Formula Terms

Term	iff	Formula list		
ft_1	$iff(ft_1)$	f_a $tf(ft_1, f_a)$ $tl(ft_1, f_a)$ $W_{importance}(f_a)$	...	f_b $tf(ft_1, f_b)$ $tl(ft_1, f_b)$ $W_{importance}(f_b)$
...	...	...	...	...
ft_i	$iff(ft_i)$	f_c $tf(ft_i, f_c)$ $tl(ft_i, f_c)$ $W_{importance}(f_c)$	...	f_d $tf(ft_i, f_d)$ $tl(ft_i, f_d)$ $W_{importance}(f_d)$

In Table 3, $iff(ft)$ is the inverted formula frequency of ft and $tf(ft, f)$ represents the frequency of ft occurring in f. How to calculate them is described detailedly in the literature [11]. $tl(ft, f)$ describes the level of ft in f. It distinguishes the same terms in different levels. Table 2 shows the tl of each formula term of $a^2 + b^2 = c^2$. $W_{importance}(f)$ is the importance value of f in a document and it will be described detailedly later. Finally, all the formula terms with their statistics information mentioned above are recorded in $index_{tf-f}$.

Context Indexer. As for the context information, the index file (see Table 4) of context terms (ct) is constructed to calculate the context score of a query (Q) and a document (D). This index is referred to as $index_{ct-d}$ hereafter.

Table 4: Index of Context Terms

Term	iff	Documents list		
ct_1	$icf(ct_1)$	d_a $tf(ct_1, d_a)$	...	d_b $tf(ct_1, d_b)$
...	...	...	...	...
ct_i	$icf(ct_i)$	d_c $tf(ct_i, d_c)$	...	d_d $tf(ct_i, d_d)$

For each context term ct, $icf(ct)$ denotes the inverted context frequency of ct, $tf(ct, d)$ represents the frequency of ct occurring in d. And the definitions of them are the same with the typical $tf - idf$ models.

Formula Importance Value. In *WikiMirs 2.0* [11], the top retrieved documents may be not desired, even though the formulae in them are the same with the formula of the query. The reason is that all the formulae in a document are treated equally in *WikiMirs 2.0*. However, different formulae usually play different roles in a document. The significant ones should be paid more attention to.

Therefore, the importance of formulae in a document is introduced to improve *WikiMirs* in this paper. The importance values of formulae in each document are calculated in the *indexer* module of the *offline* workflow and stored in $index_{tf-f}$.

In *WikiMirs 3.0*, four aspects of formula circumstances are taken into consideration to measure the importance of formulae: 1) Whether the formula occupies a whole line by itself. For a document, the leading formulae are usually on the more important positions than the embedded ones. 2) The number of formulae existing in the single document. A document contains more formulae, the importance of each formula is shared and reduced more. 3) The total length of the context paragraphs. The preceding paragraph and the following paragraph of a formula are usually the introduction or illustration of the formula and selected as the context of the formula, whose lengthes could be regarded as a rough measure of the formula importance. 4) The cited number of the formula in the document. If a formula is cited more in a document, it is possibly more important for the document. As a consequence, the formula importance value ($W_{importance}$) is defined as follows,

$$W_{importance} = \alpha \times w_l \times w_p \times \frac{1}{\ln(w_n + 1)} \times \frac{1}{w_c}, \quad (1)$$

$$w_l = \begin{cases} 1 & leading\ formula \\ 0.5 & otherwise \end{cases}, \quad (2)$$

$$w_p = \frac{length\ of\ the\ context\ paragraphs}{length\ of\ the\ document}, \quad (3)$$

where α is a heuristic coefficient to balance the influence of $W_{importance}$ in the ranking process. w_l denotes whether the formula occupies a line independently, as shown in Equation 2. w_n is equal to the number of formulae existing in the document. For each formula, w_p is defined in Equation 3. In *WikiMirs 3.0*, the context paragraphs contain the preceding paragraph and the following paragraph, which are analysed and obtained by the methods proposed in [2]. w_c is the placement number of the formula after all the formulae in the document are ranked by the cited numbers of the formulae from large to small. If two formulae have the same cited number, they have the same placement. The references of formulae in a document are detected by the way similar with the method proposed in the literature [10]. All the cited numbers of formulae in a document are initialized as 1. And the number pluses 1 once a reference of the corresponding formula is found in the body text of the document.

2.3.4 Ranker

Ranker is a core module of search engines and it directly determines the ranking results. In the searching process, first of all, the query is parsed into terms by *tokenizer*. Afterwards, the inverted index files, $index_{tf-f}$ and $index_{ct-d}$, are looked up and the matched terms are returned to calculate the similarity scores in *ranker*. Since *WikiMirs-3.0* takes both the formula and context information into consideration. A composite score ($score(Q,D)$) to measure the similarity between a query (Q) and a document (D) is proposed, as defined in Equation 4:

$$score(Q,D) = \sqrt{\frac{(score_f(Q,D)+1)^2 + (score_c(Q,D)+1)}{2}} - 1, \quad (4)$$

where $score_f(Q,D)$ is the similarity score between the formula of Q and D. $score_c(Q,D)$ is the similarity between the context of Q and D. The $score(Q,D)$ which emphasizes formula information is a approximate derivative average of $score_f(Q,D)$ and $score_c(Q,D)$. The definitions of $score_f(Q,D)$ and $score_c(Q,D)$ are given in Equation 5 and Equation 8 respectively.

$$score_f(Q,D) = \max_i \{\sum_{ft \in Q} (tf(ft,f_i) \times iff^2(ft) \times W_{f_i})\}, \quad (5)$$

$$W_{f_i} = W_{importance}(f_i) \times W_{cover}(Q,f_i) \times W_{level}(ft,Q,f_i), \quad (6)$$

$$W_{cover}(Q,f_i) = \frac{2 \times number\ of\ matched\ terms\ between\ Q\ and\ f_i}{number\ of\ terms\ of\ Q + number\ of\ terms\ f_i}, \quad (7)$$

where $tf(ft,f_i)$ and $iff(ft)$ are directly obtained from the index file, $index_{tf-f}$. W_{f_i} is the weight of f_i, as defined in Equation 6. $W_{importance}(f_i)$ denotes the formula importance value referred to Section 2.3.3. $W_{level}(ft,Q,f)$ is introduced to calculate the level distance of the matched term ft in Q and f, similar to *WikiMirs 2.0* [11]. W_{cover} is defined in Equation 7.

In *WikiMirs 3.0*, $score_c(Q,D)$ is used to evaluate the similarity between the context of a query (Q) and a document (D). It is defined in Equation 8:

$$score_c(Q,D) = \sum_{ct \in Q} (tf(ct,d_i) \times icf^2(ct) \times W_{cover}(Q,D)), \quad (8)$$

$$W_{cover}(Q,D) = \frac{number\ of\ matched\ terms\ between\ Q\ and\ D}{number\ of\ terms\ of\ Q}, \quad (9)$$

where $tf(ct,d)$ and $icf(ct)$ stored in $index_{ct-d}$ denote the term frequency and inverse context frequency of the context term (ct). $W_{cover}(Q,D)$ is the context matching score, as defined in Equation 9.

3. EXPERIMENTAL RESULTS

3.1 Dataset

A few of datasets have been utilized in the existing MIR systems, such as DLMF[3], arXiv[4], Wikipedia[5] and so on. Different from other domain-specific or academic corpuses (e.g., ArXiv), Wikipedia is widely used by users with different backgrounds and it is a public available dataset, which makes it possible to compare the performances of different MIR systems. Thus, Wikipedia is also taken as the dataset in *WikiMirs 3.0*. And the 2014-07-30 dump of Wikipedia is used in the experiments of this paper, whose size is approximately 10 GB compressed and 47 GB uncompressed. This dataset contains 14650390 webpages and 562324 mathematical formulae.

It is worth to mention that the NTCIR-11 Math Group has released an accessible dataset[6]. This dataset has been tested by many current MIR systems in the past MIR competition held by the group. However, most documents of NTCIR-11 Math dataset contain few formulae and context text. Therefore, it is unsuitable and not adopted here, while the experiments of this paper mainly focus on evaluating the effects of the context, structure and importance of formulae for MIR.

3.2 Time & Space Efficiency

WikiMirs 3.0 is implemented in Scala with the aid of Apache Lucene. Both the *offline* and the *online* workflows run on a PC with a 3.00 GHz Intel Core2 Duo E8400 CPU, 4 GB DDR3 and 150 GB SATA Disk.

For the *offline* workflow, Figure 4(a) shows the time consumption to construct the index files of different numbers of webpages. It costs about 37 minutes to produce the entire index files for the Wikipedia dataset, containing 14650390 webpages. Figure 4(b) illustrates the sizes of the formula index files ($index_{ft-f}$) and the context index files

[3]http://dlmf.nist.gov
[4]http://arxiv.org
[5]http://en.wikipedia.org/wiki/
[6]http://ntcir-math.nii.ac.jp/data/

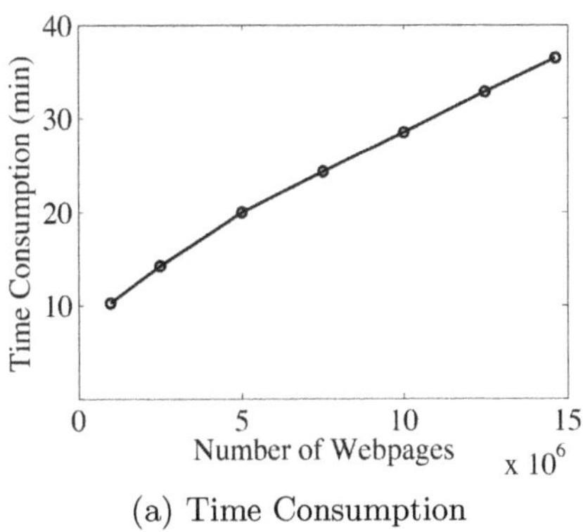

(a) Time Consumption

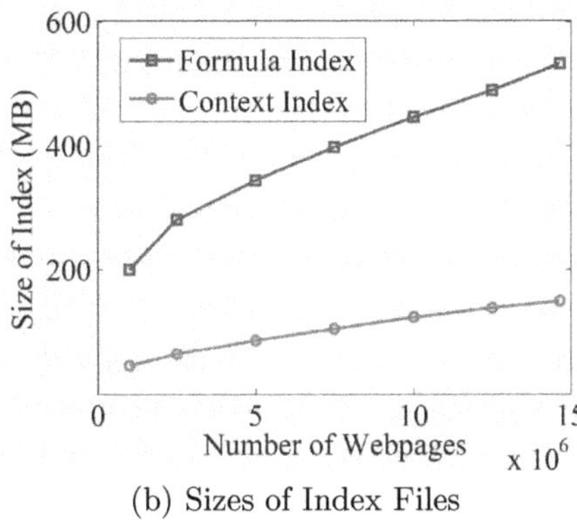

(b) Sizes of Index Files

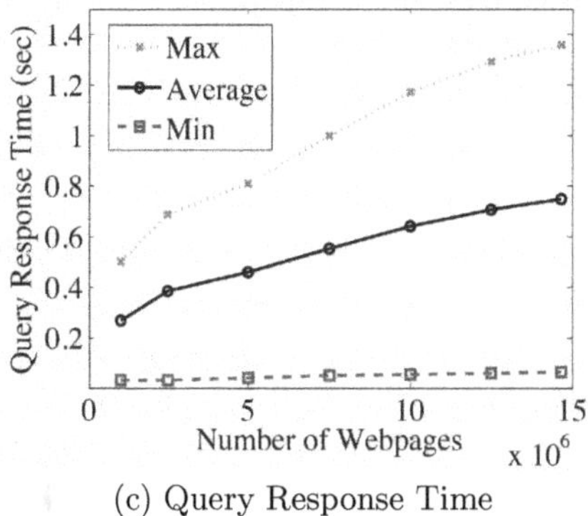

(c) Query Response Time

Figure 4: Time & Space Efficiency

($index_{ct-d}$) with increasing amount of indexed webpages. The total size of the index files ($index_{ft-f}$ and $index_{ct-d}$) is 682 MB approximately. As shown in Figure 4(a) and Figure 4(b), both the time consumption for constructing index files and the sizes of the index files grow linearly along with the number of indexed webpages. It is acceptable for a MIR system in practice.

For the *online* workflow, Figure 4(c) presents the relevance of query response time and the number of indexed webpages. The minimum, maximum and average time are measured by 52 queries. The detailed description of the queries is in Section 3.3.2. Figure 4(c) shows that the three categories of query response time increase steadily with the increasing number of indexed webpages. On the average, it costs 0.75s to respond a query on the entire Wikipedia dataset.

3.3 Accuracy

3.3.1 Compared Algorithms

In this paper, two tree-based MIR systems, MIaS [26] and *WikiMirs 2.0* [11], are implemented as baselines to evaluate the accuracy of *WikiMirs 3.0*. MIaS is a classical tree-based MIR system and it is regarded as a baseline by several existing MIR methods and systems [11]. MIaS indexes all the substructures of formulae and calculates the similarity of them. It is based on arXiv, so this paper re-implements it over Wikipedia dataset for comparison. *WikiMirs 2.0* is another tree-based indexing system, while it is run on Wikipedia.

In order to verify the effectiveness of the proposed algorithms of *WikiMirs 3.0*, only adopting the context or importance of formulae respectively, two systems with each algorithm are implemented for comparison in this paper. In *WikiMirs 3.0* $_{context}$, the context information is adopted, the importance of formulae is taken no account of. Meanwhile, *WikiMirs 3.0* $_{importance}$ represents another system, in which only importance of formulae in a document is considered. *WikiMirs 3.0* denotes the proposed system in this paper. In other words, both the two algorithms are employed in it.

In total, five systems, MIaS, *WikiMirs 2.0*, *WikiMirs 3.0-* $_{context}$, *WikiMirs 3.0* $_{importance}$, *WikiMirs 3.0*, are tested and evaluated in the experiments of this paper.

3.3.2 Query Set

In this paper, the query set contains 52 queries. 35 of them are picked up from the "Relevance Page" of Wikipedia, mentioned in [8]. The 35 formulae cover broad most kinds of formulae, such as integral, probability, set theory, etc. The other 17 queries are described in [27]. They are the most famous formulae in the world, such as Pythagorean theorem ($a^2+b^2=c^2$), Relativity ($E=mc^2$), Navier-Stokes Equation ($\rho\left(\frac{\partial \mathbf{v}}{\partial t}+\mathbf{v}\cdot\nabla\mathbf{v}\right)=-\nabla p+\nabla\cdot\mathbf{T}+f$) and so on. For further comparison, the query set along with the scores for pairs of a query and corresponding retrieved documents can be downloaded in the webpage of *WikiMirs 3.0*.

3.3.3 Evaluation Measure

The top-k documents retrieved by the five tested systems over the query set are utilized to measure their performances. Average *Precision* (P) and *Discounted Cumulative Gain* (DCG) [7] are calculated to evaluate the performance of different systems. For each of the top-k items, a relevance score ranging from 0 to 5 is given. An item is given a higher score if users think it is more relevant with the corresponding query. The score 5 means the result exactly meets the user needs and the score 0 denotes that the result is completely unrelated to the query at all. The scores are provided by five postgraduates with different majors, such as mathematics, physics, computer science, etc. P_k is determined by the number of retrieved documents ($score > n, n = 0, 1, \ldots, 4$) relevant to the query. P_k of the top-k results is defined as follows,

$$P_k = \sum_{i=1}^{k} \frac{number\ of\ relevant\ documents}{k}. \tag{10}$$

Based on the score of each retrieved document and the ranking of the documents, DCG is defined as,

$$DCG_k = \sum_{i=1}^{k} \frac{2^{score_i - 1} - 1}{\log_2 i + 1}, \tag{11}$$

where $score_i$ denotes the score of the i-th retrieved item. It reflects the rationality of the retrieved documents' order.

3.3.4 Performance of the Top-k Results

The the top-k results over P and DCG are presented in Table 5 and Table 6. In the experiments, some results of MIaS are irrelevant with the corresponding queries, especially for complicated formulae. Note that MIaS is proposed for arXIv. Therefore, the algorithms and settings of MIaS are not towards Wikipeida. This is a possible factor affecting MIaS's performance here. In *WikiMirs 2.0*, the ranking of the retrieved documents is not reasonable enough because *WikiMirs 2.0* only considers the formula information and ignores the context and the importance of formulae.

In Table 5, the P_k of the five systems is illustrated detailedly. For the top-3 retrieved documents, *WikiMirs 3.0* $_{context}$ has the most retrieved documents whose scores are above 0. *WikiMirs 3.0* $_{importance}$ performs best only when the score is greater than 1. For all the other conditions, *WikiMirs-3.0* achieves the best performances. From Table 5, it can be concluded that both the context and importance of formulae improve P_k of results and the hybrid of them performs best.

Table 5: Average Precision(P) of the Five Systems

Systems		MIaS	*2.0*[1]	*3.0*$_c$[2]	*3.0*$_i$[3]	*3.0*[4]
score > 0	P_3	0.647	0.974	**0.994**	0.951	0.987
	P_5	0.604	0.938	0.969	0.945	**0.980**
	P_{10}	0.529	0.850	0.909	0.861	**0.957**
score > 1	P_3	0.212	0.827	0.878	**0.884**	0.882
	P_5	0.200	0.773	0.812	0.815	**0.835**
	P_{10}	0.192	0.654	0.692	0.698	**0.761**
score > 2	P_3	0.122	0.647	0.660	0.693	**0.699**
	P_5	0.108	0.550	0.562	0.573	**0.604**
	P_{10}	0.100	0.419	0.460	0.475	**0.522**
score > 3	P_3	0.071	0.474	0.481	0.529	**0.550**
	P_5	0.062	0.377	0.392	0.420	**0.424**
	P_{10}	0.060	0.258	0.300	0.308	**0.324**
score > 4	P_3	0.026	0.269	0.314	0.320	**0.340**
	P_5	0.020	0.204	0.227	0.227	**0.235**
	P_{10}	0.017	0.127	0.145	0.141	**0.149**

[1] *WikiMirs 2.0* [2] *WikiMirs 3.0* $_{context}$
[3] *WikiMirs 3.0* $_{importance}$ [4] *WikiMirs 3.0*

Table 6 shows *DCG* results of the five systems. All of the three *3.0* systems' *DCG* are higher than *WikiMirs 2.0* and MIaS. It is obviously that the importance of formulae is more helpful for the ranking of the results than the context information. Furthermore, taking both the importance of formulae and the context information into consideration can achieve the most reasonable ranking results.

Table 6: DCG of the Five Systems

Systems	MIaS	*2.0*[1]	*3.0*$_c$[2]	*3.0*$_i$[3]	*3.0*[4]
DCG_3	8.164	14.600	15.641	16.559	**17.134**
DCG_5	12.377	17.291	18.387	19.257	**19.865**
DCG_{10}	17.452	20.624	22.699	23.515	**24.750**

[1] *WikiMirs 2.0* [2] *WikiMirs 3.0* $_{context}$
[3] *WikiMirs 3.0* $_{importance}$ [4] *WikiMirs 3.0*

3.3.5 Case Study

Two searching cases (two query and their top-5 results) are presented in Figure 5. They are used to illustrate concretely the benefit of the context and importance of formulae for MIR. The name of the formula is taken as its context for *WikiMirs 3.0* $_{context}$. More case studies can be downloaded online in *WikiMirs 3.0*. Each entry of the MIR systems' results consists of the title and the matched formula of the retrieved Wikipedia webpage.

Take "$E = mc^2$" as a query for MIaS, *WikiMirs 2.0* and *WikiMirs 3.0* $_{importance}$. The matched formulae in the top-5 results of the three MIR systems are all the same with the query. After looking into the webpages, it can be found that the retrieved items of *WikiMirs 3.0* $_{importance}$ are more relevant to "Relativity" than the results of the other two MIR systems. Because *WikiMirs 3.0* $_{importance}$ considers the importance of formulae, the documents whose themes are about the matched formulae are paid more attention in the system and listed in the topper place of the retrieved results.

Take "$a^2 + b^2 = c^2$" as another example. MIaS can not find the exact formula, "$a^2 + b^2 = c^2$", while *WikiMirs-2.0* finds the results containing the identical formula with the query. Search "Pythagoras's theorem, $a^2 + b^2 = c^2$" in *WikiMirs 3.0* $_{context}$. After checking the top-5 results of *WikiMirs 2.0* and *WikiMirs 3.0* $_{context}$, it is obviously that the results of top-5 of *WikiMirs 3.0* $_{context}$ are more reasonable to the query than *WikiMirs 2.0*. For instance, all the top-3 results of *WikiMirs 3.0* $_{context}$ are the relevant web page for Pythagorass theorem, while only the second record of *WikiMirs 2.0* is relevant to Pythagorass theorem. It is because that the context information is employed in *WikiMirs 3.0* $_{context}$, which helps the MIR system understand mathematical information.

4. CONCLUSIONS

In this paper, *WikiMirs 3.0* is proposed based on the previous versions of *WikiMirs*. This new system enables users to type in queries or "cut" formulae with context paragraphs as queries directly from PDF documents for searching, which is more friendly and convenient. Apart from formulae, *WikiMirs 3.0* also takes the context information of formulae into account as a supplementary. And a context index is constructed to match the context of formulae in queries and the context of formulae in documents. What's more, for the ranking of retrieved documents, the importance of formulae in a document is introduced. With the aid of it, the order of the results becomes more reasonable. The experimental results prove that both the context and importance of formulae in a document are helpful for MIR.

For the future work of MIR research, processing the contexts of formulae by natural language processing techniques is meaningful for deep understanding mathematical information need of users. Moreover, drawing on the experience of learning to rank may enhance the retrieval and ranking performance, while training data and multiple ranking features are available.

5. ACKNOWLEDGMENTS

This work is supported by the National Natural Science Foundation of China (No.61472014), the Natural Science Foundation of Beijing (No.4142023) and the Beijing Nova Program (2015). We also thank the anonymous reviewers for their valuable comments.

6. REFERENCES

[1] A. Aizawa, M. Kohlhase, I. Ounis, and M. Schubotz. Ntcir-11 math-2 task overview. In *Proceedings of NTCIR-11 Math-2 task Workshop Meeting [1]*, 2014.

[2] L. Gao, Z. Tang, X. Lin, Y. Liu, R. Qiu, and Y. Wang. Structure extraction from pdf-based book documents. In *Proceedings of the 11th annual international ACM/IEEE joint conference on Digital libraries*, pages 11–20. ACM, 2011.

[3] L. Gao, Y. Wang, L. Hao, and Z. Tang. Icst math retrieval system for ntcir-11 math-2 task. In *Proceedings of the 11th NTCIR Conference on Evaluation of Information Access Technologies*, 2014.

[4] Y. K. Giovanni, T. F. H. Goran, and A. Akiko. The mcat math retrieval system for ntcir-11 math track. In *Proceedings of the 11th NTCIR Conference on Evaluation of Information Access Technologies*, 2014.

[5] R. Hambasan, M. Kohlhase, and C. Prodescu. Mathwebsearch at ntcir-11. In *Proceedings of the 11th NTCIR Conference on Evaluation of Information Access Technologies*, 2014.

[6] X. Hu, L. Gao, X. Lin, Z. Tang, X. Lin, and J. B. Baker. Wikimirs: a mathematical information retrieval system for wikipedia. In *Proceedings of the 13th ACM/IEEE-CS joint conference on Digital libraries*, pages 11–20. ACM, 2013.

[7] K. Järvelin and J. Kekäläinen. Ir evaluation methods for retrieving highly relevant documents. In *Proceedings of the 23rd annual international ACM SIGIR conference on Research and development in information retrieval*, pages 41–48. ACM, 2000.

[8] S. Kamali and F. W. Tompa. Retrieving documents with mathematical content. In *Proceedings of the 36th international ACM SIGIR conference on Research and development in information retrieval*, pages 353–362. ACM, 2013.

[9] M. Kohlhase and I. Sucan. A search engine for mathematical formulae. In *Artificial Intelligence and Symbolic Computation*, pages 241–253. Springer, 2006.

[10] S. Li, L. Gao, Z. Tang, and Y. Yu. Cross-reference identification within a pdf document. In *IS&T/SPIE Electronic Imaging*. International Society for Optics and Photonics, 2015.

[11] X. Lin, L. Gao, X. Hu, Z. Tang, Y. Xiao, and X. Liu. A mathematics retrieval system for formulae in layout presentations. In *Proceedings of the 37th international ACM SIGIR conference on Research & development in information retrieval*, pages 697–706. ACM, 2014.

[12] A. Lipani, L. Andersson, F. Piroi, M. Lupu, and A. Hanbury. Tuw-imp at the ntcir-11 math-2. In *Proceedings of the 11th NTCIR Conference on Evaluation of Information Access Technologies*, 2014.

[13] X. Liu. Generating metadata for cyberlearning resources through information retrieval and meta-search. *Journal of the American Society for Information Science and Technology*, 64(4):771–786, 2013.

[14] C. D. Manning, P. Raghavan, and H. Schütze. *Introduction to information retrieval*, volume 1. Cambridge university press Cambridge, 2008.

[15] B. R. Miller and A. Youssef. Technical aspects of the digital library of mathematical functions. *Annals of Mathematics and Artificial Intelligence*, 38(1-3):121–136, 2003.

[16] R. Miner and R. Munavalli. An approach to mathematical search through query formulation and data normalization. In *Towards Mechanized Mathematical Assistants*, pages 342–355. Springer, 2007.

[17] J. Mišutka and L. Galamboš. Extending full text search engine for mathematical content. *Towards Digital Mathematics Library. Birmingham, United Kingdom, July 27th, 2008*, pages 55–67, 2008.

[18] T. T. Nguyen, K. Chang, and S. C. Hui. A math-aware search engine for math question answering system. In *Proceedings of the 21st ACM international conference on Information and knowledge management*, pages 724–733. ACM, 2012.

[19] T. T. Nguyen, S. C. Hui, and K. Chang. A lattice-based approach for mathematical search using formal concept analysis. *Expert Systems with Applications*, 39(5):5820–5828, 2012.

[20] N. Pattaniyil and R. Zanibbi. Combining tf-idf text retrieval with an inverted index over symbol pairs in math expressions: The tangent math search engine at ntcir 2014. In *Proceedings of the 11th NTCIR Conference on Evaluation of Information Access Technologies*, 2014.

[21] J. M. G. Pinto, S. Barthel, and W.-T. Balke. Qualibeta at the ntcir-11 math 2 task: An attempt to query math collections. In *Proceedings of the 11th NTCIR Conference on Evaluation of Information Access Technologies*, 2014.

[22] M. Ružicka, P. Sojka, and M. Líška. Math indexer and searcher under the hood: History and development of a winning strategy. In *Proceedings of the 11th NTCIR Conference on Evaluation of Information Access Technologies*, 2014.

[23] T. Schellenberg, B. Yuan, and R. Zanibbi. Layout-based substitution tree indexing and retrieval for mathematical expressions. In *IS&T/SPIE Electronic Imaging*, pages 82970I–82970I. International Society for Optics and Photonics, 2012.

[24] M. Schubotz, A. Youssef, V. Markl, H. S. Cohl, and J. J. Li. Evaluation of similarity-measure factors for formulae based on the ntcir-11 math task. In *Proceedings of the 11th NTCIR Conference on Evaluation of Information Access Technologies*, 2014.

[25] A. Singhal. Modern information retrieval: A brief overview. *IEEE Data Eng. Bull.*, 24(4):35–43, 2001.

[26] P. Sojka and M. Líška. Indexing and searching mathematics in digital libraries. In *Intelligent Computer Mathematics*, pages 228–243. Springer, 2011.

[27] I. Stewart. *In pursuit of the unknown: 17 equations that changed the world*. Basic Books, 2012.

[28] R. Zanibbi, D. Blostein, and J. R. Cordy. Recognizing mathematical expressions using tree transformation. *Pattern Analysis and Machine Intelligence, IEEE Transactions on*, 24(11):1455–1467, 2002.

Wikipedia:Reference desk/Archives/Science/2009 August 18

$E = mc^2$

Antiproton

$E = mc^2$

Sporadic fatal insomnia

$E = mc^2$

Template:General physics

$E = mc^2$

Wikipedia:Reference desk/Archives/Science/2009 December 27

$E = mc^2$

(a) MIaS for $e = mc^2$

HAL/S

$x = a^2 + b_i^2$

Wikipedia:Reference desk/Archives/Science/2006 November 30

c^2

Magnetoplasmadynamic thruster

a^2

Wikipedia:Reference desk/Archives/Science/2008 November 14

c^2

Wikipedia:Reference desk/Archives/Science/2009 August 7

$E^2 = m^2c^4 + p^2c^2$

(b) MIaS for $a^2 + b^2 = c^2$

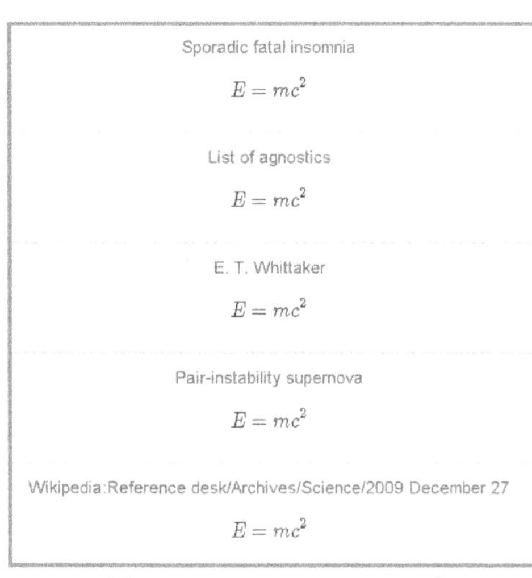

(c) WikiMirs 2.0 for $e = mc^2$

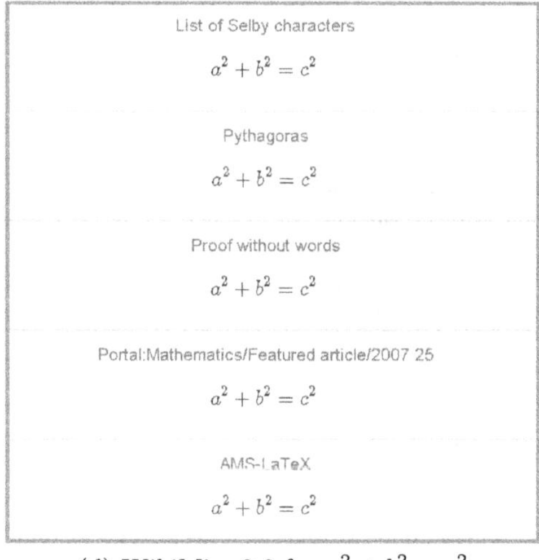

(d) WikiMirs 2.0 for $a^2 + b^2 = c^2$

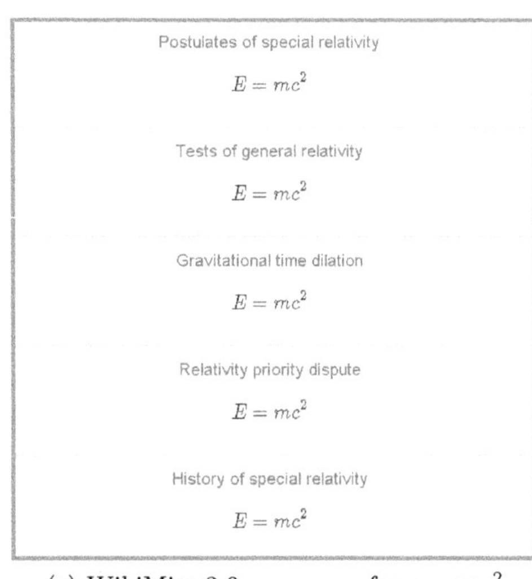

Postulates of special relativity
$E = mc^2$
Tests of general relativity
$E = mc^2$
Gravitational time dilation
$E = mc^2$
Relativity priority dispute
$E = mc^2$
History of special relativity
$E = mc^2$

(e) WikiMirs 3.0 $_{importance}$ for $e = mc^2$

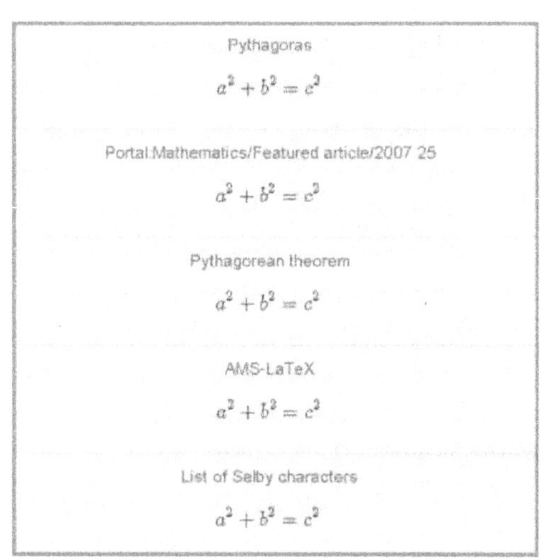

Pythagoras
$a^2 + b^2 = c^2$
Portal:Mathematics/Featured article/2007 25
$a^2 + b^2 = c^2$
Pythagorean theorem
$a^2 + b^2 = c^2$
AMS-LaTeX
$a^2 + b^2 = c^2$
List of Selby characters
$a^2 + b^2 = c^2$

(f) WikiMirs 3.0 $_{context}$ for Pythagoras's theorem, $a^2 + b^2 = c^2$

Figure 5: Two Case Studies

Topic Modeling Users' Interpretations of Songs to Inform Subject Access in Music Digital Libraries

Kahyun Choi
GSLIS
University of Illinois
MC-493, Suite 329
Champaign, IL 61820
+1.217.333.3282
ckahyu2@illinois.edu

Jin Ha Lee
Information School
University of Washington
Mary Gates Hall, Suite 370
Seattle, WA 98195
+1.206.685.0153
jinhalee@uw.edu

Craig Willis, J. Stephen Downie
GSLIS
University of Illinois
MC-493, Suite 213
Champaign, IL 61820
+1.217.333.3282
{willis8, jdownie}@illinois.edu

ABSTRACT

The assignment of subject metadata to music is useful for organizing and accessing digital music collections. Since manual subject annotation of large-scale music collections is labor-intensive, automatic methods are preferred. Topic modeling algorithms can be used to automatically identify latent topics from appropriate text sources. Candidate text sources such as song lyrics are often too poetic, resulting in lower-quality topics. Users' interpretations of song lyrics provide an alternative source. In this paper, we propose an automatic topic discovery system from web-mined user-generated interpretations of songs to provide subject access to a music digital library. We also propose and evaluate filtering techniques to identify high-quality topics. In our experiments, we use 24,436 popular songs that exist in both the Million Song Dataset and `songmeanings.com`. Topic models are generated using Latent Dirichlet Allocation (LDA). To evaluate the coherence of learned topics, we calculate the Normalized Pointwise Mutual Information (NPMI) of the top ten words in each topic based on occurrences in Wikipedia. Finally, we evaluate the resulting topics using a subset of 422 songs that have been manually assigned to six subjects. Using this system, 71% of the manually assigned subjects were correctly identified. These results demonstrate that topic modeling of song interpretations is a promising method for subject metadata enrichment in music digital libraries. It also has implications for affording similar access to collections of poetry and fiction.

Categories and Subject Descriptors

H.3.1 [Content Analysis and Indexing]: indexing methods

General Terms

Algorithms, Measurement, Performance, Experimentation

Keywords

Topic Models; Music Digital Library; Interpretations of Lyrics

1. INTRODUCTION

The subjects of songs are of great interest to music listeners. Users' strong desire to understand what songs are about is evidenced by millions of online postings discussing and arguing about different interpretations of the meanings of song lyrics. Previous studies also have found that users want subject metadata for music. Bainbridge et al. [1] analyzed 502 music-related online postings from Google Answers, now a defunct Q&A service, and found that "Lyric Story (storyline of song)" was described as one of the information needs. Lee & Downie [2] conducted a large-scale online survey showing that more than 30% of respondents would be likely to use "storyline of music" to navigate music collections, if such an option was available. However, unlike other music metadata such as title, artist, and lyrics, the subject of a song is more difficult to capture. The agent (human or mechanical) needs to comprehend and interpret the lyrics to determine what a song is about. For this reason, enriching a large-scale music digital library (MDL) with additional subject metadata calls for automatic techniques that can efficiently and effectively identify the topics of songs.

Several researchers have attempted to extract subject information from lyrics using both supervised and unsupervised algorithms. For example, Mahedero et al. [3] introduced a naïve Bayes classifier to predict the topic of songs based on lyrics. The algorithm performed well in experiments with 125 songs and five subjects, including "Love", "Violent", "Protest", "Christian", and "Drugs". Similarly, Kleedorfer et al. [4] proposed an automatic subject indexing system that analyzed lyrics using Non-negative Matrix Factorization (NMF), a topic modeling algorithm. Human evaluation of the automatically assigned topics suggests that these unsupervised methods can produce a reasonable number of "good" topics. In addition, Sasaki et al. [5] presented an interface that allows users to navigate music based on topics extracted from lyrics using Latent Dirichlet Allocation (LDA).

While lyrics generally produced positive results, the poetic nature of lyrics can make it difficult for a machine to understand their meaning [6]. Like poetry and some fiction, lyric often use nuanced and deliberately ambiguous language. An auxiliary dataset with elaborated interpretations or explanations of the lyrics may help improve the performance of the automatic systems. In our prior work [6], we demonstrated that interpretations of lyrics are more useful than lyrics themselves when automatically classifying music subjects using supervised methods. In this paper, we shift our focus from supervised methods to an unsupervised algorithm functioning as an automatic music subject discovery system. In the proposed system, a collection of web-mined interpretations of lyrics is used to first identify candidate topics. These topics are then systematically filtered to better represent the subjects of the song lyrics. We propose using prior

JCDL'15, June 21-25, 2015, Knoxville, Tennessee, USA.

ACM 978-1-4503-3594-2/15/06...$15.00
DOI: http://dx.doi.org/10.1145/2756406.2756936

topic weights and intrinsic topic coherence measurements for this filtering process.

2. THE DATA AND POSSIBLE ISSUES

2.1 Collection

We collected interpretations of lyrics from `songmeanings.com`, where music listeners share and discuss their understanding of lyrics by posting comments about millions of songs. For the experiment, we used songs that appear in both `songmeanings.com` and the Million Song Dataset (MSD)[1], a freely available music collection with a variety of useful audio features and metadata. Of the 58,649 overlapping songs in both collections, we selected 24,436 songs with at least five user interpretations to have sufficient text for our analysis.

In order to conduct an external evaluation of the automatically identified topics, we set aside 422 songs from the test collection with subject labels available from `songfacts.com`. `Songfacts.com` is a website that provides users with a number of browsing options such as subject categories annotated by music experts. From the complete set of 136 subject categories, we selected the six most popular subjects including "war", "parents", "religion", "sex", "drugs", and "heartache". This is consistent with other work [3] in automatic subject identification in music.

2.2 Issues of Lyric Interpretations

Although interpretations often contain subject information, they also contain other types of information that are not useful for browsing music in digital libraries. Examples include general music-related terms, user sentiment, and artist names.

From the preliminary results of topic modeling, we observed several groups of topics that consist of these types of collection-specific terms:

- **General terms**: topics formed around nouns and verbs that universally appear in lyrics interpretations, e.g. *song*, *lyric*, *comment*, *sing*, *music*, *interpret*, *mean*, *understand*, etc.
- **Personal taste/sentiment**: some topics made up of words that express interpreters' personal taste/preference rather than the subject of songs, such as *amaze*, *favorite*, *love*, *awesome*, etc.
- **Music-related terms**: topics mainly related with certain music-related terms, e.g., *play*, *cd*, *rock*, *verse*, etc.
- **Proper nouns**: these topics are composed of names of artists or bands, such as *Bob Dylan*, *Kurt Cobain*, *Oasis*, and *Pearl Jam*.

Some of these issues can be addressed during preprocessing. For example, personal and band names can be identified and removed using standard named-entity recognition techniques. In addition, terms with high document frequencies (DF) can also be handled by establishing a set of corpus-specific stopwords, such as "*lyric*" or "*song*". However, the DF threshold should be chosen carefully, as some important and frequently used subject-related terms might be accidently discarded.

In this work, we address the remaining problems of identifying irrelevant topics in a systematic way. We propose a topic selection technique based on prior topic weights and topic coherence measures, discussed further in section 4.3. We believe that interpretations of poetry and fiction (e.g., novels, short stories) have similar characteristics. While we are limiting ourselves to the lyric case here, we hope to investigate poetry and fiction in future work.

3. METHODS

3.1 Topic Modeling

Topic modeling has been widely used to discover latent topics in document collections [7][8][9]. Since our goal is to learn the underlying subjects of lyric interpretations, topic modeling algorithms are well-suited for this work. In general, topic modeling algorithms learn two probability distributions: one over the occurrences of words in each topic, and the other over the contribution of topics to each document. The latter topic distribution allows each document to belong to multiple topics with different probabilities. For the subjects of songs, this is more realistic than clustering techniques that allow only one latent component per item. Latent Dirichlet allocation (LDA) is a powerful generative model that further assumes *a priori* Dirichlet distributions for both the word and topic distributions [7]. In particular, in this work we focus on the latter prior for the topic distribution, which we utilize to judge the popularity of a given topic. Specifically, the Dirichlet parameter, or the prior topic weight, is a vector with elements corresponding to the topics, which tells us the global probability of drawing the multinomial topic distribution. Hence, it eventually determines the contribution of topics to documents: topics with smaller values are rarer in the collection, while at the other extreme can be said to be very popular topics that appear in almost all the documents.

3.2 Evaluation of Topic Modeling

There are two categories of evaluation techniques for topic modeling: intrinsic and extrinsic methods [8]. In this work we use both to measure the quality of the identified topics.

First, we use Pointwise Mutual Information (PMI) as an intrinsic method, as proposed by Newman et al. [8]. Unlike other intrinsic measures, such as perplexity, PMI has been found to be highly correlated with human assessment of topic coherence. This is useful when identifying topics intended for browsing in digital libraries. Newman et al. calculate the PMI of pairs of terms in LDA topic models based on their co-occurrence in Wikipedia.

In this study, we use Normalized PMI (NPMI) as implemented in the Palmetto online tool [9]. NPMI-produced values are bounded between -1 and 1 resulting from the normalization factor, $-\log p(w_i, w_j)$:

$$\mathrm{NPMI}(w_i, w_j) = \frac{\log \frac{p(w_i, w_j)}{p(w_i)p(w_j)}}{-\log p(w_i, w_j)}$$

An NPMI of -1 means the terms never occur together, 0 means independence, and 1 means the terms always occur together. Following Newman et al., we calculate the average NPMI for the top ten terms in each topic and use this as a proxy for topic coherence.

4. EXPERIMENTS

4.1 LDA Implementation

For learning topics, we use the LDA implementation in the MALLET machine learning toolkit [10]. In order to reflect the fact that some topics are more prominent than others in the collection, we conduct hyperparameter optimization. This is also known to result in generating better topics. For this experiment, we selected k=100 topics, as this is closely associated to the

[1] We focus on the common songs in both collections, because we need the metadata in MSD in future work.

number of subject categories on songfacts.com. Both intrinsic and extrinsic evaluations were performed on the resulting topics.

4.2 Preprocessing

Of the 58,649 songs with records in both songmeanings.com and MSD, only songs with five or more interpretations were used, to ensure sufficient text for topic modeling. This resulted in a collection of 24,437 songs. Only the words consisting of alphabetic letters were considered in order to filter user IDs. General stopwords[2] such as function words were eliminated to increase the quality of learned topics. In addition, terms that appear in more than 40% of the interpretations were also removed. For lemmatization, we used Morphadorner[3], which is also used by Palmetto [9]. In order to remove proper nouns, we used the named-entity recognizer unit in Morphadorner. After preprocessing, a total of 168,846 terms were left.

4.3 Intrinsic Evaluation

To assess the coherence of topics, we calculated the average NPMI of the top ten terms in each topic. As shown in Figure 1, the NPMI values range from -0.19 to 0.26 (mean= 0.07, sd=0.08). Of the 100 LDA topics, 83 have positive NPMI values, suggesting that topics are generally composed of words that are not independent. However, the NPMI values alone are not sufficient for assessing topic quality for use in automatic subject labeling.

In Figure 1, the probability of a topic in the collection is plotted against the associated topic NPMI values, sorted in descending order. A polynomial regression of the NPMI values is also plotted. From this graph, we can see that topics with very high or low probabilities in the collection also have lower NPMI values.

A sample of 12 topics with high (H), medium (M) and low (L) prior topic weights (Dirichlet parameter) are presented in Table 1, along with the associated NPMI values and the top ten topic terms. Topics with higher NPMI values are generally strongly related to potential song subjects. For example, topic M4 (NPMI: 0.24) is clearly about religion or Christianity. However, some topics are clearly outliers. For example, L3 (NPMI: 0.27) is not a subject, but a collection of Spanish terms. Topics with low NPMI values are difficult to associate with a particular subject. In general, they also have lower prior topic weights, such as L2 (NPMI=-0.19).

Most of the topics with very high prior topic weights consist of corpus-specific terms that were described in Section 2.2. The fact that they co-occur more frequently in the collection than the whole Wikipedia may be the reason for their lower NPMI values. Most of the topics with low prior topic weights tend to also have low NPMI values. The three points on the far right side of Figure 1 have very high NPMI values and low prior topic weights. Each of these topics contains non-English words in Spanish, German and French.

In the next section, we demonstrate how the LDA topic probabilities and topic NPMI values can be used to improve subject label quality in an extrinsic evaluation.

4.4 Extrinsic Evaluation

The goal of this evaluation was to determine the effect of different filtering options on the correlation of topics with the ground-truth labels from songfacts.com.

For extrinsic evaluation of the LDA topics, we constructed a ground-truth test set based on songs found in songfacts.com. The resulting collection consists of 422 songs manually labeled with the six most popular subjects. Subjects include "Heartache", "Sex", "Parents", "Religion", "Drugs", and "War". Although the number of songs is not large enough to completely evaluate the quality of all topics, we believe it is sufficient to evaluate topics associated with these six popular subjects.

Instead of manually mapping LDA topics to songfacts.com subjects, we used a majority-voting approach. For each song, we extracted the top three LDA topics. Each songfacts.com category was then mapped to the top-occurring LDA topic based on frequency.

Four different topic-filtering strategies were evaluated based on combinations of NPMI and prior topic weights. First, under the baseline condition all topics were used. In the second case, to filter topics that occur too frequently or infrequently in the collection, only those topics with a collection probability between 0.05 and 0.40 were considered. In the third case, only topics with an NPMI greater than 0.05 were considered. In the fourth and final case, only topics with both a collection probability between 0.05 and 0.40 and NPMI greater than 0.05 are considered.

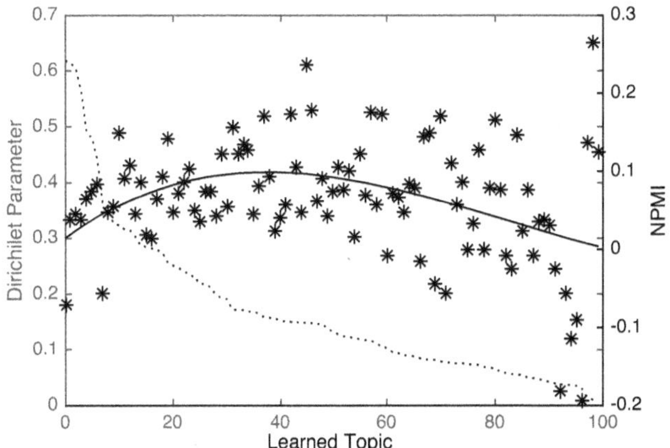

Figure 1. Prior topic weights (Dirichlet parameter) and NPMI values of LDA topics (k=100).

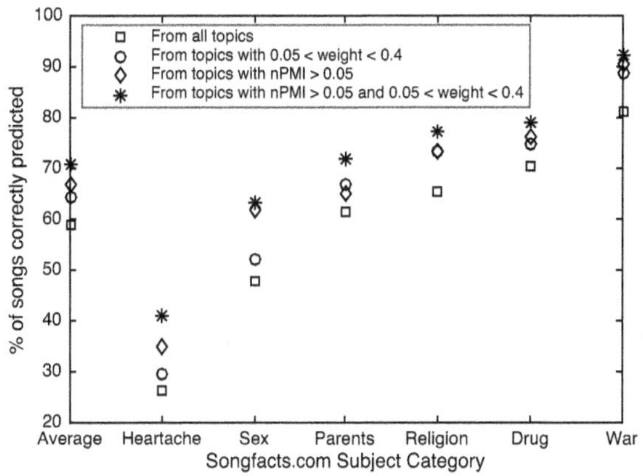

Figure 2. Extrinsic evaluation results (when we assume that top three topics are all equally important).

[2] https://code.google.com/p/stop-words/

[3] http://morphadorner.northwestern.edu/

Table 1. Selected topics from 100 learned topics

Selected Topics	Topic ID	Topic weight	NPMI	Top Words (Top 10)
High Weight	H1	0.62	*-0.07*	awesome, yeah, cd, relate, kinda, lol, total, lot, rock, play
	H2	0.61	0.04	reference, refer, sense, verse, idea, obvious, probable, kind, lot, bit
	H3	0.60	0.05	interpretation, narrator, verse, experience, place, literal, sense, point, speaker, fact
Medium Weight	M1	0.32	0.06	relationship, break, feeling, work, long, leave, girl, hurt, situation, stay
	M2	0.17	0.16	child, father, mother, parent, family, son, dad, brother, daughter, kid
	M3	0.15	0.11	sex, sexual, girl, prostitute, lust, woman, dirty, sexy, whore, desire
	M4	0.15	0.24	god, christian, religion, faith, religious, church, belief, bible, christianity, jesus
	M5	0.13	0.11	drug, addiction, heroin, high, addict, smoke, cocaine, reference, refer, coke
	M6	0.12	0.10	war, fight, soldier, bush, bomb, country, battle, kill, army, military
Low Weight	L1	0.04	*-0.09*	green, river, rise, weezer, edge, lucky, pie, bye, buy, stuff
	L2	0.03	*-0.19*	la, ghost, holly, deaf, vulture, ear, bebot, yeah, gorillaz, bounce
	L3	0.01	0.27	la, spanish, el, en, lo, se, es, mi, una, por

Figure 2 presents the percentage of songs correctly assigned to each of the six popular `songfacts.com` subject categories. The average percentage of correctly labeled songs without filtering is 59%. This increases to 71% with filtering based on a combination of NPMI and prior topic weights. This result suggests both prior topic weights and NPMI are useful criteria when assigning subjects to songs.

In one example, the dominant topic for the category 'Heartache' before filtering is topic H1 (awesome, yeah, cd...). After filtering, the primary topic for category "Heartache" is M1 (relationship, break, feeling...), which is semantically closer to the subject. For the remaining four subject categories, the dominant topic remains the same with or without filtering. "Parents" is mapped to topic M2 (child, father, mother...); "Sex" to M3 (sex, sexual, girl...); "Religion" to M4 (god, Christian, religion...); "Drugs" to M5 (drug, addiction, heroin...) and "War" to M6 (war, fight, soldier...). In all cases, the primary/dominant LDA topics include words that are semantically related to the ground-truth label and also have higher NPMI scores.

These results suggest that the proposed system is effective for detecting song subjects. In addition, the higher average accuracy when either filtering criteria were applied indicates that both criteria are useful for improving subject quality.

5. CONCLUSION

Because lyric terms are so ambiguous, we have presented a method for automatic identification of song subjects based on topic modeling of users' interpretations. We presented techniques for filtering LDA topics using topic coherence values and prior topic weights, and demonstrated how these can be applied to improve the quality of assigned subjects. Intrinsic evaluation using a topic coherence measure has been performed to automate the topic quality assessment process. Extrinsic evaluation using a small ground-truth dataset suggests that this system is effective for automatic subject analysis for possible subject access in MDL. In the future, we plan to expand this work to explore supervised topic modeling using an expanded ground-truth dataset. We also hope to find interpretation sources for poetry and fiction to explore our intuition about providing similar automatically created subject access in digital libraries consisting of these materials.

6. ACKNOWLEDGMENTS

We thank The Andrew Mellon Foundation for their financial support.

7. REFERENCES

[1] D. Bainbridge, S. J. Cunningham, and J. S. Downie, "How people describe their music information needs: A grounded theory analysis of music queries," *In Proc. of 4th Int. Soc. for Music Inform. Retrieval Conf.*, 2003, 221-222.

[2] J. H. Lee and J. S. Downie, "Survey Of Music Information Needs, Uses, And Seeking Behaviors: Preliminary Findings," In *Proc. of 5th Int. Soc. for Music Inform. Retrieval Conf.*, Barcelona, Spain, Oct. 2004, 441–446.

[3] J. P. Mahedero, Á. MartÍnez, and P. Cano, "Natural language processing of lyrics," In *Proc. of the 13th annual ACM Int. Conf. on Multimedia*, Singapore, Nov. 2005, 475-478.

[4] F. Kleedorfer, P. Knees, and T. Pohle, "Oh Oh Oh Whoah! Towards Automatic Topic Detection in Song Lyrics," *In Proc. of 9th Int. Soc. for Music Inform. Retrieval Conf.*, Philadelphia, PA, Sep. 2008, 287-292.

[5] S. Sasaki, K. Yoshii, T. Nakano, M. Goto, and S. Morishima, "LyricRadar: A Lyrics Retrieval System Based on Latent Topics of Lyrics," *In Proc. of 15th Int. Soc. for Music Inform. Retrieval Conf.*, Taipei, Taiwan, Oct. 2014, 585-590.

[6] K. Choi, J. H. Lee, and J. S. Downie, "What is this song about anyway?: Automatic classification of subject using user interpretations and lyrics," *In Proc. of the ACM/IEEE Joint Conf. on Digital Libraries*, 2014, 453-454.

[7] D. M. Blei, A. Y. Ng, and M. I. Jordan, "Latent Dirichlet Allocation," *The Journal of Machine Learning Research*, vol. *3*, 993-1022, 2003

[8] D. Newman, J. H. Lau, K. Grieser, and T. Baldwin, "Automatic evaluation of topic coherence," *In Proc. of Human Language Technologies (NAACL-HLT 2010)*, LA, CA, June, 2010, 100-108.

[9] M. Röder, A. Both, and A. Hinneburg, "Exploring the Space of Topic Coherence Measure," *In Proc. of the 8th ACM Int. Conf. on Web Search and Data Mining*, 2015.

[10] A. K. McCallum, "MALLET: A Machine Learning for Language Toolkit." http://mallet.cs.umass.edu. 2002.

Towards a Distributed Digital Library for Sign Language Content

Frank Shipman, Ricardo Gutierrez-Osuna, Tamra Shipman, Caio D. D. Monteiro, Virendra Karappa
Department of Computer Science and Engineering
Texas A&M University
College Station, TX 77843-3112
1-979-862-3216
shipman@cse.tamu.edu

ABSTRACT

The Internet provides access to content in almost all languages through a combination of crawling, indexing, and ranking capabilities. The ability to locate content on almost any topic has become expected for most users. But it is not the case for those whose primary language is a sign language. Members of this community communicate via the Internet, but they pass around links to videos via email and social media. In this paper, we describe the need for, the architecture of, and initial software components of a distributed digital library of sign language content, called SLaDL. Our initial efforts have been to develop a model of collection development that enables community involvement without assuming it. This goal necessitated the development of video processing techniques that automatically detect sign language content in video.

Categories and Subject Descriptors

H.3.7 [**Information Storage and Retrieval**]: Digital Libraries – *collection, dissemination, systems issues, user issues.*

General Terms

Algorithms, Design, Experimentation, Human Factors.

Keywords

Sign language digital library; sign language detection; digital library architecture; distributed digital library collection.

1. INTRODUCTION

General purpose and specialized digital library search engines allow Internet users to search for content on most any topic. In many cases, users can select among search engines and libraries to match their primary language. But languages that do not have a written form, including sign languages, are not well supported by the existing infrastructure.

Sign languages evolved in part independently of written language and thus do not have a one-to-one mapping to any written form [14]. For example, American Sign Language (ASL) is independent from British Sign Language (BSL) and both have a different grammar and syntax than written/spoken English. Sign languages are the primary language for many in the Deaf community, particularly for those who become deaf early in life. Those who grow up with sign language as a primary language learn English (or another written language) as a second language. A study of deaf and hard-of-hearing 17-18 year olds shows that half of the population had a lower than beginning of fourth grade reading level [5]. Thus, for a large portion of the sign language community, access to content in a written language is not a substitute for access to sign language content.

The ease of recording and sharing videos has resulted in a large quantity of sign language content being available on video sharing sites, such as YouTube. But this content is most often accessed via ad-hoc mechanisms, such as people sharing URLs to videos via email and social media. Searching for content is limited to the capabilities provided by the video sharing sites, which relies on the quality of metadata and tags. As a result, locating sign language content on a particular topic is not easy.

The next section of this paper illustrates the difficulty of locating sign language videos on particular topics. We then discuss related work and present an architecture/framework for building SLaDL, a distributed digital library for sign language content. Next, we describe the initial design and evaluation of components of the architecture. We conclude with a summary of our status and a plan of work yet to be done.

2. QUANTIFYING THE PROBLEM

A more precise understanding of sign language videos (SL videos) is valuable before discussing their location. We consider a SL video one where most content in the video can be understood through sign language. These are the videos that are of value to the sign language community. Videos of one or more signers presenting to the camera or having conversations, and videos with a sign language interpreter in picture-in-picture are the most common forms. Videos that include sign language incidentally, such as a spoken-language news report that includes a brief bit of ASL, are not useful to the community and thus not our target.

Accessing content on a particular topic is a common activity on the Internet. From personal experience (the third author's primary language is ASL) we know that there is considerable sign language content passed around from person to person but there is no "go to" place for finding ASL content on particular topics. Indeed, most do not even try to locate such content. But why?

To help answer this question we previously conducted a study to quantify how hard is it to locate content in ASL for particular topics on YouTube [13]. The topics were chosen as the top 10 news queries for 2011 from Yahoo! [12]. To locate content on

JCDL'15, June 21–25, 2015, Knoxville, Tennessee, USA.
Copyright 2015 ACM. ISBN 978-1-4503-3594-2/15/06…$15.00
DOI: http://dx.doi.org/10.1145/2756406.2756945

these topics in ASL, we generated queries that included the string phrase for the topic, e.g. "Arizona shooting" or "Arab spring", and added the query terms ASL, "sign language", or both.

Table 1. Number and percent of results in/not in sign language and on/off topic when ASL and "sign language" are included to locate content on top ten 2011 news queries on Yahoo!

	In SL	Not in SL	Total
On Topic	50 (46%)	27 (25%)	77 (70%)
Not on Topic	24 (22%)	9 (8%)	33 (30%)
Total	74 (67%)	36 (33%)	110 (100%)

The top 20 results were coded by hand to determine if they were on topic *and* in ASL. The best performance (precision=46%) was achieved when both terms (ASL and "sign language") were added to the query; see Table 1. The remaining videos returned were nearly evenly divided among videos not in sign language and videos not on topic; in total, 33% of the videos returned were not in sign language. When either term (but not both) was included, the proportion of videos not in sign language increased to 46%.

A larger, follow-up study [6] on 100 more varied and less time-limited topics (e.g. topics were the top 10 queries in 10 different categories, including topics like food, health, etc. instead of just news topics) found a lower precision (13% instead of 46%) but only 21% not in sign language; see Table 2. Though differences in topics and the availability of content in those topics are largely responsible for the difference in results, it is also possible that changes to the YouTube ranking algorithm played a role.

Table 2. Number and percent of results in/not in sign language and on/off topic when both terms (ASL and "sign language") are included in the query along with one of 100 topics.

	In SL	Not in SL	Total
On Topic	203 (13%)	38 (3%)	241 (16%)
Not on Topic	998 (66%)	279 (18%)	1277 (84%)
Total	1201 (79%)	317 (21%)	1518 (100%)

Why is the precision so low? Examination of the videos uncovers limitations of using text-based queries for locating SL videos. In particular, query terms are inherently ambiguous so the phrase "sign language" returns videos (1) in sign language, (2) about sign language, and (3) about the language used in signs, e.g., protest signs. An additional issue is the quality of the metadata used to match the query terms; text-based metadata can be idiosyncratic in video sharing and other social media sites [4][10].

The above results indicate that supporting access to sign language content from popular video sharing sites requires the development of specialized tools. Our work to date [11][7][13][6] has focused on developing video processing techniques for that purpose.

3. ARCHITECTURE

Creating a sign language digital library shares technical challenges with prior work on video digital libraries. Our focus is not on storage infrastructure and playback interfaces (capabilities that are already provided by video sharing sites) but on extracting metadata related to the language(s) used in the video. Thus, our research is more closely related to prior work on web services that support the location of video content. Among these it is worth noting TalkMiner [1], a webcast search engine that provides an alternative interface for accessing lecture videos hosted on other sites. TalkMiner includes a component for downloading video lectures from other sites, a component to generate new metadata and segment the videos, and an interface/portal with unique visualizations where users can go to locate video lectures and segments.

A challenge for SLaDL is that SL videos are hard to locate since most are uploaded with minimal metadata – as noted, the current practice among members of the SL community is to share the URL via email or social media. Thus, SLaDL needs a robust approach for locating videos to be included in the corpus. Figure 1 shows the current SLaDL architecture, which acknowledges this collection-building challenge.

In this model, content is added to SLaDL via two paths, one via human/community classification and the other via automatic classification. Both paths begin with the identification of a set of potential SL videos. These are identified by the crawler, either through the addition of query terms to the user's query request, resulting in queries much like described in Section 2, or by relationships to known SL videos (e.g. being in same YouTube channel, posted by same user, in same list of videos, etc.)

Community involvement in the creation of digital library collections is a common practice [8][3]. This path involves members of the community (1) providing the locations of SL videos (e.g. ones they have uploaded to video sharing sites), (2) identifying videos where there is evidence that they may include sign language content, and (3) voting them in/out of the library. Such a path involves a number of social issues that are not our current focus, and will not be discussed further.

The second path to building the collection is through automatic classification. This path involves a multistage process whereby potential SL videos are crawled from video sharing sites. The crawler currently uses hand-authored queries to the YouTube query interface, though future versions may exploit information such as YouTube channels, video lists co-occurrence, co-viewing statistics, etc. The important aspect of the crawler is that it creates a manageable set of videos for further processing.

Once there is a local cache of potential SL videos, a specialized classifier is used to detect sign language in these videos. This

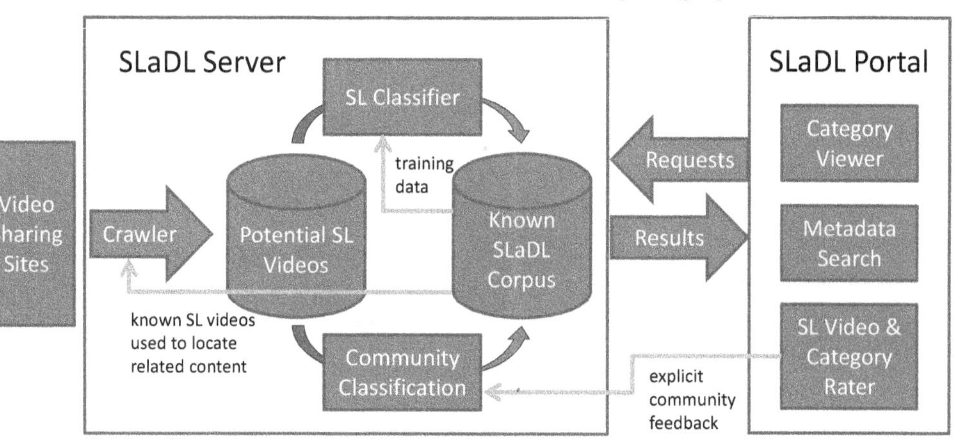

Figure 1. Architecture of the Sign Language Digital Library (SLaDL).

classification problem has been the focus of much of our activity to date and is discussed in depth in the next section.

The architecture includes feedback paths to improve the crawler and sign language classification techniques. As the known SLaDL corpus grows, the set of videos that are brought into the cache of potential SL videos will change (due to their relations to known SL videos) and the SL classifiers, which rely on machine learning techniques, will be retrained with the expanded corpus.

The SLaDL portal (see Figure 2) provides an interface for the sign language community to access and modify the collection. At present, the portal includes a category viewer to browse the collection via multiple perspectives, and a view by topic, much like the categories found in news aggregators (e.g. Google News). In coming work, metadata filters are being added to tailor views to individual users. For example, items in the collection may be filtered based on the sign language used in the video. While we cannot automatically assign the particular sign language, such metadata can be added by members of the community, or can be predicted from user comments and metadata.

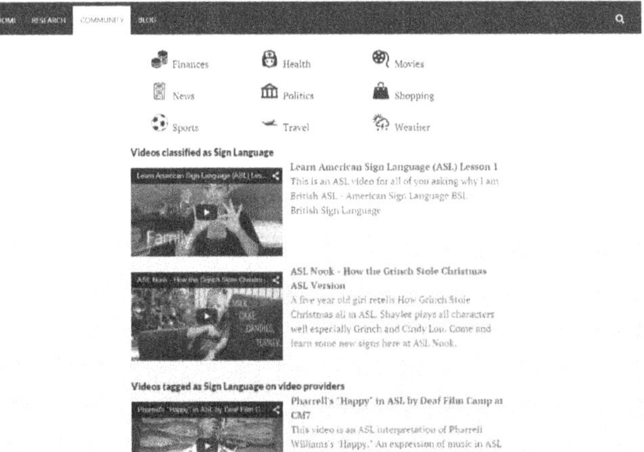

Figure 2. The SLaDL portal enables collection browsing, search, and community feedback on presented videos.

Our architecture also allows a path for mitigating the issues concerned with the initial lack of content on many topics. When users search for content on a topic, two sets of results are generated. The first set is the result of the query being compared to the videos within the known SLaDL corpus. The second set of results is generated from the list of potential SL videos (see Figure 1); these results are provided separately. In addition, the user's query may cause new requests to go to the video sharing services that add new videos to the set of potential SL videos. This happens when there are too few matching results in the potential SL video cache. In this way, expression of interest from the community helps drive the content being examined for inclusion in SLaDL by automated and/or human means.

Overall, the SLaDL architecture addresses the difficulty of locating SL videos. As with prior distributed video digital libraries, we do not store video content but only information about categories and topics that have been identified by the community and our algorithms.

4. DETECTING SIGN LANGUAGE VIDEO

Sign language is a fairly obvious activity to those around signers, since the combination of temporal structure, trajectories, velocities, hand shapes, and facial cues is hard to mistake. This observation led us to develop algorithms for the automatic detection of sign language as one path to create the SLaDL collection. While there has been prior work in identifying pauses in signing to improve bandwidth utilization [2], no prior work exists on the problem of distinguishing between videos containing sign language vs. other human gestures. The problem shares similarities with prior research on activity detection in video, in that developing a sign language detector involves selecting video or metadata features as inputs for a pattern classifier – a support vector machine (SVM) in our case.

Our video features are motivated by the fact that sign language generally happens in a region from slightly above the head (top) to the middle of the torso (bottom) and in front of or slightly to the side of the body (left/right). Our first approach [11] to characterizing activity in this region was based on this observation. The approach is illustrated in Figure 3. First, a face detector from openFrameworks [9] is used to locate people. If no faces are detected, it is unlikely that the video will have sign language content, and the process is terminated. Once at least one face is detected (Fig 3a), a dynamic background model is generated (Fig. 3c) and then used to perform foreground-background segmentation (Fig. 3d). Next, a morphological filter for the resulting content is used to remove noise so that only the larger moving objects remain (Fig. 3b). In a final step, five video features are defined from the identified foreground motion: 1) total activity in video, 2) spread of activity across video frame, 3) speed of motion, 4) symmetry of motion relative to middle of the face, and 5) amount of non-facial movement. Details on these five features and the resulting *five feature classifier (5FC)* were reported elsewhere [11].

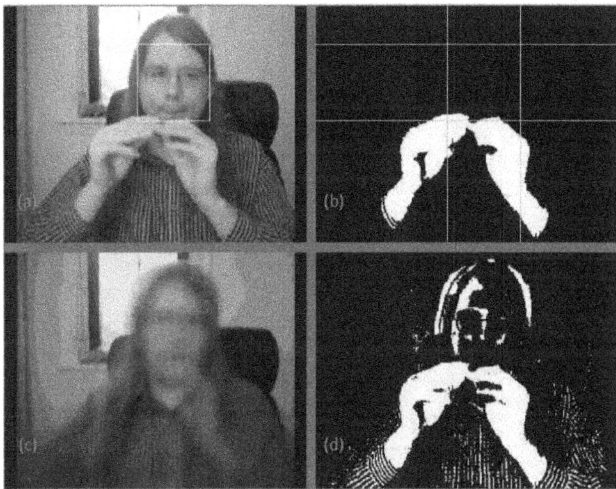

Figure 3. Identifying activity via (a) face detection in the video frame, (b) the final foreground image, (c) the computed background model and (d) the intermediate foreground image

The 5FC classifier was evaluated on a corpus containing 78 ASL, 20 BSL, and 94 likely false positive videos (e.g. elaborately gesturing reporters) with a single signer/speaker. Overall discrimination performance between SL and non-SL videos was 82% precision and 86% recall. Given the difficulty of the corpus (in practice, most YouTube videos are not of weathermen, mimes, etc.) the performance on a more representative set of videos would almost certainly be higher still. Further evaluation of the individual features showed that symmetry of motion was the most discriminatory feature. Examination of false negatives showed that many errors originate during face detection (e.g., the detector loses track of the face) rather than at the classification stage.

These initial results led us to develop a second sign language classifier. In this new approach, the face recognition module was improved by running multiple face detectors in parallel, each of which could recognize multiple faces in the video frame. A majority voting scheme was then used to determine which ones among all candidate faces would be included in the motion analysis stage. Because symmetry of motion had proven to be so valuable in the first evaluation, a *polar-motion profile (PMP)* was developed to characterize the distance and polar orientation of the motion from the center of the face [7]. Figure 4a shows the regions of interest generated for three signers, and the PMP (the probabilities for finding a foreground pixel at particular distance or orientation) for the rightmost signer. The peaks in the graphs indicate the position of the hands relative to the face.

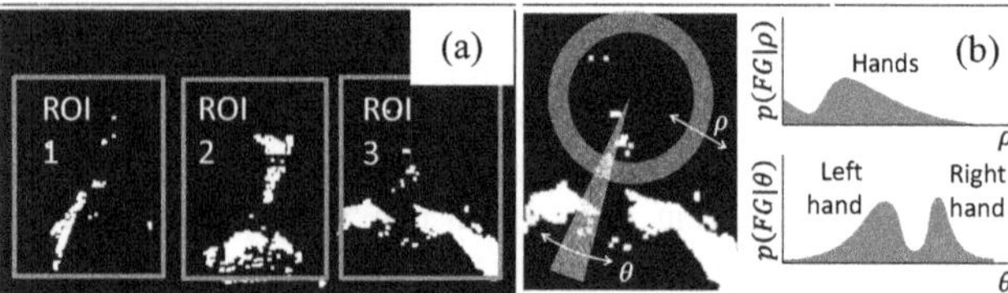

Figure 4. (a) Region of interests for the three signers in the frame. (b) PMPs for a video frame represent the probability of finding a foreground pixel.

To evaluate this second sign language classifier, a new dataset was collected that included videos with multiple signers, and also more complex backgrounds. This data set was selected based on an examination of the top 105 results from YouTube for the query "American Sign Language" and video recommendations from YouTube for these 105 results.

When applied to the original corpus, results on the PMP classifier were similar to those of the original 5FC classifier. With the second corpus, the precision of the classifiers were similar (81-82%) but the recall of the PMP classifier (94%) was significantly higher than that of the 5FC classifier (60%). This result is due to the PMP classifier's richer representation of motion, more robust face tracking, and the ability to track multiple signers.

Figure 5. Frames from videos with sign language captions.

In short, we have developed robust techniques to detect sign language in videos. But there are still classes of sign language content yet to be explored. We are currently working towards using the existing techniques to detect sign language captions, examples of which are seen in Figure 5, and segmentation of video based on the existence of sign language content.

5. DISCUSSION

Our development of a sign language library started with the goal of enabling topic-based access to the sign language content found in video sharing sites. We quantified the challenges of locating sign language content via text-based queries. Towards that goal of creating a sign language digital library, we have fashioned architecture based on the unique challenges of identifying sign language content and have developed and tested components of this architecture. A distinguishing feature of SLaDL is generating a collection through a combination of automatic classification and community feedback. While deployment and engagement are required to assess the community-feedback path, initial results from the video classifiers supports our plan to initially populate SLaDL automatically.

Topic-based access to content is very different from the term-based access provided by search engines. While there is considerable research into sign language translation, the current state of those efforts cannot be applied to the vocabulary, signing speed, context (e.g. moving backgrounds), or recording quality commonly found in shared sign language video. As a result, SLaDL focuses its video analysis efforts on detecting SL content and uses metadata analysis and community feedback when assessing finer topic-oriented distinctions.

6. REFERENCES

[1] J. Adcock, M. Cooper, L. Denoue, H. Pirsiavash, and L.A. Rowe, "TalkMiner: A lecture webcast search engine", *Proc. MM*, 2010, pp. 241-250.

[2] N. Cherniavsky, R.E. Ladner, and E.A. Riskin, "Activity detection in conversational sign language video for mobile telecommunication", *Proc. FG '08,* 2008, pp.1-6.

[3] E. Fox, et al. "Ensemble PDP-8: eight principles for distributed portals". *Proc. JCDL*, 2010, pp. 341-344.

[4] M. Heckner, T. Neubauer, and C. Wolff, "Tree, funny, to_read, google: What are tags supposed to achieve?", *Proc. of Workshop on Search in Social Media*, 2008, 3-10.

[5] J. Holt, C. Traxler, and T. Allen, *Interpreting the Scores: A User's Guide to the 9th Edition Stanford Achievement Test for Educators of Deaf and Hard-of-Hearing Students.* Gallaudet Research Institute Technical Report 97-1. Washington, DC: Gallaudet University, 1997.

[6] V. Karappa, *Detection of Sign-Language Content in Video through Polar Motion Profiles*, unpublished MS Thesis, Texas A&M University, 2014.

[7] V. Karappa, C. Monteiro, F. Shipman, and R. Gutierrez-Osuna, "Detection of sign-language content in video through polar motion profiles", *Proc. ICASSP*, 2014, pp. 1299-1303.

[8] M. Khoo, "Community design of DLESE's collections review policy: a technological frames analysis", *Proc. JCDL*, 2001, pp. 157-164.

[9] Z. Lieberman and T. Watson. openFrameworks. http://www.openframeworks.cc/ Accessed September 2011

[10] C. Marshall, "No Bull, No Spin: A comparison of tags with other forms of user metadata", *Proc. JCDL*, 2009, 241-250.

[11] C. Monteiro, R. Gutierrez-Osuna, F. Shipman. "Design and evaluation of classifier for identifying sign language videos in video sharing sites". *Proc. ASSETS*, 2012, 191-198.

[12] E. Osmeloski. *2011 Yahoo! In review: Top US searches in 30 categories.* http://searchengineland.com/2011-yahoo-in-review-top-us-searches-in-30-categories-103215.

[13] F. Shipman, R. Gutierrez-Osuna, and C. Monteiro, "Identifying sign language in video sharing sites", *ACM Trans. On Accessible Computing*, 2014, 9:1-9:14.

[14] C. Valli and C. Lucas, *Linguistics of American Sign Language: An Introduction*, Gallaudet University Press, Washington D.C., 2000.

Analyzing News Events in Non-Traditional Digital Library Collections

Martin Klein
University of California Los Angeles
Research Library
Los Angeles, CA, USA
martinklein@library.ucla.edu

Peter Broadwell
University of California Los Angeles
Research Library
Los Angeles, CA, USA
broadwell@library.ucla.edu

ABSTRACT

Digital libraries are called upon to organize, aggregate, and steward born-digital news collections. Rather than continuously building silos of such non-traditional collections, digital libraries are seeking to manage these collections in conjunction with each other in order to provide the most value to scholars. We here present the results of a preliminary study analyzing characteristics of items in two collections of digital news media: television broadcasts and social media coverage. Our findings indicate a number of factors that similar efforts will need to take into consideration when linking digital "news" collections similar to ours.

Categories and Subject Descriptors

H.3.7 [**Digital Libraries**]: Collection

1. INTRODUCTION

The role of memory organizations is increasingly defined by organizing, aggregating, and stewarding born-digital content. As such, many libraries and archives around the world are building digital collections from a plethora of independent sources, often diverse in format, disconnected, and of varying degrees of completeness. Digital libraries are now facing the task of making these "messy" collections as useful as possible to scholars. This is a challenging endeavor, and traditional analytical library tools may not be applicable to these novel types of collections. The collection of and custodianship over contemporary digital news content is a representative example of the issues entailed in the management of such non-traditional collections. The UCLA Library has assembled a wide variety of such non-traditional collections; in this paper, we focus on the following two:

NewsScape: Television news coverage of the events considered in our experiments was analyzed via the NewsScape, an online archive of news broadcasts recorded from cable and broadcast news networks in the United States as well as local television markets and international news sources [7]. The NewsScape represents an emergent type of multimedia archive that is becoming more prevalent due to advances in technologies for collecting, indexing, and presenting large amounts of multimedia data. As of this writing, the NewsScape stores and provides streaming access for research and instructional purposes to more than 244,000 hours of television news programs from 2005 to the present, recorded from 38 networks. The audio stream is indexed chronologically via its time-coded closed-caption texts, as well as official program transcriptions that are aligned with the caption texts. Words that appear on screen, such as in a story-related graphic or a rotating "news crawl" at the bottom of the screen, also are identified by the NewsScape's automatic optical character recognition tool and are tagged with their time of appearance as well as their location on screen. The more than 2.9 billion words thereby extracted from these programs are made searchable via an Apache Solr index, which is augmented with various official and computationally derived program-related metadata. Approximately 135 new recordings are added to the NewsScape each day.

Twitter capture: The UCLA library is establishing a framework to build collections of social media news coverage related to current world events. This social media capture effort currently focuses on Twitter data (tweets), but an expansion to portals such as YouTube and Flickr is planned for the near future. The social media collection framework is based on available open source tools such as Social Feed Manager (SFM) [2] and twarc [3] and provides enhancements to their functionality. For example, we have prototype implementations in place that provide archival functions to preserve embedded resources, as well as interactive real-time data visualization features.

Digital libraries have increasingly invested effort in avoiding the creation of "siloed" collections, so when building non-traditional news collections that are focused upon the same event, advanced analytical methods are required to help recognize, analyze, and (temporally) correlate different accounts of the event. In this paper, we address this challenge and provide evidence of how such analytical methods should work. We do not present mature solutions and do not showcase the required tools, but we do describe our preliminary findings which, given the nature of our two collections, concern a scenario that to the best of our knowledge has not been considered closely before. We provide a number of indicators of what similar efforts will need to take into consideration when linking news collections that have similar characteristics to those described here.

JCDL'15, June 21–25, 2015, Knoxville, Tennessee, USA.

ACM 978-1-4503-3594-2/15/06 ...$15.00.
http://dx.doi.org/10.1145/2756406.2756948 .

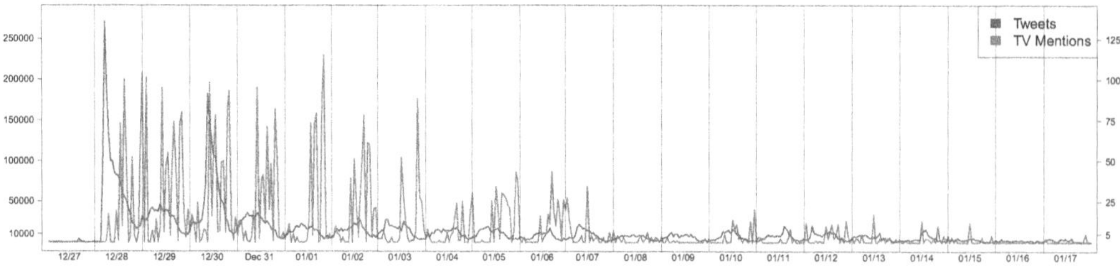

Figure 1: Frequency of tweets and television mentions

2. RELATED WORK

Previous comparisons of social media and traditional media have typically used online or digitized print sources as the representative form of the latter, largely because fully indexed, large-scale archives of audiovisual news media like the NewsScape were not available until very recently. These studies have noted, for example, that the topics discussed on Twitter generally tend to be more "entity-oriented" and those in print media more "event-oriented" [8]. Such findings are certainly of interest to digital librarians who wish to compile and cross-reference a broad spectrum of digital resources related to a particular subject. Yet television news (as well as radio and other audio-centered media) introduces a distinct set of considerations due to the challenges of indexing and characterizing time-based audiovisual content and the fact that television news coverage of events tends to unfold continuously in real-time, as is also true of the reactions to these events on Twitter and other forms of social media.

Earlier studies by students and faculty in the UCLA Digital Humanities program have investigated relationships between television news coverage as recorded in the NewsScape and social media sources, including Twitter and Reddit, focusing on events with significant coverage in both types of media, such as the April 15th, 2013 Boston Marathon bombing and the May 23rd, 2014 Isla Vista, CA killing spree [6]. These studies have found that social media and television news exhibit vastly divergent profiles in terms of the volume and topics of discussion over time. Television news coverage of a specific event tends to follow a sequential process of narrating, analyzing, and recounting the event, typically with the goal of concluding with recommendations for how similar events might be avoided in the future. Social media coverage sometimes displays a much larger range of emotional reactions, often serving as a medium for collective mourning as well as unsupported speculation and discussion of tangentially related topics. The present work expands upon such initial studies and focuses on the divergences between how social media and broadcast news respond to "news-worthy" events. With NewsScape, we now have a large-scale archive of audiovisual news media that enables us to investigate these variances and their implications for digital librarians in what, to the best of our knowledge, is an unprecedented manner and scale.

3. DATA GATHERING

We collected content about the AirAsia flight 8501 air disaster, beginning on December 27th 2014, the date of the initial disappearance of the flight. To analyze television coverage of the topic as recorded in the NewsScape, we used the archive's index to search through the time-coded metadata associated with each program for terms matching all or part of the keywords "AirAsia" and "QZ8501". This allowed us to find all news programs in which at least one of these terms appeared in the closed captioning or official transcript, indicating that it had been spoken on air, or was displayed graphically on screen and noted by the NewsScape's optical character recognition feature. We further inspected each match in the search results, associating it with the exact timecode when it was spoken or shown. We also recorded the terms immediately surrounding the matching term. We limited the surrounding terms to the closest 140 trailing and following characters, thereby approximating the length limit of a tweet and facilitating the experiments outlined below.

We used the prototype implementation of our framework based on SFM and twarc to collect social media data from Twitter. We used the same keywords for both social media collection tools as we did for NewsScape ("AirAsia" and "QZ8501") in order to obtain tweets related to the disaster. We collected a total of more than 7.3 million tweets sent from more than 1.3 million distinct Twitter users.

Both collections are temporally bound, starting on December 27th 2014 and ending on January 17th 2015. To enable convenient comparisons, all times recored from NewsScape and Twitter are in Greenwich Mean Time.

4. RESULTS

We analyze our collections from three different perspectives: we consider the timeline of events, analyze the content of the collections, and approach the notion of causality between items of both collections by investigating the sequentiality of terms that appear in one or both.

4.1 Time

Our first analysis concerns the frequency of reports about this event in the two collections over time. For the NewsScape collection, this frequency is determined by the number of times any of our keywords occur in the index over the observed period of time. For the Twitter collection, the frequency is simply the amount of tweets collected by our framework over the same period of time, given that all collected tweets contain at least one of our keywords. To display the frequency of reports over the 22-day period we considered (Dec 27th - Jan 17th) in a coherent manner, we aggregate events into hourly bins. Figure 1 displays the frequency lines for reports in both collections. The black vertical lines separate the plot into 22 days. The blue series represents all collected tweets and its values are given on the left y-axis. The red series, with values indicated by the right

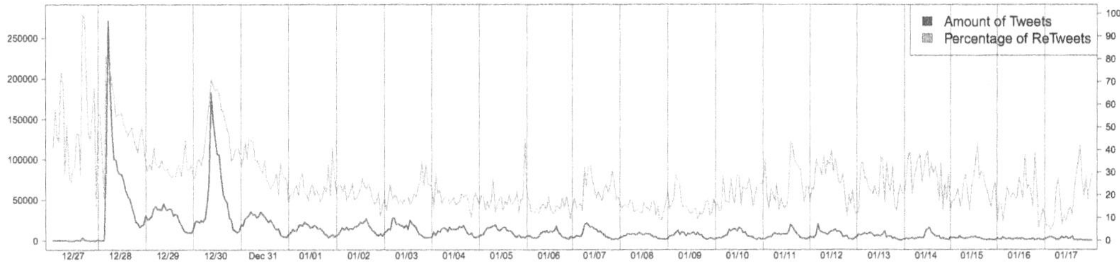

Figure 2: Frequency of total tweets and retweets

y-axis, shows all mentions or appearances of the terms on television. The Twitter series shows two significant spikes, one at 4am on December 28th (270,000 tweets) and the second on the morning of the 30th (180,000). Both spikes correlate to major events: the plane was officially declared missing at 3.41am on December 28th, and the first debris items resembling parts of a plane were spotted on December 30th. The frequency of tweets drops off after the 30th and, after a minor high point on the 31st (36,000 tweets at 4am), averages around 10,000 tweets per hour.

Interestingly, we can observe a clear delay in the television frequency series. This frequency does not increase until noon GMT on the 28th (73 mentions) and peaks around midnight (104). Unlike the frequency of tweets, the television coverage remains high throughout the 29th, likely catching up with events of the previous day, and it peaks again, together with the tweet frequency, in the morning of the 30th (98). The coverage level remains fairly high (around 70 mentions per hour) through January 3rd but then drops off late on the 7th and remains low for the rest of the observed time period. Some minor spikes can be seen on the 12th and 13th which likely correspond to the news of the flight recorders being located and recovered. The very small bump in the tweet frequency at 3pm on the 27th mirrors a significant increase in unrelated customer complaints as AirAsia had just announced the cancellation of direct flights from Melbourne to Bali, giving only one or two days' notice to customers who had purchased tickets [1].

As Figure 1 shows, the absolute numbers for occurrences of the search terms on television are much lower than the volume of tweets. The degree of "attention" paid to the story on television news (measured in matching search terms) is strongly influenced by the networks' set broadcasting schedules, which allocate a limited percentage of airtime to recent news stories, typically in the mornings and evenings, and only allow special coverage of breaking news in extreme situations. Figure 1 indicates that Twitter also is influenced by such daily patterns, though to a lesser degree. For these and other reasons, neither data set can be considered a "complete" record of reactions to the event, yet as with all other collections, it is the digital librarian's task to make it as useful to scholars as possible and, as indicated, each digital collection is more meaningful when considered in conjunction with the other, rather than singly.

4.2 Content

The total amount of tweets collected around this event (more than 7.3 million) is impressive, but our intuition tells us that this value does not translate to the same number of distinct news items. A big part of Twitter are "retweets" and

Twitter Rank	TV Rank	Term
5	162	QZ8501
31	907	prayers
34	785	thoughts
42	594	condolences
83	1,008	Reuters
154	33	CEO
291	44	questions
215	64	investigators
1,483	70	reporter
523	81	vanishes

Table 1: Terms that occur in both collections and their corresponding frequency rank

related studies [5] have indicated that users send retweets more frequently at the time of a major event. This prompted us to investigate the frequency of retweets in our collection, displayed in Figure 2. The blue series represents the tweet frequency (as seen in Figure 1) and the green series is the corresponding retweet ratio, with the percentages displayed on the right y-axis. We can observe very high retweet ratios during the spikes in event-related traffic on the 28th (80%) and 30th (71%). From the 30th onwards, the ratio is much lower and fluctuates between 10% and 40%. The high ratio on the 27th derives from other issues, namely complaints about flight cancellations and passenger rerouting.

With this information in mind, we turned to analyzing the terms that occur in both collections. Our question was whether there are terms more specific or more important to either of the collections. We discarded all non-English language tweets and applied a stop word filter before generating the list of terms that occur in both collections. The top five rows of Table 1 show examples of terms that occur rather frequently in tweets (high Twitter rank) but are mentioned much less frequently on television (lower TV rank). We observed two patterns here. First, there are terms that are more natural to the medium of Twitter than television, such as the exact flight number `QZ8501` (television news mostly referred to it as **`flight 8501`**) and references to journalistic information sources such as **`reuters`**. Secondly, we found many more emotional expressions in the Twitter collection, indicated by terms such as `prayers` and `thoughts`, compared to the TV collection. The bottom five rows show terms with the opposite frequency characteristics, i.e., they are mentioned often on television and less so in tweets. These terms are much less personal and perhaps more representative of investigative reporting, e.g., `questions` and `reporter`.

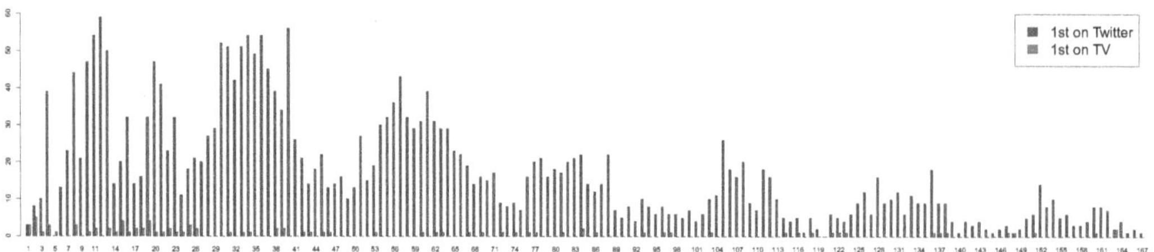

Figure 3: Sequentiality of terms in tweets and on television

4.3 Sequentiality

From the corpus of terms that occur in both collections we examined the sequence in which individual terms occur across the collections. This allows us to identify cases in which one collection introduces a term earlier than the other, and also to consider whether one of the two forms of media may have had an influence on the other. Figure 3 depicts the sequentiality of terms. The height of a blue bar represents the number of terms that occurred first on Twitter, and the height of a red bar stands for the number of terms first seen on television. The time delta is indicated on the x-axis in hours. Our first observation from Figure 3 is the dominance of blue bars, indicating that the vast majority of shared terms are mentioned on Twitter first. The first group of significant bars indicates an average delay between the appearance of a term on Twitter and on television of between 4 and 13 hours, which likely is due to the delay before television coverage of the event began, as seen in Figure 1. The terms here are those that tend to be used in the first television reports covering breaking news, e.g., `missing, breaking, officials, 155` (the number of passengers on board the plane). However, the figure also includes many terms with a Twitter-to-TV propagation delay of 30 to 40 and 55 and 65 hours. We can only hypothesize as to why these terms are mentioned so much later on television, but it is plausible that many tweets are more speculative in nature and hence contain terms such as `tale, sightings, chances` that foresee (rightly or wrongly) aspects of a story before it actually unfolds on television and in other media sources; other examples of such terms are `maintenance, routing, investigations`. Figure 3 indicates that very few terms were first mentioned on television, most of which are then mentioned on Twitter within 26 hours. The terms also tend to be of no particular significance to the news reporting, e.g., `Costello`, the name of a popular news anchor. Our results indicate that Twitter is a continuous and highly pro-active medium for commentary on breaking events, and therefore has a strong potential to affect the content of other media collections, particularly those that tend to be more conservative in their event coverage. An interesting example is the hashtag `#8501qs` which was not born on Twitter but coined by CNN. Their viewers were encouraged to send questions via Twitter by using this hashtag [4]. It has a television frequency rank of 203 but a tweet rank of only 2,716.

5. CONCLUSIONS

In this paper, we present results of our preliminary study analyzing news events in non-traditional collections. We consider two such collections, one from our online archive of television news broadcasts and the other obtained via our social media capture framework, both of which contain news coverage of a recent air disaster. Our investigation provides indicators that items of such collections can vary dramatically by frequency and content and even have the potential to influence other collections. For example, we observed a delay of at least eight hours in the television coverage of the news event compared to social media. Spikes in "attention" on Twitter seem to be correlated with real-world events, but the intensity drops quickly afterwards. Television coverage, on the other hand, tends to continue at a high level for a few days after a major event. Terms and concepts conveying human emotions seem more typical of social media and terms of a speculative nature occur on Twitter much sooner than they do on television. These indicators are relevant for librarians when making informed decisions in building such non-traditional collections.

6. REFERENCES

[1] Holidays thrown into chaos after AirAsia cancels direct Bali flights. `http://www.theage.com.au/victoria/holidays-thrown-into-chaos-after-airasia-cancels-direct-bali-flights-20141227-12eac5.html`.

[2] Social Feed Manager. `http://gwu-libraries.github.io/social-feed-manager/`.

[3] twarc. `https://github.com/edsu/twarc`.

[4] What happened to AirAsia Flight QZ8501: Your questions answered. `http://www.cnn.com/2014/12/29/world/asia/airasia-questions-answers/`.

[5] F. Chierichetti, J. Kleinberg, R. Kumar, M. Mahdian, and S. Pandey. Event detection via communication pattern analysis. In *Proceedings of ICWSM'14*, 2014.

[6] A. Pogany, A. Khan, J. Palau, M. Gawlick, S. Wong, and T. Gallati. Social Media Analytics: Twitter as Newsource during the Boston Marathon Bombings. `http://dx.doi.org/10.6084/m9.figshare.1298123`.

[7] F. Steen. The NewsScape Project: Understanding the Media through a Multimodal Perspective. Technical report, 2014. `https://idre.ucla.edu/featured/newsscape-project-understanding-media-through-multimodal-perspective`.

[8] W. Zhao, J. Jiang, J. Weng, J. He, E.-P. Lim, H. Yan, and X. Li. Comparing twitter and traditional media using topic models. In *Proceedings of ECIR'11*, pages 338–349, 2011.

Time will Tell: Temporal Linking of News Stories

Thomas Bögel
Institute of Computer Science
Heidelberg University, Germany
thomas.boegel@informatik.uni-heidelberg.de

Michael Gertz
Institute of Computer Science
Heidelberg University, Germany
gertz@informatik.uni-heidelberg.de

ABSTRACT

Readers of news articles are typically faced with the problem of getting a good understanding of a complex story covered in an article. However, as news articles mainly focus on current or recent events, they often do not provide sufficient information about the history of an event or topic, leaving the user alone in discovering and exploring other news articles that might be related to a given article. This is a time consuming and non-trivial task, and the only help provided by some news outlets is some list of related articles or a few links within an article itself. What further complicates this task is that many of today's news stories cover a wide range of topics and events even within a single article, thus leaving the realm of traditional approaches that track a single topic or event over time.

In this paper, we present a framework to link news articles based on temporal expressions that occur in the articles, following the idea "if an article refers to something in the past, then there should be an article about that something". Our approach aims to recover the chronology of one or more events and topics covered in an article, leading to an information network of articles that can be explored in a thematic and particular chronological fashion. For this, we propose a measure for the relatedness of articles that is primarily based on temporal expressions in articles but also exploits other information such as persons mentioned and keywords. We provide a comprehensive evaluation that demonstrates the functionality of our framework using a multi-source corpus of recent German news articles.

Categories and Subject Descriptors

H.4 [**Information Systems Applications**]: Miscellaneous; H.3.4 [**Information Storage and Retrieval**]: Systems and Software—*Information networks*; H.3.3 [**Information Storage and Retrieval**]: Information Search and Retrieval—*Information filtering*

JCDL'15, June 21–25, 2015, Knoxville, Tennessee, USA.

ACM 978-1-4503-3594-2/15/06 ...$15.00.
DOI: http://dx.doi.org/10.1145/2756406.2756919.

Keywords

Information networks; news networks; document similarity

1. INTRODUCTION

Many of today's news stories report on current events and topics that are complex in terms of the background the reader has to have to fully get a picture of the context of the story. Some news outlets, for select articles, provide links to related articles either within the news text itself or through an extra list of links, aiming to give the reader some more background information. However, such links often seem to be ad-hoc and do not follow any structure, such as a chronology. Take, for example, a news story that covers a recent meeting of the board of inquiry dealing with the NSA affair in Germany. Understanding statements made or actions decided by that board often require a good understanding of what happened in the past. Such historic information ideally should be covered as additional information in the article as well. In practice this is done, if at all, in a very short form and then mostly hinting to some event(s) in the past. More importantly, relevant historic information can be of diverse types and not only be related to a single topic. A good example for this is the pro-Russian unrest in the southern and eastern Ukraine with all its implications and precursors in the areas of politics and economy, to name but a few. A news article covering a recent development in that context can be related to many different topics, events, and previous stories. Getting a grasp of how it came to a recent event is difficult when only a single news article and, optionally, some ad-hoc links are provided.

Approaches that aim to recover a chain or thread of events for a news story typically focus on events within a single topic. Links to be discovered between news articles then have to be salient and coherent regarding that topic (see, e.g., [Feng and Allan, 2009, Shahaf and Guestrin, 2012]). Hierarchical topic models and document clustering approaches, e.g., [Nallapati et al., 2004], also only focus on single (composite) topics and are not able to relate individual articles that cover diverse types of events that belong to different topics. What becomes very clear for the two example stories mentioned above, however, is that a temporal ordering or a chronology of events play a crucial role in detecting link structures among news articles, an aspect mostly neglected in related approaches.

In this paper, we present a novel framework to extract links between news articles based on the "temporal relatedness" of articles. A key feature we build on for this are *temporal expressions* that occur in an article and, when normalized appropriately, hint to points in time where older articles (published at that date or timeframe) might give more details about what is being covered in the article. Especially the extraction and normalization of temporal expressions is something rarely employed in standard approaches for determining document similarity or relatedness. Our conjecture is that temporal expressions provide a good focus on what articles should be investigated regarding their relatedness to a given article, an aspect that holds in particular true for the mostly very dense style in which today's news articles are written.

We propose an approach to construct a directed *information network* of news articles from a multi-source, heterogeneous collection of news articles that capture a broad range of topics. The construction of the network, which can be performed in an iterative fashion, e.g., for a stream of news articles, is primarily based on exploiting temporal expressions, but subsequently also uses person names and keywords occurring in parts of news articles. Furthermore, instead of comparing articles in their entirety as done in traditional approaches for document or topic similarity, we exploit the structure of typical news articles (lead paragraph, explanatory paragraphs, and additional information paragraphs). A network of articles extracted that way provides an ideal tool for the exploration and analysis of articles related to a given article, allowing the user to chronologically explore links between articles.

Because of the typical network structure built from a collection of news articles, different measures known for networks can be employed to further support exploration tasks. These include aspects like centrality (hinting to articles often referenced latently through temporal expressions), connected components (chronologically sorted collections of related articles), and bibliographic coupling (hinting to duplicate articles from different news outlets). In our experimental evaluations based on a large corpus of news articles from different German news outlets, we demonstrate the functionality of the proposed framework. In particular, we show that temporal link structures indeed provide an effective means to organize and explore news articles in a chronological manner not offered by related approaches.

The remainder of the paper is structured as follows. After a review of related work in the following section, we present our model for news articles and the approach for linking articles in Section 3 and 4, respectively. In Section 5, we evaluate our system and demonstrate the functionality and utility of our framework using large collections of recent German news articles.

2. RELATED WORK

Linking news stories has been addressed from a variety of directions. Most approaches in this area tackle the problem from a viewpoint of topic detection and tracking based on various similarity metrics: [Allan, 2002] and [Nomoto, 2010], for instance, use tf-idf and language models for content words, while [Shahaf and Guestrin, 2012] determine important phrases. [Vaca et al., 2014] employ collective factorization to model the temporal evolution of news. All of these approaches compute pairwise document similarity without taking into account the thread structure of news or giving explicit background information for complex news stories.

Besides topic tracking, many approaches focus on events for document linking (e.g., [Brants et al., 2003, Kumaran and Allan, 2005, Zhu and Oates, 2012, Zhu and Oates, 2013]). This is problematic as the definition of event is vague and a story thread might consist of multiple events covering different topics. In addition, each distinct definition of event requires laborious manual annotations.

[Wang and Li, 2011] use geo-spatial information to tackle the huge amount of news stories by coarse-grained geo-spatial clustering. Geographical information in isolation might, however, not be informative enough to model the fine-grained temporal development of news stories. Creating news summaries [Yan et al., 2011] is another approach to bring structure into large document collections but – by definition – neglects detailed information about relationships between news stories. As illustrated in Section 5.5.2, creating a story thread for central articles yields both a summary of a complex news story and also a fine-grained analysis of the temporal progression of a story.

The systems described in [Nallapati et al., 2004] and [Gillenwater et al., 2012] are most similar to ours as they create a linked, threaded structure of news. [Shahaf and Guestrin, 2012] also explicitly take the link structure of news into account by using activation patterns across multiple documents for document linking. In contrast to them, we do not rely on the notion of topical salience but our network is based on temporal links prevalent in news articles to allow for a fine-grained analysis. We will show in our evaluation that salience and document similarity get less and less reliable for connecting complex stories spanning a larger time frame. [Shahaf et al., 2013] use the metaphor of metro maps for representing complex threads of stories and their relationships. While their system also tries to combat information overload by representing news in a graph-like structure, the precondition is different: our system operates on a collection of documents that cover different topics and thus might be relevant to each other or not, while their approach assumes a collection of documents for a specific user query (e.g., "Middle East"), thus pre-filtering articles and inducing structure on articles for which a certain relatedness is already known.

In addition, while there are coarse-grained multi-lingual systems (e.g., [Pouliquen et al., 2008]), to our knowledge, there is no previous system that explicitly provides a fine-grained analysis of German news texts.

3. DOCUMENT MODEL AND TIMELINES

We assume a given collection A of news articles. To apply our approach, the collection does not have to be static but new (recent) articles can be added over time. Each article $a \in A$ has a timestamp $a.ts$, a title $a.ti$, and an abstract $a.ab$. Furthermore, an article can have one or more blocks $\langle b_1, \ldots, b_n \rangle$, given in document order, where a block is a paragraph or section of the article.

Basis for our framework to link articles using temporal information are *timelines*, which can be of different granularities. The timeline of the finest granularity is of type *date*, denoted T_{date}. An element of this timeline would be a fully specified date, e.g., "2014-08-30". Coarser timelines are T_{month} (with elements such as "2014-05") and T_{year} (with elements such as "2013") and are employed as well. The document timestamp of each news article (i.e., the date when an article has been published) is anchored at T_{date}. Furthermore, with each date $t \in T_{date}$, a set of articles A_t can be associated, i.e., $A_t = \{a | a \in A, a.ts = t\}$.

We now turn to three types of functions we employ to extract information from articles that are later used in our article linkage model.

Temporal Information Extraction. Let $T = T_{date} \cup T_{month} \cup T_{year}$ be the domain of all normalized time elements of different granularities. Assume some text corresponding to the title, abstract or some block of an article. Then, the function $t : text \rightarrow 2^T$ returns a set of normalized time elements. A temporal tagger in combination with a normalization component is a realization of such a function, where the tagger discovers explicit, implicit, and relative temporal expressions in a text and maps them to a normalized, standard format (see, e.g., [Strötgen and Gertz, 2013]).

Person Names. A common task in Named-Entity Recognition is the detection of person mentions in a text and mapping respective expressions to normalized person names. Assume a set P of normalized person names. The function $p : text \rightarrow 2^P$ returns a set of person names that have been detected in a text.

Keywords. The third function we employ returns a set of keywords that occur in a text. In our approach, we consider nouns, adjectives, and verbs, all in their lemmatized form, as keywords. The function $k : text \rightarrow 2^W$ returns a set of keywords for a text, with W simply being some kind of dictionary of words.

4. ARTICLE LINKAGE MODEL

In this section, we present our model to link news articles based on temporal expressions occurring in articles. After giving the problem statement in the following Section 4.1, in Sections 4.2 and 4.3, we detail how links between pairs of articles are determined and how an information network of interlinked news articles is incrementally built. In Section 4.4, we then discuss typical properties of such an information network, tailored to news articles.

4.1 Problem Statement and Objective

Given an article $a \in A$ describing some news story, we want to determine those articles in the collection A that provide further information about what is being covered in a. While we are not looking for a story chain describing the evolution of a single event or topic over time, we are interested in what other (older) articles in A are related to a in the sense that these articles provide further information about what is being covered in article a. This notion thus subsumes a story line or chain of events. Although we do not make use of an explicit notion or representation of an event, the key assumptions underlying our framework are that (1) there is a temporal relationship between events and, more importantly, (2) such relationships are often made explicit in news articles through temporal references. That is, if an article refers to "something" in the past by means of a temporal expression, then there should be an article related to that "something". We make such relationships between articles explicit through weighted links that suitably take the different types of the information (latently) embedded in and extracted from news articles into account.

Given a corpus of news articles, through the above type of relationship a directed information network of interlinked articles is formed. For example, for a given (recent) article a directed acyclic graph can be built that shows how a (recent) story or event is related to previous events that are both "temporally related" and "relevant" with respect to the current article. How individual links are determined, and how eventually a network is built and explored will be discussed in the following.

4.2 Pairwise Article Linkage

Given an article a with its components $\langle a.ts, a.ti, a.ab, a.b_1, \ldots, a.b_n \rangle$. For the sake of explanation, we first only consider temporal expressions of type T_{date} that can be extracted from the abstract $a.ab$ and blocks $a.b_i$. Let $t(a) = t(a.ab) \cup t(b_1) \cup \ldots \cup t(b_n)$ denote all normalized date expression extracted from these $n+1$ components of the article a. For each date $t \in t(a)$, we determine the set of articles $A_t \subset A$ that have the timestamp t. We thus get a set of all articles that have a document timestamp corresponding to some temporal expression in article a. Note that not every component in a has to have a temporal expression, and the same (normalized) temporal expression can occur in more than one component. For each date $t \in t(a)$, one can consider A_t as a set of articles that are "temporally related" to the article a.

Given an article $a' \in A_t$ with timestamp t, we now determine whether also the content of a' is "relevant" to the article a, assuming that a' might provide some background information about what is covered in a as a' is already temporally related to a. For this, we do not compare the two full articles a and a' but their components as follows. For two text components c_1, c_2, the similarity is defined as follows:

$$sim(c_1, c_2) := \frac{1}{4}(\alpha_1(Jac(p_{c_1}, p_{c_2}) + Cos(p_{c_1}, p_{c_2})) + \alpha_2(Jac(k_{c_1}, k_{c_2}) + Cos(k_{c_1}, k_{c_2}))) \quad (1)$$

where p_{c_i} and k_{c_i} denote the set of persons names and keyword, respectively, extracted from text components c_i and c_j (see Section 3). Jac and Cos denote the Jaccard and Cosine similarity, respectively. We choose this formulation of a similarity measure because both metrics have successfully been used in previous work for story linking of English texts [Kumaran and Allan, 2005, Wang and Li, 2011]. We also employ a weighting of person and keyword similarity using the weights α_1 and α_2 with $\alpha_1 + \alpha_2 = 1$. This allows us to employ, e.g., a more person-centric similarity by choosing appropriate values for these weights.

To determine whether an article a' that is temporally related to an article a is also relavent from a content point of view, we introduce a measure for relevance as follows. Let $a.B_t = \{b_k, \ldots, b_l\}$ denote all components in article a that have a temporal expression mapped to time point t (the timestamp of article a'). The relevance measure $link$ is then defined as follows:

$$link(a, a') := \max_{a.b_i \in a.B_t} sim(a.b_i, a'.ab) \quad (2)$$

That is, we determine the relevance of an article a' with respect to an article a based on only the maximum similarity between the abstract of a' and each block in $a.b_i$ of a that has a temporal expression mapped to t. The rationale for choosing only the abstract of a' for comparison is that we assume the abstract of an article gives a succinct summary of an article and it mentions important terms and persons.

4.3 Network Construction, Pruning, and Support Paths

For a collection of articles, the above computation of pairwise links can be done efficiently, starting with the most recent article(s) and then proceeding in a chronological order of article timestamps. It should be noted that if for an article we consider only temporal expressions whose normalized values are less (earlier) than the article's timestamp, we obtain a directed acyclic graph, with paths leading from recent to older articles. If we also consider temporal expressions in an article a that refer to the future, then one can also compute links between a and articles whose timestamp is in $t(a)$, i.e., articles more recent than a. Such (potential) forward links can be maintained over time and investigated once new articles are added to the collection. If both types of temporal expressions are considered, then the resulting graph structure is likely to be not acyclic anymore. However, as our experiments will confirm, the amount of temporal expressions referring to the past is much larger than those referring to the future.

How to handle temporal expressions in articles coarser than of type T_{date}? Expressions of type T_{month} and the like result in time intervals. If an article contains such coarse-grained temporal references, then a pairwise linkage to those articles needs to be investigated whose timestamp lies in that temporal interval. Thus, all types of temporal expressions can be considered to build an initial *article network* $N = (A', L)$ of articles $A' \subseteq A$ linked by directed edges L between pairs of articles in A' according to Eq. (2) above.

Obviously, not every link is meaningful, namely when the value for $link(a, a')$ is below a certain threshold, say γ. Setting such a threshold is not trivial, and we will elaborate on this in Section 5. It would be straightforward to prune the network N by deleting all edges whose link value is below γ, leading to a reduced network, denoted N_γ. Instead, we make use of so-called *support paths* to keep some links with $link(a, a') < \gamma$. The idea is as follows: Assume a path $p = \langle a_1, \ldots, a_n \rangle$ where all edges have a value greater γ. All articles along that path are pairwise temporally related and also relevant with respect to their content. Assume another path $p' = \langle a_i, \ldots, a_k \rangle$ such that $a_i, a_k \in p$, that is, the first and last article in p' can be found along the path p. Figures 1(a) and (b) illustrate this case. Now assume that some links in p' have a value less than γ. Given that p provides evidence that a_i and a_k are related (because all link values along p are greater than γ), the path p' is fully kept, despite having (some) pairwise links below the threshold. In such a scenario, we call path p the *support path* for p'.

Based on the idea of support paths, given a threshold γ, a pruned network N_γ thus is obtained as follows: all edges are deleted from N that (1) are not part of a path being supported and (2) whose link value is less than γ. In Section 5, we will show that for a fairly heterogeneous collection of news articles, support paths typically consist of just a few edges (for the most simple example, see Figure 1(c)).

4.4 Properties of Article Networks

It is obvious that the larger the value for the threshold γ, the more components the network N_γ will have, because the number of support paths is reduced. The initial network N itself may have many components, namely when many articles neither contain a temporal expressions nor are temporally related to other articles. Each such article that is not linked forms a component. In a practical setting, one would choose some initial value for γ and let the user interactively increase or decrease that value to see how the network changes, e.g., what components develop when γ becomes larger.

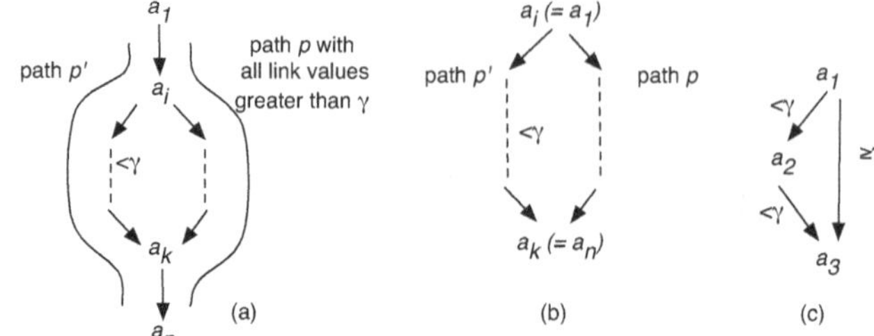

Figure 1: Examples of support paths scenarios ((a) and (b)) and most simple support path configuration found in a collection of news articles (c).

In general, an article network N_γ can be viewed as an information network specified in the form of a directed graph that may have several components. In particular, N_γ can be represented as an adjacency matrix $\mathbf{N}_\gamma$. Standard network measures [Newman, 2010] then can be obtained through matrix operations, such as in-degree centrality, which gives those articles that are often referred to by other articles (temporally and content-wise) and thus are likely to cover some key event or initial story.

Of particular interest is the *bibliographic coupling* measure known from citation networks [Newman, 2010]. In our context, bibliographic coupling of two articles a_i and a_j is the number of articles to which both are directly linked, described as $B_{ij} = \sum_{k=1}^{n} N_{ki} N_{kj} = \sum_{k=1}^{n} N_{ik}^T N_{kj}$, where N_{ij} is the ij-th element of the $(n \times n)$-matrix $\mathbf{N}_\gamma$. Articles that have a high bibliographic coupling thus are likely to be about the same event or story, or even duplicate articles, because they are related to many of the same (older) articles. In Section 5, we will show how bibliographic coupling is exploited in the context of a corpus of news articles from different news outlets.

5. EXPERIMENTS AND EVALUATION

Having presented the theory behind temporal linking and network construction, we will now present the details about our implementation, as well as optimization strategies for the resulting network in Section 5.3. Finally, the system will be evaluated formally and empirically in Section 5.5).

5.1 Description and Statistics of the Data Set

To determine the influence of data quality and size of the data set, we use two different data sets for our experiments:

NSA: A manually created data set covering a specific topic – the NSA spying scandal. We collected all articles related to the topic between 06-2013 and 08-2014 from two major German news sites, *Spiegel Online*[1] and *FAZ*[2].

[1] `www.spiegel.de/`

[2] `www.faz.net/`

	NSA	A5
articles	1155	13945
time range: begin	06/06/13	05/25/2014
time range: end	08/08/14	08/08/2014
news sources	2	5
sentences per article	41.2	32.3
exact dates (anchors)	2189	27703
articles: >0 exact dates	68%	69%
future references	5.9%	6.0%

Table 1: Data set statistics and comparison between NSA and A5 data set.

A5: A large data set automatically assembled from five major news sites (*Tagesschau*[3], *Spiegel Online, FAZ, Welt*[4], *SZ*[5]) by continuously pulling RSS streams in the categories *Politics* and *Economy* and parsing the raw HTML source using manually written rules.

A comparison of the statistics relevant to our system is given in Table 1. As our approach only links articles containing at least one temporal expression, 68% to 69% of all articles can *instantiate* a link. Note, however, that the remaining articles can be link *targets*. With only about 6% (relative to all references) being future references, only considering references to the past for linking (see Section 4.2) is a reasonable approach.

Comparing both data sets, one can see that documents in the NSA data set comprise more sentences and slightly more articles with exact dates than in the automatic data set. This is due to noise introduced by the automatic extraction process with few articles containing only photo galleries etc.

5.2 Preprocessing Pipeline

To extract temporal expressions, persons and keywords from our texts, we first apply a modular pipeline for robust information extraction at a fine-grained level based on Apache UIMA[6], performing annotations with increasing levels of complexity and allowing for easy adaptation and exchange of different base components. The pipeline consists of off-the-shelf NLP tools, such as the TreeTagger for part-of-speech tagging [Schmid, 1995] and Stanford NER for extracting person names. After person extraction, we cluster all mentions of persons that denote the same entity in the real world using similarities between names obtained by NESim [Do et al., 2009]. Our candidates for keywords are nouns, adjectives and verbs. Stop words and auxiliaries are filtered, and the lemmatized version of a token is used for a broader generalization and reduction of sparsity.

Extracting temporal expressions.

As our system strongly relies on temporal references in texts, we employ HeidelTime [Strötgen and Gertz, 2013], a multi-lingual temporal tagger that extracts and normalizes temporal expressions. The latter step is especially crucial as most of the temporal expressions are ambiguous, such as *"yesterday"* or *"last weekend"* that are only meaningful with respect to their specific context. The normalization component in HeidelTime correctly converts context-dependent temporal expressions to the concrete calendaric date (e.g., "2014-08-24") based on multiple heuristics.

Splitting documents.

The final component in our pipeline splits news articles into blocks using structural and paragraph information from the original article, such as tags within the HTML code or empty lines. Based on the information obtained by the pipeline, articles are linked as described in Section 4.2.

As a result, for an article consisting of the blocks $\langle b_1, \ldots, b_n \rangle$, the preprocessing pipeline creates a set of occurring persons $\langle p_{a1}, \ldots, p_{an} \rangle$ and keywords $\langle k_{a1}, \ldots, k_{an} \rangle$ for each block.

5.3 Network Optimization

After the network structure has been created as described in Section 4.2, we will now first study the influence of different similarity metrics and the pruning threshold γ. Having obtained a reasonable setting, we analyze the static structure of the network and validate our assumptions about necessary properties we consider important for the network to be used as an exploration tool.

Person-centric vs. balanced similarity.

To measure the effect of different weightings for person and keyword similarities – as introduced in Section 4.2 – we experiment with two different settings: a *balanced* version that assigns equal weights to person and keyword similarity ($\alpha_1 = \alpha_2 = 0.5$), as well as a *person-centric* scenario that favors person similarity ($\alpha_1 = \frac{2}{3}$, $\alpha_2 = \frac{1}{3}$).

Finding the optimal pruning threshold (γ).

As described in Section 4.2, all edges below a certain threshold γ are pruned to filter out weak links. After each pruning step, we also remove all nodes that are not connected. Figure 2 shows a histogram of edge weights – corresponding to document similarities – in the network when using the balanced and person-centric similarity metric, respectively. Most of the weights are very small, which is due to cosine similarity as a similarity metric for sparse vectors. In general, the person-centric metric yields more evenly distributed similarities. The average similarity for the balanced metric is 0.053, while it is 0.058 for the person-centric similarity metric.

To find the optimal threshold γ, we investigate its influence on the network structure, which is presented in Fig. 3 for the A5 data set. The numbers are similar for the NSA data set. Obviously, the number of edges decreases substantially with an increasing threshold, while the number of nodes decreases more slowly. This indicates that the pruning step reduces weak links between nodes but many of the nodes are still connected to other nodes. Comparing the two pairwise similarity metrics, the person-centric similarity metric yields higher overall weights and thus prunes less edges for the same threshold compared to the balanced similarity.

Setting γ to the average edge weight, more than 70% of all edges are removed from the network but only less than 6% of all the nodes. This means that removing many potentially weak edges still retains most of the nodes and thus information in the network. For the following experiments, we therefore use the respective average edge weight as our pruning threshold. The difference between the two similar-

[3]www.tagesschau.de/
[4]www.welt.de/
[5]www.sueddeutsche.de/
[6]http://uima.apache.org/

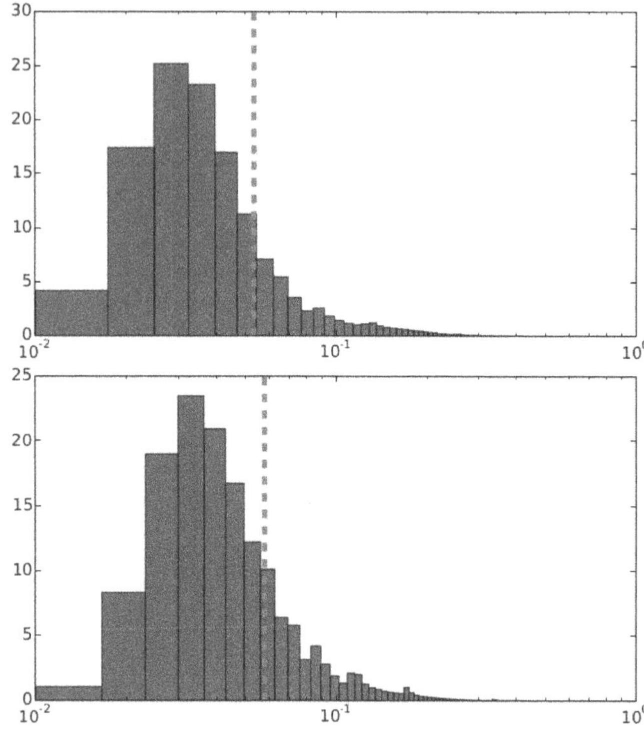

Figure 2: Distribution of edge weights (x-axis, log-scale) in the *A5* network for balanced (top) and person-centric (bottom) similarity. The dashed line represents the average similarity.

ity metrics when using the average similarity as a threshold is minor: nonetheless, the number of nodes is slightly higher for the person-centric metric, while the number of edges is slightly lower. As a loss of nodes represents a loss of information, we use the pruned network with person-centric similarities and support paths as the foundation for further data analysis. Note, however, that the choice of thresholds and similarity metrics is completely flexible and changeable by the user in an exploration interface, depending on the desired application.

Exploiting support paths as a quality indicator to block pruning (see Section 4.4) yields 30% more edges in the final network consistently across all data sets and similarity metrics. This shows that relying on single edge weights alone leads to the removal of potentially useful links as it neglects the additional information provided by the global network structure. Inspection of the data revealed that only less than 2% of all paths consist of more than 3 nodes (see Table 2).

Network statistics.

Table 2 lists statistics about the resulting networks when using the parameters described in the previous section: γ is set to the average similarity score and support paths are exploited. It is evident that the average size of components is much larger for the A5 data set (280 nodes per component) than for the NSA data set (23 nodes per component). This is mostly caused by the larger number of news sources that implicitly cite each other, resulting in more news articles that cover the same story.

	NSA	A5
nodes	668	11353
edges	1913	180138
components	63	86
cluster (communities, Sec. 5.4)	73	106
avg. nodes per component	23	280
avg. nodes per community	7	131
nodes in largest community	80	430
support paths (3 nodes)	203	19038
support paths (4 nodes)	46	3589
highest out-degree	34	230
highest in-degree	70	247

Table 2: Statistics for the information network obtained after pruning weak links as described in Section 5.3.

5.4 Investigating Story Threads

Due to the high connectedness in our information network – evident by the number of nodes per connected component – we employ strategies for clustering the entire network into smaller story threads that cover the progression of single story lines over time.

Community detection for clustering.

The number of nodes in the largest component is quite high for both data sets (cf. Table 2). To investigate the structure, we plotted the nodes and edges of the largest component of the NSA data in Figure 4. The network consists of densely connected sub-structures as well as single connections between these dense structures.

As the network structurally resembles the structure of a social network [Wasserman, 1994], we apply **community detection** to the network based on modularity optimization [Blondel et al., 2008] to cluster the network. The resulting communities – indicated by different colors in Fig. 4 – reflect these highly connected sub-structures and their relationships very well. Regarding a community as a **story thread**, the result allows a user to find pivot articles connecting two story threads.

As Table 2 shows, using community detection for clustering yields more clusters in comparison to components (106 vs. 86 for the A5 network) while maintaining connections between them at the same time.

Temporal evolution of a story thread.

Instead of using a model based on document similarity for linking stories – such as topic models or relevance models (e.g., [Lavrenko et al., 2002]) – we argue that explicit temporal expressions model the flow of complex story threads more naturally. To validate our hypothesis, we investigate the similarity between all documents within a story thread depending on the time span between pairs of articles. Our assumption is that the larger the time difference between articles within a story thread, the lower the document similarity. Document similarity is measured as described in Section 4.2.

Figure 5 illustrates the average similarity for article pairs covering a specific time span. As expected, the average document similarity decreases with increasing time spans. This shows that document similarity in isolation is not sufficient to cover evolving aspects of a more complex story but instead

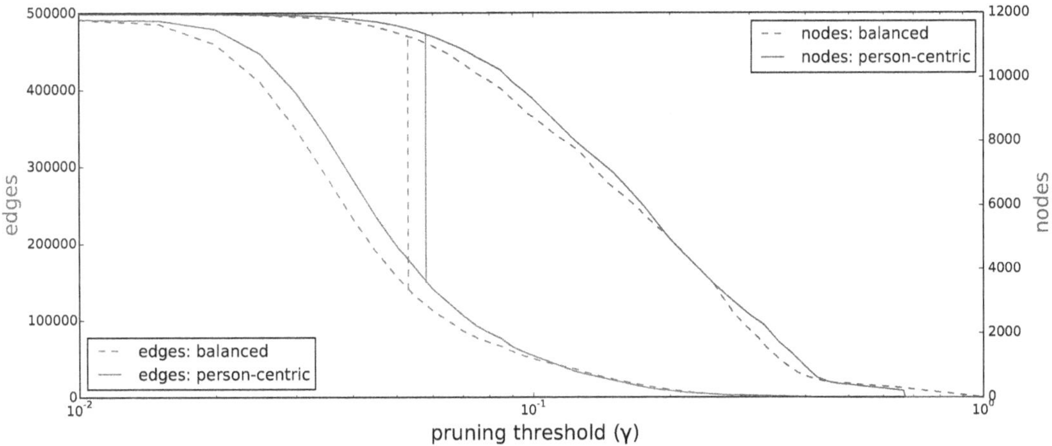

Figure 3: Influence of pruning: nodes and edges depending on γ for balanced (dashed, $\alpha_1 = \alpha_2 = 0.5$) and person-centric (solid, $\alpha_1 = \frac{2}{3}$, $\alpha_2 = \frac{1}{3}$) metric. Horizontal bars indicate the respective average similarity.

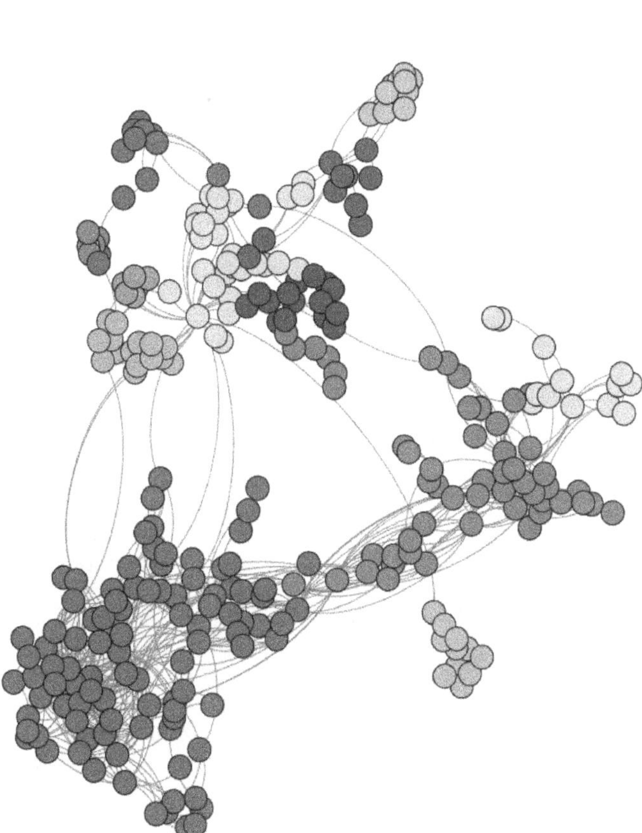

Figure 4: Structure of news articles and their connections in the largest component of the NSA information network. Colors represent different clusters based on community detection.

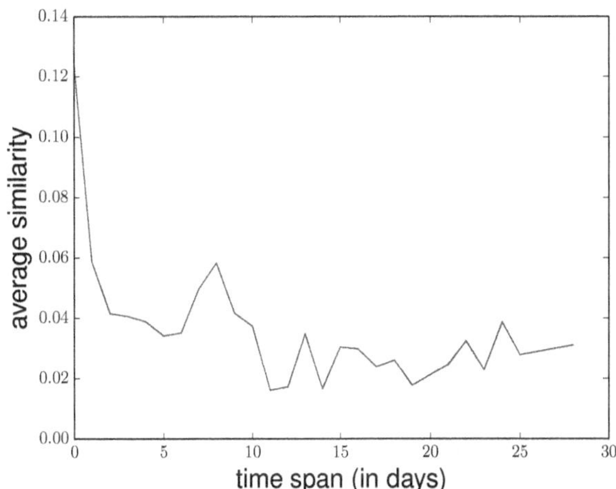

Figure 5: Average similarity within all articles of a community plotted against time span (in days) within a community.

yields story threads comprising time spans with a narrow, topically highly related collection of articles.

5.5 Evaluation and Data Exploration

As noted by [Shahaf and Guestrin, 2012], a quantitative evaluation of story linking in general is challenging due to the lack of training and evaluation data. This factor is owed to the highly subjective nature of the endeavor to link stories: similar to the field of Information Retrieval, there is no definite answer to the question of relevance. While we think that a formal evaluation is crucial, in our opinion, a more intuitive evaluation of the plausibility and practicality for using our system as an exploration interface is equally important.

Thus, we will first propose a setting to formally evaluate story linking approaches, followed by examples showing whether our system fulfills desired properties of a news exploration interface in Section 5.5.2.

	temporal links	explicit links
linked nodes	11353	4165
% of articles (coverage)	81.41%	29.87%
edges	180138	4432
↳ same news outlet	22.01%	95.17%

Table 3: Comparison of the article coverage of temporal vs. explicit links and the fraction of edges connecting articles from the same news outlet.

5.5.1 *Comparison to explicit links*

In order to evaluate whether our system links related articles that are of interest to the user, we propose a formal evaluation consisting of a comparison between the links obtained by our system and manual, **explicit** links added by the authors of an article.

As indicated in Section 1, explicit links are links within article pointing to other articles that might be of interest to the user reading the current story. As this is the typical (and oftentimes only) way of exploring related articles and because the links are manually added by the authors of an article, these links provide a good estimator of the quality of our linking approach. All comparisons between explicit and temporal links are performed with the entire A5 data set.

Article coverage.

As we regard our system as a news exploration tool that presents other, potentially interesting articles to the reader of a current news article, the overall coverage of news articles is very important. We regard as coverage the number of nodes that are connected to at least one other node (i.e. with a degree ≥ 1). If a node in the network is not connected, no valuable information about related articles can be found.

Table 3 compares how many articles are covered by the information network when using temporal links and explicit links. Using explicit links, only about one third of all articles is linked to any other article, meaning that explicit links do not provide information about related articles for the vast majority of articles. In contrast, the network constructed with our temporal linking approach covers more than 80% of all articles. But external links raise another important issue: 95% of all explicit links connect news articles published by the same news outlet – thus ignoring competitive outlets. Temporal linking circumvents this issue by linking articles to potential targets published by all news outlets on a specific date.

Evaluation of link recall.

Explicit links only represent a fraction of articles that are related. Besides the issue of competitive news outlets mentioned above, if there exists a manually created, explicit link between two articles, they are most certainly relevant to each other and should thus also be linked by our temporal linking system. It should be noted, however, that this evaluation scenario neglects near-synonym articles reporting the same news item published by different news sites: while there might not be a temporal link between two explicitly linked articles from the *same* news outlet, there might exist a link *across different* outlets.

Treating explicit links as a gold standard, we measure link recall of the temporal linking system based on the number of articles that exist in both networks. As the result in Table 4 reveals, 82% of all explicit links also exist when applying temporal links.

	temporal links
link recall	82.62%

Table 4: Evaluation of link recall for temporal linking with respect to explicit links.

Ability to group related articles.

Due to the small fraction of explicitly linked nodes, measuring precision is not very meaningful. Recall in isolation, however, does not account for erroneous edges. Thus, we measure whether our approach groups related articles together. Taking explicitly linked articles as a ground truth for a subset of articles that are related, all pairs of connected articles should be assigned to the same story thread, i.e., cluster by our system.

In fact, 87% of all articles that are connected by explicit links are assigned to the same community. This shows that our approach does not yield arbitrary links but groups related articles.

Error analysis.

Manual error analysis revealed that most of the missing links between articles are due to non-existent or unrecognized temporal expressions. While the temporal tagger HeidelTime recognizes most of the temporal expressions, certain German compounds are currently not yet recognized, such as "Montagmorgen" (Monday morning). Most of these issues will be resolved in an upcoming version of the temporal tagger. Documents without any temporal expression are more challenging to account for. Experiments to link these articles with highly similar articles that were published within the same week yield first promising results.

5.5.2 *Usage as a data exploration tool*

As already noted, we regard our system as an exploration tool for end users who can adjust the parameters for similarities and the pruning threshold γ. To judge the usefulness of the system, we thus analyze the resulting information network obtained from our experiments and check whether it fulfills the required properties of a news exploration tool.

Central articles.

Intuitively, articles with a high out-degree centrality should be overview articles that mention many other articles and thus present an overview of developments. The article with the highest out-degree in the NSA data set is titled "Timeline of a scandal"[7] and was written at the end of October 2013. It links to 34 articles in the network. The overview aspect is well-represented in the link structure as the articles comprise all major events in the course of this story, beginning with the discovery of Prism in June 2013. Again, our system is able to link articles of different aspects and topics in one story line. This shows that central articles are suitable for a quick overview of the development of a story over time and are thus a suitable starting point. In the au-

[7] `http://www.faz.net/-gpf-7irh3`: October 25, 2013

tomatic data set, there are also numerous central overview articles: the article "Conflict between the Ukraine and Russia"[8], for example, reviews the major developments in the conflict between the Ukraine and Russia.

Bibliographic coupling.

Viewing our network of news articles as a citation network with links representing explicit citations of previously written articles, we compute the co-citation between articles. Intuitively, if two articles are both cited more often in the same article, they have a strong resemblance and can thus be regarded as near-duplicates. Our information network supports this hypothesis. In the NSA data set, the two articles titled "Merkel and the spying scandal" (FAZ) and "Obama and the chancelor's cellphone" (Spiegel) describe the same story covered by two different news sites and are co-cited 30 times within following news articles. In the NSA data set, about 35% of all articles are co-cited in more than 3 articles, whereas the proportion of frequently co-cited articles is higher in the automatic data set (about 50%). This is not surprising as the automatic data set comprises more news sites with potentially redundant articles from different outlets (near duplicates).

The degree of similarity between co-cited articles varies, as some of the articles are actually paraphrased copies of a news agency report, whereas other pairs describe the same story from different points of views. Bibliographic coupling and co-citation can thus be used for an analysis of news and information flow across different news sites with respect to time (e.g., what outlet published a story first).

5.5.3 Usage scenario: background information

Another application for our exploration tool is to get background information for a specific, complex news article. Figure 6 shows a shortened version of a news network for the starting article "Argument about EU posts". The original network consists of 13 news stories. The initial article (highlighted in green) mentions multiple aspects of the debate about political EU posts that are not understandable without the corresponding background knowledge. The network gives an overview of topics related to the entire story, including, among others, the stability pact. This helps to uncover dependencies across different news stories and to better understand and judge the story at hand.

5.6 Summary of our Experiments

Having applied our document linking model (Section 4.2) to real-world data, the findings of our experiments can be summarized as follows. We first investigated the influence of the *pruning threshold* γ as well as support paths to obtain an information network for our evaluation in Section 5.3. To cluster the network structure into *story threads*, we then motivated and applied *community detection* and showed why document similarity in isolation is insufficient to model the temporal evolution of complex stories (Section 5.4).

Comparing our information network to a network structure based on explicit links in Section 5.5.1 revealed that: (a) our network captures more articles than explicit links in isolation and interlinks different news outlets, (b) temporal links reproduce the vast majority of explicit links and (c) our similarity metric in combination with community detection is suitable for grouping related articles into the same story thread. Finally, we showed several applications to demonstrate the usefulness our news information network as an exploration tool in Section 5.5.2.

Discussion.

While the presented evaluation clearly shows the functionality and performance of our approach in comparison to explicit links, we are aware of the fact that additional experiments are necessary in future. To reliably determine the applicability of our system as a news exploration tool, user studies comparing our approach with alternative methods of document linking should be employed.

6. CONCLUSIONS AND ONGOING WORK

This paper presented an approach to link news articles by taking temporal expressions in articles as starting points for linking articles. The link strength between articles is determined using document similarity metrics applied to keywords and persons. We evaluated and validated the resulting network structure for a German news corpus and presented several usage scenarios for data exploration.

We are currently working on an interface that lets users explore a news network either for a specific news article or an overview over a complex news-topic in its entirety. In addition, the current architecture provides a good starting point to exploit properties of the global information network in a joint-inference setting to enhance performance, as well as integrating additional and alternative similarity metrics based on activation patterns.

7. REFERENCES

[Allan, 2002] Allan, J. (2002). *Topic detection and tracking: event-based information organization*, volume 12. Springer.

[Blondel et al., 2008] Blondel, V. D., Guillaume, J.-L., Lambiotte, R., and Lefebvre, E. (2008). Fast unfolding of communities in large networks. *Journal of Statistical Mechanics: Theory and Experiment*, 2008(10):P10008.

[Brants et al., 2003] Brants, T., Chen, F., and Farahat, A. (2003). A system for new event detection. In *SIGIR '03*, pages 330–337.

[Do et al., 2009] Do, Q., Roth, D., Sammons, M., Tu, Y., and Vydiswaran, V. (2009). Robust, light-weight approaches to compute lexical similarity. *Computer Science Research and Technical Reports, University of Illinois.*

[Feng and Allan, 2009] Feng, A. and Allan, J. (2009). Incident threading for news passages. In *CIKM'09*, pages 1307–1316.

[Gillenwater et al., 2012] Gillenwater, J., Kulesza, A., and Taskar, B. (2012). Discovering diverse and salient threads in document collections. In *EMNLP-CoNLL 2012*, pages 710–720.

[Kumaran and Allan, 2005] Kumaran, G. and Allan, J. (2005). Using names and topics for new event detection. In *HLT/EMNLP 2005*, pages 121–128.

[Lavrenko et al., 2002] Lavrenko, V., Allan, J., DeGuzman, E., LaFlamme, D., Pollard, V., and Thomas, S. (2002). Relevance models for topic detection and tracking. In *Human Language Technology Research*, pages 115–121.

[8] `http://sz.de/1.2021629`: June 30, 2014

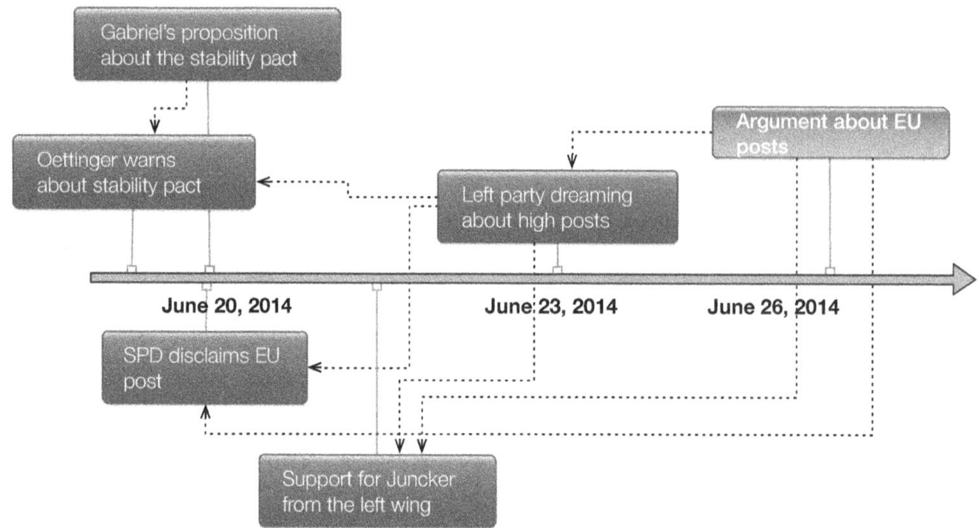

Figure 6: Sample information network demonstrating the usage of our linking approach to obtain background information for a complex topic.

[Nallapati et al., 2004] Nallapati, R., Feng, A., Peng, F., and Allan, J. (2004). Event threading within news topics. In *CIKM 2004*, pages 446–453.

[Newman, 2010] Newman, M. (2010). *Networks - An Introduction*. Oxford University Press.

[Nomoto, 2010] Nomoto, T. (2010). Two-tier similarity model for story link detection. In *CIKM'10*, pages 789–798.

[Pouliquen et al., 2008] Pouliquen, B., Steinberger, R., and Deguernel, O. (2008). Story tracking: linking similar news over time and across languages. In *MMIES '08*, pages 49–56.

[Schmid, 1995] Schmid, H. (1995). Improvements in part-of-speech tagging with an application to German. In *ACL SIGDAT-Workshop*.

[Shahaf and Guestrin, 2012] Shahaf, D. and Guestrin, C. (2012). Connecting two (or less) dots: Discovering structure in news articles. *TKDD*, 5(4):24.

[Shahaf et al., 2013] Shahaf, D., Yang, J., Suen, C., Jacobs, J., Wang, H., and Leskovec, J. (2013). Information cartography: Creating zoomable, large-scale maps of information. In *Knowledge Discovery and Data Mining*, KDD '13, pages 1097–1105.

[Strötgen and Gertz, 2013] Strötgen, J. and Gertz, M. (2013). Multilingual and cross-domain temporal tagging. *Language Resources and Evaluation*, 47(2):269–298.

[Vaca et al., 2014] Vaca, C. K., Mantrach, A., Jaimes, A., and Saerens, M. (2014). A time-based collective factorization for topic discovery and monitoring in news. In *WWW '14*, pages 527–538.

[Wang and Li, 2011] Wang, L. and Li, F. (2011). Story link detection based on event words. In *Computational Linguistics and Intelligent Text Processing*, pages 202–211. Springer.

[Wasserman, 1994] Wasserman, S. (1994). *Social network analysis: Methods and applications*, volume 8. Cambridge University Press.

[Yan et al., 2011] Yan, R., Wan, X., Otterbacher, J., Kong, L., Li, X., and Zhang, Y. (2011). Evolutionary timeline summarization: A balanced optimization framework via iterative substitution. In *SIGIR '11*, pages 745–754.

[Zhu and Oates, 2012] Zhu, X. and Oates, T. (2012). Finding story chains in newswire articles. In *Information Reuse and Integration*, pages 93–100.

[Zhu and Oates, 2013] Zhu, X. and Oates, T. (2013). Finding news story chains based on multi-dimensional event profiles. In *Open Research Areas in Information Retrieval*, pages 157–164.

Predicting Temporal Intention in Resource Sharing

Hany M. SalahEldeen
Old Dominion University
Norfolk, VA, USA
hany@cs.odu.edu

Michael L. Nelson
Old Dominion University
Norfolk, VA, USA
mln@cs.odu.edu

ABSTRACT

When users post links to web pages in Twitter there is a time delta between when the post was shared (t_{tweet}) and when it was read (t_{click}). Ideally, when this time delta is small there is often no change in the page's state. However upon reading shared content in the past and due to the dynamic nature of the web, the page's state could change and the intention of the author need to be inferred. In this work, we enhance a prior temporal intention model and tackle its shortcomings by incorporating extended linguistic feature analysis, replacing the prior textual similarity measure with semantic similarity one based on latent topic detection trained on Wikipedia English corpus, and finally by enriching and balancing the training dataset. We uncovered three different intention behaviors in respect to time: Stable Intention, Changing Intention from current to past, and Undefined intention. Using these classes and only the information available at posting time from the tweet and the current state of the resource, we correctly predict the temporal intention classification and strength with 77% accuracy.

1. INTRODUCTION

When a link to a webpage is shared in social media, authors have an implicit expectation as to what people in their social network would read when they click on that link. Authors might want the readers to view the exact same version of the page they saw when they posted (at time t_{tweet}); or they might want the readers to examine the most current version of the resource at the time of clicking on the link (t_{click}). If the time difference is small ($t_{click} - t_{tweet} \approx 0$), then the reader will not notice any discrepancy or shift in what the author intended for them to see. Unfortunately, due to the highly dynamic nature of the web it is highly likely that the intentions diverge through time either by change or loss of resources. This divergence could be highly problematic upon archiving and curating social media posts that narrate public events like the Arab Spring, Occupy Wall Street movement, natural disasters like Hurricane Sandy and others.

JCDL'15, June 21–25, 2015, Knoxville, Tennessee, USA.

DOI: http://dx.doi.org/10.1145/2756406.2756921.

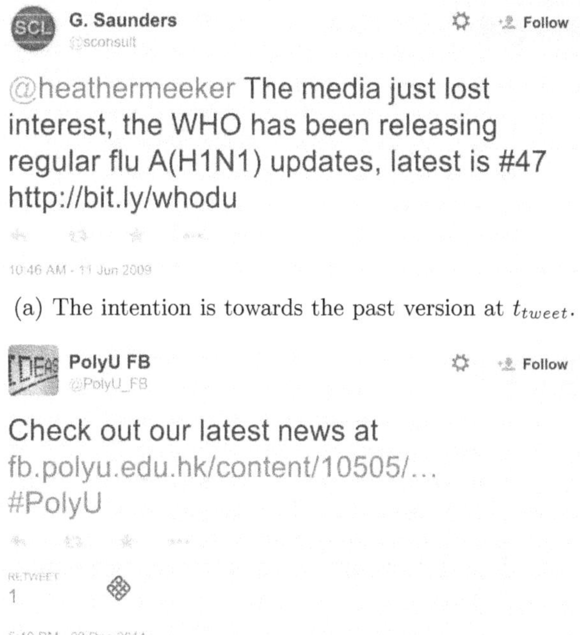

(a) The intention is towards the past version at t_{tweet}.

(b) The intention is towards the latest version at t_{click}.

Figure 1: Tweet examples for different intention classes.

Consider the tweets shown in Figure 1. In Figure 1(a) we can see that the author's intention is for a specific information resource and thus the intention is t_{tweet}. In Figure 1(b) the author wants the reader to see the latest information, so the intention is t_{click}. In this work, we build a predictive model which can effectively differentiate between each intention class at tweet-authoring time. The ability to differentiate the intention in real-time can be used to push a copy of the linked resource into a web archive (e.g., webcitation.org, archive.today, archive.org) at t_{tweet} so the link is to an archived version instead of a web version, thus ensuring what readers see is consistent with the author's intention.

In our prior work, we analyzed the temporal intention concept and were able to successfully model temporal intention by breaking it down into two simpler tasks of *content relevance* and *change*, and named it the Temporal Intention Relevance Model (TIRM) [17]. Relevance describes whether the content of the resource still matches the tweet in topicality and context, while Change means that the resource have changed in content from the initial state at the time of tweeting. The subproblems of relevance and change are more straightforward to measure and there is an abundance of prior literature addressing them in regards to textual content relevance, as well as linguistic and semantic similarity.

To illustrate TIRM, we examine two points in the life of a tweet as described earlier: 1)t_{tweet} when the author of the tweet posted it, 2) t_{click} when the reader clicks on the link to examine the resource at current time. Table 1 shows that if the resource has changed and no longer relevant, then the intention is for the past (e.g., in Figure 1(a) the author intends for readers to access the WHO page as it was at t_{tweet}), while if the resource changed but still relevant, then the intention is for the current (e.g., in Figure 1(b) the author intends for readers to access latest news page as it will be at t_{click}). The model was trained using 39 different social, archival, and textual features extracted at t_{click}.

Resource's State	Tweet and resource are: Relevant	Not Relevant
Changed	t_{click}	t_{tweet}
Not Changed	t_{tweet}	either or undefined

Table 1: Temporal Intention Relevancy Model (TIRM).

When we first started using TIRM in prediction we noticed that our model in its simplistic form had some shortcomings. One problem in judging relevance between a tweet and a linked resource is the tweet is limited to 140 characters while the resource could span thousands of characters. This highlights the need to find a better similarity measure based on the semantic similarity rather than just textual overlap. Second problem is that the model is more aggressive towards relevance due to the bias in the training dataset extracted from Mechanical Turk (80% Relevant class and 20% Non-Relevant). Therefore, prior to the prediction analysis steps we extend the model to address those problems and enhance the model.

Following the enhancement of the model, we wanted to estimate the confidence of this probabilistic classification. We are able to tell the relevance class and if the content is changed or not, but not a collective classification measure of confidence. We propose a formulation of intention based on the relevance measure from the classifier and the change measure obtained by calculating similarity between the resource's versions. We call this formulation the *Intention Strength Measure*.

With this measure, for each resource in our dataset we calculate the intention measure at 12 points in the time period spanning 3.5 years from t_{click} to t_{tweet}. Plotting those intention strength across time We devised a model to identify the intention progression from t_{click} to t_{tweet}. This modeling will enable us to predict this temporal intention at an early stage, and provide the authors with enough information to perform an educated assessment on how to successfully convey their intention to the readers at any future t_{click}. For example, in the tweet shown in Figure 1, at t_{tweet} when the author is posting a tweet with a link to the WHO Disease Outbreak News page, if it was predicted that the intention would change in the future they might push a copy of the current state of the page into one of the public archives and link to that snapshot instead of the live version.

2. RELATED WORK

Researchers also explored the problem of web content changing through time and how to predict this change [1, 4, 5, 8]. Radinsky et al. introduced a new method incorporating not only the analysis of the page changes in the past but also the usefulness of this change and how related this page under observation is to other pages and how similar they are in the types of changes they undergo [14].

Latent Dirichlet Allocation (LDA) has been used extensively in detecting latent relations between phrases and words in corpora. Rus et al. investigated LDA and Latent Semantic Analysis (LSA) in deriving meaning on word level and phrase level in large corpora [16, 12]. In conversational analysis, and perhaps in Twitter, Oliva et al. explored the concept of semantic similarity in relatively short-text and built their method based on the semantic meaning behind words along with the structural relation between those words in the short text [13]. The semantic understanding of text and the meaning behind it could be utilized in further more than textual similarity but rather in identifying usefulness of content posted in social media [11]. Beyond merely textual analysis, Chen et al. have focused on analyzing the tweets that are associated with other resources, namely image tweets [3]. In their search for content relevancy between the associated images and the text, they explored various textual, visual, and social context features. They utilized LDA in modeling and detecting textual and visual hidden topics.

LDA has been also utilized in other context as well like tweet classification. The concept of retweeting was analyzed by Wang et al. in their search for the linguistic and functional factors leading to retweeting [20]. In their work they analyzed a multitude of factors in the tweet's structure and text ranging from sentiment analysis, emoticons existence, part-of-speech (POS) tagging, named entity extraction (NE), hashtag analysis, verb tense analysis, discourse relations and phrase similarity. In our work, we adopt their approach in tweet analysis and extract similar features aiding the enhancement of our model.

3. ENHANCING TIRM

To enhance TIRM we focused on the shortcomings of the model in regards to linguistic analysis, similarity measures, and dataset balancing while utilizing the same dataset used in TIRM spanning 1,124 instances.

3.1 Linguistic Feature Analysis

Previously, 39 different features were extracted from the tweet-resource pair in regards to similarity, URL structure, social and archival existence. The results were promising but we needed a deeper analysis and understanding of the linguistic properties of the tweet-resource pair.

3.1.1 Tweet structural analysis

After filtering out the linked resource we checked the existence of user mentions, hashtags, question marks "?" (indicating a question tweet), and exclamation marks "!" (indicating an expression of strong feelings). Furthermore we utilized regular expressions, adopted from Ritter et al.'s work, in detecting emoticons in the tweets [15]. We deduced that along with the extracted sentiment from the prior experiment we will be able to capture the emotional state the author. Finally, we also checked if the tweet was a re-tweet. These simple features proved to be highly effective as six of which are present among the top 13 ranked features in information gain of the retrained model as shown by table 3 (Key: FB=Facebook, Twt=Tweet, Sim=Similarity, Cur=Current, Len=Length, Celeb=Celebrities, Pct=Percent, Init=Initial, Pos=Positive, Neg=Negative, Neu=Neutral).

3.1.2 POS tagging and Named Entity Extraction

In the prior TIRM, Wikipedia was harvested for lists of artists, actors, and singers from the English speaking world to use in detecting the existence of celebrities in the tweets. This feature proved to be highly valuable due to its corresponding high information gain. This observation led us to believe we need to further investigate named entities in tweets.

In tweet analysis, due to the rather small size of text with the lack of context and the informality in writing, tasks like Part-of-speech (POS) tagging, sentence chunking, and named entity recognition are quite challenging. Ritter et al. developed a distantly supervised approach that is tailored for tweet based analysis overcoming those challenges [15]. We adopted their labeled LDA-based POS tagger and chunker which have performed effectively against standard POS taggers on tweet datasets. Ten different types of entities are defined by Ritter's tagger as shown in table 2 along with the number of identified entities in each class across the training dataset of 1,124 instances. Furthermore, with the extracted POS tags and chunks we were able to determine if the most prominent tense in a tweet is present or past and used it as a feature too. The rationale behind this analysis is to also identify the intention of the author in discussing contemporaneous events or past ones.

3.1.3 Tweet Classification

Users tweet to convey an opinion, update a status, ask for information, sarcasm, spread jokes, and many other reasons [7]. In our search for the author's temporal intention we utilized Wang et al. work in classifying tweeting motive [20]. We adopted the first level of their two-tiered classification: Opinion, Update, Interaction, Fact, Deals, News, Others. Furthermore, and for the sake of simplicity, we utilized the largest classes of *Opinion, Update, Interaction, Others* which collectively comprised 94% of the instances in Wang et al.'s datset.

	Interaction	Update	Opinion
Relevant	69.67%	59.28%	36.99%
Non-Relevant	30.33%	40.72%	63.01%

Table 4: Tweet classification across relevancy classes

As shown in table 4, for class *Interaction*, the *Relevance* class is significantly higher than the other while in class *Opinion* the instances are more biased towards the Non-Relevant. This indicates the relation between tweet class and relevance thus we use it as a feature.

3.2 Semantic Similarity Analysis Using Latent Topic Modeling

In the prior TIRM, similarity measures were based on word overlap either by using SimHash or n-grams cosine similarity. This technique proved to be lacking upon calculating the similarity between a tweet (140 characters) and a resource which could be virtually unlimited. Similarly between two versions of a resource, where a change in the html design could be interpreted as a low similarity while in fact the content itself remained unchanged. It is worth mentioning that in this experiment we only account for non-missing resources (i.e., gives 200 OK response). In their prior experiment, we attempted to overcome the latter problem by introducing a boiler plate removal algorithm to remove the effect of change in styling and extract the main content.

To address the former we employed topic detection, as we would consider a tweet and a resource to be similar if they were both mentioning the same topic, or discussing the same point. Thus we measure similarity based on collective semantics or "aboutness" of the pair rather than textual overlap.

We use both LSA and LDA in calculating the similarities between the tweet-resource and resource-resource pairs accordingly. We considered both techniques as LSA is much faster to train while LDA has higher accuracy. We also considered utilizing Twitter based LDA models from the works of Mehrotra et al. and Zhao et al. which are more fitted to handle tweeted textual content with its embedded hashtags [10, 21]. Since we were not performing topic modeling on tweets only and we are calculating similarities between the tweet and the resource, which is written formally in most cases, traditional LDA-LSI models trained on a diverse corpus like Wikipedia seemed more suitable. Furthermore, we calculate the similarities between the resource versions (at t_{tweet} or past version, and at t_{click} or current version) and the tweet.

To prepare these models we utilize the Wikipedia Corpus in extracting the topics and features. We downloaded 4,295,020 documents spanning the English Wikipedia documents in January 2014[1]. We chose Wikipedia for training as it spans a wide variety of topics and the latent relations between them. Next we built the LDA and LSA models with 100,000 features, 672,235,199 non-zero entries in the sparse TF-IDF matrix. The LDA model in this case is an online learning LDA model developed by Hoffman et al. [6]. We get the current version of the resource, the past version, and the tweet. We convert each to latent vector space and using the model we calculate the cosine similarity. The result is

[1] http://download.wikimedia.org/enwiki/

Person	GeoLoc	TVShow	Movie	Facility	Company	Product	SportsTeam	Band	Other
233	81	18	37	19	115	42	10	62	96
Tweets with Named Entities				543	Tweets without Named Entities				581

Table 2: Named Entities instances in the dataset

#	Feature Name	Type	Extraction Method	Availability	Gain	Rank	Min	
1	**ShortURLLen**	Structural	Analyzing resource's URL	At t_{tweet}	0.1709	4	✓	The original TIRM Model with 39 Features
2	**NumArchives**	Archival	Analyzing resource's timemap	After Archival	0.1663	5	✓	
3	**URLDepth**	Structural	Analyzing resource's URL	At t_{tweet}	0.1569	10	✓	
4	**CelebInTwts**	Linguistic	Mining Wiki+Text analysis	At t_{tweet}	0.1203	11	✓	
5	**CelebInTwt**	Linguistic	Mining Wiki+Text analysis	At t_{tweet}	0.0917	22	✓	
6	**CosTwtPast**	Similarity	Cosine Similarity+BoilerPlt	After Archival	0.0877	23	✓	
7	**CosCurTwt**	Similarity	Cosine Similarity+BoilerPlt	At t_{tweet}	0.0864	24	✓	
8	**CosCurPast**	Similarity	Cosine Similarity+BoilerPlt	After Archival	0.0862	25	✓	
9	**CelebPctInTwt**	Linguistic	Mining Wiki+Text analysis	At t_{tweet}	0.0861	26	✓	
10	**TwtSimCur**	Similarity	Similarity+BoilerPlt	At t_{tweet}	0.0846	27	✓	
11	**URLLen**	Structural	Analyzing resource's URL	At t_{tweet}	0.0846	286		
12	**ReductionRate**	Structural	Analyzing resource's URL	At t_{tweet}	0.0845	29		
13	**CelebPctInTwts**	Linguistic	Mining Wiki+Text analysis	After being retweeted	0.0835	30		
14	**InfluTwtsCount**	Social	Mining Topsy API	After being retweeted	0.0835	31		
15	**SimhashCurPast**	Similarity	Simhash Similarity+BoilerPlt	After Archival	0.0799	33		
16	**MementoCount**	Archival	Analyzing resource's timemap	After Archival	0.0774	34		
17	**FBClicks**	Social	Mining FB API	After being posted on FB	0.074	35		
18	**CosCurTwts**	Similarity	Cosine Similarity+BoilerPlt	After being retweeted	0.0695	36		
19	**FBLikes**	Social	Mining FB API	After being posted on FB	0.0689	37		
20	**FBComments**	Social	Mining FB API	After being posted on FB	0.0668	38		
21	**TwtLen**	Structural	Text analysis	At t_{tweet}	0.0662	39		
22	**CosTwtsPast**	Similarity	Cosine Similarity+BoilerPlt	After Archival+retweeted	0.0569	41		
23	**SimhashCurTwts**	Similarity	Simhash Similarity+BoilerPlt	After being retweeted	0.0569	42		
24	**FBShares**	Social	Mining FB API	After being posted on FB	0.0538	44		
25	**InitContentLen**	Structural	Mining Bitly API	After being Bitly Shortened	0.0481	46		
26	**NeuSentiment**	Linguistic	NLTK Sentiment Analysis	At t_{tweet}	0.048	47		
27	**TwtSimPast**	Similarity	Similarity+BoilerPlt	After Archival	0.0475	48		
28	**BitlyClicks**	Social	Mining Bitly API	After being Bitly Shortened	0.0463	49		
29	**SimhashCurTwt**	Similarity	Simhash Similarity+BoilerPlt	At t_{tweet}	0.0438	52		
30	**CloseMemTime**	Archival	Analyzing resource's timemap	After Archival	0.0434	53		
31	**SimhashTwtpast**	Similarity	Simhash Similarity+BoilerPlt	After Archival	0.0411	55		
32	**PastCurSim**	Similarity	Similarity+BoilerPlt	After Archival	0.0376	56		
33	**PosSentiment**	Linguistic	NLTK Sentiment Analysis	At t_{tweet}	0.0356	57		
34	**SimhashTwtsPast**	Similarity	Simhash Similarity+BoilerPlt	After Archival+retweeted	0.0353	58		
35	**TwtsSimCur**	Similarity	Similarity+BoilerPlt	At t_{tweet}	0.0351	59		
36	**RetrievedTwts**	Social	Mining Topsy API	After being retweeted	0.0233	60		
37	**NegSentiment**	Linguistic	NLTK Sentiment Analysis	At t_{tweet}	0.0215	62		
38	**TotalTwtCount**	Social	Mining Topsy API	After being retweeted	0.0202	63		
39	**TwtsSimPast**	Similarity	Similarity+BoilerPlt	After Archival	0	65		
40	**UserMention**	Linguistic	Text analysis	At t_{tweet}	0.2254	1	✓	The enhancing extended features
41	**IsRetweet**	Linguistic	Text analysis	At t_{tweet}	0.2015	2	✓	
42	**Has!**	Linguistic	Text analysis	At t_{tweet}	0.1845	3	✓	
43	**GEO-LOC**	Linguistic	Named Entity Extraction	At t_{tweet}	0.1653	6	✓	
44	**Has?**	Linguistic	Text analysis	At t_{tweet}	0.1643	7	✓	
45	**PERSON**	Linguistic	Named Entity Extraction	At t_{tweet}	0.1612	8	✓	
46	**HashtagCount**	Linguistic	Counting Hashtags	At t_{tweet}	0.1602	9	✓	
47	**COMPANY**	Linguistic	Named Entity Extraction	At t_{tweet}	0.1186	12	✓	
48	**HasEmoticon**	Linguistic	Text analysis	At t_{tweet}	0.1106	13	✓	
49	**MOVIE**	Linguistic	Named Entity Extraction	At t_{tweet}	0.1085	14	✓	
50	**TVSHOW**	Linguistic	Named Entity Extraction	At t_{tweet}	0.1065	15	✓	
51	**OTHER**	Linguistic	Named Entity Extraction	At t_{tweet}	0.1056	16	✓	
52	**BAND**	Linguistic	Named Entity Extraction	At t_{tweet}	0.1016	17	✓	
53	**SPORTSTEAM**	Linguistic	Named Entity Extraction	At t_{tweet}	0.0985	18	✓	
54	**LDATwtsSimCur**	Similarity	LDA Similarity+BoilerPlt	After being retweeted	0.0945	19	✓	
55	**PRODUCT**	Linguistic	Named Entity Extraction	At t_{tweet}	0.0922	20	✓	
56	**LSATwtSimCur**	Similarity	LSA Similarity+BoilerPlt	At t_{tweet}	0.092	21	✓	
57	**LSATwtsSimCur**	Similarity	LSA Similarity+BoilerPlt	After being retweeted	0.0819	32		
58	**LSATwtSimPast**	Similarity	LSA Similarity+BoilerPlt	After Archival	0.0591	40		
59	**LSATwtsSimPast**	Similarity	LSA Similarity+BoilerPlt	After Archival+retweeted	0.0548	43		
60	**LDATwtSimCur**	Similarity	LDA Similarity+BoilerPlt	At t_{tweet}	0.0522	45		
61	**TweetClass**	Linguistic	LDA Tweet Classification	At t_{tweet}	0.0453	50		
62	**LDATwtSimPast**	Similarity	LDA Similarity+BoilerPlt	After Archival	0.0452	51		
63	**LDATwtsSimPast**	Similarity	LDA Similarity+BoilerPlt	After Archival+retweeted	0.0429	54		
64	**Tense**	Linguistic	POS tagging	At t_{tweet}	0.0223	61		
65	**FACILITY**	Linguistic	Named Entity Extraction	At t_{tweet}	0	64		

Table 3: All the features used in TIRM and after enhancement, ranked by Information Gain Ratio.

a number ranging from 0 (indicating no similarity) and 1 (identical similarity). Gensim by Řehůřek et al. was used in our LDA and LSA modeling and similarity calculations [19].

3.3 Dataset Balancing

From the prior experiment, the dataset used in training and cross validation was collected using five different Mechanical Turk voters for 1,124 instances. The instances were classified by the majority of voters to Relevant and Non-Relevant classes. Unfortunately, but yet matching intuition, the dataset collected is biased towards Relevancy (with 930 Relevant Vs. 194 Non-Relevant). This undersampling of the class Non-Relevant is causing the trained model to be more aggressive towards the Relevant class as shown in the class-based recall, precision and F-measure in table 6.

The problem of imbalanced training datasets in classification is a well-known problem. In a multitude of cases, one of the classes is significantly lower in training points than the other class(es). This causes the classifier to be overly sensitive towards one class than the other. In our analysis, the Relevant class is almost five times in magnitude than the Non-Relevant class resulting in a reduced precision and recall in the minor class. Possible solutions to this problem is by undersampling the major class (Relevant) to be nearly the same size of the minor class (Non-Relevant). This approach has a downside as we purposely dispose of good data points that could enhance the classifier. Also it reduces the size of the training dataset for the collective classes gravely.

Another approach is the Synthetic Minority Over-sampling Technique or (SMOTE) introduced by Chawla et al. [2]. By synthesizing balancing datapoints via over-sampling the minor class in the dataset and utilizing the k-nearest neighbors algorithm, they were able to enrich the training dataset iteratively by oversampling the minor class until the two classes were close in size. Their technique proved to achieve better classifier performance (in ROC space) than undersampling the major class. Given so, we utilized SMOTE with five nearest neighbors in balancing our Relevant-NonRelevant dataset iteratively then we randomized the dataset uniformly. Table 5 shows the results of retraining the classifier after enhancement.

3.4 Feature Minimization

To this point, we have collected 65 different features (39 original + 26 new) to train TIRM. Due to the associated high cost of calculating all the features, we investigate the effect of feature minimization on the trained classifier.

For each feature, there are two important factors: cost (computational power and time) and effectiveness (information gain ratio). We will assume a uniform cost and optimize in regards to information gain. We use ranker algorithm in extracting the top 25 features (as shown in table 3) in terms of information gain to retrain TIRM. Table 6 shows the 60% reduced TIRM classifier has a performance reduction of about 2%.

4. INTENTION STRENGTH

To indicate the intention class, we use the resulting relevance from the model along with change in TIRM (as illustrated in table 1). This mapping model is effective, but unfortunately, although we can deduce the intention class (being past or current) but there is no quantification of this intention strength. To overcome this, we devise a formulation of calculating the intention strength in terms of change and relevance as follows.

	Precision	Recall	F-measure
Prior TIRM			
Relevant	0.863	0.971	0.914
Non-Relevant	0.654	0.263	0.375
Weighted Avg.	0.827	0.849	0.821
TIRM after Enhancement			
Relevant	0.880	0.932	0.905
Non-Relevant	0.928	0.873	0.900
Weighted Avg.	0.904	0.903	0.903
TIRM after Minimization			
Relevant	0.849	0.939	0.892
Non-Relevant	0.932	0.834	0.880
Weighted Avg.	0.890	0.886	0.886

Table 6: Results from the previous TIRM, TIRM after enhancement, and minimization with Random Forrest Classifier

For each resource r, the similarity $\sigma_{past-current}$ is calculated using LDA similarity illustrated earlier between the two versions, the past version (at t_{tweet}) and the current version (at t_{click}). Thus, $\delta_{past-current}$ is the normalized change ranging from 0.0 to 1.0. From the classifier we extract the relevance measure $\rho(r)$ ranging from 0.0 - 1.0, where 0.0 being completely Non-Relevant, and 1.0 being completely Relevant. Referring back to the TIRM model table 1 we define the intention class $\chi(r)$ in terms of change $\delta(r)$ and relevance $\rho(r)$ as follows:

$$\chi(r) = \begin{cases} \text{Current}, & \text{if } \rho(r) > 0.5 \ \& \ \delta(r) > 0.5 \\ \text{Past}, & \text{if } \begin{cases} \rho(r) < 0.5 \ \& \ \delta(r) > 0.5 \\ \rho(r) > 0.5 \ \& \ \delta(r) < 0.5 \end{cases} \\ \text{Unknown}, & \text{otherwise} \end{cases} \tag{1}$$

After identifying the intention class $\chi(r)$, we calculate the intention magnitude or strength $|\chi(r)|$. From Figure 2 we can deduce that the point $(\rho(r_s),\ \delta(r_s)) = (1,1)$ means it is most relevant and completely changed which indicates the strongest "decided current intention" or $|\chi(r_s)| = 1$.

Point $(\rho(r_c),\ \delta(r_c)) = (0.5,0.5)$ is considered the point of confusion as it illustrates peak uncertainty of intention, or $|\chi(r_c)| = 0$. The further the new resource $(\rho(r),\ \delta(r)) =$ (x,y) from the point of confusion the stronger the intention certainty is. The furthest distance is the distance from the confusion point $(\rho(r_c),\ \delta(r_c)) = (0.5,0.5)$ to certainty point $(\rho(r_s),\ \delta(r_s)) = (1,1)$. This distance S will be used for normalization. Also the distances are Euclidean.

So to calculate $|\chi(r)|$ for the new resource $(\rho(r),\ \delta(r)) =$ (x,y) we follow equation 2.

$$|\chi(r)| = \frac{L}{L'} = \frac{\sqrt{(\rho(r) - \rho(r_c))^2 + (\delta(r) - \delta(r_c))^2}}{\sqrt{(\rho(r_s) - \rho(r_c))^2 + (\delta(r_s) - \delta(r_c))^2}} \tag{2}$$

	10-Fold Cross-Validation Testing				
	Mean Absolute Error	Relative Absolute Error	Kappa Statistic	Incorrectly Classified %	Correctly Classified %
Prior TIRM	0.22	75.77%	0.31	15.12%	84.88%
Enhanced TIRM	0.20	39.69	0.81	9.73%	90.27%

Table 5: Results of 10-fold cross-validation for TIRM prior and after the three-staged enhancement process.

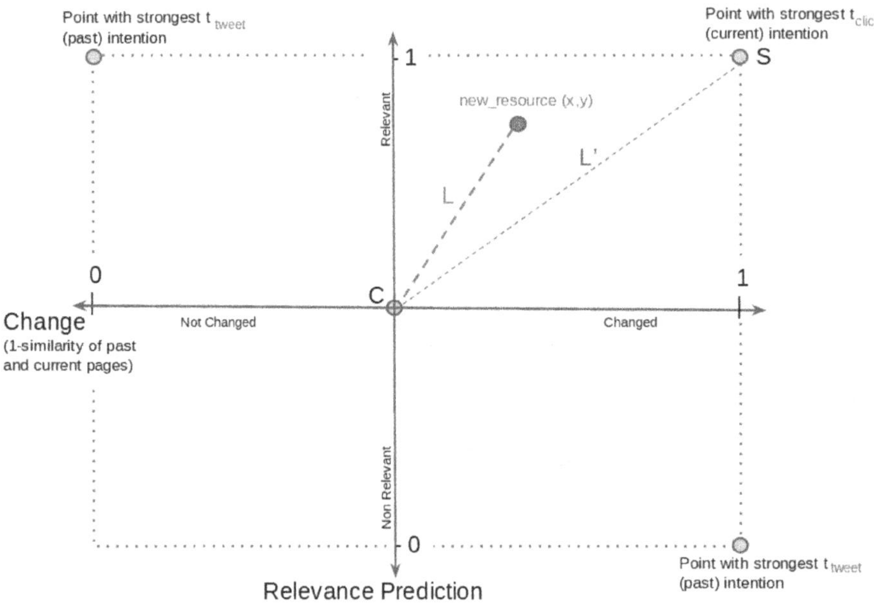

Figure 2: Intention Strength Mapping.

Or to simplify: strengthsInstances

$$|\chi(r)| = \frac{\sqrt{(\rho(r)-\frac{1}{2})^2+(\delta(r)-\frac{1}{2})^2}}{\sqrt{(1-\frac{1}{2})^2+(1-\frac{1}{2})^2}} \quad (3)$$

$$|\chi(r)| = \sqrt{2[(\rho(r)-\frac{1}{2})^2+(\delta(r)-\frac{1}{2})^2]} \quad (4)$$

Finally by merging the intention class $\chi(r)$ and the intention strength $|\chi(r)|$ we get this formula:

$$|\chi(r)| = \begin{cases} |\chi(r)| & if\ \ \chi(r) = Current \\ -|\chi(r)| & if\ \ \chi(r) = Past \\ Undefined & if\ \ \chi(r) = Unknown \end{cases} \quad (5)$$

Equation 5 summarizes $|\chi(r)|$ to be a value ranging from -1.0 to 1.0, with -1.0 being the strongest *Past* intention and 1.0 being the strongest *Current* intention. For the 1,124 instances in the dataset we calculate the corresponding intention strengths $|\chi(r_{1-1,124})|$. Figure 3 shows a histogram of the instances in each intention strength bin ranging from -1.0 to 1.0 and Figure 4 shows the sorted instances in terms of intention strength.

5. MODELING INTENTION ACROSS TIME

At this point, we are able to calculate the intention strength at the current time, and whether it is current or past, given

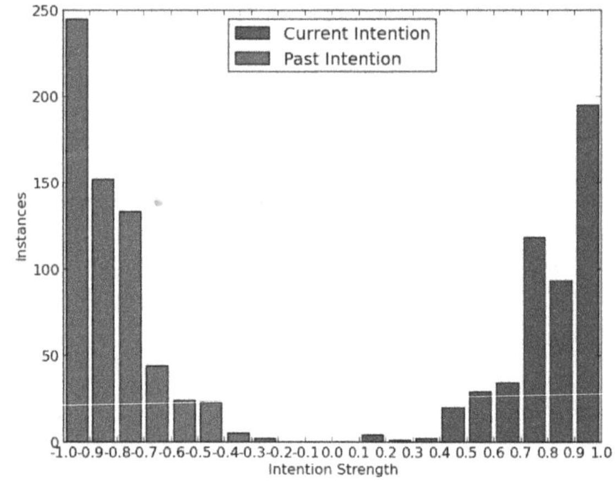

Figure 3: Histogram of the 1,124 instances in each intention strength bin.

the tweet and the resource's state at t_{tweet} and at t_{click}. The next logical question was: *Did the intention strength through the life span of the resource between t_{tweet} and t_{click} change at one point during these three and half years?*

Answering this question will put us on track of answering the ultimate question of this paper: *Would the study of how intention strength change through time give us a way*

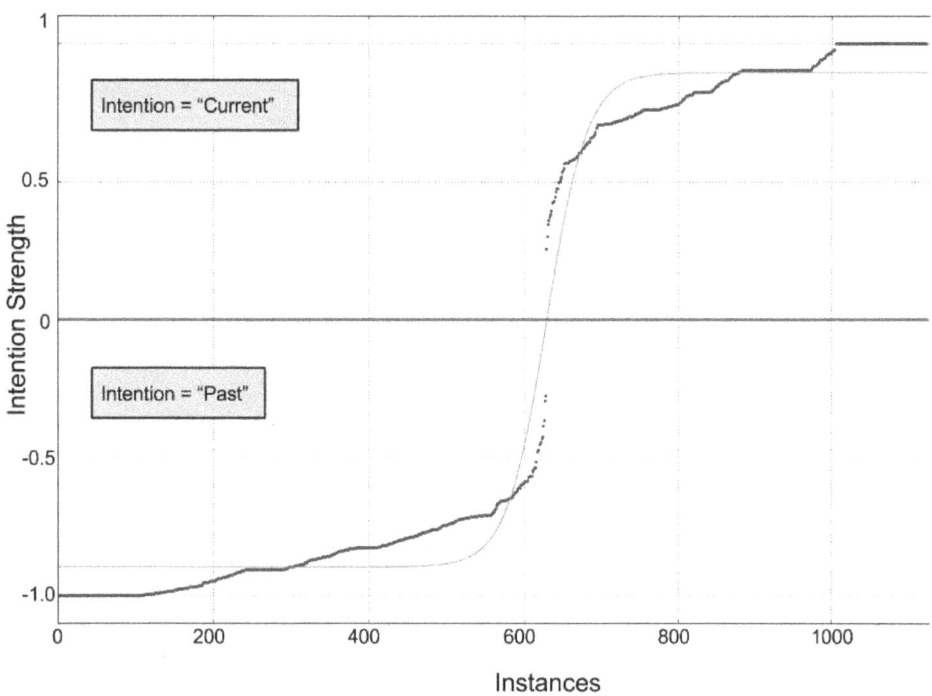

Figure 4: Intention strength across all 1,124 instances

Behavior	Example Tweet
Steady-Current	Check out our latest news at http://bit.ly/1xC7MhK #PolyU
Changing	@heathermeeker The media just lost interest, the WHO has been releasing regular flu A(H1N1) updates, latest is #47 http://bit.ly/whodu
Steady-Past	The Real Secret to Becoming a Popular Blogger http://bit.ly/16OY7q via @FreelanceSw

Table 7: Tweet examples of the behavior classes.

to predict this change at an earlier point in time, namely at posting time t_{tweet}?

In the dataset used in building the model, the 1,124 tweets were extracted from the Stanford Network Analysis Project (SNAP) Twitter dataset [9] which spanned around 476 million tweets. These instances were collected in the period from June to December of 2009. The Mechanical Turk experiment was conducted and the *current* snapshots were captured in January 2013 after about three and half years. We utilized the public archives through the Memento Framework to extract the state of the linked resource at the time of the tweet [18]. To get the past version of the resource, we extracted the closest memento to the time of posting the tweet t_{tweet}. To gauge the validity of the extracted past version, we measured the time difference between t_{tweet} and the creation time of that closest memento. The time difference between t_{tweet} and $t_{closest\_memento}$ was ranging from 3.07 minutes to 56.04 hours averaging 25.79 hours. For the sake of simplicity, we assumed these time deltas are negligible and $t_{closest\_memento} \approx t_{tweet}$. Following the same paradigm we extracted 10 mementos from the period between t_{tweet} and t_{click}:

$$t_{snapshot}(i) = \begin{cases} t_{tweet} & for \quad i = 0 \\ t_{memento}(i) & \forall i = 1...10 \\ t_{click} & for \quad i = 11 \end{cases} \tag{6}$$

Where $i = 0$ means the first snapshot which is at time of the tweet and $i = 11$ means the last snapshot at the current end time of the experiment. The ten downloaded mementos are at $i = 1 \rightarrow 10$.

The next step is to calculate the intention strength at each of those 12 points in time. Since we need to simulate the state at each time $t_{snapshot}(i)$ we need to download the state of the resource, get the Bitly clicklogs and the summation of the posted tweets up to this time. We mined the Bit.ly API to extract the clicks count to that moment $t_{snapshot}(i)$. We extracted the tweets posted till $t_{snapshot}(i)$ from Topsy.com API. This is another rationale behind using Topsy API instead of the Twitter API as the latter does not enable searching further than the indexing period (two weeks). Furthermore, we calculated all the applicable features for each snapshot as shown in Figure 5. Finally, using our prior trained model and the strength formulation we calculated $|\chi(r_i)|$ for each snapshot and plotted them across time as shown in examples in Figure 6.

6. PREDICTING TEMPORAL INTENTION AT TWEET TIME

In Figure 6, the blue points indicate the intention strength at this point in time. We noticed a steady behavior with respect to time in some cases and a changing behavior in others. This matches our intuition that users intended for the

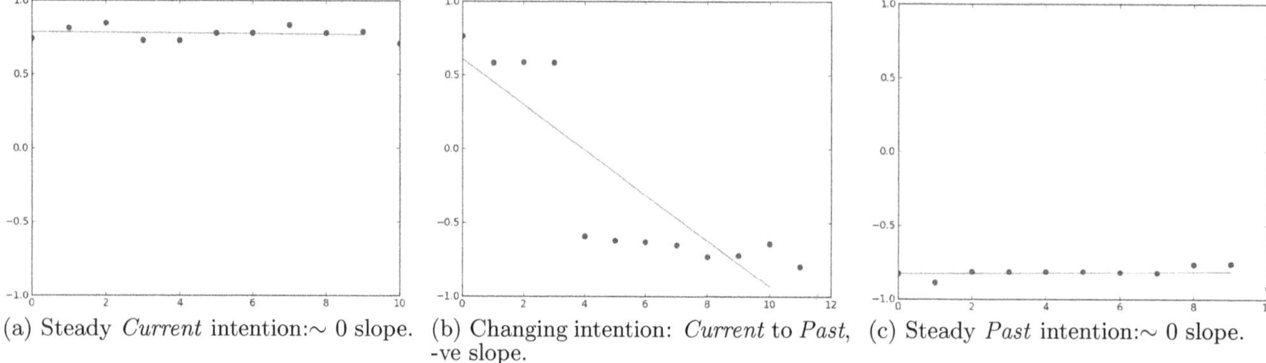

(a) Steady *Current* intention:$\sim$ 0 slope. (b) Changing intention: *Current* to *Past*, -ve slope. (c) Steady *Past* intention:$\sim$ 0 slope.

Figure 6: The resources' intention strength across time for different behavior categories.

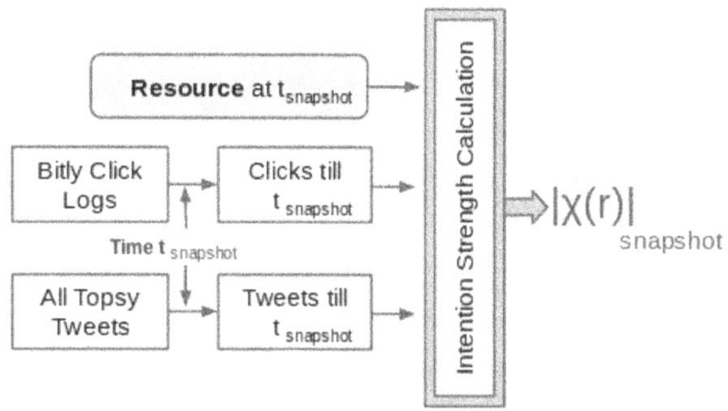

Figure 5: Intention Strength calculation per snapshot

readers to see the version at t_{click} for the first short period of time, but upon changing and updating of the resource the intention deviated to the t_{tweet} version as shown in Figure 6(b).

To further analyze this phenomena, and to differentiate the steady state from the changing one, we fitted with blue intention strength points in the graphs with the closest linear regression line (red line) to measure its progression through its slope as shown as well in Figure 6. Evidently, if the slope was negative this indicate the intention has changed from *current* to *past*. We use both the slope of the fitted regression line and the fitting error to cluster the plots into three different categories: Steady, Changing, and Unknown. The *Steady Intentional behavior* means the slope is small and the fitting error is small, this indicates a resource where the intention did not change across time. The *Changing Intentional behavior* means the slope is negative indicating a change in intention from current to past across time, with a moderate fitting error. Finally the *Unknown Intentional behavior* is where the regression line fitting error is too high or the 4th class of our TIRM model where the resource is not relevant and did not change.

Given the slope, intercept, and fitting error along with the other features, we were able to successfully train a regression classifier to automatically categorize the behavior of a resource across time into either one of these three categories. We performed a 10-fold cross-validation and the classifier correctly classified 89% of the dataset as shown in table 9. We were able to identify the behavioral class of intention given the knowledge of the state of the resource and the social network around it through time; The next step is to validate the viability of identifying these classes given only the information available at tweet time t_{tweet}.

With our model from the previous stage, we filtered out all the longitudinal temporal features and kept only the features extracted from the tweet and the current version of the resource at t_{tweet}. We retrained the classifier using these limited features and it correctly classified 77% of the dataset. This percentage is lower than the prior percentage with the full knowledge of the resource in time as expected. Moreover, it is still high enough indicating the viability of predicting the temporal intention progression given only the knowledge of the tweet at posting time and the state of the resource at t_{tweet} as shown also in tables 8 and 9.

In other words, at the time of authoring a tweet, and given only the information about the resource and the tweet available at the current time, we can predict for the author whether the intention conveyed to the readers will be consistent or will it change with 77% accuracy.

Returning to our tweet examples, in the tweet in Figure 1(a), the model predicted a change in intention from current to past with 60% probability. While in the tweet in Figure 1(b), the model predicted a 60% probability of steady-current intention. Furthermore in table 7, for the third tweet our model predicted a steady behavior with a 40% probability.

This prediction will give the author sufficient information to choose to just post the tweet or take a snapshot of the resource and push it into one of the public archives and link to that snapshot instead to maintain the consistency. This prediction will have implication on maintaining the consistency of the conveyed information on the web and will help enrich the archived content of a multitude of resources by crowdsourcing the preservation task.

	Precision	Recall	F-measure
Steady Intention	0.680	0.715	0.697
Changing Intention (Current to Past)	0.912	0.897	0.904
Undefined Intention	0.713	0.688	0.700
Weighted Avg.	0.768	0.767	0.767

Table 8: Intention behavior prediction classifier

10-Fold Cross-Validation Testing

Predicting Intention	Mean Absolute Error	Relative Absolute Error	Kappa Statistic	Incorrectly Classified %	Correctly Classified %
With all Features	0.15	34.11%	0.84	10.94%	89.06%
With the tweet and the resource at t_{tweet}	0.22	50.57%	0.65	23.32%	76.68%

Table 9: Results of 10-fold cross-validation for predicting intention behavior strength across time.

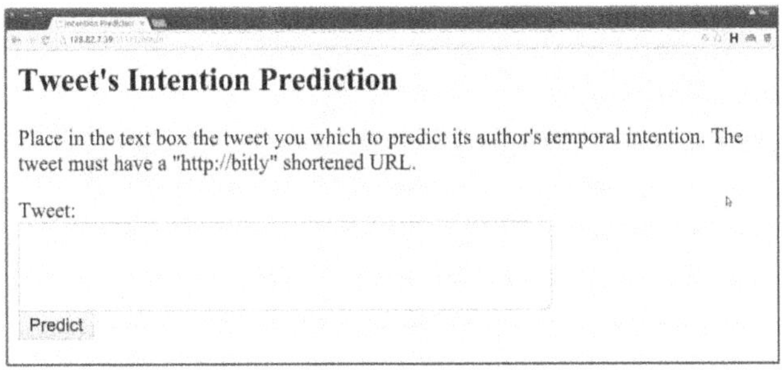

Figure 7: Intention Oracle API service

7. INTENTION ORACLE API

We built a proof-of-concept class prediction service which implements the prediction model described in section 6. The service takes a tweet with a URL shortened via Bit.ly and extracts the necessary features after downloading content and then predicts the behavioral class of the tweet. For the time being it classifies if the resource is more likely to be in a steady state of intention or a changing state of intention. The service interface is shown in Figure 7 and a sample JSON-encoded response obtained in correspondence to the three tweet examples in table 7 respectively are demonstrated in Figure 8.

8. CONCLUSIONS

In this work, we analyze the problem of temporal intention in sharing resources in social media. We adopt a prior preliminary model in analyzing users' temporal intention. This model enabled us to detect and classify relevance and map it along with the resource's change to extract the intention class of the tweet in relation to the linked resource in it. In this paper, our first contribution is by enhancing this model and addressing the short comings in regards to linguistic features analysis, balancing the training dataset, and finally using latent semantics in measuring similarity instead of merely textual resemblance. With these three stages, we were able to enhance the model considerably, especially in the Non-Relevant class, with a 0.5 improvement in F-measure and a 6% increase in total classification from the prior model upon utilizing a Random Forrest based classifier.

Our second contribution is quantifying this temporal intention based on the enhanced model. We formulate a combination of the new semantic change measure and the relevance prediction from the enhanced classifier to produce a normalized quantifiable intention strength measure ranging from -1.0 to 1.0 (past to current intention, respectively).

The third contribution is analyzing the progression of intention through time. We simulate the intention analysis over the period of 3.5 years from June 2009 to January 2013 to observe the intention strength change across time. We observe three different classes of behavior: a steady intention either in the past or current, a changing intention gradually with time from the current to past, and undefined intention. We use these observations to fit regression lines to calculate the slopes and intercepts of intention to detect the progression scheme through time.

Our fourth contribution is in predicting the temporal intention at the time of authoring a tweet. We incorporate


```
{
  "Tweet Analyzed": "Check out our latest news
  at http://bit.ly/1xC7MhK #PolyU",
  "Bitly Extracted": "http://bit.ly/1xC7MhK",
  "Original Resource URL": "http://www.fb.
  polyu.edu.hk/content/10505/index.html",
  "State": "Steady, Not changing",
  "Prediction": "Predicted Steady intention
  for the resource with 60.0% confidence",
  "Confidence": "60.0"
}

{
  "Tweet Analyzed": "@heathermeeker The media
  just lost interest, the WHO has been
  releasing regular lu A(H1N1) updates,
  latest is #47 http://bit.ly/whodu",
  "Bitly Extracted": "http://bit.ly/whodu",
  "Original Resource URL": "http://www.who.
  int/csr/don/en/",
  "State": "Unsteady, Changing",
  "Prediction": "Predicted Unsteady intention
  observed for the resource, recommend
  preservation with 60.0% confidence",
  "Confidence": "60.0"
}

{
  "Tweet Analyzed": "The Real Secret to
  Becoming a Popular Blogger http://bit.ly/
  16OY7q via @FreelanceSw",
  "Bitly Extracted": "http://bit.ly/16OY7q",
  "Original Resource URL": "http://www.
  copyblogger.com/popular-blogger/",
  "State": "Steady, Not changing",
  "Prediction": "Predicted Steady intention
  for the resource with 50.0% confidence",
  "Confidence": "50.0"
}
```


Figure 8: JSON Objects resulting from the Intention Oracle API

these features to our previous dataset across time and model the change of intention with a success of 89%. Finally we predict this change or steadiness of intention at t_{tweet} by using only the features that are readily available at t_{tweet} from both the tweet and the resource and were able to successfully predict this intention with 77% accuracy. Giving the authors enough information to aid them to either re-write the tweet with the knowledge of change or push a snapshot of the resource to one of the public archives and link to it instead, maintaining temporal consistence and enriching the archives at the same time.

Finally we demonstrate a prototype API service implementation of our intention prediction model to be utilized on tweet with links shortened via Bitly.com service.

9. ACKNOWLEDGMENT

This work was supported in part by the Library of Congress and NSF IIS-1009392. We thank the anonymous reviewers for their suggestions in regards to the strength formulation.

10. REFERENCES

[1] E. Adar, J. Teevan, S. T. Dumais, and J. L. Elsas. The Web Changes Everything: Understanding The Dynamics Of Web Content. In *WSDM '09: Proceedings Of The Second ACM International Conference On Web Search and Data Mining*, pages 282–291, 2009.

[2] N. V. Chawla, K. W. Bowyer, L. O. Hall, and W. P. Kegelmeyer. SMOTE: Synthetic Minority Over-Sampling Technique. *Journal Of Artificial Intelligence Research*, 16(1):321–357, June 2002.

[3] T. Chen, D. Lu, M.-Y. Kan, and P. Cui. Understanding and Classifying Image Tweets. In *Proceedings Of The 21st ACM International Conference On Multimedia*, MM '13, pages 781–784, New York, NY, USA, 2013. ACM.

[4] J. Cho and H. Garcia-Molina. Estimating Frequency Of Change. *ACM Transactions On Internet Technology*, 3(3):256–290, Aug. 2003.

[5] D. Fetterly, M. Manasse, M. Najork, and J. Wiener. A Large-Scale Study Of The Evolution Of Web Pages. In *WWW '03: Proceedings Of The 12th International Conference On World Wide Web*, pages 669–678, 2003.

[6] M. D. Hoffman, D. M. Blei, and F. R. Bach. Online Learning For Latent Dirichlet Allocation. In *NIPS*, pages 856–864, 2010.

[7] A. Java, X. Song, T. Finin, and B. Tseng. Why We Twitter: Understanding Microblogging Usage and Communities. In *Proceedings Of The 9th WebKDD and 1st Sna-Kdd 2007 Workshop On Web Mining and Social Network Analysis*, WebKDD/SNA-KDD '07, pages 56–65, New York, NY, USA, 2007. ACM.

[8] M. Klein and M. L. Nelson. Investigating The Change Of Web Pages' Titles Over Time. Technical Report arXiv:0907.3445, 2009.

[9] J. Leskovec and A. Krevl. Snap Datasets: Stanford Large Network Dataset Collection. `http://snap.stanford.edu/data`, June 2014.

[10] R. Mehrotra, S. Sanner, W. Buntine, and L. Xie. Improving Lda Topic Models For Microblogs Via Tweet Pooling and Automatic Labeling. In *Proceedings Of The 36th International ACM SIGIR Conference On Research and Development In Information Retrieval*, SIGIR '13, pages 889–892, New York, NY, USA, 2013. ACM.

[11] E. Momeni, K. Tao, B. Haslhofer, and G.-J. Houben. Identification Of Useful User Comments In Social Media: A Case Study On Flickr Commons. In *Proceedings Of The 13th ACM/IEEE-CS Joint Conference On Digital Libraries*, JCDL '13, pages 1–10, New York, NY, USA, 2013. ACM.

[12] N. Niraula, R. Banjade, D. Stefanescu, and V. Rus. Experiments With Semantic Similarity Measures Based On Lda and Lsa. *Statistical Language and Speech Processing*, 7978:188–199, 2013.

[13] J. Oliva, J. I. Serrano, M. D. Del Castillo, and A. Iglesias. Symss: A Syntax-Based Measure For Short-Text Semantic Similarity. *Data & Knowledge Engineering*, 70(4):390–405, 2011.

[14] K. Radinsky and P. N. Bennett. Predicting content change on the web. In *Proceedings of the Sixth ACM International Conference on Web Search and Data Mining*, WSDM '13, pages 415–424, New York, NY, USA, 2013. ACM.

[15] A. Ritter, S. Clark, Mausam, and O. Etzioni. Named Entity Recognition In Tweets: An Experimental Study. In *Proceedings Of The Conference On Empirical Methods In Natural Language Processing*, EMNLP '11, pages 1524–1534, Stroudsburg, PA, USA, 2011. Association for Computational Linguistics.

[16] V. Rus, N. Niraula, and R. Banjade. Similarity Measures Based On Latent Dirichlet Allocation. *Computational Linguistics and Intelligent Text Processing*, 7816:459–470, 2013.

[17] H. M. SalahEldeen and M. L. Nelson. Reading The Correct History?: Modeling Temporal Intention In Resource Sharing. In *Proceedings Of The 13th ACM/IEEE-CS Joint Conference On Digital Libraries*, JCDL '13, pages 257–266, New York, NY, USA, 2013. ACM.

[18] H. Van de Sompel, M. L. Nelson, R. Sanderson, L. Balakireva, S. Ainsworth, and H. Shankar. Memento: Time Travel For The Web. Technical Report arXiv:0911.1112, 2009.

[19] R. Řehůřek and P. Sojka. Software Framework For Topic Modelling With Large Corpora. In *Proceedings Of The LREC 2010 Workshop On New Challenges For NLP Frameworks*, pages 45–50, Valletta, Malta, May 2010. ELRA.

[20] A. Wang, T. Chen, and M.-Y. Kan. Re-Tweeting From A Linguistic Perspective. In *Proceedings Of The Second Workshop On Language In Social Media*, LSM '12, pages 46–55, Stroudsburg, PA, USA, 2012. Association for Computational Linguistics.

[21] W. X. Zhao, J. Jiang, J. Weng, J. He, E.-P. Lim, H. Yan, and X. Li. Comparing Twitter and Traditional Media Using Topic Models. In *Proceedings Of The 33rd European Conference On Advances In Information Retrieval*, ECIR'11, pages 338–349, Berlin, Heidelberg, 2011. Springer-Verlag.

Before the Repository: Defining the Preservation Threats to Research Data in the Lab

Stacy T. Kowalczyk
Dominican University
7900 W. Division Street
River Forest, Illinois
1-708- 524-6482
skowalczyk@dom.edu

ABSTRACT

This paper describes the results of a large survey designed to quantify the risks and threats to the preservation of the research data in the lab and to determine the mitigating actions of researchers. A total of 724 National Science Foundation awardees completed this survey. Identifying risks and threats to digital preservation has been a significant research stream. Much of this work has been within the context of a preservation technology infrastructure such as data archives for a digital repository. This study looks at the risks and threats to research data prior to its inclusion in a preservation technology infrastructure. The greatest threat to preservation is human error, followed by equipment malfunction, obsolete software, and data corruption. Lost and mislabeled media are not components in the threat taxonomies developed for repositories; however, they do represent an important threat to research data in the lab. Researchers have recognized the need to mitigate the risks inherent in maintaining digital data by implementing data management in their lab environments and have taken their responsibility as data managers seriously; however, they would still prefer to have professional data management support.

Categories and Subject Descriptors

H.3.7 Digital Libraries – *Collection;* D.4.5 [Reliability]: Backup procedures – *best practice, disaster mitigation.*

General Terms

Management, Measurement, Documentation, Reliability, Theory

Keywords

Research data; data management; repositories; digital preservation; preservation threats

1. INTRODUCTION

Computer-based technology has fundamentally changed both the practice and the output of science [8]. Virtually all scientific research and an increasing amount of humanities research is computationally-based. The result of this computational research is digital data. The process of ensuring the long-term access to this research data, that is preserving it, has become a major area of focus for libraries and research organizations.

Preserving scientific data begins with data. Data "refer[s] to any information that can be stored in digital form, including text, numbers, images, video or movies, audio, software, algorithms, equations, animations, models, simulations, etc. Such data may be generated by various means including observation, computation, or experiment" [30, p. 9]. Data can be dynamic and subject to change; or data can be stable and non-changing [23, 25]. The more volatile the data, the more difficult to manage, store, and access [10]. But even stable data changes as it is processed. Data evolves through four stages: collection, organization, presentation, and application [22]. This evolution can be described as a lifecycle. Many lifecycles make an assumption that data is eventually stored in a preservation infrastructure; that is, data is ingested into a digital repository. However, only a small amount of research data is actually managed in a preservation environment; most research data is maintained by the researcher [19]. Research is needed to describe, measure, and mitigate the "obstacles to the longevity of digital materials" [33 p. 6].

A central tenet of preservation, the process of assuring the longevity of digital content, is mitigating risks to the well-being of the digital content. Defining and categorizing the threats to digital preservation has been a significant theme in the literature. Most of these threats are discussed within the context of a repository [38]. This study investigates the preservation threats faced by researchers and the actions they take to mitigate them.

Research questions

1. What threats to preservation have caused data loss in the research environment?
2. How do researchers mitigate these risks?

There is little quantitative data about the preservation threats to research data in the lab environment. This paper reports on a large survey of National Science Foundation awardees, their experience with data loss and the decisions that they make about data management. This paper is organized as follows: a brief literature review of preservation threats, the research methodology, the survey results, and a discussion.

2. Literature Review

2.1 Preservation Threat Taxonomies

Assessing, describing, and managing risk is a significant component of preservation infrastructure management [1, 3, 15, 29, 38, 39]. The risks associated with preservation infrastructures have been defined through the literature as threats to preservation

JCDL'15, June 21-25, 2015, Knoxville, TN, USA
© 2015 ACM. ISBN 978-1-4503-3594-2/15/06…$15.00
DOI: http://dx.doi.org/10.1145/2756406.2756909

[1, 2, 3, 13, 31, 32, 38]. In the literature, these threats have been categorized in a number of ways: component failures, management failures, disasters, and attacks [2]; physical threats, technology threats, human threats, and institutional threats [1]; economic threat, human error, disasters and attacks [32].

A more nuanced taxonomy of preservation threats has been developed that differentiates between the inherent risks of technologies, described as vulnerabilities, and threats (see Table 1.) [3]. Vulnerabilities include process, data, and infrastructure; threats include disasters, attacks, management, and legislation [3].

Table 1. Taxonomy of Vulnerabilities and Threats to Preservation [3, p. 9]

Vulnerabilities	Process	Software faults Software obsolescence
	Data	Media faults Media obsolescence
	Infrastructure	Hardware faults Hardware obsolescence Communication faults Network service failures
Threats	Disasters	Natural disasters Human operational errors
	Attacks	Internal attacks External attacks
	Management	Economic failures Organizational failures
	Legislation	Legislative changes Legal requirements

2.2 Mitigating Threats

The primary threat mitigation strategy is good data management [14, 19, 25, 36]. Data management is a set of tasks and activities to plan for system backups, contingencies, process resumption, hardware and network redundancy, automatic failover, and site mirroring – all efforts to avert problems. Established and well-funded data repositories often have dedicated data management staff [16] and large data centers to manage the petabyte datasets [7, 12].

Even well run organizations with strong commitments to digital preservation and with strong technical infrastructures face many challenges including threats both to archived digital content and to the organization [38]. Research on threats faced when developing and deploying a repository for a large-scale newspaper digitizing project shows that the primary threats were media failure, hardware failure, software failures, and operator errors [20]. Research has show that the United Nations' disaster recovery plan was insufficient during Hurricane Sandy; both the primary and secondary sites were incapacitated by the storm causing the UN's Official Document System (ODS) to be unavailable for several days [6].

2.3 Threats to Data Prior to the Repository

Preservation threats have been analyzed and discussed within the context of a preservation infrastructure, such as an archival system or a data repository. However, only a small percentage of research data is submitted to repositories for long-term preservation [19]. Individual scientists are responsible to manage their own data [24, 25]. Researchers often lack the skills to be effective data managers [37]; and the self-sufficient research culture often hinders collaboration between scientists and trained data managers [5]. Rather than hiring data management experts, scientists have been using Ph.D. students as systems administrators, sacrificing a generation of new researchers [11]. The probability of long-term data management for research collections is low when the ongoing responsibility lies with an individual researcher or graduate student [19, 28].

2.4 Lost Data

Research on lost data is sparse. Two of the most famous, or perhaps infamous, examples of lost data are both from NASA. The first of these is data collected during the Apollo 11, 12, and 14 moon missions from instrumentation for collecting lunar surface environmental information. The 173 tapes of that data were misplaced by the University of Sydney's data center before they were archived or documented by NASA. In 2008, researchers realized that the data on lunar atmospheric dust could be useful for future lunar exploration research. The tapes were located but the tape drives needed to read the data were no longer available [26]. The second example is a similar story. The tapes of Neil Armstrong's first walk on the moon, along with approximately 700 other data tapes of Apollo data, were withdrawn from the National Archives in 1984 by NASA's Goddard Space Center in Maryland. These tapes are now missing [27]. Significant data, both historical and scientific, was lost.

3. Research Methodology

A survey frame of grant awardees of the National Science Foundation (NSF) from 2007 through 2010 was retrieved from the Scholarly Database [21]. A subset of 1,200 unique PIs from each of the seven NSF directorates was selected randomly for a total pool of 8,400 potential participants. Each of these 8,400 principal investigators was asked to participate via email solicitations. A total of 897 researchers started the survey, resulting in a response rate of 10.6%. Of the 897 people who started the survey, 724 completed it for a completion rate of 80.7%. The participants in this study identified affiliations with 334 unique research institutions.

Three significant demographic elements were collected in this survey: scientific domain, funding source, and size of laboratory. Scientific domain was expected to be an important factor in the research behavior of the participants. The distribution of participants among the various domains is as follows: Biological Sciences (22%), Computer and Information Science (11%), Education (4%), Engineering (13%), Geosciences (13%), Mathematical Sciences (8%), Physical Sciences (17%), and Social, Behavioral and Economic Sciences (13%).

Lab funding can influence the final disposition of data: more funding means more resources available for data management. As well, outside funding agencies can influence data decisions by mandating data management policies or repository deposit [4]. For this study, funding is considered to be a continuum from exclusively funded by the researchers' institution to exclusively funded by external granting agencies with the underlying expectation that researchers with more stable funding from their institutions would have different concerns than those whose funding must be renewed regularly. The results of this survey indicate that 85% of researchers are funded exclusively or primarily from grants. Only 8% of responders are funded exclusively or primarily from their institution.

As with funding, the size of lab or work group can have an effect on long-term data management; larger labs have more resources to manage their data [17]. Although no standard definitions of large or small labs exist, this study defines a large lab as five or more researchers while a small lab has fewer than five researchers. A large majority, 82%, works in some type of lab or group setting, with 47% in a large lab and 35% in small labs; 17% of researchers work independently without a group or lab.

The data from this survey lends itself to three major types of data analysis: general descriptive analysis, analysis of demographic subcategory significance (scientific domain, size of lab, and funding source), and textual analysis. The analysis of demographic subcategories used cross tabulations with Chi square tests for significance, one-way analysis of variance (ANOVA) tests, and bivariate correlation analysis, depending on the type of question. The p value is considered significant at .01.

4. Results

4.1 Data Loss in the Research Environment

The researchers in this study were asked to identify the causes of any known data loss based on a set of vulnerabilities and threats developed above (see Table 2). Of the 716 respondents to the question on data loss, 50% reported some type of data loss. Human based data management failures were prominent in the list of reported reasons for data loss. Direct loss through inadvertent human error was the largest cause of data loss (30%). This threat was sensitive to the size of lab (χ_2^2 = *18.329, p < .001).* Researchers in large labs were more likely to report data loss due to inadvertent human error while individual researchers and those who work in mid-sized labs were less likely to have suffered such a loss.

Table 2. Data Loss

Data Loss	Responses (1242)	Percentage (of 716 responders)
Lack of funding	36	5%
Inadvertent human error	216	30%
Malicious hacking	6	1%
Mistakenly thought data not needed	49	7%
Equipment malfunction	173	24%
Lost media	73	10%
Mislabeled media	34	5%
Equipment obsolescence	76	11%
Software no longer recognizes data	88	12%
Physical disaster	29	4%
Data corruption	91	13%
I have not lost data	355	49%
Other	21	3%

For the researchers in this study, 23% suffered data loss due to obsolescence – 11% with hardware obsolescence and 12% with software obsolescence. Obsolescence was sensitive to size of lab: software (χ_2^2 = *7.211, p = .027)* and equipment (χ_2^2 = *9.005, p = .011)* obsolescence were both more likely to be reported by large labs than individual researchers or by those in mid-sized labs. Two scientific domains, geoscience and physical science, were sensitive to equipment (χ_7^2 = *14.545, p = .042)* obsolescence.

Lack of disaster preparedness [2, 31, 32] does not seem to be a major threat to the researchers in this study, as only 4% reported loss of data due to physical disasters. Two reasonable conclusions may be drawn from this result. It is possible that the research centers and data centers in major universities have implemented business resumption plans that have mitigated this threat. It is also possible that this finding is the result of happenstance, that the participants in this study simply have not experienced a large-scale disaster.

Although malicious attack is widely accepted as a threat to preservation [1, 2, 31, 32] and is perceived as a significant and imminent threat in the literature, only 1% of the researchers in this study reported any loss due to malicious hacking. There are at least two possible explanations for the low incidence of malicious attack: one is the low reward for hacking scientific data (as opposed to credit card companies or other financial institutions), and the second is the improved security of both servers and networks at research institutions.

Of the 716 respondents, 91 (13%) experienced data loss due to corruption. Data loss due to corruption is difficult to categorize because it may have multiple causes. Data corruption can be caused by media failure, software malfunctions, and human error such as partial overwrites and poor file management. Size of lab was a significant factor in data corruption (χ_2^2 = *19.003, p < .001)*: researchers in large labs were more likely to report data loss due to corruption while individual researchers were less likely.

Equipment malfunction was the second most common cause of data loss reported in this study; 24% of the researchers reported data loss from equipment failures. Equipment malfunction was sensitive to scientific domain (χ_7^2 = *26.945, p < .001)* and to lab size (χ_2^2 = *25.914, p < .001).* Geoscientists and physical scientists were more likely to report data loss by equipment failure while computer scientists, mathematicians and educators were less likely to have lost data due to equipment failure. Researchers in large labs were more likely to report data loss due to equipment failure while individual researchers and those in mid-sized labs were less likely.

Loss of context is a major threat to preservation [18]. Data sets with minimal or no metadata are virtually lost [34, 35]. The researchers in this study confirm this finding. Mislabeled media constitutes a loss of context and metadata. In this study, it accounted for 5% of the data loss scenarios. Seven of the commenters via the "other" option reported that the lack of metadata caused a loss of access to data. All of these researchers equated the loss of access via metadata to the loss of data.

Lack of funding was reported by 5% of the respondents. Neither scientific domain nor size of lab was significant to this issue; however, funding source ($F_{4,785}$ = *.395, p = .048)* was; those researchers who were equally funded by institution and grants were more likely to report data loss by lack of funding.

Of the 716 respondents to the question on data loss, 50% reported no data loss. Individual researchers and those in mid-sized labs were more likely to report no data loss while researchers in large labs were less likely (χ_2^2 = *10.689, p = .005).* Although this could be a positive indication of data management in action, it cannot be taken as proof of good practice. As one of the commenters in the "other" option stated, "I don't *think* that I have lost data!"

4.2 Data Management Mitigation

Because data management is complex and is closely tied to the type of data, the long-term needs of the researchers, and the technologies available, it is difficult to codify and reduce best practice to a survey question. However, data management is well known to be part of the entire data lifecycle [9]. As such, the item used to understand the extent to which researchers know data management best practice measures the understanding of data management timing; that is, the question asked researchers to identify the point in the research data life cycle at which data management becomes important. A majority of researchers (55%) reported that data management is important throughout the life cycle, beginning with the creation of the data (see Table 3). An additional 17% indicated that data management should begin at the onset of data analysis, a relatively early stage in the data lifecycle. By this measure, a large majority, 72%, had a reasonable understanding of the importance of managing data early in the lifecycle. Of the 720 respondents, 151 (21%) did not convey a reasonable understanding of data management as they indicated that data management is important only as the data life cycle is concluding: 4% as the analysis is complete; 8% as research papers are written; 3% as data is archived; 4% as data is missing; and 2% are unsure.

Table 3. Data Management within the Research Lifecycle

Data Management Timing	Responses (720)	Percentage
Managing data is not important to my research.	50	7%
When the data is created.	398	55%
When the analysis begins.	121	17%
When the analysis is complete.	29	4%
When papers are being written.	56	8%
When the data needs to be archived.	23	3%
When I need to find something and can't remember where it is.	26	4%
Not sure	17	2%

Size of lab affected the perception of the need for data management within the data lifecycle *(χ^2_{12} = 25.388, p = .013)*: individual researchers were more likely to consider data management to be unimportant while those in mid-sized labs considered data management to be important when the data analysis began. Responses from researchers in large labs did not vary from the expected distribution. Scientific domain also had a significant impact this issue *(χ^2_{42} = 130.438, p < .001)*. Both computer scientists and mathematicians were more likely to find data management was unimportant to their research. Engineers were more likely to find data management was important when writing their papers. Biologists, social scientists, and educators were more likely to find data management important at data creation. Funding source was not significant *($F_{4, 693}$ = 5.850, p = .580)*.

4.2.1 Data Management Practice

A significant component of data management, and indeed data preservation, is the assurance of multiple copies of data in disparate locations. The primary method of creating multiple copies is creating backups. When asked to identify if they followed standard best practice for backing up their data, 55% of the researchers reported that they almost always did. An additional 28% of the researchers indicated that they did sometimes follow best practice. Only 8% reported that they rarely or never followed best practice for data backup. An alarming 10% said they did not know best practice (see Table 4).

Scientific domain was significant to the perceived use of best practice *(χ^2_{28} = 42.922, p = .011)*. Computer scientists and geoscientists were significantly more likely to report that they always used best practice. Engineers were more likely to report that they sometimes used best practices and were less likely to report always using best practice. Neither size of lab *(χ^2_8 = 10.883, p = .208)* nor source of funding *($F_{4, 697}$ = 3.993, p = .634)* was a significant factor.

Table 4. Use of Best Practice for Backup

Best Practice	Responses (725)	Percentage
Yes, almost always	375	52%
Sometimes	204	28%
Not generally	42	6%
No, almost never	15	2%
Not sure what is best practice	72	10%
Other	17	2%

4.2.2 Data Management Changes

The researchers were asked to identify data management practices that they would change if money were not an issue. Of the 583 responders, 55 (9%) reported through the "other" option that they would not make any changes; a typical response was as follows: "Our current system is adequate; all problems so far have been due to human error." If funding were not an issue, the remaining 91% the researchers would make different choices about the amount of data they stored, the technologies used to store that data, and the processes and staff by which they managed their data (see Table 5). The most common change researchers would institute is to hire professional staff to manage their data.

Table 5. Data Management Funding Options

Funding Options	Responses (912)	Percentage (of 583)
Choose different storage technologies	144	25%
Save more data	144	25%
Choose different data management practices	167	29%
Choose different backup strategies	181	31%
Hire professional staff to manage the data	276	47%

Only two of the options were sensitive to scientific domain: choosing different data management practices *(χ^2_7 = 16.524, p = .021)* and hiring professional staff to manage the data *(χ^2_7 = 29.788, p < .001)*. Biologists and educators were more likely to want to change both options if funding were available, while social scientists would change only data management practices and geoscientists would hire data professionals. Mathematicians and physical scientists were less likely to want to change their data management practices or to hire a data professional. Computer scientists were less likely to want to hire data professionals. Only one of the options was sensitive to the source of funding *($F_{4, 785}$ = 3.093, p = .008)*; researchers who were exclusively or primarily funded by grants were more likely to want to hire a data professional.

As seen in Table 6, all but one of the options were sensitive to size of lab. While saving more data does not vary based on size of lab, the desire to hire data professionals as well as to choose different storage technologies, different data management practices, and different backup strategies were more likely among researchers in large labs. Individual researchers and those in mid-sized labs were less likely to want to implement changes.

Table 6. Data Management Funding Options By Size of Lab

Funding Options	More Likely	Less Likely
Choose different storage technologies (χ^2_2 = 13.460, p = .001)	Large Labs	Individual Mid-size Labs
Save more data (χ^2_2 = 4.891, p = .087)	n/a	n/a
Choose different data management practices (χ^2_2 = 7.266, p = .026)	Large Labs	Individual Mid-size Labs
Choose different backup strategies (χ^2_2 = 14.167, p = .001)	Large Labs	Individual Mid-size Labs
Hire professional staff to manage the data (χ^2_2 = 6.726, p = .035)	Large Labs	Individual Mid-size Labs

4.3 Limitations

This study is intended to be a broad-based survey of research data practices. The sample frame was based on recent National Science Foundation grant awardees. Although there was broad-based participation across geographic area, institutions, and domains, the sample was skewed toward high level, established researchers in the U.S. The primary attempt to broaden the participation, a request to pass the survey on to others, was less than successful; less than 6% of respondents were outside the original sample list. Having a sample with researchers with different roles, such as graduate student or post-doc, would provide a more balanced view and perhaps more generalizable results.

5. Discussion

Preservation threats have been analyzed and discussed within the context of a preservation infrastructure, an archival system. But data is vulnerable to preservation threats long before it reaches a repository; research data can be lost or damaged from its creation. This study explores the threats to research data in the lab environment. This study found that in general, most researchers believe that they understand and implement good data management practices, and yet more than half of the researchers surveyed lost important data while under their control.

5.1 Types of Data Loss

Categorizing and comparing the actual experience of data loss to the preservation threat taxonomy can provide some additional insights. The data loss scenarios reported by the researchers in this study fit within threat taxonomy [3] described in Section 2.1. In Table 7, we can see that the threats outnumber the vulnerabilities; yet the percentages are nearly equal: 62% of data loss is due to threats, and 60% of data loss is due to vulnerabilities. The inherent vulnerabilities of digital technologies, such as failure, obsolescence, flaws, were as dangerous to the research data as were traditional threats, such as physical disasters, attacks, and economic and management failures.

Table 7. Data Loss by Threat Taxonomy

Data Loss	%	Preservation Threat Taxonomy [3]	
Malicious hacking	1%	Threat – Attacks	External Internal
Inadvertent human error	30%	Threat – Disaster	Human Operational Errors
Physical disaster (flooding, power surges, etc.)	4%	Threat – Disaster	Natural Disaster
Lack of funding	5%	Threat – Management	Economic Failures Organizational Failures
Mistakenly thought data was no longer needed	7%	Threat – Management	Organizational Failures
Lost media	10%	Threat – Management	Organizational Failures
Mislabeled media	5%	Threat – Management	Organizational Failures
Equipment malfunction	24%	Vulnerabilities – Infrastructure	Hardware Faults
Equipment obsolescence	11%	Vulnerabilities – Infrastructure	Hardware Obsolescence
Software no longer recognizes data	12%	Vulnerabilities – Process	Software Fault Software Obsolescence
Data corruption	3%	Vulnerabilities – Data Process	 Media Faults Software Faults

Management failures, including economic and organizational failures, account for 27% of the data loss. However, it would be reasonable to reclassify two of the components of management failures as human error. Do we attribute lost media and mislabeled media as a human error or a systemic error? Infrastructure, including hardware faults and obsolescence, accounts for 35% of the loss. Process, including software fault and obsolescence, accounts for 12% of data loss. Data corruption, accounts for 13% of the data loss. Disasters, including human operational errors and natural disasters, account for 34% of the data loss. This last category, disasters, seems to be overloaded with meaning; combining natural disasters, such as floods and fire, with human error can seem misleading. If the incidences of human error were removed, disasters would account for only 4% of the data loss. Based on the research presented here, creating a separate category for human error or including it as a subcategory under management would more clearly described the threats to preservation.

5.2 Lost Media

As described in section 2.4, incidents of data loss due to misplaced media have been well publicized; 10% of the researchers in this survey reported to have lost media and the data thereon. In addition, two researchers reported via the "other" option that they lost data because equipment was stolen. In the literature on preservation, the rapid rate at which removable media becomes obsolete are discussed [31]; however, the loss of the physical media is not treated as a threat. As large percentage of researchers copy their data to removable media such as CDs, DVDs, and hard drives at the end of a project [19], removable media management needs to be included in the discussion of threats to preservation.

5.3 Threat Mitigation

Several previous studies have shown that individual researchers have the primary responsibility for managing their research data [19, 25]. This study indicates researchers are aware of their responsibilities, that they understand the importance of data management, and believe that they follow best practice. However, the researchers do think that they could improve their data management practices. If funds were not a constraint, researchers would save more data, use different storage systems, back up their data more frequently. But more importantly, the researchers would hire professional staff to manage their data. This could indicate that while researchers understand their responsibilities as data managers, they would rather find someone else to take on the responsibility and do the work.

This study shows that the size of lab impacts the complexity of effectively managing data. Large labs were more likely to import problems and want to change than small labs or individual researchers; this seems reasonable: more people, more complexity, more problems. Large labs were more likely to report data loss due to human error than small labs or individual researchers. It is likely that these human errors are due to communication failures; explaining which files are "good" and should be kept and which files should be deleted can be complicated. Large labs are also more likely to have lost data due to equipment failures. As large labs are generally associated with hard sciences, it is more likely that they would have more equipment than an individual researcher. Researchers in large labs were also more likely to report implementing data management early in the research process; with multiple people and multiple pieces of equipment generating data, it is reasonable that the researchers would see the need to manage data as soon as it is created. Researchers in large labs were more likely to want to change their data management practices; again, this is a reasonable response if they have lost data and/or struggled with managing their data.

5.4 Future Work

More research needs to be done in order to understand how these threats affect data throughout the entire research lifecycle. Determining the lifecycle stage at which each threat is most probable could be used to develop policies to mitigate these threats and to promote preservation. Future studies could gather additional information about the details of threat mitigation actions. Data management is a complex process and is likely occur throughout an organization. A study could be devised to determine the levels of data management actions. That is, at what level in the organization do mitigating behaviors occur; are the responsibilities for external threat mitigation, for data backup, for disaster planning clearly delineated; and how do researchers interact with those centers of responsibility.

6. Conclusion

The assessment of the risks and threats to the preservation of research data has primarily focused on preservation infrastructure. Taxonomies and checklists abound for digital repositories. Little research has been conducted on the risks associated with data outside of the repository. This research provides new insight into the preservation threats to research data while in the research lab. As most research data does not reach preservation infrastructure such as a data archive or a digital repository, understanding the risks for this data is important. Researchers have recognized the need to mitigate the risks inherent in maintaining digital data by implementing data management in their lab environments and have taken their responsibility as data managers seriously; however, they would still prefer to have professional data management support.

7. REFERENCES

[1] Altman, M., Adams, M. O., Crabtree, J., Donakowski, D., Maynard, M. M., Pienta, A., and Young, C. H. 2009. Digital preservation through archival collaboration: The data preservation alliance for the social sciences. *American Archivist, 72*,1, 170-184.

[2] Barateiro, J., Antunes, G., Cabral, M., Borbinha, J., and Rodrigues, R. 2008. Using a Grid for digital preservation. In *Digital Libraries: Universal and Ubiquitous Access to Information,* G. Buchanan, M. Masoodian, and S. J. Cunningham, Eds. Berlin: Springer, 225-235.

[3] Barateiro, J., Antunes, G., Freitas, F., and Borbinha, J. 2010. Designing digital preservation solutions: A risk management-based approach. *International Journal of Digital Curation, 5*, 1, 4-17.

[4] Coles, S., Carr, L., and Frey, J. 2007. *Final Report: The Repository for the Laboratory*. Southampton, England: Joint Information Systems Committee (JISC) Digital Repositories Programme and the University of Southampton.

[5] Committee on Data for Science and Technology. 2002. *CODATA Workshop on Archiving Scientific and Technical (S&T) DATA Report* (Pretoria, South Africa, May 20-21) South African National Committee for CODATA, CODATA Working Group on Data Archiving and the National Research Foundation of South Africa.

[6] Emery, C. R. 2013. Preservation of IGO Documents in a Digital Environment. *DttP: Documents to the People*, *41*, 1, 7-8.

[7] Gray, J., Liu, D. T., Nieto-Santisteban, M., Szalay, A., DeWitt, D. J., and Heber, G. 2005. Scientific data management in the coming decade. *ACM SIGMOD Record*, *34*, 4, 34-41.

[8] Gray, J., Szalay, A. S., Thakar, A. R., Stoughton, C., and vandenBerg, J. 2002. *Online Scientific Data Curation, Publication, and Archiving* (Vol. 200). Redmond, WA: Microsoft Research.

[9] Green, A. G. and Gutmann, M. P. 2007. Building partnerships among social science researchers, institution-based repositories and domain specific data archives. *OCLC Systems and Services*, *23*, 1, 35-53. DOI = doi:10.1108/10650750710720757

[10] Guy, L., Kunszt, P., Laure, E., Stockinger, H., and Stockinger K. 2002. *Replica management in data grids. Global Grid Forum 5*. Edinburgh, Scotland.

[11] Hey, T. 2010. *Data-intensive scientific discovery: The fourth paradigm*. Bloomington, IN: Digital Science Center, Pervasive Technology Institute, Indiana University.

[12] Hey, T. and Trefethen, A. 2003. The data deluge: An e-science perspective. In *Grid Computing: Making the Global Infrastructure a Reality*, F. Berman, G. C. Fox, and A. J. G. Hey, Eds. Chitchester, England: John Wiley and Sons, Ltd., 809-824.

[13] Hunter, J. and Choudhury, S. 2004. A semi-automated digital preservation system based on semantic web services. *Proceedings of the 4th ACM/IEEE-CS Joint Conference on Digital Libraries* (Tucson, AZ, June 7-11). ACM and IEEE. DOI = doi:10.1145/996350.996415

[14] Jones, S., Ball, A., and Ekmekcioglu, Ç. 2008. The data audit framework: A first step in the data management challenge. *International Journal of Digital Curation*, *3*(2), 112-120.

[15] Jones, S., Ross, S., and Ruusalepp, R. 2009, Data Audit Framework Methodology, (Glasgow, HATII and Digital Curation Centre).

[16] Karasti, H., Baker, K. S., and Halkola, E. 2006. Enriching the notion of data curation in e-science: Data managing and information infrastructure in the Long Term Ecological Research (LTER) network. *Computer Supported Cooperative Work (CSCW)*, *15*(4), 321-358. Springer. DOI = doi:10.1007/s10606-006-9023-2

[17] Key Perspectives Ltd. 2010. *Data dimensions: disciplinary differences in research data sharing, reuse and long term viability*. Edinburgh, Scotland: Digital Curation Centre.

[18] Kowalczyk, S. T. 2008. Digital preservation by design. In *Handbook of Research on Global Information Technology: Management in the Digital Economy*, M. S. Raisinghani, Ed. Hershey, PA: Information Science Reference/IGI Global, 405-431.

[19] Kowalczyk, S. T. 2014. Where Does All the Data Go: Quantifying the Final Disposition of Research Data. In the *Proceeding of the 77th ASIS&T Annual Meeting (*October 31- November 5, 2014, Seattle, WA).

[20] Littman, J. 2007. Actualized preservation threats: practical lessons from chronicling America. *D-Lib Magazine*, *13*, 7.

[21] LaRowe, G., Ambre, S., Burgoon, J., Ke, W., and Börner, K. (2009). The Scholarly Database and its utility for scientometrics research . *Scientometrics*, *79*, 2, 219 - 234.

[22] Liu, L. and Chi, L. 2002. Evolutionary data quality: A theory-specific view. *Proceedings of the 7th International Conference on Information Quality, (MIT IQ Conference)*, 292-304.

[23] Lord, P. and Macdonald, A. 2003. *e-Science curation report: Data curation for e-Science in the UK: An audit to establish requirements for future curation and provision*. London, UK: Joint Information Systems Committee (JISC) Committee for the Support of Research.

[24] Lynch, C. 2008. Big data: How do your data grow? *Nature*, *455*, 7209, 28–29. Nature Publishing Group.

[25] Lyon, L. 2007. *Dealing with data: Roles, rights, responsibilities and relationships. Consultancy report*. Bath, UK: UKOLN and Joint Information Systems Committee (JISC) Committee for the Support of Research.

[26] MacBean, N. 2008. Fridge-sized tape recorder could crack lunar mysteries (November 10). *Australian Broadcast Corporation News*. Sydney, Australia.

[27] Macey, R. 2006. One giant blunder for mankind: How NASA lost moon pictures (August 5). *The Sydney Morning Herald*. Sydney, Australia.

[28] Marshall, C. C. (2008, June). From writing and analysis to the repository: taking the scholars' perspective on scholarly archiving. In *Proceedings of the 8th ACM/IEEE-CS joint conference on Digital libraries* (pp. 251-260). ACM.

[29] McHugh, A., Innocenti, P., Ross, S. and Ruusalepp, R. 2007. Risk management foundations for DLs: DRAMBORA (Digital Repository Audit Method Based on Risk Assessment). DELOS 2nd Workshop on Foundations of Digital Libraries, within ECDL conference, Budapest, Hungary, September 20, 2007

[30] National Science Board. (2005). *Long-lived digital data collections Enabling research and education in the 21st century*. Arlington, VA: National Science Board Committee on Programs and Plans, NSB-05-40.

[31] Rosenthal, D. S. H., Robertson, T. S., Lipkis, T., Reich, V., and Morabito, S. 2005. Requirements for digital preservation systems: A bottom-up approach. *D-Lib Magazine*, *11*, 11.

[32] Rosenthal, D. S., Roussopoulos, M., Giuli, T., Maniatis, P., and Baker, M. (2004). Using hard disks for digital preservation. *IS&T Archiving Conference Final Program and Proceedings (Archiving 2004)*, 249-253.

[33] Ross, S. 2007. Digital preservation, archival science and methodological foundations for digital libraries. *Proceedings of the 11th European Conference on Digital Libraries (ECDL)* (Budapest 17 September 2007). Budapest, Hungary: Springer.

[34] Rumsey, A. S. 2010. *Sustainable economics for a digital planet: Ensuring long-term access to digital information. Final report of the Blue Ribbon Task Force on Sustainable Digital Preservation and Access*. Washington, DC: National Science Foundation.

[35] Swan, A. and Brown, S. 2008. *To share or not to share: Publication and quality assurance of research data outputs: Main report*. London, UK: Research Information Network, Joint Information Systems Committee (JISC) Committee for the Support of Research, and the National Environment Research Council UK.

[36] Tam, W., Fry, J., and Probets, S. 2014. The Disciplinary Shaping of Research Data Management Practices. In *iConference 2014 Proceedings*, 721 - 728. DOI = doi:10.9776/14338

[37] Treloar, A., Groenewegen, D., and Harboe-Ree, C. C. 2007. The data curation continuum: Managing data objects in institutional repositories. *D-Lib Magazine*, *13*, 9.

[38] Vermaaten, S., Lavoie, B., and Caplan, P. 2012. Identifying Threats to Successful Digital Preservation: the SPOT Model for Risk Assessment. *D-Lib Magazine*, *18*, 9.

[39] Whyte, A., Job, D., Giles, S., and Lawrie, S. 2008. Meeting curation challenges in a neuroimaging group. *The International Journal of Digital Curation*, *3*, 1, 171 - 181.

How Well Are Arabic Websites Archived?

Lulwah M. Alkwai*, Michael L. Nelson, and Michele C. Weigle
Department of Computer Science
Old Dominion University
Norfolk, Virginia 23529 USA
{lalkwai,mln,mweigle}@cs.odu.edu

ABSTRACT

It is has long been anecdotally known that web archives and search engines favor Western and English-language sites. In this paper we quantitatively explore how well indexed and archived are Arabic language web sites. We began by sampling 15,092 unique URIs from three different website directories: DMOZ (multi-lingual), Raddadi and Star28 (both primarily Arabic language). Using language identification tools we eliminated pages not in the Arabic language (e.g., English language versions of Al-Jazeera sites) and culled the collection to 7,976 definitely Arabic language web pages. We then used these 7,976 pages and crawled the live web and web archives to produce a collection of 300,646 Arabic language pages. We discovered: 1) 46% are not archived and 31% are not indexed by Google (`www.google.com`), 2) only 14.84% of the URIs had an Arabic country code top-level domain (e.g., `.sa`) and only 10.53% had a GeoIP in an Arabic country, 3) having either only an Arabic GeoIP or only an Arabic top-level domain appears to negatively impact archiving, 4) most of the archived pages are near the top level of the site and deeper links into the site are not well-archived, 5) the presence in a directory positively impacts indexing and presence in the DMOZ directory, specifically, positively impacts archiving.

Categories and Subject Descriptors

H.3.7 [**Information Storage and Retrieval**]: Digital Libraries and Archives

General Terms

Design, Experimentation, Measurement

Keywords

Web Archiving, Indexing, Digital Preservation, Arabic Web

*Department of Computer Science and Software Engineering, University of Hail, Hail, Saudi Arabia

JCDL'15, June 21–25, 2015, Knoxville, Tennessee, USA.

ACM 978-1-4503-3594-2/15/06 ...$15.00.
http://dx.doi.org/10.1145/2756406.2756912.

1. INTRODUCTION

Arabic is the fourth most popular language on the Internet, trailing only English, Chinese, and Spanish [12]. Over the past few years, the number of Arabic-speaking Internet users has grown rapidly. In 2009, only 17% of Arabic speakers used the Internet [10], but by the end of 2013 that had increased to almost 36% (over 135 million), approaching the world average of 39% of the population using the Internet [11]. In 2010, the size of the indexed Arabic web was estimated to be about 2 billion pages [2]. It is not unreasonable to assume that Arabic online content is even larger today.

The Web is quickly becoming a repository for our cultural heritage, but studies have shown that the lifetime of webpages is short (44-100 days) [6, 13], and that resources are disappearing from the live web [14, 19]. Thus, webpages need to be preserved for future cultural and historical data mining. Web archiving is becoming recognized as an important problem [15], and several institutions, most notably the Internet Archive, have created archives to preserve websites. There are even several country and language specific archives[1], such as the BnF Web Archives (.fr domain)[2], the National Archives of the UK government (.uk domain)[3], and the Icelandic Web Archive (.is domain)[4].

The lack of focused archiving of the Arabic web motivates our study of how well Arabic language webpages are being archived today. To investigate this, we obtained a sample of URIs from Arabic web directories. For those webpages that we determined were written in Arabic, we studied several characteristics, including GeoIP location, country code top-level domain (ccTLD), URI path depth, estimated creation date, how well the page was archived, and if the page was indexed in Google. To increase the size of our dataset, we also crawled the Arabic webpages to collect more URIs to investigate.

With this study, we have found that 46% of the Arabic URIs in our collection are not archived and 31% are not indexed by Google. Further we found that a large majority of webpages with Arabic language content use generic TLDs (especially .com) and are physically located in Western countries (with over half in the US). As expected, we found that URIs with higher path depth are less likely to

[1]A list of prominent web archives is available at `http://netpreserve.org/resources/member-archives`.
[2]`http://www.bnf.fr/fr/collections_et_services/collections_departements.html`
[3]`http://www.nationalarchives.gov.uk`
[4]`http://vefsafn.is/`

Table 1: Countries with Arabic as the official language, their population, percentage of those who are Internet users, and ccTLD. Source: [11].

Country	Population (2014)	% are Internet Users	ccTLD	Note
Egypt	86,895,099	49.6%	.eg	
Algeria	38,813,722	16.5%	.dz	
Sudan	35,482,233	22.7%	.sd	
Morocco	32,987,206	56.0%	.ma	Co-official language, along with Berber.
Iraq	32,585,692	9.2%	.iq	Co-official language, along with Kurdish.
Saudi Arabia	27,345,986	60.5%	.sa	
Yemen	26,052,966	20.0%	.ye	
Syria	22,597,531	26.2%	.sy	
South Sudan	11,562,695	0%	.ss	
Tunisia	10,937,521	43.8%	.tn	
Somalia	10,428,043	1.5%	.so	Co-official language, along with Somali.
United Arab Emirates	9,206,000	88.0%	.ae	
Jordan	6,528,061	44.2%	.jo	
Libya	6,244,174	16.5%	.ly	
Lebanon	4,136,895	70.5%	.lb	
Mauritania	3,516,806	6.2%	.mr	
Oman	3,219,775	66.4%	.om	
Kuwait	2,742,711	75.5%	.kw	
Palestine	2,731,052	55.4%	.ps	
Qatar	2,123,160	85.3%	.qa	
Bahrain	1,314,089	90.0%	.bh	
Djibouti	810,179	9.5%	.dj	Co-official language, along with French.
Comoros	766,865	6.5%	.km	Co-official language, along with French and Comorian.

be archived and indexed than URIs closer to the top-level site. In addition, we found that the presence in a directory positively impacts indexing and presence in the DMOZ directory, specifically, positively impacts archiving.

2. RELATED WORK

There has been previous work on the coverage of web archives, including a study of international bias in archiving and studies of national domains. Little, though, has been done specifically in terms of Arabic language content.

In 2010, Ainsworth et al. [1] investigated how much of the web was archived. They collected a sample of URIs from four different sources (DMOZ, Delicious, Bitly, and search engine indexes). The resulting archival percentages ranged from 16% to 79%. A follow-on study in 2013 [3] showed that the archival percentages had increased from 33% to 95%. However, these studies were not focused on content from specific countries or content in specific languages.

Thelwall and Vaughn [20] studied the coverage of archiving at the Internet Archive and focused on content from four different countries: China, Singapore, Taiwan, and the United States. They found large national differences in the archive coverage of the web. This work focused on content location rather than content language and TLD.

Baeza-Yates et al. [4] characterized national web domains based on 120 million pages from 24 different countries. They found that some characteristics, such as URI path length and distribution of HTTP response codes (e.g., 200 OK, 404 Not Found, etc.), were similar across different country domains. Yet they noted that not all sites in a country use the country-code Top-Level Domain (e.g., `.us` is seldom used in the United States), so other methods for determining if a site belongs to a particular country may be required.

Gomes and Silva [8] studied the Portuguese web, including websites related to Portugal or of interest to Portuguese people. They filtered sites based on domain (`.pt`), but also acknowledged that some sites would use other TLDs (such as `.com`, `.net`, `.org`) and so also considered sites that had content in the Portuguese language.

A recent investigation into the unarchived web [9] has shown that the archived web can be a rich source of links to potentially unarchived content. In this work, we crawl archived pages to increase the size and variety of our dataset.

To further discuss web archiving, we must introduce terminology from the Memento framework. Memento [21,22] is an HTTP protocol extension which links information from multiple Web archives. We can use Memento to obtain a list of archived versions of resources, or mementos, from various different archives. In this paper, we use the following Memento terminology:

- URI-R - the original resource as it used to appear on the live Web. A URI-R may have 0 or more mementos (URI-Ms).
- URI-M - an archived snapshot of the URI-R at a specific date and time, which is called the Memento-Datetime, e.g., $URI\text{-}M_i = URI\text{-}R@t_i$.
- TimeMap - a resource that provides a list of mementos (URI-Ms) for a URI-R, ordered by their Memento-Datetimes.

3. EXPERIMENTAL SETUP

This section describes our experimental setup: selecting seed URIs, determining language, and crawling Arabic seed URIs.

3.1 Selecting Seed URIs

First, we searched for Arabic website directories and took the top three based on Alexa ranking[5]. Between March-May 2014, we collected all URIs from these three Arabic website directories: 1) the Arabic DMOZ listing, registered in US in 1999, 2) Raddadi, a well-known Arabic directory, registered in Saudi Arabia in 2000, and 3) Star28, an Arabic directory, registered in Lebanon in 2004. Table 2 shows the number of collected URIs from these three sources. We collected 15,092 unique seed URIs. Using cs.odu.edu machines we tested the existence of each seed URI on the live Web and found 11,014 that returned HTTP 200 OK status code (some after redirection). We downloaded the contents of each page that was found on the live Web.

Table 2: Seed source count

Name	URI	Initial seed URIs
DMOZ	dmoz.org/World/Arabic/	4,086
Raddadi	raddadi.com	3,271
Star28	star28.com	8,386
Total		15,743

3.2 Determining Language

Table 1, sorted by population, lists each country where Arabic is an official language, its population, the percentage of its population that are Internet users, its country code TLD, and if other languages are spoken. Although we gathered webpages from Arabic language directories, it is likely that some of these were written in other languages. We were interested in further analyzing only pages written in Arabic, so we used several methods to determine the language of each of the 11,014 live Web seed URIs.

One of the challenges is to find a reliable language test to determine language. No test will result in 100% confidence, so in order to detect the language of a webpage, we tested four different methods. The language tests we performed were as follows:

- **HTTP `Content-Language`** - If the HTTP response header contained `Content-Language:ar`, where ar is the ISO 629-2 code for Arabic, we considered the webpage to be written in Arabic.

- **HTML title tag** - The HTML title tag is often a good indicator of the language of a webpage's content [17]. We extracted the title tag of each webpage and used the guess-language Python library[6] to determine the language.

- **Trigram method** - The trigram technique uses letter trigrams, sequences of three letters, to determine language [5]. The identification is performed through basic trigram lookups paired with unicode character set recognition. We used the Python-Language-Detector tool[7], which implements the trigram method, on the extracted text from the HTML of each webpage.

- **Language detection API client** - The Language Detection API[8] is a web service that detects 106 different languages. We ran the test on the extracted text from the HTML of each webpage.

The reliability of the tests to determine if a web page is in Arabic was measured by having a native reader (the first author) quickly evaluate a sample of pages. Next, we measured the number of URIs reported as Arabic. Figure 1 shows the intersection between the four language tests. We found 872 of the URIs tested as Arabic language in all four tests. We decided to consider the webpage part of the Arabic Web if it passes any one of the language tests.

After running all of the tests on the 11,014 live webpages, we found 7,976 that passed at least one of the language tests. We consider this set to be our Arabic seed URIs.

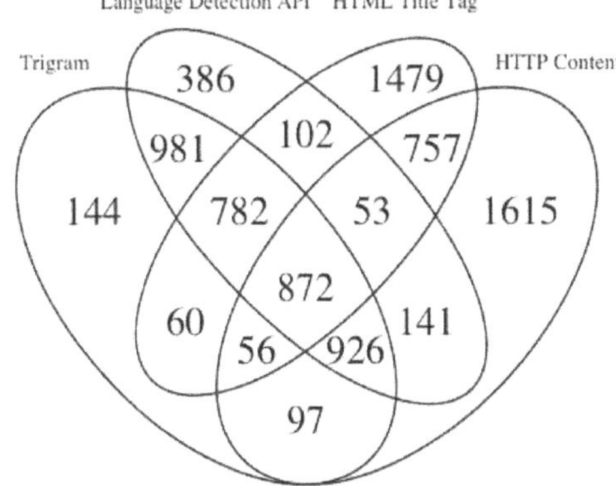

Figure 1: Language test intersection testing for Arabic language

3.3 Crawling Arabic Seed URIs

To increase the size of our dataset, we crawled the Arabic seed URIs, between January-March 2014. Our first pass was to gather additional URIs linked from the live Web versions of our seed URIs. This resulted in collecting 575,242 URIs, all of which were available on the live Web.

To gather even more URIs, we crawled the Arabic seed URIs that had at least one archived version (or, memento). We crawled the most recent memento and gathered 515,821 URIs. Of these, only 335,283 were available on the live Web.

Combining the three sets (original URIs, crawled live, and crawled archived), we obtained a total of 663,443 unique URIs. We ran each of these through our Arabic language tests, resulting in 292,670 Arabic URIs obtained from crawling our Arabic seeds.

Figures 2 and 3 show the summary of collecting Arabic URIs for seed URIs and for crawled URIs. Combining the seed URIs and crawled URIs, we collected 300,646 Arabic URIs that we analyze in the remainder of the paper.

4. RESULTS

In this section we examine the characteristics of our Arabic URI dataset. We investigate the number of unique domains, TLD and country-code TLD (ccTLD), URI path

[5]`http://www.alexa.com`

[6]`https://code.google.com/p/guess-language/`

[7]`https://github.com/decultured/Python-Language-Detector`

[8]`https://detectlanguage.com/`

depth, presence in the archive, and estimated creation date for our combined dataset. For the original Arabic seed URI dataset we also investigate the GeoIP location and presence in the Google search engine index.

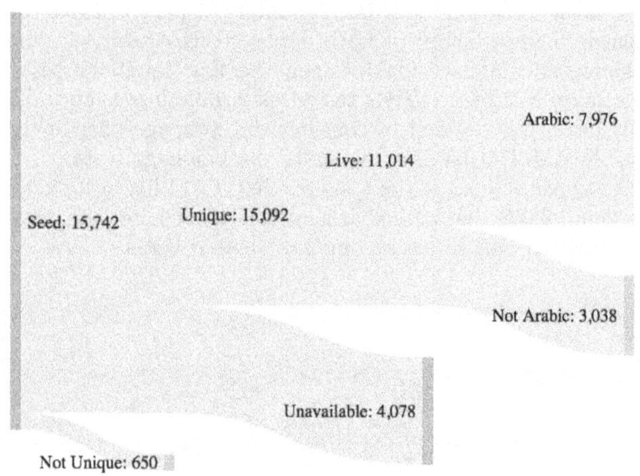

Figure 2: Seed URIs count detail

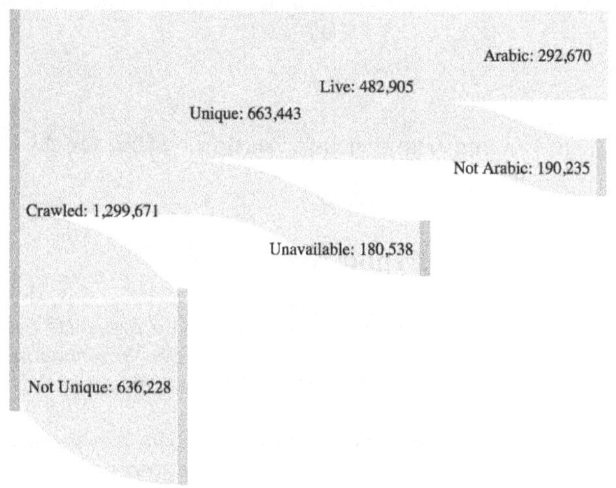

Figure 3: Crawled URIs count detail

4.1 Unique Domains

First, we investigate the number of unique domains in our dataset. Out of the 300,646 Arabic URIs, there are 17,536 unique domains. The most frequent domains are shown in Table 3. We also tested the GeoIP location of the top-level webpage of each of these domains and found that the top 16 are all located in the US. The first domain we find located in an Arabic country is the 17th most frequent.

We note that several of these top domains are popular Western sites, such as cnn.com and wikipedia.org. This indicates that the Arabic language community is already using services on Western sites that are likely to be archived.

Table 3: Most frequent domains

Rank	Domain	URIs	GeoIP Location
1	alarab.net	284	US
2	aljarida.com	248	US
3	arabic.cnn.com	245	US
4	alarabiya.net	231	US
5	ar.wikipedia.org	230	US
6	aljazeera.net	213	US
7	moheet.com	142	US
8	facebook.com	133	US
9	al-sharq.com	132	US
10	lakii.com	123	US
17	kuwaitclub.com.kw	71	Kuwait

4.2 Top Level Domains

We investigate the top level domain (TLD) and country-code TLD (ccTLD), together termed effective TLD, of the unique Arabic language domains. Generic TLDs such as .com, .net, and .org are open for any registrant. In addition to TLDs, many sites also use the two-letter ccTLD of their home country. Although a small percentage of the websites add the ccTLD, it may be a good indication of the source of the website. Table 4 shows the distribution of the top 10 effective TLDs. We also checked if the ccTLD was from a country where Arabic is an official language (listed in Table 1). Almost 58% of all URIs have a .com TLD, which is not unexpected since .com is a popular TLD and has an open registration policy. We note that the top Arabic ccTLD, .sa for Saudi Arabia, is used in fewer URIs than the generic TLDs .com, .net, and .org.

Table 5 shows the top 5 ccTLDs from Arabic-speaking countries. We found that Saudi Arabia was the most frequent Arabic ccTLD, followed by Egypt and Jordan.

Table 4: Top 10 effective TLDs

TLD	Percent
com	57.97%
net	15.07%
org	6.40%
gov.sa	1.94%
info	1.68%
edu.sa	1.27%
ws	1.16%
org.sa	0.97%
com.sa	0.80%
gov.eg	0.80%
other	11.94%

Table 5: Top 5 Arabic ccTLDs

ccTLD	Country	Percent
.sa	Saudi Arabia	5.33%
.eg	Egypt	2.00%
.jo	Jordan	2.00%
.ae	United Arab Emirates	1.06%
.kw	Kuwait	0.82%

4.3 URI Path Depth

URI path depth is an important factor in archiving, as we assume that webpages nearer to the top-level of a site are better archived than pages deeper into the site (i.e., with higher path depth). Table 6 shows the breakdown of URI path depth for our Arabic URIs. As expected, over half of the URIs have a path depth of 0 or 1, with barely 7% having a path depth greater than 3.

Table 6: Path depth of the Arabic URIs

Path Depth	Example	Percent
0	example.com	17.30%
1	example.com/a	40.42%
2	example.com/a/b	24.45%
3	example.com/a/b/c	10.81%
4+	example.com/a/b/c/d	7.02%

4.4 Presence in the Archive

Between January-March 2015, we used the Memento Framework, through the ODU CS Memento Aggregator (mementoproxy.cs.odu.edu), to determine if the URIs in our dataset are archived. For each URI, the aggregator returns a TimeMap that lists the number of mementos that exist in various archives. Overall, we found that 161,678 URIs (53.77% of our Arabic URIs) are archived (i.e., have one or more mementos). Figure 4 shows the number of mementos found for each archived URI, sorted by memento count, with a median of 16 mementos.

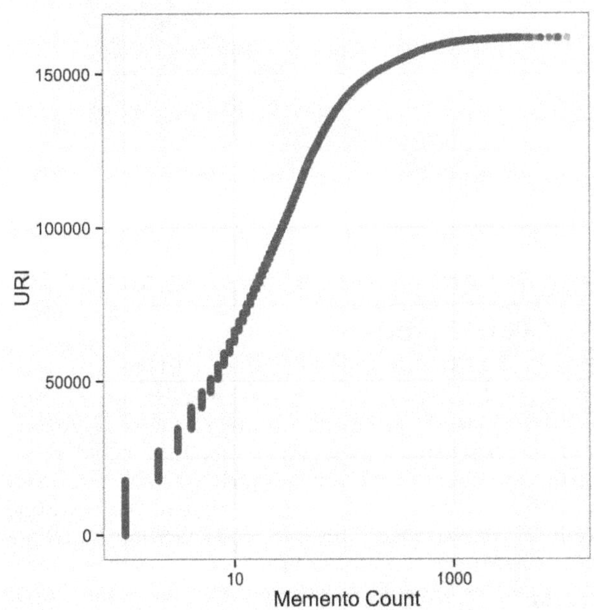

Figure 4: Memento count frequency

Table 7 lists the top 10 archived URI-Rs with the most mementos. As expected, most of these are news websites.

Figure 5 shows the number of URI-Ms with Memento-Datetimes in each year. This reveals an increasing rate of archiving in recent years, especially by the Internet Archive.

Table 7: Top 10 archived URI-Rs

URI-Rs	Memento Count	Category
gulfup.com	10,987	File Sharing
masrawy.com	9,144	Egyptian portal
arabic.cnn.com	9,022	News
aljazeera.net	8,906	News
maktoob.yahoo.com	8,478	Search Engine
shorooknews.com	7,548	News
arabnews.com	6,274	News
bbc.co.uk/arabic	6,268	News
ahram.org.eg	5,347	News
google.com.sa	4,968	Search Engine

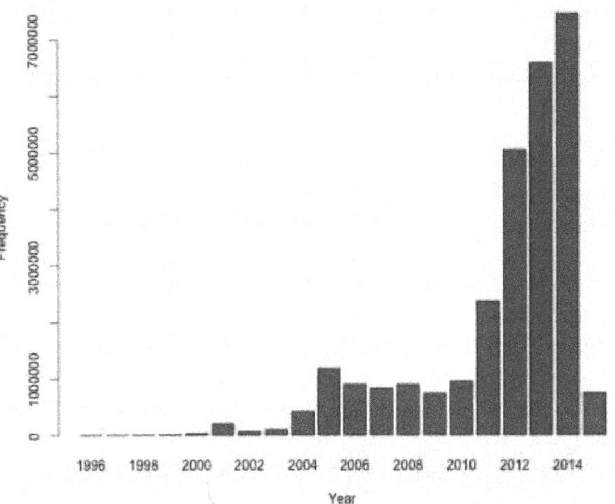

Figure 5: Number of URI-Ms in each year

Since the TimeMap identifies mementos present in multiple archives, here we present the breakdown of archives holding URIs in our Arabic dataset. Table 8 shows the percentage of archived URI-Rs that each archive holds. We found that the Internet Archive has the highest percentage by far, followed by Archive.today and Webcitation. We note that the percentages sum to greater than 100% because multiple archives can have mementos from the same original resource (URI-R).

Table 8: Archived URI-Rs present in all archives

Archive	Percent
Internet Archive	97.04%
Archive.today	6.58%
Webcitation	6.00%
Archive-It	5.49%
British Library Archive	1.06%
UK Parliament Web Archive	0.88%
Icelandic Web Archive	0.87%
UK National Archives	0.62%
Proni	0.21%
Stanford	0.11%
Total	118.86%

Next, we want to know the breakdown of the archives for all mementos (URI-M) in our data set. Table 9 shows the percentage of archived mementos that each archive holds. We found that almost 73% were in the Internet Archive and 21% were in Archive-It.

Table 9: Archived URI-Ms present in all archives

Archive	Percent
Internet Archive	72.87%
Archive-It	21.26%
Archive.today	2.14%
Webcitation	2.08%
Icelandic Web Archive	1.17%
British Library Archive	0.29%
UK Parliament Web Archive	0.10%
Proni	0.05%
UK National Archives	0.04%
Stanford	<0.01%
Total	100.00%

To determine how well a URI is archived, we can look at the timespan of the mementos (number of days between the datetimes of the first memento and last memento), but that does not indicate how often the URI was archived. These could be two endpoints with no other mementos in between, or the URI could be regularly archived over the timespan. Here, we exclude URIs that have only one memento (16,732 URIs). We calculate the average archiving period by dividing the timespan by the number of mementos for the URI. The smaller the period, the more regularly the URI was captured by the archives. In Figure 6, we show the average archiving period (in days) for each archived URI, where the URIs are sorted by archiving period, with a median of 48 days. Values less than 1 indicate that the URI is archived multiple times per day on average.

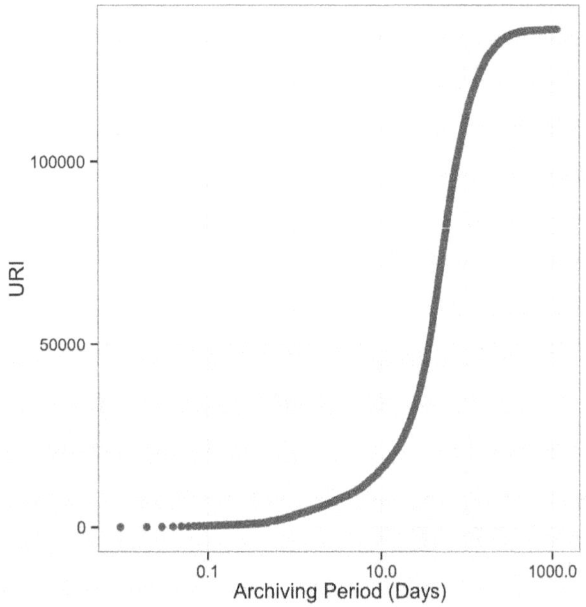

Figure 6: Average archiving period (days)

4.5 Creation Date

Another interesting characteristic of a URI is its creation date. In terms of evaluating how well our Arabic URIs have been archived, we want to verify that we have URIs of various ages to ensure that they have been around long enough to be captured. For instance, if a webpage was created in 2000, we would expect to see several mementos in the archives. However, if the webpage was just created in 2015, we would not be surprised if it had not yet been archived or archived as much.

Usually we cannot definitively determine the creation date of a webpage, but there have been several methods proposed to estimate this. We use CarbonDate [18], which looks to see when the URI was indexed in search engines, archived in public archives, and shared in social media. It then saves the oldest date found as the estimated creation date.

We applied CarbonDate to our archived Arabic data set. Figure 7 shows the frequency of estimated creation dates, with 2013 being the most frequent year. The figure also shows that our dataset contains a wide range of creation dates extending over the past 18 years.

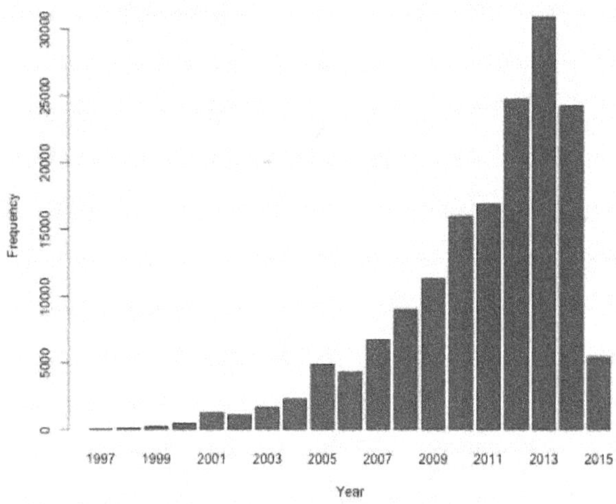

Figure 7: Creation dates for archived Arabic URIs

4.6 GeoIP Location

Earlier we looked at the ccTLD of the URIs to help determine where the hosts of the webpages might be located. Now we want to look at the GeoIP location of the IP address of the unique hostnames. First, we obtained the IP addresses of the hostnames using `nslookup`, which uses DNS to convert the hostname to its IP address. Then we used the MaxMind GeoLite2[9] database to determine location from the IP address. Which tests at 99.8% accuracy at the country level[10].

We used this method to determine GeoIP for the Arabic URI dataset (300,646 URIs). We found that less than 11% of the URIs are hosted in Arabic countries. Table 10 shows the top GeoIP locations, with Arabic countries grouped together. Table 11 shows the top 5 GeoIP locations from Arabic countries. Overall, almost 58% of the Arabic seed URIs are hosted at IP addresses in the US. Other Western coun-

[9] http://dev.maxmind.com/geoip/geoip2/geolite2/
[10] http://dev.maxmind.com/faq/how-accurate-are-the-geoip-databases/

tries, including Germany and the Netherlands, host more of the Arabic seed URIs than does Saudi Arabia, the highest contributor of the Arabic countries.

Table 10: Top GeoIP locations

Country	Percent
US	57.97%
Arabic countries	10.53%
Germany	9.75%
Netherlands	5.29%
France	4.37%
Canada	3.31%
UK	3.07%
Others	5.71%

Table 11: Top 5 Arabic GeoIP locations

Country	Percent
Saudi Arabia	4.75%
Egypt	1.97%
Jordan	1.42%
Kuwait	0.71%
UAE	0.67%

4.7 Search Engine Indexing

In addition to investigating if the Arabic URIs are archived, we are also interested to discover how well they are indexed in search engines such as Google. We used the Google Custom Search API to determine if the Arabic seed URIs are indexed by Google. We tested only the seed URIs because we were limited by the restriction of 1000 requests per day in the API. We found that only 36.2% of the Arabic seed URIs were indexed by Google. However, we note that the Google user web interface may produce different results than the Custom Search API [16].

For the Arabic seed URIs, we can indicate if they were present on the live Web, in the Google index, and present in an archive, creating a `(live, indexed, archived)` tuple. In Table 12, we show the percentage of our Arabic seed URI dataset (7,976 URIs) that fell into each permutation of the tuple. We note that all of our Arabic seeds were present on the live Web at the time of our analysis. Almost 44% of the Arabic seed URIs were both indexed and archived, while only 15% were neither indexed nor archived.

Table 12: Status of Arabic seed URIs

(Live, Indexed, Archived)	Count	Percent
(1, 1, 1)	3,457	43.34%
(1, 1, 0)	2,041	25.59%
(1, 0, 1)	1,218	15.27%
(1, 0, 0)	1,257	15.76%

5. ANALYSIS

5.1 Creation Date and First Memento

Here we want to investigate the gap between the creation date of Arabic websites and when they were first archived. We used the creation date obtained in Section 4.5 and the date of the first memento obtained in Section 4.4.

Figure 8 shows the URIs on the y-axis and the log of the delta (creation date - first memento) in days on the x-axis. We found that 19.48% of the URIs have an estimated creation date that is the same as first memento date and excluded those from the figure. For the remaining 130,184, almost 18% have creation dates over 1 year before the first memento was archived (solid vertical line).

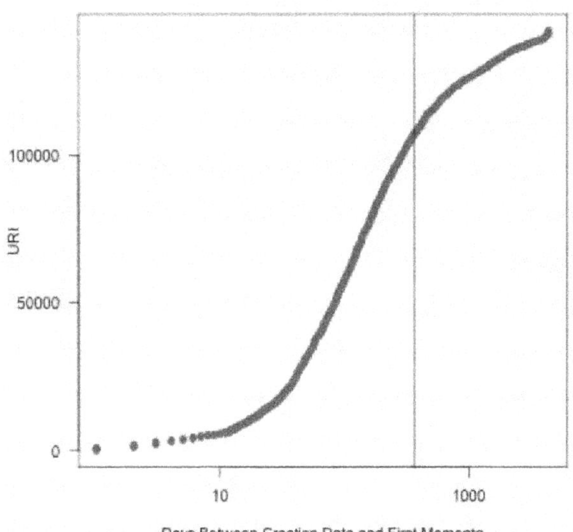

Figure 8: Difference between creation date and first memento

5.2 Archiving Based on Seed URI Source

Here we look at archiving based on seed URI source. As shown in Table 13, we found that 96% of DMOZ seed URIs are archived and that 45% of those from Raddadi and 42% from Star28 are archived. This was expected because DMOZ URIs are more likely to be found and archived [1,3]. DMOZ has historically been a source of seed URIs for indexing and archiving, at least as far back as 1999 [7].

5.3 Archiving Based on Location and ccTLD

Based on our previous results, we want to look at how many archived URIs have an Arabic ccTLD, Arabic GeoIP, or both. Table 14 shows the breakdown of the Arabic URIs that have both an Arabic ccTLD and an Arabic GeoIP, only an Arabic ccTLD, only an Arabic GeoIP, or neither Arabic ccTLD nor Arabic GeoIP. Only 33.18% of our set had evidence of location in an Arabic country (ccTLD or GeoIP), and these URIs were archived at a lower rate (34%) than URIs that had no evidence of location inside an Arabic country (65%). This finding goes with our intuition that sites hosted in Western countries would be more likely to be archived. Figure 9 shows the detail count of GeoIP location, ccTLD, both, and neither of the archived Arabic set.

Table 13: Archiving and Indexing based on Arabic seed source

Name	Total	Arabic	Percent	Archived Count	Percent	Indexed Count	Percent
DMOZ	4,086	2,904	34.43%	2,774	95.52%	2,385	82.13%
Raddadi	3,271	1,677	19.88%	762	45.44%	1,104	65.83%
Star28	8,386	3,854	45.69%	1,601	41.54%	2,514	65.23%
Total	15,743	8,435					

Table 14: Archiving based on location and ccTLD

	Total	Percent	Archived Count	Percent
Arabic ccTLD	44,609	14.84%	12,532	28.09%
Arabic GeoIP	31,671	10.53%	4,152	13.11%
Arabic GeoIP and ccTLD	23,479	7.81%	13,969	59.50%
Neither	200,887	66.82%	131,025	65.22%

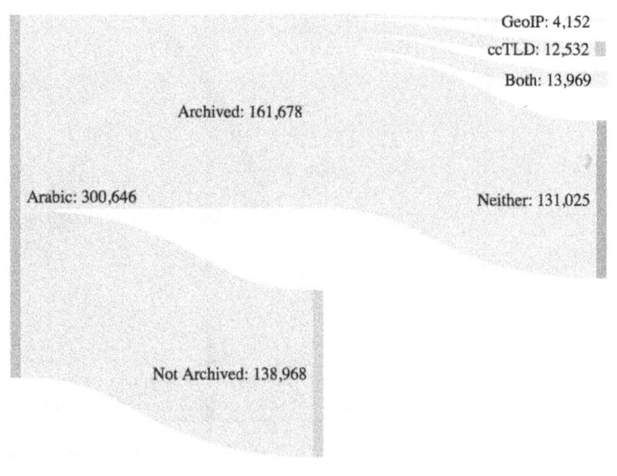

Figure 9: Arabic URIs count detail for Arabic GeoIP and ccTLD

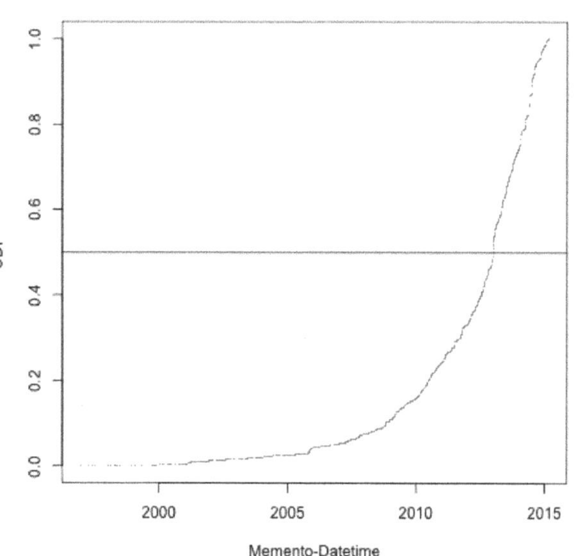

Figure 10: CDF of Memento-Datetimes both Arabic GeoIP and Arabic ccTLD

Next we wanted to statistically analyze the archived Arabic data set. Figure 10 shows the CDF of the Memento-Datetimes for the both Arabic ccTLD and Arabic GeoIP set. The CDFs for the other three sets (Arabic GeoIP, Arabic ccTLD, and neither), resulted in the same curve as observed visually. The means for the four groups (both Arabic ccTLD and Arabic GeoIP, Arabic GeoIP, Arabic ccTLD, and neither) were respectively, 0.5016, 0.5010, 0.5013 and 0.5005. To analyze these similarities further, we performed the Kolmogorov-Smirnov test to determine if the data sets are likely to be different. We compared the two sets Arabic GeoIP and Arabic ccTLD to the set with neither Arabic GeoIP nor Arabic TLD. We checked the p-value that gives us the probability of whether or not we can reject the null hypothesis, which is that two datasets have the same distribution. The D statistic is the absolute maximum distance between the CDFs of the two samples. The closer this number is to 0, the more likely it is that the two samples were drawn from the same distribution. The D value for comparing Arabic ccTLD and neither and for comparing Arabic GeoIP and neither is 0.017 and 0.014. For both $p < 0.002$, meaning that the CDFs are statistically equivalent.

Figure 11 shows the age of a URI (days since creation) vs. its number of mementos. One might think that the older the resource, the more mementos it has. In the short term (less than 3 years), this is true (see Figure 12 for detail), but for URIs over 3 years old, this is not necessarily the case because of low historical archiving rates (as shown in Figure 5).

5.4 Archiving Based on URI Path Depth

Next, we look at the effect of different URI path depths on archiving. As expected, we found that the shorter the URI path depth, the higher the rate of archiving. As shown in Table 15, we found that 86% of URIs with path depth 0 (i.e., top-level pages) were archived, with decreasing archiving rates as path depth increased. For those URIs with a path depth of greater than 3, only 32% were archived.

Table 15: Archiving based on URI path depth

Path Depth	Total	Percent	Archived Count	Percent
0	52,011	17.30%	44,880	86.29%
1	121,521	40.42%	65,001	53.49%
2	73,507	24.45%	33,497	45.57%
3	32,499	10.81%	11,585	35.65%
4+	21,108	7.02%	6,715	31.82%

Table 16: Indexing based on location and ccTLD of Arabic seed URIs

	Total	Percent	Indexed Count	Percent
Arabic ccTLD	527	6.61%	401	76.09%
Arabic GeoIP	189	2.37%	139	73.54%
Arabic GeoIP and ccTLD	481	6.03%	410	85.24%
Neither	6,779	84.99%	4,548	67.09%

Table 17: Indexing based on URI path depth of Arabic seed URIs

Path Depth	Total	Percent	Indexed Count	Percent
0	6,863	86.05%	5,120	74.60%
1	776	9.77%	302	38.91%
2	297	3.72%	53	17.85%
3+	40	0.50%	23	57.5%

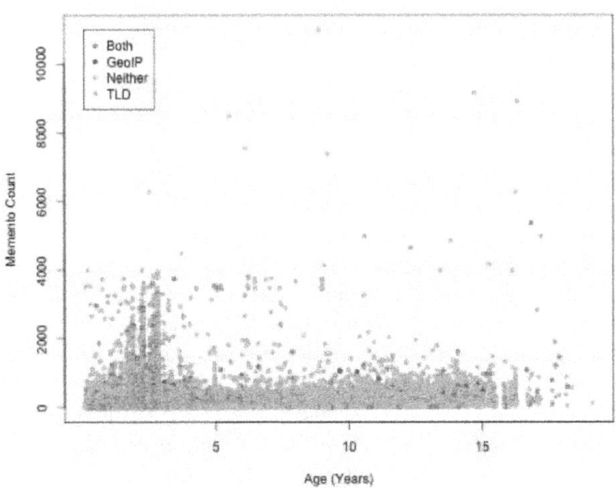

Figure 11: URI age and memento count

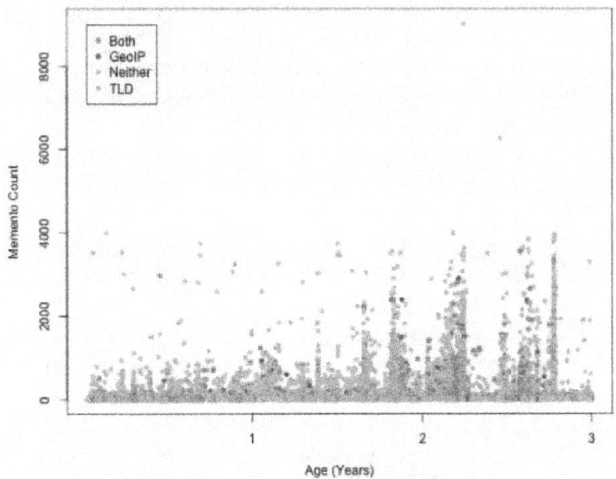

Figure 12: URI age less than three years and memento count

5.5 Indexing Based on Seed URI Source

Here we look at indexing based on seed URI source. As shown in Table 13, we found that 82% of DMOZ seed URIs are indexed by Google and that 66% of those from Raddadi and 65% from Star28 are indexed. This was expected because DMOZ URIs are more likely to be found and indexed [1,3].

5.6 Indexing Based on Location and ccTLD

So far, we have looked at how archiving is affected by location and path depth. Next we look at how these factors affect search engine indexing. Similar to what we did with archiving, here we look at how location (Arabic GeoIP and Arabic ccTLD) affects indexing. We note that, as in section 4.7, we only look at indexing for the Arabic seed URI set.

Table 16 shows the breakdown of indexing based on location. For seed URIs with both Arabic GeoIP and Arabic ccTLD, we found that 85% are indexed by Google. For those with only Arabic ccTLD, 76% were indexed, and for those with only Arabic GeoIP, 74% were indexed. We found that seed URIs that had some Arabic location (GeoIP or ccTLD) had a higher indexing rate (79%) than URIs with no Arabic location evidence (67%).

5.7 Indexing Based on URI Path Depth

Here we look at indexing based on URI path depth. As with archiving, we would expect that URIs with lower path depths would be more likely to be indexed. As shown in Table 17, we found that 74.6% of URIs with path depth 0 are indexed, and only 22.5% of the URIs with path depth of 3 or more are indexed. As with archiving, URIs closer to the top level are more likely to be indexed than those with higher path depths.

6. CONCLUSIONS

In this study, we evaluated how well Arabic webpages are archived and indexed. First we collected webpages from Arabic directories, then determined if these webpages are written in the Arabic language. After that, we crawled the seed URIs to enlarge the dataset. Then we analyze those Arabic webpages. We used four different language tests to check the webpages language, then we performed some basic data analysis, such as checking the presence on the live Web, TLD, GeoIP, URI path depth, and creation date. Then we checked if these webpages are archived and measured the archiving frequency and the gap between creation date and the first archived version. Finally, we investigated if archiving and indexing were affected by Arabic ccTLD, Arabic GeoIP, URI path depth, or creation date.

We found that 46% of the Arabic websites are not archived and that 31% were not indexed by Google. We also found that archiving and indexing appear to be affected by the TLD, GeoIP location, URI path depth, creation date, and presence in a directory. Arabic language sites having either only an Arabic GeoIP or only an Arabic top-level domain are less likely to be archived than others. URIs that are present in a directory are more likely to be indexed, and those present in the DMOZ directory are more likely to be archived. We also found that only 14.84% of the URIs had an Arabic ccTLD and only 10.53% had a GeoIP location in an Arabic country. Popular Western sites (such as facebook.com, wikipedia.org, and google.com) were in the top 10 domains found in our sample of Arabic language URIs. This seems to indicate that the Arabic language community is using services hosted on Western sites and their cultural discourse is occurring on Western sites where archiving is likely to be already taking place.

Future work will include study of comparing archiving for other languages, such as Chinese, English, and other languages. In future work, we will check if the characteristics of the language, culture, and technology have an influence the archiving results.

7. REFERENCES

[1] S. G. Ainsworth, A. Alsum, H. SalahEldeen, M. C. Weigle, and M. L. Nelson. How Much of the Web is Archived? In *Proceedings of the IEEE/ACM Joint Conference on Digital Libraries (JCDL)*, pages 133–136. ACM, 2011.

[2] A. Alarifi, M. Alghamdi, M. Zarour, B. Aloqail, H. Lraqibah, K. Alsadhan, and L. Alkwai. Estimating the Size of Arabic Indexed Web Content. *Scientific Research and Essays*, 7(28):2472–2483, 2012.

[3] A. AlSum. *Web Archive Services Framework for Tighter Integration Between the Past and Present Web*. PhD thesis, Old Dominion University, 2014.

[4] R. Baeza-Yates, C. Castillo, and E. N. Efthimiadis. Characterization of National Web Domains. *ACM Transactions on Internet Technology (TOIT)*, 7(2):9, 2007.

[5] K. R. Beesley. Language Identifier: A Computer Program for Automatic Natural-Language Identification of On-line Text. In *Proceedings of the 29th Annual Conference of the American Translators Association*, volume 47, page 54, 1988.

[6] B. E. Brewington and G. Cybenko. Keeping up with the changing web. *Computer*, 33(5):52–58, 2000.

[7] J. Cho and H. Garcia-Molina. Parallel crawlers. In *Proceedings of the 11th International Conference on World Wide Web*, pages 124–135, 2002.

[8] D. Gomes and M. J. Silva. Characterizing a National Community Web. *ACM Transactions on Internet Technology (TOIT)*, 5(3):508–531, 2005.

[9] H. C. Huurdeman, A. Ben-David, J. Kamps, T. Samar, and A. P. de Vries. Finding Pages on the Unarchived Web. In *Proceedings of the IEEE/ACM Joint Conference on Digital Libraries (JCDL)*, pages 331–340. IEEE, 2014.

[10] Internet World Stats. Arabic Speaking Internet Users Statistics. `https://web.archive.org/web/20100515122707/http://www.internetworldstats.com/stats19.htm`, 2009.

[11] Internet World Stats. Arabic Speaking Internet Users Statistics. `https://web.archive.org/web/20141002202223/http://www.internetworldstats.com/stats19.htm`, 2014.

[12] Internet World Stats. Internet World Users By Language. `https://web.archive.org/web/20141213103739/http://www.internetworldstats.com/stats7.htm`, 2014.

[13] B. Kahle. Preserving The Internet. *Scientific American*, 276(3):82–83, 1997.

[14] M. Klein, H. Van de Sompel, R. Sanderson, H. Shankar, L. Balakireva, K. Zhou, and R. Tobin. Scholarly context not found: One in five articles suffers from reference rot. *PLoS ONE*, 9(12):e115253, 2014.

[15] J. Lepore. The Cobweb: Can the Internet be Archived? *The New Yorker*, January 2015.

[16] F. McCown and M. L. Nelson. Agreeing To Disagree: Search Engines And Their Public Interfaces. In *Proceedings of the IEEE/ACM Joint Conference on Digital Libraries (JCDL)*, pages 309–318. ACM, 2007.

[17] A. Noruzi. A Study of HTML Title Tag Creation Behavior of Academic Web Sites. *The Journal of Academic Librarianship*, 33(4):501–506, 2007.

[18] H. M. SalahEldeen and M. L. Nelson. Carbon Dating the Web: Estimating the Age of Web Resources. In *Proceedings of the Temporal Web Analytics Workshop (TempWeb)*, pages 1075–1082, 2013.

[19] H. M. Salaheldeen and M. L. Nelson. Resurrecting my revolution. In *Research and Advanced Technology for Digital Libraries*, pages 333–345. Springer, 2013.

[20] M. Thelwall and L. Vaughan. A Fair History of the Web? Examining Country Balance in the Internet Archive. *Library & Information Science Research*, 26(2):162–176, 2004.

[21] H. Van de Sompel, M. L. Nelson, and R. Sanderson. HTTP framework for time-based access to resource states – Memento, Internet RFC 7089. 2013.

[22] H. Van de Sompel, M. L. Nelson, R. Sanderson, L. L. Balakireva, S. Ainsworth, and H. Shankar. Memento: Time Travel for the Web. Technical Report arXiv:0911.1112, 2009.

No More 404s: Predicting Referenced Link Rot in Scholarly Articles for Pro-Active Archiving

Ke Zhou
University of Edinburgh
Ke.Zhou@ed.ac.uk

Claire Grover
University of Edinburgh
Claire.Grover@ed.ac.uk

Martin Klein
University of California
Los Angeles
martinklein@library.ucla.edu

Richard Tobin
University of Edinburgh
richard@inf.ed.ac.uk

ABSTRACT

The citation of resources is a fundamental part of scholarly discourse. Due to the popularity of the web, there is an increasing trend for scholarly articles to reference web resources (e.g. software, data). However, due to the dynamic nature of the web, the referenced links may become inaccessible ('rotten') sometime after publication, returning a "404 Not Found" HTTP error. In this paper we first present some preliminary findings of a study of the persistence and availability of web resources referenced from papers in a large-scale scholarly repository. We reaffirm previous research that link rot is a serious problem in the scholarly world and that current web archives do not always preserve all rotten links. Therefore, a more pro-active archival solution needs to be developed to further preserve web content referenced in scholarly articles. To this end, we propose to apply machine learning techniques to train a link rot predictor for use by an archival framework to prioritise pro-active archiving of links that are more likely to be rotten. We demonstrate that we can obtain a fairly high link rot prediction AUC (0.72) with only a small set of features. By simulation, we also show that our prediction framework is more effective than current web archives for preserving links that are likely to be rotten. This work has a potential impact for the scholarly world where publishers can utilise this framework to prioritise the archiving of links for digital preservation, especially when there is a large quantity of links to be archived.

Categories and Subject Descriptors: H.5.4 [Information Interfaces and Presentation: Hypertext][Architectures, Navigation]
Keywords: Digital Preservation, Repositories, Web Persistence

1. INTRODUCTION

The citation of resources is a fundamental part of scholarly discourse. Beyond traditionally-cited published articles or books, in the digital age web-based scholarly endeavour has greatly enlarged the range of scholarly artefacts that are being published and referenced. Many of these are resources created as part of research activity such as software, datasets, presentations, videos, etc. as well as scientific workflows and ontologies. Our recent research[1] [11] has shown that in large-scale scholarly corpora, around 20% of scholarly articles have referenced web links (URLs) and the number of those referenced links is increasing over the years.

The real-time nature of the web enables immediate access to web resources and dramatically increases the speed of knowledge dissemination. At the same time however, it also poses the challenge of preserving endangered referenced web links that may become inaccessible (i.e. rotten) after publication. There are two ways in which links can be considered dysfunctional: (1) *link rot*, the content of the link is not available on the live web at its original URI anymore; or (2) *content drift*, the content of the link has changed since publication of the scholarly article. Both scenarios give rise to the risk that researchers in the future will not be able to thoroughly study the citation context of a scholarly publication. In this preliminary work, we focus solely on investigating the first type of link rot problem, i.e. the links returning a "404 Not Found" HTTP error status code. We leave the second type of reference rot problem, content drift, for future work.

In previous work, various researchers have aimed to quantify aspects of the reference rot problem [4, 7, 6]. There exist a variety of web archival services [1] (e.g. Internet Archive[2]) which aim to preserve web resources. Although these archival services largely preserve online resources [1], how well they archive referenced web resources for the scholarly world is not clear. Klein et al. [6] recently investigated this problem and found that for several large-scale scholarly collections, one out of five STM (Science, Technology, and Medicine) articles suffer from reference rot, meaning it is impossible to revisit the entire web context that surrounds them at some point after their publication. Therefore, more pro-active archival solutions for archiving links in the scholarly world are required for digital preservation for future researchers. Given the large and increasing number of links referenced in the scholarly world, we might not have the capability to archive all of them and we therefore need to prioritise some links over others. We hypothesise that *a referenced link that is more likely to become rotten should become a higher priority to be pro-actively archived.* Even if all of the links can be archived, it would still be useful to automatically suggest to publishers or authors the links that are more likely to become rotten so that action can be taken.

Our main goal in this work is to investigate whether it is possible to accurately predict link rot. We aim to answer: **Can we accurately predict referenced link rot in scholarly articles in order to prioritise pro-active archiving of links that are at risk?**

JCDL'15, June 21–25, 2015, Knoxville, Tennessee, USA.

http://dx.doi.org/10.1145/2756406.2756940 .

[1]The Hiberlink project (http://www.hiberlink.org/) is supported by the Andrew W. Mellon Foundation. We would like to thank our project partners from EDINA and Los Alamos National Laboratory Research Library for their useful feedback.

[2]https://www.archive.org/

The contributions of this paper are two-fold: **(1)** We demonstrate the feasibility of using a machine learned classification framework to accurately predict the referenced link rot problem (i.e. the likelihood that a given link will become rotten). We also analyse the impact of different features (including scholarly article features and link features) on the link rot prediction task. **(2)** In order to demonstrate the effectiveness of our link rot predictor, we simulate pro-active archiving and show that the approach outperforms current web archives in preserving rotten links.

2. RELATED WORK

Two lines of research relate to this work. One focuses on current endeavours to study and quantify the referenced link rot problem in the scholarly world. The second line focuses on reviewing current web archives and their archiving (crawling) strategies. The contributions of our work lie in our proposed machine learned link rot prediction framework and extensive analysis of the features that affect the link rot problem in the scholarly world.

Referenced Link Rot Study Over the past ten years, extensive, although typically small-scale, research has been conducted on the persistence of the resources identified by URLs cited in scholarly publications, especially journal articles. For example, the study by Lawrence [7] was seminal and indicated that only 75% of URLs were accessible in the corpus of citations he examined in 2000. It also attempted to discover if the resources that were not available at their original URL were still online at new locations. For example, Lawrence [7] used search engines to investigate the availability of 205 URLs that did not resolve and rediscovered 163 (79.7%). The studies since have all been small-scale while the extent to which the cited resources were available from archives was only comprehensively studied recently [6]. By using the Memento protocol [10] (a web archive aggregator), this research reported that the survival rate in larger STM (Science, Technology, and Medicine) corpora is at around 80%. A more detailed review of those studies can be found in [6] and our work is inspired by those studies.

Web Archive and Crawling Archiving web content is not new and there exists a variety of web archives [1] and their aggregators [10]. The way they prioritise preservation is based on several heuristics [5, 9], similar to the way in which search engines crawl web pages [2]. Different features, mostly derived from web pages and their domain, such as PageRank, etc. have been exploited. For example, current web archives [5] prioritise archiving of web pages from top ranked domains (although with only a limited number of levels). Crawling the web pages of one site at a time can be done in breadth first mode, postponing the crawling of external web pages until the corresponding sites are visited.

Unlike current web archives, the links of interest to us for preservation are referenced links within scholarly articles. As we briefly show in Section 3.1, current web archives fail to preserve all the referenced link contents for publishers and future researchers. We aim to use the features derived from both the referenced link and scholarly articles to predict link rot. This prediction is then used to assist a pro-active archive to prioritise the archiving of referenced links that are more likely to become rotten and that should therefore be preserved as early as possible.

3. LINK ROT PREDICTION

In this study, we treat link rot prediction as a binary classification problem (i.e. we classify links as "highly likely to become rotten" or not), and investigate how to use machine learning techniques to learn this. In this section, we first quantify the link rot problem, followed by presentation of our approach and evaluation results.

Table 1: The characteristics and quantification of referenced link rot of the Elsevier scholarly article collection.

Statistics and Results/Collection	Elsevier [3]
(a). Subject	variety of subjects, e.g. finance, medical
(b). Publication Type	Journal and Book Series
(c). Publication Period	1997-2012
(d). # of articles	648,388
(e). fraction of articles with links	12.1% (78,237)
(f). total # of links extracted	193,955
(g). fraction of "rotten" links	36.2% (70,270)
(h). fraction of archived links	77.5% (150,368)
(i). fraction of archived "rotten" links	62.3% (43,745)

3.1 Link Rot Quantification

By using a state-of-the-art link extraction system [11] (with high performance F-measure of 0.8) on a scholarly collection, we aim to quantify the referenced link rot problem by dereferencing the links on the live web and obtaining their archived status via Memento (a web archive aggregator). The aim here is to introduce link rot quantification (following approaches similar to previous work [6]), leaving a more thorough quantification for future work.

We use the Elsevier collection as our test set—detailed characteristics of this collection are shown in Table 1(a) to (d). We can observe that this collection is relatively large, with hundreds of thousands of scholarly articles on a variety of subjects spanning more than fifteen years. From Table 1(e) to (f), we can also see that a significant fraction of documents (12%) have referenced web links.

To quantify link rot, we probe each extracted referenced link on the live web and check its HTTP status. Since there could potentially be redirects of the links, we set a rule to allow redirects only up to a maximum of 50. We record the whole HTTP transaction chain and if this ends with a 2XX status code, we consider the link to exist (i.e. it is not rotten). Otherwise, we consider the link to be rotten. The results are shown in Table 1(g). We can observe that many links are rotten and 36.2% of the links extracted suffer from the risk of content rot. This finding reaffirms previous research [6]. Not surprisingly, we also find this problem occurs across all publication time spans and subjects. We conclude it is crucial for a digital preservation service to preserve all those referenced web links.

Using a Memento Aggregator [10] that covers nine archives, including the Internet Archive, Web Citation, the UK National Archive and the Library of Congress, we also attempt to quantify whether the links have been archived by current web archival facilities. Specifically, we retrieve a TimeMap for each of the referenced URLs. If a TimeMap cannot be retrieved, the URL is marked as not being archived, and otherwise marked as being archived. We conducted this study in March 2014 and Table 1 (h) and (i) present the results. From (h), it can be seen that for all the links extracted (Table 1 (f)), a large percentage of them (77.5%) is archived at least once over the years. However, from (i), we can observe that for the links that are rotten (Table 1 (g)) only 62.3% of them are preserved by current web archives. This implies that the remaining approximately 40% of the rotten link contents are not preserved and would not be retrievable by future researchers. We conclude, therefore, that the current digital preservation framework fails to accurately preserve all of the referenced link content in scholarly works and that a more pro-active referenced link preservation framework needs to be developed.

[3] http://www.developers.elsevier.com/cms/index

Table 2: Two types of features generated for quantifying the likelihood of link rot for machine learning in the scholarly world.

Feature	Description	Data Source
Scholarly Article Features		
Publication Subject Vector	A vector containing all the subject areas[4] of the publication where the weight of the given publication's subject is 1, otherwise 0.	meta-data
Year of Publication (distance to the present)	An integer score representing the distance (in years) from the publication year of the given publication to 2014.	meta-data
Open Access Status of the Publication	Whether the publication is open-access (1) or not (0).	meta-data
h5-index of the Journal (if available)	The h5-index of the given publication evenly distributed into 20 quality-bins.	Google Scholar Metrics[5]
Link Features		
Link Domain PageRank	The pagerank score of the given link's score, averaged over its domain based on pagerank values computed on 50 million web pages then evenly distributed into 100 quality-bins.	ClueWeb'09 dataset[6]
Link Depth	An integer score of the depths of the link (i.e. number of tokens).	URL standard tokenization[7]
Link Position Vector	A vector containing all the link positions where the weight of the given link position is 1, otherwise 0.	XML annotation
Link Type Vector	A vector containing all the link types where the weight of the given link type is 1, otherwise 0.	ODP and UClassifier[8]

3.2 Link Rot Prediction Approach

Given the severity of link rot in the referenced links in scholarly works, we aim to predict the likelihood of this link rot in order to preserve the links that are highly likely to become rotten in a pro-active archival framework. In order to train and test a machine learned link rot predictor, we need to develop various features to effectively represent the problem and train the classifier.

3.2.1 Features

We believe that two types of factors influence the likelihood of the link rot: (1) scholarly article features: the quality and the type of the scholarly publication which the link is extracted from; and (2) link features: the quality and the type of the link. The underlying hypothesis is that some of the links (e.g. from high-quality domains) originating from some scholarly publications (e.g. open-access journals) might be less susceptible to rot than others. Details of the features we extract to quantify this are presented in Table 2. The main objective of this preliminary study is to demonstrate the feasibility of our approach.

Most of the features are either available from the Elsevier collection meta-data (e.g. publication year) or from existing resources (e.g. h5-index, PageRank). To obtain the link position in the article, we extract the annotated sections within the XML format of the Elsevier collection using a stylesheet. We define a set of manual rules to transform the XML annotations to the set of document structures we are interested in. The corresponding positions we obtain are: header, footnote, figure, table, body and reference.

We also believe that link type information (specifying which resource a link refers to) could also be useful for link rot prediction. To investigate link type, we use a publicly available classification tool, UClassifier, to classify links into the taxonomy provided from the Open Directory Project (ODP)[7]. This is a machine learning classifier that is based on training data provided by ODP (textual representation of all the web pages within each category). Rather than being interested in the general topics of the link (e.g. Arts, Business, Computers, etc.), we are more interested in whether the links appear within categories that are more related to scholarly publications: software, licence, data, slides, blog, image, video and publishers. We manually label the corresponding sub-categories in the ODP with those categories. All the links that are not classified into any of the categories are given the category "Other". We also have a whitelist of publishers' website domains to determine whether a link points to a publisher website. To represent each link for learning, rather than downloading the actual content (which might be not available due to the "rot" problem), we use the textual context of each referenced link for the representation. Following one of the best performing methods from Ritchie [8] for representing citation context, we use "three sentences" around a referenced link as the textual context. Although a more comprehensive evaluation of this link type classifier would help us better estimate its effectiveness, the idea in this work is to apply current solutions. Full evaluation of our link type classifier is left for future work. We empirically demonstrate in Sec. 3.3 that this feature is useful for link rot prediction.

3.2.2 Classifier and Training

We use Support Vector Machine (SVM) learning for our classifier since SVMs are proven to perform well in other classification tasks. Specifically, we use the publicly available LIBSVM toolkit (`http://www.csie.ntu.edu.tw/~cjlin/libsvm/`) for our implementation. Study of the effectiveness of other classifiers (e.g. linear regression, random forest, etc.) is left for future work.

To train the classifier, we sample 10,000 links from the Elsevier collection and obtain the corresponding rot label (1 or 0) by probing on the live web. To avoid bias where the classifier rewards a class with more positive cases (here, the non-rotten links), our sampling approach is based on random sampling while ensuring that the two classes contain the same number of positive cases. In order to train the performance of our classifier, we perform five-fold cross validation with the sampled links using our approach. We finally report the standard AUC [3] of our trained classifier on the test set (another sampled set of 2,000 links using the same sampling approach) and we ensure that the test set does not overlap with the training set.

3.3 Evaluation

We conduct two types of evaluation: (1) the AUC of the learned link rot predictor; and (2) the effectiveness of applying the link rot predictor to a simulated archival environment.

3.3.1 Evaluating the Link Rot Predictor

The evaluation results of our link rot predictor are presented in Table 3. Specifically, we find that we can obtain an AUC of prediction up to 0.72, which is significantly better than a random prediction (0.50 AUC). Significance was tested using a sign test, where the null hypothesis is that the classifier predicts the link rot randomly with equal probability. This demonstrates that our proposed learned approach and corresponding features are feasible and effective in predicting link rot.

To further investigate the effectiveness of each feature in its contribution to the prediction, we conduct an ablation study (i.e. leave one feature type out and track the performance change). The results are shown in Table 3. A non-significant performance drop in AUC does not necessarily mean the feature captures no useful evidence, as features may be correlated. We can observe the following

[4] Elsevier contains 27 subjects from http://www.elsevier.com/journals/title/a

[5] http://scholar.google.co.uk/citations?view_op=top_venues

[6] http://boston.lti.cs.cmu.edu/clueweb09/wiki/tiki-index.php?page=PageRank

[7] http://www.ietf.org/rfc/rfc1738.txt

[8] UClassifier (http://www.uclassify.com/browse) and ODP (http://www.dmoz.org)

Table 3: Feature set contribution to link rot prediction AUC: leaving one feature type out (feature ablation study). The differences of AUC performance are calculated over "All", our classifier using all features.

Feature Variation	Feature Type	AUC	% diff
All	Both	**0.72**	
no.Publication Subject	Article	0.70	-2.8%
no.Year of Publication	Article	0.65	**-9.7%**
no.Publication Open Access Status	Article	0.72	-0.0%
no.h5-index of the Journal	Article	0.70	-2.8%
no.Link Domain PageRank	Link	0.67	**-6.9%**
no.Link.Depth	Link	0.66	**-8.3%**
no.Link Position	Link	0.71	-1.4%
no.Link Type	Link	0.69	**-4.2%**

trends: (1) In terms of feature types, in general, more link features contribute more significantly than scholarly article features. Specifically, the article feature "Year of Publication" contributes most to the prediction AUC. To explore this further, we plot the rot likelihood of extracted links according to publication year in Figure 1. We can observe that links are more likely to be rotten if they originate from older scholarly publications. Not surprisingly, the further from the time of publication, the more likely it is that an extracted link will be rotten. Note that the link creation time might potentially be correlated with the year of publication since the links are likely created prior to the scholarly articles which cite them. (2) The second and third most helpful features are link features: "Link.Depth" and "Link.Domain.PageRank". From close examination, we find that links to low quality domains and which have more depth (longer length) are more likely to rot. (3) The features which contribute least are link position and publication open access status. This implies that ease of access and the position of a link in a scholarly article do not have a big impact on link rot. It is also interesting however that the citation-based quality measure of the publication (h5-index) can also contribute to link rot prediction. This implies that links to scholarly articles, which are published in higher impact journals, are less likely to be rotten.

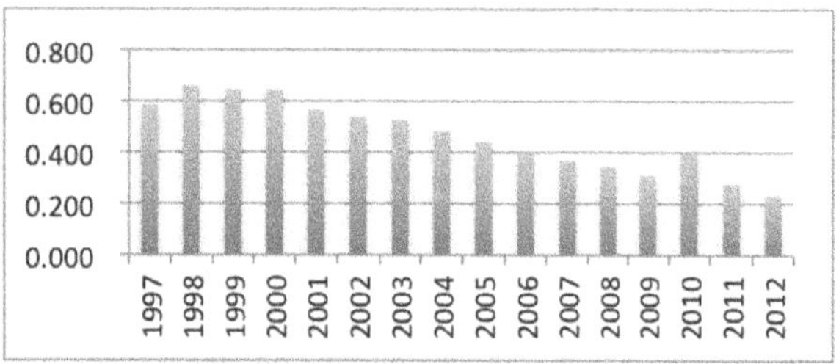

Figure 1: Time-aware analysis of likelihood of extracted links deemed to be rotten according to publication year (Elsevier).

In summary, we have analysed different features in predicting link rot and have demonstrated the feasibility of our approach.

3.3.2 Evaluating Simulated Pro-active Archiving

So far, we have demonstrated the effectiveness of predicting the likelihood of link rot. However, the utility of this learned link rot predictor in a pro-active archive for scholarly works is still to be considered. Since there are currently no pro-active archive solutions for scholarly works, we simulate one using our link rot predictor and compare its effectiveness in archiving rotten links from past publications, compared to current web archives.

We first sample a set of extracted links from all the links extracted from Elsevier (Table 1). Then we use our learned link rot predictor to predict which links are more likely to become rotten and should be prioritised for archiving. Finally, by archiving the same number of links with the current web archives, we track whether our simulated pro-active archive can preserve more links at risk of rot. The results are presented in Table 4. We can observe that compared with current archives (62.3%), our simulated pro-active archive preserved a significantly larger number of rotten links (84.8%). Although this simulation does not conform to a real-world setting, we conclude that our link rot predictor can be helpful for archiving scholarly referenced links for digital preservation.

Table 4: Evaluation of applying link rot predictor to archive rotten links, compared with current archival solution.

Results /Systems	Current Archives	Simulated Archive
fraction of archived "rotten" links	62.3%	84.8%

4. CONCLUSIONS

In this paper, we briefly quantified the referenced link rot problem in scholarly works and proposed a link rot prediction task. We reaffirm previous research that link rot is prevalent in the scholarly world and that pro-active archival solutions are required to solve this. To this end, we proposed a machine learned link rot predictor and investigated two sources of evidence for learning, i.e. link features and scholarly article features. We treat link rot prediction as a binary classification problem and use machine learning techniques (SVM) to learn a classifier. Although we have only used a limited set of essential features, we found that we can predict the link rot problem with an AUC of 0.72. We also showed that this preliminary predictor could be used alongside an archival framework to prioritise pro-actively archiving links that are more at risk of rot. We tested this in a simulated environment and showed that the simulated archival solution outperforms current web archives. Although testing this in a real-world archival setting is out of scope for this paper, we believe that with further feature engineering and classifier evaluation, this could be further improved and used in a practical setting.

Our future work includes expanding our link rot definition and investigating the more complex *content drift* aspect of the reference rot problem: the change of referenced link content over time. We would also like to study more features and conduct a more thorough evaluation of our learned link rot predictor for assisting scholarly referenced link archiving.

5. REFERENCES

[1] S. G. Ainsworth, A. Alsum, H. SalahEldeen, M. C. Weigle, and M. L. Nelson. How much of the web is archived? In *JCDL*, JCDL '11, pages 133–136, 2011.

[2] J. Cho and H. Garcia-Molina. The evolution of the web and implications for an incremental crawler. In *VLDB*, pages 200–209, 2000.

[3] T. Fawcett. An introduction to roc analysis. *Pattern recognition letters*, 27(8):861–874, 2006.

[4] D. Fetterly, M. Manasse, M. Najork, and J. Wiener. A large-scale study of the evolution of web pages. In *WWW*, pages 669–678. ACM, 2003.

[5] D. Gomes, S. Freitas, and M. J. Silva. Design and selection criteria for a national web archive. In *Research and Advanced Technology for Digital Libraries*, pages 196–207. Springer, 2006.

[6] M. Klein, H. Van de Sompel, R. Sanderson, H. Shankar, L. Balakireva, K. Zhou, and R. Tobin. Scholarly context not found: One in five articles suffers from reference rot. *PloS one*, 9(12):e115253, 2014.

[7] S. Lawrence, D. M. Pennock, G. W. Flake, R. Krovetz, F. M. Coetzee, E. Glover, F. Å. Nielsen, A. Kruger, and C. L. Giles. Persistence of web references in scientific research. *Computer*, 34(2):26–31, 2001.

[8] A. Ritchie, S. Robertson, and S. Teufel. Comparing citation contexts for information retrieval. In *CIKM*, pages 213–222. ACM, 2008.

[9] M. Spaniol, D. Denev, A. Mazeika, G. Weikum, and P. Senellart. Data quality in web archiving. In *Proceedings of the 3rd workshop on Information credibility on the web*, pages 19–26. ACM, 2009.

[10] H. Van de Sompel, M. Nelson, and R. Sanderson. Http framework for time-based access to resource states–memento, 2012.

[11] K. Zhou, R. Tobin, and C. Grover. Extraction and analysis of referenced web links in large-scale scholarly articles. In *Proceedings of the 14th ACM/IEEE-CS Joint Conference on Digital Libraries*, JCDL '14, pages 451–452, 2014.

The Problem of "Additional Content" in Video Games

Jin Ha Lee
University of Washington
Mary Gates Hall, Suite 370
Seattle, WA 98195
+1 206.685.0153
jinhalee@uw.edu

Jacob Jett
Univ. of Illinois at Urbana-Champaign
501 E. Daniel Street
Champaign, IL 61820
+1 217.244.2164
jjett2@illiniois.edu

Andrew Perti
Seattle Interactive Media Museum
305 Harrison Street
Seattle, WA 98109
+1 518.653.5864
andrew.perti@thesimm.org

ABSTRACT

Additional content for video games such as mods (modifications) or DLC (downloadable content) are increasingly prevalent in the current video game market. For cultural heritage institutions with video game collections, such content introduces various philosophical and practical challenges on multiple aspects including acquisition, description, access/use, and preservation. In this paper, we discuss these challenges and propose a solution that can alleviate the problem of managing a digital library collection including video games with additional content. While our discussion and proposed solution focus on video games, they also have broader implications for cultural heritage institutions that manage other types of digital and multimedia objects with additional content as well as serial publications.

Categories and Subject Descriptors

H.3.7 [**Information Storage and Retrieval**]: Digital Libraries – Standards, K.8.0 [**Personal Computing**]: Games

General Terms

Standardization; Theory.

Keywords

Video games; DLC; mods; digital libraries; cataloging practice; conceptual models.

1. INTRODUCTION

The concept of additional content that expands or supplements a bibliographic resource is not new to information science. Supplementary issues containing additional resources, articles, and breaking news are a well-documented feature of serial publications. Similar additional content for games emerged in the 1970s for board and paper-and-pen role-playing games, and became prevalent for video games during the 1980s as a means for adding levels and gameplay features.

Today, additional content plays an enormous role in the cultural, economic, and professional aspects of video game development and gaming communities. It is rare to find a video game which does not have some kind of additional content available for it – whether that content is in the form of official expansion packages, small downloadable extras, or fan-made modifications (mods). Clearly understanding the boundaries of and effectively describing content which does not initially come with video games at their points of purchase is a compounding problem for faithfully representing them as objects of interest in libraries and similar cultural heritage institutions. As traditional divisions between media continue to erode in the born-digital world, we see increasing parallels between additional video game content and more traditional bibliographic forms. Whether it be the video game/book mashup of the visual novel or datasets accompanying academic papers, the issue of additional content is not limited to the video game domain.

In this paper, we define the scope of additional content with regards to video games. We first briefly review previous work that remarks on the problem of additional content and situate our working definitions for DLC (downloadable content) and mods within the existing literature. We next remark on the philosophical and practical challenges that digitally distributed add-on content presents for cataloging practices. Finally, we propose a solution that can alleviate the problem in various contexts.

2. DEFINING ADDITIONAL CONTENT

To remediate potential disparities, it is necessary to define boundaries for what we consider as additional content. Our purpose is to explore only the content which improves or extends the experience of gamers beyond what a game offered at its initial point of purchase. Therefore our working definition does not encompass ordinary software patches and bug fixes that software corporations deploy during the normal lifespan of their products. While some authors categorize patches or bug fixes as a type of mod, and therefore part of additional content, such categorization is problematic. A patch released to fix bugs, or blatant problems, in our view, is not content per se. Those patches affect how the code is run, and may correct problems to improve interactions with game content, but they do not expand the content of the game. Here, we consider additional content as that which goes beyond fixing problems and glitches, such as new characters, dungeons, stories, etc. It intentionally extends the playing experience from the gamer's perspective. Our definition also does not include community efforts that do not add new content, such as aftermarket patches (i.e., mods that specifically patch a malfunctioning game) or emulation architectures.

We consider two types of additional content: mods and DLC, the former of which has a longer and better documented history within video game scholarship. A primary distinction between the two is in the development responsibility. It is universally accepted that mods are developed by members of fan communities while DLC is produced and distributed by corporate entities. Therefore, it might be natural to assume that mods are free and DLC must be paid for. However, while mods tend to be free today, this was not always the case [7], and while many DLC packages cost money, there are many examples of promotional DLC that are free with

JCDL'15, June 21 - 25, 2015, Knoxville, TN, USA

ACM 978-1-4503-3594-2/15/06…$15.00
DOI: http://dx.doi.org/10.1145/2756406.2756949

the purchase of other related merchandise [16]. The one thing that they do have in common is the required presence of the initially purchased video game that they expand.

Sometimes likened to fan fiction, mods run the gamut from minor code changes up to "total conversions" that change one game into another [13][14]. Modding culture has become so widespread that many video game communities contain sub-communities of modders, and some corporate entities provide tools such as software development kits to facilitate modding activity and the dialogue between fan developers and corporate developers [15].

Unlike mods, DLC rarely includes minor changes to the abstract mechanisms (i.e., code). The scope of DLC is similar to, yet narrower than that of mods. Most work on DLC overlooks the nature of what it adds to a game in favor of remarking on how it affects game commodification models and economics [4][9][17]. Yet with regards to content, DLC ranges from adding or altering cosmetic content (e.g., new character sprites, skins, costumes, or other minor graphic variations) to extending and expanding a game's core functionality (e.g., through the addition of new characters, new play modes, new maps, etc.). The only pronounced similarity between the various types of DLC is the method by which the content is delivered: an online download.

Although currently most common, mods and DLC are not the only ways gamers can expand their games with additional content. Developers still produce large scale expansions distributed as discs. Libraries and cultural heritage institutions have been dealing with similar situations regarding serial publications and similar bibliographic items for many decades. However, prior literature on serials cataloging also identifies challenges in establishing and maintaining bibliographic control over serials due to their instability (e.g., title change, format change) and tendency to split or merge with other serials [1][2].

3. PROBLEMS

3.1 Philosophical Challenges

A fundamental problem with additional content is how it challenges the notion of work. In the bibliographic universe, works have typically been defined as distinct intellectual or artistic creations [5]. According to this definition, an original release of a video game is a work. Adding additional content to this established work may be comparable to supplementary materials in other formats, such as monographs or films. However for games, additional content can significantly change the gameplay and the narrative itself, resulting in a more substantial deviation from the original work.

Use of DLC as a marketing tool [16] and its distribution as a separate consumer product complicates the issue. For instance, official strategy guides for *Disgaea D2: A Brighter Darkness* and *Ni No Kuni* include redeemable codes for DLC such as new characters. Games like *Disney Infinity* or *Skylanders* encourage players to purchase figurines of additional characters, which use embedded ID tags to import the figure as a playable character in the game. If there is always the possibility to create new DLC that can significantly change the gameplay experience, and it can be distributed as separate information objects, can we really consider any game as a complete work?

The optional nature of additional content also raises issues, as it allows multiple game players to play different variations of the work. If the mods or DLC substantially alter the game experience, can we really say that players are playing the same game?[1]

Mods and DLC can fundamentally alter game content, and thus create new works. But at what point does the distinction of a new work arise? The lack of boundaries for works presents a significant challenge, as there are currently no itemized lists or numbers of changes that need to occur before a mod or a game with DLC is considered a new game. Or, perhaps usage criteria are a more appropriate evaluation of work boundaries: maybe a mod can simply be considered a new game if it is widely used and popular. There are some cases where mods are more popular and well-known than the original games themselves (e.g., *Counter-Strike*, a mod for *Half-Life*; *Dota (Defense of the Ancients)*, a mod for *Warcraft III: Reign of Chaos*).

3.2 Practical Challenges

3.2.1 Acquisition

Distribution methods for additional content have evolved from physical carriers like disks distributed via retail stores or mail-order, to digital distribution platforms like Xbox Live, Steam, PlayStation Network, etc. Each method offers unique challenges. Availability issues abound for both physical and digital carriers for additional content as both may only be available for a limited time and are often withdrawn from publication for a variety of reasons. Official distributors of content do not keep or offer access to records regarding additional content, and user-generated information is also often incomplete and uncontrolled. Another complicating factor is the need for the original game. In most cases, the original game must be present to access its additional content. Unless an organization takes steps to acquire everything, they risk losing the ability to access and play the additional content at all. Also, DLC is increasingly only available via specific consoles, defying any precise distinction from the original game. Much additional content is not offered for free, especially DLC, which will quickly deplete the acquisition budget. Even if availability was not an issue, problems of selection remain. Should organizations acquire all of the content associated with a game? The continued proliferation makes full acquisition unlikely. What criteria for collection development should be used to facilitate selection judgments, considering the end user's best interest?

3.2.2 Characterization and Description

Lack of vocabulary and clear definitional boundaries bring challenges for description of additional content. Due to the rapid development and transformation of games and their distribution methods, many gamers and other affiliated users do not understand or agree upon distinctions among different kinds of additional content. Therefore, there is no standard controlled vocabulary within the game industry or user communities that defines and describes these different kinds of additional content. This harkens back to the philosophical questions regarding delineations among works. The lack of any formally or popularly established demarcations raises questions about attributes of description (such as title, creator, genre, etc.) that are assigned at the work level. Mods and DLC often have different creators than their original games, which may range from large corporate teams

[1] Cf, Suits, (1978) The Grasshopper for full discussions of the intrinsic nature of games.

to individual fans and players. Attributing creation information to additional content is difficult in and of itself, but it also signifies implications for treating additional content as separate works.

In addition to these standard descriptive elements, additional content also requires a thorough and accurate description of system requirements, compatibility, and conflicts between it and the game it modifies. Games often need updates to apply DLC or function with a particular mod. Moreover, some mods require other mods in order to work, while some mods will not work with other mods. These requirements comprise critical description necessary for users to select and obtain desirable functional content.

3.2.3 Access, Use, and Preservation

The variety of distribution methods previously discussed has a significant impact on the ability to access, use and preserve additional content for games. In addition to the physical/digital divide, the multiplicity of platform architectures means that platform-specific workflows must be devised to restore additional content to a usable state. Over the years, developers have used a large number of different strategies to store and deploy the code that bears additional content on end users machines. Among these methods are files on physical media (disks), separate additional content folders, or as customizations within a user profile. This makes it difficult to discern what portion of the data, once accessible, is the additional content in contrast to the game itself. The large variety of access mechanisms affects the ability of cultural heritage institutions to prescribe a one-size-fits-all method or framework that allows use of additional content.

The variety of carriers, distribution methods, and access mechanisms also present technical and legal hurdles to preserving additional game content. Physical media like floppy and optical discs contain a variety of copy protection measures, preventing their migration to sustainable digital infrastructures for preservation. Digitally distributed content has a particularly unique set of constraints, as the user typically has no way to access the file(s) from which the additional content stems. Accessing this content may be hindered due to system-level encryption which writes information to the system's hard disk in a completely undiscernible format.

3.3 A Proposed Solution

To reconcile some of the aforementioned issues that additional content presents for cultural heritage institutions, we propose a new model (Figure 1) that better defines and represents additional content and its related descriptive information [6]. This model is designed to represent video games as they are published across various markets. This model addresses the work issue by creating a specific separate entity for additional content, defining it as content that is published after the initial publication of a video game. Specific attributes are then assigned to this entity, with controlled vocabulary of community accepted terms for each attribute. Formal metadata records can easily be crafted that will represent the information captured by the model.

This solution solves many of the issues with regards to capturing information that is relevant to collecting and describing additional content for video games. Within the confines of the model, it becomes easy to delineate between content that is a mod, DLC, or some other form of expansion. For instance, *Sid Meyer's Civilization V (CiV)* has a very large and active modding community. The additional content module of the video game conceptual model allows the following descriptive information to be captured for each mod – Name/Title, Type (i.e., that it is a mod rather than DLC or an expansion), and the version/configuration requirements that are necessary for it to work.

To give two illustrations, consider the *CiV* expansion, *Gods & Kings*: the expansion has the title *Gods & Kings*, it is an "expansion" rather than being DLC or a mod, and it only requires

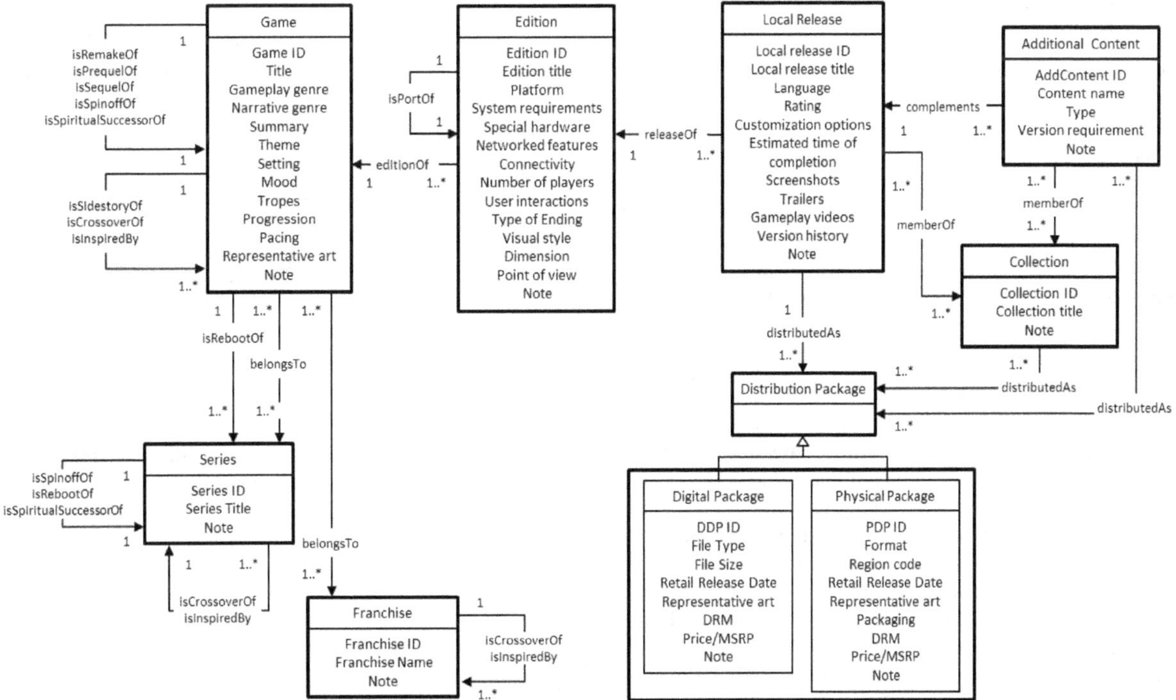

Figure 1. Video Game Conceptual Model (excluding the Agent entity; modified from [6])

the latest version of the base game to work. In contrast, consider the "Camera Rotation" mod for *CiV*. Using the attributes suggested in the model, we would record the title as *CameraRotation*, note that it is a "mod", and finally remark that it has the following requirements: *CiV*, *Gods & Kings*, and another mod called *Civ V Unofficial Patch for Civilization V: Gods & Kings*.

Despite the effectiveness of this solution, some challenges persist. One issue is that it abandons the FRBR framework [5] that has risen to become the primary conceptual model for bibliographic entities. A growing number of studies demonstrate that FRBR does not fit non-text media forms well [3][8][10][11][12], and is especially limited in representing serial publications and objects with multiple versions (which share many similarities with additional game content) [1][2]. Therefore, a conceptual model specific to the video games will better support the needs of users of game collections at cultural heritage institutions.

While the model does separate established additional content from a game itself, it cannot solve the underlying philosophical issue of when and how to determine that separation. This is an issue that only community best practices can solve. A good rule of thumb to start with is that mods which are total conversions, such as *Dota*, constitute instances of new games rather than additional content for the game they are based upon.

Beyond the inability to solve the issue of when a mod is actually a new game rather than additional content, applying the conceptual model raises the problematic issue of perpetual cataloging. Additional content changes a work from a relatively static bibliographic entity into a more amorphous and constantly evolving one. As more and more additional content is created, more and more descriptions and records must be created as well, creating a cycle of continuous maintenance. Such efforts are not new to the information professions, but rather the expected norm in specialties like serials cataloging. As additional content becomes more prevalent, video games are becoming more analogous to serials than to monographs.

Deriving a formal metadata record format from the conceptual model is only one possible approach. Another direction would be to develop a linked data ontology from the conceptual model. With this approach, the labor for controlled vocabulary development and the recording of individual instances of games is distributed across the entire stakeholder community. Existing linked data ontologies such as BIBFRAME, schema.org, or freebase may be viable alternatives. As such a comparison is not the primary purpose of this paper and we have limited space, we will leave this question to be explored in the future.

4. CONCLUSION AND FUTURE WORK

In this paper, we discussed various problems and challenges posed to cultural heritage institutions with video game collections by the increasing prevalence of additional content for video games. The issues discussed here, although centered on video games, also apply to other media with additional content in e-publication areas. Without a descriptive standard and best practice guidelines for dealing with additional content for video games and other distributed media, cultural heritage institutions risk the ability to successfully acquire, describe, and preserve their collection and ensure future use. In our future work, we plan to continue evaluating and refining the video game conceptual model by applying it to real video games and their additional content. We will also compare and evaluate the applicability of existing linked data ontologies for representing video games with additional content.

5. ACKNOWLEDGMENTS

We thank Rachel Ivy Clarke and Simone Sacchi for their valuable input. This research is supported by the University of Washington, Office of Research.

6. REFERENCES

[1] Allgood, J. E. 2007. Serials and multiple versions, or the inexorable trend toward work-level displays. *Library Resources & Technical Services (LRTS)*, 51, 3, 160-178.

[2] Antelman, K. 2004. Identifying the serial work as a bibliographic entity. *LRTS*, 48, 4, 238-255.

[3] Baca, M. & Clarke, S. (2007). FRBR and Works of Art, Architecture, and Material Culture. In *Understanding FRBR* (pp. 103-110). Westport, CT: Libraries Unlimited.

[4] Dey, D. and Lahiri, A. 2014. Versioning of Video Games: Go Vertical in a Horizontal Market? (June 6, 2014). DOI= http://dx.doi.org/10.2139/ssrn.2066194

[5] IFLA Study Group on the FRBR, IFLA Section on Cataloging. 2009. *Functional requirements for bibliographic records: Final report*. K.G. Saur Verlag, München.

[6] Jett, J., Sacchi, S., Lee, J. H., and Clarke, R. (in press). A conceptual model for video games and interactive media. *JASIST*. http://hdl.handle.net/2142/73848

[7] Kow, Y. M. and Nardi, B. 2010. Who owns the mods? *First Monday*, 15, 3.

[8] Lee, J. H. 2010. Analysis of user needs and information features in natural language queries seeking music information. *JASIST*, 61, 5, 1025-1045.

[9] Lizardi, R. 2012. DLC: Perpetual commodification of video game. *Democratic Communiqué*, 25, 1, (Spring 2012).

[10] McDonough, J., Olendorf, R., Kirschenbaum, M., et al. 2010. *Preserving Virtual Worlds Final Report*. http://hdl.handle.net/2142/17097

[11] Miller, D. and Le Boeuf, P. 2005. "Such stuff as dreams are made on": How does FRBR fit performing arts? *CCQ*, 39, 3-4, 151-178.

[12] Nicolas, Y. 2005. Folklore requirements for bibliographic records: oral traditions and FRBR. *CCQ*, 39, 3-4, 179-195.

[13] Nieborg, D. B. 2005. Am I mod or not? – An analysis of first person shooter modification culture. *Creative Gamers Seminar*. http://www.gamespace.nl/content/DBNieborg2005_CreativeGamers.pdf

[14] Postigo, H. 2007. Of mods and modders: chasing down the value of fan-based digital game modifications. *Games and Culture*, 2, 4, 300-313.

[15] Scacchi, W. 2010. Computer game mods, modders, modding, and the mod scene. *First Monday*, 15, 5.

[16] Steirer, G. 2010. DLC as Marketing Tool. http://cultural productionblog.com/?p=280

[17] Tyni, H. and Sotamaa, O. 2011. Extended or exhausted: how console DLC keeps the player on the rail. In *Proceedings of MindTrek '11*, 311-313.

Using Transactional Web Archives To Handle Server Errors

Zhiwu Xie[1], Prashant Chandrasekar[2], and Edward A. Fox[2]
[1]University Libraries and [2]Department of Computer Science
Virginia Polytechnic Institute and State University
Blacksburg, VA
{zhiwuxie, peecee, fox@vt.edu }

ABSTRACT

We describe a web archiving application that handles server errors using the most recently archived representation of the requested web resource. The application is developed as an Apache module. It leverages the transactional web archiving tool SiteStory, which archives all previously accessed representations of web resources originating from a website. This application helps to improve the website's quality of service by temporarily masking server errors from the end user and gaining precious time for the system administrator to debug and recover from server failures. By providing pertinent support to website operations, we aim to reduce the resistance to transactional web archiving, which in turn may lead to a better coverage of web history.

Categories and Subject Descriptors

H.3.7 [**Information Storage and Retrieval**]: Digital Libraries

Keywords

Digital preservation; transactional web archiving; SiteStory; Memento.

1. INTRODUCTION

By estimates [1][2], existing web archives barely scratch the surface of the total web history. The low coverage may partially be attributed to the crawler-based archiving approach predominantly used by these archives. A web crawler can only archive the content it actively fetches through the scheduled crawling. However, the change of web resources is inherently unpredictable, making it extremely difficult to interleave the crawling schedule with the changes. Observing the politeness policy further limits the crawler's ability to track changes.

More comprehensive web history may be collected by involving more stakeholders through transactional web archiving [3]. A transaction is initiated by the user of a website. The archive sits between the user and the origin server and passively collects and archives the responses used to fulfill the user requests. The collective response to all these requests is a close approximation to a website's full history, or at least its memorable portion.

JCDL'15, June 21-25, 2015, Knoxville, TN, USA
ACM 978-1-4503-3594-2/15/06.
http://dx.doi.org/10.1145/2756406.2756955

Despite its advantages, archiving web transactions requires cooperation from the website owner. Only the origin server has information about all requests and responses; therefore the archive needs to be part of it. But it is not easy to engage website operations staff and convince them of the archive's value. Typical IT operations are preoccupied with their immediate needs and pay little attention to services whose benefits are longer term. It is therefore crucial for us to expand the value proposition of web archiving beyond the pledged altruistic cause and make transactional web archives immediately useful to day-to-day IT operations.

In this paper we present a web archiving application intended to improve website uptime, a core quality of service indicator for web operations. It takes the most recently archived representation of a web resource to handle application server failures. Webmasters benefit from this application because they gain precious time to recover from application server failures without disrupting the majority of their users' web experience. Archivists also benefit from it because the fine archival granularity resulting from transactional archiving is impossible to attain otherwise.

2. ARCHITECTURE

Figure 1 illustrates the architecture of this archiving application. It assumes the typical 3-tier web application made up of 1) a front-end server, assumed to be Apache, 2) an application server, and 3) an optional database server.

The system includes SiteStory [4], a transactional web archiving tool developed by Los Alamos National Laboratory. SiteStory has two components: mod_sitestory, an Apache module installed and configured as part of the Apache frontend server, and SiteStory Web Archive, a Java application run in a Tomcat container that uses Berkeley DB to store the archived web content.

The application developed in this project, mod_uws, is similar to mod_sitestory in that it is also an Apache module. It handles web disruptions that generate HTTP 5xx error codes. These errors usually occur behind the frontend, and result from application server failure, internal network congestion and disruption, and database server bottlenecks and failures. These problems are not uncommon, and are of great concern to webmasters. When these errors occur, we assume the frontend server is still alive and working properly to generate HTTP 5xx codes. This assumption is realistic because the commonly used gateway servers, e.g., Apache, are designed to handle high workloads and have well-designed scaling capabilities. They have been battle-hardened, and usually are more mature and robust than the other components in a web deployment.

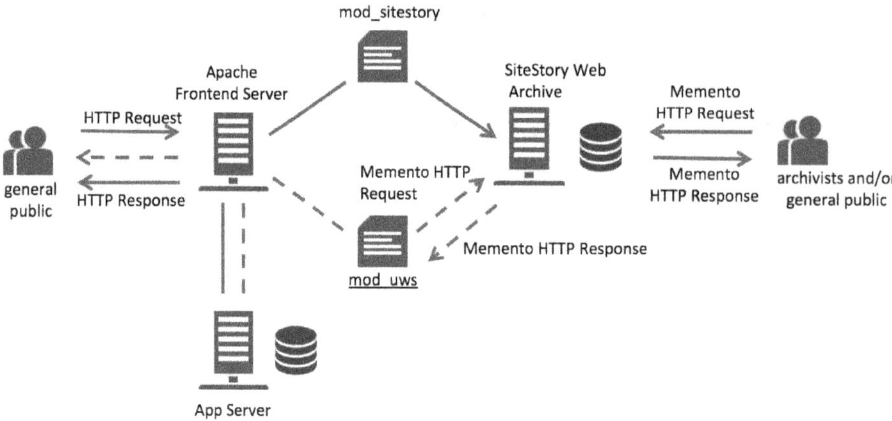

Figure 1. Architecture

In Figure 1 the solid line denotes the transactional archiving workflow under normal working conditions, while the dotted line presents the error-handling mode when an error occurs and an HTTP 5xx response triggers our application.

As explained in [4], under normal working conditions all HTTP 200 responses are sent in parallel to both the website user and the SiteStory web archive. This archive therefore always contains the most recent server state until an error occurs. At that point an HTTP 5xx response normally would have to be sent back to the requester through the Apache frontend server. However, instead, mod_uws will detect the error, become active, and intercept the 5xx response. Then mod_uws will send a Memento request [5] to the SiteStory archive to retrieve the most recently archived copy of the requested URI. This copy will be sent back to the requester with appropriate HTTP headers modified, hence masking the server error from end users. Although currently not implemented, in theory once mod_uws is activated, it may adaptively manage any subsequent requests using algorithms like exponential backoff. This would help flatten any potential peak load and allow the application server to recover from bottlenecks.

We developed mod_uws at the level of frontend server in order to make it agnostic to various programming languages, development tools, web frameworks, and database products used to build the website. This ensures the broadest possible adoption base. Any web operation using Apache HTTP server can easily integrate and benefit from this application without significantly modifying its deployment and configurations.

3. FUTURE WORK

It has been shown that using SiteStory does not significantly affect the performance of Apache HTTP server [6]. We will soon publish the performance test results showing how the current implementation of mod_uws affects Apache. We will also attempt to put the Memento request and response function into an external application in the hope of lessening the performance impact of mod_uws on Apache.

Larger web operations usually deploy a load balancer in front of many Apache servers. This provides us with the opportunity to move both SiteStory and the error handling application one level up to the load balancer to further improve the archiving efficiency and the ease of deployment.

4. ACKNOWLEDGMENTS

This work is supported in part by the Web Archiving Incentive Awards, funded as part of Columbia University Libraries' 2013 Mellon Grant for Collaborations in Web Content Archiving.

5. REFERENCES

[1] SalahEldeen, H.M. and Nelson, M.L. 2012. Losing My Revolution: How Many Resources Shared on Social Media Have Been Lost? *Theory and Practice of Digital Libraries*. P. Zaphiris, G. Buchanan, E. Rasmussen, and F. Loizides, eds. Springer Berlin Heidelberg. 125–137.

[2] Ainsworth, S.G., AlSum, A., SalahEldeen, H., Weigle, M.C. and Nelson, M.L. 2012. How Much of the Web Is Archived? *arXiv:1212.6177 [cs]*. (Dec. 2012).

[3] Masanès, J. ed. 2006. *Web Archiving*. Springer.

[4] SiteStory Web Archive: http://mementoweb.github.io/SiteStory/index.html. Accessed: 2015-02-01.

[5] Van de Sompel, H., Nelson, M. and Sanderson, R. 2013. *HTTP Framework for Time-Based Access to Resource States–Memento*. IETF RFC 7089.

[6] Brunelle, J.F., Nelson, M.L., Balakireva, L., Sanderson, R. and Van de Sompel, H. 2013. Evaluating the SiteStory Transactional Web Archive with the ApacheBench Tool. *Research and Advanced Technology for Digital Libraries*. T. Aalberg, C. Papatheodorou, M. Dobreva, G. Tsakonas, and C.J. Farrugia, eds. Springer Berlin Heidelberg. 204–215.

Mobile Mink: Merging Mobile and Desktop Archived Webs

Wesley Jordan[1], Mat Kelly[2], Justin F. Brunelle[2,3], Laura Vobrak[1], Michele C. Weigle[2], and Michael L. Nelson[2]
[1] New Horizons Regional Education Center Governor's School for Science and Technology
[2] Old Dominion University, Department of Computer Science
[3] The MITRE Corporation

ABSTRACT

We describe the mobile app *Mobile Mink* which extends Mink, a browser extension that integrates the live and archived web. Mobile Mink discovers mobile and desktop URIs and provides the user an aggregated TimeMap of both mobile and desktop mementos. Mobile Mink also allows users to submit mobile and desktop URIs for archiving at the Internet Archive and Archive.today. Mobile Mink helps to increase the archival coverage of the growing mobile web.

Categories and Subject Descriptors

H.3.7 [**Online Information Services**]: Digital Libraries

General Terms

Design; Experimentation; Measurement

Keywords

Web Archiving; Digital Preservation; Memento; TimeMaps

1. INTRODUCTION

Mink [4] is a browser extension for Google Chrome that more closely integrates the past and present web. Mink uses the Memento framework [8] to present archived versions of visited pages to the user, allowing the users to seamlessly navigate between the archived and live web.

Memento is a framework that standardizes Web archive access and terminology. Live web resources are identified by URI-R. Archived versions of URI-Rs are called *mementos* and are identified by URI-M. Memento TimeMaps are machine-readable lists of mementos (at the level of single-archives or aggregation-of-archives) sorted by archival date.

While Mink works well in the traditional, desktop-oriented web, the mobile web continues to be less prominent in the archives. This phenomenon persists even as mobile devices grow in power, use, and ubiquity and the mobile web continues to grow and become more prevalent [9]. Because of their prevalence on the web, it is increasingly important to archive mobile resources and representations. However, because mobile resources are not always directly linked from their desktop counterparts, it is difficult for crawlers to find pages in the mobile web [2].

Mobile Mink is a mobile application that – in the same way Mink integrated the past and present desktop webs – bridges the mobile and desktop webs. Mobile Mink uses URI permutations to discover mobile and desktop versions of the same resource. Mobile Mink provides the user an aggregate TimeMap of mobile and desktop mementos, and provides the opportunity to submit the mobile and desktop URI-Rs to the Save Page Now service at the Internet Archive [6] and Archive.today [1].

2. AGGREGATE TIMEMAPS

Mobile Mink is an Android application that is currently in development and will be released for download in the Google Play app store. Much like its desktop browser parent, Mobile Mink offers a TimeMap of mementos that allows the user to navigate between the past and present webs. Mobile Mink also allows the user to submit mobile and desktop URI-Rs to be archived by archival services.

When using a web browser native to the Android operating system, the user is presented with an expandable menu in the top right of the browser window (called a "view as list"). Selecting this sign opens a menu of options, one of which is the option to "Share" the page (Figure 1(a)). Mobile Mink adds the option to "View Mementos" of the currently viewed page to the list of sharing options (Figure 1(b)).

Selecting the option of viewing mementos begins the process of discovering mobile and desktop URIs of the current URI-R. First, Mobile Mink identifies the URI-R of the currently viewed page. Mobile Mink identifies the URI-R as either a desktop URI or a mobile URI. Second, if the URI is a desktop URI, Mobile Mink translates the URI to a mobile URI; if the URI is a mobile URI, Mobile Mink translates the URI to a desktop URI. We use the same URI modifications as in Schneider and McCown's work [7] and test for the mobile URI's existence on the live web (i.e., returns an HTTP 200 response) and in the archives (returns a TimeMap of cardinality > 0 from the Memento aggregator).

Note that our previous research demonstrated that differentiating between the mobile and desktop versions of a page can be difficult if the same URI is used to identify the mobile and desktop representations, and only content-negotiation based on the user-agent is used by the server to

JCDL'15, June 21–25, 2015, Knoxville, Tennessee, USA.
ACM 978-1-4503-3594-2/15/06.
http://dx.doi.org/10.1145/2756406.2756956.

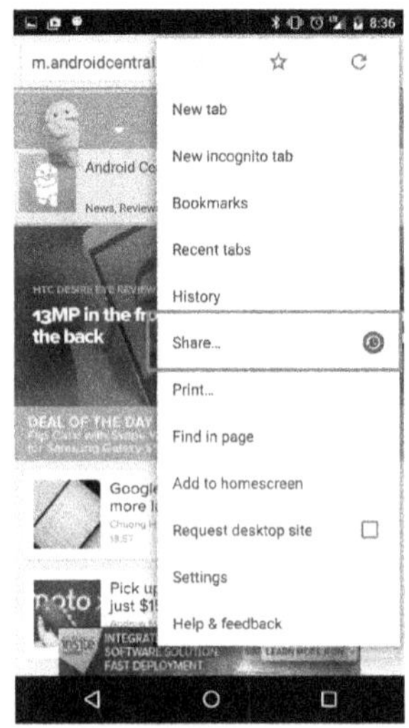

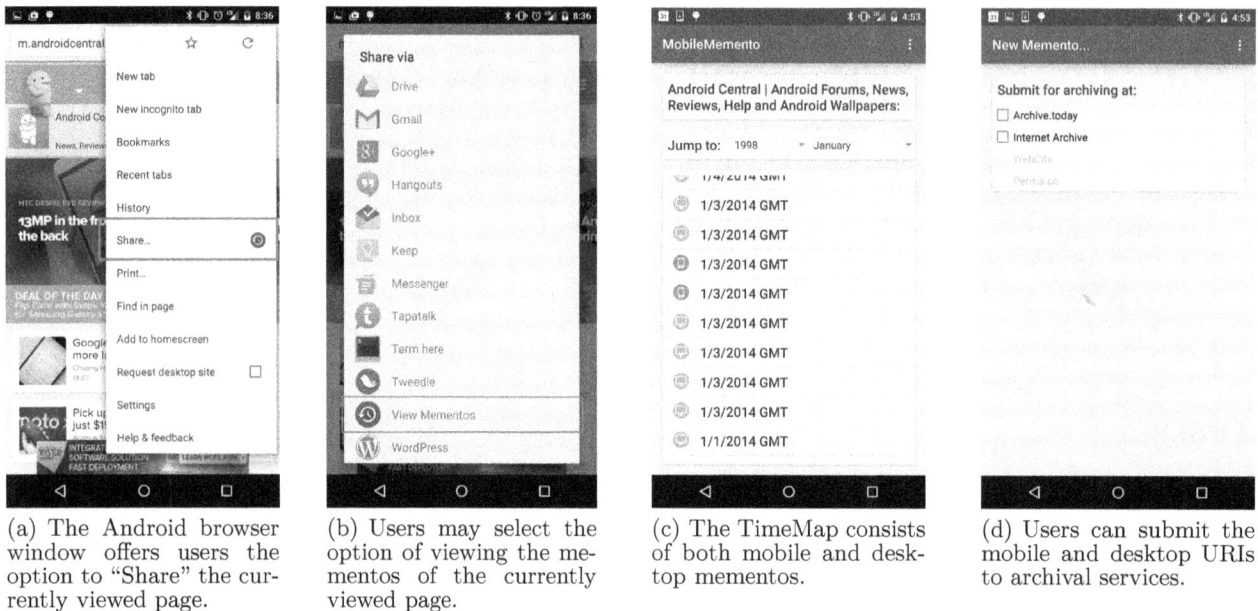

(a) The Android browser window offers users the option to "Share" the currently viewed page.

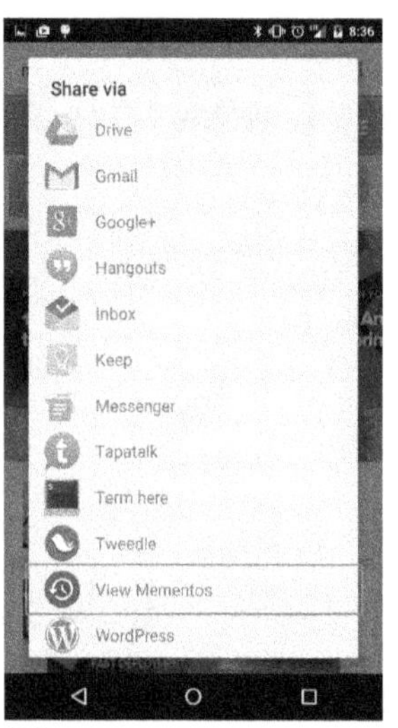

(b) Users may select the option of viewing the mementos of the currently viewed page.

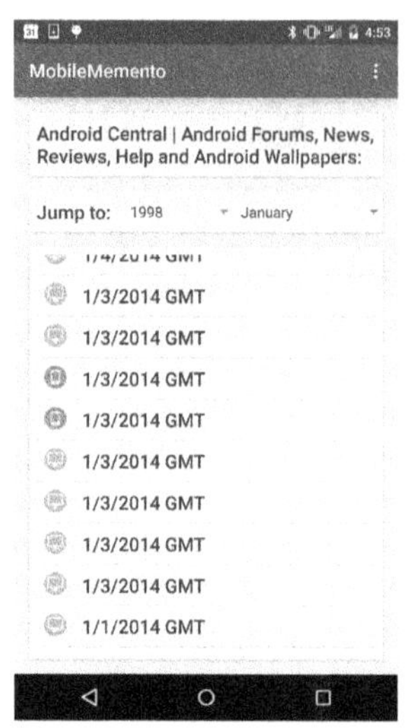

(c) The TimeMap consists of both mobile and desktop mementos.

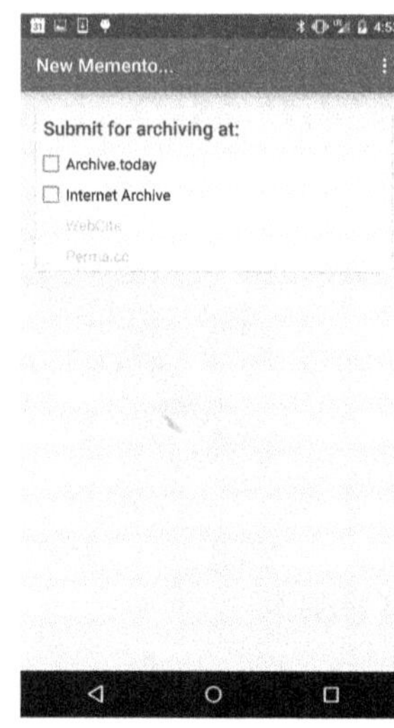

(d) Users can submit the mobile and desktop URIs to archival services.

Figure 1: Using existing Android browser features to view the TimeMap of the currently viewed page.

decide whether to return a mobile or desktop representation [3]. Content-negotiation is out of the scope of this work, and we focus solely on differentiations by URI. Other methods of mobile representation discovery are available [5].

With the URI-Rs of the mobile and desktop resources identified, we get the TimeMaps of both URI-Rs (e.g., `m.androidcentral.com/` and `www.androidcentral.com/`). Mobile Mink compiles an aggregate TimeMap of both mobile and desktop mementos that is sorted by archival datetime and has icons indicating the mobile and desktop mementos by a mobile phone and PC icon, respectively (Figure 1(c)). We include mementos of all permutations of mobile and desktop URIs in the TimeMap because the mobile URIs may have changed over time (e.g., migrating from m.example.com to mobile.example.com). Selecting a memento from the list redirects the user's browser to the URI-M.

3. ARCHIVING MOBILE URI-RS

To ensure both the mobile and desktop representations exist in the archives, Mobile Mink allows the user to submit both URI-Rs to the Internet Archive's Save Page Now service and Archive.today (Figure 1(d)). Before the submission, Mobile Mink ensures that both URI-Rs return an HTTP 200 when dereferenced on the live web to prevent the attempted archiving of resources that do not exist.

With this utility, Mobile Mink offers a way for users to actively curate mobile versions of pages they visit, even when crawlers and archival services cannot find them. With this feature, users can help archive the mobile web.

4. ACKNOWLEDGMENTS

This work supported in part by the NEH HK-50181. This work was performed as part of Wesley Jordan's mentorship at The MITRE Corporation. The author's affiliation with The MITRE Corporation is provided for identification purposes only, and is not intended to convey or imply MITRE's concurrence with, or support for, the positions, opinions or viewpoints expressed by the author.

5. REFERENCES

[1] Archive.today. Archive.today. `http://archive.today/`, 2013. `http://archive.today/`.

[2] A. Jindal, C. Crutchfield, S. Goel, R. Kolluri, and R. Jain. The mobile web is structurally different. In *INFOCOM Workshops 2008, IEEE*, pages 1–6, 2008.

[3] M. Kelly, J. F. Brunelle, M. C. Weigle, and M. L. Nelson. A method for identifying dynamic representations in the archives. *D-Lib Magazine*, 19(11/12), November/December 2013.

[4] M. Kelly, M. L. Nelson, and M. C. Weigle. Mink: Integrating the Live and Archived Web Viewing Experience Using Web Browsers and Memento . In *DL '14*, September 2014.

[5] F. McCown, M. Yarbrough, and K. Enlow. Tools for discovering and archiving the mobile web. *D-Lib Magazine*, 21(3/4), March/April 2015.

[6] A. Rossi. Fixing Broken Links on the Internet. `https://blog.archive.org/2013/10/25/fixing-broken-links/`, 2013.

[7] R. Schneider and F. McCown. First Steps in Archiving the Mobile Web: Automated Discovery of Mobile Websites. In *JCDL '13*, pages 53–56, 2013.

[8] H. Van de Sompel, M. L. Nelson, R. Sanderson, L. L. Balakireva, S. Ainsworth, and H. Shankar. Memento: Time Travel for the Web. Technical Report arXiv:0911.1112, Los Alamos National Laboratory, 2009.

[9] B. V. Wakode, D. N. Choudhari, and V. M. Thakare. Accessing Web Content on Mobile Devices: Relevance, State of the Art and Future Direction. *International Journal of Computer Science & Applications (TIJCSA)*, 1(4):16–21, 2012.

Combination Effects of Word-based and Extended Co-citation Search Algorithms

Masaki Eto
Gakushuin Women's College
Tokyo, Japan
masaki.eto@gakushuin.ac.jp

ABSTRACT

In the field of academic document search, citations are often used for measuring implicit relationships between documents. Recently, some studies have attempted to extend co-citation searching. However, these studies mainly focus on comparisons of traditional co-citation and extended co-citation search methods; combination effects of word-based and extended co-citation search algorithms have not yet been sufficiently evaluated. This paper empirically evaluates the search performance of the combination search by using a test collection comprising about 152,000 documents and a metric 'precision at *k*.' The experimental results indicate that the combination search outperforms two baseline methods: a word-based search and a combination search of word-based and traditional co-citation search algorithms.

Categories and Subject Descriptors

H.3.3 [**Information Search and Retrieval**]: Retrieval models

Keywords

Co-citation, Context, Hybrid, Random walk with restart, TF-IDF

1. INTRODUCTION

In the field of academic document search, citations are often used for measuring implicit relationships between documents. Co-citation, which is defined as a linkage between a pair of documents concurrently cited by a third document, has so far been used to enhance search performances. Recently, some studies have attempted to extend co-citation searching for improving both the recall and the precision, as enough machine-readable documents are easily available and huge amount of citation information can be processed at high speed. However, these studies mainly focus on comparisons of traditional co-citation and extended co-citation search methods; combination effects of word-based and extended co-citation search algorithms have not yet been sufficiently evaluated. This paper empirically evaluates the search performance of the combination of the two search algorithms.

2. EXTENDED CO-CITATION

The differences between traditional and extended co-citations are shown in Figure 1. This figure shows a network composed of document nodes connected by undirected co-citation linkages. On this network, a search query is a seed document known to be relevant to the information needs of a user.

For improving the recall, the scope of target documents is enlarged (e.g., [2]). That is, the traditional co-citation searching tries to find documents which are one edge hop from the seed document whereas the extended co-citation searching detects documents which are one or more hops from the seed (the experiment described in this paper uses up to three hops).

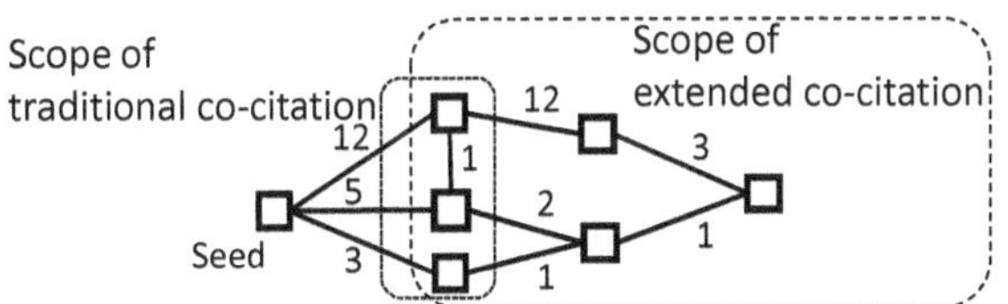

Figure 1. Traditional and extended co-citations.

For improving the precision, the process of computing edge weights can be refined (e.g., [1], [3]). Traditionally, a weight of each edge, i.e., strength of the co-citation linkage, is computed based on the number of documents citing both nodes as:

$$w(d_1, d_2) = cociting(d_1, d_2) \tag{1}$$

where d_1 and d_2 are co-cited documents, and $cociting(d_1,d_2)$ indicates the total number of documents co-citing d_1 and d_2 in a document set. Meanwhile, an edge weight of extended co-citation is specified by context-based co-citations obtained by parsing the full text of the citing documents. In the computation of each weight, strong context-based co-citations are discerned from weak ones; if references to the two documents appear within a paragraph, the context-based co-citation is classified as 'strong,' whereas if references to the two documents appear across two paragraphs, the context-based co-citation is classified as 'weak.' Therefore, the weight of extended co-citation is given by:

$$w(d_1, d_2) = strong\_cociting(d_1, d_2)v + weak\_cociting(d_1, d_2) \tag{2}$$

where $strong\_cociting(d_1,d_2)$ is the number of co-citing documents that cite d_1 and d_2 in a strong context, $weak\_cociting(d_1,d_2)$ is the number of co-citing documents that cite d_1 and d_2 in a weak context, and v is a parameter for balancing the two components.

3. Combination Search

3.1 Source Search Algorithms

3.1.1 Extended Co-citation Search

To calculate document scores, the extended co-citation search method [2] uses Random Walk with Restart (RWR), which is one of the latest algorithms for computing similarities between nodes on a network (e.g., [4]). The algorithm iteratively investigates the entire network to calculate the similarity between a seed node and each node in a network. Specifically, the walker starts at a seed node, then either proceeds to the connected node based on a transition probability calculated by edge weights, or returns to the seed node. Then the long-term visit rate of each node can be used as a document score; these rates are given by the steady-state of Eq. (3):

$$\vec{p} = (1-r)\widetilde{W}\vec{p} + r\vec{s} \tag{3}$$

JCDL'15, June 21-25, 2015, Knoxville, TN, USA
ACM 978-1-4503-3594-2/15/06.
http://dx.doi.org/10.1145/2756406.2756957

where $\vec{p}$ is an n-dimensional vector (n is the number of nodes in a network), r is a return probability, $\widetilde{W}$ is a transition probability matrix, and $\vec{s}$ is an n-dimensional vector with 1 for the seed node and 0 for the rest.

3.1.2 Word-based Search

In the case of word-based search methods, a full-text search method that targets all documents in a document set is conducted for the title words of the query document. In this study, the tf-idf retrieval function of the Indri search engine developed in the Lemur Project was used.

3.2 Merging the Results of Search Methods

The combination search merges the results of the word-based and the extended co-citation search methods by using reciprocal numbers, and the score of document d is calculated as:

$$Score(d) = \frac{1}{word\_rank(d)}\alpha + \frac{1}{cocitation\_rank(d)}(1-\alpha) \quad (4)$$

where $word\_rank(d)$ is the rank of d given by the word-based search and $co\text{-}citation\_rank(d)$ is the rank of d given by the extended co-citation search. Also, α indicates a mixture ratio between the two search methods; this paper uses 11 different values of α from 0.0 to 1.0.

4. EXPERIMENTS

4.1 Experimental Settings

This experiment was conducted on the test collection used in [2]. The test collection is based on the Open Access Subset of PubMed Central, and is composed of about 152,000 documents. The test collection contained 50 seed documents selected randomly from all documents under two conditions: a seed document cited by 30 or more other documents, and the number of documents within one hop from the seed is 100 or more (the conditions are needed for co-citation search methods to work in real situations). In this test collection, whether a document is relevant is determined by the degree to which it shares *MeSH Descriptors* with the seed document; documents having 25% or more descriptors assigned to a seed document are identified as relevant documents.

To conduct search runs for the extended co-citation search method, the parameter v of Eq. (2) is set at 10 and the parameter r of Eq. (3) is set at 0.3, because the search with these values indicated the best search performance in the experiment by [2].

4.2 Possibilities of the Extended Co-citation

This experiment explores whether the extended co-citation search method actually detects relevant documents which cannot be found by the word-based search method. To clarify the possibilities of extended co-citation, search runs for the simplest traditional co-citation search method were also conducted. This traditional search method ranks the target documents by using the weight of each edge connected to the seed (see Fig. 1). That is, the weight calculated by Eq. (1) is directly used as a document score.

Figure 2 shows average numbers of relevant documents uniquely included in the top N documents by each co-citation search method in the comparisons with the top 1,000 documents by the word-based search method. As shown in this figure, both co-citation search methods can detect unique relevant documents. However, it is clear that the traditional co-citation search method may not detect sufficient numbers of relevant documents. Specifically, the result by the traditional co-citation search method tended to reach its peak, because the number of detected documents in many search runs was fewer than N when N was large.

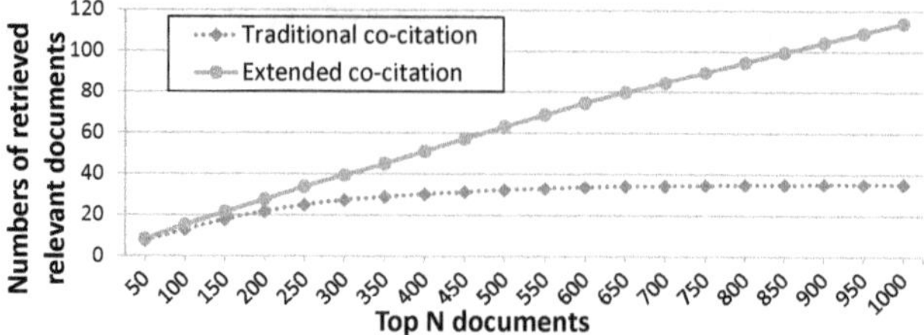

Figure 2. Average numbers of relevant documents detected uniquely by co-citation search methods.

4.3 Evaluations of the Combination Search

To evaluate the proposed search method, i.e., the combination of the word-based and extended co-citation search algorithms, this experiment used two baseline methods: the word-based search and a combination of the word-based and simplest traditional co-citation search algorithms by Eq. (4). In addition, this experiment adopted 'precision at k,' i.e., a precision of the top k documents, as a metric for evaluating the search performance.

Table 1. Average scores of precision at k.

	Baseline 1	Baseline 2	Proposed
	Word-based	Word-based + traditional co-citation	Word-based + extended co-citation
P@10	0.364	0.430 (α = 0.4)	0.442 (α = 0.4)
P@30	0.282	0.366 (α = 0.3)	0.368 (α = 0.3)
P@50	0.260	0.316 (α = 0.2)	0.339* (α = 0.1)
P@100	0.234	0.266 (α = 0.6)	0.287* (α = 0.1)
P@500	0.157	0.173 (α = 0.2)	0.193** (α = 0.2)
P@1000	0.133	0.142 (α = 0.6)	0.161* (α = 0.3)

* $p < 0.05$, ** $p < 0.01$

Table 1 indicates results of Baseline 1, results of the best scores of Baseline 2 and the proposed method, and results of the paired t-test between Baseline 2 and the proposed method. As shown in this table, the proposed method outperformed the two baseline methods.

5. CONCLUSION

This paper explored the combination effects of the word-based and the extended co-citation search algorithms. The experimental results indicate that the extended co-citation searching has high potential and the combination search can improve the search performance.

6. ACKNOWLEDGMENTS

This work was supported by JSPS KAKENHI Grant Number 26730163.

7. REFERENCES

[1] Eto, M. 2013. Evaluations of context-based co-citation searching, *Scientometrics* 94, 2, 651-673.

[2] Eto, M. 2014. Document retrieval method using random walk with restart on weighted co-citation network, In *Proceedings of the 77th ASIS&T Annual Meeting.*

[3] Gipp, B. and Beel, J. 2009. Citation proximity analysis (CPA) - A new approach for identifying related work based on co-citation analysis. In *Proceedings of the 12th ISSI Conference*. 2, 571-575.

[4] Tong, H., Faloutsos, C. and Pan, J. 2008. Random walk with restart: fast solutions and applications. *Knowledge and Information Systems*, 14, 3, 327-346.

Studying Chinese-English Mixed Language Queries from the User Perspectives

Hengyi Fu
School of Information
Florida State University
142 Collegiate Loop, FL 32306
hf13c@my.fsu.edu

Shuheng Wu
Graduate School of Library and Information Studies
Queens College, City University of New York
65-30 Kissena Blvd., Flushing, NY 11367
shuheng.wu@qc.cuny.edu

ABSTRACT

With the increasing number of multilingual webpages on the Internet, cross-language information retrieval has become an important research issue. Using Activity Theory as a theoretical framework, this study employs semi-structured interviews with key informants who are frequent users of Chinese-English mixed language queries in web searching. The findings present the context of and reasons for using Chinese-English mixed language queries, which can inform the design of cross-language controlled vocabularies and information retrieval systems.

Categories and Subject Descriptors

H.3.3 [**Information Storage And Retrieval**]: Information Search and Retrieval – *query formulation*

General Terms

Performance, Human Factors, Languages.

Keywords

Mixed language queries; cross-language information retrieval; search behavior.

1. INTRODUCTION

Cross-language information retrieval (CLIR) has emerged as an important research area since the amount of multilingual web resources is increasing rapidly. In CLIR, queries are translated from the source language to the target language, and the original and translated queries are used to retrieve documents in both the source and targeted languages. The assumption behind such mechanism is that queries are *consistently* used in one language. This mechanism works well when the user is monolingual looking for information in a certain language. However, the user of a CLIR system may be bilingual to some extent. In cultures where people speak both Chinese and English, using mixed language is a common phenomenon. For example, Hong Kong people typically speak Cantonese with English words. When conducting web searching, they often use Chinese-English mixed language queries to approximate their information need. This phenomenon, called *code-switching*, has become a focus of research in sociology, psycholinguistics, and linguistics [1].

A mixed language consists of sentences or terms mostly in the primary language with some words in a secondary language. A *mixed language query* is a search query including words mixed from two or more languages. For example, the query "Transformers 影评" is a Chinese-English mixed language query that a user created to look for reviews about the Transformers series. Researches on Chinese search engines found that using Chinese-English mixed language queries

JCDL'15, June 21–25, 2015, Knoxville, Tennessee, USA.
ACM 978-1-4503-3594-2/15/06.
http://dx.doi.org/10.1145/2756406.2756958

became more frequent in recent years [2]. However, very few studies have addressed why and how people use mixed language queries in web searching. In our previous studies, we examined the topics and user intents of Chinese-English mixed language queries, and developed a typology of English terms used in those queries [3, 4]. In this poster we report the findings about the context (i.e., activities) in which users employed Chinese-English mixed language queries and why they preferred to those queries. The findings can inform librarians, information scientists, and IR system designers of the needs, requirements, and approaches to enhance cross-language controlled vocabularies, and improve search engines to provide users with more relevant results.

2. RESEARCH DESIGN

Activity Theory is a meta-theory for studying human behavior in a specific context [5]. To examine how and why users employ mixed language queries in web searching, this study used Activity Theory as a methodological framework to help develop the following research questions:

RQ1: In what activities do users employ Chinese-English mixed language queries? What are the objectives of these activities? What are the tools that users employ in these activities?
RQ2: Why do users employ Chinese-English mixed language queries?

To answer these research questions, this study conducted qualitative semi-structured interviews [6] with 8 key informants who identified themselves as frequent users of Chinese-English mixed language queries and engaged in various professions, such as professor, software engineer, mechanical engineer, music librarian, and commercial consultant. All informants were native Chinese speakers living all over the world, including mainland China, Taiwan, Hong Kong, Japan, Australia, Europe, and the United States. Interviews were conducted online between October 2014 and December 2014. Interview times ranged from 19 to 32 minutes with an average length of 26 minutes. All of the interviews were audiorecorded, transcribed, and coded using NVivo 10. Two researchers independently coded all of the interviews to identify major themes for each research question. After comparing, discussing, and resolving any differences in their coding, the researchers created a codebook and used it to recode all of the data.

3. FINGINGS

3.1 Activities and Objectives

The data analysis found that the activities of Chinese-English mixed language query users can be categorized into three types: recreation, work-related, and academic searching. Recreation searching included, but was not limited to, looking for a specific celebrity, place, book, movie, game, brand, product, and company originated in the Anglosphere. All informants mentioned that they had the experience of using mixed language queries to look for lyrics of English songs or reviews of books, games, movies, or products in Chinese. Work-related searching activities were varied by informants' professions and their communities. For example, the software engineer used mixed language queries to search for downloadable software or solutions to programming errors. The music librarian used mixed language queries to search for background information in Chinese about the western music materials (e.g., madrigal) that she was cataloging. Informants working in academia employed mixed language queries to know about the English translation of specific terminologies or how the Chinese research community translated or used certain neologism. For example, a professor in industry engineering used mixed language queries to search for scholarly papers to learn about the English translation of a terminology and how it was used in academic writing.

Although informants applied mixed language queries for different objectives, they can be summarized into three broad categories: (a) to obtain high quality search results, (b) to retrieve webpages in Chinese to save their reading time and effort, and (c) to obtain webpages provided by certain communities. For example, one of the informants stated, "I use mixed language queries to retrieve Chinese webpages about certain concepts originated from the English world because English-only queries will take me to English-only pages, which increase my reading time."

3.2 Tools

Informants mentioned the tools that they used in those searching activities including Baidu, Google, and Google's language setting. Informants selected different tools for specific searching activities depending on their objectives and communities. Most informants indicated that they mainly used Baidu for recreation searching and to look for local resources in mainland China. However, Google was considered more useful for work-related searching and retrieving resources outside of mainland China, such as webpages in traditional Chinese characters. The data analysis found that contradictions existed between the objectives of those searching activities and tools. According to Activity Theory, *contradictions* refer to any historically accumulated tensions or inabilities within or between activity systems, playing a central role in changing and developing activities [5]. Some informants believed that Baidu did not index webpages in traditional Chinese characters and English published outside of mainland China, and thus failed to help them achieve completeness (or recall) in search results. Some informants pointed out that despite Google as their favorite search engine for multilingual IR, it was unavailable in mainland China and less efficient in retrieving local Chinese resources. Five out of eight informants used Google's language setting function before, but none of them regarded it useful to meet their objective of retrieving webpages in Chinese, as the function was difficult to locate and the returned webpages containing English only. One of the informants doubted the usefulness of Google's language setting function, which would translate returned webpages to Chinese instead of retrieving pages that contain Chinese.

3.3 Why Mixed Language Queries

The second research question was analyzed from two perspectives: why to use English terms and why to use Chinese terms in those mixed language queries. Informants revealed that the reasons for using Chinese terms included: (a) directing results to webpages in Chinese, (b) limiting results to certain areas, (c) unaware of corresponding English terms, and (d) retrieving resources provided by certain communities. One of the informants explained, "Since now I live in Australia, if I search certain product review in mixed language like the product name in English and "评论" (i.e., review in Chinese), I have more chances to get review pages written by Australian Chinese."

The reasons provided by informants for employing English terms are more diverse, including but were not limited to: (a) they did not know or were uncertain of the Chinese translations of those English terms (e.g., error messages in programming), (b) there were no corresponding Chinese translations (e.g., MH370, Python, C++), (c) various or no official Chinese translations existed (e.g., English personal names), (d) the English terms were used more widely in the Chinese communities (e.g., NBA, PSP), (e) the Chinese translations were hard to memorize or write, (f) the English terms were coined by Chinese, and (g) certain terminologies were too new to have Chinese translations (e.g., community informatics, social computing). One of the informants emphasized that, "When the first time I knew these concepts, like NBA and iPhone, they were expressed in English and are much more popular in both web searching and oral expression. Although they are technically in a foreign language, I feel that they are like Chinese terms to me." All informants implied that using English terms in their mixed language queries could help obtain high quality (e.g., relevant, complete, current, and secure) results. One of the informants explained, "Because the English term has multiple versions of Chinese translation, I'm not sure which one is official or more popular. In that case using a Chinese term will reduce the number of hits or get less relevant results." Another informant stated that using English terms in his queries when searching for business information could ensure more secure results, "For big companies like Sony, it's fine to use their Chinese translations to locate the official website. However, for some niche brands, you assume to increase the chance to be directed to some fake or phishing sites if using their Chinese translations."

4. CONCLUSION AND FUTURE STUDIES

This poster reports the context of and reasons for using Chinese-English mixed language queries from the user perspectives, which could be expanded to other languages that would improve the search engine design. The contradictions identified from this study can inform the development of discovery platforms for multilingual content. Future research includes collecting more interview data and developing a thesaurus of English terms used in CLIR to enhance traditional or monolingual controlled vocabularies. Since this study collected interview data from native Chinese speakers, it will be interesting to examine how other populations (e.g., Chinese learners) use English-Chinese mixed language queries in web searching.

5. REFERENCES

[1] Auer, P. 1998. *Code-Switching in conversation: Language, interaction, and identify*. Routledge, London.

[2] Chau, M., Fang, X., and Yang, C. C. 2007. Web searching in Chinese: A study of a search engine in Hong Kong. *Journal of the American Society for Information Science and Technology*. 58, 7 (May. 2007), 1044-1054.

[3] Fu, H., and Wu, S. 2014. Analyzing Chinese-English mixed language queries in a Web search engine. In *Proceedings of the 77th Annual Meeting of the Association for Information Science and Technology* (Seattle, USA, November 01–05, 2014).

[4] Fu, H., and Wu, S. 2015. Determining the user intent of Chinese-English mixed language queries based on search logs. *Proceedings of iConference 2015* (Newport Beach, USA, March 24-27, 2015).

[5] Engeström, Y. 1990. *Learning, working and imagining: Twelve studies in activity theory*. Helsinki: Orienta-Konsultit Oy.

[6] Kvale, S., and Brinkmann, S. 2009. *Interviews: Learning the craft of qualitative research interviewing*. Sage, Thousand Oaks.

Content Analysis of Social Tags Generated by Health Consumers

Soohyung Joo
University of Kentucky
Lexington, KY 40506
soohyung.joo@uky.edu

Yunseon Choi
Southern Connecticut State University
New Haven, CT 06515
choiy1@southernect.edu

ABSTRACT
This poster presents preliminary findings of user tag analysis in the domain of consumer health information. To obtain user terms, 36,205 tags from 38 consumer health information sites were collected from delicious.com. Content analysis was applied to identify the dimensions and types of the collected tags. The preliminary findings showed that user generated tags covers a variety of aspects of health information, ranging from general terms, subject terms, knowledge type, and to audience. General terms and subject terms were observed dominantly by showing 31.7% and 22.8% respectively.

Categories and Subject Descriptors
H3.1. Content Analysis and Indexing

General Terms
Documentation

Keywords
Social tagging; consumer health information; qualitative analysis

1. INTRODUCTION
This poster is part of a larger project that intends to develop a multi-faceted information architecture design for consumer health information by analyzing user generated terms. Health information for consumers should be able to be provided to lay people without difficulty. However, the growing amount of health information on the Web has increased concern about effective access to quality health information because terminology, currently used for organizing health information, is generated by professionals and it would not be familiar to users. The previous study on indexing consistency revealed relatively low consistency in medical and health information subjects between users and professional indexers [1]. Studies also show that most health information users have low levels of health literacy which means that users are not able to access health information effectively and understand the information [2]. As an initial step to understand user terms, we identified dimensions and types of social tags in consumer health information. Researchers have identified various types of social tags in different environments. For example, Sen et al. [3] classified social tags into three levels, factual, subjective, and personal focusing on users' search tasks. Pu and Chang [4] extracted different types of social tags considering related factors such as personal, content, situational, and social factors using Q-method and factor analysis. Golder and Huberman [5] categorized seven functions of tags, such as what it is about, what it is, and who owns it. However, less research has explored dimensions and types of tags in consumer health information. This study intends to identify the dimensions and types of user tags in the domain of health information to understand users' preferences on terms and intention in tagging practices in organizing health information.

JCDL'15, June 21–25, 2015, Knoxville, Tennessee, USA.
ACM 978-1-4503-3594-2/15/06.
http://dx.doi.org/10.1145/2756406.2756959

2. RESEARCH QUESTIONS
RQ1. What are the dimensions and types of tags that users use to describe consumer health information?
RQ2. How do tagging practices differ by health information areas?

3. METHODOLOGY
This study categorizes social tags assigned in thirty-eight sites, which are recommended as reliable health information sources by Consumer and Patient Health Information Section (CAPHIS). Tags for each site were extracted from delicious.com, and the collected data (36,205 tags from 38 health information sites) were analyzed qualitatively using open coding method, which is the process of breaking down, examining, comparing, conceptualizing, and categorizing unstructured textual transcripts [6]. We present preliminary results identifying the dimensions and types of tags in health information organization. To answer the RQ1, two researchers conducted a content analysis. Inter-coder reliability turned out 91.8% between the two coders. For RQ2, a cross-tabulation analysis was applied using Chi-square test to examine how user tag dimensions would differ by website type.

4. RESULTS
4.1 Dimensions and Types of Tags in Consumer Health Information Sites
The results highlight that user terms tend to be general as about one-thirds of the terms fell into the category of general terms, such as "health," "medical," and "healthinfo." As users usually have less domain knowledge compared to experts, their terms remain as general, not offering specific enough representation of the site.

About 22% of the observed terms represent topics or subjects of medical areas such as diseases, symptoms, treatments, and drugs. In particular, tags related to drugs (10.1%) and well-being (4.0%) were frequently observed. This implies that consumer-level users are interested in healthy life and drug information while using online health sites. Approximately 19% of tags were associated to resource type while 9.2% were used to indicate knowledge type and source. This reveals social tags could function as defining resource and knowledge characteristics from the user perspective. Then, 11.7% of tag terms reflect the audiences of the sites. Among them, tags concerning age group (5.0%) were frequently observed than other audience types. Specifically, most tags occurred in the age group were related to children and kids. This result reaffirms previous findings reporting parents' preference of Internet health sites and increase of online resource use for their children care [7].

4.2 Tagging Practice by Health Information Area

As to RQ2, we found that the proportions of tag dimensions differed by health information area as shown in Table 2 (Chi-square = 8435.48 (*df*=25); p<.001). In general health information sites (e.g. WebMD), the proportions of general and resource/media type terms were relatively high accounting for 39.3% and 25.1% respectively, whereas audience related terms (4.3%) were lower. Conversely, in the Websites customized to specific groups such as kids, seniors, and women, audience related tags were frequently observed (kids 36.6%; seniors 21.6%; women 27.8%). In drug information sites, tags in the topic type were frequently observed since users were likely to tag drug related terms for these sites.

Table 1. Dimensions of and Types of Social Tags in Consumer Health Resources on the Web

Dimension	Type	Example	Freq.	%.
General	General	health, medical	11,495	31.7%
Topic/ Subjects	Disease	diabetes, cancer	665	1.8%
	Symptom	pain, skinailment	525	1.5%
	Department	dental, Obstetrics	582	1.6%
	Treatment	physicaltheraphy	575	1.6%
	Drugs	Rx, prescription	3,656	10.1%
	Well-being	wellness, exercise	1,459	4.0%
	Nutrition	healthnutrition	592	1.6%
	Doctors	physicians	64	0.2%
	Insurance/ finance	insurance	151	0.4%
Resource/ Media	Media	magazine, news	488	1.30%
	Communica-tion	socialnetworking	118	0.30%
	File format	images, video	82	0.20%
	References	tools, guide	5,723	15.80%
	Dictionary	encyclopedia	406	1.10%
	Languages/ countries	English, Spanish	158	0.40%
Knowledge type/ Information Source	Scholarly/ research	science, academic	1,197	3.3%
	Educational	education, teaching	1,056	2.9%
	Source	NLM, NIH, aarp	1,088	3.0%
Website	Title	mayo, medlineplus	546	1.5%
	Type	portal, health2.0	178	0.5%
	Functions	searchengine	555	1.5%
	Cost	free, opensource	102	0.3%
Audience	Age	kid, senior, teen	1,813	5.0%
	Gender	women, men	668	1.8%
	Level	consumer, patient	1,391	3.8%
	Group	family	368	1.0%
User Feedback	Evaluation	useful, reliable	44	0.1%
Others	Stop words	of, for, the	99	0.3%
	Not judgeable	eme4401, 8fold	361	1.0%
Total		Total	36,205	100.0%

5. CONCLUSION

This study has made a significant contribution to analyzing social tags of the health information domain qualitatively by employing the open coding and conducting content analysis of tags. The findings show that users' vocabulary covers a variety of aspects of health information although a large amount of tags (31.7%) were general terms. User terms reflected different categories, such as topic/subject, knowledge type, website related information, and audience type. Moreover, this study found that users' tagging types would differ by health information areas. The findings of this study have implications for developing information architecture of online consumer health information. Furthermore, since tags themselves do not provide explicit evidence of user intention, our next step in this line of research will be investigating users' cognitive intention and motivation of tagging to better understand indexing practices from the perspective of users.

Table 2. Tagging practice by health information area

	General Info	Children	Senior	Women	Men	Drug
General terms	39.3%	25.8%	27.8%	38.2%	46.0%	31.4%
Topic/ Subject	15.6%	11.7%	31.6%	15.3%	25.5%	37.7%
Resource/ Media	25.1%	12.1%	7.8%	11.8%	14.1%	19.3%
Knowledge type	11.4%	12.3%	8.7%	6.3%	2.0%	3.5%
Website	4.3%	1.4%	2.5%	0.6%	0.9%	5.9%
Audience	4.3%	36.6%	21.6%	27.8%	11.5%	2.2%

6. REFERENCES

[1] Y. Choi. Traditional versus Emerging Knowledge Organization Systems: Consistency of Subject Indexing of the Web by Indexers and Taggers. *Proceedings of ASIST annual meeting.* 2010.

[2] L.A. Ferguson and R. Pawlak. Health literacy: the road to improved health outcomes 2011, *International Journal of Nursing Practice*, 7(2): 123–129. 2011.

[3] S. Sen, S. Lam, A.M. Rashid, D. Cosley, D. Frankowski, J. Osterhouse, M. Harper, & J. Riedl. Tagging, communites, vocabulary, evolution. Proceedings of CSCW'06. 2006.

[4] H. Pu & C. Chang. An empirical study on the sociality of tag selection on social bookmarking services. *Proceedings of ASIST annual meeting,* 2009.

[5] S. Golder & B.A. Huberman. Usage patterns of collaborative tagging systems. *Journal of Information Science*, 32(2), 198-208. 2006.

[6] A. Strauss & J. M. Corbin. *Basics of qualitative research: Grounded theory procedures and techniques.* Sage Publications, Inc. 1990

[7] K. Khoo, P. Bolt, F. E. Babl, E., S. Jury & R. D. Goldman. Health information seeking by parents in the Internet age. *Journal of paediatrics and child health*, 44(7-8), 419-423. 2008

Automatic Classification of Research Documents using Textual Entailment

Bolanle Adefowoke Ojokoh[1]
Department of Computer Science,
Federal University of Technology,
Akure, Ondo State, Nigeria
+2347030538346
bolanleojokoh@yahoo.com

Olatunji Mumini Omisore[2,*]
Centre for Info Technology and
Systems, University of Lagos,
Akoka-Yaba, Lagos State, Nigeria
+2347031967847
ootsorewilly@gmail.com

Oluwarotimi Williams Samuel[3]
Biomedical Engineering & Health Tech.,
Shenzhen Institute of Advanced Tech.
CAS, Shenzhen, Guangdong, China
+8615814491870.
timitex92@gmail.com

ABSTRACT
Exploring the accumulative nature of Internet documents has become a rising issue that requires systematic ways to construct what we need from what we have. Manual and semi-manual document classification techniques have facilitated retrieval and maintenance of document repositories for easy access; however, they are customarily painstaking and labor-intensive. Herein, we propose a document classification model using automatic access of natural language meaning. The model is made up of application, business, and storage layers. The business layer, as a core component, automatically extracts sentences containing keywords from research documents and classifies them using the geometrical similarity of their sentential entailments.

Categories and Subject Descriptors
H.3.2 **[Information Storage]**: Record classification; H.3.4 **[Information Storage and Retrieval]**: Content Analysis and Indexing; H.3.7 **[Digital Libraries]:** Document Classification

General Terms
Design; Algorithms

Keywords
Document Classification, Textual Entailment, Keyword, Semantic Analyzer, Natural Language Processing.

1. INTRODUCTION
The speedy growth of information in the modern world often leads people to organize textual materials in ways that are not easy to access. Until the advent of digital catalogues, card cataloguing was the traditional way of organizing lists of resources and their location within a large library for easy access and maintenance [1]. This interest has led to significant efforts to define and refine ways of arranging books on shelves with unrestricted efforts to single disciplines or intellectual traditions. Yet, the approaches are very tedious and time consuming. The tremendous growth and usage of information has led to the problem of information overload in which users find it difficult to locate the right information at the right time [2,3]. However, standard library classification schemes are used to accomplish this goal though some flaws like vocabulary ambiguities, inherent with natural languages, create severe issues like increased inaccuracy in the classification process.

Document classification is a systematic and consistent way of facilitating the storage, retrieval, maintenance and disposal of documents (in any form) using text categorization techniques. Such techniques hold a great interest for researchers in machine learning by providing excellent benchmarks for different techniques and methodologies [4]. However, the majority of categorization techniques available today involve manual or algorithmic assignment of documents to some classes that best describe their content. Manual classification, used in library science, engages a human expert who performs painstaking and labor-intensive classification tasks, while an algorithmic approach is trained to automatically classify resources [4] though with minimal human intervention. Automatic access of natural language in document retrieval is yet to be implemented effectively; even prominent search engines often present search results in rough approximates [5]. Frequencies of terms occurring in such documents are taken as clues to their meaning and approximation is concluded upon after performing minimal linguistic processes to identify word contents like nouns, verbs and adjectives in indexed documents but cannot bring optimality.

Document classification has been of interest in different areas like iconographic medical diagnosis [6], sentiment analysis, and web page classification [7]. We, herein, propose a textual entailment recognizer for automatic classification of research documents.

2. TER CLASSIFICATION MODEL
The Textual Entailment Recognizer (TER) is designed for automatic classification of research documents. The model, shown in Fig. 1, is a three-layer architecture with application, business, and storage layers. The application layer consists of interface for crawling documents and viewing results. The business layer has an inbuilt complexity because important operations of the model are performed there and therefore, it is properly described later. The storage layer houses the data repository which is composed of models, policies, rules or standards that govern how data is collected, stored, arranged in a data-mart for efficient utilization.

System-specific functionalities like management of document and keywords, and recognition of entailment are performed at business layer. The logical layer is constituted by document manager, keyword manager, and entailment recognizer. The keyword manager retrieves keywords that are tied to documents in data repository. Since the ability to understand and analyze data

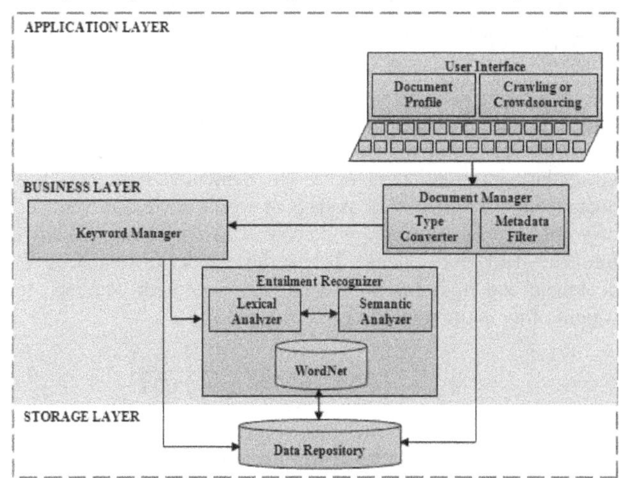

Figure 1. TER for Automatic Classification of Documents

JCDL'15, June 21-25, 2015, Knoxville, TN, USA
ACM 978-1-4503-3594-2/15/06.
http://dx.doi.org/10.1145/2756406.2756960

gives opportunity to derive maximum value from stored information and a number of research documents do not have keyword section, semantic orientation of words in documents can be used to describe their relationships. The classical *tf-idf* approach in [8] is straightforward and less intuitive since it only gives idea about the general distribution of terms amongst documents of all categories. The keyword manager utilized a modified *tf-idf* by localizing document *idf* to extract frequent terms in the document while very frequent ones are filtered based on principle of maximum entropy with testable information. A term is a keyword of a document with frequency more than a critical threshold value (α) that depends on settings.

$$\text{freq}(\text{t},\text{d}) = \begin{cases} 0 & if\, t \in d \\ nt\,.\,log\left(\frac{1}{n}\right) & otherwise \end{cases} \quad \text{Eq. 1}$$

where $\boldsymbol{nt}$ is number of times term $\boldsymbol{t}$ appeared in document **d**, and $\boldsymbol{n}$ is the number of terms with higher frequency in document **d**.

Lexical analyzer preprocesses (stemmed) documents in the repository to reduce different grammatical forms of words to root form. This reduces inflectional and derivationally related forms of a word to a common base form in order to improve recall without compromising the precision of documents fetched. Stemming is done by co-occurrence word counting with variants automatically conflated. The abstract and body sections of each document are tokenized into sentential forms while sentences where keywords are found are extracted to compute lexical similarity. However, minimum edit distance, given as Eq. 2, is used to transform text-hypothesis sentences to a uniform lexical structure.

$$D(t,h) = \sum_{i=1}^{max\,(l(t),l(h))} \begin{pmatrix} w_t(i) = w_h(i) & 0 \\ othersie & x \end{pmatrix} \quad \text{Eq. 2}$$

where $l(t), l(h)$ are lengths of text and hypothesis; $max\,(l(t), l(h))$ is the sentence with higher length; $w_t(i)$ is i^{th} word of text and x is the cost of operation.

Finally, lexical similarity is observed to find pair of dictionary senses with greatest word overlap in dictionary definitions of two (or more) sentences. This process is known as disambiguation.

$$\text{Word Overlap} = \frac{\text{word}_t \cup \text{word}_h}{len(\text{h}) + len(\text{t})} \quad \text{Eq. 3}$$

A final component is the semantic analyzer that determines the entailment of a document in another. The idea here is to calculate the distance between a document of interest against other documents based on their contextual meaning as opposed to ordinary structural similarity observed during lexical analysis. This component observes the entailment level found in the structured text-hypothesis using word vector approach [9]. The approach utilizes geometrical primitives as directed lines built from points to represent words in a sentence.

The analyzer performs candidature entailment check for each word in the text/hypothesis sentence pair with the aid of vocabulary information in WordNet. Sentential fragments from documents are represented as bags of words such that frequency of words in each sentence is computed as its inverse document frequency (idf) per sentence. If N is the number of sentences in a document and n_i is the number of sentences with word w_i, the weight of w_i in the sentence is:

$$idf_{w_i} = log\left(\frac{N}{n_i + 1.001}\right) \quad Eq. 4$$

The idea here is that terms that occur less in a sentence have higher score and can effectively discriminate the content of a particular document. Given sentence S_t from document d as text and S_h from d' as hypothesis, an entailment score of S_t in S_h is determined by comparing sum of weights of all terms that appear in both S_t and S_h to sum of weights of terms in S_h, as in Eq. 5.

$$entscore(S_t, S_h) = \frac{\sum_{w \in (S_t, S_h)} idf(w)}{\sum_{w \in S_h} idf(w)} \quad \text{Eq. 5}$$

The entailment score varies from 0 to 1, providing an approximate entailment judgment between two sentences. The score of each sentence-pair is a vector representing the entailment relationship of cross join of all sentences in the research documents. For instance, suppose we have n documents to be classified based on a document of interest d_i using their vector representation, a common origin [a,b,c]. The nearness of other documents d_1, say [x,y,z] that is a line from [0,0,0] through [x,y,z], is an angle theta, that indicates the entailment level of in d_1 and d_i. The angle varies according to how close they are. Finally, the research documents are classified based on cosine of their theta values, making $\cos(\theta)$ a powerful predictor of document category. If the two documents are identical in terms of sentential entailment, they would appear as collinear vectors in Fig 2 with a $\cos(\theta)$=1 but if they are completely different, the vectors would be orthogonal with $\cos(\theta) = 0$.

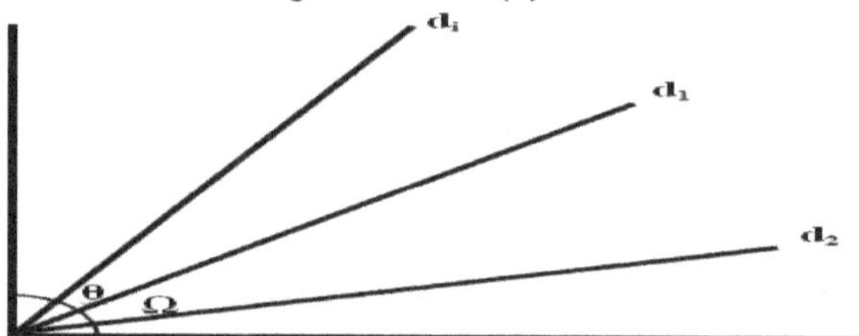

Fig 2: Angular Representation of Documents

3. CONCLUSION

The potentials of Internet repositories have been identified with emphasis on their use to manage and preserve scholarly intellectual resources and assets for long-term access and use. And then, issues regarding information overload have impeded the retrieval of such resources thus misleading information searchers. Having successfully proposed TER for automatic document classification, implementing the model for validation will identify multiple avenues for further exploration.

The conceptual approach can achieve classification of some documents around the features of a certain document. In a future work, we shall test the classification performance of this model.

4. REFERENCES

[1] Onwuchekwa, E. and Jegede, O. 2011. Information Retrieval Methods in Libraries and Information Centers, *International Multidisciplinary Journal*, Vol. 5(6), No. 23, 108-120

[2] Omisore O. and Samuel O. 2014. Personalized Recommender System for Digital Libraries. *International Journal of Web-Based Learning and Teaching Technologies*, Vol 9 (1), No. 2, 18-32.

[3] Ojokoh B., Omisore O., Samuel O. and Ogunniyi T. 2012. A Fuzzy Logic Based Personalized Recommender System. *Int. J.of Computer Science and Information Technology & Security*, Vol 2(5), 1008-15.

[4] Alessandro Z. 2005, *Text Mining and Its Applications*. WIT Press. Southampton, UK, pp.109-129.

[5] Pang, B and Lee L. 2008. Using very simple statistics for review search: An exploration, *Int. Conference on Computational Linguistics*, Poster.

[6] Radev D. R.,Muthukrishnan P., Qazvinian V. 2013. ACL Anthology Network Corpus", *Language Resources and Evaluation*, Springer.

[7] Qi, X. and Davison B. 2009. Web Page Classification: Features and Algorithms.*ACM Computing Surveys*, 41(2) 1-31.

[8] Paltoglou G. and Thelwall M. 2010. A Study of Information Retrieval Weighting Schemes for Sentiment Analysis, *48th Annual Meeting of Association for Computational Linguistics*, Uppsala, Sweden, pp. 1386–95.

[9] Parker R, Williams R, Nitse S. and Tay-Albert M. 2008. Use of Normalized Word Vector Approach in Document Classification for an LKMC, *Issues in Informing Science and Information Technology*, Vol 5, 513-524

Case Study of Waiting List on WPLC Digital Library

Wooseob Jeong
University of Wisconsin-Milwaukee
School of Information Studies
Milwaukee, WI 53201-0413 USA
1-414-229-6167
wjj8612@uwm.edu

Hyejung Han
University of Wisconsin-Milwaukee
School of Information Studies
Milwaukee, WI 53201-0413 USA
1-414-229-3492
hanh@uwm.edu

Laura Ridenour
University of Wisconsin-Milwaukee
School of Information Studies
Milwaukee, WI 53201-0413 USA
1-414-229-3492
ridenour@uwm.edu

ABSTRACT

With the increasing popularity of e-books and audiobooks provided by public libraries in the U.S., the demand does not seem to be met with sufficient supply, as many popular titles require months of waiting time. In this study, we collected data from the Wisconsin Public Library Consortium's digital libraries service once a day for more than two months for selected popular titles. This data reflects the current supply and demand of popular titles in public libraries' digital library services. Based on our data analysis and observation, we suggest ways to achieve faster circulation, which ultimately allows for better services to library users.

Categories and Subject Descriptors

H.3.7 [**Information Storage and Retrieval**]: Digital Libraries – collection, user issues.

General Terms

Management, Design, Human Factors

Keywords

digital libraries; e-books; audiobooks; public libraries; circulation.

1. INTRODUCTION

According to the 2014 e-book survey by Library Journal, there is still a larger demand for paper books than for e-books in public libraries in the U.S [1]. However, the length of waiting list on many OverDrive digital library sites for American public libraries details the demand for e-books. Waiting periods for popular e-book and audiobook titles are easily two months, which either reflects a high demand for popular e-books and audiobooks, or low numbers of available e-book and audiobook titles. A major advantage of digital libraries is their availability, regardless of time and location. Availability is an important element of evaluation of digital libraries [2], but current e-book and audiobook services do not capitalize on the essential accessibility of digital library services. The Wisconsin Public Library Consortium (WPLC) uses OverDrive for their digital library book title holdings.

JCDL'15, June 21–25, 2015, Knoxville, Tennessee, USA.
ACM 978-1-4503-3594-2/15/06.
http://dx.doi.org/10.1145/2756406.2756961

2. RESEARCH QUESTION

Many studies examining the quality of library collection management have been conducted, but few studies have been conducted on public libraries' digital collections and use. This study aims to begin to investigate this emerging area by collecting data on wait time in the WPLC queue for popular book titles in either e-book or audiobook format. The difference in waiting time by format (e-books vs. audiobooks) and the correlation between waiting time and the length of titles are also examined.

3. METHODOLOGY

Data was collected on a daily basis from three individual user from November 15, 2014, to January 19, 2015, at approximately 10:00pm each day, via the WPLC Digital Library website. Each account requested the same popular book titles from the digital collection. Thirty-seven e-book titles and twenty-five audiobook titles were requested[1].

For each title, the waiting reduction rate (WRR), or how much each copy affected in reducing the waiting line per day was calculated. WRR is calculated by dividing the number of spots gained (DN) during the whole waiting period by the outcome of multiplication of the number of copies of a title available in the collection (C) and the number of days in the waiting period (DA). In other words, WRR = DN/(C*DA). During the data collection period, the number of available copies of several books changed; extremely popular titles increased numbers of titles available for circulation, while titles with less demand decreased numbers available. This mechanism helps cope with the changes in demand for different titles. To accommodate the change in availability, a separate WRR was calculated for titles affected by fluctuating numbers; this WRR reflected the changed (either increased or decreased) availability of a title, the corresponding wait time, and the number of spots gained in the waiting queue.

WRR shows each title's average change in the waiting line per day. It should be noted that if a title had changes in the number of copies in the collection, as descried in the previous section, separate waiting reduction rate was calculated for different numbers of available copies with the matching waiting period. With the available WRR data, a t-test was conducted to see if there is any difference in WRR between two formats (e-books vs. audiobooks), and correlation coefficients were calculated to identify any relationship between WRR and the length of each title.

[1] The data set will be available on our poster display and by requests via email.

4. RESULTS

4.1 Waiting reduction rate by format

Forty-three different WRRs existed in each group (e-books vs. audiobooks). The mean rate for e-books was 0.1255, while that of audiobooks was 0.1382, which may imply that the waiting time for audiobooks is slightly shorter than that of the waiting time for e-books. It is speculated that the shorter maximum lending period for audiobooks (14 days) may contribute the observed difference. However, a t-test calculated using SPSS software indicated there is no significant difference between two groups statistically, $t(84)=.604$, $p>.05$.

4.2 Waiting reduction rate by length of title

A Pearson product-moment correlation coefficient was computed to assess the relationship between the length of titles and their waiting time. Overall, across the two formats, there is no statistically significant relationship between WRR and the length of titles [$r = 0.190$, $n = 86$, $p = 0.080$]. Neither the e-book group nor the audiobook group showed any statistically significant relationship respectively.

5. DISCUSSION

5.1 Difference between e-books and audiobooks

The average reading speed is around 250 to 300 words per minute, but most people only feel comfortable listening to 150 to 160 words per minute [3], which makes the reading an e-book much faster than listening to the same title as an audiobook. That being said, a distinct advantage of audiobooks is that they allow the reader to multitask their consumption of book material with activities such as driving and chores. Considering these two "conflicting" factors, different maximum lending periods between two formats do not much make sense.

5.2 Waiting time and length of titles

It would be reasonable to predict that shorter titles could be circulated faster than much longer ones; however, our data did not show any significant relationship between WWR and length of titles. We assume the lack of returned titles is due to the inherent nature of e-book lending: once the lending period has lapsed, the title is removed from their device, requiring no effort on their part to return the title as it is automatically removed from their reading device. The current interface requires that borrowers return titles via Amazon.com or OverDrive's app, which is cumbersome. It would be useful, if the reading/listening device or app could handle the returning process without requiring users exit the application or use a different device. This would allow easier returning of the finished titles before the expiration of the lending period, and eventually help increase circulation speed of the titles.

5.3 Options for speeding up the waiting time

There are several ways to increase the circulation speed of materials from digital libraries. First, limits on the number of days of lending may help to get faster circulation. Philadelphia Free Library's decision of reducing the maximum of lending period from 21 days to 14 days was well publicized. Recent policy change in Wisconsin Public Library Consortium's lending period for extremely popular titles was shortened to 14 days after data collection for this study was concluded. This shortening of the lending period reflects the approach to increase circulation speed of these titles.

We recommend that a shorter lending period should be combined with other aspects of lending, such as limits on the maximum number of checked-out items and items on hold per patron account, in order to more effectively improve electronic circulation. An informal survey of lending policy shows a wide range of allowance of checked-out items, from 3 to 30, but most libraries put the maximum of 10 items. Many libraries justified this policy based on their lending policy for printed materials. Given the popular lending period of 21 days for e-books and long waiting lists for readers, 10 items seems too generous. In reality, it is not easy to simultaneously read 10 books for the purpose of leisure. Based on our observations, we suggest reducing the number of maximum items checked out with a reasonable lending period. This way, much more efficient circulation can be achieved for e-books and audiobooks while reducing the cost associated with acquiring more copies of titles, particularly in this era of perpetual budget pressure.

5.4 Holds-to-copy ratio

The majority of public libraries are trying to maintain 6:1 holds-to-copy ratio in their digital collections, with a very small number of them with 5:1 or 7:1 [1]. However, according to the calculated waiting reduction rate in this study, a 6:1 holds-to-copy ratio is not ideal for great access to digital collections. For example, if you have 1 copy of a title and 6 people on the waiting list, the last person in the line will obtain the copy after a four-month waiting period assuming a lending period of 21 days (again, not many users return their copies earlier than the maximum lending period).

6. CONCLUSION

The Library Journal's annual survey of Ebook Usage in U.S. Public Libraries has provided valuable information about the trend in e-book services for last five years. Unfortunately, the survey does not include a separate analysis of audiobook usage; as this area of digital consumption is increasing with the number of users, we consider this integral to understanding the entire picture of digital collection usage and recommend including a separate analysis in future annual surveys. This case study attempted to cover these two types of media with daily data spanning more than two months. We believe this study provides useful insights and suggestions for public libraries' to provide better service, improving wait times and availability for both e-books and audiobooks.

7. REFERENCES

[1] Library Journal. 2015. *2014 Survey of Ebook Usage in U.S. Public Libraries*: http://www.thedigitalshift.com/research/ebook-usage-u-s-public-libraries-2014-report/

[2] Tefko, S. 2000. Digital library evaluation: Toward evolution of concepts. *Library Trends* 49, 2, 350-369.

[3] Human Factors International. 2000. Human interaction speed. *Newsletter.* August. http://www.humanfactors.com/newsletters/human_interaction_speeds.asp

Analyzing Tagging Patterns by Integrating Visual Analytics with the Inferential Test

Yunseon Choi
Southern Connecticut State University
501 Crescent Street, New Haven, CT 06515
choiy1@southernect.edu

ABSTRACT
Due to the large volume and complexity of data, exploring data using visual analytics has become more helpful to interpret and analyze it. The box plot is one of graphical ways and is the most common technique for presenting and summarizing statistics. In this paper, we focus on discussing the tagging patterns by integrating visualization assessment using the box plot with the Shapiro-Wilk test.

Categories and Subject Descriptors
I.6 Simulation and Modeling

General Terms
Measurement

Keywords
Social tagging; data analytics; data visualization

1. INTRODUCTION
Social tagging is described as "user-generated keywords" [1]. Since tags indicate users' perspectives and descriptions in indexing resources, they have been suggested as a means to improve search and retrieval of resources on the web. Several researchers have discussed social tagging behavior and its usefulness for classification or retrieval [2]. Choi [3] focuses on bridging the gap of insufficiency of studies on vocabulary analysis by comparing user-generated tags with professional-generated index terms regarding web resources. The comparison of users' tags and indexers' keywords has been promoted by analyzing indexing consistency [4][5]. This paper is part of a larger project which aims to analyze indexing consistency of social tagging. We employed Vector Space Model (VSM) based similarity measures to analyze indexing consistency. Wolfram and Olson [6] applied the concept of document space in the VSM into the terms assigned by a group of indexers to a document, and defined an Indexer/Tagger Space. Wolfram and Olson proposed a method, the Inter-indexer Consistency Density (ICD) by calculating the distance between each indexer/tagger's resulting vector and the indexing centroid (or average vector across all indexers/taggers).

We adopted Wolfram and Olson's formula with different VSM based measures: Adjusted Euclidean distance metric, Dot product similarity, and Cosine similarity. Using three different VSM measures intend to produce a more convincing and valuable analysis and to decrease possible bias by each measure.

JCDL'15, June 21–25, 2015, Knoxville, Tennessee, USA.
ACM 978-1-4503-3594-2/15/06.
http://dx.doi.org/10.1145/2756406.2756962

On the other hand, due to the large volume and complexity of data, exploring data using visual analytics has become more helpful to interpret and analyze it. There are several data visualization methods for graphically presenting statistics, such as charts, line graphs, tables, and graphical plots. Graphical plots present information in a pictorial way which allows for making data interpretation quick and easy [7]. The box plot is one of graphical ways and is the most common technique for presenting and summarizing statistics. In this paper, we focus on discussing the tagging patterns by integrating visualization assessment using the box plot with the inferential test. The following research questions will be answered in this study: Is tagging tendency is normally distributed or skewed? Are there any unusual observations in tagging patterns?

2. METHODOLOGY
Social tags were collected from Delicous.com and 31,319 tags were collected from 113 web documents which were randomly sampled. The analysis of indexing consistency was conducted by using three measures (Euclidean distance, dot product, and cosine).

Adjusted Euclidean distance metric
The similarity as measured by the Euclidean distance metric [8] is inversely proportional to the Euclidean distance. Thus, sign minus one (-1) is put in front of the formula to make this metric proportional to the similarity:
$Similarity(I_i, C) = -Dist(I_i, C)$
This is equal to:
$-Dist(I_i, C) = -|C - I_i|$

Dot product similarity
Dot product based similarity is represented by:
$Similarity\ (I_i, C) = I_i \cdot C$

Cosine similarity is measured by the cosine of the angle between two vectors of the same dimensions. The cosine similarity (θ) is represented using a dot product and magnitude as:

= ―――

$|I_i|$ = vector norm of I_i
|C| = vector norm of vector Centroid
θ = angle between vector I_i and vector C

where I_i and C are two vectors of attributes and I_i ·C is the dot product of vectors.

To interpret the distribution of a dataset of tagging consistency, the box plot was used. A box plot indicates the lower quartile (25%), the median (50%) and upper quartile (75%). A box plot also indicates "outliers". Any data observation which lies more than 1.5 times the inter-quartile range (the difference between the upper and lower quartiles) is considered an outlier. Furthermore, in order to conduct in-depth investigation of the observed distribution of tag data, that is, to see whether tagging consistency in Delicious is normally distributed or not, the test of normality was conducted. This study used the Shapiro-Wilk test [9] which is appropriate when the sample size is between 3 and 2000. The Shapiro-Wilk test calculates a W statistic [10]:

$$W = \frac{\left(\sum_{i=1}^{n} a_i x_{(i)}\right)^2}{\sum_{i=1}^{n}(x_i - \bar{x})^2}$$

$x_{(i)}$: the ordered sample values ($x_{(1)}$ is the smallest)
a_i : constants generated from the means, variances and covariances of the order statistics of a sample of size n from a normal distribution

The null hypothesis for this test is that the data are normally distributed.

3. RESULTS

The tendency of the tagging consistency in Delicious was graphically explained as illustrated in Figure 1.

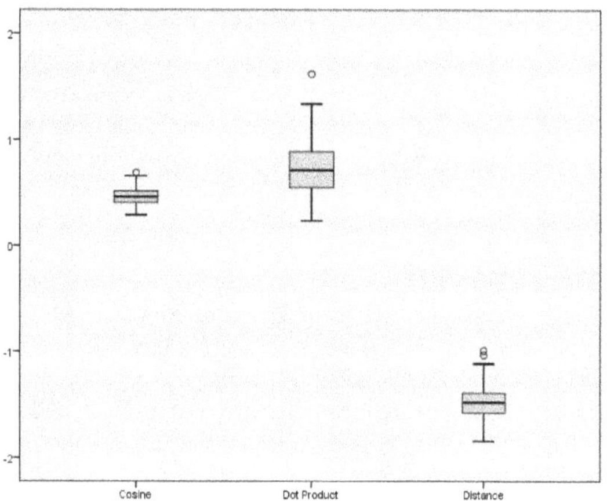

Figure 1. A box plot of tagging patterns in Delicious

In Figure 1, the middle black line is the median, the shaded region shows middle 50 % of consistency values, and outliers are represented by open dots. The box plot indicates the minimum value excluding outliers by connecting it to the box with a horizontal line or "whisker". Also, it indicates the maximum value excluding outliers by extending above the box with a "whisker". Furthermore, it is possible to understand the distribution of sets of data by looking at the lengths of the whiskers on both sides of the box and the position of the median within the box. It is noticeable that in the case of dot product measure, the whisker associated with the upper quartile is larger than the whisker associated the lower quartile. In these cases, therefore, we could detect possible skewness in the data.

Table 1. The results of normality test on tagging consistency

	Shapiro-Wilk		
	Statistic	df	Sig.
Distance	.988	113	.433
Cosine	.989	113	.503
Dot product	.971	113	**.016**

(α level: 0.05)

On the other hand, Table 1 shows the results of normality on tagging at Delicious. The chosen alpha level is 0.05 and the p-value (0.016) in the Dot product is less than 0.05. So, the null hypothesis that the data are normally distributed was rejected. It was demonstrated that in dot product measure, tagging consistency was not normally distributed while tagging consistency in the cosine similarity and distance metrics measures derived from normal distributions.

5. CONCLUSION

This study has demonstrated how tagging patterns could be analyzed by integrating visual presentation of dataset with the inferential test. The box plot method was used to pictorially represent the dataset of tagging. The Shapiro-Wilk test was additionally conducted to inferentially test whether the dataset of tagging in Delicious is normally distributed or not. The findings showed that tagging patterns differed among VSM similarities. In the dot product measure, we could detect possible skewness in the data. The interpreted data from the box plot was reconfirmed by the results of the Shapiro-Wilk test which demonstrated that in dot product measure, tagging consistency was not normally distributed while tagging consistency in the cosine similarity and distance metrics measures derived from normal distributions.

6. ACKNOWLEDGEMENTS

This paper derives from my University of Illinois doctoral dissertation entitled "Usefulness of Social Tagging in Organizing and Providing Access to the Web: An Analysis of Indexing Consistency and Quality." I am deeply grateful to my dissertation committee. Dr. Linda C. Smith was the chairperson of that committee, which included Dr. Allen Renear, Dr. Miles Efron, and Dr. John Unsworth.

7. REFERENCES

[1] J. Trant. Studying social tagging and folksonomy: A review and framework. *Journal of Digital Information,* 10 (1). 2009.

[2] P. Heymann, G. Koutrika, and Garcia-Molina, H. Can Social Bookmarking Improve Web Search? *Proceedings of the 1st International Conference on Web Search and Data Mining.* 2008.

[3] Y. Choi. Traditional versus Emerging Knowledge Organization Systems: Consistency of Subject Indexing of the Web by Indexers and Taggers. *Proceedings of the Annual Meeting of the American Society for Information Science.* 2010.

[4] Y. Choi. Social Indexing: A Solution to the Challenges of Current Information Organization. In *New Directions in Information Organization.* Emerald Group Publishing Limited. 2013.

[5] Y. Choi. A Complete Assessment of Tagging Quality: A Consolidated Methodology. *Journal of the Association for Information Science and Technology (JASIS&T).* 2014.

[6] D. Wolfram and H.A. Olson. A method for comparing large scale inter-indexer consistency using IR modeling. *Proceedings of the 35th Annual Conference of the Canadian Association for Information Science.* 2007.

[7] Potter K. Methods for presenting statistical information: the box plot. In: Hagan H, Kerren A, Dannemann P, eds. *Visualization of Large and Unstructured Data Sets,* GI-Edition Lecture. Notes in Informatics (LNI). 2006.

[8] T. Kohonen. *Self-Organizing Maps.* Berlin: Springer-Verlag. 1995.

[9] S. S. Shapiro and M. B. Wilk. An analysis of variance test for normality (complete samples). *Biometrika,* 52(3/4): 591-611. 1965.

[10] A. V. Pearson and H. O. Hartley. *Biometrica Tables for Statisticians, Vol 2,* Cambridge, England: Cambridge University Press. 1972.

ConfAssist: A Conflict Resolution Framework for Assisting the Categorization of Computer Science Conferences

Mayank Singh, Tanmoy Chakraborty, Animesh Mukherjee, Pawan Goyal
Department of Computer Science and Engineering
Indian Institute of Technology, Kharagpur, WB, India
{mayank.singh,its_tanmoy,animeshm,pawang}@cse.iitkgp.ernet.in

ABSTRACT

Classifying publication venues into top-tier or non top-tier is quite subjective and can be debatable at times. In this paper, we propose *ConfAssist*, a novel assisting framework for conference categorization that aims to address the limitations in the existing systems and portals for venue classification. We identify various features related to the stability of conferences that might help us separate a top-tier conference from the rest of the lot. While there are many clear cases where expert agreement can be almost immediately achieved as to whether a conference is a top-tier or not, there are equally many cases that can result in a conflict even among the experts. *ConfAssist* tries to serve as an aid in such cases by increasing the confidence of the experts in their decision. A human judgment survey was conducted with 28 domain experts. The results were quite impressive with 91.6% classification accuracy.

Categories and Subject Descriptors

H.4 [**Information Systems Applications**]: Miscellaneous

Keywords

Venue classification; Diversity Index; Stability; Conflict resolution

1. INTRODUCTION

The scientific community has always been demanding for better algorithms, metrics and features for scientific venue ranking and categorization. The existing systems and portals for venue classification, however, have several limitations such as no clear demarcation between categories and no description of main intuitions behind such classification. Ranking systems use h-index and impact factor based metrics, which in turn are debatable. Studies on recommending appropriate publication venues to the researcher for their research paper have explored author's network of related co-authors [4] as well as topic and writing-style information [5]. A similar study [3] suggests that the prestige of a venue depends on several factors such as sponsorship by national or international professional organization, reputation of publisher etc. Another study on wellness of software engineering conferences uses features like author and program committee (PC) stability, prestige etc. [2].

JCDL'15, June 21–25, 2015, Knoxville, Tennessee, USA.
ACM 978-1-4503-3594-2/15/06.
http://dx.doi.org/10.1145/2756406.2756963

In this paper, we present *ConfAssist* which is a novel conflict resolution framework that can assist experts to resolve conflicts in deciding whether a conference is a top-tier or not by expressing how (dis)similar the conference is to other well accepted top-tier/ non top-tier conferences. This paper tries to answer some of the very pertinent questions: ***1.*** *What are the underlying features behind the popularity of conferences?* ***2.*** *How can these features be meaningfully used to predict the category of a given conference?*

2. DATASET

This paper uses the dataset (see [1]), crawled from Microsoft Academic Search. For our study, we consider papers published from 1999 to 2010 for 92 conferences. A benchmark is built from systems that provide conference categorizations. We consider 4 such systems and compile categories for each of the 92 conferences. A conference is eligible for consideration, if it is present in atleast 3 systems. 73 out of the 92 conferences satisfied this criteria. Out of these 73 conferences, we call a conference as non-conflicting (NC) if it has been labeled using the same category in all the systems, otherwise it is called a conflicting conference (CC). Overall, the set NC contains 37 conferences with 28 labeled as top-tier and 9 labeled as non top-tier.

3. FEATURES AND ANALYSIS

We select 9 different features and study the dynamics of the conferences in terms of how these parameters change over the years.

i) Conference Reference Diversity Index (CRDI) measures how diversified are the fields referred to by the papers published in a conference.

ii) Conference Keyword Diversity Index (CKDI) represents the diversity in the paper keywords.

iii) Conference Author Diversity Index (CADI) corresponds to what fraction of authors with diversified research interests publish in a conference.

iv) Proportion of New Authors (PNA) explores whether the fraction of papers with new authors is roughly the same over the years for the conference.

v) Conference Author Publication Age Diversity Index (CAAI) represents whether the top-tier conferences have more inclination towards maintaining similar publication-age diversity (or diversity in terms of publication experience of the authors) over time.

vi) Degree Diversity Index (DDI) presents the fluctuations in the overall collaborative behavior of the authors in the conference.

vii) Edge Strength Diversity Index (EDI) shows the fluctuations in the choice of the co-authors for a given author in a conference.

viii) Average Closeness centrality (ACC) represents the closeness of an author to other authors in terms of collaboration.

ix) Average Betweenness Centrality (ABC) measures the "importance" of each author in the collaboration network of the authors publishing in a conference.

For each of these 9 features, we use 3 different parameters: the mean, the median and the standard deviation of consecutive year difference (Δ) of raw values.

***Comparing top-tier and non top-tier using features*:** Figure 1 presents comparison between INFOCOM (top-tier) and IWQoS (non top-tier) using 3 features, CAAI, DDI and ACC on a yearly scale. One observation is that in majority of features, values are much higher for INFOCOM than for IWQoS. This plot clearly shows that for non top-tier conferences, raw values over the years are very fluctuating, thus they give rise to high mean and standard deviation in the year-wise differences.

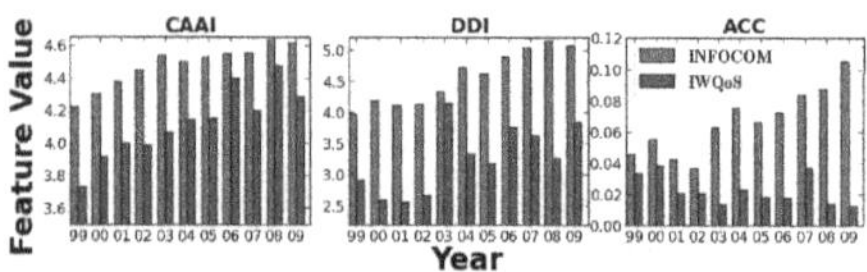

Figure 1: Comparison between INFOCOM (top-tier) and IWQoS (non top-tier) raw feature values using CAAI, DDI and ACC.

***Fieldwise comparison of representative conferences*:** We compare feature values of top-tier conferences with non top-tier in each field. Figure 2 shows plots for 4 computer science fields. For the sake of visualization, we divide our features into three buckets, features 1-9, 10-18 and 19-27. One straightforward observation is that at least for the first two buckets, the feature values for top-tier conferences are lower than those for the non top-tier. Figure 3 presents plots of two conflicting conferences, ICALP and ECIR, compared against the representative conferences of their fields, *Algorithms and Theory* and *Information Retrieval* respectively. At least for the most discriminative features, the feature values for these conferences lie between the features values of the top-tier and the non top-tier conferences in their field. At the same time, for the medium discriminative features, the values of the conflicting conferences is sometimes even higher than the non top-tier conferences.

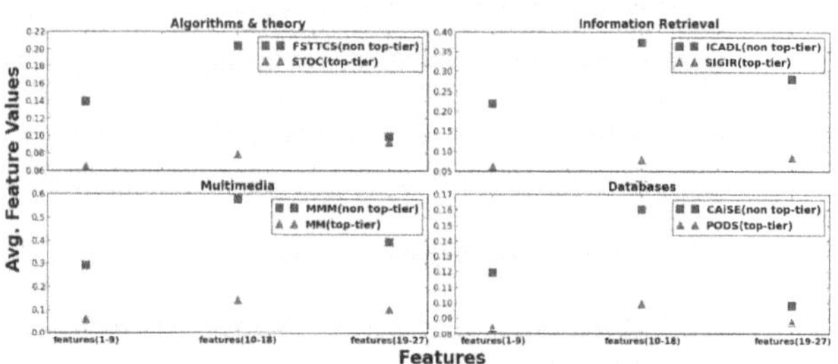

Figure 2: Comparison of feature values of top-tier and non top-tier in four computer science fields.

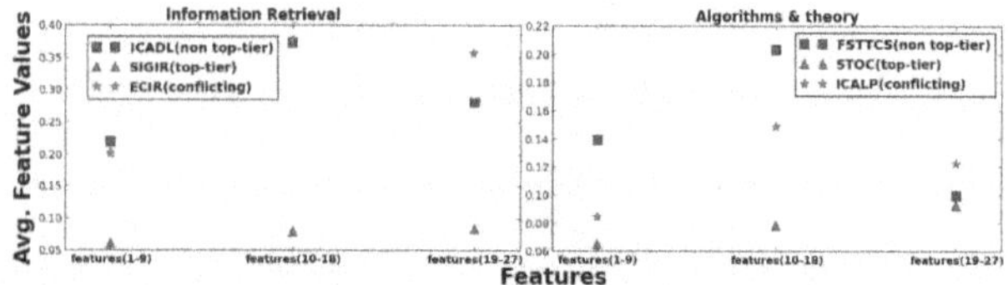

Figure 3: Comparison of feature values of conflicting conferences with top-tier and non top-tier for two CS fields.

***Comparison of newly starting conferences with top-tier and non top-tier*:** We also made an attempt to compare a newly starting conference (for example, JCDL, started in 2001) with top-tier and non top-tier conferences. Figure 4 shows comparison of year-wise profile for JCDL with the average values for all the top-tier and non top-tier using two features, namely ΔPNA and ΔABC. As noted from the left panel, the initial ΔPNA values for JCDL are closely matching with that of the non top-tier conferences. However, after the year 2003, the fluctuation in PNA values is low, even much lower than the average values for the top-tier conferences. The right panel in Figure 4 shows fluctuations in consecutive values of ΔABC. Here, the values for JCDL are below the top-tier average from the beginning. Further analysis on dataset shows that JCDL is slowly promoting the increase in the raw ABC values by allowing higher proportion of bridging authors till 2008, then a sudden drop and again rise in next consecutive years.

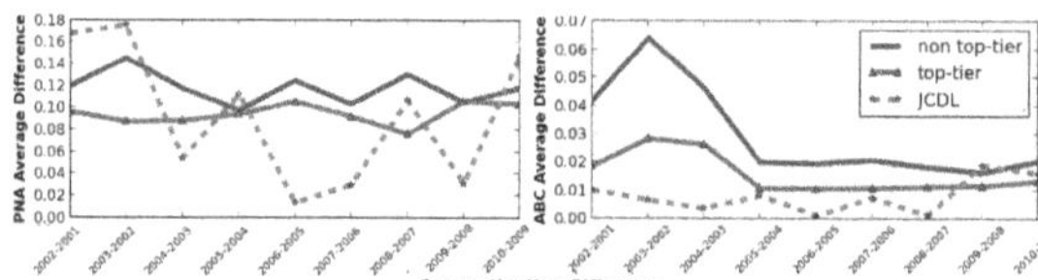

Figure 4: Comparison of year-wise profile for JCDL and average of all top-tier and non top-tier.

4. EXPERIMENTS

The main idea behind this experiment is to predict a category for a conference based on the nearest matching conference from the ground truth dataset. The set NC was taken as the gold-standard to classify any conflicting conference in the set CC. Since the number of top-tier conferences (28) in this set is 3 times the number of non top-tier conferences (9), we created 5 NC sub-sets each having 9 non top-tier and 9 random top-tier conferences. We ran kNN on each of the 5 NC subsets and in each run, we classified a conference in set CC as top-tier, if at-least 4 nearest neighbors are top-tier, otherwise it is classified as a non-top-tier. Finally, a conference is categorized based on the majority from the 5 runs of kNN.

To evaluate the results obtained by our system for this conflicting set, we conduct an online survey[1]. Out of 525 responses, 363 (69.1%) matched our classification results. Considering the majority voting for each conference, 33 out of 36 (91.6%) conferences were correctly classified, 2 were incorrectly classified, while 1 got equal number of matching and non-matching votes. JCDL got 62% votes in favor of top-tier. 148 out of the 226 responses felt more confident about their choice after seeing our results.

5. REFERENCES

[1] T. Chakraborty, S. Kumar, P. Goyal, N. Ganguly, and A. Mukherjee. Towards a stratified learning approach to predict future citation counts. In *Digital Libraries*, 2014.

[2] B. Vasilescu, A. Serebrenik, T. Mens, M. G. van den Brand, and E. Pek. How healthy are software engineering conferences? *Science of Computer Programming*, 89, Part C:251–272, 2014.

[3] R. E. West and P. J. Rich. Rigor, impact and prestige: A proposed framework for evaluating scholarly publications. *Innovative Higher Education*, 37:359–371, 2012.

[4] F. Xia, N. Y. Asabere, J. J. Rodrigues, F. Basso, N. Deonauth, and W. Wang. Socially-aware venue recommendation for conference participants. In *UIC/ATC*, pages 134–141, 2013.

[5] Z. Yang and B. D. Davison. Venue recommendation: Submitting your paper with style. In *ICMLA*, volume 1, pages 681–686, 2012.

[1]Further Reference and online survey, available at `http://cse.iitkgp.ac.in/resgrp/cnerg/evaluation/JCDL/`.

Combining Classifiers and User Feedback for Disambiguating Author Names

Emilia A. de Souza
Departamento de Computação
Universidade Federal de Ouro Preto
Ouro Preto, Brazil
emilia.alvess@gmail.com

Anderson A. Ferreira
Departamento de Computação
Universidade Federal de Ouro Preto
Ouro Preto, Brazil
ferreira@iceb.ufop.br

Marcos André Gonçalves
Departamento de Ciência da Computação
Universidade Federal de Minas Gerais
Belo Horizonte, Brazil
mgoncalv@dcc.ufmg.br

ABSTRACT

Historically, supervised methods have been the most effective ones for author name disambiguation tasks. In here, we propose a specific manner to combine supervised techniques along with user feedback. Although, we use supervised techniques, the only user effort is to provide feedback on results since initial training data is automatically generated. Our experiments show gains up to 20% in the disambiguation performance against representative baselines.

Categories and Subject Descriptors

H.3.7 [**Information Storage and Retrieval**]: Digital Libraries

General Terms

Algorithms, Measurement

Keywords

Author name disambiguation; ensemble classifiers

1. INTRODUCTION

Author name ambiguity is a hard problem [3, 4]. To solve it, an automated method may be applied to a collection of bibliographic citations, splitting them into several partitions where each one should contain all and only all citations of a given author. In this paper, we propose a supervised method to solve the author name ambiguity problem by combining the results of several classifiers along with user feedback to improve the disambiguation effectiveness. In this method, the only user effort is to provide feedback on the results since initial training examples are automatically generated.

2. PROPOSED METHOD

Figure 1 provides an overview of the proposed method. Next, we describe each of its steps in more details.

JCDL'15, June 21–25, 2015, Knoxville, Tennessee, USA.
ACM 978-1-4503-3594-2/15/06.
http://dx.doi.org/10.1145/2756406.2756964 .

Step 1 - Generating Pure Clusters.

Step 1 aims at producing pure clusters for the next steps using the author and coauthor attributes, as in [1, 5]. We use coauthorship relations among citations in order to group together those belonging to a same author. In addition, we also put in the same cluster citations with very similar work and publication venue titles. This step produces pure but fragmented clusters which will be merged by the next steps.

Step 2 - Generating Training Examples.

We select, from the clusters produced in Step 1, those more likely to belong to different authors. Among the selected clusters, citations in the same cluster are considered as belonging to the same author while those in different clusters are considered from different authors. Each training example corresponds to pairwise comparison, using different similarity functions, between the attributes of citations in the same (class 1) and in different clusters (class 0).

Step 3 - Combining Classifiers.

Due to the larger number of negative training examples (i.e., class 0) the classifiers have a natural bias towards predicting this class. On the other hand, when they make a positive decision (i,e., class = 1), they are rarely wrongly. Thus, we propose to use a simple but very effective (for the disambiguation problem, at least) manner to combine results of different classifiers aimed at inducing more positive classifications. Our combiner classifier $\mathcal{F}$ predicts class = 1 if any individual classifier also predicts class 1; otherwise $\mathcal{F}$ the prediction is 0.

Checking the Similarity Between Clusters.

When comparing two clusters, if the ratio between the number of records predicted as class 1 and the total number of records (aka, t_{cr}) is equal or higher than the automatic threshold $\%_{min}$, both clusters are fused, being considered as belonging to the same author.

Generating Automatic Threshold Values.

We propose the following way to automatically determine the threshold value $\%_{min}$ for comparing clusters: $\%_{min} = \frac{1}{log_2\left(c*\left(|L_i|*|L_j|\right)\right)}$, where $|L_i|$ and $|L_j|$ are the number of references in clusters L_i and L_j, respectively. The constant c avoids a denominator equals to 0.

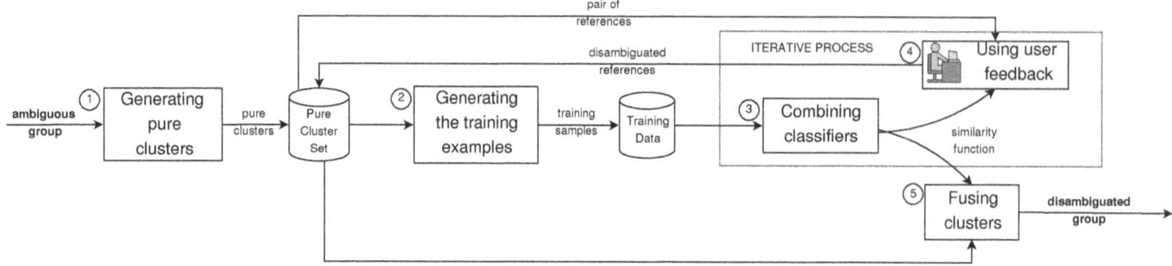

Figure 1: An overview of our proposed method.

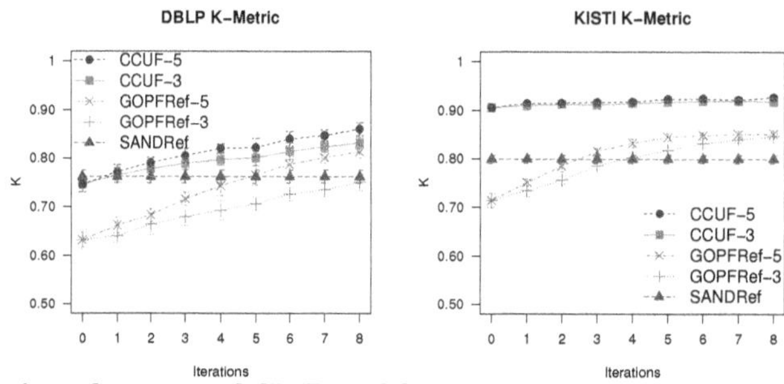

Figure 2: Comparison between CCUF and baselines in the DBLP and KISTI collections

Step 4 - Using User Feedback.

The method exploits user feedback in an iterative way. In each iteration, we ask the user whether two clusters of citations belong to the same author based on the top-n most doubtful comparisons. If the answer is positive, both clusters are fused; otherwise they remain separated and are not compared anymore. For this, we consider the comparisons with the ratio t_{cr} closer to the automatic threshold $\%_{min}$ as the most doubtful ones.

Step 5 - Fusing Clusters..

Step 5 aims at fusing clusters belonging to the same author, decreasing fragmentation. It pairwisely compares the clusters and, if two clusters are considered similar, they are fused. We use our combined classifier $\mathcal{F}$, t_{cr} and $\%_{min}$ as defined in Step 3. Two clusters are similar, when $t_{cr} \geq \%_{min}$.

3. EXPERIMENTAL EVALUATION

We use two collections derived from the Computer Science Bibliography (DBLP), DBLP and KISTI, SANDRef [2] and GOPRef [6] as baselines, and the K metrics [3] to evaluate the methods. We use Support Vector Machines (SVM), K-Nearest Neighbor (KNN) and Random Forest (RF) as classifiers in our third step. The methods were executed ten times and compared with a confidence interval of 99% (t-test).

Comparison of our method with the baselines.

Figure 2 shows the comparison of our method, hereafter referred to as CCUF, with SANDRef and GOPFRef in the DBLP and KISTI collections. In each iteration, the user labels 3 (CCUF-3 and GOPFRef-3) or 5 (CCUF-5 and GOPFRef-5) comparisons for CCUF and authors for GOPFRef. In the DBLP collection, under the K metric, CCUF-3 and CCUF-5 improve their performance over the version without user feedback in around 11% and 15%, respectively. CCUF outperforms SANDRef after only 3 iterations under the K metric while outperforming GOPFRef-3 in all iterations. In the KISTI collection, CCUF outperforms all baselines in all iterations labeling 3 or 5 comparisons per iteration. The result obtained by CCUF without user feedback is very good, K=0.905. Thus, the gains after 8 iterations are smaller than in the DBLP collection.

4. CONCLUSIONS

In this paper, we propose a new author name disambiguation method that efficiently combines results of 3 classifiers and includes user feedback. Our method outperforms feedback-based baselines by large margins with few iterations and very low labeling effort.

Acknowledgments

This work has been supported by InWeb and by grants from CAPES, CNPq and FAPEMIG.

References

[1] R. G. Cota, A. A. Ferreira, M. A. Gonçalves, A. H. F. Laender, and C. Nascimento. An unsupervised heuristic-based hierarchical method for name disambiguation in bibliographic citations. *JASIST*, 61(9):1853–1870, 2010.

[2] A. A. Ferreira, T. M. Machado, and M. A. Gonçalves. Improving author name disambiguation with user relevance feedback. *JIDM*, 3(3):332–347, 2012.

[3] A. A. Ferreira, M. A. Gonçalves, and A. H. F. Laender. A Brief Survey of Automatic Methods for Author Name Disambiguation. *SIGMOD Record*, 41(2):15–26, 2012b.

[4] A. A. Ferreira, M. A. Gonçalves, and A. H. F. Laender. Disambiguating author names using minimum bibliographic information. *World Digital Libraries*, 7(1):71–84, 2014.

[5] A. A. Ferreira, A. Veloso, M. A. Gonçalves, and A. H. Laender. Self-training author name disambiguation for information scarce scenarios. *JASIST*, 65(6):1257–1278, 2014.

[6] T. A. Godoi, R. da Silva Torres, A. M. B. R. Carvalho, M. A. Gonçalves, A. A. Ferreira, W. Fan, and E. A. Fox. A relevance feedback approach for the author name disambiguation problem. In *JCDL*, pages 209–218, 2013.

Using the Business Model Canvas to Support a Risk Assessment Method for Digital Curation

Diogo Proença
IST/INESC-ID
Rua Alves Redol, 9
1000-029 Lisboa
diogo.proenca@tecnico.ulisboa.pt

Ahmad Nadali
IST/INESC-ID
Rua Alves Redol, 9
1000-029 Lisboa
ahmad.nadali@tecnico.ulisboa.pt

José Borbinha
IST/INESC-ID
Rua Alves Redol, 9
1000-029 Lisboa
jlb@tecnico.ulisboa.pt

ABSTRACT

This poster presents a pragmatic risk assessment method based on best practice from the ISO 31000 family of standards regarding risk management. The method proposed is supported by established risk management concepts that can be applied to help a data repository to gain awareness of the risks and costs of the controls for the identified risks. In simple terms the technique that supports this method is a pragmatic risk registry that can be used to identify risks from a Business Model Canvas of an organization. A Business Model Canvas is a model used in strategic management to document existing business models and develop new ones.

Categories and Subject Descriptors

H.1 [**Information Systems**]: Models and Principles; J.1 Administrative Data Processing Government; K.6.4 Management of computing and Information Systems

General Terms

Management, Security, Standardization, Verification.

Keywords

Risk Assessment; Digital Curation; Business Model Canvas.

1. INTRODUCTION

The purpose of this research is to make good use of risk management [3] concepts to raise awareness of repository costs of digital curation. Costs are what we have to give up for controls, which in turn are the measures that we have to put in practice to minimize loss or to maximize gain. In that sense, a control is anything we are considering applying to either minimize negative impacts or to take advantage of opportunities to produce value and thus bring gains. However, we must also agree that, in most of the usual digital curation scenarios, it is usually very difficult to estimate the absolute value of an asset. For that reason, we are here ignoring the measurement of value, and focusing only in the identification of controls as the source of costs.

JCDL'15, June 21–25, 2015, Knoxville, Tennessee, USA.
ACM 978-1-4503-3594-2/15/06.
http://dx.doi.org/10.1145/2756406.2756965

The technique behind this method (depicted in Figure 1) analyses an archive with the support of a risk registry and is based on Business Model Canvas (BMC) [4]. A BMC allows organizations to fill their business model in a visual canvas that allows for easy understanding of their business in nine building blocks. The motivation behind it is to understand both what can positively affect the value propositions of your business (opportunities) and what can negatively affect those same value propositions (risks).

The idea is to identify and understand the risks and their impact (positive and negative) on each of the nine building blocks of the BMC. We demonstrate how the BMC technique can be used in the method above to find risks and then controls for those risks. This in turn makes it possible to estimate the related costs as part of the overall costs of curation. Digital curation "involves maintaining, preserving and adding value to digital research data throughout its lifecycle. The active management of research data reduces threats to their long-term research value and mitigates the risk of digital obsolescence." [2] The main steps done are:

1. Formulation of related risk questions: for each of the building blocks of BMC some questions are provided to facilitate the identification of risks for each of the building blocks.
2. Generic Risks and Controls for the Generic BMC: after the formulation of the risk questions, the next step is to identify the related risks, and then the respective controls.

Generic risks and controls were identified after analyzing the results of the DRAMBORA [1] report. The risks and controls that better align with the generic BMC model were selected.

The result is a generic BMC, depicted in Figure 2, based on the Open Archival Information System (OAIS) [5], with an associated generic registry of risk questions and common related controls, relevant for the domain of digital curation to cost evaluation. The pragmatic method was applied to estimate costs of curation focusing on risks and controls to three case studies: two data archives and one web archive. The details on the two case studies, generic BMCs and risk registry can be found at http://4ctoolset.sysresearch.org/.

2. ACKNOWLEDGEMENTS

This work was supported by national funds through Fundação para a Ciência e a Tecnologia (FCT) with references UID/CEC/50021/2013 and EXCL/EEI- ESS/0257/2012 (DataStorm), and by the project 4C, co-funded by the EU under FP7 under grant agreement no. 600471.

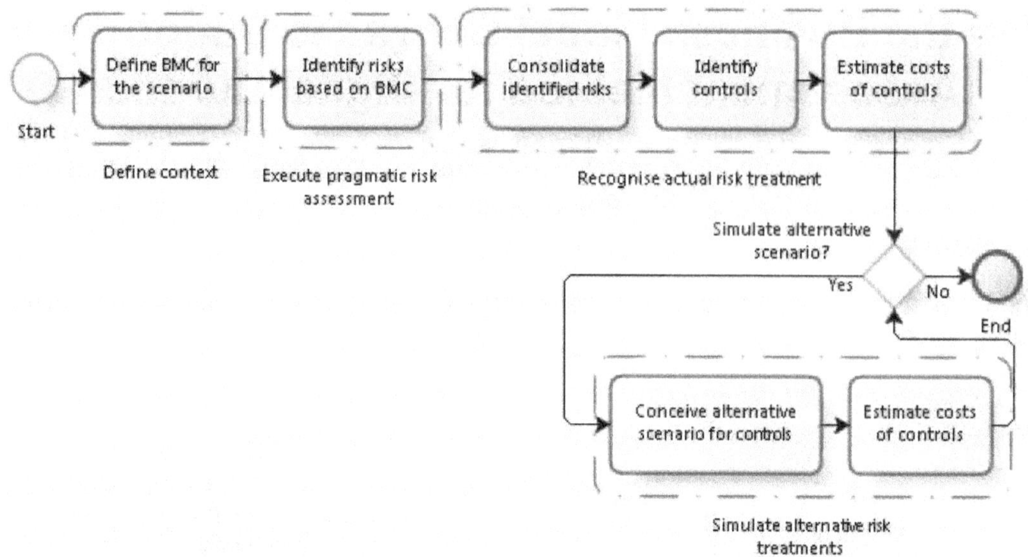

Figure 1: BPMN diagram of the pragmatic method to estimate costs of curation focusing on risks and controls

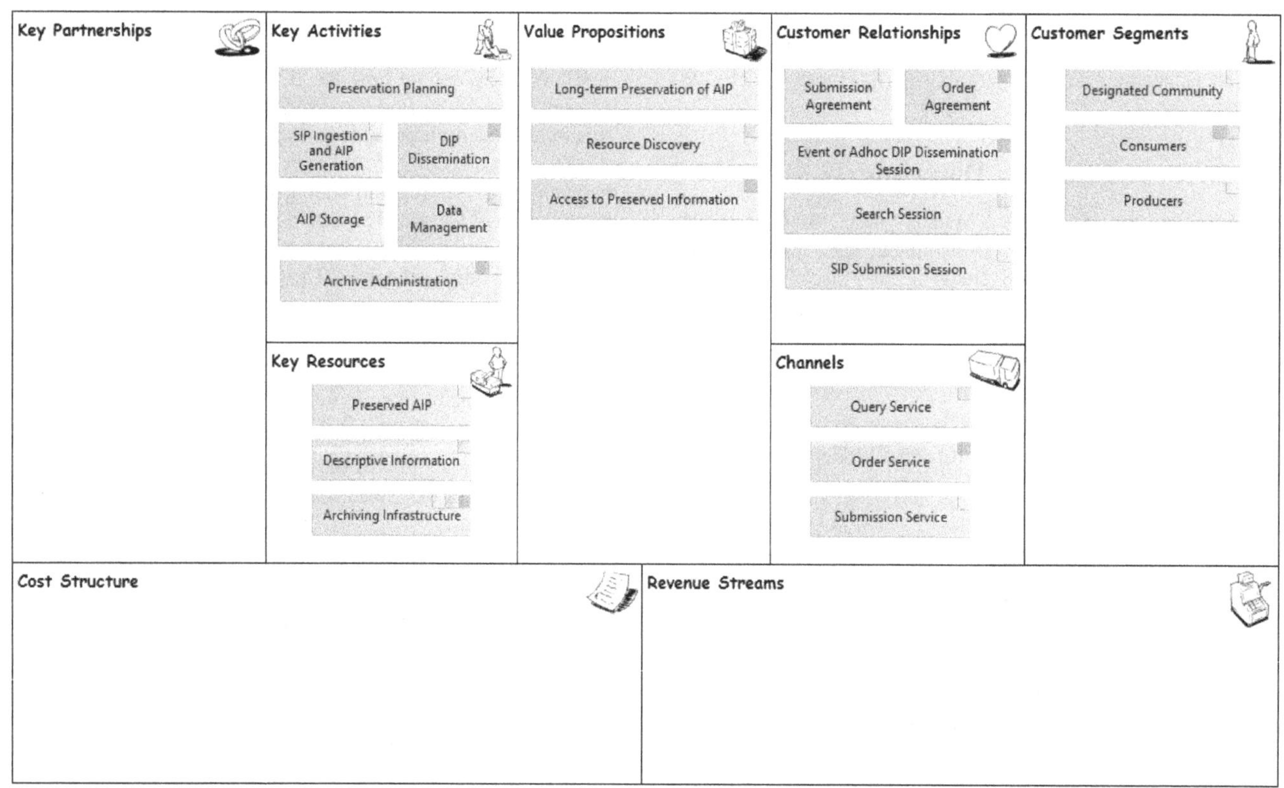

Figure 2: Generic BMC for Digital Curation based on the OAIS

3. REFERENCES

[1] Digital Curation Centre and Digital Preservation Europe, (February 2007), "DCC and DPE Digital Repository Audit Method Based on Risk Assessment, v1.0.", retrieved 22.03.2014, from http://www.repositoryaudit.eu/download

[2] Digital Curation Centre, "What is digital curation?". [Online]. Available: http://www.dcc.ac.uk/digital-curation/what-digital-curation

[3] ISO/FDIS 31000:2009(E): Risk Management—Principles and guidelines.

[4] A. Osterwalder, "Business Model Generation", Alexander Osterwalder & Yves Pigneur, 2009.

[5] The Consultative Committee for Space Data Systems, Space data and information transfer systems – Open archival information system – Reference model – Magenta Book. June 2012. CCSDS 650.0-M-2.

Grading Degradation in an Institutionally Managed Repository

Luis Meneses, Sampath Jayarathna, Richard Furuta and Frank Shipman

Center for the Study of Digital Libraries and Department of Computer Science and Engineering
Texas A&M University
College Station, TX 77843-3112 USA
(ldmm, sampath, furuta, shipman)@cse.tamu.edu

ABSTRACT

It is not unusual for digital collections to degrade and suffer from problems associated with unexpected change. In an analysis of the ACM conference list, we found that categorizing the degree of change affecting a digital collection over time is a difficult task. More specifically, we found that categorizing this degree of change is not a binary problem where documents are either unchanged or they have changed so dramatically that they do not fit within the scope of the collection. It is, in part, a characterization of the intent of the change. In this work, we examine and categorize the various degrees of change that digital documents endure within the boundaries of an institutionally managed repository.

Categories and Subject Descriptors

H.3.7 [**Information Storage and Retrieval**]: Digital Libraries – *collection, systems issues, user issues.*

General Terms

Management, Design, Reliability, Experimentation, Verification

ywords

Web resource management; distributed collections; web change classification

1. INTRODUCTION

Imagine a library filled with books that have missing pages. It might seem as overly exaggerated, but that metaphor can be used to depict the state of the digital repositories that have been affected by unexpected change. We have found that electronic resources can change, both intentionally and unintentionally, because of different factors and circumstances. Change can occur because of deliberate actions on part of the collector, unexpected events or may be due to other uncontrollable factors.

However, Web documents are not static resources and a certain degree of change is expected from them [1]. For example – and taking into account the specific infrastructure of Walden's Paths [2], where decentralized collections are stored and represented as traversable paths containing multiple nodes and documents – we have observed that Web resources suffer from changes in content, layout, presentation and location. However, as members of a larger assembly, these documents are expected to either change little over time or mutate harmoniously and accordingly with the other documents in order to preserve the semantic meaning and systematic order of the collection.

Additionally, distributed collections that are hosted in institutional repositories operate under the assumption that they are more resilient and able to withstand change. Because of their focus on long-term storage, these repositories have different attributes and operate under different principles when compared to the Web as a whole. Surprisingly, we have found these features – which are often found in digital repositories emphasizing in long-term storage – do not fully preserve the referenced documents and make them impervious to change. For example, as of 9/27/2014 the ACM Digital Library had 15 unique links referencing the different sites in the JCDL conference series and 8 of them report errors or point to the wrong content.

More so, we also found that categorizing the degree of change affecting the documents in a digital collection over time is not a binary problem where documents are either unchanged or they have changed so dramatically that they do not fit within the scope of the collection. Previous work on this topic has and relied on methods based on response codes, monitoring the fluctuation in file sizes and analyzing the documents content. However, we believe there is growing need for a categorization framework that will allow us to tag and sort documents that have been affected by different amounts of change.

2. GRADING DEGRADATION

The corpus for our study is the Association for Computing Machinery list of conference proceedings (http://dl.acm.org/proceedings.cfm), which we retrieved on 9/27/2014 and used as our starting point. Then we followed each hyperlink to a metadata page that displayed basic information for each corresponding conference and workshop, which in turn allowed us to extract the external URLs. As a result of this procedure, we were able to extract 6086 URLs – out of which 2001 were unique.

We then proceeded to inspect and categorize the 1492 pages that were retrieved with a successful HTTP response code. We categorized these pages into three categories by evaluating the relationship between the anchor text and the corresponding retrieved page. As a result of this categorization, we found that 917 pages were "clearly correct" and 531 were incorrect. Additionally, we were unable to evaluate 44 pages because their contents didn't provide us enough information to make an accurate assessment.

Then we analyzed the 531 pages that were incorrect in an effort to understand how conference sites degrade over time. The coding

JCDL'15, June 21–25, 2015, Knoxville, Tennessee, USA.
ACM 978-1-4503-3594-2/15/06.

scheme evolved through examination of the particular collection rather than using a pre-defined classification scheme. In the end, nine categories were used to classify the "incorrect" pages, which we list in (approximate) order of severity. These nine groups provide insight regarding the different stages that conference pages go through until they are ultimately abandoned:

1. **Kind of correct:** (197 entries) Pages that contain related content, but they do not fully match the semantic concept encapsulated in the anchor text. When taking into account conference proceedings, these pages often link to a different year in the conference series. For example: Anchor text "Conference X 2006" references the Conference X 2009 site.
2. **University/institution pages:** (36 entries) These are cases that surface when a site has been taken down, but the server configuration redirects the user to its parent institution. In cases dealing with conference sites, servers would usually redirect the user to the website of the University that hosted the conference or to a related professional organization.
3. **Directory listings pages:** (18 entries) Pages displaying a listing of files or a "Hello World" page. Probably caused by an error in the server configuration. In these cases, the original content looks to still be available but the new web server does not recognize homepage.html as a default page to view for this URL.
4. **Blank pages:** (141 entries) Pages that returned no content.
5. **Failed redirects:** (30 entries)
6. **Error pages:** (17 entries) Pages that specifically state that an error has occurred.
7. **Pages in a different language:** (32 entries) Pages that didn't match the language found in the anchor text. Most of these pages were in a language different than English.
8. **Domain for sale pages:** (17 entries) Pages that indicated that the domain name registration has lapsed and it is being sold by a registrar, or taken over by a third party in order to profit from the sale.
9. **Deceiving pages:** (43 entries) Pages that have been taken over by a third party. The content displayed in these pages is totally unrelated to the original purpose of the site. We believe many of these pages were not created to deceive users, but as an attempt to manipulate the PageRank algorithm [3].

Many of these links still lead to information related to the original purpose but clearly not to the originally intended materials. There are a number of categories that result when no content is available depending on how the servers are configured – blank pages, failed redirects, some directory listings, error pages, and university/institutional pages. In some of these cases, these pages can be detected with previous work on identifying Soft 404 error pages [4, 5]. The remaining pages are perhaps the most problematic, when the web address has been taken over and is either for sale or being used for other purposes.

3. DISCUSSION

The analysis of the conference website links within the ACM Digital Library shows that institutional archives are not immune to the challenges of distributed collection management. Upon our initial assessment, 404 HTTP errors were more prevalent in our corpus. However, upon further inspection we found that 36% of the pages that were supposed to be correct as reported by their HTTP response code were actually incorrect. For us this is a clear indication that the correctness of a web page is relative and that there is a growing need for methods to categorize and locate likely problematic resources that might require the attention of collection managers.

Being able to distinguish between the "kind of correct" and "deceiving" pages is important to collection managers. So, why are the documents in the "deceiving pages" category created? Although the pages in this category are very diverse in content and presentation, they do share two characteristics. First, the number of links that point to other pages within the site is much greater than the number of out-links. On average, pages in the "deceiving" category had 66 links, which is more than twice the average in the "correct" and "kind of correct" categories (20 and 27 links respectively). And second, the domain names that host these pages once belonged to a reputable institution for number of years (i.e., a conference series) before being abandoned. Consequently, these abandoned domain names have value – not necessarily due to current network traffic but in the perception of their authority/validity. We could hypothesize that these pages are created to manipulate pageRank scores by utilizing a large number of links from a page that once had a high PageRank but has been taken over by a third party. This problem becomes increasingly interesting when we consider that the cost of creating a web page is small and that some search engines (most notably Google) do not share the overall rankings for their indexed sites, which can lead some parties to abuse these malicious techniques.

Our research focuses on investigating methods to detect unexpected changes in Web documents within a collection. However, the degree of change that we are focusing on falls within a specific range: not as subtle as a few terms substitutions in the body of a Web page and not as dramatic causing servers to report errors explicitly. Detecting the instances that fall between these two extreme cases is difficult and therefore requires the assistance of a classification system.

4. ACKNOWLEDGMENTS

This work was supported in part by National Science Foundation grants DUE–0840715 and DUE–1044212.

5. REFERENCES

[1] P. L. Bogen, R. Furuta, and F. Shipman, "A quantitative evaluation of techniques for detection of abnormal change events in blogs," presented at the Proceedings of the 12th ACM/IEEE-CS joint conference on Digital Libraries, Washington, DC, USA, 2012.

[2] P. Dave, U. P. Karadkar, R. Furuta, L. Francisco-Revilla, F. Shipman, S. Dash, *et al.*, "Browsing intricately interconnected paths," in *Proceedings of the fourteenth ACM conference on Hypertext and hypermedia - HYPERTEXT '03*, Nottingham, UK, 2003, pp. 95 - 103.

[3] L. Page, S. Brin, R. Motwani, and T. Winograd, "The PageRank citation ranking: Bringing order to the web," Stanford University1999.

[4] Z. Bar-Yossef, A. Z. Broder, R. Kumar, and A. Tomkins, "Sic transit gloria telae: towards an understanding of the web's decay," in *Proceedings of the 13th international conference on World Wide Web*, New York, NY, USA, 2004.

[5] L. Meneses, R. Furuta, and F. M. Shipman, "Identifying "Soft 404" Error Pages: Analyzing the Lexical Signatures of Documents in Distributed Collections," in *Proceedings of Theory and Practice of Digital Libraries 2012*, Paphos, Cyprus, 2012.

Automatically Generating a Concept Hierarchy with Graphs*

Pucktada Treeratpituk†
Ministry of Science and Technology
Bangkok, Thailand
pucktada@gmail.com

Madian Khabsa
Pennsylvania State University
University Park, PA, USA
madian@psu.edu

C. Lee Giles
Pennsylvania State University
University Park, PA, USA
giles@ist.psu.edu

ABSTRACT

We propose a novel graph-based approach for constructing concept hierarchy from a large text corpus. Our algorithm incorporates both statistical co-occurrences and lexical similarity in optimizing the structure of the taxonomy. To automatically generate topic-dependent taxonomies from a large text corpus, we first extracts topical terms and their relationships from the corpus. The algorithm then constructs a weighted graph representing topics and their associations. A graph partitioning algorithm is then used to recursively partition the topic graph into a taxonomy. For evaluation, we apply our approach to articles, primarily computer science, in the CiteSeerX digital library and search engine.

Categories and Subject Descriptors

H.3.3 [[**Information Storage and Retrieval**]: Information Search and Retrieval

1. INTRODUCTION

A taxonomy organizes concepts into a hierarchical structure, where broad concepts are at the top of the hierarchy and more specific concepts are further down. Large document collections are often organized into taxonomies, e.g. the Library of Congress and MEDLINE, because taxonomies enhance both search and browse features. In addition, a taxonomy also serves as a summary of a collection's content. Generally, taxonomies are manually created and maintained by domain experts, which is extremely time-consuming and costly. As a consequence, they are often incomplete and quickly become outdated, especially in a rapidly evolving domain like computer science. Thus, it is highly desirable to be able to generate taxonomies automatically.

There are two approaches to taxonomy generation: the query-independent approach, where one global taxonomy is constructed for the whole corpus , and the query-dependent approach, where a taxonomy is created for each query. Our approach present here focuses only on the query-dependent approach. Prior techniques used for automatic taxonomy generation can be grouped into three main categories: pattern-based, clustering-based, and knowledge source methods. Clustering-based methods hierarchically cluster topics based on similarity measures.

Our approach for taxonomy generation presented in this paper falls under the clustering-based methods. Specifically, we propose a novel graph-based algorithm, called GraBTax (Graph-Based Taxonomy Generation), for automatically constructing a query dependent taxonomy from a corpus. Our proposed algorithm has the following attractive characteristics. First, it incorporates both statistical co-occurrence and lexical similarity in determining the relationship between topics; the framework is also flexible enough to be extended to include other features. Second, the algorithm tries to construct a balanced taxonomy, where each topic is divided into distinct subtopics but of a similar generality level, though graph partitioning optimization. It also does not rely on any external knowledge sources. Thus, it could be easily applied to multiple domains. Furthermore, our algorithm can build a taxonomy from scratch, given a root node, because it automatically extracts the terms. For evaluation, we apply the algorithm to generate taxonomies for topics in computer science using papers from CiteSeer^X digital library.

2. TAXONOMY GENERATION

The GraBTax algorithm can be decomposed into three main parts: topic extraction, graph construction and topic-dependent taxonomy generation. The first two steps are carried out offline, while the last step is carried out at query-time on a per-query basis.

2.1 Extracting Topics

Our algorithm makes one strong assumption regarding the nature of the data. It assumes that given enough number of documents, any meaningful topic will appear in multiple times in the document titles. And vice versa, if a term/phrase does not appear in any titles, then it does not warrant being included in a taxonomy. To construct the set of candidate topics, first, the algorithm separately generates word-level bigrams, trigrams and quadgrams that appear at least 3 times in titles of papers in CiteSeerX. The list of bigrams, trigrams and fourgrams are then merged together to create one single list of ngrams. These are selected as candidate topics. For each topic pair, its co-occurrence within the document abstract is also computed.

2.2 Constructing the Topic Association Graph

Once we extract the set of topics and their co-occurrence, we then construct the topic association graph. The topic association graph is defined as an undirected weighted graph, $G = (T, E)$, where both vertices and edges have weights. Each topic t_i is a vertex in G ($\forall_i \; t_i \in T$). There exists an edge between the topic t_i and the topic t_j ($e_{ij} \in E$) if and only if t_i co-occurs with t_j in a document. Let the **strength** s_i denote the weight for the vertex t_i, where

*A longer version is available in [4]

†Work done while at PSU

JCDL'15, June 21–25, 2015, Knoxville, Tennessee, USA.
ACM 978-1-4503-3594-2/15/06.
http://dx.doi.org/10.1145/2756406.2756967.

s_i is computed as: $s_i = \sum_{e_{ij} \in E} count(t_i, t_j)$ where $count(t_i, t_j)$ is the number of documents that t_i and t_j co-occur in the title and document abstract. The strength of a topic, is simply the sum of all its co-occurrences representing that topic's importance. In addition to the strength measure, we also compute the degree for each vertex t_i, denoted by k_i, which is just the total number of edges associated with the vertex t_i.

Let w_{ij} be the weight of the edge e_{ij} between the topic t_i and the topic t_j. The weight w_{ij} depends not only on the co-occurrence between t_i and t_j, but also on their lexical similarity. More precisely, an edge weight w_{ij} is defined as:

$w_{ij} = 1 + \lambda_1 1_{(rank(t_i|t_j)=1 \text{ OR } rank(t_j|t_i)=1)} + \lambda_2 jac(t_i, t_j)] \times count(t_i, t_j)$

where

$1_{cond} = 1$ if *cond* is true, and 0 otherwise

$rank(t_i|t_j) = |\{ t_h \mid s_j < s_h \text{ and } Pr(t_h|t_j) > Pr(t_i|t_j) \}| + 1$

jac(t_i, t_j) = Jaccard similarity between t_i and t_j

$rank(t_i|t_j)$, the rank of t_i for t_j, is one plus the number of the topics with higher probability than t_i given t_j, not counting the topics that have lower strength than t_j. If t_i has the highest conditional probability given t_j, then the rank of t_i for t_j is 1. The relative weights to given each type of similarity (λ_1 and λ_2) are currently set heuristically.

2.3 Selecting the Topic-Specific Subgraph

Given a query topic t_0, first, a query-specific subgraph is selected from the topic association graph. This process determines which topics are to be included in the final taxonomy. Let $G_0 = (T_0, E_0)$ denote the topic-specific subgraph for the query t_0, the set of vertices (T_0) and edges (E_0) for the subgraph G_0 are defined as follow: $T_0 = \{ t_i \in T \mid rank(t_0|t_i) \leq r_{max} \text{ and } k_i \geq k_{min} \text{ and } s_i \geq s_{min} \}$ and $E_0 = \{ e_{ij} \in E \mid t_i, t_j \in T_0 \}$

The threshold constant k_{min} and s_{min} denote the minimum degree and the minimum strength of topics to be selected respectively. They regulate the specificity of topics to be included in a taxonomy. Lowering either k_{min} or s_{min} allows the taxonomy to include more specific concepts. Similarly, by increasing them, only broader topics will be included, resulting in a smaller taxonomy. On the other hand, the threshold r_{max} (the maximum rank) controls the relative-specificity with respect to the query topic t_0. With low value of r_{max}, only topics strongly related to the query topic will be included and vice versa. Also, note that the definition of $rank(t_0|t_i)$ permits that only the topics with lower strength than t_0 to be included in the subgraph for t_0.

2.4 Partitioning the Subgraph

Once the subgraph G_0 for the query topic t_0 is selected, the graph partitioning algorithm is applied to partition the subgraph into a taxonomy. First, all topics in the subgraph G_0, excluding the query topic, are divided into partitions. Within each partition, a topic vertex is selected to be the label of the partition. These label topics become the first-level subtopics of the query topic t_0 in the taxonomy. Then for each partition, all edges associated with its label topic are removed and the partition is further divided to generate the second-level subtopics. The partitioning is carried out recursively until a stopping criteria heuristic is met, which is when the number of topics in the partition is less than a minimum threshold or the intra-partition connectivity is zero.

The number of partitions at each level is determined by the number of vertices in the parent partition. Let $n(G')$ denote the number of sub-partitions to split a parent partition $G' = (T', E')$ into, then

$$n(G') = \begin{cases} \lfloor (|T'|/\beta) \rfloor & \text{if } |T'| < \alpha \\ \alpha/\beta & \text{otherwise} \end{cases}$$

Query Topic	#Topics	GraBTax		HAC
		P	SP	SP
computer graphics	200	0.88	0.68	0.42
information retrieval	200	0.90	0.72	0.48
artificial intelligence	185	0.77	0.63	0.46
semantic web	161	0.86	0.68	0.40
machine translation	128	0.97	0.71	0.44
social network	82	0.88	0.69	0.45
Average	159.33	0.88	0.69	0.44

Table 1: Precision (P) and Semantic Precision (SP) for each of the six query topics

where α and β are constants. In our implementation, $\alpha = 200$ and $\beta = 20$. GraBTax uses the multi-level graph partitioning algorithm, proposed in [3, 2], to find the optimal partitioning that minimizes the edge-cut while keeping the vertex strength balanced. After a topic is partitioned into multiple subtopic partitions, a topic from each partition is selected as its partition label. We pick the topic with the highest total connection to other topics in the same cluster to be the partition label.

3. EVALUATION

Two metrics are used to assess the quality of a taxonomy: Precision (P) and Semantic Precision (SP). ***Precision*** is defined as the number of relevant topics to the root divided by the total number of topics in the taxonomy. While ***Semantic Precision*** is equal to the number of relevant topics that are under their correct parents divided by the total number of topics in the taxonomy.

For evaluation, six well-known topics in computer science were selected to be the query topics. Since to manually evaluate the full taxonomy for each query topic would take too much time, we restrict the maximum number of topics in each taxonomy to be 200. The threshold r_{max}, k_{min} and s_{min} in the subgraph selection step are set as 3, 10, 20 respectively. The exact number of topics included for each query topic is shown in Table 1. All 6 taxonomies contain up to 5 levels of subtopics.

Three graduate students in computer science were asked to manually assess the relevancy and the semantic relevancy of each topic in all 6 taxonomies produced by GraBTax. Their assessments are then averaged and are used to compute Precision and Semantic Precision for each taxonomy. In addition, we also make a comparison with a hierarchal agglomerative clustering method (HAC) as the baseline approach, similar to [1]. Precision and Semantic Precision for both GraBTax and HAC are shown in Table 1. Since HAC uses the set of topics generated by GraBTax as the input, the Precision values are the same as GraBTax's. In general, the Precision values are quite high for all queries, implying that most topics in the generated taxonomies are relevant to the query topic.

4. REFERENCES

[1] T. Fountain and M. Lapata. Taxonomy induction using hierarchical random graphs. In *NAACL HLT*, pages 466–476. ACL, 2012.

[2] G. Karypis and V. Kumar. Multilevel algorithms for multi-constraint graph partitioning. *Proceedings of the 1998 ACM/IEEE conference on Supercomputing (CDROM)*.

[3] G. Karypis and V. Kumar. A fast and high quality multilevel scheme for partitioning irregular graphs. *SIAM Journal on Scientific Computing*, Jan 1999.

[4] P. Treeratpituk, M. Khabsa, and C. L. Giles. Graph-based approach to automatic taxonomy generation (grabtax). *arXiv preprint arXiv:1307.1718*, 2013.

Taxonomy Induction and Taxonomy-based Recommendations for Online Courses

Shuo Yang, Yansong Feng*, Lei Zou, Aixia Jia, Dongyan Zhao
ICST, Peking University, Beijing, China
yangshuo1991, fengyansong, zoulei, jiaaixia, zhaodongyan@pku.edu.cn

ABSTRACT
Taxonomy is a useful and ubiquitous way to organize knowledge. As online education attracting more and more attention, organizing lecture notes or exercises, from different online sources, in a more structured form has become an effective way to navigate users to better access course materials. However, it is expensive and time consuming to manually annotate large amounts of corpora to build a detailed taxonomy. In this paper, we propose a taxonomy induction framework with limited human involvement. We also show that the constructed taxonomy can be used to improve lecture notes/exercises recommendations.

Keywords
Online Education; Knowledge Concepts; Term Extraction; Taxonomy Induction; Personalized Recommendation.

1. INTRODUCTION
Recent years have witnessed of rapid development of online education. It would be of great convenience and importance for users, if cross-sourced resources (e.g., lecture notes/exercises) can be correlated and better organized, e.g., in a form of taxonomy. Especially, a detailed taxonomy and organized multi-sourced course materials will provide users an overview of the concepts, or even personalized recommendations.

However, it is impossible to perform it process manually, which is expensive and time consuming. In literature, terms extraction problem is usually solved via human created patterns [1], but when it comes to Chinese, expressions are more complex and hard to capture. There are work [1] concerning taxonomy induction based on manual patterns, which can cover only a small proportion of complex linguistic phenomena. Fu and Guo [2] proposed a method to learn taxonomy structure via word embedding. This method needs lots of hierarchical links as its training data. In our situation, hierarchical information is limited.

In this paper, we propose a term extraction approach, an unsupervised taxonomy induction method and a novel bottom-up approach to recommend lecture notes/exercises for knowledge concepts. We illustrate our system in figure 1.

2. METHOD
2.1 Task Definition
Given a subject, our task is to construct taxonomy for this subject. We choose ***English Grammar for Junior School (in Chinese)*** as our target subject. Additionally, we design a taxonomy based recommendation algorithm to provide resources recommendations.

JCDL'15, June 21–25, 2015, Knoxville, Tennessee, USA.
ACM 978-1-4503-3594-2/15/06.
http://dx.doi.org/10.1145/2756406.2756968

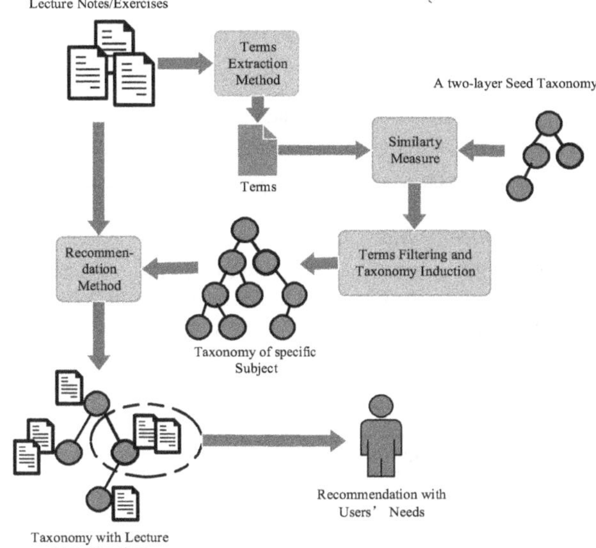

Figure 1: Framework of our algorithm

2.2 Terms Extraction
Traditional pattern based terms extraction method is often of low recall in Chinese, however, sequence labeling methods provide an ideal way to capture complex linguistic phenomena in Chinese. We label the lecture notes automatically by making use of terms extracted from a course syllabus. This paper use the BIO scheme to prepare the training data, which represents that the current word is at the beginning, inside or out of a term, respectively. We use Conditional Random Field (CRFs) [3] to solve this problem.

2.3 Taxonomy Induction
2.3.1 Adding Sub-Concepts
If a term is a hyponym of another, there are two kinds of linguistic phenomena:

a. Surface coverage: in Chinese terminology, hyponyms are often the sub-sequence of their hypernyms. The similarity of the surface coverage of term x and y is represented as $e(x,y)$.
b. Pointwise Mutual Information: a hyponym usually appears in the same paragraph with its hypernym. We uses PMI(x ,y) to measure the likelihood that term x is the sub-concept of term y. The probability is defined as:

$$s_1(x,y) = \frac{e(x,y) + PMI(x,y)}{2}$$

*Yansong Feng is the corresponding author.

2.3.2 Adding Sibling Concepts

The similarity of terms can be measured by the cosine similarity of their semantic vectors. Sibling concepts may appear in the similar contexts. The likelihood is defined as:

$$s_2(x,y) = \frac{\sum_{k \in U_y} vector(x) \cdot vector(y)}{|U_y|}$$

In this formula, $vector(x)$ is the word embedding representation [4] of term x. U_y is the sub-concepts set of term y.

2.3.3 Scoring

Combining the two aspects mentioned above, we define the probability that term x is the hyponym of term y:

$$hypo(x,y) = \alpha_y s_1(x,y) + \beta_y s_2(x,y)$$

where α_y and β_y are automatically adjustable, when the taxonomy grows larger, the sibling relation weights higher than hierarchical relation and vice versa, where $\alpha_y = \frac{b}{|U_y|+b}$, $\beta_y = 1 - \alpha_y$.

2.3.4 Taxonomy Induction

We calculate the most probable hypernym for each term, add the term with the highest probability to taxonomy. If the hyponym-hypernym probability hypo(x, y) of term x and its most probable hypernym y is below a threshold θ, we discard it. Then we re-calculate the likelihood of the remaining terms, until there is no term remaining. Our algorithm is described as Algorithm 1.

Algorithm 1 Taxonomy Induction

```
Input:
  The remaining terms set R which is not on taxonomy.
  The terms set T in present taxonomy.
While R≠∅
  For each x ∈ R, y ∈ T
    Calculate hypo(x, y).
    Find x's most probable hypernym hyper(x).
  For each x ∈ R
    Find x with the highest hypo(x, hyper(x)).
  If hypo(x, hyper(x)) ≥ θ
    Add x to T, as a sub-concept of hyper(x).
  Else discard x from R.
```

2.4 Taxonomy-based Recommendations

In this section, we propose an algorithm to recommend lecture notes/exercises for each concept. We use TF-IDF algorithm to measure the importance of each concept. When recommending lecture notes/exercises, a concept appears in this note describes itself as well as its ancestor-concepts (described in Algorithm 2).

3. EXPERIMENTS

3.1 Methodology

We evaluate the quality of taxonomy directly. Two judges are asked to label {30, 50, 100} links samples uniformly generated from the top {50, 200, 500} links, according to their confidences, added by our method.

Then we recommend the lecture notes/exercises based on the knowledge concepts. And ask judges to grade the results.

3.2 Taxonomy Evaluation

We categorize links suggested by our system into four categories: C1, correct links; C2, missing interlayer concept; C3, one-step errors, suggest two sibling concepts or reverse the relation; C4, incorrect relation. C2 and C3 indicate that the algorithm suggests some links inappropriate but correlative. We use |C1|/|C| to calculate the precision, |C1+C2+C3|/|C| to evaluate the relevance precision. Our method outperforms the three baselines, including method only consider PMI, surface coverage or semantic similarity (table 1 and table 2). The taxonomy is shown on http://59.108.48.28/taxonomy.html.

Algorithm 2 Taxonomy-based Recommendation

```
Input:
  Lecture note/exercise NE.
  Taxonomy T.
  A decay factor 0 ≤ σ < 1.
Find out terms list L appear in NE.
For each x ∈ T  Set Value(x) = 0.
For each x ∈ L
  Calculate TF-IDF(x).
  Value(x) = Value(x)+TF-IDF(x).
  Find ancestors set A={a_1, a_2, ...} of x in taxonomy, a_i is the i-step ancestor of x.
  For each a_i ∈ A
    Value(a_i) = Value(a_i) +σ^i ×TF-IDF(x).
Sort T by the Value function, choose the top k concepts, and match NE to them.
```

#Link	PMI	Edit	Semantic	E+S+PMI
50	0.3	0.37	0.27	0.77
150	0.28	0.34	0.26	0.66
500	0.24	0.3	0.19	0.54

Table 1: Precision compared with baselines.

#Links	PMI	Edit	Semantic	E+S+PMI
50	0.53	0.5	0.5	0.87
150	0.68	0.46	0.44	0.86
500	0.54	0.42	0.42	0.81

Table 2: Relevance precision compared with baselines.

3.3 Recommendations Evaluation

For further estimation, we recommend lecture notes/exercises for each concept and compare our model with the conventional TF-IDF method. We pick out 50 terms randomly and show the notes/exercises recommended to the judges, and ask them to score our recommendations from 1 to 3 (shown in table 3).

Method	Score	Proportion of 3 scores
TF-IDF	1.83	0.25
Our Method	2.57	0.7

Table 3: Recommendation results comparison.

Acknowledgement

This work was supported by National High-Tech R&D Program (No.2015AA015403) and NSFC under Grant No. 61370055, 61202233, 61272344.

4. REFERENCES

[1] Zornitsa Kozareva and Eduard Hovy. A semi-supervised method to learn and construct taxonomies using the web. *In Proceedings of EMNLP 2010*, pages 1110–1118.

[2] Fu R, Guo J, Qin B, et al. Learning semantic hierarchies via word embedding. *In Proceedings of ACL*, volume 1.

[3] Lafferty J, McCallum A, Pereira F C N. Conditional random fields: Probabilistic models for segmenting and labeling sequence data. *In Proceedings of ICML*, pp. 282–289, 2001.

[4] Mikolov T, Chen K, Corrado G, et al. Efficient estimation of word representations in vector space, *arXiv preprint arXiv:1301.3781*, 2013.

Analyzing User Requests for Anime Recommendations

Jin Ha Lee, Yuna Shim
University of Washington
Mary Gates Hall, Suite 370
Seattle, WA 98195
+1 206.685.0153
jinhalee@uw.edu, yunas@uw.edu

Jacob Jett
Center for Informatics Research in Science & Scholarship
Graduate School of Library & Information Science
501 E. Daniel St., Champaign, IL 61820
+1 217.244.2164
jjett2@illinois.edu

ABSTRACT

Anime is increasingly becoming recognized as an important commercial product and cultural artifact. However, little is known regarding users' information needs and behavior related to anime. This study specifically attempts to improve our understanding of how people seek anime recommendations. We analyzed 546 user questions in natural language, collected from a Korean Q&A website Naver Knowledge-iN, where users are asking for anime recommendations. The findings suggest the importance of establishing robust metadata for the seven commonly used features for anime recommenders (i.e., title, genre, artistic style, story, character description, series title, and mood) in digital libraries, as well as allowing users to specify known anime and series titles as examples for seeking similar items, or examples of the kinds of items to be excluded.

Categories and Subject Descriptors

H.3.7 Digital Libraries: User Issues; H.5.1 Multimedia Information Systems: Animations

General Terms

Human Factors.

Keywords

Anime; User; Recommendation; Metadata.

1. INTRODUCTION

Anime (i.e., Japanese Animation) emerged from Japan's strong heritage of comics in the 1960s and has been part of mainstream Japanese culture since the 1970s. Its global popularity has been gradually increasing [10], owing to successful filmmakers such as Miyazaki Hayao and steady penetration into broadcast marketplaces (e.g., Cartoon Network's Toonami). As anime's user base is continuing to grow in the global market, it is important to provide users from different regions and cultures with efficient ways to seek anime information to facilitate the discovery of new titles. However, little research has been done on cross-cultural users' information needs or seeking behavior around anime. Therefore we do not have enough empirical user data to derive design requirements for an effective anime recommender with cross-cultural considerations, resulting in reduced discoverability.

This study attempts to address this gap and aims to improve our understanding on cross-cultural anime users' information needs and behavior, in particular, when they seek recommendations. We specifically seek to answer the following research question: Which information features do people describe and how do they describe them when seeking anime recommendations?

JCDL'15, June 21–25, 2015, Knoxville, TN, USA.
ACM 978-1-4503-3594-2/15/06.
http://dx.doi.org/10.1145/2756406.2756969

2. BACKGROUND AND PRIOR WORK

Anime is a rich and complex form of multimedia, consisting of various components such as images, sound, speech and text [7]. Although there are a number of studies focusing on organization of and access to movies (e.g., [2],[8]), anime, as a cross-cultural information resource, is different from conventional movies in terms of genres, characters, and content, and thus poses unique search/discovery challenges for users. Among these challenges are:

- exact title (*Shingeki no Kyojin* vs. *Attack on Titan*),
- names of cast members,
- unique genres (e.g., *スーパーロボット (Super Robot)*), and
- cross-medium visual styles (e.g., shōnen, shōjo)

Previous studies on multimedia information retrieval systems and their users found that user queries tend to be shorter and less formulated than queries in traditional information retrieval systems because of the lack of web searching mechanisms and representational congruity [4]. This may also be the case for anime related queries. For this reason, rather than attempting to analyze search queries in a particular anime website(s), we chose to collect users' natural language questions from relevant Q&A websites. Several prior studies have successfully analyzed and utilized user questions for automatic classification of queries [3], to understand users' motivations for participation [9], and to investigate how they seek music information [6]. We also chose to analyze online user questions rather than observe how they conduct an artificial search task in an experimental setting in order to understand how they behave in a real-life search setting.

3. STUDY DESIGN AND METHOD

Content analysis of user questions was adopted as the main method for this research [5]. The user questions were collected from Naver Knowledge-iN, the largest online Q&A community in South Korea. Naver limits the number of questions that are viewable, and thus we mined the maximum number of questions retrievable using a combination of keywords such as 애니, 애니메이션, 추천 (anime, animation, recommend(ation)). A total of 1,326 questions were collected in 2013, and we manually filtered out the irrelevant questions that were not seeking anime recommendations (e.g., known-item searches). After examination, 546 were deemed relevant. A typical question looks like: "I am looking for fantasy action anime, over 50 episodes with a bright tone (unlike *D.Gray-man* or *Black Butler*)." All the examples of user questions presented here are translated by the first author who is fluent in both English and Korean.

The questions in the dataset were coded over 11 months through an iterative process of coding sub-samples and refining the codebook. In order to test the intercoder reliability of the features, two coders independently coded 100 queries based on the revised codebook. The coded data were transformed into a binary representation based on the absence (0) and presence (1) of each feature, and Krippendorff's alpha-coefficient was calculated. The global alpha-coefficient value of all features was .81 exceeding the minimum value of .8 to be considered reliable [5].

4. RESULTS AND DISCUSSION

4.1 Features of Anime in Users' Questions

In total, 13 features of anime were identified in more than five questions. Table 1 shows the features with their definition, count of questions containing each feature, and percentage over the number of questions. The number of features commonly used was relatively small; users tended to heavily rely on a handful of top ranked features. Anime title was the most frequently used term, and series title was also commonly used. Several features describing the content of anime such as genre, style, story, character description, and mood were also highly ranked. The other six features were used in less than five percent of all questions. The "other" category included features like person or corporate names, availability of anime, edition information, etc.

Table 1. Features of anime mentioned in user questions

Feature	Description	#	%
title	Name of anime titles	294	53.85
genre	Genre/theme of the anime	193	35.35
style	Description of artistic style of the anime	83	15.20
story	Story, narrative, or plot of the anime	73	13.37
character description	Characters' personalities or traits portrayed in the anime	59	10.81
series	Name of anime series	52	9.52
mood	Overall tone or atmosphere of the anime	47	8.61
audience	Intended audience of the anime	26	4.76
temporal information	Specific year or a range of years when the anime is published	19	3.48
length	Number of episodes (for TV series) or running time (for movies)	18	3.30
scene	Description of a specific kind of scene wanted (e.g., hot spring scene, kiss scene)	13	2.38
character-name	Names of specific anime characters (e.g., Naruto, Lelouch)	8	1.47
format	Distribution medium of the anime	8	1.47
other	Other characteristics	10	1.83

Among the lessons derived from the results of this study, relevant to the development of an anime recommendation service are:

1) similarity-based relationships among anime titles are extremely important to users
2) narrative genre-labels, theme-labels, and mood terms vary considerably across cultures creating a complex topical landscape for users to navigate (e.g., unique terms like 먼치킨 (munchkin), 백합 (baekhap))
3) artistic style of anime is prominently featured in user questions, yet its description tends to be generic, and
4) descriptions of overall story/narrative or specific characters are also commonly used (e.g., *"protagonist's talent gets noticed by a renowned person…and everyone else gets jealous"*)

4.2 Other Contextual Information

In addition to the information features of anime found in questions, context particular to each user was prominently featured in many of the questions. These questions included qualitative information such as: personal tastes and contextual information about themselves (appeared in 163 questions), reaction (appeared in 102 questions), criteria for exclusion (appeared in 140 questions), and instructions for recommenders (e.g., provide images or short summaries) (appeared in 112 questions).

5. CONCLUSION

The findings of our analysis of 546 user questions suggest that there is a need for robust metadata that better captures and describes anime content features such as genre, artistic style, story, character types, and mood. Such metadata would support a more well-rounded recommendation service that improves users' abilities to expand their queries beyond known-title searching strategies. While users have a deep and descriptive understanding of genre and mood labels, the vocabulary used to express artistic styles remains simple and their information needs were frequently more qualitative and contextually sensitive than ordinary library metadata and recommenders services typically support (e.g., their personal tastes). In our future work, we plan to establish user-centered taxonomies of genre, mood, and trope based on the description given in user questions so that it can be used to facilitate discovery of anime in digital libraries. We also plan to conduct semi-structured interviews to learn more about how users seek and evaluate anime recommendations, involving users from different cultural backgrounds to identify any cross-cultural differences or challenges that may exist.

6. REFERENCES

[1] Bloch, D. A. and Kraemer, H. C. 1989. 2x2 kappa coefficients: measures of agreement or association. *Biometrics,* 45, 269-287.

[2] Cameron, A. 2010. Approaches to cataloguing moving image: some practical experiences. *Catalogue & Index*, 159, 2-4.

[3] Harper, F. M., Moy, D. and Konstan, J. A. 2009. Facts or friends?: distinguishing informational and conversational questions in social Q&A sites. In *Proc. CHI,* ACM, 759-768.

[4] Jansen, B. J., Goodrum, A. and Spink, A. 2000. Searching for multimedia: analysis of audio, video and image Web queries. World Wide Web 3, 4, 249-254.

[5] Krippendorff, K. 2004. *Content analysis: an introduction to its methodology*. Sage, Thousand Oaks, CA.

[6] Lee, J. H. 2010. Analysis of user needs and information features in natural language queries seeking music information. *JASIST,* 61, 5, 1025-1045.

[7] Maghrebi, H. and David, A. 2006. Toward a model for the representation of multimedia information based on users' needs: economic intelligence approach. In *Proceedings of m-ICTE*, 195-200.

[8] Martins, P., Langlois, T. and Chambel, T. 2011. MovieClouds: content-based overviews and exploratory browsing of movies. In *Proc. MindTrek '11,* ACM, 133-140.

[9] Nam, K. K., Ackerman, M. S. and Adamic, L. A. 2009. Questions in, knowledge in?: a study of Naver's question answering community. In *Proc. CHI*, ACM, 779-788.

[10] Poitras, G. 2008. Contemporary anime in Japanese pop culture. In *Japanese visual culture: Explorations in the world of manga and anime*. M.E. Sharpe, Armonk, N.Y.

Computationally Supported Collection-level Descriptions in Large Heterogeneous Metadata Aggregations

Unmil P. Karadkar
Karen Wickett
School of Information
The University of Texas at Austin
1616 Guadalupe St. Ste. 5.202
Austin, TX 78701-1213 USA
+1-512-471-9292
{unmil,wickett}@ischool.utexas.edu

Madhura Parikh
Department of Computer Science
The University of Texas at Austin
2317 Speedway, Stop D9500
Austin, TX 78712
mparikh@cs.utexas.edu

Richard Furuta, Joshua Sheehy
Meghanath Reddy Junnutula
Jeremy Tzou
Department of CSE and Center for the Study of Digital Libraries
Texas A&M University
College Station, TX 77843
+1-979-845-3839
furuta@cse.tamu.edu

ABSTRACT
The Computational Collection Description project is developing mechanisms for generating field-specific collection-level descriptors from item values. Using the Digital Public Library of America (DPLA) as a sample data set, we describe a flexible, extensible architecture for processing field-level values, an augmented Collection class to record the generated metadata, and our early results of enhancements for a DPLA collection.

Categories and Subject Descriptors
H.3.7 [**Information Storage and Retrieval**]: Digital Libraries – *collection, systems issues;* H.2.1 [**Database Management**]: Logical Design – *data models.*

General Terms
Algorithms, Design, Experimentation.

Keywords
Computational collection descriptions; collection-level metadata; field propagation rules.

1. INTRODUCTION
Large metadata aggregations have come of age with high-visibility examples such as the Digital Public Library of America (DPLA, http://dp.la) and Europeana (http://www.europeana.eu/). These Web portals enable their audience to access cultural heritage materials belonging to large and small institutions. While the contributing institutions organize their holdings in collections and report the collection membership to these aggregators, the item-centric portal interfaces do not display the collection details. In addition to providing context, collection-level metadata serves a range of functions including assessment of item relevance, presenting information about the host institution, managing search results [8], and facilitating collection interoperability [3].

The Computational Collection Descriptions (CCD) project is developing mechanisms for enhancing collection metadata from item-level values. Our modular architecture supports the development of customized pipelines for processing field-specific values such as subjects and dates. The generated metadata is stored locally using a DPLA-compatible data model with the intention of providing access to this data to the DPLA user community.

JCDL '15, June 21–25, 2015, Knoxville, Tennessee, USA.
ACM 978-1-4503-3594-2/15/06.
http://dx.doi.org/10.1145/2756406.2756970

2. COMPUTATIONAL COLLECTION DESCRIPTIONS
Archives, libraries, and museums differ in their approaches toward describing collection-level metadata [6]. Archives have a long history of developing rich collection descriptions, articulating collection provenance, acquisition and processing, scope, size, subjects, and organization through finding aids [1]. In contrast, DPLA only harvests item-level metadata from providers, whether these are archives, libraries or museums. Collection-level metadata is harvested only when included as a part of item metadata. Processed metadata is made available via a RESTful application programming interface (API) as JSON-LD in order to facilitate third-party application development. The DPLA hosts objects belonging to over 1,300 institutions, contributed via 29 hubs. In spite of collection fields being optional in the DPLA metadata application profile (MAP) and minimally described via titles and a free-text description [2], the aggregation expresses over 10,000 collections with item membership ranging between a few items and over 250,000, thus highlighting the significance of collection-level descriptions for data providers.

While the contributing institutions are better positioned to provide authoritative collection-level metadata, these organizations are already stretched thin and do not possess the resources to provide additional details [7]. In light of this reality, the CCD project is exploring semi-automatic mechanisms for generating collection-level metadata, focusing on the following research directions:

- generating collection-level data using item metadata
- assessing the quality of generated collection-level data
- enhancing digital aggregations with collection-level metadata
- supporting collection managers in developing rich, informative descriptions

We aim to generate metadata that corresponds to a collection's scope, size, and subjects. Our approach is designed to be robust enough to harness data of varying quality both in terms of density (number of available values) as well as the formats used for encoding these values (for example, dates expressed as m/d/y or d-m-y). We adopt established processing methods from domains such as information retrieval, geo-spatial information systems (GIS), and adapt these when demanded by the nature of our document corpus.

Figure 1 illustrates the CCD architecture. DPLA items express collection membership using the collection's unique id. Our architecture employs flexible, incremental development of field-specific processing pipelines. Each pipeline follows similar steps, which include extraction and aggregation of values in particular fields. These aggregated values serve as the source data for deriving collection-level values, which are stored in the Collection Description. While the sequence of operations is identical for the three pipelines shown in figure 1, the specifics of processing within each deriver are data-dependent, and hence distinct from each other. For example, collection-level dates include the earliest and latest values, signifying the temporal coverage of the collection, subject values include clusters generated by k-means clustering, and the spatial pipeline includes a rule for retrieving the geographic boundaries of the collection. In addition to those described here, new rules can be developed to enhance the deriver capabilities. Each new rule generates a collection-level value, which is stored in the extended Collection class.

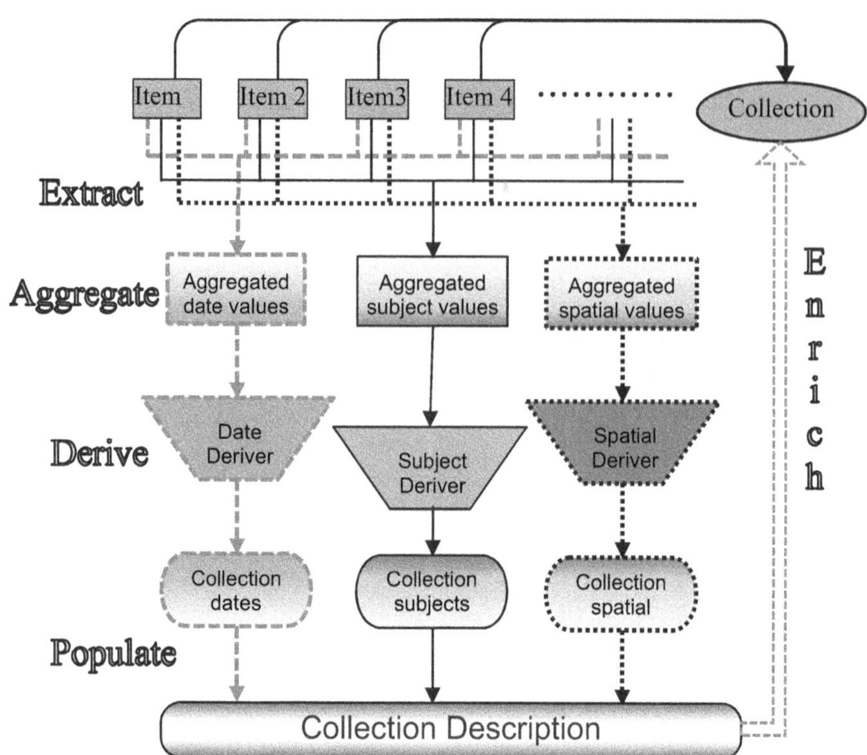

Figure 1. Computational collection description system architecture.

The extensions to the Collection class are designed to be consistent with the DPLA MAP and are stored in the collectionResource object, which parallels item-level the sourceResource object at the item level. Sample extensions to this class include Begin date (.collectionResource.date.begin), Subjects (.collectionResource. subjects), and Geographic boundaries (collectionResource.spatial. boundary). Our extensions to the DPLA Collection class are based on well-known schema elements wherever possible. For example, the Geographic Convex Boundary and subjects map to corresponding properties in DCMI terms, while the date properties map to elements in the Europeana data model. While the generated data is currently stored locally, we hope to integrate our collection-level descriptions with those of the DPLA's, indicated by the enrichment operation in figure 1.

3. CONCLUSION

We have presented a flexible, extensible architecture and the early results of our approach for generating field-specific collection-level metadata from corresponding item-level values with the twin goals of enhancing the infrastructure available for humanities scholarship and improving the visibility of smaller but stronger collections in large aggregations. As our mechanism processes existing metadata, the outcomes are strongly dependent on the quality and volume of the base metadata. Our brief experience with using the DPLA data has yielded surprising results in terms of the variation in data formats as well as data density. One collection contained 35 different date formats (id: 3f0e282f7fed21d7790fce877faf11d7). While this collection will help us enrich our date filters, such variety highlights issues of data consistency in the DPLA's corpus.

Efforts of data providers, hubs—such as the North Carolina Digital Heritage Center—and the DPLA are focused on streamlining the ingestion pipeline [4,5]. However, the DPLA's freely available API enables external developers to create tools that augment this rich and varied data set.

4. ACKNOWLEDGMENTS

Research support: Temple Teaching Fellowship by the iSchool at UT Austin; Mark Matienzo and Gretchen Gueguen, DPLA; System development: Nan Guo, Ruoying Li, Jiexian Li, and Zeyuan Zhu.

5. REFERENCES

1. Bourdon, F., Catapano, T., McDonough, J., et al. EAD 2002 Schema - EAD Official Site. 2002. http://www.loc.gov/ead/eadschema.html.
2. Digital Public Library of America. Metadata Application Profile, Version 3.1. 2014. http://dp.la/info/wp-content/uploads/2013/04/DPLA-MAP-V3.1-2.pdf.
3. Dunn, H. Collection Level Description - the Museum Perspective. *D-Lib Magazine 6*, 2000. http://www.dlib.org/dlib/september00/dunn/09dunn.html.
4. Gregory, L. and Williams, S. On Being a Hub: Some Details behind Providing Metadata for the Digital Public Library of America. *D-Lib Magazine 20*, 2014. http://www.dlib.org/dlib/july14/gregory/07gregory.html.
5. Matienzo, M. and Rudersdorf, A. The Digital Public Library of America Ingestion Ecosystem: Lessons Learned After One Year of Large-Scale Collaborative Metadata Aggregation. *2014 Proc. Intl. Conf. on Dublin Core and Metadata Applications*, Dublin Core Metadata Initative (2014), 12–21.
6. Miller, P. Collected Wisdom: Some Cross-domain Issues of Collection Level Description. *D-Lib Magazine 6*, 2009. http://www.dlib.org/dlib/september00/miller/09miller.html.
7. Sweet, M. and Thomas, D. Archives Described at Collection Level. *D-Lib Magazine 6*, 2000. http://www.dlib.org/dlib/september00/sweet/09sweet.html.
8. Wickett, K., Issac, A., Doerr, M., Fenlon, K., Meghini, C., and Palmer, C. Representing Cultural Collections in Digital Aggregation and Exchange Environments. *D-Lib Magazine 20*, 2014. http://www.dlib.org/dlib/may14/wickett/05wickett.html.

Read Between the Lines: A Machine Learning Approach for Disambiguating the Geo-location of Tweets

Sunshin Lee Mohamed Farag Tarek Kanan Edward A. Fox

Digital Library Research Laboratory
Department of Computer Science
Virginia Tech, Blacksburg, VA 24061
{sslee777, mmagdy, tarekk, fox}@vt.edu

ABSTRACT

This paper describes a Machine Learning (ML) approach for extracting named entities and disambiguating the location of tweets based on those named entities and related content. We conducted experiments with tweets (e.g., about potholes), and found significant improvement in disambiguating tweet locations using a ML algorithm along with the Stanford NER. Adding state information predicted by our classifiers increases the possibility to find the state-level geo-location unambiguously by up to 80%.

Categories and Subject Descriptors

H.2.8 [**Database Management**]: Database applications-Data mining; J.4 [Computer Application]: Social and Behavioral Sciences; H.3.7 [Digital Libraries]: Collection

General Terms

Algorithms, Measurement, and Experimentation.

Keywords

Digital Library; Disambiguation; Geospatial Information; Machine Learning; Microtext; Named Entity Recognition

1. INTRODUCTION

Geospatial information has become more significant due to an increased usage of mobile devices such as smartphones and tablets, as well as micro-blogging services such as Twitter.

Some researchers use tweets as a human or social sensor for event detection, for example finding an earthquake's location [1], estimating a typhoon's trajectory [1], or detecting a water main break [5]. Some researchers extract knowledge such as person, organization, date, location, etc. from web documents [2]. Martins et al. [4] disambiguate location by estimating the distance between the true geospatial location and candidate geospatial locations. A content-based approach to geo-locating Twitter users was proposed by Cheng et al. [3]. They used a language model to identify the city-level location based on the content of the user's tweets, even in the absence of any other geospatial cues, placing 51% of Twitter users within 100 miles of their actual location.

JCDL'15, June 21–25, 2015, Knoxville, Tennessee, USA.
ACM 978-1-4503-3594-2/15/06.
http://dx.doi.org/10.1145/2756406.2756971

In order to determine the location corresponding to each event it is crucial to unambiguously geotag each tweet. However, finding a tweet's location is a difficult task: 1) Most users prefer to provide geospatial information by stating it in the contents of the tweet rather than lose privacy by enabling GPS (latitude, longitude) information. 2) When people communicate, they may not mention what they already know. To overcome these problems, we determine tweet locations through analysis of geospatial named entities (geonames). Our intuition is that implicit information such as the state location name of a tweet may help to minimize the ambiguity of the tweet's location.

Our main approach is introduced in Section 2. In Section 3, we present our dataset and experimental results.

2. DISAMBIGUATING GEO-LOCATION OF TWEETS

Geonames are found through geospatial name extraction from preprocessed tweets using a named entity recognizer (NER). Using the extracted geonames, a ML algorithm predicts the tweet's implicit state location and adds it to the tweet's list of geonames. Combined information (geonames and predicted state) is sent to the geocoding API to get the location of the tweet.

To find a geo-location for a tweet, we extract location information from a tweet's text. We used a state-of-the-art NER: Stanford NER version 3.4.0 with its default 3-class (location, person, and organization) model trained on the CoNLL dataset.

To predict the implicit location of a tweet using ML, we built training and testing datasets for an ML algorithm. We used Weka to build and apply our classifier. Building a good training dataset is essential when applying an ML algorithm. We tried to find an automated way to build a training dataset, and we realized that we could get an unambiguous geo-location if we have complete location information. After sending geonames extracted from a tweet's text to a geocoding API, we receive a list of possible locations in return. We can build a training dataset using just those geonames, so we have unambiguous geo-location pairs. Multi-class classification for 51 classes is a difficult problem. Therefore we transformed the multi-class (or multinomial) classification problem into a binary class classification problem. The training set for each state is created using extracted geonames as a feature and geo-coded location (state name) as a target class (target state and others).

With geonames extracted from tweet text and implicit state information predicted by a classifier based on those geonames, we can find a tweet location by sending to the geocoding API, which can return both formatted addresses and geographic coordinates.

3. EXPERIMENTS

3.1 Dataset

To collect data from Twitter.com, we used *yourTwapperKeeper*[1], which is an open source tool for collecting tweets. For our experiment, we selected a dataset (keyword: Pothole). The pothole dataset has 324,849 tweets from 2013-04-02 to 2014-06-25. We removed the re-tweets: all tweets starting with 'RT' (113,430); there were 211,419 tweets remaining.

To extract geospatial named entities from tweet text, we used Stanford NER and finally had 37,129 tweets that have geographical named entities out of 211,419 non-RT tweets. After sending geonames to the Google Geocoding API, we found 12,918 (34.8%) tweets that have unambiguous geo-location (returned one geo-location only) and 24,211 (65.2%) tweets that have ambiguous geo-locations (returned more than one geo-locations) or foreign geo-location.

With the tweets (12,918) that have unambiguous geo-location, we built a training dataset for 50 states (plus Washington D.C.) in the U.S.A. The states with more than 1,000 tweets are Illinois (IL, 1,765), Michigan (MI, 1,644), New York (NY, 1,194), and Pennsylvania (1,138). An average state has 253 tweets. The median is 93 while the minimum is 7 (for New Mexico).

To build a testing dataset, we selected the 3 most frequent states: Illinois, New York, and Pennsylvania. After selecting 804 tweets randomly for testing, from ambiguous tweets where their geo-location could be Illinois, New York, or Pennsylvania, we tagged the correct state label manually for each tweet instead of ambiguous (multiple) states of geo-locations. In this experiment, we also used the top frequent states, PA (114), IL (57), and NY (23) for testing. We ignored MI (117), MA (48) since most of their tweets come from pothole reporting systems (MI: Grand Rapids, and MA: Boston).

To evaluate the quality of a tweet's location, we used precision, recall, and F1 measures to evaluate our classifier. The precision measures how many of the geo-locations that an algorithm finds are correct, while recall measures how many of the correct geo-locations are found. The F1 measure aims for balance between precision and recall.

3.2 Location Disambiguation

Using extracted geoname as a feature and geo-location (state name) as a target class, we trained a state classifier. We used 3 ML classifiers, Support Vector Machine (SVM), Naïve Bayes (NB), and Random Forest (RF).

With 10-fold cross validation, we measured precision, recall, and F1. Note that all measures are only for each state, not for the other class. SVM and RF show good performance on all measures for all states (0.985~0.999). On the other hand, NB shows good performance on precision (0.994~1.000), poor on recall (0.493~0.816), and moderate on F1 (0.660~0.899).

We also predicted implicit state information from geonames using SVM, NB, and RF. Table 1 reports the precision, recall, and F1 on the test (unseen) dataset using 3 ML classifiers for 3 states.

[1] https://github.com/540co/yourTwapperKeeper

Table 1. Results for 3 states on test datasets

ML	Measure	PA	IL	NY
Dataset	# of tweets	114	57	23
SVM	Precision	0.978	0.667	0.545
	Recall	**0.798**	**0.737**	**0.261**
	F1	0.879	0.700	0.353
NB	Precision	1.000	0.933	1.000
	Recall	**0.456**	**0.246**	**0.087**
	F1	0.627	0.389	0.160
RF	Precision	0.989	0.764	0.750
	Recall	**0.798**	**0.737**	**0.130**
	F1	0.883	0.750	0.222

Note that all measures are only for each state, not for the other class. For the PA and IL datasets, NB and RF show good performance on all measures, but NB is not good on recall on the PA dataset and poor on the IL dataset. For the NY dataset (with only 23 tweets), all classifiers show poor performance on recall.

We can find tweet locations by sending those enriched geonames to the Google Geocoding API. We then received formatted addresses including state name from the geocoding API. According to Table 1, recall for PA using RF is 0.798, which means it finds about 80% more (out of 114 tweets) by adding predicted state information to ambiguous geonames.

4. CONCLUSION

Our experiments showed significant improvement in disambiguating tweet's locations using the ML algorithm along with the Stanford NER. We found that we are able to predict correctly implicit state information based on geospatial named entities using a Random Forest (RF) classifier with precision of 0.989, recall 0.798, and F1 of 0.883, for Pennsylvania. We also found that adding implicit state information that is predicted by our classifier increases the possibility to find state-level geo-location unambiguously by up to 80%.

5. ACKNOWLEDGMENTS

This publication was made possible by NPRP Grant No. 4-029-1-007 from the Qatar National Research Fund (a member of Qatar Foundation) and the National Science Foundation under Grant No. IIS-1319578. The statements made herein are solely the responsibility of the authors.

6. REFERENCES

[1] Sakaki, T., Okazaki, M., Matsuo, Y. 2010. Earthquake shakes Twitter users: real-time event detection by social sensors. WWW2010 (April 2010), 851-860.

[2] Alani, H., Kim, S., Millard, D. E., Weal, M. J., Hall, W., Lewis, P. H., Shadbolt, N. R. 2000. Automatic ontology-based knowledge extraction from Web documents. Intelligent Systems. 18, 1 (2000), 14-21.

[3] Cheng, Z., Caverlee, J., Lee, K. 2010. You Are Where You Tweet: A Content-Based Approach to Geo-locating Twitter Users. CIKM 2010 (New York, USA, 2010), 759–768.

[4] Martins, B. Anastacio, I., Calado, P. 2010. A Machine Learning Approach for Resolving Place References in Text - Springer. Geospatial Thinking (2010), 221-236.

[5] Lee, S. Elsherbiny, N., Fox, E. A. 2012. A digital library for water main break identification and visualization. JCDL2012 (Jun. 2012), 335-33

Modeling Faceted Browsing with Category Theory to Support Interoperability and Reuse

Daniel R. Harris
University of Kentucky
Center for Clinical and Translational Science
Lexington, Kentucky 40506
daniel.harris@uky.edu

ABSTRACT

Faceted browsing has become ubiquitous with modern digital libraries and online search engines, yet the process is still difficult to abstractly model in a manner that supports the development of interoperable and reusable interfaces. Existing efforts in facet modeling are based upon set theory, formal concept analysis, and light-weight ontologies, but in many regards, they are implementations of faceted browsing rather than a specification of the basic, underlying structures and interactions. We propose category theory as a theoretical foundation for faceted browsing and demonstrate how the interactive process can be mathematically abstracted in a way that naturally supports interoperability and reuse.

Categories and Subject Descriptors

H.3.1 [**Information Storage and Retrieval**]: Content Analysis and Indexing—*Abstracting methods*

1. INTRODUCTION

Faceted browsing (also called faceted search or faceted navigation) is an exploratory search model, where facets assist in the navigation of search results [3]. Facets are simply attributes attached to the actual objects being explored. An example of a facet attached to a book could be its genre or publication date. The design of the system's underlying model directly impacts the user's ability to filter, rank, and interact with the facets; in fact, some models contain no interactivity [6]. Wei et al. observed three major theoretical foundations behind current research of facet models: set theory, formal concept analysis, and lightweight ontologies [6]. Facet modeling focuses on the formal representation of faceted data and the interactive consequences that follow when using that model.

The motivation for choosing category theory began when designing the next phase of DELVE [2], our framework for creating visualizations for browsing biomedical literature. Specifically, we encountered difficultly in modeling DELVE's ability to create numerous visualizations, which are either controlled by facets or contain faceted structures. The volume of existing work for faceted browsing systems lends itself to a higher degree of abstraction, where existing works can become interoperable and reusable in new research settings. We will demonstrate that category theory is an appropriate framework for developing such abstractions by establishing facets and faceted taxonomies as categories. Only basic knowledge of category theory[1, 5] is needed to understand our modeling techniques.

Definition 1. A category $\mathcal{C}$ consists of the following: (1) A collection of objects, $Ob(\mathcal{C})$. (2) A collection of morphisms (also called arrows): for every pair $x, y \in Ob(\mathcal{C})$, there exists a set $Hom_{\mathcal{C}}(x, y)$ that contains morphisms from x to y [5]; a morphism $f \in Hom_{\mathcal{C}}(x, y)$ is of the form $f : x \to y$, where x is the domain and y is the codomain of f. (3) For every object $x \in Ob(\mathcal{C})$, the identity morphism, $id_x \in Hom_{\mathcal{C}}(x, x)$, exists. (4) For $x, y, z \in Ob(\mathcal{C})$, the composition function is defined as follows: $\circ : Hom_{\mathcal{C}}(y, z) \times Hom_{\mathcal{C}}(x, y) \to Hom_{\mathcal{C}}(x, z)$. Lastly, given 1-4, identity and association laws must hold for morphisms.

In our model, we will relate the concept of a facet to an existing, well-known category: **Rel**, the category with sets as objects and relations as morphisms [1]. A relation $f : X \to Y \in Hom_{\mathbf{Rel}}(X, Y)$ is a subset of $X \times Y$. In other words, any subset of $X \times Y$ is a relation from X to Y. Any binary relation is allowed, but most examples demonstrate the utility of '$<$, "$\leq$", and "$\subseteq$". We must also introduce another well-known category: **Cat**, the category of small categories[1]. The objects of **Cat** are small categories and the morphisms are functors (mappings between categories).

2. A CATEGORY-THEORETIC MODEL

We wish to be as general as possible in our abstractions so that any system with any faceted taxonomy can be modeled, regardless of the particular nuances of the facets and intra-facet relationships. The faceted taxonomy presented in an interface can contain several unrelated (or disjoint) sub-facets.

Definition 2. A facet type (a facet i and its related sub-facets) of a faceted taxonomy is a sub-category of **Rel**, the category of sets as objects and relations as morphisms. Let's call this sub-category $\mathbf{Facet}_i$ and let $Ob(\mathbf{Facet}_i) = Ob(\mathbf{Rel})$ and let the morphisms be the relations that correspond only to the $\subseteq$-relations. The identity and composition definitions are just copied from **Rel**.

JCDL'15, June 21–25, 2015, Knoxville, Tennessee, USA.
ACM 978-1-4503-3594-2/15/06.
http://dx.doi.org/10.1145/2756406.2756972.

In other words, $\mathbf{Facet}_i$ is just a slimmer version of **Rel**, where we know exactly what binary relation is being used to order the facets. The $\subseteq$-relation is powerful for specification: it allows for facets to be ordered by inclusion, which can model any structure where x is categorically related to y; this is a pivotal component to most faceted implementations. Given a facet, we also need to describe how any selection within a facet can be modeled. We simply discard any undesirable objects (and their corresponding morphisms) to create a new category that represents a focused collection of facets.

Definition 3. A subcategory $\mathbf{Focus}_i \subseteq \mathbf{Facet}_i$[1] can be constructed to represent a focused selection for $\mathbf{Facet}_i$.

Definition 4. Let **FacetTax** be a category that represents a faceted taxonomy, whose objects are the disjoint union of $\mathbf{Facet}_i$ categories. In other words, let $Ob(\mathbf{FacetTax}) = \bigsqcup_{i=1}^{n} \mathbf{Facet}_i$, where $n = |Ob(\mathbf{FacetTax})|$. The morphisms of **FacetTax** are functors (mappings between categories) of the form $Hom_{\mathbf{FacetTax}}(\mathcal{C}, \mathcal{D}) = \{F : \mathcal{C} \rightarrow \mathcal{D}\}$.

We don't have to formally prove that **FacetTax** is a true category because it is simply a sub-category of **Cat**, the category of categories. The complexity of a faceted system varies by interface, but typically includes the ability to select (or focus) and de-select (or negate) facets within a facet type. The collective effort across all facets are then used to filter the faceted knowledge presented.

Definition 5. A facet universe, U, is the n-ary product [1] within the **FacetTax** category, defined as $\prod_{i=1}^{n} \mathbf{Facet}_i$, where $n = |Ob(\mathbf{FacetTax})|$. The n coordinates of U are projection functors $P_j : \prod \mathbf{Facet}_i \rightarrow \mathbf{Facet}_j$, where $j = 1, \ldots, n$ is the jth projection of the n-ary product.

Note that since $\mathbf{Focus}_i \subseteq \mathbf{Facet}_i$, there exists a restricted universe $U_{\subseteq} \subseteq U$ where every facet is potentially reduced to a focused subset. The act of querying the universe is essentially constructing this restricted universe $U_{\subseteq}$. A high-level overview of the interactions between $\mathbf{Facet}_i$, $\mathbf{Focus}_i$, and queries in the **FacetTax** category is found in Fig. 1.

Definition 6. A faceted query, Q, is the modified n-ary product[1] within the **FacetTax** category, defined as $\prod_{i=1}^{n} \mathbf{Focus}_i$, where $n = |Ob(\mathbf{FacetTax})|$. The n coordinates of Q are similarly defined as projection functors $P_j : \prod \mathbf{Focus}_i \rightarrow \mathbf{Focus}_j$.

3. UTILITY AND FUTURE WORK

An example faceted browsing technique, dynamic taxonomies [4], constructs taxonomies with *is-a* relationships by dynamically calculating the deep extension of a node: $\text{deepExtension}(C) = \{d | d \in \text{shallowExtension}(C\prime) \wedge (C\prime = C \vee C\prime \text{ is a descendant of } C)\}$, where the shallow extension contains the direct descendants of C. Both shallow extension and *descendant-of* relationships are expressible as binary relations and, in particular, are expressible with the binary relations of **FacetTax**'s **Facet** categories.

Our model is capable of capturing different faceted structures: lists, hierarchies, trees, graphs, and lattices. These structures can be put into the same abstract framework to support interoperability between systems (or parts of systems). When designing a system where different structures interact with one another, the notation and representations become cumbersome. The burden of writing consistent abstractions with different structures is removed by using category theory.

We are applying our model to the next stage of our interface, DELVE [2], to help represent faceted structures that help create or control other faceted structures. We wish to continue our model to include the exploratory search phase of faceted browsing. Our modeling technique of interoperable faceted objects enables the quick release and integration of new visualizations into the DELVE system.

[1] $A \subseteq B$ is commonly used denote that A is a subcategory of B, despite neither A nor B being an actual set [5].

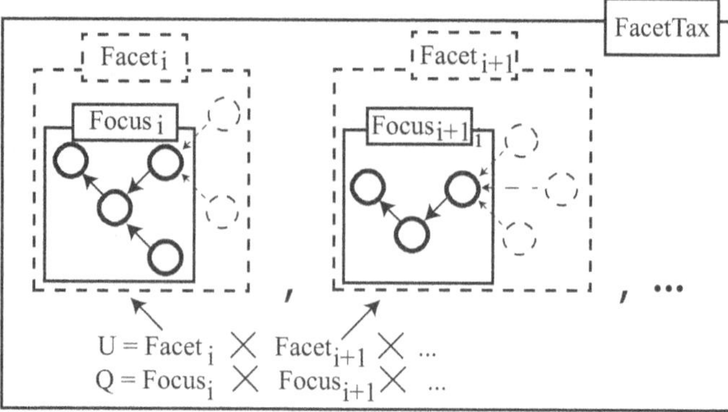

Figure 1: A high-level overview of FacetTax, $\mathbf{Facet}_i$, $\mathbf{Focus}_i$, and queries with focused subcategories.

4. ACKNOWLEDGMENTS

The project described was supported by the National Center for Research Resources and the National Center for Advancing Translational Sciences, National Institutes of Health, through Grant UL1TR000117. The content is solely the responsibility of the authors and does not necessarily represent the official views of the NIH.

5. REFERENCES

[1] M. Barr and C. Wells. *Category theory for computing science.* Prentice Hall New York, 1990.

[2] D. R. Harris, R. Kavuluru, S. Yu, R. Theakston, J. W. Jaromczyk, and T. R. Johnson. Delve: A document exploration and visualization engine. In *Proceedings of the Summit on Clinical Research Informatics*, page 179. AMIA, 2014.

[3] M. A. Hearst. Clustering versus faceted categories for information exploration. *Communications of the ACM*, 49(4):59–61, 2006.

[4] G. M. Sacco and Y. Tzitzikas. *Dynamic taxonomies and faceted search: theory, practice, and experience.* Springer, 2009.

[5] D. I. Spivak. *Category Theory for the Sciences.* MIT Press, 2014.

[6] B. Wei, J. Liu, Q. Zheng, W. Zhang, X. Fu, and B. Feng. A survey of faceted search. *Journal of Web engineering*, 12(1-2):41–64, 2013.

An Instrument for Merging of Bibliographic Databases

Anna Knyazeva
Institute of Computational Technologies
Tomsk, Russian Federation
aknjazeva@ict.nsc.ru

Oleg Kolobov
Institute of High Current Electronics
Tomsk, Russian Federation
okolobov@gmail.com

Fjodor Tatarsky
Tomsk Polytechnic University
Tomsk, Russian Federation
fjodor.tatarsky@gmail.com

Igor Turchanovsky
Institute of Computational Technologies
Tomsk, Russian Federation
tur@hcei.tsc.ru

ABSTRACT

The process of merging two or more library catalogues is considered in this paper. It's necessary to solve the problem of duplicate detection and merging into one database instead of simple union of different resources. The toolbox *Cflib* for duplicate detection and merging has been developed by us. It's based on standard principles of record linkage and has quite simple architecture.

Categories and Subject Descriptors

H.3.3 [**Information Storage and Retrieval**]: Information Search and Retrieval; H.3.7 [**Information Storage and Retrieval**]: Digital Libraries

General Terms

Algorithms

Keywords

Record Linkage, Duplicate Detection, Authority Records, Bibliographic Records

1. INTRODUCTION

Simple union of resources is when we collect all data together without any analysis. As result of simple union of two library catalogs we get records duplicates and lose some links between records. We can correct this by merging authority records and then by merging bibliographic records. It's important to collect all links between authority and bibliographic records. Each authority record refers to certain object mentioned in bibliographic data (person, organization, subject heading etc.). Publications (articles, monographies, preprints etc.) are described in bibliographic records.

JCDL'15, June 21–25, 2015, Knoxville, Tennessee, USA.
ACM 978-1-4503-3594-2/15/06.
http://dx.doi.org/10.1145/2756406.2756973.

The problem of duplicate detection and merging arises during the process of union several library catalogs. The problem of merging authority and bibliographic records is considered in this paper. We use some principles generated in VIAF (Virtual International Authority File) [1]. For example, we use Extended Authority Records (EARs), try to account indirect information about person etc.

We've started to develop a toolbox Cflib for merging library resources. Users of Cflib can build their own record linkage models by varying rules and tuning parameters of system.

2. OUR APPROACH

2.1 Data description

We deal with data of several small catalogs (bibliography and authority databases of 20 libraries). In total we have about 300 000 bibliographic records and about 10 000 authority records. All records were translated to format RUSMARC. RUSMARC is a russian bibliographic format, based on UNIMARC [2]. But not all of records are valid for this format because of errors.

RUSMARC is highly structured format of data. It contains strict instructions about every field of record. But sometimes inaccurate or automatic creation of records leads to errors in filling the fields. The example (Table 1) shows how it can happen. The name of Kafka's novella ("The Metamorphosis") is specified in the initials field instead of letter "F".

Original records are in Russian language. They were translated into English for convenience. We have 6 different records for one person with different quality. In fact there are even more records for Franz Kafka (24 records instead of 6 as in Table 1). We put all strict duplicates together. Merging of strict duplicates is technical and not complicated task. This also applies to bibliographic records. One article can be described in several libraries and so we can get several different records.

2.2 Cflib

The toolbox described in this paper was initially developed us for Institute's CRIS (Institute of Computational Technologies) [3]. We've modificated it for work with bibliographic data and extended its functionality.

Table 1: Franz Kafka's authority records

№	Field	Value	in English
1	surname	Кафка	Kafka
	initials	Ф.	F.
	name	Франц	Franz
	addition	австр. писатель	austr. writer
	dates	1883-1924	1883-1924
2	surname	Кафка	Kafka
	initials	Ф.	F.
	name	Франц	Franz
3	surname	Кафка	Kafka
	name	Франц	Franz
4	surname	Кафка	Kafka
	initials	Ф.	F.
	addition	писатель	writer
5	surname	КАФКА ФРАНЦ (ПИСАТЕЛЬ)	KAFKA FRANZ (WRITER)
	addition	О НЕМ	ABOUT HIM
6	surname	КАФКА Ф.	KAFKA F.
	initials	("Превращение")	("The Metamorphosis")

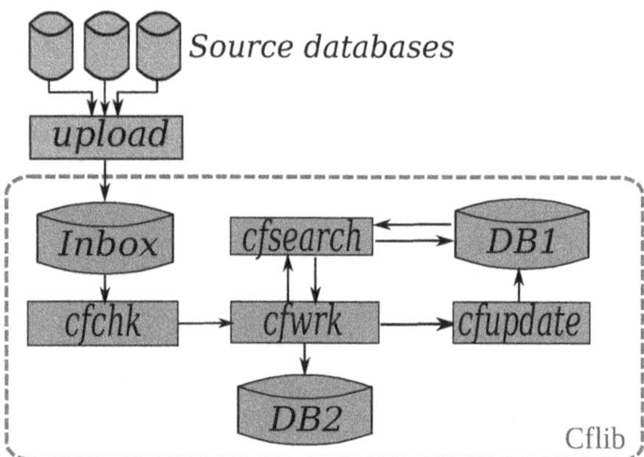

Figure 1: The Cflib architecture

Cflib based on standard record linkage system architecture [4, 5]. Most popular principles of record linkage are used in it.

2.2.1 *The Cflib architecture*

The Cflib architecture is shown on Figure 1. The Cflib includes 3 databases (*Inbox*, *DB1* and *DB2*) and 4 modules. Authority databases are not part of Cflib, these databases have to be merged. Upload module is used for union of databases. It marks records so we know which database every record come from.

Inbox is the temporal database which contain all records from databases at start. It's empty when the work has been finished. *DB1* is a result of work. At finish this database contains merged records for persons. *DB2* is database for records which can't be operated. It's used for analysis and future work.

All modules can perform different tasks depending on current stage of work. But main idea of every module is preserved. The *cfchk* performs data preprocessing and filtering. Then the cfsearh chooses potential duplicates or candidates for linking based on current record. The *cfwrk* is responsible for records comparison. The *cfupdate* changes records and adds new ones into database *DB1* if it's necessary.

The *cfsearch* determines which records in database *DB1* will be compared with current record. There are two posible methods for search in Cflib: exact matching and bi-grams. The user can choose one of them.

The comparison of two records consists of several stages. Firstly we check a strict equality between them. It means checking basic information about persons. We exclude technical information about holder of records and so on. Then we check fuzzy equality of records. This stage of comparison is determined by rules. The user can formulate rules as combination of functions for string comparison and critical values for them. Two fuzzy string comparison functions are used in Cflib this moment: Edit distance and Bi-gramms. We plan to include more functions later.

The work of *cfupdate* depends of the result of comparison. If current record is unique (is not duplicate), it has to be uploaded to database as is. Maybe there is another record in result database which refer to this person or work. In this case updating module has to add some information in existing record. Mainly such additional information is current record's identifier.

3. CONCLUSIONS

The problem of merging data created in different libraries has been considered. This problem is common in case of pool resources at several libraries. In such case a lot of fuzzy duplicates among authority and bibliography records appear This article describes work in progress. We wish to consider more functions for fuzzy string matching and more experiments. The Cflib toolbox can be used for duplicates detection among bibliographic records or for authority control separately. It also can be used for merging library resources on the whole when all stages are performed in described order.

4. REFERENCES

[1] M. F. Loesch. VIAF (the virtual international authority file) – http://viaf.org. *Technical Services Quarterly*, 28(2):255–256, feb 2011.

[2] A. Hopkinson, editor. *UNIMARC Manual*. Walter de Gruyter – K. G. Saur, jan 2008.

[3] A. Knyazeva, I. Turchanovsky, O. Kolobov, and O. Zhizhimov. Experience of person identification for cris-systems. In *Selected Papers of XVI All-Russian Scientific Conference "Digital libraries: Advanced Methods and Technologies, Digital Collections"*, oct 2014.

[4] P. Jurczyk, J. J. Lu, L. Xiong, J. D. Cragan, and A. Correa. Fine-grained record integration and linkage tool. *Birth Defect Res A*, 82(11):822–829, nov 2008.

[5] M. Elfeky, V. Verykios, and A. Elmagarmid. TAILOR: a record linkage toolbox. In *Proceedings 18th International Conference on Data Engineering*. IEEE Comput. Soc, 2002.

Databrary: Enabling Sharing and Reuse of Research Video

Dylan A. Simon
Databrary Project
New York University
New York, NY, USA
dylan@databrary.org

Andrew S. Gordon
Databrary Project
New York University
New York, NY, USA
drew@databrary.org

Lisa Steiger
Databrary Project
New York University
New York, NY, USA
lisa@databrary.org

Rick O. Gilmore
Department of Psychology
Penn State
University Park, PA, USA
rogilmore@psu.edu

ABSTRACT

Video and audio recordings serve as a primary data source in many fields, especially in the social and behavioral sciences. Recordings present unique opportunities for reuse and reanalysis for novel scientific purposes, but also present challenges related to respecting the privacy of individuals depicted. Databrary is a web-based service for sharing and reusing the video data created by researchers in the developmental and learning sciences. By investigating how researchers organize, analyze, and mine their own recordings, we have implemented a system that empowers researchers to capture, store, and share recordings in a standardized way. This demo will provide a tour through the Databrary service, highlighting how it promotes storage, management, sharing, and reuse of research data, controls access privileges to restricted human subject data, and facilitates browsing and discoverability of datasets.

Categories and Subject Descriptors

H.2.8 [**Database Management**]: Database Applications—*scientific databases, image databases*; H.3.5 [**Information Storage and Retrieval**]: Online Information Systems—*data sharing, web-based services*

General Terms

Design; Standardization

Keywords

Data sharing; open science; video; psychology; developmental science

JCDL'15, June 21–25, 2015, Knoxville, Tennessee, USA.
ACM 978-1-4503-3594-2/15/06.
http://dx.doi.org/10.1145/2756406.2756951.

1. INTRODUCTION

Video and audio recordings serve as a primary data source for scientific research in psychology, linguistics, education, anthropology, and many other disciplines. They are, in contrast to other timeseries data, human-consumable and largely self-documenting. This allows recordings collected in one context to be used by others for different purposes with minimal explanation. Moreover, video and audio recordings are often analyzed without the use of sophisticated tools as human observers can directly glean much of the data's richness.

While video data have many benefits, they also contain highly identifiable aspects of depicted human participants: recordings contain participants' faces and voices, and their names are often spoken aloud. Because of this, sharing video data presents challenges related to the privacy of human subjects. In contrast to other forms of data that are non-identifiable or can be easily de-identified, video data cannot be easily de-identified without significantly diminishing its value and richness. Therefore, any solution for video sharing must provide a policy and access framework to ensure appropriate protection of research participants.

Despite their inherent reusability, researchers rarely share recordings with others, due largely to entrenched practices and perceived privacy requirements. This lack of sharing prevents others from extracting the full value out of recordings and impedes scientific discovery. To address this problem, the Databrary project[1] aims to build tools and policies that facilitate repurposing and reuse of recordings without placing undue burden on data contributors. We have created a web-based data library to store and organize recordings and to capture contextual information necessary for reuse in standardized ways.

Our approach is to focus on video and audio recordings in a particular research domain, and build appropriate structured and unstructured resources around this core. We designed the system by investigating how researchers studying human development and education organize their own data, deriving from those observations a unifying set of principles for organizing contextual metadata. We aimed to design a system that facilitates the capture, standardization, discovery, and understanding of data to enable reuse of recordings for novel purposes at an unprecedented scale.

[1]https://databrary.org/

2. REPOSITORY DETAILS

Databrary began accepting contributions in early 2014 and opened for general use in October 2014. As of April 2015, it hosts 7,300 video files totaling 2,400 hours of recordings along with 2,600 additional files. These files make up 3,100 study sessions and are covered by 2,000 metadata records (including 1,800 individual participants). Data originate from 35 individual contributors across 25 different universities. Fifty universities have granted access to the repository to over 95 researchers.

Databrary is an open-source web application[2], featuring a responsive user interface, a JSON API, and high-performance video streaming. Databrary stores at least two versions of each item of Databrary video content: a copy for access, and the received original file. The access copy is generated by automatically transcoding the uploaded file to a standard format to enable cross-platform HTML5-based streaming and downloading for off-line access, currently H.264/AAC in an MPEG-4 container for video.

3. DATA MANAGEMENT

Focusing on a particular research domain allows us to develop tools informed by how the intended community of users currently works, while accommodating the specific privacy concerns for data that often have a high disclosure risk. We have created a set of data management features that empower researchers to actively manage their own projects—to upload data with accompanying metadata—as each study unfolds. These features include a spreadsheet interface for entering, editing, and viewing the metadata for all sessions related to a study. Session-level metadata might include participant details, tasks in the experiment, permission levels, study groups, or conditions, and serves the purpose of providing ways to browse and search for specific video data in Databrary. We have found that most researchers use desktop spreadsheets for managing data in their own labs, making the interface and functionality intuitive to users.

We have also implemented a timeline for uploading, viewing, and tagging video assets related to sessions. The timeline view is designed to look and operate like video editing software commonly used in many research labs. A common practice for researchers in this domain who make use of video data is to have multiple, parallel camera views, or a sequence of recordings documenting the same study session. The timeline view then allows users to upload video files, position them to reflect the temporal order of each video collected, and annotate video sections with user-generated tags.

Providing a targeted user interface to meet the existing and evolving needs of our user base allows us to control and standardize the means of data entry and thus achieve a greater amount of normalization in the data from the outset, through liberal use of visualization, auto-completion, and suggestions. In turn, this adds convenience and functionality for researchers over existing practices and alleviates storage burdens.

In addition, because video data involving human subjects is identifiable, we have built the access checks necessary to honor the participant consents under which the data were collected. User registration for gaining access to Databrary involves an authorization process by which site users are verified to be faculty, students, or researchers affiliated with an educational institution. Users are required to review and sign an access agreement stating that they will treat the data they are able to access through Databrary in a manner that complies with the ethical handling of research data involving human subjects[3]. Finally, contributors are offered the ability to set permission levels for files and groups of files that allow them to fine-tune who has access to their data.

4. DISCOVERY AND REUSE

Databrary's mission is not merely the storage and management of research data, but also to make these data discoverable by other researchers and to facilitate their reuse. Currently we support text searching over the entire repository, and we plan to continue to implement more refined searches that allows faceting of search results based on session metadata such as participant details, tasks involved in the experiment, study conditions, and context. Additionally, Databrary allows for the annotation of videos and video segments with tags, which can serve as an index point for more refined search functionality.

We aim to allow data to be reused in future studies, cited in scholarly communication, as well as used to aid in scientific and educational presentations. To promote using datasets as a bibliographic source, each dataset comes with a formatted citation, a persistent URI, and soon will also be assigned a Digital Object Identifier (DOI) for referencing in scholarly publications and presentations. Based on input from site users we have also built in the ability to excerpt or highlight clips from videos in such a way that they might serve as an exemplar clip for the dataset—providing users unfamiliar with a dataset a quick summary of what is contained therein—or be used in the classroom as an education tool or at professional conferences.

As we continue to gather feedback from our user base, we not only see Databrary as a tool that facilitates the standardized management of research data, but also as an opportunity to enhance the ability for academics to communicate about and bolster their own research. We have already addressed the basic upload, data management, and storage needs of our target community, and have sufficiently answered the question of how to protect sensitive video data while providing wider opportunities to share those data. Going forward, we hope to focus more on developing the tools for searching, discovering, and reusing those data, allowing researchers to work with their data in ways they had not previously imagined.

Acknowledgments

This work was supported by the NSF (BCS-1238599) and the NICHD (U01-HD-076595-01). The authors gratefully acknowledge the NYU Libraries for their valuable advice and consultation.

[2]http://github.com/databrary/databrary

[3]http://databrary.org/access/policies/agreement.html

The RMap Project: Capturing and Preserving Associations Amongst Multi-Part Distributed Publications

Karen L. Hanson
Portico
100 Campus Drive, Suite 100
Princeton, NJ 08540
+1 609-986-2282
karen.hanson@ithaka.org

Tim DiLauro
Johns Hopkins University
3400 N. Charles Street / MSEL
Baltimore, MD 21218
+1 410-929-3722
tim.dilauro@jhu.org

Mark Donoghue
IEEE
445 Hoes Lane
Piscataway, NJ 08854
+1 732-562-6045
m.donoghue@ieee.org

ABSTRACT

The goal of the RMap Project is to create a prototype service that can capture and preserve maps of relationships amongst the increasingly distributed components (article, data, software, workflow objects, multimedia, etc.) that comprise the new model for scholarly publication. The demonstration will provide a tour of some of the features of the initial web service prototype. This will include examples of Distributed Scholarly Complex Objects (DiSCOs) and associated provenance data in RMap, as well as some of the options that users might have for interacting with the framework.

Categories and Subject Descriptors

H.3.5 [**Information Systems**]: Online Information Services – *web-based services, data sharing.* H.3.7 [**Information Systems**]: Digital Libraries – *collection, dissemination.*

General Terms

Management, Documentation, Standardization.

Keywords

Publishing workflows; linked data; data publishing; semantic web; REST API; digital preservation; scholarly communication; digital scholarship

1. BACKGROUND

In recent years, the content that comprises the scholarly record has become more dynamic and less "bounded." Formerly, even digital artifacts of the scholarly record were more or less discrete objects, such as journal articles or books, usually encapsulated in a single file. Increasingly, the primary unit of scholarly communication is evolving into a multi-part distributed object that often includes data and software [3] (see Figure 1).

As one indicator of this trend, we see publishers working to adopt new approaches for dealing with these forms of publication. The movement towards publishing and citing datasets as standalone objects has been particularly prominent in recent years, and is but one component of an ongoing shift in scholarly publishing.

Further, the many, and dynamic, relationships amongst the components comprising a distributed scholarly complex object are first class objects in themselves. Not only does the scholarly community require preservation of publication, data, and other artifacts of scholarly research (whether preserved separately or together), it also requires the preservation of the relationships amongst them. In addition, in the scholarly environment, proper preservation also mandates models and information graphs that account for the provenance of the assertions of those relationships.

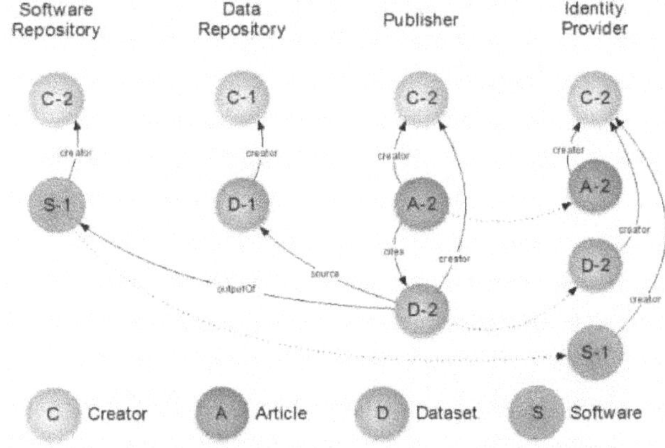

Figure 1 Multi-part Distributed Publication

2. THE RMAP PROJECT

The RMap Project[1] is a two-year Alfred P. Sloan Foundation[2]-funded initiative undertaken by the Data Conservancy[3], Portico[4], and IEEE[5]. The goal of the project is to create a prototype service that can assemble the maps of relationships amongst the distributed components of a modern scholarly publication, and preserve those maps over the long term.

The project builds on the features of the semantic web [1] and linked data[6], adopting concepts from the Open Archives Initiative Object Reuse and Exchange (OAI-ORE).[7] To simplify integration with publishing and scholarly workflows, RMap employs a RESTful (Representational State Transfer) API [2] and makes use

JCDL '15, June 21–25, 2015, Knoxville, Tennessee, USA.
ACM 978-1-4503-3594-2/15/06.
http://dx.doi.org/10.1145/2756406.2756952

[1] http://rmap-project.info/rmap/

[2] http://www.sloan.org/

[3] http://dataconservancy.org/

[4] http://www.portico.org/

[5] http://www.ieee.org/

[6] http://www.w3.org/standards/semanticweb/data

[7] http://www.openarchives.org/ore/

of existing well-known vocabularies (e.g. Dublin Core[8], Friend of a Friend[9], Open Provenance Model[10]) in its data model.

2.1 Objectives

The RMap Service will record and preserve links amongst the artifacts of scholarly communication and those who create, modify, employ, and annotate them. Its purpose in doing so is to facilitate the discovery and reuse of those artifacts, to demonstrate the impact and reuse of research, to make those demonstrations available to those making curatorial decisions about collection and preservation of digital research artifacts such as software and workflows, and to inform those curatorial and other choices with solid provenance information about the representations in RMap.

Key design objectives of the RMap service in support of these goals are to

- support assertions from a broad set of contributors
- integrate with Linked Data
- leverage existing data from other scholarly publishing stakeholders (publishers, identifier providers, identity authorities, data and software repositories)
- provide some support for resources lacking identifiers

2.2 Data Model

Major components of the data model, constructed upon the Resource Description Framework (RDF)[11] concepts of resources, triples and graphs, are *Statements*, *DiSCOs*, *Agents*, and *Events*.

RMap *Statements* are essentially reified RDF triples and map closely to the class of *RDF Statement*. In addition to an identifier they provide status, and Event (provenance) information.

RMap *DiSCOs* (Distributed Scholarly Complex Objects) are graphs representing aggregations of related scholarly resources (see Figure 2). For example: A single DiSCO might represent, an article, its related datasets, and software – as well as any useful context metadata describing those resources. DiSCOs also have an associated identifier, status, and Event (provenance) information.

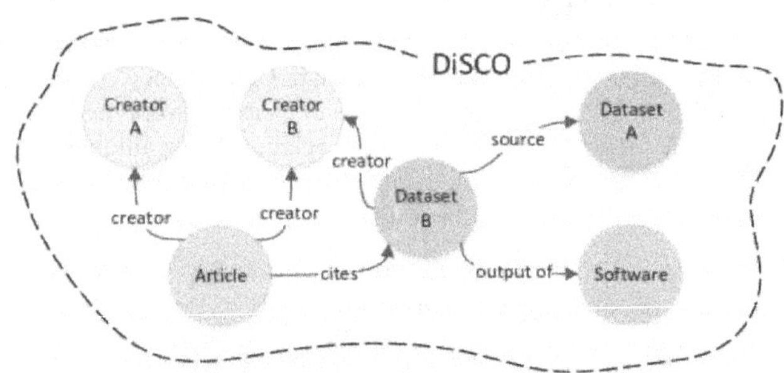

Figure 2. Example of a DiSCO

An RMap *Agent* is a person or thing (or group of these) responsible for some action. In RMap this can include, but is not limited to, authors, funders, publishers, and administrators. RMap distinguishes between scholarly agents (e.g., author, funder, publisher, data processing software) and system agents (RMap component, user, etc.).

An RMap *Event* captures provenance within RMap. This includes the system agent responsible for a particular activity, the activity itself, the timeframe thereof, and the associated context. Linked, for example, to a DiSCO at the time of its creation or update, Events make it possible to trace the provenance of all assertions within and about a DiSCO.

2.3 REST API

The primary interface for accessing the RMap database is a REST API. The features of a RESTful API include programming language independence and conformance to web architecture metaphors. Both are important in facilitating the integration of the RMap service into heterogeneous publisher, researcher, funder, and other institutional workflows.

3. CONCLUSIONS

By being part of publisher, researcher, funder, and other scholarly workflows and by aggregating data from multiple sources, RMap aims to support third party discovery as well as facilitate the capture of information about scholarly artifacts that is not easily captured elsewhere.

4. ACKNOWLEDGMENTS

The RMap Project is funded by the Alfred P. Sloan Foundation. The authors wish to acknowledge the contributions of their RMap project colleagues: Sayeed Choudhury, Johns Hopkins University, The Sheridan Libraries, Associate Dean for Research Data Management; Kate Wittenberg, Managing Director, Portico; Gerry Grenier, Senior Director, Publishing Technologies, IEEE, Portico colleagues Jabin White, Sheila Morrissey, Vinay Cheruku, Amy Kirchhoff, John Meyer, Stephanie Orphan; and IEEE colleagues Renny Guida, Ken Rawson, Ken Moore.

5. REFERENCES

[1] Berners-Lee, T., Hendler, J., and Lassila, O. (2001). The semantic web. *Scientific American*, *284*(5), 28-37.

[2] Fielding, R. T. 2000. "Architectural Styles and the Design of Network-based Software Architectures". Dissertation. University of California, Irvine. Retrieved 26 January 2015 from https://www.ics.uci.edu/~fielding/pubs/dissertation/fielding_dissertation.pdf

[3] Lavoie, B., Childress, E., Erway, R., Faniel, I., Malpas, C., Schaffner, J., and van der Werf, Titia. 2014. The Evolving Scholarly Record. Dublin, Ohio: OCLC Research. Retrieved 26 January 2015 from http://www.oclc.org/content/dam/research/publications/library/2014/oclcresearch-evolving-scholarly-record-2014.pdf

[8] http://dublincore.org/specifications/

[9] http://xmlns.com/foaf/spec/

[10] http://openprovenance.org/

[11] http://www.w3.org/TR/rdf11-concepts/

$5e^{x+y}$: Searching over Mathematical Content in Digital Libraries

Arthur Oviedo
EPFL, Switzerland.
arthur.oviedo@alumni.epfl.ch

Nikos Kasioumis
CERN, Switzerland.
nikos.kasioumis@cern.ch

Karl Aberer
EPFL, Switzerland.
karl.aberer@epfl.ch

ABSTRACT

This paper presents $5e^{x+y}$, a system that is able to extract, index and query mathematical content expressed as mathematical expressions, complementing the CERN Document Server (CDS)[5]. We present the most important aspects of its design, our approach to model the relevant features of the mathematical content, and provide a demonstration of its searching capabilities.

Categories and Subject Descriptors

H.3.3 [**Information Storage and Retrieval**]: Information Search and Retrieval

Keywords

Mathematical Information Retrieval

1. INTRODUCTION

CDS (CERN Document Server) is the institutional digital repository developed and used at CERN[2]. It contains more than 1,000,000 records and stores more than 400,000 full text documents, organized in different collections among published articles, books and preprints. Invenio[6] is the open-source digital library software platform behind CDS and it is developed in parallel to CDS at CERN. Besides CDS, Invenio supports around thirty scientific institutions worldwide including INSPIRE (a collaboration between Fermilab, CERN, DESY and SLAC), EPFL and ILO. A considerable amount of the full text documents on CDS contains mathematical content. The Preprints collection alone contains more than 700,000 records, harvesting documents from services like ArXiV[4] where most of the documents are in the areas of physics, mathematics and statistics which are very rich in this type of content. Even though Invenio provides a powerful search engine that allows users to query records using different fields like author or keywords, it is not suitable for mathematical content. $5e^{x+y}$ is developed as a first attempt to address this limitation by allowing querying for records based on mathematical expressions. Compared to existing systems in the context of Mathematical Information Retrieval (MIR), our system improves on them by modelling mathematical expressions using 2 distinct set of features and relying on specialized tools to manipulate and analyse them.

JCDL'15 June 21-25, 2015, Knoxville, TN, USA
ACM 978-1-4503-3594-2/15/06
http://dx.doi.org/10.1145/2756406.2756953.

2. SYSTEM OVERVIEW

In this section we provide a general overview of the main design points of $5e^{x+y}$. A more detailed description of the system can be found in [10].

2.1 Features Extraction

Our initial focus in the project was to define a good set of features that we could extract and index from our equations. We divide them into two different categories: notational and structural features. The notational features relate to the actual naming and representation of the different elements of the equation. The selected format for representation and internal processing of the equations was MathML. This language allows for easier processing because of its markup nature and has a stronger support from the W3C among other communities. For the notational features we extract the leaf elements of the equation: variables, numbers and operators represented by the <mi>, <mn> and <mo> tags respectively. In addition, we index 2-grams and 3-grams of symbol-operator and symbol-operator-symbol sequences.

We perform some processing of these tokens such as normalizing and decomposing of complex characters. This allows us to partially match characters with different unicode points but similar or equal visual rendering. For instance LATIN CAPITAL LETTER A WITH RING ABOVE with code 0xc5 and ANGSTROM SIGN with code 0x212b both are rendered as Å and can both be used to refer to the Angstrom measurement unit. Following this example, we index both the original token <mi>Å</mi> and the normalized form <mi>Å</mi> <mi>A</mi>.For operators which are semantically related such as comparison, integrals and arithmetic, we apply another set of rules since their unicode characters do not provide an easy way to match them. For example the INTEGRAL character with code 0x222b generates the tokens <mo>∫</mo> and INT_OP and the CONTOUR INTEGRAL character with code 0x222e generates the tokens <mo>∮ </mo> and INT_OP. In this way, both have a partial matching in the second token.

The second set of features relate to the structure of the equation. Two different properties of mathematical equations impose additional challenges for a MIR system. First, variables can be used indistinguishably and any character set can be used to represent the same equation. For example, $f(t) = vt + c$ and $g(x) = ac + b$ can represent the same linear equation, however the context in which each variable is used follows certain conventions. To address this issue, we relied on pattern matching, a very powerful feature that current Computer Algebra Systems (CAS) provide. We integrated Mathematica[8] into our system, to perform pattern matching on the equations and identify occurrences within a predefined set of patterns. This allows us to detect if the equation contains certain types of common algebraic structures. For instance, the pattern `a_.x^ 2 + b_.x + c_.` is used to identify a quadratic expression. This mechanism is very powerful since _.x represents any type of expression, not only a single term.

An additional challenge mathematical equations pose is the fact that a given equality can be rewritten in multiple ways taking into account properties of the different operators like associativity, distributivity and commutativity among others. Our approach relies once more in the features provided by Mathematica: we perform the `Simplify` operation which applies a set of predefined rules on a given equation with the goal of providing a canonical representation.

2.2 System architecture

$5e^{x+y}$ is implemented on top of the Lucene/Solr [3] framework. We expanded the default schema with several fields, the most important ones being: the `math_notational_field` which stores all the described tokens and n-grams, the `math_structural_field` which stores the occurrences of predefined algebraic structures and the `filename` which is used to store the file/record where the particular equation was found.

In order to extend Lucene with the new use case, our work extends some of the base classes. `MultiplePatternTokenizer` is in charge of producing a stream of tokens from a single equation. These tokens are identified by applying multiple regular expressions. `UnicodeNormalizingFilter` applies the unicode normalizing transformation described above. `SynonymExpandingFilter` expands operators, using a manually computed table based on [9], with the category they belong to. Finally `StructuralPatternsTokenizer` provides the pattern matching functionality by establishing communication with Mathematica's `Kernel Link` API.

To integrate $5e^{x+y}$ with Invenio, we used the `solrpy` library which communicates with an instance of Solr running $5e^{x+y}$ as a plugin. Since Solr provides different integrating mechanisms with external systems, $5e^{x+y}$ can be easily be incorporated into different digital libraries.

3. DEMONSTRATION

As part of the demonstration of $5e^{x+y}$, we present a demo instance of the Invenio software with the mathematical equations search functionality. The user can access the mathematical search functionality through a link in the main page. Once there, the user is presented with a classic search functionality where they can input an equation. The equation can be expressed in either LaTeXor MathML. To ease the writing of LaTeXcode, we include an online editor[7] that renders the input as the user types it. LaTeXcode is usually more familiar to users, however, the internal representation

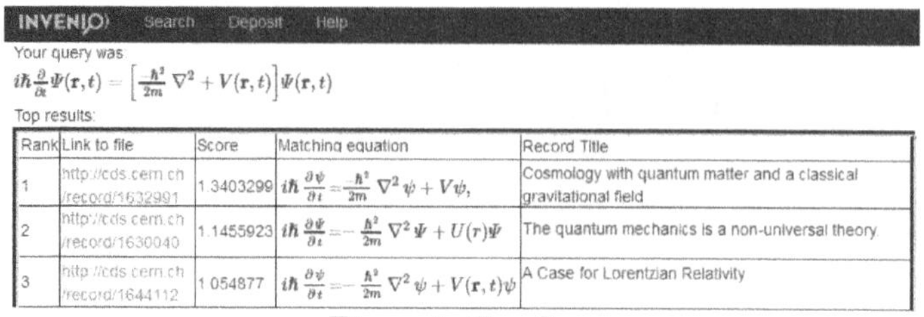

INVENIO Search Deposit Help

Your query was:

$i\hbar\frac{\partial}{\partial t}\Psi(\mathbf{r},t) = \left[\frac{-\hbar^2}{2m}\nabla^2 + V(\mathbf{r},t)\right]\Psi(\mathbf{r},t)$

Top results:

Rank	Link to file	Score	Matching equation	Record Title
1	http://cds.cern.ch /record/1632991	1.3403299	$i\hbar\frac{\partial\psi}{\partial t} = \frac{-\hbar^2}{2m}\nabla^2\psi + V\psi,$	Cosmology with quantum matter and a classical gravitational field
2	http://cds.cern.ch /record/1630040	1.1455923	$i\hbar\frac{\partial\Psi}{\partial t} = -\frac{\hbar^2}{2m}\nabla^2\Psi + U(r)\Psi$	The quantum mechanics is a non-universal theory
3	http://cds.cern.ch /record/1644112	1.054877	$i\hbar\frac{\partial\psi}{\partial t} = -\frac{\hbar^2}{2m}\nabla^2\psi + V(\mathbf{r},t)\psi$	A Case for Lorentzian Relativity

Figure 1: Result page.

is in MathML as previously explained. The translation from LaTeXto MathML is done through the third party library SnuggleTex[1] that has some shortcomings, so we allow users to input the query in MathML as well. When the query is ready, the user can click the submit button and the system then performs the search. Once the system has performed the lookup and produced the results, they are presented to the user. The system displays the 20 results with the highest score. Each result shows the matched equation snippet, the title of the record containing the given equation and the link to the record as it can be observed in Figure 1.

4. CONCLUSIONS

In this demonstration, we focused on a limitation of CDS, and how our system, $5e^{x+y}$, provides efficient and precise searching capabilities over mathematical content. We presented our approach to model mathematical equations in terms of two different types of features. We extended the Lucene/Solr framework to handle specific type of content and through the Mathematica CAS we were able to include powerful functionalities such as pattern matching and equation simplification to our system, improving the quality of the results. Finally we presented our integration mechanism with the Invenio software through the solarpy library.

5. AVAILABILITY

Both the Invenio software and the $5e^{x+y}$ module are open-source software available through GPL Licence. Invenio can be downloaded from `http://invenio-software.org/`. $5e^{x+y}$ can be downloaded from `https://github.com/arthoviedo/cern_math_explorer`.

6. REFERENCES

[1] Snuggletex (1.2.2). http://www2.ph.ed.ac.uk/snuggletex/documentation/overview-and-features.html.

[2] About cern, 2014. http://home.web.cern.ch/about.

[3] Apache solr/lucene., 2014. http://lucene.apache.org/solr.

[4] arxiv.org e-print archive, 2014. http://arxiv.org.

[5] Cern document server, 2014. http://cds.cern.ch/.

[6] Invenio, 2014. http://invenio-software.org/.

[7] Online latex editor, 2014. http://www.codecogs.com/latex/eqneditor.php.

[8] Wolfram mathematica, 2014. http://www.wolfram.com/mathematica//.

[9] X. Lee. Unicode: Math symbols, 2010. http://xahlee.info/comp/unicode_math_operators.html.

[10] A. Oviedo, N. Kaisoumis, and K. Aberer. $5e^{x+y}$: A math-aware search engine for cds. CERN Document Server. http://cds.cern.ch/record/1670010?ln=en.

Reconstruction of the US First Website

Ahmed AlSum
Stanford University
Stanford CA, USA
aalsum@stanford.edu

ABSTRACT

The Web idea started on 1989 with a proposal from Sir Tim Berners-Lee. The first US website has been developed at SLAC[1] on 1991. This early version of the Web and the subsequent updates until 1998 have been preserved by SLAC archive and history office for many years. In this paper, we discuss the strategy and techniques to reconstruct this early website and make it available through Stanford Web Archive Portal[2].

Categories and Subject Descriptors

H.3.7 [**Digital Libraries**]: Systems issues

General Terms

Experimentation

Keywords

Web Archiving

1. INTRODUCTION

Sir Tim Berners-Lee invented the WorldWideWeb in 1989 [2]. On 1991, Paul Kunz from SLAC National Accelerator Laboratory implemented the first website in US to enable researchers to access two major databases SPIRES and BINLIST. SLAC archives and history office[3] preserved periodical copies of this website between 1991 until 1998. In May 2014, Stanford Web Archiving Service received a copy of this backup to convert the original list of scattered files into an accessible and browsable website with temporal navigation through Stanford Web Archiving Portal that depends on Open Wayback 2.0. This paper will explain the technical challenges and the procedural that we used to convert and index the SLAC archive backup into the Open Wayback software.

Acquiring the content preserved by third party in the general web archives is a common source of data. For example, the Portuguese web archive accepts web materials that have been saved by other contributors [1]. The Portuguese web archives asks the submitter to provide: the website address, the content address, and the content dates.

2. RECONSTRUCTION METHODOLOGY

Our strategy depended on determining three pieces of information for each page: page content C, timestamp T, and URI R.

- The page content C refers to the actual file that is backup by the SLAC archive.
- The captured timestamp T is the date/time that the page with content C appeared on the Web with URI R. This timestamp is determined based on the last-modified date of this file as defined by listing command file in the context directory in the UNIX backup system.
- The URI R is the uri that is used to locate the page with content C on the Web. The mechanism to determine the URI R is discussed in the next section,

2.1 Tools

We used `wget`[4] with warc option to convert the preserved webpages content C to WARC file. `wget` command generates CDX file that is used to index the content into the Open Wayback software. We modified the automatic generated CDX file to include the actual URI R and the historical timestamp T. We replayed the archived website using customized version of Open Wayback 2.0[5].

2.2 Crawling the Archive

The SLAC's archive was a set of flat files that are not compatible with Open Wayback that requires the content in ARC or WARC format. The first step was converting the flat files paths into URIs by parsing the backup context files to extract the candidate page URIs. Then, we fed this list to `wget` unix command to download it in WARC output. We moved generated WARC to Open Wayback data store as content source. We modified the generated CDX to add the historical URI and timestamp.

[1] `http://www.slac.stanford.edu`
[2] `https://swap.stanford.edu/`
[3] `http://www.slac.stanford.edu/history/earlyweb/index.shtml`

[4] `https://www.gnu.org/software/wget/`
[5] `https://github.com/iipc/openwayback`

JCDL'15, June 21–25, 2015, Knoxville, Tennessee, USA.
ACM 978-1-4503-3594-2/15/06.
http://dx.doi.org/10.1145/2756406.2756954

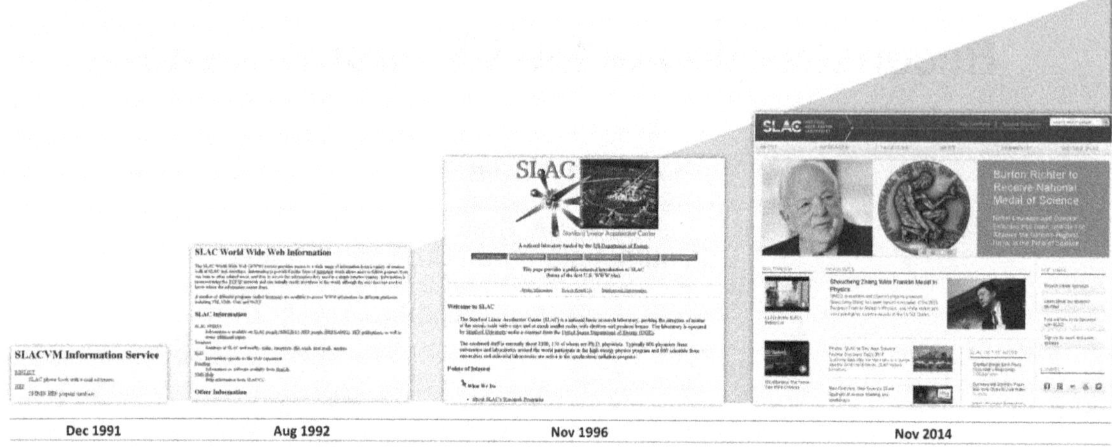

Figure 1: The evolution of SLAC homepage through time.

Table 1: The number of reconstructed URIs per year.

1991	1992	1993	1994	1995	1996	1997	1998
52	119	356	663	5264	4911	2026	2378

2.3 URL Challenge

In these early days of the Web, the concept of page hierarchy and homepage were not well established. We discovered that between 1991 to 1995, the pages were organized in one level depth only, so we can not use the directory structure to predict the URI. In order to determine what URIs were used to locate for these pages in the past, we applied various techniques:

- Inlinks from the collection itself - we extracted outlinks from all pages and tried to match these links with available pages. We used the page name as a key.
- Search Engines - we queried the popular search engines with the predicted URL to find an evidence for these URLs.
- Source code documentation - the early WWW engineers were eager to document their activities and decisions in www.history[6], such as installing new servers and migrating the pages from domain to another. We read these notes to get insights about technical decisions. Moreover, we had to read the comments in the page source code.
- The Internet Archive Wayback Machine was another source for historical URL, specifically after 1995 when there were available captures for slac.stanford.edu.
- Publications - there are a few publications that talk about the development of the early Web. Some of these publications included links to old URLs.
- Interviews with SLAC staff - we conducted a couple of interviews with the engineers who were involved with the SLAC earliest websites.

[6] `https://swap.stanford.edu/19951003000000/http://slacvm.slac.stanford.edu/FIND/www.history`

After defining the URI for each page, we wrote ruby scripts that mapped SLAC archive URI to the actual URI in the past.

2.4 Results

Figure 1 shows the evolution of the SLAC homepage through time. Table 1 lists the number of reconstructed URIs per year. In order to verify the accuracy of the construction process, we shared the initial site with the early WWW engineers to receive their feedback.

2.5 Limitations

The first limitation was the ability to modify the webpages, even though some of the pages had syntax error or broken links that could be fixed easily because we wanted to let the user browsing the web as it appeared in the past, even if it appeared broken. The second limitation was that the early design of the website was to query the SPIRES and BINLIST databases. Web archiving access methodologies right now do not support retrieval of dynamic webpages.

3. CONCLUSION

In this paper, we give an overview about the restoration process of SLAC first website. The strategy focuses on crawling the actual content using wget, then indexing it with the actual URI and the right timestamp. We provided this guidelines to help other archivists in dealing with nonstandard web archive materials that require to be replayed by the Wayback Machine.

4. REFERENCES

[1] Supplying historical Portuguese web contents. http://sobre.arquivo.pt/how-to-participate/supplying-historical-portuguese-web-contents?set_language=en, 2013.

[2] T. Berners-Lee. Information Management: A Proposal. Technical report, CERN, 1990.

Lifelong Digital Libraries

Cathal Gurrin
Dublin City University
Glasnevin, Dublin 9, Ireland
cgurrin@computing.dcu.ie

Frank Hopfgartner
University of Glasgow
11 University Gardens, Glasgow G12 8QH, UK
frank.hopfgartner@glasgow.ac.uk

ABSTRACT

The organisation of personal data is receiving increasing research attention due to the challenges that are faced in gathering, enriching, searching and visualising this data. Given the increasing quantities of personal data being gathered by individuals, the concept of a lifelong digital library of rich multimedia and sensory content for every individual is becoming a reality. This panel brought together researchers from different parts of the information retrieval and digital libraries community to debate the opportunities and challenges for researchers in this new and challenging area.

Categories and Subject Descriptors

H [**Information Systems**]: General; H.3.7 [**Digital Libraries**]: Collection

General Terms

Experimentation, Human Factors

Keywords

panel, lifelogging, lifelong personal data

1. INTRODUCTION

Recent technological advances have introduced new types of sensors (informational sensors, physical sensors) and devices (for example Google Glass or Apple's iWatch) which allow the individual to compile vast archives of personal data. Captured over a long period of time, these heterogeneous digital libraries can provide a detailed picture of the activities of an individual and will require search, summarisation and knowledge extraction tools to make them valuable.

Therefore it comes as no surprise that Lifelong Digital Libraries are receiving increasing attention within the research community . An example is *NTCIR Lifelog*[1], a new evaluation task at NTCIR-12 that focuses on the evaluation of personal digital libraries, commonly referred to as lifelogs. Apart from technical challenges arising from gathering and accessing such vast amount of data (see [1] for a detailed discussion of these challenges), various additional aspects need to be considered that are concerned with the impact on these new technological advances both for individuals as well as for society as a whole.

This panel discussion aimed to bring this topic to the attention of the JCDL audience and motivate some of the key research challenges that the community will need to address in the coming years. The main questions discussed include:

- What are the main technical challenges for the creation and access to personal digital archives?
- How to make progress towards making personal digital libraries easier for an individual to manage and extract value from?
- What are the most promising current approaches to maintain and access such archives?
- In which areas are further technical advances required to improve access to such archives?
- How best to motivate and encourage research in the area?
- How to deal with privacy and data security challenges that arise when such archives become commonplace?
- What ethical issues arise from the creation of such archives?
- Who should own these archives and where should the data be hosted?
- How to ensure digital preservation of such archives?
- What are the concerns and expectations of the research community towards this area in the years to come?
- What will personal digital libraries look like in ten years time?

After each panel member introduced themselves, their research and expertise, they individually shared their point of view on these topics. In addition, the chairman encouraged and welcomed input and questions from the floor.

2. REFERENCES

[1] C. Gurrin, A. F. Smeaton, and A. R. Doherty. Lifelogging: Personal big data. *Foundations and Trends in Information Retrieval*, 8(1):1–125, 2014.

[1] `http://ntcir-lifelog.computing.dcu.ie/`

JCDL'15, June 21–25, 2015, Knoxville, Tennessee, USA.
Copyright © 2015 ACM 978-1-4503-3594-2/15/06.
http://dx.doi.org/10.1145/2756406.2756974.

Organizational Strategies for Cultural Heritage Preservation

Moderator: Paul Logasa Bogen II
Google Inc.
Seattle, WA
plbogen@google.com

ABSTRACT

Cultural Heritage content is increasingly being both created digitally and digitized. Preserving this content has been a much discussed and debated question in the Digital Libraries and Digital Humanities communities. Many concerns have been raised around the organizational challenges. Centralized preservation is often praised for unified access and consistency, but at the same are criticized for their reliance on the continued interest of a smaller number of maintainers. Alternatively, decentralized preservation leads to better longevity but often at a cost of consistency or ease of access. Beyond this question, there are many other organizational issues. Such as the role of states and commercial entities in preservation; and, dealing with concerns about ownership, privacy and acceptable use of materials. This panel will discuss these issues with the goal of finding a balance between these often conflicting approaches.

Categories and Subject Descriptors

H.3.7 [**Digital Libraries**]: Collection

K.4.3 [**Organizational Impacts**]

General Terms

Management, Design, Economics, Reliability, Security, Human Factors, Standardization, Legal Aspects

Keywords

Digital Libraries; Cultural Heritage; Preservation

Panelists

- Katherine Skinner
  Executive Director
  Educopia Institute
- Piotr Adamczyk
  Program Manager
  Google Cultural Institute
- Unmil Karadkar
  Assistant Professor
  School of Information
  The University of Texas at Austin

JCDL'15, June 21--25, 2015, Knoxville, Tennessee, USA.
Copyright 2015 ACM 10.1145/2756406.2756975…$15.00.
http://dx.doi.org/10.1145/2756406.2756975

Introduction to Digital Libraries

Edward A. Fox
Virginia Tech
Dept. of Computer Science
Blacksburg, VA 24061 USA
+1-540-231-5113
fox@vt.edu

ABSTRACT

This tutorial is a thorough and deep introduction to the DL field, providing a firm foundation: covering key concepts and terminology, as well as services, systems, technologies, methods, standards, projects, issues, and practices. It introduces and builds upon a firm theoretical foundation (starting with the '5S' set of intuitive aspects: Streams, Structures, Spaces, Scenarios, Societies), giving careful definitions and explanations of all the key parts of a 'minimal digital library', and expanding from that basis to cover key DL issues. Illustrations come from a set of case studies. Attendees will be exposed to four Morgan & Claypool books that elaborate on 5S, 2012-2014. Complementing the coverage of '5S' will be an overview of key aspects of the DELOS Reference Model and DL.org activities. Further, use of a Hadoop cluster supporting DLs will be described.

Categories and Subject Descriptors

H.3.7 [**Information Storage and Retrieval**]: Digital Libraries – *Collection, Dissemination, Standards, Systems issues, User issues*.

General Terms

Algorithms, Management, Documentation, Performance, Design, Experimentation, Human Factors, Standardization, Legal Aspects.

Keywords

5S; Societies; Scenarios; Spaces; Structures; Streams.

1. INTRODUCTION

Highlights of this tutorial include the applications of digital libraries [1] and the underlying technologies [2], which include: Exploration, Evaluation, Integration, Complex Objects, Annotation/Subdocuments, Ontologies, Classification, Text Extraction, Security, Content-based Image Retrieval, Education, Social Networks, Bioinformatics/eScience/Simulation, and Geospatial Information.

Supporting all of those are integration methods, along with suitable schemes for evaluation [3]. By discussing all these topics we make clear that the 5S framework provides a comprehensive theoretical foundation for the field of digital libraries [4].

JCDL'15, June 21-25, 2015, Knoxville, TN, USA
ACM 978-1-4503-3594-2/15/06.
http://dx.doi.org/10.1145/2756406.2756927

2. DL TEACHING AND LEARNING

Educational resources from an US National Science Foundation funded grant to develop DL curriculum (see http://curric.dlib.vt.edu/) will be presented, including descriptions (aimed at teachers and learners) of the more than 30 major modules and sub-modules that cover the core DL topics and related topics (e.g., those used to teach in both undergraduate and graduate courses at Virginia Tech). Most of the modules have been reviewed, revised, field tested, and used at several locations. Further, NSF TUES support has aided integration of digital library coverage in each of 3 courses: Digital Libraries, Information Retrieval, and Computational Linguistics. Part of this involved problem-project based learning, with large collections and a Hadoop cluster. Based on the above, the discussion will be tailored to the interests of the attendees.

3. ACKNOWLEDGMENTS

Thanks go to NSF for support through grants CCF-1032677; DUE-0121679, 0435059, 0840719, 1141209; and IIS-0325579, 0535057, 0535060, 0910183, 0910465, 0916733. Thanks go to the National Inst. of Justice for NCJ 239049 and to QNRF for support through NPRP 4-029-1-007. The opinions expressed in this document are solely those of the author.

4. REFERENCES

[1] Fox, E.A., and Leidig, J.P. 2014. Digital Library Applications: CBIR, Education, Social Networks, eScience/Simulation, and GIS. Morgan & Claypool Publishers, San Francisco, ISBN 9781627050326, http://dx.doi.org/10.2200/S00565ED1V01Y201401ICR032

[2] Fox, E.A., and Torres, R. 2014. Digital Library Technologies: Complex Objects, Annotation, Ontologies, Classification, Extraction, and Security. Morgan & Claypool Publishers, San Francisco, ISBN 9781627050302, http://dx.doi.org/10.2200/S00566ED1V01Y201401ICR033

[3] Shen, R., Goncalves, M.A., and Fox, E.A. 2013. Key Issues Regarding Digital Libraries: Evaluation and Integration. Morgan & Claypool Publishers, San Francisco, ISBN 9781608459124, http://dx.doi.org/10.2200/S00474ED1V01Y201301ICR026

[4] Fox, E.A., Goncalves, M.A., and Shen, R. 2012. Theoretical Foundations for Digital Libraries: The 5S (Societies, Scenarios, Spaces, Structures, Streams) Approach. Morgan & Claypool Publishers, San Francisco, ISBN 9781608459100, http://dx.doi.org/10.2200/S00434ED1V01Y201207ICR022, https://sites.google.com/a/morganclaypool.com/dlibrary/

Digital Data Curation Essentials for Data Scientists and Data Curators and Librarians

Helen R. Tibbo
University of North Carolina at Chapel Hill
Manning Hall, Room 201
Chapel Hill, NC 27599-3360
1-919-962-8063
tibbbo@ils.unc.edu

Carolyn Hank
University of Tennessee
420B Communications Bldg
Knoxville, TN 37996-0341
1-865-974-4049
chank@utk.edu

ABSTRACT
This paper describes a detailed description of a full-day data digital curation tutorial held at *JCDL'15*.

Categories and Subject Descriptors
E.m [**Data**]: Miscellaneous
H.3.7 [**Information Storage and Retrieval**]: Digital Libraries

General Terms
Management, documentation

Keywords
Data management planning; life cycle; preservation

1. INTRODUCTION
As major funding agencies, publishers, and research institutions continue to issue data sharing, management, and archiving policies in increasing numbers, it is necessary for data scientists and information professionals, including data curators and data librarians, to "skill up to do data" by gaining the knowledge, skills, and competencies necessary to confront their growing—and increasingly complex—data management needs. With lecture, discussion, and hands-on exercises, this tutorial will explore the obligations of researchers to manage their data, identify the attributes of data that add to the complexity of data curation tasks, and introduce a range of standards, tools and resources available to help data scientists and librarians effectively implement data management and curation services. Further, as an essential aspect of data management planning is ensuring data is made available for future access and use, depositing data to an appropriate data or digital repository is either a required or highly recommended outcome. This tutorial will also explore submission agreements that enable such deposits through making clear the expectations, roles, and responsibilities of data scientists and repository managers.

JCDL'15, June 21–25, 2015, Knoxville, Tennessee, USA.
ACM 978-1-4503-3594-2/15/06.
http://dx.doi.org/10.1145/2756406.2756928

2. DETAILED TOPICAL OUTLINE

2.1 Issues in Digital Curation
An overview of essential terminology and the data life cycle, from conceptualization and pre-creation through disposition for shared understanding. A review of current issues around data curation including funding agency and publisher policies, the open access movement, and eScience trends that have made it necessary for library leaders to provide data curation services.

2.2 Standards Overview
An introduction to various data types and applicable standards and best practices for data curation. An overview of functional components and stakeholder roles in the Open Archival Information System (OAIS) Reference Model, with particular emphasis on the OAIS ingest function, reflecting roles and requirements of Producer-Archive Interface Methodology Abstract Standard (PAIMAS).

2.3 Data Management Planning
Exploration of tools and resources for archiving, preserving, and providing access to data in accordance with standards and best practices. Includes review of the impetus for and approaches to data management planning for research data, an overview of the specific role of data curator and data scientist, and identification of leading disciplinary digital data repositories.

2.4 Submission Agreements
Exploration of submission agreements, including where submission agreements fit within a digital data repository's overall policy framework, identification of mandatory, recommended and optional elements of submission agreement forms with attention to language, legal and technical considerations. Overview of strategies and tips for effective communication and interaction between data scientists (producers) and data curators (repository managers).

2.5 Conclusion and Discussion
Summary discussion of concepts, principles, techniques, and recommendations discussed. Overview of data curation tools and services available to data curators and data scientists for guiding additional self-directed learning post-tutorial.

3. TARGET AUDIENCE

This full-day tutorial is designed for an audience with introductory or intermediate levels of understanding or experience in data management planning, digital data curation, and/or digital or data repositories. It is designed to accommodate members of the producer and consumer communities (data scientists) as well as digital repository managers. This is intentional so as to foster engaging discussion among these distinct stakeholder groups, particularly in regard to roles and expectations. Targeted audience members may be working in libraries, archives, government agencies, corporations, or other organizations responsible for archiving, preserving, and providing access to research data. Specific professionals targeted in this tutorial (1) Data scientists, including researchers from Oak Ridge National Laboratory; (2) Digital curators or digital librarians; and (3) Data curators or data curation librarians.

4. LEARNING OBJECTIVES

By the end of this tutorial, it is expected participants will be able to:

- Recognize different types of data and data curation issues specific to those types of data.
- Discuss established and emerging standards and best practice for data curation.
- Understand funding agency and publisher policies, standard community practices, and other issues driving the need for digital data curation.
- Identify available tools and services to assist with data curation tasks.
- Identify essential elements of an effective data management plan based on hands-on experience.
- Identify components of effective submission agreement forms.
- Identify critical planning steps for negotiating deposits to a digital or data repository as a producer.
- Identify critical planning steps for negotiating deposits to a digital or data repository as a digital curator or digital librarian.

5. PRESENTER BIOS

Dr. Helen R. Tibbo is an Alumni Distinguished Professor in the School of Information and Library Science (SILS) at the University of North Carolina at Chapel Hill. She leads the Archives and Records Management and Digital Curation programs at SILS and has been PI for numerous grant-funded projects including DigCCurr I and II, ESOPI-21 and ESOPI2, Closing the Digital Curation Gap, and most recently, CRADLE. Her primary interests are how best to educating a digital curation stewardship workforce, institutional repositories, and audit and certification of trustworthy repositories.

Dr. Carolyn Hank is an Assistant Professor at the School of Information Sciences at the University of Tennessee, Knoxville (UTK). She received her Ph.D. from the School of Information and Library Science (SILS) at the University of North Carolina at Chapel Hill (UNC-CH), where she served as the project manager for the DigCCurr I project from 2007-200, and program manager for the UNC-CH Digital Curation/Institutional Repository Committee (2005-2008) and Carolina Digital Repository (2008-2009). At UTK she teaches graduate-level courses in digital curation, human information interactions, and research methods.

6. ACKNOWLEDGMENTS

This tutorial is being offered, in part, through the CRADLE (Curating Research Assets and Data Using Lifecycle Education) project, sponsored by the Institute of Museum and Library Services, under award #RE-06-13-0052-13.

7. SELECT RELATED TUTORIALS

(Tibbo) *Curating Research Assets and Data Using Lifecycle Education* at the 78th Annual Meeting of the Society of American Archivists (August 11, 2014)

(Tibbo and Hank) *Digital Curation and Digital Preservation: A Introduction* at JCDL 2007 (June 19, 2007)

Topic Exploration with the HTRC Data Capsule for Non-Consumptive Research

Jaimie Murdock
Indiana University
jammurdo@indiana.edu

Jiaan Zeng
Indiana University
jiaazeng@indiana.edu

Robert H. McDonald
Indiana University
rhmcdona@indiana.edu

ABSTRACT

In this half-day tutorial, we will show 1) how the HathiTrust Research Center (HTRC) Data Capsule can be used for non-consumptive research over collection of texts and 2) how integrated tools for LDA topic modeling and visualization can be used to drive formulation of new research questions. Participants will be given an account in the HTRC Data Capsule and taught how to use the workset manager to create a corpus, and then use the VM's secure mode to download texts and analyze their contents.

Categories and Subject Descriptors

C.2.4 [**Computer Communication Systems**]: Distributed systems; H.3.7 [**Information Systems**]: Digital libraries; I.2.7 [**Natural Language Processing**]: Text analysis

Keywords

topic modeling, non-consupmtive use, data capsules

1. A NON-CONSUMPTIVE WORKFLOW

As large-scale digitization projects have grown to include both copyrighted and public domain works, legal consensus was built for the "non-expressive use" of text, including text mining over copyrighted works to produce analysis of a large corpus (see *Authors Guild v. HathiTrust*). The HathiTrust Research Center (HTRC)[1] Data Capsule [4] enables this "non-consumptive" use. In this tutorial, we present a five-stage research pipeline for non-consumptive textual analysis: from initial corpus curation to modeling and visualization with tools developed by the InPhO Project[2].

First, a collection of HathiTrust IDs is created using either the plain-text bibliography parser of the InPhO Corpus Builder or the search capacities of the HathiTrust Workset Creator (Figure 1, blue boxes). Then, the HTRC Data Capsule is switched to *secure mode* in which network and file system access is highly constrained to protect copyrighted texts (Figure 1, yellow boxes). At this point, the volumes may be downloaded to the Data Capsule. These are modeled by Latent Dirichlet Allocation (LDA) [1] and visualized through the InPhO Topic Explorer [2] (Figure 1, top). Additional programmatic access to the models is provided by automatically-generated IPython/Jupyter Notebooks [3].

[1] `http://hathitrust.org/htrc/`

[2] `http://inpho.cogs.indiana.edu/`

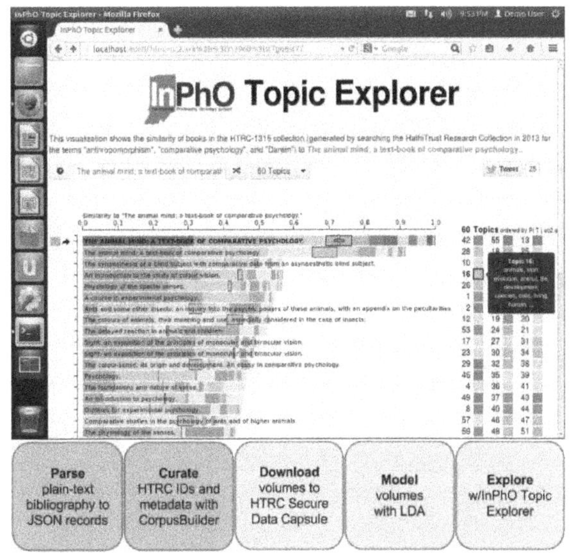

Figure 1: *Top* — The InPhO Topic Explorer in the HTRC Data Capsule. *Bottom* — Topic exploration workflow: blue nodes may be completed in maintenance mode; yellow nodes require secure mode.

2. REFERENCES

[1] D. M. Blei, A. Y. Ng, and M. I. Jordan. Latent Dirichlet Allocation. *Journal of Machine Learning Research*, 3:993–1022, 2003.

[2] J. Murdock and C. Allen. Visualization techniques for topic model checking. In *Proceedings of the 29th AAAI Conference on Artificial Intelligence (AAAI-15)*, 2015.

[3] F. Pérez and B. E. Granger. IPython: a system for interactive scientific computing, May 2007.

[4] J. Zeng, G. Ruan, A. Crowell, A. Prakash, and B. Plale. Cloud computing data capsules for non-consumptiveuse of texts. In *Proceedings of the 5th ACM Workshop on Scientific Cloud Computing*, ScienceCloud '14, pages 9–16, 2014.

JCDL'15, June 21–25, 2015, Knoxville, Tennessee, USA.
ACM 978-1-4503-3594-2/15/06.
http://dx.doi.org/10.1145/2756406.2756929.

Automatic Methods for Disambiguating Author Names in Bibliographic Data Repositories

Anderson A. Ferreira[1] Marcos André Gonçalves[2] Alberto H. F. Laender[2]

[1]Departamento de Computação
Universidade Federal de Ouro Preto
Ouro Preto, Brazil
ferreira@iceb.ufop.br

[2]Departamento de Ciência da Computação
Universidade Federal de Minas Gerais
Belo Horizonte, Brazil
{mgoncalv,laender}@dcc.ufmg.br

ABSTRACT

Name ambiguity in the context of bibliographic citation records is a hard problem that affects the quality of services and content in digital libraries and similar systems. This problem occurs when an author publishes works under distinct names or distinct authors publish works under similar names. The challenges of dealing with author name ambiguity have led to a myriad of name disambiguation methods. In this tutorial, we characterize such methods by means of a proposed taxonomy, present an overview of some of the most representative ones and discuss open challenges.

Categories and Subject Descriptors

H.3.3 [**Information Search and Retrieval**]: Information Search and Retrieval; H.3.7 [**Information Storage and Retrieval**]: Digital Libraries

General Terms

Algorithms, Measurement

Keywords

Ambiguity author names; disambiguation methods

1. INTRODUCTION

Name ambiguity in the context of bibliographic citation records is a hard problem that affects the quality of services and content in digital libraries (DLs) and similar systems. This problem occurs when an author publishes works under distinct names or distinct authors publish works under similar names. The author name ambiguity challenges have led to a myriad of disambiguation methods.

This tutorial is divided in two parts. The first part is based on our survey, entitled "A Brief Survey of Automatic Methods for Author Name Disambiguation", which was published in SIGMOD Record in June 2012 [7]. In this introductory part, we contextualize the problem, present a formal definition for it and propose a general taxonomy for characterizing the automatic author name disambiguation methods proposed in the literature. Then, we briefly describe some of these methods according to our taxonomy and discuss open research challenges. In the second part, we address some of our solutions for the problem. First, we present HHC - Heuristic-based Hierarchical Clustering [3]. HHC disambiguates a set of citation records by successively fusing clusters of citation records with similar author names based on a real-world heuristic applied to their citation attributes. Then, we present SAND - Self-training Associative Name Disambiguator [9, 8]. SAND is a three-step self-training method for author name disambiguation that requires no manual labeling and no parameterization (in real world scenarios). Finally, we present INDi - Incremental unsupervised Name Disambiguation [2]. INDi is an unsupervised incremental method that aims to disambiguate only the new ambiguous citation records inserted into a disambiguated DL. We conclude this second part by presenting SyGAR [6], a tool for generating synthetic collections that allows the simulation of several realistic scenarios to support the evaluation of disambiguation methods.

JCDL'15, June 21–25, 2015, Knoxville, Tennessee, USA.
ACM 978-1-4503-3594-2/15/06.
http://dx.doi.org/10.1145/2756406.2756930 .

2. PROPOSED TAXONOMY

In [7], we proposed a hierarchical taxonomy for grouping the most representative automatic author name disambiguation methods found in the literature. According to our taxonomy, the methods may be classified following the main type of exploited approach: *author grouping* [3, 9, 11, 12, 14, 13, 16, 17], which tries to group the references to the same author using some type of similarity among reference attributes, or *author assignment* [1, 4, 8, 10, 15, 18], which aims at directly assigning the references to their respective authors. Alternatively, the methods may be grouped according to the evidence explored in the disambiguation task: the citation attributes (only), web information, or implicit data that can be extracted from the available information.

3. OVERVIEW OF THE METHODS

In this tutorial, we present an overview of our three most representative methods [5], namely, HHC - Heuristic-based Hierarchical Clustering, SAND - Self-training Associative Name Disambiguator and INDi - Incremental unsupervised Name Disambiguation.

HHC [3] is based on a general heuristic that considers two real-world assumptions: (1) very rarely two authors with similar names and sharing a common co-author are two different persons in the real world and (2) authors tend to publish in the same subjects and publication venues for a considerable portion of their careers. HHC works in two steps. In the first step, it groups citation records with similar author names into clusters based on the coauthorship relations existing among the records. Then, in the second step, it fuses the initially created clusters based on the similarity of their work or publication venue titles. This process continues until no more clusters can be fused. The final result is a list of clusters with their respective citation records.

SAND [9, 8] is a self-training method that divides the disambiguation task in three steps. Step 1 (*author grouping*) aims to automatically create pure clusters of citation records. SAND obtains pure clusters by exploiting coauthorship relations among the records. SAND considers that a citation record and a cluster share co-authors if both have at least one similar co-author name whose last name is not popular (i.e., it is not a common last name) or if they have at least two similar co-author names (popular or not). Step 2 (*cluster selection*) aims to select, from clusters produced by Step 1, the ones belonging to distinct authors for composing the training data used by Step 3. We select the dissimilar clusters with the largest number of citation records. The citation records from these selected clusters are inserted into the training data D, along with the author label of the corresponding cluster. Step 3 (*author assignment*) uses the set of examples D to produce a disambiguation function for predicting the correct author of the unselected clusters, based on a lazy associative classifier [19]. SAND detects authors without a representative cluster in the training data D and includes them in D. It also increases the coverage of D by exploiting reliable predictions.

INDi [2] is an incremental author name disambiguation method aimed at determining the authors of new citation records as they get added to a DL. As such, it need not be applied to the whole DL at once to disambiguate it, thus preserving eventual manual corrections previously done. INDi includes specific heuristics to check whether author names of new citation records refer to pre-existing authors in the DL or to new ones (authors with no citation records in the DL). These heuristics are meant to disambiguate new citation records by prioritizing the assignment of such records to the correct author instead of assigning the doubtful record to an existing author with a probability of error. INDi attempts to disambiguate the new citation records by looking for an existing author whose records in the DL include a similar author name, at least one common co-author, and similar work or publication venue titles. For cases in which the new citation record does not include co-authors or all existing records in a group of an existing similar author do not include any co-authors, it does not perform the co-author check, but raises similarity thresholds for publication venue and work title. When this checking procedure fails, the citation record is considered as belonging to a new author.

4. CONCLUDING REMARKS

Author name ambiguity is a hard problem that affects the quality of services and content in DLs. Thus, at the end of this tutorial, we expect the participants will have understood the challenges of this problem and learned about some of the existing solutions.

Acknowledgments

This work has been supported by InWeb and by the authors' individual grants from CAPES, CNPq and FAPEMIG.

References

[1] I. Bhattacharya and L. Getoor. A Latent Dirichlet Model for Unsupervised Entity Resolution. In *SDM*, 2006.

[2] A. P. Carvalho, A. A. Ferreira, A. H. F. Laender, and M. A. Gonçalves. Incremental Unsupervised Name Disambiguation in Cleaned Digital Libraries. *JIDM*, 2(3):289–304, 2011.

[3] R. G. Cota, A. A. Ferreira, M. A. Gonçalves, A. H. F. Laender, and C. Nascimento. An unsupervised heuristic-based hierarchical method for name disambiguation in bibliographic citations. *JASIST*, 61(9):1853–1870, 2010.

[4] L. V. B. Esperidião, A. A. Ferreira, A. H. F. Laender, M. A. Gonçalves, D. M. Gomes, A. I. Tavares, and G. T. de Assis. Reducing Fragmentation in Incremental Author Name Disambiguation. *JIDM*, 5(3):293–307, 2014.

[5] A. A. Ferreira, M. A. Gonçalves, and A. H. F. Laender. Disambiguating author names using minimum bibliographic information. *World Digital Libraries*, 7(1):71–84, 2014.

[6] A. A. Ferreira, M. A. Gonçalves, J. M. Almeida, A. H. F. Laender, and A. Veloso. A tool for generating synthetic authorship records for evaluating author name disambiguation methods. *Information Sciences*, 206:42–62, 2012.

[7] A. A. Ferreira, M. A. Gonçalves, and A. H. F. Laender. A Brief Survey of Automatic Methods for Author Name Disambiguation. *SIGMOD Record*, 41(2):15–26, 2012.

[8] A. A. Ferreira, A. Veloso, M. A. Gonçalves, and A. H. F. Laender. Self-training author name disambiguation for information scarce scenarios. *JASIST*, 65(6):1257–1278, 2014.

[9] A. A. Ferreira, A. Veloso, M. A. Gonçalves, and A. H. F. Laender. Effective self-training author name disambiguation in scholarly digital libraries. In *JCDL*, pages 39–48, 2010.

[10] H. Han, C. L. Giles, H. Zha, C. Li, and K. Tsioutsiouliklis. Two Supervised Learning Approaches for Name Disambiguation in Author Citations. In *JCDL*, pages 296–305, 2004.

[11] J. Huang, S. Ertekin, and C. L. Giles. Efficient Name Disambiguation for Large-Scale Databases. In *PKDD*, pages 536–544, 2006.

[12] I.-S. Kang, S.-H. Na, S. Lee, H. Jung, P. Kim, W.-K. Sung, and J.-H. Lee. On co-authorship for author disambiguation. *IPM*, 45(1):84–97, 2009.

[13] A. F. Santana, M. A. Gonçalves, A. H. F. Laender, and A. A. Ferreira. Combining Domain-specific Heuristics for Author Name Disambiguation. In *JCDL*, pages 173–182, 2014.

[14] Y. Song, J. Huang, I. G. Councill, J. Li, and C. L. Giles. Efficient Topic-based Unsupervised Name Disambiguation. In *JCDL*, pages 342–351, 2007.

[15] J. Tang, A. C. M. Fong, B. Wang, and J. Zhang. A unified probabilistic framework for name disambiguation in digital library. *TKDE*, 24(6):975–987, 2012.

[16] V. I. Torvik and N. R. Smalheiser. Author name disambiguation in medline. *TKDD*, 3(3):1–29, 2009.

[17] P. Treeratpituk and C. L. Giles. Disambiguating Authors in Academic Publications using Random Forests. In *JCDL*, pages 39–48, 2009.

[18] A. Veloso, A. A. Ferreira, M. A. Gonçalves, A. H. Laender, and W. Meira Jr. Cost-effective on-demand associative author name disambiguation. *IPM*, 48(4):680 – 697, 2012.

[19] A. Veloso, W. M. Jr., M. A. Gonçalves, and M. J. Zaki. Multi-label lazy associative classification. In *PKDD*, pages 605–612, 2007.

WOSP2015: 4th International Workshop on Mining Scientific Publications

Petr Knoth
Knowledge Media institute
The Open University
Milton Keynes, UK
petr.knoth@open.ac.uk

Kris Jack
Mendeley Ltd.
London, UK
kris.jack@mendeley.com

Lucas Anastasiou
Knowledge Media institute
The Open University
Milton Keynes, UK
lucas.anastasiou@open.ac.uk

Nuno Freire
The European Library
Hague, The Netherlands
nuno.freire@kb.nl

Nancy Pontika
Knowledge Media institute
The Open University
Milton Keynes, UK
nancy.pontika@open.ac.uk

Drahomira Herrmannova
Knowledge Media institute
The Open University
Milton Keynes, UK
drahomira.herrmannova@open.ac.uk

Categories and Subject Descriptors
H.3 [**Information Storage and Retrieval**]

General Terms
Algorithms, Management, Design

Keywords
Scientific Publication Datasets, Text Mining, Data Mining, Natural Language Processing

1. INTRODUCTION
Digital libraries that store scientific publications are becoming increasingly central to the research process. They are not only used for traditional tasks, such as finding and storing research outputs, but also as a source for discovering new research trends or evaluating research excellence. With the current growth of scientific publications deposited in digital libraries, it is no longer sufficient to provide only access to content. To aid research, it is especially important to leverage the potential of text and data mining technologies to improve the process of how research is being done.

This workshop aims to bring together people from different backgrounds who: (a) are interested in analysing and mining databases of scientific publications, (b) develop systems that enable such analysis and mining of scientific databases (especially those who run databases of publications) or (c) who develop novel technologies that improve the way research is being done.

JCDL'15, June 21-25, 2015, Knoxville, TN, USA
ACM 978-1-4503-3594-2/15/06.
http://dx.doi.org/10.1145/2756406.2756932

2. TOPICS
The topics of the workshop will be organised around the following themes:

1. The whole ecosystem of infrastructures including repositories, aggregators, text-and data-mining facilities, impact monitoring tools, datasets, services and APIs that enable analysis of large volumes of scientific publications.
2. Semantic enrichment of scientific publications by means of text and data mining, crowdsourcing or other methods.
3. Analysis of large databases of scientific publications to identify research trends, high impact, cross-fertilisation between disciplines, research excellence etc.

Topics of interest relevant to theme 1 include but are not limited to:

- *Infrastructures including repositories, aggregators, text-and data-mining facilities, impact monitoring tools, datasets,, services and APIs for accessing scientific publications and/or research data.* The existence of datasets, services, systems and APIs (in particular those that are open) providing access to large volumes of scientific publications and research data, is an essential prerequisite for being able to research and develop new technologies that can transform the way people do research. We invite papers presenting innovative approaches to the development of these systems that enable people to access databases and carry out their analysis. Papers addressing Open Access are of special interest. We also welcome submissions discussing the technical aspects of supporting Open Science, in particular reproducibility of research, sharing of scientific workflows and linking research data with publications. Finally, we also invite papers discussing issues and current challenges in the design of these systems.

Topics of interest relevant to theme 2 include but are not limited to:

- *Novel information extraction and text-mining approaches to semantic enrichment of publications.* This might range from mining publication structure, such as title, abstract, authors, citation information etc. to more challenging tasks, such as extracting names of applied methods, research questions (or scientific gaps), identifying parts of the scholarly discourse structure etc.

- *Automatic categorization and clustering of scientific publications.* Methods that can automatically categorize publications according to an established subject-based classification/taxonomy (such as Library of Congress classification, UNESCO thesaurus, DOAJ subject classification, Library of Congress Subject Headings) are of particular interest. Other approaches might involve automatic clustering or classification of research publications according to various criteria.
- *New methods and models for connecting and interlinking scientific publications.* Scientific publications in digital libraries are not isolated islands. Connecting publications using explicitly defined citations is very restrictive and has many disadvantages. We are interested in innovative technologies that can automatically connect and interlink publications or parts of publications according to various criteria, such as semantic similarity, contradiction, argument support or other relationship types.
- *Models for semantically representing and annotating publications.* This topic is related to the aspect of semantically modeling publications and scholarly discourse. Models that are practical with respect to the state-of-the-art in Natural Language Processing (NLP) technologies are of a special interest.
- *Semantically enriching/annotating publications by crowdsourcing.* Crowdsourcing can be used in innovative ways to annotate publications with richer metadata or to approve/disapprove annotations created using text-mining or other approaches. We welcome papers that address the following questions: (a) what incentives should be provided to motivate users in contributing, (b) how to apply crowdsourcing in the specialized domains of scientific publications, (c) what tasks in the domain of organising scientific publications is crowdsourcing suitable for and where it might fail, other relevant crowdsourcing topics relevant to the domain of scientific publications.

Topics of interest relevant to theme 3 include but are not limited to:

- *New methods, models and innovative approaches for measuring impact of publications.* The most widely used metrics for measuring impact are based on citations. However, counting citations not taking into account the publication content and the qualitative nature of the citation. In addition, there is a delay between the publication and the measurable impact in citations. We in particular encourage papers addressing new ways of evaluating publications' impact beyond standard citation measures.
- *New methods for measuring performance of researchers.* Methods for assessing impact of a publication can be often extended to methods that can assess the impact of individual researchers. However, there are also other criteria for measuring impact in addition to publications, such as the development and publication of research data, economical and market impact that should also be taken into account. We welcome papers addressing these aspects.
- *Evaluating impact of research groups.* The same as for impact of individuals holds for research communities.
- *Methods for identifying research trends and cross-fertilization between research disciplines.* Identifying research trends should allow discovering newly emerging disciplines or it should help to explain why certain fields are attracting the attention of a wider research community. Such monitoring is important for research funders and governments in order to be able to quickly respond to new developments. We invite papers discussing new methods for identifying trends and cross-fertilization between research disciplines using methods ranging from social network analysis and text- and data-mining to innovative visualization approaches.
- *Application and case studies of mining from scientific databases and publications.* New methods and models developed for mining from scientific publications can be applied in many different scenarios, such as improving access to scientific publications, providing exploratory search in digital collections, identifying experts. We encourage papers describing innovative approaches that use scientific publications and data to solve real-world problems.
- *Improving the infrastructure of repositories to support the development and integration of new impact and performance metrics.* New ways of improving the repository infrastructure can include, for example, tracking accesses and downloads, researcher profiling and the interlinking of repository data with external services.. These can be in turn used for developing new impact metrics. We welcome papers addressing these issues.

3. SPECIAL OPEN PUBLICATIONS DATASET TRACK

This year we would like to invite the workshop participants to makes use of the CORE publications dataset containing large volume of research publications from a wide variety of research areas. The dataset contains not only full-texts, but also an enriched version of publications' metadata. This dataset provides a framework for developing and testing methods and tools addressing the workshop topics. The use of this dataset is not mandatory, however it is encouraged.

4. EXPECTED AUDIENCE

The workshop on Mining Scientific Publications aims to bring together researchers, digital library developers and practitioners from government and industry to address the current challenges in the domain of mining scientific publications.

5. PREVIOUS ORGANISATION

The 1st International Workshop on Mining Scientific Publications (http://core-project.kmi.open.ac.uk/jcdl2012/) was previously held in conjunction with JCDL 2012. The 2nd run of this workshop was held in conjunction with JCDL 2013 (http://core-project.kmi.open.ac.uk/jcdl2013/). The third run was especially popular and was associated with DL2014 in London (http://core-project.kmi.open.ac.uk/dl2013/). All runs of the workshop have been extremely successful in terms of attracting submissions and participants from leading institutions in the area including Cambridge University, British Library, Elsevier Labs, National Library of Medicine, Library of Congress, University of Pennsylvania (CiteSeerX), Know-Center Graz, University of Athens (OpenAIRE project) and Mendeley.

6. FORMAT

We plan this workshop as a one whole-day event. The workshop is organized this year for the forth time (the three previous workshops were also in association with JCDL) and is planned to take place yearly. The workshop will consist of two invited talks, a series of presentations followed by a short discussion, a short work in groups session dedicated to addressing specific issues in the field and a final round table discussion at the end of the day. The workshop participants will be also encouraged to visit and experience demonstrations that will be presented during coffee breaks. In the evening, the workshop participants will have the possibility to attend an informal dinner.

7. SUBMISSION FORMAT

We invite submissions related to the workshop's topics. Long papers should not exceed 8 pages and short papers should not exceed 4 pages of the ACM style. Furthermore, we welcome demo presentations of systems or methods. A demonstration submission should consist of a maximum two-page description of the system, method or tool to be demonstrated. All submissions will be uploaded to EasyChair for a peer-review.

8. PEER REVIEW

All submissions will be peer-reviewed and meta-reviewed by members of the Programme Committee. Each publication will be assigned a score and the best publications will be selected. In this sense, the process will be the same as in the last years.

9. PUBLICATION

We will closely work with D-Lib to publish accepted short and full papers as a special issue. The proceedings of the special issues from the last years are available at:

http://www.dlib.org/dlib/july12/07contents.html

http://www.dlib.org/dlib/september13/09contents.html

http://www.dlib.org/dlib/november14/11contents.html

10. ORGANIZING COMMITTEE

Petr Knoth, Knowledge Media institute, The Open University, UK

Kris Jack, Mendeley Ltd., UK

Nuno Freire, The European Library, The Netherlands

Drahomira Herrmannova, Knowledge Media institute, The Open University, UK

Nancy Pontika, Knowledge Media institute, The Open University, UK

Lucas Anastasiou, Knowledge Media institute, The Open University, UK

11. PROGRAMME COMMITTEE

The Programme Committee will be officially established shortly after the acceptance of the workshop. The Programmme Committee will likely consist of its members from the last years and additional new members. The following people are expected to form the Programme Committee:

Bruno Martins, Technical University of Lisbon(IST), Portugal

Eloy Rodrigues, University of Minho, Portugal

Francesco Osborne, Knowledge Media institute, The Open University, UK

Iryna Gurevych, Darmstadt University of Technology, Germany

Martin Klein, Los Alamos National Laboratory, USA

Natalia Manola, University of Athens, Greece

Paolo Manghi, ISTI-CNR (DRIVER, OpenAIRE), Italy

Pável Calado, Technical University of Lisbon(IST), Portugal

Robert M. Patton, Oak Ridge National Laboratory, USA

Robert Sanderson, Digital Library Systems and Services, Stanford, USA

Roman Kern, Know Center Graz, Austria

Zdenek Zdrahal, Knowledge Media institute, The Open University, UK

Tanja Urbancic, Jožef Stefan Institute, Slovenia

Wojtek Sylwestrzak, University of Warsaw, Poland

Stelio Piperidis, Institute for Language and Speech processing (META-SHARE), Athena Research Center, Greece

Ziqi Zhang, Department of Computer Science, University of Sheffield, UK

12. WORKSHOP WEBPAGE & DISSEMINATION

The workshop web page will be deployed maximum one week after the workshop acceptance. The workshop will be then disseminated through a number of channels including WikiCFP, Twitter, Facebook and the mailing lists of The European Library/Europeana, Jisc, OpenAIRE, UKCoRR, META-SHARE, OpenMinTeD, Mendeley and others.

We expect the keynote presentations to address the issues of developing a) e-Infratsructures for text and data mining of research papers and b) large open citation databases to help bibliometrics researchers.

Web Archiving and Digital Libraries (WADL)

Edward A. Fox
Virginia Tech
Dept. of Computer Science
Blacksburg, VA 24061 USA
+1-540-231-5113
fox@vt.edu

Zhiwu Xie
Virginia Tech
University Libraries
Blacksburg, VA 24061 USA
+1-540-231-4453
zhiwuxie@vt.edu

ABSTRACT
This workshop will explore integration of Web archiving and digital libraries, so the complete life cycle involved is covered: creation/authoring, uploading/publishing in the Web (2.0), (focused) crawling, indexing, exploration (searching, browsing), ..., archiving (of events). It will include particular coverage of current topics of interest:, big data, mobile web archiving, and systems (e.g., Memento, SiteStory, Uninterruptible Web Service).

Categories and Subject Descriptors
H.3.5 [**Information Storage and Retrieval**]: Online Information Services – *Web-based services.* H.3.6 [**Information Storage and Retrieval**]: Library Automation – *Large text archives.* H.3.7 [**Information Storage and Retrieval**]: Digital Libraries – Collection, Standards, Systems issues.

General Terms
Management, Standardization.

Keywords
Web archiving; Internet Archive.

1. INTRODUCTION
The objectives of this workshop are to:

- continue to build the community of people integrating Web archiving with digital libraries;
- help attendees learn about useful methods, systems, and software in this area;
- help chart future research and practice in this area, so more and higher quality Web archiving occurs; and
- promote synergistic efforts including collaborative projects and proposals.

2. RELATED WORK
The most recent related workshop, WIRE, focused on research leading to or making use of archives that preserve Internet content [1]. The first workshop on Web Archiving and Digital Libraries, WADL, led to a summary [2] after a group responded to the call for meeting [3] as part of the JCDL 2013 workshop program. An earlier similar workshop at a prior JCDL took place in Ottawa in 2011 [4], partly as a result of the emergence of a cooperative to explore Web archiving [5]. Broader in scope are the international activities for Internet preservation [6], including a 2015 meeting.

JCDL'15, June 21–25, 2015, Knoxville, Tennessee, USA.
ACM 978-1-4503-3594-2/15/06.
http://dx.doi.org/10.1145/2756406.2756934

3. TOPICS
This workshop will cover all topics of interest, including but not limited to:

Archiving (events)	Big data	Classification
Community building	Crawling (focused)	Curation, Q/C
Databases / collections	Discovery	Extraction/analysis
Filling gaps	Globalization	Linking archives
Metadata	Mobile devices	Network science
Preservation	Resource description	Social sciences
Standards, protocols	Systems, tools	Tweet connections

4. ACKNOWLEDGMENTS
Our thanks go to NSF for support through IIS 1319578 and to QNRF for support through NPRP 4-029-1-007. The opinions expressed in this document are solely our own. Thanks also go to the JCDL organizing committee, and to the WADL organizing committee: Jefferson Bailey, Prashant Chandrasekar, Mohamed Magdy Farig, Vinay Goel, and Martin Weber.

5. REFERENCES
[1] Weber, M., Lazer, D., Carpenter-Negulescu, K., and Kosterich, A. 2014. *Working with Internet Archives for Research* (WIRE 2014 Workshop, Cambridge, MA, June 17-18, 2014). http://wp.comminfo.rutgers.edu/nsfia/

[2] Fox, E.A. and Farag, M.M. 2013. *Report on the Workshop on Web Archiving and Digital Libraries* (WADL 2013), WADL Workshop Report, ACM SIGIR Forum, 47(2): 128-133. http://sigir.org/files/forum/2013D/p128.pdf

[3] Fox, E.A. 2013. *Web Archiving and Digital Libraries* (WADL 2013). Virginia Tech CTRnet announcement, http://www.ctrnet.net/sites/default/files/JCDL2013Workshop WebArchiving20130603.pdf

[4] Garcia-Molina, H., McCown, F., Nelson, M., and Paepcke, A. 2011. Web Archive Globalization Workshop. In conjunction with JCDL 2011, Ottawa, Canada, June 16-17. http://cs.harding.edu/wag2011/

[5] Garcia-Molina, H., McCown, F., Nelson, M., and Paepcke, A. 2011. Web Archive Cooperative Making Web Archives Useful Today, Supported by the NSF (1009916), Stanford University, http://infolab.stanford.edu/wac/

[6] IIPC. International Internet Preservation Consortium. 2015. Homepage http://netpreserve.org/

Author Index

www.ingramcontent.com/pod-product-compliance
Lightning Source LLC
Chambersburg PA
CBHW080927220326
41598CB00034B/5708
9781450338776